Tele-learning in a Digital World
The Future of Distance Learning

To Jef, my core connection..

Tele-learning in a Digital World

The Future of Distance Learning

Dr Betty Collis

Faculty of Educational Science and Technology
Twente University
The Netherlands

INTERNATIONAL THOMSON COMPUTER PRESS

I(T)P An International Thomson Publishing Company

London • Bonn • Boston • Johannesburg • Madrid • Melbourne • Mexico City • New York • Paris
Singapore • Tokyo • Toronto • Albany, NY • Belmont, CA • Cincinnati, OH • Detroit, MI

Tele-learning in a Digital World
The Future of Distance Learning

Copyright © 1996 International Thomson Computer Press

I(T)P   A division of International Thomson Publishing Inc.
The ITP logo is a trademark under licence.

For more information, contact:

International Thomson Computer Press
Berkshire House
168–173 High Holborn
London WC1V 7AA
UK

International Thomson Computer Press
20 Park Plaza
Suite 1001
Boston, MA 02116
USA

Imprints of International Thomson Publishing

International Thomson Publishing GmbH
Königswinterer Straße 418
53227 Bonn
Germany

International Thomson Publishing Asia
221 Henderson Road #05–10
Henderson Building
Singapore 0315

Thomas Nelson Australia
102 Dodds Street
South Melbourne, 3205
Victoria
Australia

International Thomson Publishing Japan
Hirakawacho Kyowa Building, 3F
2–2–1 Hirakawacho
Chiyoda-ku, 102 Tokyo
Japan

Nelson Canada
1120 Birchmount Road
Scarborough, Ontario
Canada M1K 5G4

International Thomson Editores
Campos Eliseos 385, Piso 7
Col. Polenco
11560 Mexico D. F. Mexico

International Thomson Publishing South Africa
PO Box 2459
Halfway House
1685 South Africa

International Thomson Publishing France
1, rue St. Georges
75 009 Paris
France

British Library Cataloguing-in-Publication Data
A catalogue record for this book is available from the British Library

Library of Congress Cataloging-in-Publication Data
A catalog record for this book is available from the Library of Congress

First Printed 1996
Reprinted 1997, 1999

ISBN 1–85032–157–4

Cover Designed by Button Eventures
Printed in the UK by Selwood Printing Ltd., Burgess Hill

Contents

List of boxes

Chapter 9

Chapter 10

List of tables

Looking forward

The theme of this book is *making connections*. It is a book about action, the action of learning through connecting to resources (both human and stored) through communication technologies. However, the book is not about learning in isolation, but about the people who are involved in tele-learning, where they work and plan and study and think. And because people do not work and learn in isolation but always embedded in many different contexts, this book is also about institutions and workplaces, and how they are involved in the evolution of tele-learning. Evolution is another key word: evolution of technologies, of pedagogies, even of our concepts of learning and teaching and the educational enterprise.

Throughout the book, examples and facts are the basis of each of the perspectives on tele-learning that are brought forward. But in the last chapter, Chapter 10, the tone of the book changes, from one of observation and analysis to one of prediction. Those predictions, about not only the future of tele-learning but also the future of the learning process, context, and enterprise, could perhaps be left, like a good mystery novel, as a secret until the reader reaches the end of the book.

But one of the changes in learning that this book documents is that learning is becoming more of a process of making links and connections than of working through someone else's way of developing a thought. Therefore, for those who want to know where my own ideas about tele-learning are going before they decide to embark on the journey of this book, here are the predictions from Chapter 10. Presenting them out of context here is a risk, in that the reasoning to support the predictions is accumulated through the intervening pages of the book. But it is also a demonstration of some of the risks in an increasingly hyperlinked world: risks of jumping in rather than building-up, of telling one's message in a sound-bite rather than in a reflective analysis. Despite this risk, here are the predictions from Chapter 10.

PREDICTIONS ABOUT TECHNOLOGIES

PREDICTION 1: The Network Computer: An Ubiquitous Learning-Station

Advances in technology—distribution technologies, user-access platforms, and client-server architectures—will make it possible for tele-learners to use the same "learn-station" for both real-time and asynchronous interactions and for their choice of combinations of text, video, sound and graphics. This learn-station will be affordable and portable because it will primarily function as a client or network computer, downloading temporarily what it needs locally but mainly working off network resources.

PREDICTION 2: CONTROLLED, AND WITH A PRICE TAG...

Just as the technology will give tele-learners the possibility of choosing from multiple types of representation forms, choosing among vast numbers of central sources, and choosing to make connections with any of a wide range of human contacts, so too will the technology be used to control access to these resources and to support a uniform way to make learners pay for this access.

PREDICTION 3: "WEBWARE" AS THE BREAKTHROUGH TECHNOLOGY FOR TELE-LEARNING

The World Wide Web and its various tools and access technologies ("Webware"), *circa* 1995 and their subsequent generations, are the breakthrough technologies for many forms of tele-learning—together forming the environment that can support and stimulate tele-learning for individual learners, in the teacher-led classroom, and in the course-at-a-distance.

Prediction 4: The Evolving Internet and WWW

Central sources for tele-learning in the year 2005 will be the future generations of 1995 WWW servers. Subscribers at their "learn stations" will work and communicate through client environments that are evolutions of the WWW clients of the mid 1990s; multimedia resources will be accessed and delivered through interconnected distributed systems, by innovations such as multicasting and other aspects of network technologies. Separate applications ranging from video-conferencing and video-on-demand to ftp and computer conferencing, will all be entered via a WWW-like hyperlinked structure and through a common type of user interface evolving from the browsers of 1995.

The "information highway" will emerge out of the Internet system of the mid 1990s, but with adequate speed and bandwidth to support multi-point multi-media connectivity. "Intranets" within organizations with transparent gateways to an inter-networked system will be standard. As the Internet is a network of networks, The WWW will be a web of webs.

Predictions Relating to the Educational Enterprise and to Learning

Prediction 5: New Communities, New Knowledge Utilities

Two of the most significant changes to education involving tele-learning will be the increasing importance of virtual communities to complement face-to-face relationships in learning, and the increasing use of "knowledge utilities", particularly through hyperlinked distributed environments such as the 1990s WWW, to complement the textbook and the teacher as major information sources. Distributed intelligence, through the integration of distributed resources and human expertise, will be the way to confront the inadequacies of individual competency in an increasingly complex world.

Prediction 6: Secondary School and Enrichment

Teachers, and later on, secondary school students will come to routinely access distributed multi-media resources for resource materials, and will make occasional contacts with distributed experts for feedback and motivation. "Virtual field trips" will be part of the secondary-school experience, but more and more, will be associated with individual learning outside of the school setting.

PREDICTION 7: YOUNG CHILDREN AND CREATIVITY

When elementary schools are able to get comfortable to access both intranet and internet systems, their students will be the learners making particularly creative use of the WWW and its successors.

PREDICTION 8: FROM TRAINING INNOVATION TO PEDAGOGICAL RE-ENGINEERING

Training departments in businesses will lead the way in increased use of multi-media networks for more-efficient one-to-one tutoring and access to multi-media training materials, on the job and just-in-time. These conceptions of educational efficiency will be gradually reflected in "pedagogical re-engineering", particularly in post-secondary institutions, changing the profile of learning experiences.

PREDICTION 9: THE TELE-LEARNING LANDSCAPE OVERALL...

- In post-secondary education, the use of the WWW and its successors and other forms of networking will increase both quantitatively and imaginatively. Video-on-demand will have important educational applications.
- Elementary schools will make use of tele-learning for creative enrichment. Secondary schools will make use of tele-learning to extend learning opportunities. In both these cases, however enrichment will occur without substantial "re-engineering" of instructional approach.
- It will be in various training and professional development settings and in post-secondary institutions that the most radical pedagogical re-engineering will take place, toward just-in-time learning and learning-on-the-job and away from the concept of learning as "going to a course". The concept of distance will loose meaning, in terms of many learning experiences at the post-secondary level.

PREDICTION 10: FOR MANY INSTITUTIONS, NOT YET A RADICAL CHANGE...

Despite the changes that will be occuring, the majority of schools and post-secondary education institutions and training centers will be operating in 2005, structurally, in ways similar to their organizations in 1995.

PREDICTION 11: COMPETITION FOR ESTABLISHED EDUCATION

Although institutional organizations will be slow to change from a structural point of view, schools as well as post-secondary institutions will be forced to compete with each other and with market-place course providers for student enrollment. Schools will still function as they do now, but students will increasingly pick and choose where and what they learn, and from whom. Tele-learning technologies will make this choice process possible. This competition will stimulate change.

PREDICTION 12: TOWARD A NEW PARADIGM...

Tele-learning, connecting to resources and people via communication technologies, will be an important instrument of a new paradigm of educational organization and of a new social conception of learning, in ways similar to those accompanying the printing press and the popularization of books some centuries before.

PREDICTION 13: THE TEACHER STAYS CENTRAL

Competition will heighten the importance of good teaching (or tutoring, or guiding). Teachers will be still be important to tele-learning, and for those in organized educational settings and taking courses, the teacher will remain the central, critical variable in the organization and impact of the learning experience.

PREDICTION 14: A PARADOX...

The organization of education as we now know it, in its current paradigm, will continue; society will demand common standards and legitimization at the same time that society demands life-long learning and competence among its citizens. Society will want well-run and orderly schools at the same time as it wants universal access to interconnectivity for learning purposes. These sorts of contradictions will cause great tensions. Society will want freedom of expression and opportunity, but also quality control of experience and product.

PREDICTION CLUSTER 15: OVERALL, IMPORTANT CHANGES WILL BE THAT...

- Tele-learning will blur the distinction between expert and non-expert in the learning context;
- Tele-learning will support competition and diversity in institution, course, resource and teacher selection;
- Tele-learning will lead to a break with the dominance of the textbook and pre-determined curriculum toward an expectation that part of learning is to sort between a wide range of resources, extracting and synthesizing from many sources rather than mastering what one person or team has written.
- Assessment and evaluation will have to evolve to handle the individual's intellectual discoveries that are not known in advance to a test developer.
- Being an effective teacher in a tele-learning world will require skill and insight into linking: linking of persons, of ideas, of concepts; and of helping one's students, and one's self, see an idea or person as part of a learning web whose boundaries are continually changing, and whose attributes vary depending on one's vantage point.

So, this was a preview of the end of the book. But for those who like to start at the beginning, Chapter 1 is more orderly presentation of the perspective and content of the book, including the definition of the tele-learning that is at the core of all that is discussed.

Tele-learning is defined as:

...Making connections,
among persons and stored resources,
through communication technologies
for learning-related purposes.

Thus making connections, perhaps through the Internet and the World Wide Web, perhaps through one- or two-way video instruction, perhaps through computer conferencing, perhaps through interactive television, perhaps through desktop multi-media conferencing, and perhaps through combinations of these, is what this book is about...

1 Tele-learning: current scenarios and this book

In this chapter we introduce "tele-learning" and also this book. We set the scene through a brief look at some of the many different aspects of tele-learning that are important to teaching and learning. We look a bit at their technologies, but we look most at the people who are using those technologies. Welcome to the book and to our virtual excursion. . . .

This is a book about tele-learning. Intuitively, you probably already have a mental picture of what this term implies. Here are some possibilities of what you may be thinking, if you visualize in terms of technology-related categories.

Educational television, broadcasting, documentaries; people watching high-quality productions and presentations via a monitor

Computer-based communication, computers with a network connection, probably with Internet e-mail access: an individual reading and sending messages, reading and perhaps responding to other people's discussions or text materials

The World Wide Web: an individual scanning WWW pages, looking for information, printing or downloading interesting materials, and sending a message to persons associated with the pages

Computer-based communication, computers with a network connection, probably with Internet e-mail access: a class of students cooperating with another class of students on a joint project

Interactive television; compressed interactive video, video conferencing: people watching a monitor and talking with the people they are watching

A school, where there is one computer with a network connection: The teacher preparing lesson materials by capturing screens and downloading

A multi-media computer with a video window connected to a high-speed network: The professional working on a report getting advice from her colleague while they study the same document on their respective computer screens

Printed study materials and a telephone: The distance-education student making contact with his tutor and some fellow learners via audio conferencing

The university lecture hall, with a network-connected computer and a large-screen projection device: The instructor illustrating a lecture with visuals and simulations from remote locations, accessed through the WWW

The World Wide Web and e-mail: An instructor presenting materials for her course via a WWW site, and communicating with her students via e-mail

But when you are confronted with the term "tele-learning", perhaps you think not in terms of technologies but of concepts and big ideas.

TELE-LEARNING

Being there, while being here!

Just-in-time learning

Schools transformed into learning centres, with teachers as guides and fellow learners

Global Learning and Global Citizens

Learning independent of time and space

Lectures on demand, learn when and how you want...

Learning at the workplace

The Information Superhighway where every learner has an on ramp...

Global communities, networking as mentoring

Virtual libraries, field trips, museums

The World Wide Web...your own home(page) in cyberspace

A new kind of learner: in control, in communication

The electronic university... Schools without walls...

New colleagues, new perspectives, new possibilities...

Learning on the Information Superhighway...

Or maybe you are not disposed to these types of words and thoughts but instead you think of the enterprise of education in more utilitarian terms. You might respond to the phrase "tele-learning" with one of the following reactions:

- Will it improve cost effectiveness?
- Will it save travel costs because learners can remain at home or the workplace?
- Through it, can we reach more learners with the same staff?

- Through it, can we compensate for limited resources?
- Through it, can we deal with problems of geographic dispersion?
- Through it, can we reduce strain on physical facilities of the institution as more students stay at home to study?

OR. . .

maybe when you hear "tele-learning", your reaction is of a different nature altogether:

Tele-learning?
A bandwagon (again...)
A frill...
A fad...
A hype...

This book relates to all of these perspectives, the practical, the visionary, and the skeptical. It is one of our assertions that tele-learning is exciting and important *because* it can be viewed in so many different ways and at so many different levels of implications.

■ 1.1 THREE MESSAGES. . .

What can you expect in this book, then? This chapter gives a frame, a purpose, and an overview. We begin with an expansion of the types of educational scenarios shown at the start of this chapter, to further set the stage for thinking about tele-learning not in a certain way, but in many ways. Then we define tele-learning, and introduce three basic messages that flow through the entire book. The chapter concludes by discussing the book itself, how it is organized and what the purpose of writing this book even is, in an age of "tele-this" and "virtual-that". But before we go any further, what are the three basic messages of the book? We can express them in terms of three key phrases:

Tele-learning is:
A multi-faceted phenomena
A multi-player phenomena
A pedagogical phenomena

Read on, for a first look at these ideas. . .

■ 1.2 SCENARIOS FOR TELE-LEARNING

What did you think of when you were confronted with the words "tele-learning" at the beginning of this chapter? In this section we give some mini-scenarios that anticipate the contents of this book. Like the boxes at the start of this chapter, these scenarios are only sketches, to give a flavour of the diversity and possibilities of tele-learning before beginning to consider them more carefully. Let's look then at some sketches of tele-learning, all of which are happening, in 1995, in different ways and manifestations, in countries around the world. No one country, no one pedagogical approach, no one institution, no one person, no one technology, no one type of educational organization dominates tele-learning: that is part of its opportunity and challenge.

■ 1.2.1 WHAT ARE SOME TELE-LEARNING SCENARIOS?

Returning to your own mental model of tele-learning: What comes to your mind?

DISTANCE EDUCATION, TELEVISION-TYPE MODEL?

Perhaps you picture a group of persons in a room with a television monitor and a microphone, watching an expert in a far-away city as she teaches a course that seems directly aimed at the group. Occasionally the expert asks a question. The group members look to each other, briefly converse, and then one of them answers, through a microphone in their room. The instructor congratulates the group on the insightful question and answers immediately.

DISTANCE EDUCATION, LEARNING- MATERIALS MODEL?

Or perhaps you have a different thought? This time you picture yourself, enrolled in a distance-teaching university and busy, at home in the evening, with self-study of a package of learning materials. This package, which was delivered through the mail, includes a reader, workbooks, a study guide, a set of audio tapes, a video cassette, and some computer software for self-assessment on some of the concepts in the course through a drill-and-practice program. You see yourself ready to send in one of your assignments, so you log on through your computer and modem to the telephone number of a computer at your university, and when connected you first read a message from your tutor with comments on the last assignment, then transfer your current assignment through the phone lines to the tutor. Before you log off, you also send a message to your tutor, asking her both for some practical information and also indicating that you didn't understand the ideas in one of the exercises you have just submitted and hope that she will give you specific feedback if what you wrote was wrong.

GLOBAL PROJECTS MODEL?

Some of you, when you are confronted with the term "tele-learning" may be picturing something quite different indeed. When you think of tele-learning, perhaps you are picturing students in a secondary school, studying about topical issues such as those relating to the environment, and as one of their study activities, making a connection via e-mail to groups of students in two other countries. They are making this connection so that they can exchange data (including text and photographs) via the Internet with each other relating to that issue in their own communities, and work together on a common report.

CREATIVITY-ON-THE-WWW MODEL?

Or maybe some others of you are picturing something of quite a different nature: Young children, making their own World Wide Web pages, in which they publish short stories they have written, and illustrated with their own sketches. They invite comment on their stories through a form embedded in the template they are using for their pages, and then their teacher links the pages to the Web site maintained by their school. This site also includes a variety of other pages, some for parent–teacher interaction, some for other displays of student work, some for information about upcoming school events.

PROFESSIONAL DEVELOPMENT VIA APPLICATION SHARING?

But there are many more possibilities for your reaction to the word "tele-learning". Perhaps you are picturing yourself as a company manager, needing to learn how to handle a complicated new accounting package whose use is being required for all branch managers in your company? If this is your mental picture, you may see yourself going to a desktop video-conferencing unit in your building, and having a personalized learning session with a colleague in another branch of the company. Your colleague is already familiar with the new package, and has arranged to work through it with you during a 30-minute session application-sharing session. During this session, you both see, and share, the same package on your respective computers, you both can talk to each other, and you can see each other in small video windows at the top-right of your screen displays.

COURSE DELIVERY VIA THE WWW?

In 1995 many more persons became involved in tele-learning, through the use of the WWW as an environment for learning in higher education. Perhaps you picture this context when you hear the phrase "tele-learning"? You think of an instructor in a WWW-supported course who not only integrates her course materials with supplementary references and resources but also with links to valuable additional sources of discussion and information, all through the WWW site she has set up. In addition, you think of her using the WWW site as a frame for communication about the course materials with the students and with outside experts. You think of her experimenting with other possibilities that can be integrated into the site, such as embedding applications packages, or tutorials or case-study materials. Many of the case materials that she links to she has herself found and downloaded from another site on the WWW. She participates in a LISTSERV relevant to instructors in her area, and heard about the case-study material from the list.

LEARNING VIA THE OPINIONS OF OTHERS?

But for many thousands of persons in 1995 tele-learning probably means something quite different from any of the above. If you are one of this group, tele-learning doesn't mean taking a course; it means finding a group of persons interested in a topic that interests you, and learning from them, through reading their contributions to newsgroups and discussion lists, and through occasionally expressing your own ideas to them. Such learning may be with members of your own local community, engaged in debate about new regional laws and issues; with members of your professional community, associated with each other by discipline, not geography; or with members of newly forming "virtual communities", associated by a common interest and a common curiosity about each others experiences and opinions.

LEARNING BY NETWORKING?

When one interacts with others in one's profession, either as peers or in a mentor relationship, other valuable types of tele-learning occur. Perhaps peer networking is what you think of when you hear the phrase tele-learning? This would not be surprising, because for an increasing number of professionals, learning via networking is becoming a central aspect of their own professional lives and development. If you are one of these persons, "tele-learning" is for you probably most associated with this form of professional interaction.

And there are many more scenarios that will occur to different persons when they see the term "tele-learning". Some of the scenarios are generally familiar, others less so. The scenarios can range in complexity from "neat examples" for teaching a certain lesson, to metaphors for an "underlying information space in which we communicate and learn" (Lange, 1995, p. 32). All of the above scenarios, and others, will be illustrated in this book, because a major message of the text is that "tele-learning" is a multi-faceted phenomena with many manifestations.

■ 1.3 TELE-LEARNING: A DEFINITION

The mini-scenarios in Section 1.2 can help us anticipate what is intended by our definition of tele-learning for this book. In Chapter 2 we develop a definition in a more formal, careful way, with an emphasis on technologies and communication theory. Here, however, we are content to be more intuitive.

THE DEFINITION

Tele-learning is:
 making connections
 among persons and resources
 through communication technologies
 for learning-related purposes

Each part of this definition is amplified throughout the book.

■ 1.3.1 THE COMPONENTS

It is useful to comment on the main aspects of our definition of tele-learning, because many will have to enlarge their perspectives about tele-learning to get into the spirit of this book.

MAKING CONNECTIONS...

"Making connections" implies interactivity and deliberateness; thus we exclude from our domain of tele-learning non-purposeful flicking through television channels showing "educational programming" or clicking of links within World Wide Web pages, and the casual watching or reading that may occur as a result. The "making of connections" implies deliberate intellectual engagement. However, it does not have to imply talking or writing or button pushing or question answering or any other particular form of interaction. What matters is that cognitive connectivity is occuring. The making-of-connections may occur within a course organized by an educational institution, but it does not have to be within a course framework. There may be a teacher involved when the learner makes connections, but this also does not have to be the case. In all cases, however, both a cognitive as well as a technical connection occurs. The tele-learner is purposefully engaged in learning.

AMONG PERSONS AND RESOURCES...

The "persons" with whom a connection is made in a tele-learning situation may be experts, may be strangers, may be fellow learners, may be instructors, or may be anyone with an opinion about the particular learning domain. Persons may also be resources, if their experiences and comments can be of learning value to someone else. But resources can also be stored on different media in different representational forms, such as text, electronic datasets, graphics, photographs, analog or digital audio, analog or digital video, or in the case of multi-media, various combinations of these. In addition, persons can create resources, and resources can generate more resources (see the "Answer Web" in Chapter 8), or help to locate more persons who can be appropriate as learning connections. The persons and resources involved in tele-learning may be beyond what the learner could have access to in her ordinary learning context. But they may also be the same persons and resources, but made accessible in different ways and at different times than before, through tele-learning environments.

THROUGH COMMUNICATION TECHNOLOGIES

To be called tele-learning in the definition of this book, making connections among persons or resources occurs in part or entirely through communication channels that involve transmission of signals through the air or through some combination of wires, cable or fiber-optic networks, or through some combination of all of these. More and more, to make a connection between various points in a tele-learning situation, some combination of or even all of these communication channels are involved. In 1995, however, the interconnectivity of channels is far from established. By defining tele-learning as involving signal transmission through air, wires, cables, or fibre we are aware that we delimit tele-learning to 1995 distribution technologies. In the future, other possibilities may evolve that we are not considering now (sonic waves through the surface of the earth?).

FOR LEARNING-RELATED PURPOSES

Tele-learning is different than "edutainment" or tele-working, or tele-shopping, but its boundaries with these as well as "tele-discussions" or "tele-collaborative work" or other "teles" (which in 1995 are proliferating in the newspapers and other media) are less clear. Tele-learning has to do with learning, but it can involve those who support others in tele-learning, as well as actual learners and teachers themselves.

With this definition (which will be elaborated and illustrated throughout the book, beginning with a closer look at its technical aspects in Chapter 2), the first of our major assertions about tele-learning can be seen: tele-learning is a multi-faceted phenomenon.

■ 1.4 TELE-LEARNING: A MULTI-FACETED PHENOMENON

The major point of this chapter, and this book, is that all of the examples indicated in this chapter, and many others, are all aspects of what can be called "tele-learning". Box 1.1 emphasizes some of these facets:

Box 1.1

Tele-learning

- can take place in different ways
- in different settings
- with or without a teacher being involved
- within different sorts of instructional organization, including within a course or without a course being involved at all
- among different levels and types of learners
- via a variety of technologies
- and through a variety of pedagogies and learning approaches
- and for a variety of philosophical and strategic motivations

---

Tele-learning is already well established in many combinations of these possibilities, and just emerging in others. In this book, with examples from around the world, we hope to communicate this broad view of tele-learning. Thus, Box 1.2 expands Objective 1 for this book.

Box 1.2

Objective 1 for this book: To think of tele-learning as a multi-faceted phenomenon

By:

- Identifying different strands of tele-learning from a technological perspective, in particular those which might be called "television/video" types and those which might be called "network/Internet" types, and to see how these are converging
- Identifying different strands of tele-learning from a learning-organization perspective, including its use with classes that meet face-to-face, with class members that meet at a distance from one another, with individuals taking a course at their own pace and place; and with individuals who are learning outside of any organized course
- Identifying different functional emphases for tele-learning, including as a method of extending and enriching communication, as a tool for access to distributed resources, and as a learning environment to support collaborative and creative work
- Identifying different theories relating to the nature of learning that can be seen in different tele-learning settings, such as self-responsibility and self-motivated learning, the importance of the social construction of learning, or the importance of careful instructional design and effective lesson presentation

> • Identifying different tools, instruments, and environments for tele-learning such as video-conferencing systems (with or without computers being involved), on-line network services, WWW sites, computer-conferencing software, broadcast television, interactive television, the Internet, integrated hardware–software systems, e-mail systems, audio-conferencing, audio-graphics systems, shared workspaces, desktop multi-media systems, as well as telephone and fax

But it is not only the functions and manifestations of tele-learning that are diverse; so are the many different groups of persons that are involved in tele-learning. Another way to look at the tele-learning world is through the eyes of those involved with it.

■ 1.5 TELE-LEARNING: A MULTI-PLAYER PHENOMENON

Many professionals, particularly educational technologists, are involved in tele-learning support and delivery; and many learners and instructors and administrators and support persons are involved in the different forms of tele-learning activities. The number of both persons and forms is increasing rapidly. In this book we focus on these different sets of players and their needs and interests with respect to tele-learning. Who are tele-learning players? See Box 1.3.

Box 1.3

Tele-learning players and their major focuses

- Parents, concerned about the appropriateness and learning value of tele-learning for their children
- Families, learning together outside of school-assigned activities
- Citizens, learning about current issues in their various communities
- Learners in elementary and secondary schools, on the one hand concerned about help for their schoolwork and assignments, and on the other, just motivated to learn beyond what they are asked to do by their teachers
- Teachers in elementary and secondary schools, looking to enrich and extend what they offer to their students
- Decision makers involved with technology support for schools, districts, regions, and even countries, who must make decisions about tele-learning engagement and opportunities
- Educational technologists involved in the support of teachers, schools, and regions for various forms of tele-learning
- Teacher educators, preparing teachers or working with practicing teachers
- Professionals, increasing their own development through networking and through other means of independently constructed learning

- Adults, wishing to learn outside the setting of being a student in an educational institution
- Trainees in industry and other vocational settings
- Students in higher-education institutions
- Instructors in post-secondary education institutions, balancing teaching with research and professional activities
- Decision makers concerned with the infrastructure for tele-learning in post-secondary education institutions and training centres
- Educational technologists as designers of instructional materials and courses
- Educational technologists as designers of innovative tools and environments for tele-learning
- Educational technologists as support and service providers for teachers and learners involved in tele-learning
- Educational technologists as teachers of new generations of tele-learning professionals

In this book, we look at tele-learning through the perspectives of all these different players. What is particularly interesting is that the same person can be in different roles with respect to tele-learning at the same time: as for example, teacher and learner, educational technologist and instructor, instructor and designer of learning materials, etc. Thus a second objective of the book relates to multi-player awareness and is expanded in Box 1.4. Box 1.4 also indicates the major organizational decision of the book: to look at tele-learning through the eyes of different groups of persons. Thus Box 1.4 not only summarizes major players with respect to tele-learning but also indicates the chapters in the book that relate to the perspectives of those players.

Box 1.4

Book Objective 2: To be aware of tele-learning as a multi-player phenomenon

To become better aware of how tele-learning presents different problems, benefits and issues and requires different competencies of the different groups of those involved with tele-learning, in particular

- the independent learner, child or adult, at home (Chapter 3)
- the professional learner, at her desk or workplace (Chapter 4)
- the teacher in the elementary or secondary school (Chapter 5)
- the instructor in the post-secondary institution (Chapter 6)
- the decision maker involved with decisions about infrastructure, policy and support of tele-learning in a school, post-secondary institution, region or country (Chapter 7)
- the educational technologist involved in the design and development of courses, learning materials, tools, and innovative instrumentations for tele-learning settings (Chapter 8)

- the educational technologist involved in the support, service and education of others involved with tele-learning (Chapter 9)
- the educational technologist as researcher and visionary with respect to tele-learning (Chapters 8–10)

But functions and people are only two of the perspectives that we bring to tele-learning. The "learning" part of tele-learning is in many cases closely related to an instructional or teaching aspect. Those who design, deliver, and guide tele-learning experiences and resources are being enormously challenged to reconsider and re-engineer their own instructional practices. Thus a third layer of this book relates to tele-learning as a pedagogical phenomenon.

■ 1.6 TELE-LEARNING: A PEDAGOGICAL PHENOMENON

Athird objective for this book relates to the identification of new pedagogies and new approaches to education that can be associated with tele-learning, and in some cases, that can only occur because of tele-learning. But tele-learning is not only "new pedagogies", it is also enriched ways of carrying out familiar pedagogical approaches. We could call the first case "Doing things differently" and the second case "Doing things the same, but better" (or at least potentially better). Both of these require some system for defining what it is that a teacher or instructor does when she conceptualizes her instructional approach to a course.

■ 1.6.1 INSTRUCTIONAL COMPONENTS FOR COURSE DELIVERY

We describe, in Chapter 5, a way of analyzing one's pedagogical approach based on thinking of an overall learning experience (such as a course) as being typically composed of some combination of the following components shown in Box 1.5:

Box 1.5

Instructional components that can be combined to produce a lesson or course

1. Teacher presentation of concepts and information
2. Communication between teacher and student or between student and student about the learning content

> 3. Communication in the form of a discussion among more than two persons about the learning materials
> 4. Self-study, primarily involving reading
> 5. Individual practice and consolidation activities, such as exercises or essays, with some form of feedback
> 6. Group activities
> 7. Assessment and testing activities

For example, the teacher in a "traditional" elementary-school classroom is likely to do #1 only in short bits, to do #2 informally and in an on-going way, to plan daily variations of #5 and to a lesser degree #4, and to occasionally plan for #6 and #7. In contrast, the instructor in a post-secondary institution delivering a course via compressed video with two-way interaction to learners at a remote site may plan carefully for #1 and #2 during the live sessions, will assign #4 for times between the interactive sessions, and may plan for one or two events in #5 and #7 between and/or after the interactive sessions.

Although the boundaries may overlap, such as when questions and answers are exchanged during a presentation of concepts (thus Category #2 inside of Category #1), in general it seems that courses can be operationally expressed as some weighted combination of the seven categories in Box 1.5. In some settings, one or more of the categories may have a value of zero. If we think of the learning experience from the point of view of the learner as expressed in terms of a unit of time overall, then we might see the following "pedagogical profiles" for the two examples discussed in the previous parragraph, plus two other familiar instructional settings, in the way expressed in Table 1.1.

One of the ways to think about tele-learning is to ask how one of the specific components of a course represented by the rows in Table 1.1, can be made better, without changing the overall balance of the components. We could call this "pedagogical enrichment".

■ 1.6.2 DOING THE SAME THINGS, BUT (PERHAPS) BETTER: PEDAGOGICAL ENRICHMENT VIA TELE-LEARNING

The teacher may wish to maintain the pedagogical profile of a course, but to enrich what goes on within one or more of the components within the course, via tele-learning. In the elementary-school example in Table 1.1, the children may do a different type of group activity, one that involves children in another classroom, via tele-learning. In the secondary-classroom example, the teacher may give the students a handout to accompany a lesson presentation that includes up-to-date

Table 1.1 Pedagogical profiles of four instructional situations, with percentage of total learner time spent in each instructional component

Instructional Component	Elementary-classroom example	Secondary-classroom setting	Two-way video example	Distance education setting, based on learning materials
1. Presentation by teacher	10% of learner's time	25%	15%	
2. Communication between teacher and student	10%	5%	5%	
3. Group discussion			5%	
4. Self-study, by reading	10%	10%	30%	50%
5. Individual practice and assignment	30%	25%	30%	50%
6. Group work	15%			
7. Examination	5%	15%		
8. Other	20%	20%	15%	

information the teacher obtained the evening before, from various Internet resources. In the two-way video example in Table 1.1, the learner during self-study may be accessing and studying resource materials that she obtains herself from many different locations via the use of a WWW search engine as a tele-learning tool, instead of only studying pre-set materials in the prescribed textbook. In the distance-education setting based on a learning-materials model, the student may be able to access a WWW site that supports the course he is studying and through this site interact with some simulation software that reinforces concepts in the course. This would give a different dimension to the 50% of the course allocated to individual practice.

In each case, the overall pedagogical profile of the course in terms of balance among instructional components may stay the same, but the richness of a component is increased via tele-learning.

■ 1.6.3 DOING THINGS DIFFERENTLY: PEDAGOGICAL RE-ENGINEERING

Tele-learning can be used to do more than enrich existing pedagogical practice; it can be used to change the balance among components within that practice, or to bring new combinations of components that did not emerge before or perhaps were not even possible before. In the examples in Table 1.1, the "0%" for group discussion in learning-material based distance education can be changed to, perhaps, 15% of the learner's total time, through the addition of computer conferencing. The learner in the two-way video situation can add personal asynchronous communication with the instructor and can add asynchronous discussion among her classmates and the instructor together to the pedagogical balance of the course experience again through the integration of computer conferencing as a instructional component of the course. In the two-way video example, this would change the balance among instructional components of the course, by increasing the percentage in Categories #2 and #3 and thus reducing the relative importance of some of the other categories.

Throughout this book, we look at different ways in which instructional activities can be adapted in both their balance and combination through tele-learning. We can call this "pedagogical re-engineering".

This pedagogical discussion relates to the third general objective for this book which we expand in Box 1.6:

Box 1.6

Objective 3: To see tele-learning as both pedagogical enrichment and pedagogical re-engineering

By...

- Identifying examples in a variety of learning contexts of how tele-learning can be used to either enrich and deepen one or more of basic instructional-strategy categories, or can be used to re-engineer the balance of learner time and involvement among the categories.
- Identifying how the World Wide Web in particular is emerging as an environment for both pedagogical enrichment and pedagogical re-engineering

Thornburg (1995) expresses these ideas of pedagogical enrichment and pedagogical re-engineering succinctly when he says:

Tele-learning allows us:
to do the same things, but differently...
but also,
to do things differently.

Both of these aspects are important; we give many different examples throughout the book.

In this section, we have given our, somewhat intuitive, definition of tele-learning, and identified the three major goals of this book. In the next section, we look more closely at the book itself.

■ 1.7 A BOOK ON TELE-LEARNING? WHY? AND FOR WHO?

It may seem counter-intuitive to write a thick *book* about innovating educational delivery through tele-learning. In this section we explain how the book is integrated with a WWW site, and how more generally tele-learning does not threaten the book as a medium but can enrich and expand the book's applications. We also suggest more specifically who is intended as the target audience of the book, suggest different ways the book can be used as a learning resource, and highlight an important aspect of the book: its international orientation.

■ 1.7.1 WHY A BOOK?

On first glance, it may seem that a book about tele-learning is a strange combination of medium and topic. Looking at the seven instructional-strategy categories in Section 1.1, however, it is clear that tele-learning can be part of a learning experience that also includes other very familiar components, such as books, lectures, and face-to-face activities. Each medium has its own strengths.

EXTENDING THE BOOK...
However, this book will also be extended by a WWW site, to give the opportunity to update the WWW sites that are mentioned in the book and to communicate directly with the author in the context of a particular aspect of the book. Throughout the book, addresses of interesting WWW sites, active in late 1995, are given, in the full knowledge that in the course of time, some of these sites will disappear and better examples will emerge. They are here as examples of 1995 practice. Updated examples will be given in the WWW site approxi-

mately each six months, based on input from readers. The location of the WWW site accompanying this book is: URL `http://www.itcpmedia.com`.

Thus the WWW site associated with the book will not only present a hyperlinked overview also allow the book to be conveniently updated, and expanded not only through the author but through the input of others.

This, by the way, is one of the many ways in which the WWW can be a tool for pedagogical re-engineering. Self-study reading material, such as a book, can be made into interactive example material and a focus for communication, through associating a book with a WWW site.

■ 1.7.2 WHO IS THE MAIN AUDIENCE FOR THIS BOOK?

In terms of quantity of relevant material, one of the main audiences for this book are educational technologists, particularly those who also teach courses in educational technology (or its various associated domains) and supervise graduate work and research in educational technology. Such persons go by many different names in their different countries and organizations; Box 1.7 repeats Box 8.1 from Chapter 8, in which overlapping terminology for educational technologists is identified:

Box 1. 7

Educational technologists and overlapping classifications

Educational media specialists
Educational communications specialists
Educational communication and technology specialist
Educational materials developers
Educational software designers
Computers in education specialists
Educational library media specialists
Educational information technology specialists
Education and training systems designers
Learning technologists
Educational media and technology specialists
Educational media services specialists
Instructional technologies
Instructional media specialists
Instructional systems design specialists
Instructional resources specialists
Instructional developers
Instructional systems designers
Instruction and performance technologies

In this book, for simplicity, we use the term educational technologist throughout, but ask the reader to make a mental translation into the terminology that seems more familiar in his or her context and language. Whatever they are called, persons in work categories related to those listed in Box 1.7 are a main target group for this book. This is also my own home-base group.

The professional educational technologist is likely to find directly relevant materials in many if not all of the chapters of this book, but the book is also intended in its various parts for other major groups of tele-learning participants. In Table 1.2 we suggest various combinations of sections of the book for persons in the groups listed as tele-learning players in Box 1.3.

Table 1.2 Chapters of interest for different tele-learning participants

Group\Chapter	1	2	3	4	5	6	7	8	9	10
Parents	x		x		x					x
Families (adults and children, at home)	x		x		x					x
Citizens	x		x	x						x
Teachers in elementary and secondary schools	x		x	x	x				x	x
Decision makers involved with technology for schools, districts, regions	x	x			x		x		x	x
Teacher educators	x			x	x	x			x	x
Professionals, wishing to increase their own development				x						x
Instructors in higher education	x	x		x		x	x	x	x	x

Decision makers concerned with infrastructure for tele-learning in higher education and training	x	x				x		x	
Trainers	x	x			x	x		x	
Educational technologists as designers of instructional materials	x	x	x				x	x	
Educational technologists as designers of innovative tools and environments	x	x	x				x	x	
Educational technologists as support and service providers	x	x		x		x		x	x
Educational technologists as instructors of educational	x	x	x		x			x	x

Although a common glossary appears at the back of the book, the chapters can be read in a relatively independent manner, anticipating a modular approach for reading the book. There is cross-referencing among the chapters, but they can be read in any order. Each chapter has its own link in the WWW site accompanying the book, where the experiences related in the chapters can be linked to others and continually expanded. An extensive reference list is contained at the end of the book.

■ 1.7.3 How to use the book?

The book is intended to be used in four distinct but overlapping ways.

To read, for interest!

The book can, of course, just be read, as a commentary and a personally experienced inventory.

To use as a textbook

The book is also meant to be used in post-secondary courses relating to tele-learning, such as those taken by pre-service teachers who will focus probably on Chapter 5; or those taken by experienced teachers perhaps at the graduate level in university settings, who might supplement Chapter 5 with Chapters 4, 9 and 10. Specialists in educational technology could use Chapters 2, 8 and 9 as text material in graduate-level courses, and specialists in educational administration and policy could find Chapters 2 and 7 useful. Chapter 10 can be read by itself, as a basis for discussion or reflection or debate, or be included in the readings for any of the types of post-secondary courses just indicated.

To use as a reference

Researchers can find the references useful throughout the book. Graduate students particularly who are looking for up-to-date references reflecting a broad international spread will appreciate the resources that are assembled here. Practitioners can find the many examples and references also useful. There are approximately 1,000 references cited throughout the book, the great majority of which are from 1994 and 1995, as well as references to hundreds of WWW sites visited while the book was in preparation. The references are chosen deliberately, out of a much larger collection of possibilities, to reflect a balance in themselves between research and practice, and internationally.

The Interfaces

In addition to the chapters, there is a brief section between each chapter that serves as a sort of interface between the chapters. Each of these relates to a particular topic that a reader may like to see summarized concisely outside of the specific tele-learning content. Box 1.8 shows the topics covered in these Interface Sections.

Box 1.8

"Interface" topics

Between Chapters...

1 & 2:   **Interface 1.** The Internet: Everyone Connected with Everything?
2 & 3:   **Interface 2.** The World Wide Web: Technologies and Metaphors
3 & 4:   **Interface 3.** The World Wide Web: New Developments
4 & 5:   **Interface 4.** Read/Written a Good Book Lately? New Forms of Publication
5 & 6:   **Interface 5.** Providing an On-Ramp: Network Service Organizations
6 & 7:   **Interface 6.** Doing It In Style: Design Guidelines for WWW Environments
7 & 8:   **Interface 7.** The Internet from a Global Perspective: Culture, Circumstances and Technology
8 & 9:   **Interface 8.** Meet You On Line: Being a Learning Group at a Distance
9 & 10:   **Interface 9.** Look What My Students Did! : The WWW as a Learning Tool

The references for these Interface Sections are grouped separately at the end of the book.

■ 1.7.4 WHY AN INTERNATIONAL OVERVIEW?

A final point of emphasis in this book is its orientation not only to a broad range of technical possibilities for tele-learning, to a broad range of participants in tele-learning, and to a broad range of ideas for pedagogical enrichment and re-engineering via tele-learning, but also to a broad range of countries and cultures in terms of the experiences cited and references used throughout the book.

This book is not over-balanced in terms of any one country, nor does it assume the dominant form of tele-learning in a particular country must be or should be the dominant form elsewhere. While the book is the work of a single author, the ideas and perspectives of literally about two thousand persons from over fifty countries have influenced what is written. Many of these persons are indicated in the references given in the book. I have made a special effort to demonstrate the diversity of tele-learning and tele-learning expertise by bringing in this international approach. A careful effort has been made to remain culturally unbiased. The internationalism of the book makes it suitable for instruction and reflection wherever an English-language text is appropriate.

The tele-learning phenomena is a vibrant example of how much we can learn from each other, when geographic distance looses meaning. It is hoped that this book reflects this.

■ 1.8 AND WHAT IS MY OWN PHILOSOPHY ABOUT TELE-LEARNING?

I will close Chapter 1 with a personal statement, and then not return to my voice again until Chapter 10. What do I believe about learning, and about tele-learning? Some of my most powerful beliefs are in Box 1.9:

Box 1.9

My beliefs about tele-learning

- I believe connectivity to be vital to learning; connecting me to persons and resources that stretch my thinking and the walls of my room and mind, the corridors of my experience, and the materials in my file cabinets. I live in The Netherlands: my mind lives all over. I talk through my fingers and my keyboard every day to colleagues who are to me real, not virtual, and also to my students who I also see face-to-face and who are very real. I am absorbing through my eyes and ears an incredible amount of new ideas
- I believe that an exciting amount of creative energy is now occurring in the tele-learning domain, particularly in 1995 with the WWW, that is unlike anything I have seen in the educational technology domain in the 30 years since I started using an overhead projector in my teaching as a way to extend my pedagogical capabilities via technology
- I believe that tele-learning can facilitate better learning and better teaching in face-to-face settings as well as in distributed settings
- I believe, with the rapid convergence of technologies occurring in society coupled with changes in social and economic aspects of society, that the role of tele-learning in a new paradigm of education can be predicted (and I dare to do this in Chapter 10)
- But even in the here-and-now, in 1996, I believe tele-learning can extend learning and the pedagogy of learning in many exciting ways
- And I believe the educational technologist has a powerful opportunity to not only make a contribution to tele-learning but take a leadership role within it

---

The above are beliefs; there are also things I feel quite confident in saying. Some of these are in Box 1.10.

Box 1.10

My framework for tele-learning

- Beside what I believe, I also know that integrating any innovation into learning and teaching is difficult, that access to tele-learning technology is still difficult for most of us, and that tele-learning means I spend more time, not less, with my own learning and that of my students

- I know that being a change agent without seeming to be a bandwagon jumper requires a careful balance of realism and vision
- I know that personal contact, not with the world, but with individuals who matter to you is so very important, not only to tele-learning but to one's life
- And I know that I learn much from my students, all of whom get to experience my continual experiments with tele-learning in my own teaching, and teach me about the potential and limitations of my ideas

So, these things together shape my message about tele-learning in this book.

INTERFACE 1: THE INTERNET

CONNECTING EVERYBODY TO EVERYTHING?

THE INTERNET: WHAT IS IT?

The Internet is an inter-network of computer networks—many, many networks—connected through gateways and sharing two important characteristics.

The first of these is that all these networks agree to use the same conventions to decide how data will be moved between programs, how messages will be moved, and how errors will be handled. These conventions are called **protocols.** The system of protocols shared by networks in the Internet system is called **TCP/IP** (Transmission Control Protocol/Internet Protocol), which were developed in 1974 by Robert Kahn and Vinton G. Cerf, two Americans. The voluntary agreement of networks around the world to use this protocol makes the Internet possible.

The second important characteristic that all the networks in the Internet system share is a common way of addressing messages, and a common way of identifying computers connected to the Internet. Each computer that accesses the Internet has its own Internet Protocol **(IP) address**, made up of four numbers, each one less than 256, such as 137.113.10.35. Luckily, because such strings of numbers are hard to handle and recognize, the computers in the Internet system also represent their IP addresses with **domain** names. Domain names can have many parts, each separated by a period, and in a particular order:

- Left-most, the name given to the specific computer through which an individual connects to the Internet
- Right-most, the highest-level domain to which the computer is associated, usually a country or one of a limited number of categories, such as com for commercial.

For example, the domain name for the computer by which I am connected to the Internet is:

```
edte.utwente.nl
```

where edte is the name of the server in my faculty ("edte" was chosen as a short form of **E**ducational **Te**chnology), utwente is the name for the my university's network system to which our faculty LAN is connected, and nl stands for The Netherlands.

And who decides all these names and conventions? Again, it is voluntary. The Internet Domain System, through a number of computers around the world each responsible for keeping track of which computers are in its geographical area, converts domain names into actual IP addresses and moves messages along. A new computer that wishes to be connected as part of the system needs to register itself with this system. In June of 1995, new domain-name requests were being handled by this system at the rate of 1.2 per minute. The Internet Network Information Centre (INTERNIC) serves as the registrar for domains.

In summary, the Internet is not really a "the" at all, but a network of networks. Some of these are primary networks which are called **backbones.** Sometimes these networks use fiber-optic cable or even satellites that relay data over radio channels. The data are "chunked" as packets, given a heading indicating their destination, and computers along the network determine how best to route the data along from link to link.

WHO IS USING THE INTERNET?

If we could freeze time at a split-second, we could list and count all the computers with names in the Internet domain system. But as this amount is changing every portion of a minute, no number will remain accurate by the time it written down or stated. Also there is no real way to estimate the number of users of the Internet, each with their own address. Why? Because many of the computers with an IP addresses on the Internet are in fact hosts to which many other local computers can connect. Each host organization keeps track of its own set of users authorized to connect to that host and determines its own way to give those users each a personal address. In my institution, we currently use our last names if there are no redundancies. Thus my own address is:

collis@edte.utwente.nl

Because there is no registry anywhere asking each of the millions of host computers how many unique addresses are associated with that host, nobody knows. All we can do is make projections, based on samples and surveys and averages. Some of these projections (in 1995):

- Between July 1994 to July 1995, the number of registered hosts connected to the Internet rose from 3.2 million to 6.6 million; based on this the projection is made that by 1999 there will be 120,000,000 hosts and given a certain average number of persons with addresses per host, it is estimated that "everyone on earth will be on the Internet by 2004".
- In 1995 about 4 million of the Internet's hosts are in the US, the rest in about 100 other countries, but aggregate growth is higher outside the US than within. Hosts in Western Europe doubled in the year ending in July 1995 (from 730,000 hosts to 1,400,000 hosts).
- The world leader in Internet penetration is Finland; on a per-capita basis Finland, Norway and Sweden are among the top five countries in the world relative to the number of computers connected to the Internet. It is also estimated (1995) that 37 million persons aged 16 and above in the US and Canada have access to the Internet.
- The com (commercial) domain has been the fastest growing domain since 1993 and is the largest domain (as of July 1995).
- Internet users tend to be male, upscale socio-economically and to have university degrees.
- Internet users average 5 hours and 28 minutes per week on the Internet.

WHAT ARE USERS DOING WHEN THEY ARE CONNECTED TO THE INTERNET?

Basically, there are only a limited number of applications or tools or services available on the Internet. These include:

- Remote login (telnet)
- File transfer (ftp)
- Electronic mail (e-mail)
- Network news (newsgroups)
- Real-time communication (Internet Relay Chat)
- Information systems (such as Gopher and WWW)

The major change in what users are doing with the Internet has been the skyrocketing growth of the **World Wide Web** in 1994 and 1995. In terms of percentage of packets of data and of bytes, the WWW became in 1995 the highest-volume service in terms of use on the Internet.

The WWW (see **Interface 2**) and e-mail are seen as the applications driving the growth of the Internet, and most pointing to the Internet's major applications in the future: **personal communication** and **electronic hyperlinked publication.**

WHAT ISSUES AND DEVELOPMENTS ARE MOST IMPORTANT IN THE FUTURE OF THE INTERNET?

With respect to issues relating to the Internet and emerging or seen as critical in 1995 are:

- Dealing with the growth of the Internet
- Dealing with the growth of commercial use of the Internet
- Maintaining adequate security for data, computers, and users
- Controlling what those in one's domain can access or do with the Internet; protecting children and citizens from information perceived as harmful; balancing this with freedom of expression
- Paying for adequate services: Who pays, and for what?
- Dealing with issues of ownership and copyright
- Determining who has access, and who should be in the position to make these decisions

With respect to technical developments, major growth areas aside from those directly related to the WWW (see **Interface 3**) include:

- Handling multi-media including real-time audio and video via multi-casting
- Meeting the increasing demands for higher bandwidth and higher speed
- Accessing the Internet through a variety of entry possibilities, such as through BBSs
- Integrating tools and tasks for the user through a common interface.
- Microsoft's Corporation's commitment to the Internet as "the primary driver of all new work we are doing throughout the product line."

References relevant for the Interface sections are grouped at the end of the book.

2 Tele-learning: what are the technologies for being connected?

It can sometimes seem that there are a bewildering variety of terms and technologies associated with "tele-learning". In this chapter we give an overview of the technologies associated with tele-learning by first seeing them in terms of three main categories: technologies to transform a message, technologies to transmit a message, and technologies to receive a message. We then pay attention to some specific aspects of two streams of development in tele-learning technologies: the video-technology stream, from broadcast signals to digital compressed-video conferencing; and the data-communication stream, from the simplest forms of bulletin-board systems and e-mail to the 1995 phenomena, the World Wide Web. We look particularly at the emerging convergence of technologies into desktop multi-media conferencing that can bring text, graphics, hyperlinked applications, and audio-video communication all into the same desktop computer. For all these technologies throughout the chapter, we consider the implications for tele- learning. We then move to the four participant perspectives that we use for the bulk of this book—the individual learner, the teacher or instructor in an educational institution, the educational decision maker, and the educational technologist—and sketch the combination of tele-learning technologies and communication forms that have been of most relevance to them in the past, at the present, and in the future.

The chapter thus serves as a birds-eye view of the technological landscape of the book. It is the only chapter that focuses on technology itself; the rest of the book focuses on people and what they do, through technologies, in a tele-learning world.

▓ **2.1 The core components: transform, transmit, receive**

▓ **2.2 Video technologies for tele-learning systems: From tv to tele-presence**

▓ **2.3 Network tele-learning technologies: from a BBS to the WWW**

▓ **2.4 Combining technologies: desktop multi-media conferencing systems**

▓ **2.5 Tele-learning technologies through the eyes of the user...**

Objectives

After this chapter you should be able to:

● Explain how technologies can affect the communication process in learning

● Be aware of three major generic categories for tele-learning technologies: technologies to transform a message into a form ready for analog or digital transmission; transmission technologies, including those for video technologies and those for networks of various bandwidths; and reception technologies

● Explain what is meant by the "video-stream" and the "computer-stream" of tele-learning technologies

● Identify some main developments in video technologies relevant to tele-learning, including broadcast television, interactive television, and digital compressed video instruction

● Discuss the implications of supporting two-way interactivity for video-stream tele-learning technologies

● Explain characteristics of networks for data transmission in terms of bandwidth, speed, and the physical natures of the networks (wire, cable, fibre)

● Identify some main developments in computer-network technologies and applications most relevant to tele-learning, from dial-in bulletin-board systems , e-mail, and computer conferencing, to the Internet and the client-server architecture and tools for the World Wide Web

- Describe the Internet and the World Wide Web in terms of network technologies

- Compare different tele-learning technologies in terms of control, ease of access, costs, and implications for the learning setting

- Consider tele-learning technologies from the perspectives of an individual learner, a teacher or instructor in an educational institution, an educational decision maker, and an educational technologist, and note the tele-learning technologies that are most relevant to them in the past and present

■ 2.1 THE CORE COMPONENTS: TRANSFORM, TRANSMIT, RECEIVE

As we define it, tele-learning involves some form of connectivity and connectivity can also be expressed as communication. In this chapter, we look closely at technology and its effect on communication as the background of all the tele-learning applications that we discuss throughout the rest of the book. Let us begin this technological journey with a human problem: How do I communicate to you so that you receive the message that I intend?

■ 2.1.1 TECHNOLOGIES AND THEIR EFFECT ON COMMUNICATION

In classic communication theory, communication occurs when a message goes through some sort of transmission process and is received at its destination in as close to its intended meaning as possible (Shannon and Weaver, 1949). Loss of intended meaning due to the communication technologies involved can occur in each step of this process: in the way the message gets transformed by the sender in order to send it, in noise that affects the transmission process, and in loss of data or distorted data as it is obtained by the receiver. Let us start with an extended example which anticipates the impact of tele-learning technologies in the learning process.

LOOSING MEANING WHEN TRANSFORMING

In communication with only the technologies of pencil and paper involved, the intention of the sender may be constrained by being only able to be expressed in symbols captured on paper. This constraint may be even worse if the pencil available is dull or has no eraser, or if the paper available is limited in quantity or is a colour which makes the pencil marks hard to read. The technologies that we use to transform our thoughts and ideas to a form that can be transmitted always have the potential to constrain and distort our intended meaning.

Part of the risk of loss of meaning rests in the skill of the sender in using the technologies involved in the transformation process—a skilled writer does better with her word processor than a less-talented writer—and much effort has gone into the process of making our "idea-transformation" technologies as helpful as possible to allow us to express ourselves as we intended. We can edit video and audio, we can revise drawings, we can edit text, all with editing technologies that in theory help the idea-transformation process. In fact however, many times these technologies thwart our sense of expression, because of the inherit nature of the technology itself. If I want to sing to express my happiness, I am fundamentally constrained if all I have to transform my thoughts is a word processor.

LOOSING MEANING DURING TRANSMISSION

Once my ideas are transformed into some sort of signal that can be transmitted, they have to be transmitted to get to their destination. Technologies can cause distortion here as well. Sometimes this distortion comes because the size and shape of my transformed message do not fit what the available carrier can handle: I have expressed myself in a wonderful song recorded on audiotape, but my limited-service postal service only accepts letters up to 20 grams. Or maybe it is not the lack of capacity of the carrier, but difficulty in getting access to what the carrier could offer: I express myself in a beautiful self-portrait, but cannot fit it into the mailbox in order to send it. And of course, the transmission technologies can also fail: my letter gets lost in the mail, my portrait gets damaged in processing.

LOOSING MEANING IN RECEIVING

The risk-filled life-story of my message is still not over once it arrives at the house of my intended receiver. Perhaps the address is a postal box, and my self-portrait can't fit in it. Or perhaps the address is a general code for a block of offices, and the message must still be sorted properly so that it eventually gets to my recipient. Perhaps, when she gets my audiotape, my recipient cannot listen to it because it is on a size of tape that she cannot fit in her audio playback unit. Or perhaps she does not have an audio playback unit and will have to travel to the house of her sister in another region of the city before she can listen to the tape, and she cannot leave work to do this, and she will have problems finding the time to get to her sister's house when her sister is home because their working hours are very different.

TELE-LEARNING: TECHNOLOGIES AND THEIR RISKS

The above anecdotes were chosen to anticipate some of the many problems associated with the technologies of tele-learning. The core idea of tele-learning—making connections through communication technologies—means that the technologies involved will shape and affect all of our connectivity. In this section, we look at the three aspects of communication that we described intuitively in the above anecdotes, but this time explicitly with respect to tele-learning. To do this, we will take a bird's eye view of the communication process in tele-learning, such a high-up birds' eye view that we simplify the process to three global phases: (a) the initiator of a message moves from her ideas to the transformation of those ideas in a form ready to transmit; (b) the transmission occurs through some kind of channel; and (c) those receiving the message must use various technologies to re-process and be able to access the message through their eyes and/or ears.

Each phase of this connectivity involves many different kinds of technologies (a) to transform and send, (b) to transmit, and (c) to receive, possibly to transform again and even to send again in order to finally deliver the message to the receiver in a form that s/he can process. We illustrate these phases in an intuitive way in the next sections. The illustrations here are not meant to serve as full technical definitions; at the end of the chapter we will indicate a selection of resources useful for that purpose for those involved in tele-learning from a more-technical perspective.

■ 2.1.2 TECHNOLOGIES TO TRANSFORM AND SEND

The first set of technologies we will consider are technologies for the sender or creator of a message, to help her transform what she wants to say or show or otherwise express into a form (a "signal") by which it can be transmitted, and to somehow "move" that signal so that it is "sent out". Boxes 2.1 and 2.2 illustrate some examples:

Box 2.1

Capturing a lecture and sending (broadcasting, transmitting, etc.) the signal out

Example 1: I am a teacher and want to teach a remote group of learners about a certain subject via broadcast television. The major technologies needed to capture what I am saying and showing are a television or video camera and microphones. Then some additional technology is needed, that usually includes transmission through coaxial cable, to move the signal from the television camera to the transmission facilities that will send the signal out.

Box 2.2

Supplementing course materials with a distribution list

Example 2: I am a university instructor and want to supplement my course by putting the students onto an e-mail distribution list and regularly sending them additional resources as well as extra comments from myself. This strategy is particularly useful as the course is about a topic for which there is not an adequate textbook because of rapid changes in the field (i.e., technologies for tele-learning!), and thus I would like to forward to the students the edited contents of a number of useful professional discussion groups and distribution lists which I myself receive. I also want to send them some materials that I have written myself, that include a fair amount of graphics and screen displays, and sending these electronically is much more efficient than making multiple printed copies. The distribution-list approach is also helpful, in that many of the students live at a distance from the campus, and only come in for the actual scheduled course sessions.

What I need to do is use my mailer program to set up a distribution list with the e-mail addresses of all my students. Then, when I want to send some material to them, I must edit the material on my word processor, and if I want to preserve the formatting and graphics, I must save it in a format appropriate for transmission and reception. Usually this involves encoding it in some way. I need a utility on my mailer programme to do this. I also need to experiment with different formats for saving my file and different utilities for encoding it, because I am aware that my students have many different types of word processors and de-coding utilities on their various mailer systems.

TECHNOLOGIES CONSTRAIN AS THEY TRANSFORM...

As the illustrations in Boxes 2.1 and 2.2 begin to suggest, there are many different technologies that can be involved in this "transform-and-send" phase of tele-learning. Someone has something they want to communicate, but the message has to be put into a form that will go through the air or through wires, cables or fibres. This means the message has to be captured as some form of signal or series of signals. Many different technologies can be involved in the processing of the message, included storage technologies (most often videotapes or computer disks) and signal-editing technologies.

And the words that are used in the above two examples reflect the different language and terminology that may be used by those involved with audio-video messages compared to those involved with computer-network messages. What are some of these differences?

Audio-video: concern for images and their quality

Those involved with audio-video use terms such as shoot, take, tape, zoom, pan, and broadcast (for a good overview, see Wetzel, Radtke and Stern (1994); see also

Chapter 8). They talk about transmitting or bringing a video tape to a transmission facility, they talk about microphones, cameras and lens and about cables. As they capture and edit, they are concerned about sound quality, about light and shade, about colour quality and about fades or transitions from one view to another. The reality that they capture is visual and audial; while it may be that it is words that are being heard, those words are profoundly integrated in what the eye of the receiver is meant to see as she or he listens to those words. Of course, text may appear as titling on the final image that is to be received or may be part of what is being captured by the television or video camera; in this case, the text must be minimal in quantity in order to be legible. Text basically serves a labeling function, as a supplement to what is being said and seen.

Computer-based: concern for text and its processing

Those involved with computer-network messages use different language to express their transformation processes and technologies. They talk about files and saving and backups and printouts. They capture their ideas via typing, letter by letter, through their keyboards or occasionally scanning. Frequently they reproduce what has been previously entered, by cut-and-pasting, or otherwise inserting or editing previously entered material. Everything must be in digital form; thus a picture must be scanned, or generated by a software package in some way. The editors they use are in themselves software applications, accessed via the same computer as the entry of the original message. When the "creation" task is finished, the file or set of files must be sent through the network via network and data-communication software. Files can be downloaded or uploaded from the network. It is becoming more and more possible to insert complex graphics in a computer-generated message, and also, with the appropriate hardware, software, and input peripherals to include video and audio in a computer file made on an "ordinary" computer. The storage requirements of digitized audio and video, however, are high, as is the network capacity needed to send those huge files from one computer to another. Thus the majority of computer-based messages are predominately text with some digitized visuals.

Transforming in real-time and with a team

And there are other variables in the message-transformation process that are directly related to the technologies used for the transformation, although they are not the technologies themselves. For example, when and how does one use the transformation technologies?

In general, those wishing to communicate via audio-video technologies often need many specialists to be involved in the process. Some must work the camera and microphones, others may be involved in the editing of the taped signals, others in the handling of the technologies used to transmit the live-transmission of edited signals from camera or editing equipment to the medium through which they are going to be transmitted. It is possible to sit in front of a console with a camera and microphone mounted on or near the console, and have one's image and voice picked up and transmitted with no one else in the room (we will talk about this when we discuss the various forms of video-conferencing) and it is possible to send the captured signal without any form of storage and editing, as is also the case with video-conferencing, but very often specialist technicians are involved and present when the original message is being communicated. Another set of technologies and technicians may be needed if the signal is to be compressed before it is sent (see Section 2.2.4, for more about compressed video technologies).

Transforming in private, and over time

With the creation of computer-based messages, in contrast, the act of creating and editing the message is often a personal enterprise, as personal as writing and typing. Revision may involve only the author's fingertips. Periods of time may elapse while the message itself is being expressed, unlike the real-time situation being captured by an audio-visual message. And, although humans are certainly involved in the maintenance of servers and local-area networks and wide-area network connections, the process of creating and sending one's message via computer-based networking often occurs without another human being overtly involved in the process.

IMPLICATIONS FOR TELE-LEARNING?

These differences in the technical process of capturing a message, processing it, and sending it out are very important to the different manifestations of tele-learning. They relate to control aspects: quality control as well as personal control over the expression of one's message. They relate to cost aspects, the capital investment needed to get started, the cost of personnel and equipment per communicated message. They relate to what is communicated as well as how; as McLuhan said in 1964, "The medium is the message". As we say throughout this book, the pedagogy of tele-learning in a audio-video situation where the voice and image are the main carriers of meaning has many differences from the pedagogy of tele-learning in a text-dominant situation, where the keyboard is the channel through which one expresses one's self. But fundamental to all forms of tele-learning is that intentions must be transformed, with various technologies, to either analog or digital signals, in order to be ready for transmission. This transformation process very much shapes and constrains what has happened to the original intention of the communication act.

For more information...

For more information about digital and analog signals, or any of the technical terms used in this chapter, see the Glossary, in which these terms are defined and explained. There are also general references listed in the reference section at the end of the book which can be helpful for more extensive technical definitions. In contrast, if this chapter were published as a WWW document, clicking on a term could bring the definition immediately up; with further clicking, cross-references to examples throughout the book could be immediately examined, and examples outside the confines of the book could also be visited. This is a good example of how the technology in which a message is transformed, in this case, paper and book vs a hyperlinked transformation approach via the WWW, can affect what the sender can offer to explain her meaning.

■ 2.1.3 TECHNOLOGIES TO TRANSMIT

Once the signal is processed into either a digital or analog form, the connectivity aspect of tele-learning comes into focus. The signal must move from one location to another (point-to-point) or to others (multi-point, in network terms; broadcast range or footprint in audio-video terms). Everyone reading either the technology or media or financial columns of newspapers in 1995 knows that a major evolution in control and ownership of broadcast frequencies, airwaves, satellite space, cabling systems, telephone-line and network systems, and other forms of distribution channels is taking place. Computer signals can be sent by satellite transmission; audio-video signals can be processed by compression technologies and sent through the telephone lines, and different forms of networks and network technologies allow parallel signals to be sent at the same time, video along with computer data, through the same conduit. Some useful overall sources of information for the evolution of transmission technologies can be found in computer magazines (see, for example, Reinhardt, 1994), newsmagazines (such as Elmer-DeWit, 1993), educational-technology journals (see for example Galbreath, 1995a, b) and of course on the WWW, such as Kegel, 1996, at

```
URL http://www.alumni.caltech.edu/~dank/isdn
```

Boxes 2.3 and 2.4 carry our two examples from Boxes 2.1 and 2.2 forward, to illustrate the transmission process in tele-learning.

Box 2.3

Transmitting the audio-video message

Example 1: The signal with my lesson may stay in analog form and be broadcast through the air, or be uplinked to a satellite which in turn sends it further, or be sent through a closed-circuit system of cabling or some other form of cable system. Or the signal with my lesson may at some point in the transmission be digitized and then further transmitted through digital telephone systems or ISDN networks. It may be transmitted through optical fibre. In any case my message arrives within seconds of when those involved with its transmission send it.

Box 2.4

Transmitting the computer-text message

Example 2: The local-area network to which my computer is connected is connected itself via a router to high-speed network internetworked with the Internet system. When I have completed processing my message, I attach it as a file to a general message that I also send to the students, pointing out to them, as I would in a lecture, what the intention is of this new reading material. My message, with its attachment, is then sent to each of the e-mail addresses of the students in my course. Many of them live on campus, but others live some distance away. All receive the message at the same time.

TRANSMISSION TECHNOLOGIES: THROUGH THE AIR

The most common one-way distribution systems for analog video data are broadcasting over standard UHF and VHF channels, satellite broadcasting, transmission via microwave systems, and direct-broadcast satellite systems (DBS). Barker (1992) and Kitchen and Hughes (1992) are among many sources for more information about these transmission technologies. The following is a brief summary.

Broadcast television

Broadcast television involves the transmission of video and audio over standard UHF and VHF television channels (for a good overview, see Hartwig, 1990). Typically cable is used to bring the signals from a receiving station to their final destination on the monitor of the viewer.

Satellite broadcasting

Satellite broadcasting involves the transmission of a broadcast signal from an earth station via an uplink to a satellite, where the signal is processed by a transponder, and sent, via a downlink, to a receiving dish. The process works by first having a satellite available and then having time booked on that satellite for one's signal.

There are in general two types of satellites, geosynchronous and low-altitude. Geosynchronous satellites orbit at a sufficiently high altitude so that they are always visible to their receiving dishes and thus can sustain two-way communication. Low-altitude satellites cannot maintain their position over a receive station for more than short time intervals so thus are more appropriate for "store-and-forward" broadcasting rather than interactivity. This is an important distinction from a tele-learning perspective.

Whatever the type of satellite, earth stations relay their uplink signals to a device called a transponder on the satellite (most satellites have between 12 to 24 of these). These transponders also have variations in terms of the frequency band in which they operate: for example, C-band and Ku-band. Each type of frequency needs a different type of receive dish and each has its own set of relative strengths and limitations.

Microwave systems

Microwave systems operate within various frequency bands and require a clear line-of-sight transmission between sender and receiver—thus not even a hill or a tree!

DBS systems

Direct-broadcast satellite (DBS) systems (as the term suggests, broadcasting directly from a satellite into the receive dishes of their subscribers), developed as competition to cable distribution systems. Programmers wanted to provide as many channels as possible to their subscribers and found the answer through the technique of compressing the broadcast signal so that eight programs could reside in the transmission space previously required for one. This technology is called direct-broadcast satellite and is an example of the use of compression technologies to handle analog video more efficiently. We talk more about compressed video in Section 2.2.4.

TRANSMISSION SYSTEMS: THROUGH A "PIPELINE"

When we use the term "through a pipeline", we are informally grouping together a wide range of network types and capacities and of network-access technologies. For this section, useful references include Fritz (1995), Furht (1994), Galbreath (1995b), Heldman, (1993), Mason and Bacsich (1994), Gilster (1993), Stallings (1992) and Swadley (1994). Again, we give only an overview here.

Network types: by physical nature, bandwidth and speed

In general we can distinguish networks in terms of bandwidth, meaning the amount of data that the medium can transmit in a given amount of time. If we think of a network as a pipeline, then bandwidth refers to the transmission capacity of the pipeline, (or to visualize things, rather like the old algebra problems where the learner is asked to calculate how long it would take to drain the water out of bathtubs with different diameter drains). Networks are frequently described as narrowband, wideband, and broadband. Table 2.1 highlights some distinctions.

Table 2.1 Narrow, wide, and broadband networks and some characteristics

Bandwidth	Physical characteristics	Speed	Technologies for tele-learning applications
Narrowband	Copper wire	64,000 bits per second	Voice, data transmission, email, fax, inquiry-and-response between terminal/client and host/server, some graphics transmission
Wideband	Copper wire,	fibre64K – 1.5 Mb/s	High-quality images, complex data blocks, CAD/CAM and graphic display networks, Picturephone, video conference, wide-area networks, computer-to-computer networks
Broadband	Fibre	50 Mb/s and multiples of this	High definition television, video-conferencing, and other image handling (medical imaging)

Moving from text to multi-media: not only bandwidth

The transition between data communications to multi-media communications requires a number of adjustments in addition to bandwidth. Traffic can be steady (constant bitstreams sent over the network in the correct order with virtually no delays), necessary for file transfer, video-conferencing, and interactive visualizations; or bursty, (where packets of data can be delayed or not transmitted in the correct order but are reassembled with minimum interruption to the end user). Bursty transmission is tolerable for e-mail, voice transmission, remote multi-media data base access, and collaborative group work (Vetler and Du, 1993, give some good diagrams of this; Elmer-Dewitt, 1993; Galbreath, 1995b; and Reinhardt, 1994 are good summaries as well).

Latency is also important, the time between when a signal leaves the origination point and when it arrives at the destination point. Latency variation causes jitter, which becomes unacceptable in audio-video transmissions. A critical difference is that data transfer is characterized by point-to-point distribution, while multi-media communication typically requires multi-point communication and multi-casting, where a single signal is replicated and sent to multiple destinations in a way that does not require multiple, point-to-point transmissions.

Access technologies

A critical aspect of network transmission relates to different access technologies, particularly leased lines, ISDN networks, and ATM technology. Useful references here are Bacsich (1994), Derfler (1990), Jacobs (1994), and Poole (1992). Box 2.5 summarizes some main points.

Box 2.5

Network access technologies

- Leased lines (at 1,544Mbps or 56kbps), are a traditional, if costly way to connect branches to a main-site LAN (local area network).
- ISDN enables digital transmission over the copper-wire pairs already installed for analog local telephone service. It provides end-to-end digital transmission particularly in the "local loop" between the home and institution as the end point and the telephone company's central office, as most modern telephone systems are already digital in their major transmission channels. With ISDN, voice, data and video can be carried simultaneously, although the quality of the video signal can vary. ISDN has been available for more than a decade as a technology, but has made slow progress in acceptance, partly because of a lack of standardization and partly because of the relative lack of interest among national telephone companies to "compete" with their existing voice-network services. In 1994, 19 countries had deployed a national ISDN network or networks sufficiently like ISDN to interoperate with them, with 12 of them in Europe and the remaining being Canada, Australia, New Zealand, Singapore, Hong Kong, Japan, and the US (Bacsich, 1994).

> ● ATM (or Asynchronous Transfer Mode) technology is compatible with existing wiring and protocols, and operates in a way that allows the integrated movement of voice, video and data as well as both constant and variable-bit traffic. ATM is predicted to be the network technology of the future (Galbreath, 1995b). However, products and services to make use of this technology are not much available, particularly for asynchronous applications; (see, Poole, 1995).

The Internet

We have already given an overview of the Internet in **Interface 1**, between Chapter 1 and this chapter, so here we will only repeat that the Internet is the international network of computer networks, based on their common use of a set of standards known as the TCP/IP protocol. Many different references abound; for example Swadley, 1994, as well as paper-based journals, both popular and scientific. The best source of information about the Internet, however, is via the WWW, where a search made in July 1995 with the keywords "Internet" and "beginners" brought more than 200 links to a broad variety of manuals, tutorials, discussion materials, and even multi-media software to download and use as simulation materials for self study.

For the non-technician, is it enough to know that TCP/IP standards provide:

● A common way of providing addresses (xx@xx.[xx].[xx].domain), for example, `collis@edte.utwente.nl` where the nl stands for the domain name of The Netherlands
● A common use of protocols predominately for e-mail, for remote log-in, and for file transfer

With these components, those with Internet access can send and receive personally addressed communication, can log-on to a remote computer through their own computers, can send and receive requests from other computers, and can send and receive files. This modest-sounding set of functions allows, as of July 1995, more than 6.6 million hosts, each connected to a number of computers in its own local network, to communicate commonly with each other, and to use the core applications in a way that is seamless to the user. A good overall reference of numbers about the Internet, such as how many host computers per country are part of the Internet system, can be found at:

Netword Wizards (1995)
`URL http://www.nw.com/zone/WWW/top.html`

For interesting miscellaneous information about Internet developments, see:

The Internet Index (Treese, 1995)
URL http://www.openmarket.com/intindex

Throughout this book, the power of the increased level of connectivity to the Internet in the first decade of 1990 will be continually noted in the many tele-learning examples that make use of the Internet as a carrier network. The particular phenomenon of the World Wide Web will be discussed in Section 2.3.2, as well as **Interface** sections 2, 3, 6, and 9, and illustrated throughout the book.

Thus there are some major distinctions about transmission channels that are important to tele-learning. The simplest distinction is "air or pipeline". Another distinction, as was shown in Table 2.1, is carrier capacity: how much can be carried, in terms of volume of signal. In 1995, the carrier capacity issue is still vital. Traditional telephone lines ("POTS"—"plain old telephone system") are severely limited in their capacity to carry bandwidth-hungry signals, such as video or even photographs let alone graphics for which quality is critical such as aerial surveys or X-rays. Even access to the WWW is extremely slow and frustrating for those with graphical user interfaces and slow modem connections.

Thus, generally, those who want video or who want simultaneous transmission of voice and data, are constrained if all they have access to for transmission are traditional networks. (Compressed video is a popular, partial, solution to this constraint; see Section 2.2.)

And there are many other important issues relating to transmission channels and tele-learning, such as those relating to who is given access to the transmission possibilities. Who decides what they must pay?

MAJOR DISTINCTIONS IN TRANSMISSION CHANNELS

Control and access

In 1995, the Internet system has become available to millions of persons who can themselves choose to send a transmission whenever they like. In contrast, there are few available systems for self-initiated audio-video transmissions although the number of persons with access to digital data services such as ISDN networks is increasing. For audio-video transmissions, in 1995 at least, the majority of transmission transactions are under the control of utilities or consortia or groups who make the usually significant investment in "buying satellite time" or buying time on a broadcast network. Closed-circuit video systems are well-established; and once an institution has made the commitment to and investment in closed-circuit television, then those authorized within the institution can make use of it. "Being authorized" however, even with an in-house closed circuit system, is not as easy as having a computer account and then sending an e-mail communication;

with a computer account to a system connected to the Internet, anyone can send a tele-learning message.

Costs

Costs are extremely complicated to isolate in tele-learning situations. For example, television transmission can be cost-efficient compared to numbers of learners reached, if the infrastructure is in place for the transmission to occur, if there are is a critical mass of learners that are being reached, and if extra personnel are not needed to provide personal support to these extra learners. Computer-network transmission can be cost-efficient regardless of the number of learners to be reached, if the infrastructure is in place for the transmission to occur. The cost of setting up and maintaining those infrastructures, with their transponders and satellites and towers and routers and switches and servers, and all the specialists involved with these technologies, and all the connectivity costs involved in giving senders and receivers access to the transmissions are very hard to delimit, and thus very hard to compare.

IMPLICATIONS FOR TELE-LEARNING?

In Section 2.4 we look more closely at the implications of being able to send audio-video and text signals simultaneously through the same channels from a technical perspective; and at various places throughout the book, from a tele-learning perspective. For now, however, the main questions to remember about transmission channels are (a) who controls the transmission, the sender or "middlemen"? (b) How does the channel capacity constrain the message being transmitted? (c) How much technical and human complexity is involved in making use of the channel in order to send a message? (d) How much does it cost to transmit a message and who pays for what?

■ 2.1.4 TECHNOLOGIES TO RECEIVE

There is usually not a single channel connecting the device by which a message is sent and the device through which the receiver will see and hear, or read and/or print the incoming message. Even at the receive end there may be many intermediary technologies. A broadcast audio-video signal may have to move from its receive station at a cablehead and be re-processed before it can move from cablehead to curb to home or classroom and then to the monitor which the learner will view. The signal may have to enter an institution and get further split among locations in the institution. A computer text-based message may have to move through various gateways and routers and servers to get to the mailbox of its intended receiver. In any case, technologies may be used to intercept and store the signal, on videotape or computer disk, so that the receiver can in effect choose when he wishes to access and view the message. There are many links in these chains of technologies, some of which are illustrated in the continuation of our two examples, in Boxes 2.6 and 2.7.

Box 2.6

Receiving the audio-video signal

Example 1: My signal needs to be received, perhaps by a satellite dish, perhaps by some other type of reception technology, and if it arrives in a digital form, it needs to be re-converted into an analog form. Then this audio-video analog signal has to get to the monitors of my distant students so that they can see and hear me by watching their own monitors. There are various technologies involved in this, especially if the signal has been compressed and thus must be decompressed.

Box 2.7

Receiving and processing the message

Example 2: My students need to be able to connect, via their own computers, to a network that is in turn connected to the Internet system. In addition to the software that they will need to connect to their own network and the software that is needed by their network in turn to connect to the Internet system, my students will also need to have software to de-code my attachments, if necessary, within their mailer systems. They will also need access to a printer because of the time and physical burdens in reading large amounts of text material from the screen. They probably will download my files, save them in a directories on their hard drives, and make a print copy of some of the material for their own study-material collections.

FLEXIBILITY IN RECEIVING, AND ITS IMPLICATIONS

A major distinction here is the flexibility with which the receiver of the computer message can deal with the message that has been sent, compared to the flexibility of the receiver of the audio-video transmission even if this receiver tapes the transmission on videotape for more-flexible watching at a later period. But increase in flexibility for the receiver, in either example, brings an extra require-ment in technology. Those taping a television or television-type transmission need access to video-recording equipment, both before, during and after the transmission, and need to know how to efficiently use the equipment. Those receiving a computer message need to have access to a computer and a network computer account, need to know how to use network and mailer software, may need to know how to handle the de-coding of attachments, will need adequate computer skills to manage their files and directories and will need adequate storage and print capacity to work effectively. And each individual must have these receiver-capabilities, both technical and human, if network tele-learning reception is involved. In contrast, with the taping of a video transmission, it may be that the taping is done for an entire school or region, with the organization of the taping and indexing process done by professionals in a district media centre (see Chapter 9).

MONITORS: THE WINDOWS TO TELE-LEARNING

In both of our examples, a common element is that the receiver of the message is receiving it via a monitor—a television-type monitor or a computer monitor. The nature of these monitors and their visibility also has a major influence on tele-learning.

Do the constraints of computer monitors mean that network tele-learning is only for individuals?

The monitor to which learners attend for audio-video transmissions is attended to as a television monitor: those receiving watch and listen, in a group as well as individually. The monitor to which learners attend for text-dominant computer-network transmissions, such as our distribution-list example, is attended to as a computer monitor, something the individual reads by sitting closely to it. The assumption is usually that the receiver of a computer message will receive that message as an individual and process that message as an individual, whereas the receiver of an audio-video transmission may be watching by himself or may be watching as part of a group. This individual-only assumption needs to be challenged with regard to computer-network tele-learning, as we will show in Chapters 5 and 6, but requires still some more technology to succeed in that challenge.

Adding another type of connectivity: projecting the message to a group

To make the reception of a computer-based signal part of a large-group learning situation, some kind of additional connectivity is needed, this time to a projection device that will project the contents of the computer screen so that a number of learners can see them, even a classroom of learners. Many examples of this whole-class approach to network-based tele-learning occur in this book. However, the technology of this last component of connectivity is still hard to realize, both technically and organizationally. Institutions may have dozens of computers, even all connected to a network, but no facility for the teacher or instructor, in her classroom or lecture hall, to connect a computer to the network and to a projection device and use resources from the network as demonstration resources during a class session. As we will see in Chapters 5 and 6, a major breakthrough in tele-learning is coming from being able to project computer-screen reception via a projection device so that a larger group can see the contents of the screen at the same time, and the instructor can use the display for demonstration during face-to-face teaching. Even with projection however, text-dense screens are not appropriate for group reception. And as another point, the sort of monitor available for reception may not be compatible with both analog audio-video signal and digital computer signals, thus necessitating two different types of output devices in the same room if two different types of signal streams are to be received.

IMPLICATIONS FOR TELE-LEARNING?

The differences in how one atttends to the message being received—as watcher and listener individually or in a group, or as reader and text-processor as an individual—are critical to what occurs in a tele-learning experience. The difference between reception intended for one person and reception intended for a group is also critical.

In Section 2.1, we have taken a bird's eye view of the overall landscape of technologies that affect tele-learning. We did this deliberately, to illustrate the idea that tele-learning technologies, despite their diversity, can be seen in general and integrated categories. We see, for example, educational television and the WWW as part of an overall whole. But there is a strong tendency in the tele-learning field that persons involved are associated with one or the other of the dominant streams of technological development that we have illustrated in the two sets of examples that ran throughout Sections 2.2–2.4: what we can call in simple terms, the video stream and the network stream. Thus, in Sections 2.2 and 2.3 we look at each of these streams in more detail.

■ 2.2 VIDEO TECHNOLOGIES FOR TELE-LEARNING SYSTEMS: FROM TV TO TELE-PRESENCE

When you were asked to bring up a mental image of tele-learning at the start of this book, did you picture a group of learners watching a television monitor? If you did, you are representative of those involved with the stream of tele-learning technology development that is based on audio-video communication, voice and video. For many people, this stream is synonymous with terms such as "tele-teaching" or "distance-learning technologies" (this is particularly so in the US; see for example, US Congress, Office of Technology Assessment, 1995, pp. 109–110).

In this book, we see the "video-stream" of tele-learning as part of the larger tele-learning whole. Its technological history is important to summarize as well as its future to anticipate. We begin with a basic pedagogical question in video-stream tele-learning, and follow the influence of this question in the evolution of the technologies used for instruction, from one-way educational television to two-way digital compressed video. Core references for this section include: Bates (1984a), Hakes, Cochenour, Rezabek and Sachs (1995), Meyer (1992) and US Congress, Office of Technology Assessment (1995).

■ 2.2.1 INTERACTIVITY IN VIDEO-STREAM TELE-LEARNING: IS TWO-WAY MORE DESIRABLE?

Frequently, video-stream tele-learning technologies are categorized as being one-way or two-way. This means, does the signal only flow in one direction, or can those at the one or multiple receive sites for the signal also be part of the communication? Using the telephone is the most familiar example of two-way interaction: in video terms, however, the most common example is not two-way but rather is broadcast television, with one-way transmission. Considerable efforts, both pedagogically and technically, have been and are being made to increase two-way interaction possibilities for video-stream tele-learning, based on the assumption that adding this "natural" aspect of two-way real-time communication is unquestionably desirable. However, before discussing the technologies involved in one-way television, interactive television, and two-way compressed video, it is useful to reflect on our basic assumptions about interactivity in tele-learning.

INTERACTIVITY AND LEARNING

We begin with stating an important observation: one-way transmission in itself does not have to imply passivity on the part of the receiver. Foursslund, 1992, for example, summaries research from a number of countries, in which the influence of culture on the seriousness with which children attend to educational television, and the influence that this seriousness has on their learning, is well documented. Salomon, in his many articles (see for example, 1983) presents a theoretical framework for learning from any technology: that the "amount of invested mental effort" is a major variable. Being able to speak out and ask a question while watching a television broadcast does not necessarily mean that more invested mental effort is occurring than would be the case if a learner instead made a note to herself about the question, and after reflecting on it, asks someone (not necessarily the television speaker) for clarification at some later period, if she still does not understand. We discuss this more thoroughly in Chapter 8.

But it is important to note these issues relating to interactivity here as a counterpoint to the frequently expressed or implied assumption in video-stream developments in tele-learning: that two-way video is to be preferred above one-way transmission because as good a quality learning experience will not occur if the receiver is not able to ask questions of the sender or engage in communication as naturally as possible (i.e., by being seen and heard) with the speaker. Learning is a complex business and interaction can be intense within the head of the learner as she reads, or listens, or watches, or shuts her eyes and reflects. Learners can be in a face-to-face setting, and for reasons of personality or class size or teacher characteristics, rarely ask the teacher direct questions and rarely engage in structured group discussions; yet learning can and does still occur. And conversely, questions can be disruptive, discussions can be unprofitable or dominated by a few persons, in any setting, face-to-face or tele.

IT DEPENDS...

As usual in learning, the "best technology" depends on the circumstances, and on the teacher (see Chapter 5 and 8).

■ 2.2.2 ONE-WAY EDUCATIONAL TELEVISION: THE MOST WIDESPREAD FORM OF TELE-LEARNING

Educational television has been a well-organized enterprise in countries throughout the world for many decades. Bates (1984a), for example, noted that in 1982 in the UK almost all schools and higher-education institutions made educational use of television; an average of 85 hours a week of specifically educational broadcasts were transmitted on national networks at times when schools were open; and that over 15 million individual copies of learners' workbooks and teachers' notes were sold to schools and colleges to accompany the use of educational television. Meyer (1992) gives an overview of the extensive experience of 28 European, North African, and Middle East countries with educational broadcasting to schools and notes the diversity of relationships that educational broadcasters have developed with educational authorities in the various countries. In Italy, the Consorzio Nettuno has, during 1992–1995, delivered over 2,000 hours of lectures to universities throughout Italy, broadcasting via the national television network during late-night periods. Learners set the timers on their video recorders and tape the lessons during the night for watching when convenient (Garito, 1995). Box 2.8 shows some data from a recent US inventory about educational television in schools:

Box 2.8

Television reception in US schools

- Nearly every school in the country has (in 1995) at least one TV set for use in its instructional program
- The mean number of sets per school was 12 in 1991
- In 1993, there were slightly more than four television sets for every 10 full-time teachers
- In 1993, 41% of teachers reporting having a television set in their own classrooms
- Between 1991 and 1993 there was a 25% increase in the proportion of schools with direct cable connections so that about 75% of all schools have a cable connection
- As of 1993, 50% of all school districts reported having a satellite dish to obtain a broader variety of programming than that offered by the local cable distributor
- The majority of schools make use of one-way video technologies; only about 20% of districts support two-way video. (US Congress, Office of Technology Assessment, 1995, p. 105)

We discuss the tele-learning aspects of one-way video broadcasting from the teacher's perspective in Chapters 5 and 6, with examples from many countries throughout the world. For the focus of this chapter, we can see that the major practical barriers to tele-learning with these broadcast transmissions are the equipment costs, (in)compatibilities involved at send and receive sites and for the transmission medium itself. The major benefit is transmission over long distances (except for microwave) and the transmission of good-quality, professionally prepared audio-video-learning materials.

RADIO, TOO...

Broadcast radio is another relatively old transmission technology and like television has a long history of educational applications. Radio broadcasting of audio transmission, either live or pre-recorded, is a fully worthy form of tele-learning and especially so in regions where a radio signal is the only affordable transmission channel to remote destinations (Bates, 1995). However, it is not so widely used in current tele-learning situations, at least in terms of information being circulated in written reports in journals, presentations at international educational-technology conferences, or information sources on the WWW, and thus, with respect to one-way transmission, we generally will be referring only to one-way video in this book. Also, when we refer to video technologies, we will mean video with audio accompanying the video.

For more information about current applications of one-way video transmission or educational television, a good suggestion is to browse a summary of WWW sites about educational television, for example,

Yahoo
URL http://www.yahoo.com/Education/Television/

■ 2.2.3 MAKING ONE-WAY TRANSMISSION INTERACTIVE: INTERACTIVE TELEVISION

To supplement the one-way nature of educational television (the most typical name for one-way video tele-learning), different methods and technologies are frequently used in schools, higher-education and training to add interactivity and communication to the watching process. Despite the observation that good learning can occur through quietly attending with subsequent reflection or by having the opportunity to stop a videotape of a television broadcast, rewind it and re-watch difficult-to-understand sequences, in many cases it is pedagogically desirable to blend communication and person-to-person interactivity with the viewing of a television broadcast (examples occur throughout Chapters 5–8). We look at three basic approaches to this broadcast-supplement process, from their technological aspects.

ADDING INTERACTIVITY TO BROADCASTS THROUGH MULTIPLE-MEDIA

With one-way video transmissions coming into face-to-face school settings, interactivity is often supplied within the local classroom, through the classroom teacher developing a range of learning experiences including preparatory study activities before the watching of the one-way transmission and follow-up discussions after. This is one of the reasons teachers make such heavy use of video recorders (VCR): teachers appreciate the opportunity to first view a broadcast, decide on its feasibility for their classes, and develop learning activities around it. (In Chapter 5 we show a number of ways that innovative learning activities can be developed around quality educational broadcasting.) This approach is a human solution for adding interactivity to a broadcast, but many times educational technologists associated with the broadcast have helped this teacher-led process along by supplying integrated support materials, often of a multi-media nature, for use before and after the broadcast. Thus the technologies here are the video recorder, and supplementary media which are most typically print but can include computer software and even hands-on equipment (such as measuring instruments for science activities so that learners can carry out demonstrations they have watched on a broadcast).

ADDING A TELE-LEARNING ASPECT FOR INTERACTIVITY

In addition to the sort of integrated activities we have just discussed, educational television broadcasts are frequently being supplemented by other forms of tele-learning. As an example, in The Netherlands, a "multiple-media" learning experience was developed in combination with the national curriculum institute, the national educational-television agency, and the telephone company to conceptually integrate the use of a series of television broadcasts, print materials, computer software, and network-based activities for an overall learning unit (Lepeltak and Collis, 1993). In the US an advanced-credit course in being offered to hundreds of practicing teachers in which occasional television broadcasts are combined with extensive use of the Internet for contact and collaborative work among the participants between the broadcasts (D'Ignazio, 1995; see also Chapter 9). In the UK, the BBC (British Broadcasting Company) integrates its television offerings not only with traditional print materials but also with interactive network-based activities of both the communication and WWW variety. In Chapter 5 we describe other examples, from the US, of how educational television services are making use of commercial on-line services to stimulate innovative lesson development around their various broadcasts. These lesson-support opportunities can range from the teacher being able to download topical materials about the broadcast from a network service, to the teacher and the students being able to participate in various moderated computer-conference discussions about the topic of the broadcasts via the network service. In some cases, there are even field-trips organized through the network service that complement the theme of the original broadcasts and extend the learning experience.

INTERACTIVITY THROUGH REAL-TIME TECHNOLOGIES

The above examples involve technologies used for interactivity before or after the one-way video broadcast. In addition, a great deal of experience has developed with the use of technologies that allow real-time interaction with the speakers in a one-way broadcast. These technologies include telephone (single voice and speaker phones) and faxes, and sometimes the use of e-mail. However, few classrooms (in 1995) that are equipped to handle video-stream tele-learning are also equipped to handle computer-stream tele-learning, and thus sending an e-mail message while watching a broadcast is still not likely to occur. This will change as the connectivity of classrooms increases; a phenomenon we discuss in Chapter 7.

■ 2.2.4 COMPRESSED DIGITAL VIDEO: TWO-WAY VIDEO FOR INSTRUCTION

A major variation on one-way video is two-way video, made possible by technologies that enable live, two-way auditory and visual signals to be transmitted simultaneously among sites. Although it is possible to have two-way transmission with either analog or digital signals, the costs and complications of two-way analog video are high. The main reason for this is that video demands a very high amount of bandwidth for transmission.

TOO MUCH FOR THE PIPELINES...

One affordable approach to bringing two-way video to a learning situation would be to send the video through a regular telephone line or through access technologies such as leased lines or ISDN networks (see Table 2.1). But although attractive in many applications, not just tele-learning, the simple answer in practical terms for affordable pipelines was that this can't be feasibly done—it takes the equivalent of about 100 analog lines to transmit one full-motion video stream. All sorts of techniques have been tried out, such as freeze-frame transmission of separate pictures, but with limited or no success.

CODECS AND COMPRESSION

However, things have changed and are changing. One of the reasons is the development of techniques to change analog signals to digital signals, and compress them enormously so they require much less bandwidth in the transmission channels through which they must pass. Compression is the process of reducing the representation of information without reducing the information itself. This process thus lowers the time or space necessary to store or to transmit the information. With video, compression involves processing analog video signals digitally, and then removing signals that are not necessary when "describing" subsequent frames of a visual presentation, i.e., information that has not changed since the previous frame. This process, however, has its price and the price is jerkiness in the visual displays that are transmitted, particularly when motion occurs. Also audio signals may not be completely synchronized with the compressed video visuals.

Compressed digital video technologies and their implementation

The primary technological device for compressed video is called a codec which stands for "coder/decoder". A codec is something like a modem, only in reverse. A codec takes analog signals such as video, digitizes and compresses them and transmits them to a partner codec at the receiving end which decompresses the signal and further prepares it so that it can be viewed on a monitor by the receivers. Transmission lines must thus be digital lines. Regular television requires 90 Mb/p to transmit information between sites; compressed video techniques (as typical figures in 1995) reduce this bandwidth need to between 112 kb/p and 1.544 Mb/p for both the audio and compressed video signals between sites. With increases in compression techniques the low end of this range can accommodate acceptable-quality video for many tele-learning applications.

However, audio quality is less flexible in terms of what is acceptable in tele-learning than video quality (Sachs, 1995). The audio component of a compressed video system may travel with the video component, and thus require some (typically 16 kb/p or 64 kb/p) of the overall available bandwidth. When video transmission requires high bandwidth itself, the tendency to reduce the bandwidth for the audio component, and thus to reduce the quality of the audio, has serious implications for tele-learning. "Out-of-band" solutions for the audio, that is, sending the audio through a parallel transmission line, frees up the bandwidth for the compressed video but brings in other technical issues, such as synchronizing the audio and video at the receive end, and generally handling two different line connections.

Besides these problems related to bandwidth, there are at least two other major sets of technological problems to deal with using compressed-video systems: compatibility and interfacing with the transmission line.

Incompatibility

One set of difficulties for the compressed-video user comes not from the compression process in theory, but from the fact that different codec manufacturers have different compression algorithms to provide better-and-better quality video transmission at lower and lower bandwidths: it is not the result of the competition that is a problem for the user, but the lack of standardization and interoperability which characterizes all this competitive development. Problems come even between partner units made by the same manufacturer (for summaries, see Galbreath, 1995a; Luther, 1991; Sachs, 1995).

Interfacing with the transmission lines

Unless the compressed-video system owns or leases its own set of transmission lines, the compressed-video signal must generally travel through the switched networks usually owned or regulated by the regional or national telephone company. There are many different types of digital phone service possibilities, varying in terms of bandwidth and number of channels provided and costing strategy. Standard ISDN services, for example, typically involve two 64 kb/p channels and a third channel for additional signals, while a basic digital phone line will only offer one channel which may be 56 kb/p in some countries and 64 kb/p in others (see Bacsich, 1994). This latter point illustrates the difficulties that occur when more than one telephone company is involved in a transmission; regulations generally prohibit local or regional providers to move outside their territories to help a tele-learning participant whose partner participant in a compressed-video application is outside the first service-provider's range. Finally, there are technical issues involved with getting the compressed-video signal from the codec and onto a digital transmission line, and vice versa. These technologies involved with this process have different names and characteristics, such as multiplexers, inverse multiplexers, and terminal adapters (see Sachs, 1995).

Other technical issues

In addition to technologies related to transmission there are also technical issues to consider with the original transformation of light waves into video signals when video is originally captured by a camera. The quality of the camera and the lens used to capture images is important, as is the camera's location, as the field of view handled by different manufacturers' cameras differ considerably. Many features are available to relate to camera control, such as zoom, and remote focusing and switching. The lighting in the room is also important.

And there are many issues relating to the audio component of compressed-video systems. Audio systems can be either half-duplex or full-duplex. The former allows audio signals in only one direction at a time, the latter allows parties at both ends of the connection to speak at the same time. While this is more natural for communication, it brings the problem of echo, in which one's own audio signal is echoed back from the partner site, creating a disruptive time-lagged echo effect. To deal with this problem, further equipment is needed: special echo-cancellation technology.

Finally, there are more technical problems involved when multi-point connectivity is desired with compressed video. These relate to the multi-point switch that is required, and, as could be predicted, multi-point switches come in many varieties and are far from standardized.

DESPITE THE TECHNICAL CHALLENGES...

Despite the technical complexity of digital compressed video systems, many institutions or companies with fixed partner sites and with a desire to regularly make use of real-time, two-way communication sessions with simultaneous two-way auditory and video signals, are making the commitment to compressed video installations and equipping each site with the specialized and compatible equipment that is needed for the interconnection. Hakes and her colleagues (1995) give the profiles of 66 US organizations making use of compressed video for either instruction or conferencing. The institutions include 27 higher-education institutions or their affiliates, 7 systems involving school systems, and the rest relating to government, medical or commercial settings. In comparing their 66 profiled institutions with the 46 they had surveyed in 1993, the authors note trends toward lower transmission rates, and more use of rollabout units that can be used in regular classrooms or meeting rooms instead of only in specially constructed studio-type environments.

AND A FINAL INFLUENCE ON TELE-LEARNING?

This difference-in-location possibility for compressed video equipment also affects the use of the equipment for tele-learning. A fixed-location system in a large classroom or lecture hall is easier to envision in terms of using the connectivity for lecture-type tele-learning than it is for more personal discussions or conferencing among a few persons at each end of the transmission. The teacher in a lecture hall-like location, with or without a face-to-face class present, is more likely to lecture, and to make use of the compressed video system to extend the opportunity for learners in remote sites to feel part of the face-to-face classroom. While this could in turn mean that all learners, face-to-face and remote, are involved in group discussions or in activities even though seated in a lecture hall, more often the pedagogical approach for this sort of environment is: teacher lectures and explains, learners watch and listen and have the occasional chance to ask questions or be asked questions.

In contrast, roll-about units that can go into a smaller seminar room can be more appropriate to the learning needs of a small group of persons on one or both ends of the transmission interacting more frequently and naturally with those on the other end, such as might occur with a teacher at one end of a seminar table and the learners seated around the other end. The newest innovation in compressed video, desktop video-conferencing, which brings the video signal in through a computer not a monitor or television receiver, has even more implications for tele-learning variety; we come back to this in Section 2.4.

Desktop video (or multi-media) conferencing has another important characteristic: it represents the intersection between the video stream of tele-learning technologies and the network stream. However, before we get to this intersection point, we next turn our attention to some major aspects of the evolution of the network stream.

■ 2.3 NETWORK TELE-LEARNING TECHNOLOGIES: FROM A BBS TO THE WWW

In Table 2.1 we illustrated one aspect of network evolution, that of bandwidth and its influence on what is carried through the network as well as the applications that can be supported by the network. In this section we highlight the applications themselves, and in particular those which have the most application to tele-learning. The applications are further elaborated throughout the rest of this book. Here, we look first at basic applications that relate to communication, then at applications that relate to information access, and finally at the combination of these focuses.

■ 2.3.1 TECHNOLOGIES FOR COMPUTER-MEDIATED COMMUNICATION: TALKING THROUGH YOUR FINGERS

While in the last section, our participants were generally talking to video cameras and attending to television-type monitors, in this section our participants are generally seated at computers and "talking through their fingers" when they interact with computer-based tele-learning systems. (As we will illustrate in Chapters 5 and 6, this is not the only possibility; with projection equipment and some creativity, computer-based tele-learning can be used in whole-class settings, in a number of powerful ways). However, the most typical uses of what we are calling for simplicity "computer-type tele-learning" in the mid-1990s involve individuals with their fingers on keyboards and their eyes busy with reading from the monitor or from printouts.

REAL-TIME COMPUTER-BASED COMMUNICATION
It is certainly possible, even with 1995 technology, to use computer-type tele-learning for real-time communication. We mention two variations here.

Chat

For text-only communication, there are "chat" functions, whereby all those logged on and accepting a certain "invitation" can enter lines of text and see those lines appear as sequential entries in a rolling script visible to all who are participating. The entry into the sequence is generally based on when the individual presses her return key, which means that the conceptual integration of the messages usually leaves much to be desired. However, most of the use of chat is just that—informal chat—and thus not of much relevance to tele-learning other than indirectly, as a way to increase rapport among communicants.

MOOs

Despite this rather silly name, MOOs (or Multi-User Object-Oriented Environments) are starting to be looked at for tele-learning applications, not so much in the context of formal courses, but for informal and professional learning (see Chapter 4). MOOs (circa 1995) are text-based environments, in which each participants can take a certain role and the environment can be set up so that a kind of role playing is encouraged. This role-playing takes place in real-time, and when MOOs are used professionally, the time of interaction is announced ahead of time, and participants prepare for their use of the technology. The approach is sometimes being used for "interact with the expert" sessions prior to a conference presentation, as one example (see Chapter 4).

From a technological perspective, MOOs make use of the Internet and some special software tools which are available through the Internet. For example, a client program ("Virtual Places") has been available since early 1995 that allows users to communicate using real-time audio and/or text chat at WWW sites running a particular server, so that distributed groups can talk among themselves as they visit those sites. For more information and some educational examples, see:

"Virtual Places"
URL http://www.vplaces.com/index.htm

Audio and video on the Internet, circa 1995

Advances in technology are making it possible to send audio and video, in relatively small amounts, through the Internet in 1995 and even before then. The application CU-SeeME which was developed at Cornell University in the US has been in use for a number of years and allows persons using computers equipped to handle audio and video to communicate with each other in real time. REALAudio is a development for the WWW that makes the handling of audio much more realistic in terms of computer, storage, and network requirements than before possible. However, audio and video via ordinary networks, particularly the local LANs or modems to which end-user computers are connected, are not much suited, or not at all suited, for multi-media networking, for the same bandwidth reasons we discussed with respect to the video-stream of technologies in Section 2.2. Thus we will leave multi-media networking, and real-time multi-media communication until Section 2.4, when we look at the convergence of the video- and computer- streams of tele-learning technologies.

This leaves us with asynchronous text-based communication via computers as the form of tele-learning technology to preview here. We will do this by looking at e-mail systems, conferencing systems, and bulletin-board systems, although sometimes the functionalities of these systems overlap. Good overall sources for these topics are Mason (1994) and Kaye (1992a).

E-MAIL SYSTEMS

E-mail systems as communication environments are well known, and have a broad application. In general, e-mail systems provide the user with software that allows her to create out-going messages, read and process in-coming messages, and respond to in-coming messages in a variety of ways. Also important to e-mail is the ability to attach files to a message, to open attached files that are received, and to forward messages, or edited versions of messages, to other recipients.

Editing and tele-learning

This editing aspect is particularly important; it means that at least some of the text-handling capabilities we are familiar with in word processing are now more-and-more commonly available in mail systems themselves. We can cut and paste from different documents on our (electronic) desktops or in our (electronic) clipboards; we can create new documents out of portions of other documents received by mail as well as made outside of mail environments. All of these text-handling capabilities are increasing the possibilities of e-mail systems for the dissemination of learning materials. Also, they are increasing the possibilities for collaborative writing and other forms of work among distributed participants. We discuss these aspects further in Chapters 4 and 6.

Addressing possibilities and tele-learning

Another set of functionalities in e-mail systems that are important to tele-learning are the various ways such systems allow us to send messages to lists of persons through a single address. Such distribution lists can be small and personal: the members of a group working together on a project. The distribution lists can be specific to a course, with the names of all those involved in the course included. The lists can be maintained via special software such as LISTSERV or MAJOR-DOMO, which allows all those on the list to send messages to all others on the list through the same single address. And there are many other functionalities that make communication efficient and powerful, all based on the core standardization of addressing that is at the centre of interconnectivity with network systems and particularly with the Internet.

COMPUTER CONFERENCING TECHNOLOGIES

Computer-conferencing environments add (most) of the functionalities of e-mail systems to the additional benefit of allowing designated groups of users access to common, shared data bases of previously-sent messages. While this can be simulated through the practice of everyone keeping all messages organized in mail-folder directories with the same names of directories and files, the computer-conferencing environment not only takes care of the organization and maintenance of the shared environments centrally, but also, with graphic-user-interface systems, visualizes the communication organization in a helpful way for tele-learning applications.

The special functionalities in computer-conferencing and their impact on tele-learning are discussed in some detail in Chapters 6 and 8 as well as through many different references with additional information. Some functionalities that are particularly valuable include flags to indicate new messages in different conferences; the "thread" feature which allows one to read in sequence messages which were sent as follow-ups to other messages; the "history" feature which allows a user to see the names of everyone who has read, or read and responded to, a message; and the "resumé" function which allows each participant to conveniently make available a small biography and photo of him or herself. The latter feature is not only important for classes at a distance, but for face-to-face classes with many students who only meet together in occasional lecture-hall sessions and participate in the rest of the course in small groups through computer-conferencing.

BULLETIN BOARD SYSTEMS

Bulletin-board systems (BBSs) are older forms of integrated communication and information environments, similar to computer-conferencing environments but more oriented toward the delivery of previously categorized information than the building-up of integrated sets of messages from group communication. However, this is a difference in degree more than function. Most importantly technically about BBSs in their less-sophisticated forms is that individuals without much special equipment or without special permission could and can set up a BBS environment and support as many dial-in callers as available phone lines. With advances in technologies, BBSs are becoming accessible in a variety of ways, including via the Internet.

BBSs: Anticipating the WWW?

While conferencing environments make sense with a well-organized group, BBSs reflect the orientation of being open to their public, which may be a previously defined group with log-on passwords or may be anyone interested in the theme of the BBS. Although BBSs have someone or some number of persons responsible for the environment, both technically and in content and quality, the extent to which this quality- and content-control occurs varies widely. In many ways BBSs, in spirit and function, anticipate the World Wide Web.

■ 2.3.2 CLIENTS AND SERVERS: THE WEB

We discuss the WWW, its technology and new developments, and aspects of designing learning materials for it, in **Interface Sections 2, 3, 6 and 9**. Here we anticipate those discussions with a general overview of the WWW as a tele-learning technology.

SERVER-CLIENT ARCHITECTURE

Where the WWW first differs fundamentally from BBSs is in its client-server architecture. This key idea relates to computers running Web server software responding to computers running Web client software, when those "client" computers send a message to a server asking for a particular document. (There are, in mid 1995, at least 35 different server-software packages available, from free versions downloadable from the Internet to more-complex and well-supported commercially available versions; see Duncan, 1995b.) Every WWW document is identified by its unique address (its "URL", universal resource locator). A Web server uses the so-called "HTTP Protocol" to listen to requests from browsers on client computers. It then delivers an electronic copy of the requested file and any images that are referenced in that file to the client. The server makes this transmission and then terminates the connection. The server can also be set up to handle commands other than URL requests from client browsers, such as scripts relating to forms and other kinds of interactivity.

One of the remarkable aspects of the WWW is this type of client-server approach, so that connections to a busy server as transacted as quickly as possible (valuable for servers with 50,000 requests per day!). Thus the frustrations of busy signals for older versions of dial-in BBSs are much reduced on the WWW, but certainly not eliminated. The WWW is the victim of its own success and high-access sites are frequently busy, especially at certain hours of the day.

For more information about WWW architecture, the best source is the WWW itself, where large amounts of information are accumulating. For a start, two of the key locations are at NCSA in the US, a pioneer location in the development of the WWW technology, and the World Wide Web consortium both good sources of up-to-date technical information about the WWW.

NCSA:
URL http://www.ncsa.uiuc.edu/SDG/Software/

W3C (The World Wibe Web Consortium)
URL http://www.w3.org/pub/WWW

Browser software

The client, or browser, software used for asking servers for certain documents (these do not have to be WWW documents, they can also be files from other services such as FTP (file transfer protocol) or Gopher (another information system on the Internet)) has another main function. It interprets the document and images it receives from the server to which it has made a request, and then formats and displays the document on the screen of the browser computer. The browser also provides the user with many other functionalities, increasing by the week in 1995, to help her manipulate and make use of the WWW document which has been loaded: including building a bookmark collection in which the URL of the document and its title are retained in the user's personal collection and can be clicked for later re-access without the user having to type in the original URL; seeing the source HTML code of the document; printing the document; and using the document interactively, to move to its indicated links, respond to its embedded forms, and use its other interactivity options.

The developments in browser software in 1994 and 1995 have been an enormously important technical stimulation for tele-learning. The fact that these browsers have emerged as freely available tools, downloadable through the Internet, and that they use an intuitive, point-and-click, attractive, consistent, user interface for the access of a diverse universe of documents is central to this importance.

The best way to obtain up-to-date information on browsers is to look at their own information sources, for example, those for MOSAIC and NetScape:

NetScape:

URL `http://home.netscape.com`

Of course there are many printed sources as well; for example Ayre and Reichard (1995), Kent (1995) and Lemay (1995) (See also **Interface 2**, following this chapter; and Chapter 8.)

▓ 2.4 COMBINING TECHNOLOGIES: DESKTOP MULTI-MEDIA CONFERENCING SYSTEMS

We have talked about tele-learning technologies from a generic view in this chapter—as technologies involved in the transformation, transmission, and reception of learning-related communications. Within this generic view, we have looked more specifically at some aspects of the so-called video-stream of tele-learning technologies and some aspects of the computer stream. We have noted a number of times that a technical convergence is becoming possible in these streams, at least from the point of view of real-time video and audio being possible via computers because of advances in computing, in compression techniques for digitization of video, and in network speed, bandwidth and access technologies. In this section we look more closely at the technologies of desktop multi-media conferencing systems as a way to conclude our technological overview of tele-learning technologies.

▓ 2.4.1 DESKTOP MULTI-MEDIA CONFERENCING: THE TECHNOLOGY

Systems by which, through the same computer interface, the user can access asynchronous network applications such as computer conferencing, e-mail, and the WWW, as well as work in real time collaboratively with a distant partner on a shared document or shared application and can see and hear this partner as this interaction occurs are called desktop multi-media conferencing systems. We discuss these in more detail in Chapter 8, including the results of an evaluation study performed on a 1994 version of such a system, in terms of its potential for tele-learning.

From a technical perspective, such systems in 1995 require compressed video technology; at least wideband networking (ISDN is most frequently being used); a computer with enough memory, power and speed to handle heavy-duty multi-media applications; special software; a camera and microphone mounted on one's computer; a speaker system with the computer; and...a partner with a compatible system to which one can connect.

(I might also note that other attributes are required, such as patience and persistence, because desktop multi-media systems are still in their early days in terms of marketplace usage in 1995 and many difficulties and challenges confront the ordinary tele-learner who is trying to set up and make such a system work. The source of this comment? Personal experience....)

PROBLEMS?

What are these problems? Shouldn't all the communication needs be easier once they are all handled in one computer, on one desktop?

The problems relate fundamentally to lack of interoperability, limiting not only the number of potential partners but also the base of experienced users to turn to for peer-to-peer help; and the difficulties of connecting a desktop system to an adequate network, such as currently an ISDN network, for its signal transmission. Interoperability, or its lack, relates to how the computers involved initiate and set up a communication, and how they handle video compressions. Because there is relatively so little progress in ISDN connectivity over regions and countries, as well as within many countries, a number of competitor versions of digital desktop multi-media conferencing are also on the market. These competitors are not only incompatible with each other in terms of technology, but also make use of many different approaches to video-conferencing. Some emphasis data-sharing, shared-notebook annotations, and file-transfer applications for connected computers and restrict the video-conferencing aspects to a small video window with jerky talking heads (Salamone, 1995) Others emphasize the "tele-presence" aspects of working together at a distance and focus on the video-conferencing aspects of the systems. This video-conferencing usually requires ISDN networks, but can take place over ordinary telephone lines, although with predictable limitations.

Some want the document sharing more than the video...

For those, usually from computer backgrounds, for whom document sharing is a dominant motivation for desktop collaboration, the small video window is not even particularly interesting in comparison to having real-time audio interaction combined with application sharing (Davis, 1994). In Davis' experiments, video was not even used, only audio contact and document sharing through one ISDN-line. This is, in fact, an extension of audio-graphics conferencing, which has a relatively long history of use in certain countries, particularly Australia (see Oliver and Reeves, 1995; also see Chapters 6 and 7).

Audio-graphics conferencing, in its "traditional" form requires the simultaneous use of two telephone connections, one for an ordinary point-to-point voice connection, and the second for a computer-to-computer connection in which special software allows the same screen to be shown on all the computers involved (there can be more than two) and other functionalities relating to who is in control of the screen. This kind of combination functionality, sometimes called audio conferencing with a shared-workspace (Heeren, 1995), has been studied extensively in Australia and in scattered locations elsewhere (Gray and O'Grady, 1993).

IMPROVEMENTS...

But nonetheless, desktop multi-media conferencing is solidifying as a technology. A. Davis (1995) reports that by the end of 1995 a standard should be agreed among desktop video-conference system suppliers for how desktop conferencing should work over regular telephone lines, and over ISDN networks. This means an agreement to use the same compression algorithms, which should stop vendors from fighting competitive wars on the basis of their respective algorithms, and turn their attention to pricing and service. The fight between an emphasis on data-conferencing, with audio and video used in support of data conferencing, and an emphasis on video-conferencing, with computer applications used as support to people talking and listening to each other, remains. How this fight will resolve is not at all clear in late 1995; it relates to core differences in the background and philosophy of different tele-learning participants.

■ 2.5 TELE-LEARNING TECHNOLOGIES THROUGH THE EYES OF THE USER...

Our bird's eye view in this chapter has focused on technology, but this is a book for people, people using tele-learning and making decisions about tele-learning and supporting tele-learners. What do they see from their respective bird's-eye views? To answer this, we will briefly comment on what aspects of tele-learning technology have had most impact in the past on four different groups of persons involved with tele-learning, which aspects are most relevant in the present, and which technologies may be likely to be most important in the future.

The four groups are those which form of the focus of Chapters 3–9 of the book:

- The individual learner, the family or the professional

- The teacher or instructor in an educational institution
- The decision maker for tele-learning infrastructure in an educational institution or region
- The educational technologist

The present-relevance view is expanded in the following chapters of the book; the future-relevance view is predicted in Chapter 10.

■ 2.5.1 THE INDIVIDUAL TELE-LEARNER

We focus on two groups of "individual" tele-learners, using tele-learning outside the framework of established courses or educational institutions: the family and the professional. By the individual learner, we mean the person who wishes to learn something, not because she is enrolled in a course but because she is self-motivated. The learning may be directly related to her work or study, but the critical point is that she chooses to learn, and that the learning is not specifically structured for her by a teacher or instructor or trainer.

THE FAMILY

Motivations for tele-learning

What is the payoff for individual learner in the home and family? Pleasure, new ideas and interests, new personal contacts, but also more tangibly, information just-in-time for a task or personal problems. Parents want good extracurricular learning materials and experiences for their children, and wish themselves to learn about, in varying degrees of depth, topics varying from facts about local issues to information useful for family choices and activities and information useful for their own self-study and self-development. Children want extra resources to help them with their homework and school projects, but also can be motivated in learning for its own sake, if they are self-motivated in a topic and its presentation is interesting.

Major conditions for tele-learning

Tele-learning will be based on free choice in terms of time and involvement in the tele-learning activity and thus must be attractive and easily accessible. Tele-learning activities must be based around the sorts of technologies a family could reasonably expect to have access to in the home. And costs should be minimal.

Past and present technological emphases for tele-learning

Until recently, obtaining a learning experience from educational television was generally the only viable form of tele-learning for the family, and it continues to have valuable potential. However, a major new development is home access to the WWW, as well as other network services, for both parents and children. Community networks and network discussion groups may grow in importance for some members of families; participation in these can be a learning experience.

PROFESSIONALS

By professional group, we mean a group somehow related to one's profession or work. The group itself may be not explicitly organized (all persons interested in art history) or it may be tightly organized (a particular professional society, such as an organization of mathematics teachers); the notion of membership may be only informal (all people who are interested in environmental issues because those issues have some relationship to their professional life); or explicit (are you a member of the Environmental Management Professional Association? Are you known by name?)

Motivations for tele-learning

Tele-learning can be thought of as a method of professional development, where the motivation is clear: to gain something of value for one's work/professional life in an efficient way. The professional finds the sense of belonging to a "virtual community" a professionally useful one.

Major conditions for tele-learning

Tele-learning experiences will take place sporadically and informally, most likely at the individual's workplace or home, and most likely when he or she can find the time to take advantage of them.

Past and present technological emphases for tele-learning

In the past, the main ways the professional continued her life-long learning was to read professional literature, talk to one's colleagues, and attend the occasional profession conference. None of these involved tele-learning in any substantial way.

However, this has rapidly changed. E-mail, distribution lists, LISTSERVs and even certain newsgroups, organized by persons in one's profession, have become major sources of professional growth, both in terms of information and contact. Networking among an extended group of peers is extremely valuable for the exchange of new ideas and targeted help. Alternative forms of publications are bringing new resources into the hands of professionals through their desktops, virtual libraries and hyperlinked on-line journals and documents are rapidly changing the way the professional meets his learning needs. Conferences still are important, but the Internet supports interaction before and after the conference among the speakers and colleagues, and allows new and richer forms of access to conference materials. The Internet is the major technology. The need to occasionally work collaboratively with other active members of one's professional group on the group's business can involve audio or computer conferencing.

■ 2.5.2 THE TEACHER OR INSTRUCTOR

In this category we look at those directly involved in the process of course delivery in a educational institution. We particularly focus on teachers in elementary and secondary education and instructors in post-secondary education.

Motivations for tele-learning

The main motivations for tele-learning in the K-12 sector seem to be: to enrich existing learning settings by making new sorts of learning projects and activities possible; to expand the resources available to a student and class and school; and to compensate for "deficiencies" in educational opportunity, sometimes for an entire school or region because of lack of specialist teachers or the inability of students in a school to have access to educational opportunities because of the size or location of a school.

In contrast to the K-12 sector, major reasons for introducing tele-learning in traditional post-secondary settings may be to make the existing course-delivery process more effective and efficient, and to make one's institution's course offerings available to a broader audience.

Conditions for tele-learning

In the school sector, the teacher is constrained by lack of access to network-type tele-learning resources, either computers or connectivity or funding for connectivity. She is more likely to have classroom access to television, either broadcast or closed circuit. In the secondary school, the teacher is further constrained by time tables and lack of flexibility in content and time.

In the post-secondary sector, the instructor is constrained by lack of time, lack of reward for innovative teaching, and lack of access to tele-learning resources in the lecture hall or seminar room. She is also not likely to have had any training in pedagogy, so adapting her teaching is a matter of instinct more than theory. However, both she and her students may have good access to networks, particularly to the Internet and its services.

Past and present technological emphases for tele-learning

For the school sector: The motivation of enrichment of the learning experience has long been met by television, and now is being increasingly addressed by Internet-based projects. The motivation to expand the resources available to students for their on-going work as well as for new kinds of learning experiences has also been addressed by educational television, but now increasingly is being met by Internet-based activities, including the WWW and teacher-structured contacts via the Internet and other networks. The motivation to compensate for the lack of specialist teaching has been and still is a major motivation for video-stream tele-learning in schools, generally with broadcast-type lessons from an "expert teacher" outside of the school. While one-way broadcast with tele-phone- or fax-based response communication maintains important, digital com-pressed video instruction is gaining in impact.

For post-secondary instructors One way to make the learning process more effective and efficient in traditional post-secondary education is to provide students with on-going access to resource materials and support materials for their courses and independent studies. The WWW is serving this purpose at many higher education institutions. Another way of making existing learning more effective in higher education is to provide a way for more flexible communication with the instructor. Thus computer communications involving e-mail and com-puter conferencing are rapidly becoming important in post-secondary education, not only for information, but also for teaching and discussion.

Also, in order to reach more students, many post-secondary institutions are developing more and more of their courses in a "distance mode" where at least some of the regular face-to-face expectation of a course is replaced by various forms of flexible delivery. (In the US it is estimated that 30% of higher-education institutions were already engaged in 1994 in some form of distance delivery involving broadcast or video or audio-conferencing, and another 28% were planning to introduce it by 1995; Cotton, 1995.) An increase in the number of courses offered via the Internet is rapidly occurring, especially via the WWW. We discuss them in Chapter 6 and 9.

■ 2.5.3 THE INSTITUTIONAL DECISION MAKER

A third group of persons deeply interested in tele-learning are those who must make the decisions about what forms of tele-learning will be supported in their institutions or regions, and to what extent.

Major motivations for an interest in tele-learning

The infrastructure for tele-learning in an institution or region is complex and expensive, not only in its initial capitalization but in its on-going support and utilization. Rooms, wires, satellite receive dishes, new cabling, issues relating to network security and appropriate use, all of these are now part of the decision making process of decision makers at all levels of education. Decision makers must be well enough informed to make decisions about tele-learning based on costs-vs-effectiveness and payoff comparisons, and to identify strategies to increase the effective use of tele-learning facilities that are already in place in their institutions.

Past and present emphases for tele-learning

Many educational decision makers have equated distance education with video-type tele-learning, and have focused their strategic decisions around video technologies. However, the importance of networking to the institution or region, and the relationship of local networks to Internet access, are becoming more and more important for decision makers to confront. (For a good discussion about school and district networking options, see Newman, Bernstein and Reese, 1992; see also Chapter 7.)

■ 2.5.4 THE EDUCATIONAL TECHNOLOGIST

As we indicated in Chapter 1, we define educational technologists broadly, as those who are professionally involved in the design, delivery, support, and evaluation of technological applications in education, including instructional technology and research activities.

Motivations for tele-learning

As with educational decision makers, educational technologists must be informed about all aspects of tele-learning because tele-learning is becoming such a pervasive aspect of educational delivery.

Major conditions for tele-learning

Educational technologists may themselves have only had experience in one of the streams of tele-learning technologies, video or computer, and will have to catch up on experiences and skills relating to the other stream.

Past and present technological emphases for tele-learning

Educational technologists are being called upon to be solid sources of support for tele-learning, participants in the design of the software and electronic materials for tele-learning, specialists in the more-general design of learning materials and methods for tele-learning, researchers in a wide range of issues relating to tele-learning, and specialists in the training and support of teachers for tele-learning. Some of them may have focused on a few of these aspects in the past, but again, either for video-stream or computer-stream tele-learning rather than for both.

So, with this connection between technologies and humans, the end of the technological-overview chapter is reached. From now on, the human perspectives will dominate!

WHAT IS THE WORLD WIDE WEB?

The World Wide Web (**WWW** or **the Web**) is a collection of protocols and standards to access information on networks, and in particular, on the Internet. These standards and protocols define a particular kind of information-delivery system called a **distributed hypermedia** system.

The Web is primarily defined by three standards: **URLs (Universal Resource Locators**, providing a consistent and simple addressing scheme for different protocols); **HTTP (Hypertext Transfer Protocol**, defining a four-part transaction to deliver requested information from a server to a client); **and HTML (Hypertext Markup Language**, defining areas of text in a document by tagging them functionally and creating hypertext links between documents or pieces of documents).

URLs can specify protocols relating to, among others, ftp (file retrieval), newsgroups, Gopher menus, and HTTP documents. The format of a URL is:

```
protocol://server-name:
port/path
```

as for example,

```
http://www.w3.org/hypertext/
WWW/History.html
```

which indicates a HTTP document located on the server with domain address "www.w3.org" and found by going first to the directory "hypertext" on that server, then to the subdirectory "WWW" within the directory "hypertext" and then finding the specific file called "History.html". The extension "html" shows that the file has been processed into hypertext markup language. This particular HTTP (or Web) document is, by the way, the history of the WWW written by its developers.

HOW DOES THE WWW WORK?

The Web works under a **client-server model**. A **Web server** is a program running on a computer whose purpose is to serve documents to other computers when asked. A Web client is a program that both interfaces with the user and requests documents from a server as the user asks for them. This is a four-step procedure:

- Client connects to server through the server address information from a URL request
- Client specifies a particular document from the path information in the same URL request
- Server sends back a response with

status code and the requested document if it is available

- Either client or server ends the connection

Its efficiency is that it is a **stateless procedure**, one that does not retain any information about a connection from request to request, and a **connectionless** protocol, in that any time a client wants to fetch a document it must establish a new connection to the HTTP server on which that document resides. While these aspects allow a server to respond quickly to (sometimes tens of thousands) of requests per day, they also mean that special external techniques must be applied to maintain the state of a connection (important for personalized interactivity) and that a HTML page with many **inline images** can take a long time to load, as each image resides in a different file and must be called up in its own four-step procedure.

WHAT ARE MAIN ACRONYMS AND TERMINOLOGY FOR THE WEB?

In addition to those already mentioned—WWW, URL, HTTP, HTML, HTTP (or Web) server, hypertext, inline images (or graphics)—there are many other words and concepts about the WWW that are necessary to know in order to be an informed user of the Web. These include:

- **Browsers**, mouse-driven software interfaces to the WWW to allow computers to function as WWW clients
- WWW **documents** and **pages**, separate files coded in HTML
- **Hyperlinks**, "hotspots" within HTML

documents that can be clicked by the user to cause a jump to another document or resource. A hyperlink has two aspects: what the user sees (either marked with colour, underlined, or surrounded by a special border if a bitmap); and what the user doesn't need to see (the URL of the document or resource requested). This URL resides in the source HTML for the document but may or may not be visible on the user interface of the browser.

- **Home pages**: a document displayed at startup of a set of hyperlinked documents.
- **External viewers**: Utility programs, increasingly becoming integrated in browsers, to allow handling of images, sound, animation, and video within WWW documents
- **Navigation**: Following links from document to document. If the navigation is in the sense of making choices as one goes along, it is called browsing. If the navigation is based on specific requests, it involves search tools of various sorts.

And finally, it should be noted that the term "**WWW**" can be defined and used in a variety of ways:

- **Metaphorically**, an embodiment of human knowledge; cyberspace; webspace; an anarchy that works, a cultural revolution, or even, "a World-Wide Waste of time"
- **Semantically**, a universe of network-accessible information
- **Historically**, the name of a project proposed by Tim Berners-Lee, at CERN, the European Particle Physics Institute at Geneva Switzerland in 1989
- **Componentially**, a body of software

and a set of protocols and conventions

- Exhaustively, a global, interactive, dynamic, cross-platform, distributed, graphical hypertext information system that runs over the Internet but can also run on any set of computers that can communicate with each other

WHAT ARE IMPORTANT FEATURES OF WWW BROWSERS?

For the user, browser programs are very important as they serve as his or her interface to the Web as well as to other protocols. Dozens of browser programs are in use and new ones are continually emerging, but the dominant one in 1995 is *Netscape Navigator* (Netscape Communications Corp. Mountain View, CA; URL

```
http://home.netscape.com/
```

Important features of a WWW browser are:

- Allows **multiple simultaneous connections,** for faster loading.
- User control over graphics **display** and **layout** aspects.
- Can **save** displayed WWW documents on user's disk or **print** them on user's printer.
- Offers functions so that the user can add a current URL to his or her personal hotlist or set of **bookmark**s, and can use the hotlist interactively.
- Offers a local page **cache,** so that pages loaded during a session can be revisited locally without return to their server site.

- Provides a **history** log of URLs of sites visited during a session and **forward/back** movement to those sites.
- Offers support for **forms,** through which user can send a message or response.
- Supports **newsgroup** functionalities and (limited) **e-mail** functions (generally send-only).
- Includes **search** tools and capability.

HOW CAN WE FIND WHAT WE WANT?

A strength of the WWW is that anyone can be a WWW publisher, but this is also a serious problem, both in terms of quality expectation and also in terms of the user finding URLs that are useful to his or her needs. How can a user find a proverbial "needle in the haystack"?

- By going to sites that function as catalogues to collections of sites
- By using a tool or engine that searches **robot-generated web indices** or other forms of databases

Navigation tools can search by subject, by keyword, by concept, by location, by type of resource, by name of person, and within newsgroups and other non-HTML resources as well as HMTL resources.

There are also many collections of search engines, for example:

```
URL http://www.stir.ac.uk/
websites/search/search.html
```

HOW MANY WWW SITES ARE THERE?

In February of 1995 it was estimated there were 27,000 sites and that this population will double every 53 days. The current number of sites can be checked by accessing various information sites on the WWW such as

URL `http://www.yahoo.com/`
`Computers_and_Internet/`
`Internet/World_Wide_Web/`
`Statistics_and_Demographics/`

3 | Tele-learning and the family

The way that the general public is most likely to first encounter tele-learning is as a concept or metaphor, bound up in the current hype about the "information highway" and "cyberspace". Yet behind the metaphors serious issues are at stake with respect to informal, self-directed learning and these issues will cut across whatever happens with tele-learning in the formal educational institution. Although learning via television has long been a form of tele-learning in families, the issues and implications of children, and parents, being able to access the Internet and the WWW at home as well as other public and private network services, outside the filter of the school, are so far-reaching and so new that in this chapter we focus in this chapter only on computer-network tele-learning. Many examples, from family excursions to Virtual Museums to opportunities for creative expression and community debate, all from the home, are illustrated. On a more conceptual level, the implications of tele-learning at home are considered relative to the nature of the learning process and the way "education" is organized and controlled in society. What does this all mean to the parent and the teacher and school? Will the "rich get richer?" Is this real learning??

The answer to the last question is "Yes". The answer to the second-to-last question is, unfortunately, probably also "Yes". What should parents do? Read on. . .

■ 3.1 Networked tele-learning in the home: hype or new ways of learning?

■ 3.2 Tele-learning applications for the home: new ways of being informed and involved

■ 3.3 New tools to transcend distance

■ 3.4 New tools and opportunities for self-directed learning

■ 3.5 Tele-learning activities based on individual creativity

■ 3.6 Issues relating to tele-learning and the family

Objectives

After this chapter you should be able to:

- Be aware of the increasing social expectation concerning tele-learning for individual learning in the home and family, and of some critical demographics that relate to the increased possibilities for tele-learning in the home

- Identify four major categories of network tele-learning for the family: Being informed and involved, transcending distance, obtaining new tools for self-directed learning, and obtaining new tools and opportunities for creative self-expression

- Consider new definitions for the community, the library, the museum, the newspaper and magazine and even the school given increased access to tele-learning in the home

- Identify major cognitive and practical skills and competencies needed for informal tele-learning

- Consider the implications of "virtual excursions" and cross-cultural communication on society's conception of "school" and its physical boundaries

- Identify and reflect on major issues relating to informal, self-directed learning in the home, including: access and cost issues and their relation to equity of tele-learning opportunity, quality-control and accountability issues and their relation to freedom of expression, and issues relating to ownership of ideas and resources

■ 3.1 NETWORKED TELE-LEARNING IN THE HOME: HYPE OR NEW WAYS OF LEARNING?

When we talk about tele-learning and the family and tele-learning in the home, we are speaking broadly, referring not only to a specific location—the home—or not only to a specific collection of persons—the family—but also to the more-general idea of informal learning, outside the boundaries and definition of a formal educational organization. We are referring to learning freely chosen and freely engaged in, self-motivated learning for which the results are a mix of self-stimulation, self-satisfaction, and concrete payoff .

But we do focus mostly on the family, parents and children, and what the implications of new forms of tele-learning have for them. Tele-learning with computers currently requires a considerable investment in equipment and for access, for which someone must pay, before it can be experienced. The willingness, and ability, of parents to make a commitment to tele-learning in their homes will be increasingly important to their children in the future. This in turn relates to equity issues of important social significance.

We begin this chapter by first directly confronting the hype about tele-learning, and then introducing what we see as four major opportunities for tele-learning at home via the Internet or major on-line services. These opportunities, which we elaborate in Sections 3.2–3.5, are:

- New ways of being informed and involved
- New ways to transcend distance
- New tools for self-directed learning and problem solving
- New opportunities for creative expression

We appreciate very much the learning potential of television in the home and the fact that parents can and do stimulate and structure family viewing so that learning does occur. However, because of the many new issues and new forms of learning that are now available to the family through a home computer, we restrict ourselves in this chapter to computer-type tele-learning. Also, we further restrict ourselves here to what is feasible for families in 1996—if they have a computer and modem, and time and money.... Thus tele-learning in this chapter is happening through the home computer, and through the fingers and mouse-clicks of the user.

■ 3.1.1 HYPE OR VISION?

First of all, let's confront straight on a lurking thought that many may be having: Isn't this all a fad, being pushed by some combination of those who will make money on the home network market and the "Internet Cowboys" who see the Internet as the equivalent of freedom and the open road (and maybe even the Holy Grail)?

FREEDOM AND NIRVANA?

It is certainly not wrong to be skeptical because it is not hard to find examples of hype relating to tele-learning in the home. In countries throughout the world, magazines and newspapers routinely carry advertisements saying:

> 5 minutes to freedom: Instant Internet Access
> Directions to the Future: The Internet
> Are you lost in cyberspace? Get a roadmap to the future
> Open doors you never knew existed...

NEW WORDS...NEW METAPHORS

And, magazines and newspapers indicate that not only a new vocabulary has entered into the vernacular, but also a new culture with its own norms and mechanisms. Serious academic writers such as Harasim (1993) and popular sociologists such as Rheingold (1993) talk about "global communities" and "homesteading on the electronic frontier". We read that we are moving inexorably into a "cybersociety" (S. Jones, 1995) where our senses of self and community are changing. For some, the vision is positive and empowering: "cyberspace" is a space where "rookies and experts all can feel welcome", where "old-timers in cyberland" are willing and delighted to initiate neophytes and "newbies" (Netguide, 1995, p. 8).

And not only is cyberspace this nirvana of happy human relations, it is also, for many, synonymous with "freedom of speech and expression", with limitless resources available to all. If this cyberspace is the Internet or the "information superhighway" or the "infobahn" (European version) or only a visionary metaphor is often unclear.

POLITICALLY CORRECT?

But whatever it is, its motivational power relative to the public imagination is clear. Political leaders at the highest levels in countries around the world are calling for access for all (to whatever the "super information highway" actually is); the right of access to it is argued as a fundamental freedom (see, for example, in Canada, IHAC, 1995); the vehicle by which inequities in, among other things, educational opportunities can be bridged.

For example, in the European Community, a "trans-European Network for Education and Training" that will bring equity in educational opportunity to the learner wherever she is and whatever her circumstances (the pronoun is chosen advisedly here, in that the housebound rural female is seen as a particular target) has been a motivator of discussions and research programs since 1990 (see Collis & De Vries, 1993, for an overview). As another example the "Women on the Internet" Project, coordinated from Turkey, involves funding from various multinational agencies to support initiatives to help women from North African and Middle-Eastern countries onto "The Net" and away from the constraints of their male-dominated societies.

INTERNETMANIA?

The Internet itself is frequently seen by the general public in this sort of powerful, visionary way.

> *...the Internet is such a powerful force, it will change everything irreversibly...All culture will move through the Internet...Our culture will have to fit its structure or cease to exist...or be marginalized at the very least...(Berger, 1995, p. 22)*

> *The Internet..."is similar to what the library was 100 years ago, or the telegraph. It will be bigger and better than television. We're not talking about a 500-channel medium. We're talking about 250,000 channels that speak across all borders. It represents who we are, how we act, transact business and engage in relationships. The Internet is about information empowerment. I think it will change world culture."(Wolff, 1995a, p. A8).*

And projects such as the Blacksburg Electronic Village in the US, conceived in 1993 by Bell Atlantic Telephone and Virginia Tech University, where 12,000 people have been given Internet access (defined as being "linked to the information highway") are reported in the press as "totally transforming life", "showing what life will be like for all Americans in a few years", "bringing results beyond anyone's belief!", "bringing the whole town together. . . professors who are now friends with farmers", "folks are just one big happy family!", . . . and, particularly significant for tele-learning, "children are broadening their horizons. . .".

The above example is not isolated or extreme. I have a thick folder from 1995 alone of similar newspaper accounts from many different countries and certainly almost all the European countries, that show the pervasiveness of the public belief of the importance of being able to "get on" the information highway.

■ 3.1.2 RELATING THE HYPE/VISION TO TELE-LEARNING

This all seems a different world than that we anticipated in Chapter 2 of this book, where we attempted to categorize tele-learning technologies in terms of communication theory and technical evolution. Do people who work with the technologies in Chapter 2, as technical scientists or educational technologists, recognize the "cyberspace" of the newspapers and the global-community visionaries?

NEEDING EACH OTHER...

It is a major thesis of this book that the tele-learning domain discussed in Chapter 2 and the domain that is now becoming familiar to the public in terms of the metaphorical information highway have a critical relation to each other. Not only the evolution of the computer-stream of tele-learning technologies but also the coming convergence of video- and computer streams into network and desktop multi-media systems, require the availability of pervasive and powerful computer networks, and of public access to a wide variety of resources and communication possibilities. Without the social and political (and commercial) push that seems to need a level of hype in order to create a public momentum, the infrastructure needed to bring networking possibilities to the public and the massive investment needed to organize network-available resources are less likely to occur.

MOMENTUM IS IMPORTANT...

Without political and commercial momentum, fueled by and fueling social pressure, broad-scale affordable access to tele-learning will not occur. And we who are educators cannot make the infrastructure for affordable tele-learning occur through our analysis of its educational value alone: we need the power of the marketplace and of social demand to produce the technological infrastructure that we need.

And without standards for access, and affordable access, practical bottlenecks will constrain the development of tele-learning scenarios and limit their applicability to only a fortunate few.

A key example of this is the issue of public, affordable access to the Internet.

■ 3.1.3 PUBLIC ACCESS TO THE INTERNET

GROWTH IN NUMBERS IS ENORMOUS

Public discovery of the Internet in 1994 and more specifically the WWW in 1995 has brought an explosion of demand for public access to the Internet system in countries around the world. In Interface 1 we have already given an overview of Internet usage and its rapid growth; it is sufficient here to note just a few indicators, such as those in Table 3.1.

Table 3.1 Host computers on the Internet, by domain, January 1995 and July 1995, and January 1996

Domain	January 1995	July 1995	January 1996
com	1,316,966	1,743,390	2,430,954
edu	1,133,502	1,411,013	1,793,491
UK	241,191	291,258	451,750
gov	209,345	273,855	312,330
de (Germany)	207,717	350,707	452,997
ca (Canada)	186,722	262,644	372,891
mil	175,961	224,778	258,791
au (Australia)	161,166	207,426	309,562
org	154,578	201,905	265,327
net	150,299	300,481	758,597
jp (Japan)	96,632	159,776	269,327
fr (France)	93,041	113,974	137,217
nl (The Netherlands)	89,227	135,462	174,888

Source: Network Wizards, 1996, (http://www.nw.com/zone/WWW/report.html)

By "domains" are meant designations about the owners of the addresses, usually by country initials, with the exception of the US. The domain "edu" is used primarily in the US to identify educational sites. The domain "mil" and the domain "gov" are US military and governmental addresses. The domains "com", "org", and "net" are international and stand for commercial, organization, and network. Hosts are computers with a distinct address on the Internet; a host may itself be a server for a large number of internetworked computers, such as in a local-area network. There are more than 90 countries with their own Internet domain; only the top seven (or eight, if we count the US as the sum of various domains) appear in Table 3.1. Table 3.1 gives only an impression of growth (such data can be easily found on the Internet): In 1992 the total number of hosts worldwide was 727,000. This number is changing by about 120% every year. For some locations for these sorts of growth data, see Box 3.1.

DEMOGRAPHICS OF THE INTERNET USER

The demographics of the Internet access are also changing quickly. According to two consumer surveys conducted on the Internet in fall 1994 and spring 1995 (Chatterlee, Gupta and Pitkow, 1995), with the number of responses to various

---

Box 3.1

Locations for data about the Internet

Network Wizards:
URL http://www.nw.com/

The Internet Index:
URL http://www.openmarket.com/intindex/

The Internet Society:
URL http://info.isoc.org/indextxt.html

---

sections of the survey ranging from 2,100 to 13,000, meaningful demographic shifts took place within that six-month time period. The most telling seems to be the type of computer used to access the Internet:

- Fall 1994, 44% accessed the Internet through UNIX workstations, found at universities and corporate research settings, while 29% accessed through standard PCs
- Spring 1995, 8% accessed through UNIX workstations while 52% accessed through standard PCs

The implication of this is important: within half a year, dominance of usage swung away from researchers in technical academic departments in universities, with heavy-duty computers, to "ordinary" people, with desk top computers at home or school or wherever their desks happen to be.

Profiles of users

And the profile of the typical user of the Internet is changing, too, from male academics to males working for a company. Two-thirds of users in 1995 are male, according to various surveys, the average age is 18 to 35, the average educational level is above average, and so is the average income (Investor's Business Daily, 1995, p. A8). For a representative of these user surveys, try:

Georgia Tech GVU Survey of Web Users:
URL http://www.cc.gatech.edu/gvu/user_surveys

ACCESS: YOU NEED A WAY TO GET ON AND IN...

When you couple data about Internet usage with other relevant data (there is more to home tele-learning than the Internet, after all), such as subscriptions to commercial on-line services which may offer via their subscriptions access to the Internet, the numbers of people and families who, through their home computers, can access on-line resources in 1995 is considerable. The predictions are that as many as 15 million Europeans will subscribe to on-line services by the year 2000, above those with direct Internet access through their work or homes (Business Week, 1995a).

And the bottom line of network tele-learning in the home is a computer (there can be exceptions, of specially made terminals for example, such as those throughout France as part of the Minitel initiative). Data show home computer use to continue to grow throughout the world. As examples, estimates are that in 1995 nearly one-half of all US households have a home computer (Fields, 1995), and in The Netherlands, over 80% of students and staff involved in higher-education have personal computers at home, a quarter of whom make use of a modem to connect to their institutional network with in turn connects to the national backbone network which in turn connects to the Internet. And by 1997, in The Netherlands, the goal is that all middle-level vocational schools and their staff and students (approximately equivalent to the community college sector in the US) will have a direct connection (Zwart, 1995).

MOMENTUM FOR AT-HOME TELE-LEARNING

These demographic data are important because they are indicators that Internet use is moving from a technical setting in the university to also include the home and the individual user. This, intertwined with the strong growth in commercial on-line services in many countries, especially when those services offer Internet access as one of their features, has within a very short period of time brought a new dimension of possibilities for tele-learning in the home.

But what are home users doing with all this connectivity?

▓ 3.1.4 RELATION TO TELE-LEARNING AND THE FAMILY?

There are many things that family members are doing with network access from the home, many of which would not be defined as tele-learning. Just as with watching television, the use of on-line connectivity can be primarily for entertainment, either by browsing, chatting with like-minded strangers via newsgroups, or surreptitiously browsing forbidden domains. Or, unlike television, network connectivity from the home may be specifically utilized for "tele-working", being connected with one's physical workplace or colleagues while remaining in one's residence. Tele-working is a growing phenomena around the world, being taken seriously by employers, unions, governments, and commercial vendors (see for example, Seymour, 1995).

However, in individual tele-learning, the boundary between browsing and chatting and learning may be easily passed, because of the lack of need to involve a formal educational institution in the process. The intention to learn, the effort to learn, the accomplishment of learning, the process of learning itself, are what matters, and these are what we are interested in with tele-learning and the family in this chapter.

In Table 3.2 we expand the four main possibilities that we see for home tele-learning. Following this, we take each possibility cluster as the focus of a separate section of this chapter. For each of the categories, the technologies involved are e-mail, the WWW, and the various services provided by the on-line network service to which the family may subscribe.

Table 3.2 Tele-learning possibilities for the home and family

Tele-learning category	Realized by... (examples)
Being informed and involved	—Community BBSs, nets —Individualized information —Digital newspapers and magazines
Transcending distance	—Virtual museums —Virtual excursions —Language practice and cross-cultural communication
Tools for self-directed learning	—Virtual libraries —Learning through games and motivational activities —General-purpose learning tools —Content-specific learning materials
Creative expression	—Contribute to organized WWW sites for creative expression —Create Web pages

■ 3.2 TELE-LEARNING APPLICATIONS FOR THE HOME: NEW WAYS OF BEING INFORMED AND INVOLVED

In this section we examine three new ways of being informed and involved that are made possible by networked communication and information environments and that are important to the informal learning of the individual learner in the home. These three categories can be called "community nets", where the emphasis is on local interaction and awareness and perhaps a sort-of grassroots democracy; information sites and newsgroups targeted on special topics; and new forms of mass media, particularly new forms of newspapers and magazines. This section can only give an overview of these topics as general areas and a few, sample, sources as illustration. Part of the strength of these new ways of being informed is their quantity and vibrancy: we cannot capture these characteristics in a section or even a book and whatever we choose as today's interesting examples will be superseded by many new candidates by literally the next day. This is where the popular energy of the Internet is most broadspread and strong in 1995. The tools are primarily BBS systems; the WWW for those who seek attractively organized, hyperlinked, up-to-date information; and newsgroups, for those who prefer their information coming from the comments of others.

■ 3.2.1 COMMUNITY NETS

A community net (which may be called by other names, such as Digital City or a FreeNet) is an computer-networked environment, perhaps a BBS, perhaps a Web site, that is organized in a way that the local inhabitants of an area are encouraged to come to the site for local information and for the opportunity to make their opinions known about local events. Within this simple description there are hundreds of examples and variations.

TWO CORE MOTIVATIONS

The core motivation for a "community net" reflects the position and perhaps philosophy of those who initiate and maintain it (see D. Schuler, 1995, for a comprehensive US summary). For many years, community nets have functioned, as dial-in BBSs (bulletin-board systems), primarily as volunteer and small-scale efforts whose intention is some mixture of inexpensive information provision and communication facilitation, with an emphasis on the latter. More recently, these grass-roots BBSs have been parallel by more formally organized collections of information, often by local government or service agencies. Here the focus becomes much more one of providing continual access to up-to-date information of use to the community. The new iteration of community nets makes use of the WWW, and these two philosophies—bottom-up, citizens' self-expression vs top-down, well-organized and useful information— are very much in evidence. A few examples and some reflections follow. . . .

BULLETIN BOARD SYSTEMS

The idea of a community network is not new; local dial-in bulletin-board systems have been in operation and flourishing for more than a decade. In the WWW site:

```
URL http://www.vni.net/thedirectory/telnet.htm
```

information about BBSs can be found and hundreds of specific examples, with direct links, are given. The cost of most is only that of the phone charges needed to connect the subscriber to the board. Interestedly, BBSs are beginning to offer WWW access through a local BBS, which will broadly increase WWW use as it will provide private users an inexpensive entry into the WWW (Vaughan-Nichols, 1995).

One line of evolution: more information, less communication

There has been an evolution in BBSs over the years, particularly as sources of community learning. Earlier versions were characterized by frustratingly limited technology on one hand, and passionate expressions of opinion by a relatively few number of contributors on the other, something like call-in radio talk shows. As the information-provision aspects of call-in systems became better identified by community services and governments, many different varieties of information-system type call-in provision have emerged, typically with more secure and better-organized information but less tolerance for freedom of expression.

As learning resources, such dial-in systems have the capacity and occasionally do offer significant quantities of relevant information, downloadable for the cost of a local telephone call (once one discounts the cost of the computer and modem and communications software needed to make this connection). The extent to which information relates to tele-learning is hard to say: it is like asking how much do citizens learn from their local libraries?

Gophers

A significant breakthrough in community information provision occurred with the movement away from the general limitations of dial-in BBSs toward more flexible information-organization services, particularly through Gopher systems.

Gopher systems allow the organization of information in efficient, hierarchical layers, through which a searcher can move down or up until a relevant title is discovered. Then a click of the title allows access to what can be a very large text file, downloadable to the disk of the accessor. Gopher systems are accessible in great quantity via the Internet; however from the community-learning perspective, Internet-wide access does not have to be available. Local Gopher systems can run as local information systems and there are many examples of vibrant use (see Schuler, 1994, 1995). However, the spontaneity of self-expression, or of any individual expression, is sometimes lost, unless that expression is captured in a text file that is available, through selection of its title, from the available collection. Like a large civic archive, there may be fascinating gems of local history, from which some dedicated local archivists can learn much; or there may be information valuable to current decision making about issues important to a community, which would benefit its citizens if they had access to it in a form attractive to them.

Another line of evolution: more communication, less information

While one stream of community networks moved toward more efficient provision of larger amounts of information, another stream moved in the opposite direction, toward more and more encouragement of self-expression. While both streams are important to an informed citizenry, the self-expression advocates are sometimes extreme in their view that freedom of speech is what freedom, and thus what community nets, should be about. In this perspective "Control" and "top down" are offensive concepts, the opportunity to be heard is more important than the accuracy, quality or reasonableness of what is heard. Quality is left to the judgment of those who are speaking. Out of this stream have emerged thousands of newsgroups and distribution lists, many of them still reflecting roots in community networks.

Implications for tele-learning?

We emphasize these two lines of evolution because they are perhaps most clear to trace in the evolution of community networks from 1985 to 1995, but also because they are two lines of development, with two sets of issues and philosophies, that underlie much of what people think of and expect from the Internet itself. They affect the public's expectations about networks and the Internet in particular as tele-learning environments; those expectations can be in considerable collision, as we will see in different ways throughout this book. Box 3.2 summarizes the difference between these two lines of evolution.

Box 3.2

The issue of control and quality

- Should the environments be professionally organized, accurate, useful sources of information, *thus maintained by specialists (a library model)? or*
- Should the environments provide the user with the tools to debate, contribute, and create through being able to make and be connected with others and with a wide range of resources, *not just those selected by specialists (a communication model)?*

As in many other applications of networks, it is the WWW which is revolutionizing community networks, partly because it has the capacity to allow both the library and communication models to reside in the same integrated environment, and partly because its attractive, easy-to-use interface has lowered the entry threshold for new users, and has stimulated them to want to enter.

COMMUNITY NETS ... THE WWW EVOLUTION

Throughout the world, in 1994 and 1995, literally thousands of "community networks" residing as WWW pages have emerged. By going to the location:

City Free Nets
URL http://www.city.net/

or consulting the references in Schuler (1995), the extent of these community networks can be seen. In the City Free Nets site, the human browser can choose from continent or country or state or province or region and can find literally hundreds of active links to community networks organized as WWW sites. In The Netherlands, for example, many cities and local regions have WWW pages, usually established by the local municipality or chamber of commerce. The philosophical orientation of these is typically more that of information provision than of free expression, but an important evolution is occurring in three significant ways.

The community net and new levels of relevance, accessibility and attractiveness
Community networks bring together information pertinent to informed participation in the democratic processes of a community. Such sources are available, in countries around the world, for not only the local and regional level but also the national levels. In the US, for example, the federal government has been making tens of thousands of its databases, documents, graphics files and other such information available via the Internet. This information ranges from job

opportunities, environmental information, medical and health-related information, travel and economic data. A sampling of US-relevant information is given
in Box 3.3.

Box 3.3

Sampling of US-focused WWW sites with community-relevant information

"Thomas" (after Thomas Jefferson), full text of any bill introduced in Congress since 1992:
URL `http://thomas.loc.gov`

"Fedworld", how tax money is spent:
URL `http://www.fedworld.gov`

"Senator E. Kennedy's Home Page", legislation affecting Massachusetts:
URL `http://www.senate.gov/member/ma/kennedy/general/`

For a general discussion about such information provision in the US, see Gaffin
(1993). However, for an up-to-date overview, use any WWW search tool (see
Interface 2 for information about WWW searching). Search terms such as *[country
of interest], government* and *information* are a good way to start.

The example in Box 3.3 was US-oriented, but similar examples are increasingly
available in other countries, often more technically sophisticated to those based
in the US because of the need to express their sites in a variety of languages. As
a good example, the Commission of the European Community operates a broad-
ranging site of information about initiatives and new developments, many of
them directly relevant to trans-European tele-learning. The site can be accessed
in any of 15 languages spoken by citizens in the Community; one chooses from
clicking on the flag of one's choice. To see this site, visit:

Commission of the European Community, Information for Citizens
URL `http://europa.eu.int`

Open access to information is not only a key to individual tele-learning but to
the health of communities themselves. Thomas Jefferson, one of the architects of
the government system in the US, noted long ago:

> . . . I know of no safe depository of the ultimate power of the society but the
> people themselves, and if we think them not enlightened enough to exercise their
> control with a wholesome discretion, the remedy is not to take it from them, but
> to inform their discretion (quoted in Schuler, 1994, p. 38)

This is where individual tele-learning and community networks intersect.

The community net to stimulate reaction and feedback

Another way that information provision is being transformed by tele-learning technologies relates to the backgrounds of those who are pioneers in the design of new forms of community networks. It is often the case that community WWW sites, at least in their pioneer phases, are conceptualized and constructed by persons working within the local municipality but coming to their task in their personal histories from a communication- and expression-oriented motivation. They may work in the city hall, but they are fascinated by the Internet and its possibilities for stimulating user engagement. They emphasize the use of forms throughout their WWW pages, to encourage citizen input and reaction; they see the environment as a way to bring the opinions of the community forward to the local decision makers. They see the WWW site as a community-learning environment. The "Political Participation Project" is a model of how a Web site can be organized to stimulate informed discussion about local issues. The site also provides access to politically relevant sites on the Web more generally, in order to "improve political participation of all kinds". The location of this site is:

Political Participation as a Model for a Local WWW Site:
URL http://www.ai.mit.edu/projects/ppp/home.html

Another interesting example occurred during a major election in Canada in October 1995. In the province of Quebec, citizens went to the polls to decide if they wished independence from Canada ("Oui!") or if they wished to stay part of Canada ("Non"). Two WWW sites were set up, one for the Oui side and one for the Non side, and vigourous debates took place. (In the real election, the "Non" side won, but very narrowly, by 50.6% to 49.4%, with over 93% of eligible voters casting a vote.)

The community net as a new metaphor for community

It is not only that the WWW allows the conceptual integration of information with reaction and feedback, it also because of its hyperlinked nature and support of attractive layout and graphics that it is providing a fertile soil for the emergence of a new metaphor of community interaction: the so-called Digital City. This term "Digital City" has become very popular in The Netherlands, through the pioneering work of the Amsterdam Digital City site, which not only brought the possibilities of a new form of community network to the attention of the Dutch public, but also the new metaphor of a community whose citizens can wander freely into communication with their fellow citizens, from school child to city councilmen, and can find useful, up-to-date, relevant information all in the same environment. The Amsterdam Digital City site can be found at:

Amsterdam Digital City
URL http://www.dds.nl/

THE POWER OF A METAPHOR

The power of this metaphor is not to be underestimated. It has captured and mobilized the public imagination in The Netherlands, for example, stimulating the desire of individuals, through their homes, to be able to have an Internet connection like no other single motivation. It has fueled political decision making, and the telephone company, to aggressively look for ways to lower the costs and complexities of individual access to the Internet from the home. It has triggered a change in mentality in The Netherlands about networks and especially the Internet that has changed the possibilities for individual tele-learning.

These possibilities can only be met if people can get connected, from their homes, comfortably and affordably. The possibilities of individual tele-learning will only begin to be taken seriously by society when society as a whole gains experience with both the library-model and the communication-model of network organization and feels that experience is valuable. We discuss this more in Section 3.6.

As a final note, it is interesting that one of the main designers of the Amsterdam Digital City site is an educational technologist, a graduate of our own faculty. His motivation for becoming involved with the site was that he sees the environment as a public location for open and flexible learning, as an environment for tele-learning and more generally, as a new kind of learning environment. This is an example of the impact that educational technologists are bringing to the creative design of new tele-learning environments and tools; we discuss many examples of this in Chapter 8.

■ 3.2.2 INFORMATION SITES AND NEWSGROUPS FOR TARGETED INFORMATION

Government issues are only one of literally millions of focuses of interest that can be addressed through information available via the Internet system. As one other example, parents interested in issues affecting their children's learning have always looked for ways to find relevant information. These ways can be enhanced by sources such as those found in Table 3.3, which were found after less than one minute search time with a WWW search tool (over 600 resources were found using the search terms "parents" and "education").

Table 3.3 Sample of learning resources useful to parents available through the Internet

Location	Description
`Newsgroup:` `misc.kids.computer`	Discussion among parents of appropriate uses of computers for children and of experiences with software
`http://www.childsoft.com/` `childsoft`	Reviews of educational software programs for home use, with screen displays; demo materials can be downloaded
`http://www.ucalgary.ca/` `1%7Edkbrown/`	Guide to children's literature, with many links to specific sites and with suggestions for helping one's child read and use the site

`http://www.ed.gov/pubs/`
`parents/Reading/`
`index.html`
	Reading-encouragement activities for parents to do with their children

`http://www.ed.gov/`	Source materials for national (US) debate on connecting education to the "information superhighway" and for an "electronic town hall" discussion on the relationship between time and learning in schools. Parents can also participate in the various debates if they have access to a receive station for corresponding satellite broadcasts
`http://www.ils.nwu.edu/` `~e_for_e`	Electronic hypermedia book, "Engines for Education", discussing how information technology can assist in the reform of schools

`http://http.cs.berkeley.edu/`
`students/wicse/`
`parents.html`
	Links to a wide range of information useful for parents and children, such as links to books about parenting, links to sites about

	boy and girl-scout information, links to areas for parents to exchange experiences and information, and a link to a page with 500 more links relevant to "Kids and Parents on the Web"
`http://farnsworth.mit.edu/`	Extensive information about projects relating to participation in initiatives relevant to education and the national information infrastructure (in the US)
`http://www.stpauls.edu/`	Web site maintained by a local school, indicating its curriculum, philosophy and other features; example of how a school can mount its own Web site for parents wishing to make a decision about which school their child should attend, or wishing to have good information about their child's present school
`email to: edpol-d-request` `Subscribe edpol-d`	A listserv in the form of a moderated discussion list for parents and others interested in educational policy related to the present and future of k-12 networking
`http://bucky.aa.kic.edu/`	Information and issues relating to persons with disabilities

Another good example is a site with extensive information about considerations for local schools with regard to their "information infrastructures" (Huntley, 1995). This site, which can be extremely useful for school and district decision makers (see Chapter 7) as well as parents who wish to make a well-informed contribution to discussions and debates about infrastructure options, can be found at the "Local Information Infrastructure" site:

Local Information Infrastructure site:
URL
`http://copernicus.bbn.com:70/testbed2/LII/lii_desc.html`

NEW DIMENSIONS...

What is so special about such collections of resources? Haven't concerned parents always been able to find information relevant to the education of their children? Yes, but...there are qualitative and quantitative differences.

Quantitative differences

The quantitative differences show up in the fact that hundreds of these resources can not only be located but potentially be in the hands of the searcher within literally a few minutes, and with no more cost than the cost of the Internet connection (and whatever extra fees a local service provider may choose to levy for downloading).

Qualitative differences

The qualitative difference is not only that material is sometimes interactive, sometimes comprised of multiple media, most likely more up-to-date than print material found in libraries and often hyper-linked directly to other relevant resources, but most critically that parents can frequently choose to ask a question, via e-mail, of the source of a document, or participate in a discussion relating to the issues of focus in the site. And all this from their own home computer.

IS THIS TELE-LEARNING?

Is this tele-learning?

Yes!

Defined differently to be sure from learning demarcated by a curriculum and supervised by a teacher in a formal school setting, but learning nonetheless, informal, self-directed, self-constructed learning, relevant to the task and situation of the learner. Such learning also occurs in libraries and via books and discussions with friends, but now it can be amplified far beyond one's local resources, via tele-learning.

■ 3.2.3 NEW FORMS OF MASS MEDIA

Newspapers, magazines, television and radio are important tools for self-directed learning. Network-available versions of newspapers and magazines are offering alternative forms of publication that can bring both quantitative and qualitative additions to the learning value of these media. Why? What is better than being able to curl up in bed with a good book? Or reading a good magazine while waiting for your train? Or watching a well-done television documentary from the comfort of your living room?

Nothing, if we only think about bed and waiting rooms and watching.

But if we think in terms of added value, of added possibilities and motivational impact, then network-alternatives or supplements of traditional media are a serious and exciting new environment for individual tele-learning. In Chapter 4 and the Interface section (**Interface 4**) we look at some aspects of electronic publishing from a professional perspective, professionals as tele-learners and professionals in the business of producing these new forms of mass media. In this chapter, however, we are focusing on the family, parents and children. What are some aspects of new forms of mass media that have the most potential for them as individual tele-learners?

We see two important dimensions: interactivity, and being able to follow up information in a personally relevant way.

INTERACTIVITY AND FOLLOW-UP

Interactivity and the ability to choose from a variety of types of immediate follow-up are the two features which are being added to electronic supplements of mass media that we see as most important to individual tele-learning. A learner studying an "on-line" supplement to a newspaper or journal can choose to follow-up some aspects of items, and if the site is organized well, can access a wide variety of background and associated material, including persons, related to a particular story. A learner watching a television documentary can go to an on-line supplement to that story and have the same follow-up options. This extra material may be:

- Multi-media, even brief video and audio clips can now be received via networks on certain types of home computers, and this capacity will expand rapidly (see Chapter 2 and Chapter 10)
- Presented at the level of detail that the learner wishes
- Interactive, inviting learners to become participants in a discussion or reaction to some aspects of the content of the original message, for example to vote for or otherwise comment on issues and other aspects of the original material
- Of an auxiliary nature, materials such as software, that can be immediately downloaded from an on-line page
- Discussion groups relating to the selected item, which may include the chance to interact with the author of an article or the central figure of a broadcast

- Links that relate the original item to a long chain of related items
- Links to specialized associated information (for example, if an article is about an upcoming election, information about where to go to vote in a given area could be available to those for whom it is relevant)
- Tools that allow the tele-learner to cut and paste segments from the original material or follow-up material into a personalized format for the unique needs of the individual
- Organized in a way that invites the tele-learner to submit his or her own information, perhaps even his or her own Web documents, for subsequent publication

Box 3.4 gives the URLs of just a few of the hundreds (perhaps thousands) of on-line newspapers and magazines, available through the Internet (and thus, in 1995 at least, freely), offering different combinations of the above features to their readers. Perhaps "requesters" will come to be a better name than readers, as those who are now making use of these options often spend more time on following-up additional choices or writing their own ideas than on actually reading the original material.

Box 3.4

Examples of electronic supplements to print-based magazines and newspapers

Page Name: Interactive Canadian History Magazine
URL: `http://heritage.excite.sfu.ca/hpost.html`

Page Name: Der Spiegel (popular German magazine)
URL: `http://spiegel.nda.net/nda/spiegel/`

Page Name: Mecklermedia Computer Magazines
URL: `http://www.ziff.com/`

Page Name: San Jose Mercury On-Line (typical of multimedia version of a daily newspaper)
URL: `http://www.sjmercury.com/`

Page Name: Web Newspaper List (list of links to commerical newspapers developing Web editions)
URL: `http://www.jou.ufl.edu/commres/webjou.htm`

Downloading software and following links: examples of added value

A particularly useful feature of the on-line versions of computer-related magazines is that the reader can immediately download software (at least demo versions) mentioned in the articles and can follow links indicated to further information about the software or user experiences with the software. As another example, if the reader goes to the electronic version of the computer magazine *PC Magazine* for 14 July 1995 which is available at the location:

```
http://www.pcmag.com/
```

she can see not only a copy of the article *"PC Magazine: Top 100 Web Sites"* (Willmott, 1995) which is also available in the standard print form of the magazine, but she can also choose any of those "top 100" sites, click on the words that describe them in the on-line article, and immediately go to the actual site via the World Wide Web. In addition, she can click on the browser feature "Add bookmark", which lets her return to that site without ever having to type in its URL.

DYNAMIC READING

Thus reading becomes not only more selective and interactive, but also *dynamic*, facilitating the construction of one's own, new, integrated electronic resource (the tele-learner's personal Bookmark Page) based around sources and links that are available in an electronic version of an article.

Bookmarks...A powerful tool for constructing a personal and sharable annotation

Bookmarks as generated by WWW browsers are in fact an emerging new form of taking notes, with a number of added-value features not before available. For one, the reader can immediately follow-up what the author is offering as references, which may be useful both for deepening the reader's understanding, but also for verifying the interpretation of the author herself. In any case, a valuable reference can be clicked as a personal bookmark, and thus became a dynamic form of note taking.

In addition, personal bookmark collections can be shared with others by downloading the bookmark file and sending or otherwise giving it to someone else, another way to add new dimensions to the impact of an initial media resource.

Personal annotation will emerge as more and more important to individual tele-learning in other ways, as technologies converge in our homes and desktops (see Chapter 2). Heppel, for example, predicts a "learning layer" incorporated into interactivity, including television, "so that people can annotate what they see and hear". Heppel sees this as a way that "the colliding worlds of the PC and TV can learn from each other" (Heppel, 1995); we see it as another way that individual tele-learning will gain in power and appeal as tele-learning technologies for the home continue to converge.

Digging deeply, and with your own kind of shovel...

Reading is also more tailored and up-to-date with distributed hypermedia publication forms than it can be in print form (or broadcast form) because of the many links that can be chosen and activated based on the learner's interests and on the learner's preferred way of obtaining extra information—in text, in pictures, even in audio or video forms. Sometimes, for example, a picture is worth the proverbial 1,000 words, but other times you prefer to have those 1,000 words rather than a picture. It depends on the learner and the content involved. In individual tele-learning, without a teacher as a mediator to filter and tailor information, it is important that the learner has the tools and capacity to make choices about tailoring his or her information.

Let's look at an example. Box 3.5 shows the path taken by a home tele-learner the day after a severe earthquake struck Japan in early 1995. This tele-learner had read a brief comment about the earthquake in the local newspaper, and had noted terrible-sounding data about the damage caused, but couldn't really visualize what those numbers meant in terms of human impact. This was particularly motivating to me (because that's who this particular tele-learner was), because I had just received an e-mail message the day before from a colleague in Japan with whom I was working on a paper, and I wondered if the earthquake was anywhere near his home. The column in the newspaper couldn't give me these types of information and I only had a few minutes before I had to go to work. So I began at a general-purpose topic page available on the Web (there are many) and proceeded as shown in the Box 3.5:

Box 3.5

Personalizing the detail of information

1. I went to my bookmark collection in my WWW browser and clicked on one of my handy general sources as a beginning point:
   `http://www.w3.org/hypertext/DataSources/bySubject/Overview.html`

2. I decided to chose the topic <Environment>, not because it was the ideal choice, but I happened to spot it and I thought perhaps that is one of the perspectives I might find valuable. Clicking this linked me to the URL:
   `http://ecosys.drdr.virginia.edu/Evironment.html`

3. Well, was this going to be useful or not? I saw the topic <Earth Sciences> and clicked it. This linked me to the URL:

   `http://www.geo.ucalgary.ca/VL-EarthSciences.html`

4. Hum, I am now in Canada, not Japan. Clearly a poor choice of initial topics, but I know from experience that useful connections often can occur to compensate for weak choices that I made earlier. And here is maybe one: I saw the topic <Current Events> and chose it. This linked me to a file with the URL:

   `http://www-vl-es.geo.ucalgary.ca/VL/html/es-current.html`

5. Ah-ha! I saw an entry from the day before, directly from Japan. I clicked it (<94/01/17 South Hyogo Earthquake Information>). This linked me to the site with URL:

   `http://www.riken.go.jp/news/earthquake/html`

6. Now I was in a collection of articles and images from Japan itself about the earthquake, not just material filtered through Western news sources! From many alternatives I chose one relating to the city where my colleague works: <Disaster and Reconstruction of KOBE City with photo images mirrored from Kobe City University of Foreign Studies>. This linked me to the associated file with URL:

   `http://www.riken.go.jp/news/kobe-city/whatsnew/disaster.html`

7. Here I found many photographs taken by Japanese directly at the site of the quake. I could make my own choice as to what I wanted to see from this original-source collection. I chose: <the area devasted by the fire>. This linked me to the location

   `http://www.riken.go.jp/news/kobe-city/whatsnew/images/map.gif`

8. After about 15 seconds loading time I had a high-quality photograph on my screen. I spent a few more minutes making further choices in this site where there were many more photographs to be selected, all from the day after the earthquake. If I had wished, I could (at least technically) capture any of these photographs by pressing the "screen capture" key on my computer. (This puts a copy of what is on the screen into my clipboard. From the clipboard, I could later edit it and insert it into my own word processing document, or into my own Web page. However, for the issues relating to copyright and ownership, see Section 3.6.4!). Most WWW browsers also support easy downloading of distributed images and HTML files.

Thus, in about 10 minutes, I was able to follow-up my own learning need in a way tailored to my own circumstances (visuals relating to a certain city). I could do this without leaving my room after I read an initial article that motivated my follow-up. I could do this in a way that went around the filters and choices that had been made by newspaper editors in my region to see what persons at the actual site of the earthquake were seeing (and the photographs meant that we communicated to each other without the problem of language).

I got the level and type of follow-up I wanted, when I wanted it, through my own choices. These are key aspects of individual tele-learning.

ISSUES—WHO OWNS THE INFORMATION?

The example in Box 3.5 also anticipates a major issue about the power of being able to capture and self-tailor dynamic learning resources brought into the tele-learner's client computer as a result of a request to a distant server—the issue of ownership and *plagiarism.* We come back to this in Section 3.6.4. Should I as a teacher have been able to capture those photographs, insert them into a word-processing or presentation package (through literally six or seven clicks on my mouse) and then use them with my students in a class discussion? Yes, that seems reasonable, and is in fact one of the major implications of tele-learning for the classroom teacher with a traditional face-to-face teaching situation and without classroom access to networking (see Chapter 5). But, what if I as the teacher make printouts of these photos and distribute them to my students, so they can see and study the details better? Probably still all right, in most persons' eyes. But what if I send the file electronically, over the network, to my students as I typically do when I want to efficiently disseminate class materials to them (see Chapter 6)? Still fair? Probably. But what if one of my students forwards the file to her boyfriend, who is a free-lance journalist? All she has to do is click "forward"...And then what if he publishes it in the local newspaper? Is this fair? Many more people are learning from the images, but the chain has moved far from its source, some unnamed Japanese photographer whose images were included as part of a research collection by a scholarly agency in Japan.

And the whole chain of events above rests on the confidence that those original photographs were accurate. Who verified this? Perhaps the one I selected was mis-labeled, or even a fraud. Editorial control also brings with it reader confidence with traditional mass media: the more we can go to the "voice of the people" the more chance there is that we happen to listen to someone whose voice is not one which should be transmitted. Editors can still operate as a quality-control filter with "voice-of-the-people" collections of opinion and information, but the scale, quantity, and immediacy of digital streams of input make this sort of filtering at a human level difficult.

Personal input of the news...

An interesting example of this is happening in The Netherlands, where a national broadcasting company has augmented its television and radio services by an innovative WWW site in which citizens can contribute not only their own comments to world and local events but also their own video clips, which are then available to all through the WWW page (if the receiver has a computer that can handle multi-media, see Chapter 2). In this way, the broadcaster advertises that "everyone is welcome as a correspondent to the W.E.B. World Receiver" (Berg, 1995), but a selection process is still in place.

To see this site, or submit a contribution, visit:

W.E.B.World Receiver (Berg, 1995)
```
URL http://www.vpro.nl/www/vpro-
digitaal/web-world-receiver
```

This is where tele-learning in its freedom will, and is, bumping into unstoppable repercussions. Because as soon as I have the freedom to follow-up and tailor information so that it better suits my own learning needs, so do the next persons in the chain. And the digitization of the whole process means that the chain has no stopping point.

Smart searching, vs having information well organized for you...

The example in Box 3.5 also demonstrates another key issue in individual tele-learning: the tension between having a professionally organized (and filtered) collection of information and having the freedom, with the demands of that freedom, to search for one's self. The method I followed in Box 3.5 is in fact a typical method of searching for information on the WWW—sequential strategic choices from alternative links to associated sites.

Such an approach can work if you start well, if you make good choices all along, and if the interlinked body of resources is large enough so that you eventually come to a good choice of location. However, these are large "ifs". (We discuss this more thoroughly in Section 3.6.2.)

Getting help...

It is more efficient, and possibly more effective, if the tele-learner uses WWW search tools (which we also discuss in **Interface 2**). However, another way of searching for links is to use a tool called a "robot" (sometimes called an intelligent agent, although the use of the word intelligent is rather narrow), or to ask a service to do the searching for you. Librarians have always helped the needy searcher: now electronic resources such as "electronic librarians" can be found at many locations on the WWW, and increasingly, at a cost. Box 3.6 gives a few examples of search sources useful for home tele-learning:

Box 3.6

WWW search tools and services for home tele-learning

"NewsPage" search-support service:
http://www.newspage.com/
"...*NewsPage filters over 15,000 stories from over 500 news sources every night, and categorizes them by topic. Bookmark the topics you like, and NewsPage goes to work. Every day by 8:00 am you'll receive news on only those topics that match your interest. Scan concise briefs in seconds, then drill down to get the whole story." (Individual, Inc., 1995, p. 51). If the reader wishes to "drill down" to the full text of the selected articles there is a fee involved.*

Yanoff's Special Internet Connections (Yanoff, 1995)
URL: http://www.uwm.edu/Mirror/inet.services.html

Magellan: McKinley's Internet Directory (The McKinley Group, 1995)
URL http://www.mckinley.com/
...*Nicely organized description of hits, to help the user make a decision as to go further or not*

Yahoo
URL http://www.yahoo.com/yahoo
...*Nicely laid out and simple to use, with both lists of topics and the capacity for entering key words*

CUSI
URL http://pubweb.nexor.co.uk/public/cusi/cusi.html
...*Enter your search words once, and many different serarch engines are used to give you your hits*

Lycos (Carnegie Mellon University, 1995)
URL http://www.lycos.com
....*Lycos is a popular catalog of the Internet system, searching not only WWW sites but also Gopher and ftp, building a big database of everything it finds (in July 1995 this was 4,24 million WWW pages..) With Lycos, you enter your key words and immediately get a clickable list of as many hits as you want (ten is the default, weighted in terms of how important your key words are in the site).*

The whole business of getting help in finding the places and persons to which you want to connect for individual tele-learning is a major growth area, both scientifically and commercially. As an example, a search that I did on the WWW using the keyword "web" and "search engines" in July 1995 identified within a few seconds 2,417 documents! So-called "robots, wanderers, and spiders", see, for example:

WWW Robots, Wanderers, and Spiders (Koster, 1995):
URL `http://web.nexor.co.uk/mak/doc/robots/robots.html`

are at the intersection of computer science and big business, of the conflict between personal freedom and control, because they provide tools for anyone to find most anything once it is accessible via the Internet, a capability that has wide-ranging consequences. The implications of this for parents and children are also thought-provoking.

TELE-LEARNING: NEW WAYS OF CONNECTING WITH INFORMATION

Thus, tele-learning, with its new ways of being informed and involved with learning resources, even to the point of creating them yourself, has exciting possibilities for the individual tele-learner, and raises many issues.

As the examples in Section 3.2 illustrate, integrated communication and information resources, particularly those available via the WWW, provide a powerful platform for new ways of being informed and involved for the home learner. It is becomes only coincidental if the information one learns from is in one's local area, geographically, or far away: what matters to the tele-learner is that he or she can find what is needed, in a form that is appropriate, pursue an idea as far as desired, interact with it or communicate about it, and repeat this loop many times, all within affordable time and cost limits, perhaps within a range of minutes.

Sometimes, however, it is not the case that the tele-learner doesn't care where s/he goes in order to make connections: sometimes indeed a particular destination and its characteristics are of primary importance in a tele-learning session for the home learner. We discuss two aspects of destination-specific tele-learning in the next section.

■ 3.3 NEW TOOLS TO TRANSCEND DISTANCE

By transcending distance, we mean staying home in your body but going somewhere else, in your senses and your imagination. Of course, people have been doing this as long as there have been good story-tellers, as long as people have been able to dream. But technologies such as television and radio and the telephone have already changed the impact of distance in our lives in profound ways compared to the memory that distance had to our grandparents.

What is new about tele-learning with relation to distance?

In this section, we will look at two ways to transcend distance for the home-based tele-learner that we think are particularly interesting: making "virtual excursions" and using the communication and information resources available on a network such as the Internet to have some kind of a "global village" experience.

While both of these terms, "virtual excursions"(or virtual anything) and "global village" may sound like clichés, they are in fact important ways that parents and children together can share tele-learning experiences which at the very least will be interesting and informative, and beyond that may contribute to a changing perception of other cultures.

■ 3.3.1 THE VIRTUAL EXCURSION

We are using this term as a metaphoric name for the idea that interactive, network-accessible sites involving connections with images, words, photos, or video and also connections with people, can be so organized that a distant accessor of those resources gets some of the feeling of actually being in the location. Books and television documentaries make this possible to a certain degree, but the interactivity, the choices available to the visitor, and the possibility to communicate with "real people" at the real site that are now available to the tele-learner particularly through the WWW, bring a new dimension to these virtual excursions.

TRAVEL IS BROADENING... (INTELLECTUALLY)

Excursions to tourist areas are common on the Internet, and can have considerable learning value, especially if family members experience them together, discuss their experiences, and reinforce them with other learning inputs. (Of course, it is up to the family members if they see traveling as a learning experience, or not. These sorts of resources will not take a family with no interest in learning and change them overnight into the opposite, but for a family that does see learning possibilities in travel and vacations, tele-learning can enormously amplify those possibilities.) The Web locations in Box 3.7 are typical 1995 possibilities. They can be visited in the sense of preparing virtually for a real visit, or as virtual destinations in themselves.

Box 3.7

Turning traveling into a learning experience

W3 Servers Overview, by Country
URL http://www.w3.org/hypertext/DataSources/WWW/Servers.html
...A good starting point. countries, regions, and states from all over the world are listed, when one is selected there is usually a clickable map from which many different virtual locations can be visited

Searching Countries by Yahoo:
URL: http://www.yahoo.com/Government/Countries
...Starting any search with "http://www.yahoo.com" is a good idea for families, as topics are listed alphabetically and in logical categories, and there are thousands of up-to-date links

Visit Canada and the Canadian Parliament
URL http://www.parl.gc.ca
...Take an online tour of the National Parliament, learn the history of the national anthem as you listen to it in its different languages,

Visit the new South Africa
URL: http://www.ctcc.gov.za
...with a virtual tour book with many links both to historical and geographical information

Learn about Hong Kong
URL: http://www.hongkong.org
...History and tourism, combined with financial and statistical information

Visit the Rain Forest in Brazil
URL: http://www.escape.com/jvgkny/Brasil.Web.html
...And blend cultural insights with current news and a spelling tutorial for Portugese

And see why Paris is the City of Lights
URL: http://www.paris.org

VIRTUAL MUSEUMS: LET YOUR FINGERS DO THE WALKING...

The most consistent tele-learning value of virtual excursions seems to be associated with *virtual museums*. These are typically Web sites, organized to mimic or even improve upon what one would see in a walking tour of a museum. Multimedia aspects of these sites are important to the learning value. Among the many examples (a Web search with the search term "museum" found 18,687 sites, and with the search term "virtual museum" found 269 sites) are those shown in Table 3.4. It is a good idea to take a look at some of them first, to better understand our argument that a virtual tour to many of these museums not only brings many opportunities to the family that could never be otherwise experienced, but can also offer benefits that enrich or even surpass what happens when a family goes to a museum for a "real" visit. As "almost every museum in the world" has constructed a WWW page, mostly during 1995, as a way to extend learning experiences available through their services (Noack, 1995) all we can do here is sample a handful for the potential they offer. Interestingly, it is not usually professional educational technologists who are involved with the creative explosive of learning experiences being offered through virtual museum sites associated with actual museums. We look more at this sort of phenomena in Chapter 9.

Table 3.4 A Sample of Virtual Museums on the WWW

Museum	URL
Dinosaur Hall, University of California at Berkeley	`http://ucmp1.berkeley.edu/exhibittext/dinosaur.html`
Honolulu Community College Dinosaur Exhibit	`http://www.hcc.hawaii.edu/dinos/dinos.1.html`
Louvre Museum	`http://www.emf.net/wm/net`
Institute of Physics, Naples, Italy: Early Instruments	`http://hp133.na.infn.it/Museum/Museum.html`
Natural History Museum of Los Angeles County	`http://www.lam.mus.ca.us/lacmnh`
Franklin Institute Science Museum	`http://sln.fi.edu/tfi/welcome.html`
TheWeb Museum	`http://mistral.enst.fr/pioch/louvre`
The Vatican Museum	`http://sunsite.unc.edu/expo/vatican.exhibit/Vatican.exhibit.html`

New sites appear by the day, and the creativity of learning value and interactive possibilities associated with virtual museums in WWW sites is increasing faster than any single innovation in learning environments of which I am aware.

The "Web Museum" entry in Table 3.4 is an example of a virtual site that offers the combination of many more resources than could ever be possible in a real site. The Web Museum began as private activity in 1994 through one person in Paris (Pioch, 1995) and has grown to an enormous collection of museums, galleries, and individual artists, with many interactive activities as well as museum-collection visits possible. Another example of this type is the site of the OTIS Project which allows the virtual visitor to not only browse art by a large number of categories but also is host to collaborative projects among artists, creating art together over the Internet. See

The OTIS Project
URL `http://www.sito.org`

Is there a "real" OTIS Museum somewhere? Does it matter?

ADDING COMMUNICATION TO A VISIT

When there are real museums associated with the virtual museum, a typical virtual museum excursion will usually include options to investigate what's new at the actual museum as well as the electronic museum service. There is also often the electronic equivalent of visiting the museum's bookshop.

More substantially, there may be opportunities to directly ask a question, via e-mail, to a specialist in the museum, to participate in a survey, or to make general-information choices, such as seeing a floor plan of the museum or finding out if a particular topic or artist or event is represented in the museum. While it is often possible to find a face-to-face someone in a real museum to whom a question can be addressed, the opportunity to actually participate in a face-to-face discussion with a professional associated with a museum is quite unlikely, especially for the family on a vacation on a busy Sunday afternoon. Thus a virtual visit, through which asynchronous communication with staff can occur, can bring added value to being there.

BETTER THAN BEING THERE...

This added value can further increase through the number of areas in the (virtual) museum that are available for browsing. Choosing any one of these will bring more detailed information, perhaps including graphics that can be downloaded onto one's personal computer for private use. Sometimes there is a more interactive opportunity, usually in science museums, where the virtual excursion goer can make some of the same choices he or she would make in a hand's on visit with regard to a particular exhibition, and then see the results as well as read (or sometimes hear) an explanation. For example, the WWW site of the Australian National University in association with the Australian National Gallery includes an interactive tutorial on the history of prints, with examples of new prints in development, as they are being created by artists, so that tele-learners can see the design process from start to finish. The artists also talk about their work, and sound files are provided alongside the images (Bruntlett, 1995). See:

Australian National University Art Serve
URL http://rubens.anu.edu.au

Again, this is the individualization of depth, breadth, and medium that network tele-learning, and its 1995 form the WWW, offers to the family which makes it such a rich learning opportunity.

A virtual excursion amounts to much of the same intellectual payoff as going to the actual museum, and in fact may have added value in that one's interest can be directly targeted without a long walk through other areas of the museum, one can directly ask questions to a specialist and expect a written response, and one can generally download representative material from an area of interest for further study or archival purposes.

Such virtual excursion opportunities are becoming very popular for tele-learning in the home. On one commercial on-line service in the US, for example, offering a virtual excursion to the US Smithsonian Museum, 20 graphic images of famous Americans had been made available for free downloading on a certain day in the summer and by the next morning, the five most popular had already been downloaded nearly 500 times. Because this was during the summer vacation, these requests were probably not the result of school projects, but instead represented individual tele-learning. And this was a commercial service; tens of thousands of art reproductions available from virtual museums on the Internet, at least in 1995, are offered at no charge. The quality is not for hanging in your living room, but for parents and children as home tele-learners, the quality can be adequate for good learning experiences.

To let your fingers do the walking...? Choose some of the suggestions in Box 3.8, but better, use a search tool on the WWW and choose among the more up-to-date variety.

Box 3.8

Where to go? Families and virtual museums

Worldwide Guide to Museums and Cultural Resources
URL `http://www.usc.edu/lacmnh/webmuseums/`

Museums on the Web
URL `http://curry.edschool.virginia.edu/lha5w/museum/`

The Web Museum Network
URL `http://www.emf.net/wm/net/`
...This site, whose server is in Paris, links to an interesting variety of Web Museums in Europe, South American and Asia as well as North America

Yahoo Search: Museums
URL `http://www.yahoo/com/Art/Museums/`

Yahoo Search: Museums
URL `http://www.yahoo.com/yahoo/Science/Museums_and_Exhibits/`

If a parent is confronted with a child saying "There's nothing to do today" on a rainy Sunday afternoon, and the parent has tele-learning options as these only a mouse click away, then some remarkable new tele-learning alternatives are there for the choosing.

■ 3.3.2 OTHER VIRTUAL EXCURSION DESTINATIONS

Virtual excursions can be to other destinations besides museums or virtual museums. Destinations can be locations of historic or scientific interest, and can even be locations not available as real destinations, such as space, or simulated experiences not available to a real visitor. Box 3.9 identifies a few of these sorts of excursion destinations, all freely available via WWW on the Internet in 1995. Many more (thousands?) of such possibilities exist via regional educational network services and commercial on-line services.

Box 3.9

Virtual excursion destinations

Bradford Robotic TeleScope, UK.
URL http://www.eia.brad.ac.uk/rti/index.html
...Send a request for what you want the telescope to observe; completed jobs and images sent back the next day

Earth Viewer
URL http://www.fourmilab.ch/earthview/vplanet.html
...Take "photos" of the earth from interactive positions in space

Mayaquest
URL: http:// mayaquest.mecc.com/mayaguest.html
...Resource centre through which thousands of children from around the world could participate in an interactive learning experience with excavators at a Maya site as they were working over a two-month period

The Electronic Zoo
URL http://netvet.wustl.edu/e-zoo.htm

The Visible Human
URL http://www.nlm.nih.gov/research/visible
...Three-dimension slices of human biology (parental discretion needed here but informative for older family members)

THE VALUE? DEPENDS ON...

Of course, as is the case when the family goes on a real visit, these virtual excursion opportunities may end up being only superficial learning experiences. This is always a possibility with individualized learning, be it from books or WWW sites. What one gets out of a learning opportunity, when this is not structured and motivated by a teacher or educational institution, depends on one's own motivation and learning skills, and is constrained by the time and resources available to the individual. The family must really support (and must be able to afford to support) the value of a virtual excursion if children in the family incur connection changes for every minute that the excursion takes place. These are major issues relating to equity and feasibility of individual tele-learning in the home; we will discuss them further in Section 3.6.

■ 3.3.3 'GLOBAL VILLAGE' EXPERIENCES

The old expression "travel is broadening" is of course a cliché but like many clichés has core relevance. Travel can be a learning experience, not only at the factual level (as was the case with many of the URLs we indicated in Section 3.3.1), but also at another level, more deeply: at the level of coming to a better perspective about one's own place in the world, about other cultures and their values and customs, and about how to more effectively prepare for an increasingly international orientation in work and in society.

The importance, especially for children, of becoming less provincial in their worldview, of acquiring some skills and competencies for international, cross-cultural interactions, and of generally being aware of major barriers to effective cross-cultural communication, is not only a matter of personal enrichment but increasingly a necessity for functional literacy in the workplace.

Thus a very important benefit of electronic communication and of integrated electronic environments for communication and information is the ease, even the transparency, with which a tele-learner can move in and out of sites and contacts in other countries and cultures. This is a major, important, benefit of a home connection to the Internet, in that more than half the Internet nodes are now outside the US and it is just as easy and no more costly to access communication points and integrated learning environments on the other side of one's world as in one's own region. The power of this, the potential to influence a child's perception of the world, is considerable. In the next three subsections, we look at only a small sample of the many opportunities for global-village experiences available to the home tele-learner with an Internet connection.

Being a cross-cultural traveler

As a conceptually simple start, children can use the Internet for atlas-like information about the rest of the world, but with benefits of interactivity and potential communication that a printed atlas cannot supply. A major source of these is:

WWW City Net
URL `http://www.city.net/countries`

From here, thousands of cities from around the world can be selected, not only for information, as we saw earlier in Section 3.3.1, but with the express intention of cross-cultural awareness and even communication possibilities.

One of many examples is:

The Great Adventure
URL
`http://www.cmcc.muse.digital.ca/cmc/cmceng/childeng.html`

At this site, children can plan a trip and design their own itineraries, via interactive floorplans and a wealth of hyperlinked information. There is an option to participate in French as well as English, and a general link to United Nations information. Each of the 24 numbered options that the child can choose from in the interactive floorplans for his cultural excursion is a link to an interactive activity or at least a additional source of information, with visuals and text. Any of the materials in the overall site can be downloaded to the family's personal computer and printed out for future reference.

BEING A CROSS-CULTURAL COMMUNICATOR

Opportunities for children

The opportunity to communicate with a child from another culture, if a common language can be found, can be a powerful learning experience. Such communication is not likely to happen by chance, but needs an organizing structure. Many such structures to help children to find each other for communication purposes are available on the WWW, such as the sample from 1995 shown in Box 3.10.

Box 3.10

Cross-cultural communication possibilities for children

The Canadian Kids Page
URL: `http://www.OnRamp.ca/`

The Global Show and Tell
URL: `http:// emma.manymedia.com/show-n-tell/sites.html`

Cyber Kids
URL `http://www.mtlake.com/cyberkids`
...*An online magazine through which children can tell about themselves and find "keypals" for further communications*

Global Youth Forum
URL `http://www.sfc.keio.ac.jp/laszlo/SEICHO/SEICHO/index-e.html`
...*Young persons from more than 100 countries can express their concerns on local environmental issues on this moderated list that was set up to provide a way for student opinions to be heard at a UNEP Global Forum on the Environment*

Cross-cultural experiences for older tele-learners

Not only children can use tele-learning technologies for cross-cultural learning experiences with a focus on communication skills. Many opportunities are available for older learners as well. Again, the range is vast. Examples include Web sites that are primarily informational such as the sample in Box 3.11.

Box 3.11

Cross-cultural information sites, for adults

The Living Library of the United Nations
URL: `http://www.undcp.or.at/unlinks.html`

The Russian and East European Internet Resources Page (REESweb) [multi-languages]
URL: `http://www.pitt.edu/~cjp/rsecon.html`

Information and Misconceptions about Japan
URL: `http://bronze.ucs.indiana.edu:80/~tanaka/`

Latin America General Information
URL: `http://lanic.utexas.edu/la/region.html`

And these are only four of hundreds, (perhaps thousands) of examples similar to those shown in Box 3.11. Resnick (1995), for example has identified a broad range available for Latin America, and Jegede (1995), for Africa. Sites such as "Intercultural Communication" from the University of Arkansas bring together many possibilities

Intercultural Communication
URL
`http://www.uark.edu/depts/comminfo/www/intercultural.html`

This site offers links to 56 further sites (as of July 1995) such as Aboriginal Studies, Cross-Cultural Communication-Southeast Asia, Culture and Society of Mexico, Japan Centre for Intercultural Communication, Muslim Resources on the Net, Race and Racism, and Trans-Cultural Study Guide, each of which is a rich further source of links and communication possibilities for adults.

CROSS-CULTURAL TELE-LEARNING VIA COMMUNICATION

While the above examples focused on a combination of information and communication possibilities, many opportunities exist on the Internet via Usenet newsgroups (and are also available through many regional and commercial services) for adults to participate in discussions about events and cultural issues relating to countries and cultures throughout the world. There are literally hundreds of such discussion groups, some moderated, some not. Examples include:

misc.news.bosnia
soc.culture.japan
soc.culture.china

As one of so-many examples of the vibrancy of such discussion forums, during a one-week period in 1995 more than 800 persons contributed to the newsgroup *soc.culture.china*, including 47 messages threaded as a discussion around one particular event in Chinese–Japanese history.

Like communication in a hallway or conference centre or cocktail party, the learning value of such fora depends a great deal on who is there and with whom one finds to communicate, as well as on how well one personally communicates and what shared interest motivates the discussion. Tele-learning will not supply a magic to make dull people bright communicators, but it can provide the opportunity for people to converse in a reflective way, at their own time and place, and increase the odds enormously that one can transcend one's personal situation and find a new range of stimulating communication partners.

For some persons, the opportunity to talk via networks will evolve into a substantial tele-learning opportunity. However, much of the time, talk will be not much more than talk, unless it was motivated by a learning need in the first place.

However, a third way that tele-learning relates to cross-cultural communication and transcending distances is to offer tools and support for learning the languages one might need for this communication. Here the learning needs are specific, and the chance of valuable tele-learning occurring is high.

LANGUAGE-LEARNING RESOURCES

A particularly useful focus for home tele-learning is language learning, especially when personal motivation is strong. We discuss the more-general area of self-motivated structured learning activities via at-home tele-learning in Section 3.4; here we will only mention a few sites more generally useful for language learning in a cross-cultural framework.

A major example is the "Human-Languages Page", a project making available information about the languages of the world, including dictionaries, connections to linguistic institutions and to multilingual resources of a wide variety, and spoken samples of languages as well as language tutorials (T. Jones, 1995).

The Human-Languages Page:

URL http://www.willamette.edu/tjones/Language-Page.html

Sixty-eight languages are given as major groupings of links in this enormous site (as of June 1995), including sign language, Esperanto and Latin as well as dialects such as Breton and Catalan and non-Roman character languages such as Arabic, Bulgarian, Hindi and Hebrew. An important aspect of this site is that the tele-learner can choose to interact with the entire site in any one of 11 languages.

Expressing one's self in a second language

Finally, an important aspect of "Global Village" participation is the ability to express one's self in more than one's mother tongue. For millions around the world, this means becoming fluent in English. As an opportunity for persons learning English as a second language to publish their English writing as well as find more information about self-study English-learning resources, there is now at least one electronic, hyperlinked magazine available via the Internet to which anyone who is an ESL/EFL (English as a second-language or foreign-language) student or professional can submit potential items for publication consideration. This magazine is called EXCHANGE and is maintained at the University of Illinois at Urbana-Champaign. Its location is:

EXCHANGE

URL http://www.ed.uiuc.edu/exchange/exchange.html

This is only one example of the sort of new opportunities for self-directed tele-learning available via a network, particularly the Internet, that is most relevant for the individual learner, in the home, with the flexibility of time and choice and with a personal motivation to learn.

In the next section, let us look at possibilities to address such a motivation in concrete terms: What if the home tele-learner wants to "take a course" or some other well-structured experience, to overtly "learn" a certain body of knowledge? What is available? What is its quality? Does it count, as "real" learning?

■ 3.4 NEW TOOLS AND OPPORTUNITIES FOR SELF-DIRECTED LEARNING

The possibilities here can be classified in many ways. We will consider four: (a) tools for general-purpose learning support, (b) learning-oriented games and activities for children, (c) tutorial or modular learning materials, and (d) access to course-like tele-learning sequences.

■ 3.4.1 TOOLS FOR GENERAL-PURPOSE LEARNING SUPPORT

Of course, families typically have some sort of general-purpose resources, usually in print form, available to them, either in their homes or from a public library. These include dictionaries, thesauri, atlases, and collections of information in the specific areas in which family members are interested. These general resources in print form continue to be important, but tele-learning offers down-loadable access to many others, which is at the least a convenience but may also make tools and resources available in the home that could not be otherwise conveniently obtained.

SEARCH TOOLS

Perhaps the most powerful type of general-purpose tool available to the home tele-learner is an electronic search tool, to move quickly around distributed electronic resources on the Internet and particularly the WWW and indicate those useful to a person's needs. Fortunately for the Internet user, such search tools are one of the most rapidly growing sets of resources available. There are tools for searching WWW servers as well as tools for searching the other sorts of resources available on the Internet such as Gopher servers, newsgroups, ftp sites and others. And there are tools to search for the right tool! Sometimes search tools are called "search engines".

> *A recent use of one of the many search engines for the WWW, with the search terms:*
> *<web> and <search engines>*
> *sent, within approximately 10 seconds, a clickable list of 2,417 Web sites relating to this topic*

And these search tools are changing by the day. Changes relate to making them more powerful and more easy to use (see **Interface 2**). We have already discussed search tools in this Interface and listed a useful collection for home tele-learning in Box 3.6; thus we will not repeat URLs here. Fortunately, it is not necessary for the home-tele-learner to have 2,417 search tools to find Web sites. Having one good tool as a starting point is enough, particularly one that children can use as well as adults, such as Yahoo.

Newsgroups also have search tools, allowing the tele-learner to search the archives of many groups by topic or author and to ignore categories of entries. Often these tools are integrated into the newsreader software that is being used; and there are many, many of these as well.

Books and print sources

Finally, there are books and manuals about all these tools, also available on the Internet, for example as Web sites:

Information Sources: The Internet: Services and Tools:
URL `http://ccadfa.cc.adfa.oz.au/cmc.html`

and as text files that can be requested by email, as for example the "Nettools Guide to Network Resource Tools", produced by the CERN staff in Switzerland and available in response to an email message sent to:

`listserv@earncc.bitnet`
with the message: *GET NETTOOLS TXT*

The manual is then sent automatically to the requester, who can decide in his or her own environment how much to retain on disk or printout form.

HOWEVER, USING A TOOL REQUIRES SKILL...

Search tools generally require the searcher to enter keywords representing his or her wishes, an intellectual task that is far from easy (see Section 3.6.2). There are other general-purpose tools available that make the search process more like going to the library or like making consecutive selections from page after page of increasingly focused menus. We discuss some of these in the next subsections.

■ 3.4.2 VIRTUAL LIBRARIES AND THEIR SEARCH TOOLS

The concept of a virtual library is an interesting one (see Chapter 4). Sometimes the term refers to the possibility of distant access to an existing library's card-catalogue-type resources which are already in digital form for many libraries. Other times the term refers to a "library" that has no physical location, other than as a server on a computer. Fox, Akscyn, Furuta, and Leggett, 1995, give a good introduction to the evolution of digital libraries, which we refer to considerably in Chapter 4. For here, in Chapter 3 with our home learners, let us just accept the virtual-library phenomenon without much more explanation: many libraries can be accessed by members of the public from their home computers.

DISTANT ACCESS TO "REAL" LIBRARIES

This is an old and familiar category for on-line resources. Literally hundreds of university libraries and national libraries are accessible via the Internet. Box 3.12 shows a few of these library sites.

Box 3.12

Links to libraries, accessible via the WWW

Libweb
URL `http://sunsite.berkeley.edu/Libweb/`
...Links to hundreds of individual university libraries

The British Library
URL `http://portico.bl.uk`

The Library of Congress
URL `http://www.loc.gov/`

And of course individual libraries can be directly accessed via their URLs. The Internet makes access of libraries outside one's home country as direct as local libraries, another aspect contributing to the increase of an individual's cross-cultural orientation (see Section 3.3). The Danish Technical library is just a random example of one of hundreds of non-US libraries available for access to home tele-learners.

Danish Technical Library
URL `http://www.dtv.dk/library/index_d.htm`

VIRTUAL LIBRARIES

The "virtual library" existing nowhere but on the server of a computer, is a particularly useful tele-learning tool. Sometimes called "libraries without walls" (see, for example, Clement, 1994), this category refers to collections that reside in databases, knowledge bases, Gopher sites and the World Wide Web (again, see the excellent special issue of the *Communications of the ACM*, April 1995, edited by Fox, Akscyn, Furuta and Leggett, for many examples of both traditional and virtual libraries).

These virtual libraries often are organized by presenting the requester a long list of category descriptions in alphabetical order. When one of these is selected, another list appears, and so on. Among the many virtual library sites available, some of the most useful in 1995 are listed in Box 3.13.

Box 3.13

Virtual libraries

The WWW Virtual Library
URL: `http://www.w3.org/hypertext/DataSources/bySubject/Overview.html`

The Online Computer Library Center Inc.
URL: `http://www.oclc.org`

The Internet Public Library
URL `http://ipl.sils.umich.edu`
...Includes tutorials on how to use the Internet to find information

Ask ERIC
URL `http://ericir.syr.edu`
...Particularly oriented towards learning materials and educational research in the US

Yahoo: Virtual Libraries
`http://www.yahoo.com/`

Kids Web
URL `http://www.npac.syr.edu:80/textbook/kidsweb/`
...Oriented toward children, with images for motivation

As an example of how these virtual libraries work, the Yahoo site begins with a list of main categories and the number of sites which are associated with that category. The Yahoo site began when two graduate students at Stanford University compared their own WWW-browser bookmark lists (see Section 3.2) and decided to put them into a database capable of responding to queries by listing hits as ready-to-click links. Their site proved incredibly popular and within about eight months in 1994 their database contained approximately 25,000 Web entries, visited by more than 25,000 host computers each week with about 500,000 hits per day (data from the end of 1994; see Taylor, 1995).

OTHER ORGANIZED ENTRY POINTS TO RESOURCES

The number of organized entry points to collections of subject-related sites is probably not known to anyone, as it increases any time anyone generates a "hotlist" page from the bookmarks in his or her Internet browser program. Thus each family can develop their own set of organized entry points to WWW sites, and can develop different ones based on different topics of interest.

But among the many organized entry point sites with grouped links ready to choose from that are available on the WWW in 1995 are some general-purpose sites for children that are useful to note for the tele-learning family. These include the sample shown in Box 3.14:

Box 3.14

A sample of WWW entry-points for children

Kid's Page
URL: `http://riceinfo.rice.edu/armadillo/Rice/Resources/kids.html`

KID List
URL: `http://www.clark.net/pub/journalism/kid.html`

Uncle Bob's Kid's Page
URL: `http://gagme.wwa.com/boba/kids.html#skip`

Latitude 28 Schoolhouse
URL: `http://www.packet.net/schoolhouse/`

Interpaedia
URL `http://www.hmc.edu/`
...An on-line encyclopedia

Kid's Internet Delight
URL `http://www.pointcom.com/gifs/reviews/11_19024.htm`

Each of the above offers an extensive set of links to other WWW pages appropriate to children, as well as to sites with learning-oriented games, adventures and downloadable educational software and offering opportunities for pen-pal type communications.

OTHER REFERENCE SOURCES

Finally, there are many resource-specific collections now available for searching on the Internet, such as the following location for an on-line version of the *Encyclopedia Britannica*:

Encyclopedia Britannica:
URL `http://web.eb.com/eb.html`

Publishers are particularly interested in alternative publication approaches for their so-called "folio products" that will enhance the market position of their products rather than compete with them, as we discussed in Section 3.2.4 (see also Moonen, 1995b). These alternative or supplementary forms of electronic publication are valuable tele-learning reference resources. Also interesting is the way that various broadcasting companies, both radio and television, are now offering associated Web pages, which are intended to bring added value to the broadcasting products. For example, the BBC (British Broadcasting Company in the UK) offers such a page called the "BBC Networking Club" at:

BBC Broadcasting Club:
`http://www.bbcnc.org.uk/`

where one of the intentions is to integrate informal learning opportunities available through the various media (television, radio and the Internet integrated service). All such services are targeted at the individual tele-learner in the home, parents and children.

IMPORTANCE OF SELF-HELP AND TOOLS

Thus the many different ways of organizing and offering support for finding resources and communication partners on the Internet is, in itself, a major contribution to tele-learning, not only in the family but in general. The value to the family and the individual learner more generally is particularly strong: without a teacher to structure and suggest and steer, the home learner is centrally reliant on his or her own search skills. Having good search tools and knowing how to use them is thus a major aspect of tele-learning. The difficulties in expecting children, and parents, to have good search skills and make wise search decisions are of course another matter (see Section 3.6.2)

But while searching can be difficult, and requires adequate persistence to keep going, a different situation occurs when tele-learning takes place hidden within games and game-like motivational learning activities for children. We look at some of these in the next section.

■ 3.4.3 LEARNING-ORIENTED GAMES AND MOTIVATIONAL LEARNING ACTIVITIES

Another important category of new tools and opportunities for tele-learning for the family is interactive on-line sites, mostly again on the WWW, that present learning-oriented games and puzzles and play-like activities with a learning purpose. As before, there are hundreds (thousands?) of these. Some of the diversity are noted in Box 3.15.

Box 3.15

Educational games and motivational learning activities via tele-learning

The Ultimate Children's Internet Site
URL: `http://www.vividus.com/ucis.html`
Links to many other sites for children

Kid's Corner
URL: `http://www.ot.com/kids`
...With games, interactive stories, and gallery for display of children's submitted art

Lego Home Page
URL: `http://legowww.homepages.com/`
...Tricks and models for making things with Lego, plus discussion groups

Shareware Central
URL: `http://www.intac.com/dversch/swc.html`
...Educational software and games for children, downloadable

Diplomacy
`judge@morrolan.eff.org`
...For adults, a historical strategy game called Diplomacy, played with partners at a distance, where players send in their commands via email messages to a "judge server" that processes the command, calculates the restuls, and sends the results to all the players via email

Telerobot
URL: `http://telerobot.mech.uwa.edu.au`
...Control a robotic arm that manipulates objects in Australia

Wide World Web Contest
URL `http://www.zippo.com/contest/4/intro.htm`
...Example of "treasure hunt" game, where participants are given questions for which they must find answers, somewhere, on the Internet; answers are given on a specified date. Sometimes such contests have real prizes

Myers-Briggs Personality Test
URL: `http://sunsite.unc.edu/personality/keirsey.html`
...For adults, immediate scoring of interactive test form and immediate comparison of one's own personality-test results with those of all other site visitors, plus large amount of serious information on interpreting the results. I like this one myself, it is rather fun to compare myself with the others who have taken the test and whose results are combined for the summary statistics

City of Bits: Space, Place, and the Infobahn
URL: `http://www-mitpress.mit.edu/City_of_Bits/`
...Socially interactive book, where adult readers dialogue with author directly through the hyperlinked text

Tele-learning at home, without the imposed discipline of school, teachers, and evaluation, must rely on the individual being motivated to learn. While much of this must come from the individual, the level of intrinsic motivational appeal of an interactive resource is also critical. Examples as we have shown here are carefully designed to incorporate such appeal, and provide learning experiences at the same time.

But sometimes the learning task is clear and the home tele-learner is motivated, such as a young person wishing to improve his skill, quickly and efficiently, in a foreign language before going on a exchange course. For these people, the Internet offers a powerful way to find and use some forms of self-guided structured, learning materials. We look at one electronic category and one human category!

▪ 3.4.4 (HUMAN) TUTORIAL OR MODULAR LEARNING MATERIALS

The examples shown so far in Chapter 3 tended to be somewhat episodic and even coincidental in their learning value; tele-learning children are likely to visit a site like:

Kibpub
URL `http://en-garde.com/kidpub/intro.html`

...Site for children to publish their own writing and get comments on it

because they find it appealing to see if their work is published on the Internet, rather than that they consciously set out to improve their skills in writing for an audience. However, in many cases the home tele-learner knows that he or she wishes to reach a certain level of attainment in a particular skill domain, and thus comes to the tele-learning setting with a clear learning objective in mind and the willingness to work long enough to reach his or her self-determined level of achievement. The latter sorts of experiences require good structure and feedback mechanisms in the learning materials. This is a design challenge with individual tele-learning.

COMPUTER-BASED TUTORIAL MATERIALS

Electronic learning materials should have some structure, some feedback mechanism, and some self-assessment capacity. These sorts of resources also can be found on distributed networks such as the Internet, although less often than information collections and innovative environments for exploratory learning, such as virtual museums.

Perhaps the most common category of tutorial-sort resources available over the Internet is resources for language instruction. The capacity to have some form of interactive audio in the resources significantly extends the practice and feedback aspects of self-directed language learning. Box 3.16 names a sample of sites that provide access to a range of language-tutorial materials via the WWW.

Box 3.16

Sample of tutorials for language learning on the WWW

Traveler's Japanese
URL: http://www.ntt.jp/japan/japanese

Resources for learning Russian and German
URL: http://www2.uncg.edu/lixlpurc

Foreign Language Resources
URL: http://www.itp.berkeley.edu/thorne/HumanResources.html
...*Overall entry point for language-learning sites*

French tutorial sites
URL: http://parthe.lpthe.jussieu.fr/info_autres_fr.html

La Red Científica Peruna
URL: http://www.rcp.net.pe
...*Links to Spanish-speaking sites throughout Latin America many with language-practice orientation*

HUMAN TUTORS

An intriguing new dimension to self-learning is the opportunity to conveniently engage a human tutor for at least some feedback and perhaps incentive via a network. The home tele-learner has a number of resources to choose from that organize personal access between the learner and a distant tutor. The interaction between the two is usually by e-mail; thus the convenience of staying at home and studying when you want it is still generally maintained. Not all tutoring services are free, although access to them for initial information (or to offer one's own services as a tutor) generally are open. On the Internet, one example of such a service is:

Study-help, Tutoring, Homework, Learning, School
URL http://www.scot.net/%7Ehmwkhelp/Study-Help.html

where a Web-based form is offered both to the prospective tutor and learner seeking a tutor, and the WWW site serves as an intermediary between the two. Tutors are classified as to a large variety of subjects and also age group preferences, six categories including K-5, 6-8, 9-12, collegiate, graduate, and adult/ continuing.

Motivational value

The motivational appeal of getting feedback via a network tutor has been shown to be of value, particularly in increasing time on task, not only for individual learners but also for students in regular educational settings having access to "telecommunications tutors" for help, feedback and perhaps most importantly, contact and motivation on their homework (Mountain, 1992). For children, and also for adults depending on personal characteristics, it is probably better that a tutor be of the learner's own language group and aware of the background of the learner as far as is pertinent to the subject to be tutored. Thus tutor services for children are better organized through local organizations of tutors, than through the child working with a person not familiar with the local context and curriculum (and perhaps not speaking the same way as the child, even if in the same mother tongue). For older learners, these concerns lessen in intensity, but never fade entirely.

■ 3.4.5 COURSE-LENGTH LEARNING SEQUENCES VIA HOME TELE-LEARNING

Occasionally the home tele-learner will be so motivated to systematically cover a body of learning material that he or she may wish to participate in an entire course. On-line courses offered by traditional higher education institutions are mushrooming (see Chapters 7 and 9), so one approach is for the potential tele-learner to make contact with one of these organizations. As such courses are discussed in detail in Chapter 8, and also because taking a course implies the willingness of the individual tele-learner to work under the structure and requirements of an outside body and thus give up much of his or her individual decision-making about tele-learning, we do not include it in this chapter.

However, many course-like programs are available to the home tele-learner, via the Internet but also via educational television. The tele-learner may pay some fee for accompanying print-based learning materials and to cover the costs of an opportunity to contact a human for feedback and motivation if she wishes to participate formally in these programs.

Educational television is well established throughout the world, including variants intended for the self-motivated adult (see Chapters 2, 5, and 8). Tele-learning viewers can learn without any commitment or expense (if they subscribe to a reception service, cable or satellite that brings the broadcast into their homes) but they forego the chance for recognition for their learning, or for help or feedback or other forms of interaction. Similarly, tele-learners are increasingly finding courses on the Internet (so far, the free ones are mostly about using the Internet) in which they can also participate with the same range of commitment and interactivity as with educational television. One source of these sort of "open" courses on the Internet in 1995 is:

Globewide Network Academy (GNA, 1995)
```
http://uu-gna.mit.edu:8001/uu-gna/index.html
```

The GNA is a non-profit corporation whose immediate goal is to "create a marketplace for courses as well as to offer administrative and technical services to organizations and individuals who are presenting online courses" (GNA, 1995). GNA brokers courses, puts out a newsletter, and provides a framework for a range of Internet-based learning activities. The target audience is described as individuals who are interested in the exchange of ideas through the Internet (see also Ellsworth, 1994, and Chapters 6, 7, and 8).

MOO-U?

The "Virtual Online University" is another such organization, that offers support for some real-time interaction among participants in a so-called MOO (Multi-User Object-Oriented environment). A MOO is a communication-support environment accessible through the Internet which supports multi-participant, simultaneous discussion (called real-time chat) but within a structured environment, structured not only by a moderator but by a room- or area-like metaphor used for the context in which participants interact. MOOs were identified in Chapter 2.

The MOO site for the Virtual Online Environment is accessed by telnet to the address:

Virtual Online University
```
URL telnet://falcon.cit.cornell.edu 8888
with password: <connect guest>
```

But looking at participation in structured courses, be they by traditional universities offered in non-traditional ways, or by new sorts of tele-learning brokers such as the last examples, is farther than we want to go in this chapter. Here we want to stay with the family: child and parents providing their own self-direction in at-home tele-learning.

There is one more category of activities to note: opportunities for creative expression as tele-learning experiences via networks and particularly the 1995 WWW. We look at some on these in the next section.

■ 3.5 TELE-LEARNING ACTIVITIES BASED ON INDIVIDUAL CREATIVITY

The WWW contains many self-made sketches, usually on people's home pages. Is doing this sort of thing a learning activity? It can be. It also serves as an introduction to the last section of our various categories of individual tele-learning for the family

A child's sketch is a good example of two different categories of creative expression that can be stimulated by the WWW and its resources. One relates to the availability of channels through which one's creative work can be expressed and made public to an external audience, perhaps for feedback. The other is through the opportunity to create one's own homepage on the WWW.

■ 3.5.1 CHANNELS FOR CREATIVE EXPRESSION

Opportunities for creative expression on the Internet vary from the open-pages of newsgroups to very structured experiences on the WWW. In Table 3.5 we give a sampling, just to show some of the possibilities in 1995 sites of WWW-based opportunities for creative expression that might be attractive to families as tele-learners.

And these are just some examples: the last two entries, for example, are time-sensitive events, whose creative involvement required participating during the target time of the activity. We included those in Table 3.5 just as examples: there will be many others in the foreseeable future.

What these sorts of events do is provide a framework, a stimulus, for creative expression and communication, an opportunity to connect one's self and one's work to that of others in many different parts of the world. Is this a learning experience?

Yes!

The above examples were made easy to participate in through someone else's efforts to set up a structure. For many persons, however, the most open-ended and most stimulating form of self-expression available on the WWW is the opportunity to create one's own home page or set of pages. We discuss in Chapters 5, 6, and 9 many examples of students and instructors doing this, in the

Table 3.5 Creative environments on the WWW for families

URL	Description
Carlos' Coloring Book URL `http://www.ravenna.com/` `coloring`	For children: Paint-by-numbers on the Internet; send your results to family and friends
CyberKids URL `http://www.mtlake.com` `/cyberkids/`	For children: Create your own stories and artwork and see them "published"
Help Build a Theme Park URL `http://www.itp.tsoa.nyu.edu/` `~alumni/dlasday/`	For both parents and children: Specific design parameters and guildelines for submission to an on-line gallery of designs for a virtual theme park
Live WWW Event Comics: Make enquiries to `dg16512@is.nyu.edu`	For young people: Participate in a live WWW event around a European comic strip festival
A Day in the Life of Cyberspace URL `http://www.1010.org/`	For parents and children: Send in contributions, pictures, sounds, or words, about people "whose lives have been touched deeply by digital media and the Net" for a "Day in the Life of" page to be revealed on 10 October 1995

context of their ordinary teaching, or their "re-engineered pedagogy". In this chapter however, we are outside of teachers and schools, we are looking at individual learners, parents and children, who just for pleasure and stimulation are involved in tele-learning. So let's close this long section with some comments on making your own home page as a family learning activity.

■ 3.5.2 MAKING YOUR OWN WWW PAGES

To begin with, it is not hard to make your own WWW pages. This fact lies behind the huge amount of innovative tele-learning activities going on through WWW pages in 1995 (again, see the rest of the chapters of this book). A home tele-learner can do creative, attractive home pages. How? The following steps get anyone with a computer and a network connection going:

1. Download some HTML conversion software from the WWW
Choose a tool such as

Web Wizard
`http://www.halycon.com/Webwizard/welcome.htm`

Of the many dozens of tools that are freely available in 1995, the above example is typical of those with good help functions to work the learner through the steps that are needed to get going. And these steps get more and more transparent with each new wave of conversion tools. Of course, commercial tools are now coming on the market; these will be easier, fancier, and they will cost money....

2. Plan your page
Designing a homepage, such as all design activities, can and should be a thorough and well-considered process. There are many books and downloadable sets of guidelines for the design of effective WWW pages; we list some of the guidelines we find must important for tele-learning in **Interface 8**. Good sources for design guidelines include (among many) Aronson (1994), and

Creating WWW Pages Which Deliver (McKenzie, 1995)
`URL http://www.pacificrim.net/~mckenzie/homesweet.html`

3. Use the conversion software to enter HTML codes in your text
HTML is the name of the code used to transform your text into WWW material. The process of entering this code has now become very simple, at least at beginning levels. It is similar to using a word processor: simply highlighting what you want after you have typed it, and choosing among the menu commands relating to HTML tags for structure, for title and headings, for links, for links and images, paragraph separators, and for character formatting. (There are other tags as well, such as for forms, signatures, horizontal lines, etc., but beginners don't need them). Among many references to help with this procedure are Lemay (1995), Silberman (1995), and:

A Beginner's Guide to HTML
URL `http://www.ncsa.uiuc.edu/General/Internet/WWW/`
`HTMLPrimer.html`

and

CU_HTML.DOT (a document template for Microsoft Word for Windows word processor; Wong & Lam, 1995)
URL `http://www.cuhk.hk/csc/cu_html/cu_html.htm`

4. Organize and install your HTML files onto a computer that has WWW server software (also downloadable from the WWW)

The server may be provided by your school, work or network provider, or there are also commercial Web server services that will "rent" you space for your pages and the network connection to the Internet. You need some method for transferring your files onto the server site and generally you are charged a flat monthly fee (see Lemay (1995), Chapter 11 for a simple discussion). Most likely, you will just ask the person at your workplace who handles the WWW site administration how you can install your page, and then you won't have to worry further about it. Commercial on-line services are now offering home-page templates and support to their customers; see for example:

Prodigy EZ Home Page Creator
URL `http://www.prodigy.com (for information)`

Of course, making WWW pages is like any other skill, playing a piano or painting a picture. There is plenty of room for improvement once you get started! The remarkable thing about WWW pages, the feature that has unleashed the creative juices of so many thousands of ordinary individual tele-learners at home and in schools and universities in 1995, is that fact that the threshold to begin is relatively simple and the effects a beginner can get are satisfying, even very satisfying, even beautiful.

As an example, with not much more instruction that I have just written above, I told a group of my students how to find the resources on the WWW and to find resources they could use to teach themselves to make WWW pages. Within a few days, literally, they made the pages that can be found at:

Home Pages, Students in the course "On-Line Learning" (Collis, 1995b, see also **Interface 9** and Chapter 9)
URL `http://www.to.utwente.nl/ism/online95/campus/rooms.html`

In 1994 the first elementary school made its own home page. In 1995 the number of personal home pages is totally unknown on the WWW, but it must be in the tens of thousands. Families, parents and children, can do it together, the modern equivalent of making a scrapbook or building something beautiful and personal and interesting. What's especially nice is the children will probably catch on to it faster than the parents. "The Web can serve as a family album and hall of fame" (Seltzer, 1995); the process of creating this entity, whatever its motivation, is a tele-learning experience associated with what I believe will become part of the functional literacy of the 21st century—making connections in a hyperlinked world (see Chapter 10).

Considerable time has been spent in this chapter to illustrate the possibilities for tele-learning in the family setting. But many issues accompany the possibilities, some of them educational, some of them social and ethical. All of the issues affect the development of tele-learning in the family. We consider a range of these issues in the following section. We also note how these issues affect not only the home-based tele-learner but also the teacher in the traditional institution, the educational decision maker, and especially the educational technologist.

■ 3.6 ISSUES RELATING TO TELE-LEARNING AND THE FAMILY

So far we have discussed the good news—the many positive and exciting opportunities for tele-learning that are even now available to the family with a computer, modem, and good Internet connection.

But it is not euphoria.

There are many serious issues confronting the development of tele-learning in the family. We discuss seven sets of them in this section. These issues and a brief comment about the implications of the issues are summarized in Table 3.6 before they are discussed in more depth in the remainder of this section.

■ 3.6.1 ISSUES RELATING TO THE NATURE OF LEARNING

There are two major questions here with respect to all forms of self-directed learning, including tele-learning in the family:

Is this really learning?, and

To make it really learning, is it realistic to think individuals have the motivation, persistence, and study skills without teachers and institutions?

Table 3.6 Issues for tele-learning and the family

Issue	Main impact on tele-learning
1. **Learning-value issues**	1. Is this really learning? Conversely, is it realistic to expect individuals to learn this way?
2. **Skills and competencies for handling the environment**	2. What skills and competencies at the meta-level and at the specific level are needed to function productively? How does a family learn them? How does a family get help?
3. **Issues relating to the electronic environment itself**	3. Should the family subscribe to a commercial service? How important is the user interface through which computer-based tele-learning occurs?
4. **Cost and access issues**	4. How much does it cost for family tele-learning? Who pays? How is access possible?
5. **Which scenarios for tele-learning?**	5. What is involved in the choice for one of different tele-learning approaches? When is "traditional self -study" better than tele-learning?
6. **Social-ethical issues**	6. What are the implications of inequitable access to tele-learning in the home? Will the rich get richer? What are issues relating to censorship and quality control? What are issues relating to ownership and plagiarism? What are the implications of so much English-language materials for non-English language countries? Are there dangers of cultural imperialism?
7. **Legitimacy issues**	7. What happens when the "traditional educational establishment" is asked to recognize tele-learning as meaningful?

IS IT REALLY LEARNING?

This is a core and serious question. What is learning? Through centuries of the so-called industrial-approach to learning (see Chapter 10), we have come to expect that learning is something that happens in school or in an institution, under the organization of a specialist, and occurs when certain tests are passed or when the specialist otherwise says competency has been reached.

There are, of course, good reasons for the professionalization of learning (the major ones of these relevant to tele-learning in the family will be highlighted in the next subsection). But have we as a society got to a point where we do not think it "really counts" as learning if it is not in school, if it is not "on the test"?

Educational theorists however are increasingly saying that students must be empowered, that they must accept responsibility for their own learning, that the student must learn, above all, to be an effective decision maker about his or her own learning process (see for example, Jonassen, 1995, and Ward and Davis, 1994). Tele-learning in the home is a testbed for such ideas, ideas that are supported by learning theorists who see learning as a constructivist activity, fundamentally an individual experience and an experience in which the individual must have real self-responsibility (Jonassen, 1995).

And society itself is increasingly recognizing the inevitability of life-long learning, of learning that takes place outside the domain of formal schooling and is responsive to the needs of the workplace or problem situation (see Chapter 9). In addition, those needs are changing so rapidly themselves that formal education cannot expect to adequately "train" students during their initial school experience.

Students, instead, must be taught to be self-directed learners, learners of the sort described in this chapter.

Thus, yes, these sorts of tele-learning experiences, in the family, outside of school and teachers and courses and textbooks, can be "real" learning.

IS IT REALISTIC TO EXPECT THAT PEOPLE WILL LEARN THIS WAY?

Part of the reason that curricula and schools and teachers operate as they do now is that, apparently, the individual learner on his or her own is not as good a decision maker about what to learn as the curriculum specialist, and about how to learn it and if it is learned adequately as the teacher. Educational television and libraries are already available, as are books in great quantities; yet society still assumes learners need the structure of an institution and curriculum and textbook, and the guidance and management and motivation of a teacher. How much of the hard work of learning will occur without these? Will on-line resources and educational television be taken as the basis for serious, persistent learning?

These are questions that reflect the opposite side of the coin to the first questions in this subsection. The answer seems to be that it is not a matter of extremes:

> *...tele-learning will not replace the school and teacher and curriculum but augment them, extend them, enrich them, and offer learning experiences not available through them.*

Tele-learning in the home will sometimes run parallel to learning in the formal institution but will also have a life of its own. How rich that life of its own will be is largely dependent on issues discussed in Sections 3.6.2, 3.6.3, and 3.6.4. How rich the aspect of tele-learning is that parallels what is occurring in the educational institution for an individual is highly influenced by the teacher and the decision makers in that institution. (We discuss this in various ways in Chapters 5, 6, 7 and 10).

■ 3.6.2 ISSUES RELATING TO THE SKILLS AND COMPETENCIES NEEDED FOR TELE-LEARNING IN THE HOME

We will discuss these issues from four perspectives: (a) What meta-skills are needed for handling the tele-learning opportunities described in this chapter? (b) What specific skills and competencies are needed? (c) How does a family learn these skills? (d) Where do they go for help?

WHAT META-SKILLS ARE NEEDED?

The issue of what "information literacy" is appropriate for functioning in an "information society" has been discussed for nearly a decade. Doyle summarizes the literature in this area by identifying an information-literate person as one who:

- Recognizes that accurate and complete information is the basis for intelligent decision making
- Recognizes the need for information
- Formulates questions based on information needs
- Identifies potential sources of information
- Develops successful search strategies
- Accesses sources of information including computer-based and other technologies
- Evaluates information

- Organizes information for practice application
- Integrates new information into an existing body of knowledge
- Uses information in critical thinking and problem solving (Doyle, 1992)

It is clear that all of these competencies are required to at least some degree in order to effectively handle the resources now available for tele-learning in the home. In fact, the resources available on the Internet provide a benchmark testcase for information-literacy competency.

Information literacy and self-directed learning
Information literacy is parallel in many ways to what are described as "the skills of self-directed learning" (Wilson, 1994). These include the abilities to:

- Develop and be in touch with curiosities
- Diagnose one's learning needs
- Identify human, material, and experiential resources for accomplishing various kinds of learning goals
- Design a play of strategies for making use of appropriate learning resources effectively
- Carry out a learning plan (p. 255)

Home learner tele-learning opportunities such as those described in this chapter again represent benchmark testcases for these abilities.

How to develop information literacy in our children (and ourselves)?
Assuming we agree with lists of competencies such as these, there is still the question of how to develop them. This is, partially a matter for parents, partially for school, and partially for the individual. Tele-learning is now bringing the individual many more opportunities for practice and self-evaluation of effectiveness in these competencies. If these opportunities will be translated into cognitive skill development is not possible to say; at least there is rich opportunity for practice through the sorts of tele-learning activities described in this chapter and book.

SPECIFIC SKILLS FOR TELE-LEARNING
It is clear that a specific skill for functioning with computer-based tele-learning is handling the computer itself and the software associated with a particular task or environment. That is one of the reasons why the design of that software and particularly its user interface are so important (see Section 3.6.3). But also, it is clear that the tele-learner needs to think in terms of key words, needs to develop search strategies, needs to learn how to communicate concisely and accurately,

perhaps to someone whose mother tongue is not the same as his own, and needs to self-monitor his own activities, keeping track of what occurred before when backtracking or trouble-shooting are necessary (which they frequently are).

And there are many other practical skills associated with tele-learning: how to retrieve, sometimes unpack or decode, save, print and store resources; how to reuse them in other electronic environments; how to keep track of resources; how to deal with multi-media resources; how to efficiently remember where various resources can be found and how to get to them.

These skills are never mastered, only continually improved, and practice is the only way for this improvement.

HOW DOES A FAMILY GET STARTED IN DEVELOPING THESE SKILLS?

There is no easy answer, other than practice. Fortunately, use of the many self-help resources and on-line help tools that are becoming available provide a gentle way for practice, gentle compared to even two years ago on the Internet.

Social support

And an interesting sort of social cooperation is also developing around the use of Internet resources. "Internet cafes" are opening in Europe and the US, where people can drop in, pay for a certain amount of connect time to the Internet, and meanwhile help each other on how to proceed (Rifkin, 1995). Questions sent to authors of WWW sites and to distribution lists usually get a helpful response; there is, still, a spirit of contribution around much of what goes on through the Internet, something that may fade as the commercial discovery of its potential continues. But in 1995, it is still, often, a nice experience to "ask for help" via some Internet site and get it, from strangers who recognize your problem as one they have had themselves and reply back with some ideas or advice. This sounds over-romantic, and of course it doesn't happen all the time, but for some reason, it still does happen—people help each other.

Getting started? Still difficult for the ordinary family

But the question of getting started and getting help, despite what was just said, remains a major weak link of individual tele-learning;

...it still is not easy to get started, and often it is not easy to get beyond a particular technical problem.

Even with the rapidly growing business of on-line help (both commercial and voluntary) the process of self-learning on the Internet is frequently difficult. How the "ordinary family" with limited computer-handling skills, is to proceed is not clear. Financial resources available make a difference here, as commercial services give value for money in terms of help and support. Even more fundamentally, one must feel competent enough about what is going on, or going wrong, to know what questions to ask even the friendliest of support desks.

■ 3.6.3 Costs

A major issue in family tele-learning is costs. For most people, the sorts of activities described in this chapter, if carried out in the home, will cost money— continually and substantially.

Technology costs

The cost of setting up a home-based tele-learning environment is substantial (modem, printer, a computer, basic connection service charges, adequate storage; see Seymour, 1995, for a list of 12 components, each with a significant price tag). Gradually families in the more-developed world are acquiring home computers, but often not of the capacity to handle multi-media tele-learning activities. Nor do they have the network capacity (see Chapter 2), especially if their link to the Internet is through their copper-wire telephone line and/or they have a slow modem.

Should the family pay for an intermediary service?

Costs also are manifested in another aspect of tele-learning. The usage complexities described in Section 3.6.2 can be greatly reduced by subscribing to a well-run on-line service, buffering the family from many of the demands of actually handling the Internet. Also, a well-run on-line service can be a central point for help requests from the family and for start-up support. Sometimes such services are subsidized by the Ministry of Education in a country or the Department of Education in a state or province or an agency at the regional level. This is an important contribution that a central educational agency can make; we discuss examples in some detail in Chapter 7 (see Veen, Collis, De Vries, and Vogelzang, 1994, for an overview in Europe; and Kurshan, Harrington and Milbury, 1994, for an overview in the US).

Costs as a social divider

But if the family must choose itself to pay for a well-run support and filter service for their tele-learning needs, then they must also be able to pay.

Costs are not only a personal family constraint; they also relate to a serious social issue.

■ 3.6.4 SOCIAL AND ETHICAL ISSUES

In this category we can identify (a) equity issues, (b) issues related to censorship and freedom of expression, (c) issues relating to ownership and plagiarism of ideas and material, and (d) issues related to cultural imperialism.

EQUITY ISSUES

The "rich get richer" is a serious and moral problem (Jegede, 1995). If the tele-learning experiences described in this chapter are important to the intellectual development of the individual and his or her future in the workplace, then the gap between those who can afford and handle such resources and those who cannot is a human problem, a social problem, even a social timebomb.

Data indicate that about 80% of the users of the WWW (in 1995) are males, with a technical background and a degree from higher education, and with an average income (in US dollars) of about $65,000 (see, for example, Chatterjee, Gupta, and Pitkow, 1995, and Section 3.1). This is not the demographic profile of the persons in any country or society.

If one is committed to equal opportunity with respect to education throughout society (one of the motivations for tele-learning in general, see Chapter 1), then individual tele-learning may be going in the wrong direction.

CENSORSHIP AND QUALITY CONTROL

Perhaps more than any issue, the question of "allowing" material judged by some or many to be offensive to be available via a network source is a major point of discussion, and even of political weight. The Internet system, as it is owned by no one and just as accessible to persons in countries with very different religious and political values than one's own country, cannot in itself be quality assured or politically controlled. We must depend on the willingness of local sites to control themselves and control what comes into them, on individuals to be reasonable and self-censuring. As more and more home learners are accessing the Internet directly, a protective buffer of a local service organization is not available. And as more and more people can access the Internet and make their own WWW pages (remember how easy it is), more and more people of the sort one does not want to invite into one's home will come unrestricted into the minds of our children. Unless we as parents watch and supervise. While this has positive aspects of togetherness, it is unmanageable the more successful individual tele-learning becomes. This dilemma is a serious one for families and society. A good discussion about parental Internet control is available at:

Parental Control (Safdar, 1995)
URL http://www.vtw.org/ipcfag

Self-responsibility or society's...?

It would seem that this is a classic case of individual self-responsibility—don't look at it if you happen to find it, monitor what your children do, (for example, a recent family magazine in the US advised parents to not let any child less than nine years old use the Internet), look for ways to attach a rating label to resources or to attach a "chip" or install a software filter of some sort to your desktop that uses pattern-matching "to ferret out sexual content reading packets as they arrive" (Swaine, 1995, p. 141). In the US in the summer of 1995, for example, members of the US Congress began to attack the Internet because of the "widespread availability of graphic sexual material available" and a consortium of companies involved with Internet-related hardware and software quickly responded with the announcement of plans to "create rating systems similiar to those used in the movie and videogame business to warn of violent or sexual content"(Markoff, 1995, p. 25).

However, when pornography is involved, when racist and anti-Semitic advocacy is involved, when violence and hate are endorsed, even by a tiny minority of users of the Internet, the willingness of many families to "open up" to network-type tele-learning will be constrained.

> *The choice may be toward a more-controlled and filtered environment, which again requires subsidization or personal payment or both, and which looses some of the opportunity for free and equal access to resources and self-expression that the tele-learning examples in the first part of this chapter extol.*

These are complex issues indeed.

OWNERSHIP AND PLAGIARISM

What goes on with regard to personal ownership on material on a WWW site or retrieved from other on-line resources? How does its creator and owner maintain rights and profit? When any screen can be captured and inserted in one's own local document, plagiarism and issues of intellectual ownership are serious.

One response is to increasingly place on-line resources under the control of fee-for-use services; another is to only put on the Internet material you don't value enough to care if it is used without permission or payment by others.

Both these are happening now; the implications are important for tele-learning in the home.

CULTURAL IMPERIALISM

If an English-speaking person wishes to communicate with persons in another country, should he assume or hope they will understand English? What if they don't?

The dominance of the English language and "Western culture" on the Internet system is seen in a number of cultures as a source of concern; sufficient concern to bar or limit access for persons in their countries. These are political issues, but not only so. If we are all to be "citizens of a global village", whose rules and norms dominate that village? Whose language does the leader speak? Perhaps it should be Chinese?

If we never think about or worry about this question, then we may in fact be part of a problem we do not even realize. But we will.

The question of culture, cultural dominance and cultural survival will become increasingly important for all of us in our interconnected economies and futures.

It is already of critical importance to many in the world (Jegede, 1995). Those living in English-speaking countries where the population is not sensitized to the implications of language and culture will be at a critical disadvantage in a multi-cultural, multi-lingual world.

■ 3.6.5 SOFTWARE AND USER INTERFACES

There is a great deal of professional evidence that the design of the user interface through which a person interacts with a computer has a serious impact on the nature of that interaction (we discuss this in detail in Chapter 8). Thus the software through which a family interacts with an on-line environment is important. However, there is not much discussion of this outside the technical literature. A recent article in a computer magazine entitled "Usability Face Off" (Hackman and Montgomery, 1995) is an example of the sort of attention that this aspect of tele-learning should be getting by family decision makers. In this article, standard criteria for usability testing well-known to professional software developers are brought to the family tele-learner's attention, and applied to a number of commercially available software packages for Internet access. These usability criteria (called by different terms in the Hackman and Montgomery article) include:

- Help-system attributes
- Consistency
- Learnability
- User satisfaction

- Functionality
- Navigation support (Nielsen, 1993)

The packages evaluated differed substantially. As these factors in turn have a major impact on how users can handle a computer system, there is clearly an important concern here. (Again, we come back to this in Chapter 8).

■ 3.6.6 CHOICE OF TELE-LEARNING FOR THE FAMILY: YES OR NO?

Given all these considerations, families must decide themselves if tele-learning involving Internet-based activities and resources are feasible for them at the current time. There is also tele-learning by educational television, which is widely available and often at no extra cost or equipment requirement to what the family already own and use daily. Families could do much to improve the learning value of television among themselves.

And there is the alternative of no tele-learning at all in the family.

In many countries, families are "voting with their feet" (or with their check-books), indicating that they would value "distance learning" and the searching of reference materials as among the most important aspects of "getting on the infobahn" (Piller, 1994). Statistics of various degrees of comprehensiveness indicate that a steady growth in the number of home-based subscriptions to on-line access services is occurring throughout the world. Families seem to want to get connected, they seem to have high expectations for networked tele-learning.

In the near future, as we indicated in Chapter 2 and will further discuss in Chapter 10, through-the-air and through-the-wires/cables/fibre distinctions for transmission of tele-learning communications will gradually fade. More and more progress is being made toward a transmission infrastructure that can carry television, multi-media data communication from computers, and voice at the same time, through the same transmission channels, into the same receive-equipment into the home. When this evolves, a question not much influenced by tele-learning considerations but by politics and economics, by turfwars among the major players in the telephone, cable television, and media industries, many of the equity issues and capitalization problems confronting a family decision for tele-learning in 1995 will no longer be so substantial.

For the next few years, however, many families will not be able to choose computer-mediated tele-learning, no matter how convinced they are of its value.

■ 3.6.7 LEGITIMIZATION: IS THIS REALLY LEARNING?

And a final issue, one that will be discussed again throughout this book, is one of legitimacy. Where are the boundaries between tele-learning and "regular learning"? Where will accountability and legitimization reside? If a family member, working hard on her own, uses a variety of resources, tele- and not, to learn a body of material to a satisfactory standard, will her school or university or employer give her "credit" for it? Will it count?

Is tele-learning at home real learning? I hope that my arguments throughout this chapter explain my answer to this question: YES!

Individual tele-learning is occurring and will continue to grow. What will be the role of schools and teachers, of decision makers in educational institutions? Of educational technologists? What will be its impact?

These questions are re-addressed, with my tentative answers, in Chapter 10.

NEW DEVELOPMENTS, CIRCA 1995

Although the WWW and its browsers, as available in 1995, have brought tremendous new possibilities into distributed information systems, there is a parallel surge of new developments which is likely to continue for a number of years. Some of the motivations for new developments relate to limitations of the 1995-versions of WWW, such as:

- Links are the only structuring mechanism (leading to a "world wide spaghetti").
- Links can dangle and be inconsistent.
- There are thousands of individual WWW "empires" with no real overall organization or search potential. A site is difficult to generate or maintain.
- The WWW is read-only: servers provide, users browse and ask.
- Search facilities are non-standard.
- Bookmarks are saved locally by client, assessible only there.

In response to each of these problems, and others, a wealth of new developments are emerging. Some of these are particular features, others relate more to a new version of HTML (HTML 3), others to new developments in the way images, video and sound can be used, others in browser developments. But of particular interest are **conceptual developments**:

- The Web as an environment where *everyone can be a publisher*.
- The Web as an environment for electronic publishers to *build communities*.
- The Web as an environment for *doing business*.
- The Web as a platform for *collaborative communication*.

It is interesting that these conceptualizations of the WWW may result in similar new tools and functionalities but applied in very different ways, as for example the capacity for **write-able documents** which is important for collaborative communication may also be exploited by electronic publishers, but with a critical difference in who controls the extent to which areas of pages can be writeable. The freedom wanted by the collaborative team will not be the security and control wanted by those in business transactions, although both want new tools for interactivity.

FEATURES AND FUNCTIONALITIES

Among the many features and functionalities emerging for exploitation on the WWW are:

- Using Web servers as platform-**independent front ends to on-line data bases**, providing the user with up-to-the-minute information. This approach involves both a Web server and a SQL database server, themselves linked by a SQL database client.

- Using **"dynamic document"** functionalities, such as "server push" in which the connection between a server and client is held open and new data objects replace old data objects on the user's browser. This allows, among others, animation effects.
- Uses of the Common Gateway Interface (CGI) protocol, to **scripts** for **clickable image maps**; to serve as **gateways** between servers, to reformat the information found on these various servers, and return it to the user; to add apparent **interactivity** to server-client exchanges; to deal with **forms** and the handling of input to forms; to allow multiple users to **submit data** into a database; and to facilitate **user-user communication** through re-formating and storing of input to discussion groups.
- Sending **Web pages via e-mail** for those who just want to read the content.
- Allowing **multilevel tables of contents** for the same document so that two views of a document can be seen at the same time.
- Allowing **downloading of software** for a time-monitored period of evaluation.
- New developments in **spiders and robots** which roam the WWW and automatically index sites.

What does this all mean to the user? That pages are becoming more technically sophisticated, involve more complex programming, and that the distinctions among WWW pages and e-mail, newsgroups, groupware, and interactive software are rapidly blurring.

NEW DEVELOPMENTS IN HTML

Not surprisedly, HTML is evolving continuously. **HTML 3.0,** being finalized in late 1995, will support:

- More **control over graphics and display** for the creator of WWW pages
- New possibilities for **overlaying text** on graphics and for **flowing text** around in-line images.
- **Stationary logos and navigation bars** that don't disappear when a page is scrolled.
- Permission for browsers to **annotate forms.**
- New flexibilities with automatically sized **tables.**
- New elements for generating **footnotes and abstracts.**
- Support for **mathematical typesetting.**

NEW DEVELOPMENTS IN HANDLING MULTI-MEDIA

The capacities to handle audio and video in WWW sites are rapidly developing. Particularly interesting is the emerging **"Virtual Reality Markup Language" (VRML)** which is aimed at allowing users to navigate in three dimensional space, rather than two. The predictions are the VRML will lead to a 3-D Web where the home page will be replaced by the home space. The application of 3-D graphics for still images, embedded animations and the creation of 3-D virtual worlds for games will drive a market for these developments.

Another major area of WWW development in late 1995 is **audio applications**. Audio compression and decompressions techniques are being applied to add audio clips to WWW documents in ways that are increasingly practical. RealAudio and other tools are making broadcast audio over the Internet feasible.

NEW DEVELOPMENTS IN BROWSERS AND LANGUAGES

New versions of browsers with new features are continually emerging in 1995, competing with each other for creativity, anticipation and integration of HTML 3.0, and security provision. Innovations include allowing the user to **customize** aspects of storage and navigation, to allow personal **annotation** of pages, to see incoming **images** and download multiple images at the same time, and to handle various **drag-and-drop operations** among applications and HTML pages. Features to improve the **ease of developing** or editing a page are also strengthening; to improve **searching capacity** from directly within the browser, and for searching through (over 7,000) **newsgroup**s and interacting with those you select are also available.

But perhaps most powerful are the features related to the *Java programming language and the HotJava browser (from Sun Microsystems, URL http://www.sun.com).* HotJava **interprets embedded application <APP> tags** by downloading and executing the specified program within the WWW environment. The specified program can be an interactive game, animation or sound files, or any other interactive program. Also, when a file or application requires particular **viewers,** such as for

video, Java anticipates this and calls these viewers up automatically. Third-party developments are being encouraged to develop extensions to Java to continually enhance its product. For more information, see:

```
URL http://java.sun.com/
```

NEW DEVELOPMENTS IN AUTHORING

Two powerful lines of development in publishing and authoring are occurring in 1995. One relates to the move toward the automation of text documents into HTML documents through continual advances in **editors,** editors within word processing packages, and tools to check and verify HTML pages and their embedded links.

The second move relates to advances **in document formattting**, particularly through Adobe Acrobat's Portable Document Format (PDF):

```
URL
http://www.adobe.com/Acrobat/
```

which is moving into a position of competition or co-existence with HTML in terms of being able to embed links to either Acrobat files or HTML files within Acrobat files themselves. The great strength of Acrobat is control over formatting, such as with desktop publishing.

THE NEXT GENERATION OF HYPERLINKED NETWORK SYSTEM 5: HYPER-G?

Finally, 1995 is also seeing the emergence of a "new generation" of network architecture, the "**Hyper-G**" environment, which is seen by its developers as qualitatively different from the WWW network environment although building upon much of its strengths. Most of the new developments described in Interface 3 are realized in various ways in Hyper-G.

The **Interface Section References** at the back of the book give useful URLs for overviews of WWW developments.

4 Tele-learning and the professional

Professional learning refers to the on-going learning that adults engage in to do their work and to improve their work-related knowledge and skills. What is a profession, precisely? I do not attempt to delimit this. But what this chapter deals with are the people whose professional identity involves life-long learning, not organized and specified by one's employer but shaped and delimited by one's self. The main traditional information resources for professional learning are one's books, reports, and personal files; journals; material from conferences; and—human contacts. Tele-learning, particularly through electronic networks, is bringing a new range and form to these traditional sources.

In this chapter I discuss the implications of tele-learning to two major generic categories of professional learning—through stored information and through human contact. Many topics are discussed, in particular, with respect to information: Who are the new gatekeepers for professional information? What are new forms of traditional professional information provision, such as journals and conferences? How do the new forms of publication and communication integrate with the traditional? Where is the added value? Where is the quality control and who decides? With respect to communication: How can communication among a group of peers be captured as knowledge and information for others? What is professional networking and how do we learn from it? When the professional can talk to anyone, and everyone can publish, how do I find and identify what is valuable to my own professional learning needs?

This is the flavour of this chapter.

■ **4.1 What is professional (tele)-learning?**

■ **4.2 New ways of information dissemination and exchange: traditional information providers**

■ **4.3 New suppliers of professional information for tele-learning**

■ **4.4 Professional information creation**

■ **4.5 New forms of professional networking**

■ **4.6 Conclusions: tele-learning and the professional**

Objectives

After this chapter you should be able to:

- Distinguish professional learning from formal learning and informal learning

- Identify ways in which tele-learning through computer networks is affecting traditional forms of information dissemination and exchange among professionals, particularly with respect to libraries, professional journals and conferences

- Be aware of different meanings of the term "network" as they apply to professional learning

- Identify some relationships between human networking, electronic networks, network organizations, and tele-learning

- Describe examples of the terms "the digital library", "electronic journals", "the learning organization" and "intellectual teamwork" and relate the examples and the terms themselves to tele-learning

- Be aware of the uses being made of various electronic tools and environments for professional tele-learning: listservs, distribution lists, newsgroups, e-mail tools, computer conferencing, WWW sites, file transfer, and some new directions for these tools in the future

- As an example of a professional group which is actively becoming engaged in professional tele-learning, identify various forms of professional tele-learning for teachers particularly through networking

> ● Reflect on two major sets of issues related to tele-learning for professionals: issues related to gatekeepers and quality control, and issues related to the efficient and productive use of communication: What are the implications of these for the field, and for yourself?

■ 4.1 WHAT IS PROFESSIONAL (TELE)-LEARNING?

The term "professional learning" is perhaps not immediately clear. A first task of this section is to sketch what, and who, I mean as the focus of this chapter. Let me do it in a few words, and then spend the rest of this Section 4.1 making it more and more specific.

■ 4.1.1 A PERSONAL INTRODUCTION: LIFE-LONG LEARNING IS MORE THAN A CLICHÉ

"Professional learning" takes place not in courses, not in training centres, but in the on-going intellectual life of the professional. For example, how do I learn?

NOT FROM COURSES

It has been many years since I took a course, in any way, from anyone (maybe this is not something I should make public!). Yet I know I am learning, all the time, so much so that, in fact, this book is spilling out because of all that I have learned in just the last few years.

And how does my learning occur? I read. I talk to colleagues with good ideas and experiences. I go to professional conferences. I even organize professional conferences. And I read even more.

I READ...

What do I read? Academic journals, conference proceedings, documents that my colleagues send me, sometimes in the ordinary mail, mostly via the Internet, useful articles I find on LISTSERVs to which I subscribe, and increasingly in 1995, articles and documents I find through clicking intriguing links in WWW sites and downloading reports, papers, and reflections from others in my profession.

I COMMUNICATE...

And how do I communicate? Hardly ever on the telephone: my colleagues are all over the world, our time zones and time schedules and styles of working do not fit with telephone communication. Nor do the sorts of things I want to say of substance to learning fit with a telephone conversation. But I do talk with my colleagues, sometimes hours in a day, sometimes more, by the uses I make of the communication possibilities of the Internet. Occasionally I go to a face-to-face event, and talk in face-to-face style, but increasingly I find face-to-face events are not learning experiences, but organizational experiences: finding my colleagues so we can determine how, and about what, we will get really in contact with each other—via the Internet.

I LEARN...

Because as a professional, I am involved in life-long, never-ending learning. I can't stop, I wouldn't want to stop, learning. Learning is part of what I am. To paraphrase Descartes, "I learn, therefore I am...".

Now, what are the main characteristics of my life-long learning? I am self-motivated and self-monitored: no one tells me to start, stop, or how to proceed. I am the judge of what and who are relevant for my learning. Sometimes I know I have a specific learning need, other times I just know I want to know more. I need tools and resources and ways to make contact with those people and documents relevant to my learning. It has come to be that tele-learning is a core aspect of my everyday life, not only for me, but also for many of my colleagues.

INDIVIDUAL, AND PROFESSIONAL

In Chapter 3, we took the viewpoint of the family; of course, members of a family may also be professionals and many of the categories of interest in Chapter 3 can be re-cast in terms of the level and frames of interest of the professional in Chapter 4, such as new forms of electronic publication, and search tools for WWW as efficient location of resources. I come back to a number of these aspects of tele-learning in this chapter, but in a different context and through a different optic. One's life as a professional, and life as a parent, sometimes overlap and sometimes use the same tools with regard to tele-learning. But of course, the focuses, the tone and style, the criteria for evaluating relevance, take on different hues for tele-learning in the family and for tele-learning as a professional. So it is to the latter perspective that we turn in this chapter. In Chapter 3 I was talking to parents; in Chapter 4 I am talking to my colleagues. If my colleagues are themselves parents or not, is not relevant to this chapter.

A DEFINITION

Now, on to a more professional tone and style. I begin with a useful definition of professional learning:

> *...Professional learning refers to the on-going learning that adults engage in to do their work and improve their work-related knowledge and skills. In fact, for many professionals, learning is the central aspect of their work. Like informal learning, it is mainly self-directed; but unlike formal or informal learning, it is focused on a specific field closely linked to job performance, aims to be comprehensive, and is acquired and applied longitudinally.* (Marchionini & Maurer, 1995, pp. 68–69)

From this definition I can extract a number of important aspects of professional learning: Who does it refer to and what are their major characteristics? How is it different from other forms of learning? How does it occur? What are criteria for success? I will address these questions in Section 4.1, as well as the more global question: What is professional tele-learning?

■ 4.1.2 Who is engaged in professional learning and what are their major characteristics?

From Marchionini and Maurer's definition, it is clear that we are focusing on adults, with a professional occupation, and thus identified by both their background preparation and their current work definition and setting. For these persons, professional learning is not for pleasure and self-motivation, as informal learning in the family may be, although of course the professional learners may well experience pleasure as they are learning or from the results of their learning. Professional learning is not about an arbitrary range of topics; it is closely connected to the professional's intellectual tasks and problems.

In addition, the way the professional learner learns is an important aspect of professional learning. As the personal anecdote at the start of this chapter indicated, professional learning is self-directed. The professional decides him or herself what to read, with whom to communicate, how much to say, and what conferences to attend and what aspects of one's field to pay most attention to as learning targets. Steeples (1993) notes that learner control and independence are key aspects in making learning meaningful for professional learners; there must be a blend of learning with one's on-going activities to allow context and experience to be utilised in a way relevant to the specific situation of the professional. This makes the boundary for professionals between doing one's work and learning often impossible to specify.

THE LEARNING ORGANIZATION AND THE INDIVIDUAL LEARNER
Steeples notes another interesting characteristic of professional learners; they may work together with others on a task or collaborate informally to explore areas of

common interest, but even when working in a group the primary result for the individual relates to one's own work context, one's own professional goals. This distinction is easier to see when looking at professionals involved in a transitory activity such as a research project or a conference. It becomes less clear as the work organizations of professionals become more conscious of being "learning organizations" with implicit or explicit commitment to concepts and practices such as those listed in Box 4.1.

Box 4.1

The Learning Organization:

- A learning approach to strategy
- Inter-organizational learning
- Learning culture and climate
- Self-development opportunities for all
- Adaptable, with reward flexibility
- Committed to informative, collaborative interaction (Burgoyne, 1992)

This approach, in theory at least, is becoming widespread in organizational or human-resource management circles: the importance of moving from a "bureaucratic to a networked organization" (Nasta, 1994) is seen as essential for optimizing the human capital in an organization. An immediate consequence of such a managerial orientation is a "paradigm shift" away from "training" and toward life-long, just-in-time learning (Gardiol, Boder and Peraya, 1993; Landry, 1994).

Thus professional learning is based on the principles of self-control and independence, with choices based on what one feels will be useful in one's job performance. While it may be largely self-motivated, organizational cultures themselves are expecting it more and more in the professionals working for those organizations. However, regardless of the mix of motivations, the self-regulated aspects of professional learning mean that it is complex and unique mix of personal and situational circumstances for each individual involved.

■ 4.1.2 HOW IS PROFESSIONAL LEARNING DIFFERENT FROM OTHER FORMS OF LEARNING?

From what has been said so far, the answer to this question is probably predictable. However, it is useful, in anticipation of the positioning of professional tele-learning in the spectrum of tele-learning, to look more systematically at three categories of differences between professional learning and other forms of learning. Again, Marchionini and Maurer (1995) are a helpful reference in this, through their categorization of learning into three general forms: formal learning, informal learning, and professional learning.

FORMAL VS PROFESSIONAL LEARNING

Formal learning can be defined as what occurs in educational institutions, under the general control and structure of the teacher, the curriculum, and the institution itself. In plain terms, formal learning occurs when one "takes a course". The course may be of a short-term nature, it may be taught by a trainer, it may consist of self-study materials that are studied in one's home in the evening. The key idea is that the learner does what is specified by someone else, in specific or global terms, within the framework of a course, or workshop, or module.

Of course, professionals can and do take courses, go to workshops, and take part in other sorts of structured learning activities; generally they make the decision based on their own determination of what is useful to them for their work performance. When the decision to "take a course" is made by the professional, the learning involved moves out of the frame of reference for this chapter; the professional then chooses to become a student. In this chapter, the focus will stay on "on-going, comprehensive learning ... that is acquired and applied longitudinally" (Marchionini & Maurer, 1995, p. 69). I address the course-taking, or formal learning, experience for adults in Chapter 6.

PROFESSIONAL VS INFORMAL LEARNING

Professional learning also differs from informal learning, such as discussed in Chapter 3, in that professional learning is limited in its focus by the individual's work needs, rather than by his or her broader interests. Of course, the professional at home may turn to his or her computer or television or book and engage in professional learning, but probably as a subset of all the other things that are being done at that family computer or in front of the family television set.

Private vs public

But there are other distinctions as well between professional learning and informal learning. Nipper (1989), for example, notes the following:

- The home environment is, socially speaking, a private environment, where the learners are seen as individuals acting in accordance with their personal and private educational objectives.

● The professional environment is a public or semi-public environment, where the learners are seen in their professional and vocational roles, and where the individual or social profiles are a function of the professional identities. The professional learner is pursuing professional objectives which may or may not correspond to private objectives, but which are defined by the professional function of the learner. (p. 69).

Difference in communication styles

Nipper makes a further distinction between the communication styles of the informal, home-based learner and the professional learner. More often, the communication style of the professional learner can be characterized as a "memo" style, while that of the informal learner as a "letter" style, with differences as shown in Box 4.2.

Box 4.2

Communication style differences between informal and professional learners

Memo Style, Professional Learner	Letter Style, Informal Learner
Subject triggered	Process triggered
Short and to the point	Long, diffuse and associative
Neutral	Personal
Passive	Dynamic
Formatted	Messy, unformatted

Of course, these are generalizations, but Nipper's observation that professional learners expect that they may be seen as mirroring the standards for public communication of their organizations and of their professional community—a concern not burdening the informal home learner—is an important one. Also, Nipper notes that professional learners must be highly sensitive to time and cost factors if engaging in professional learning at the workplace. Discussions with one's colleagues, trips to the library, periods spent reading a book, conference attendance, must be squeezed into short intervals, handled at the same time as the individual's "real" work is completed. The informal learner, in contrast, has only her free time and personal costs to consider (not insignificant considerations, of course).

Professional learning: the organization pays, in indirect ways

Here is a tremendous advantage for some professional learners compared to informal learners (or compared to other professional learners). Some professionals are fortunate enough that their workplace subsidizes their off-hours use of networks or other communication technologies. Those associated with universities are the most consistently fortunate in this respect, compared to many other categories of professionals such as dentists or nurses or accountants or most school teachers.

Communication within boundaries

Aside from the cost aspects, Nipper notes another consequence of the difference in communication style between (many) professional learners and (many) informal learners: the informal learner may be more inclined to be sociable and personal, engaging in small talk that "can overshadow objectives, disintegrate discussions and impose low discipline...the environment can become sloppy..." (p. 70). In general, this kind of communication, while it certainly occurs among professionals when they interact informally, does not tend to occur when they write to each other or address each other as professionals.

I will come back to these observations about communication style throughout this chapter as they are important to the professional tele-learning context.

■ 4.1.4 HOW DOES PROFESSIONAL LEARNING TRADITIONALLY OCCUR?

Professional learning in one sense is as old as apprenticeship and modeling, as old as learning by doing as one sees one's significant others doing. However, to anticipate our context of tele-learning, I will delimit the discussion in this chapter to professional-learning needs related to information and communication, as opposed to a fuller-range of learning-on-the-job possibilities, which can include intervals of "student-type" activities. Professional-learning needs related to information and communication traditionally are met in two major ways: through reading and filing, in a way useful to ones' self, print materials of various sorts; and through contacts with colleagues. These are discussed generally here, in ways that anticipate important continuities and distinctions for professional tele-learning.

PRINTED MATERIALS FOR PROFESSIONAL LEARNING

The major categories of printed materials for professional learning are books, professional journals, reports, and fugitive materials. Some of these materials may have been acquired from informal sources, such as in-house papers written by a colleague. However, most will represent the output of some sort of professional validation process, via the referees for a journal, the editors for a book, the professionals in an organization or association related to one's field. Conference papers also represent the result of professional gatekeeping, although to various degrees of scrutiny.

Acquiring information resources, traditional professional learning

And through what channels does the professional traditionally acquire these printed resources? Generally, through book stores or publishers' representatives, through the recommendations of his or her colleagues, through displays and handouts at conferences, through conference proceedings, through being sent something in the mail either on request or unsolicited, through serving as a reviewer ones' self, through subscriptions to journals, through membership in a professional society, and through going to a professional library.

Constraints and confidence level

In each of these cases the traditional professional learner is constrained by his or her resources, both in terms of access range and availability and financial constraints. What the professional does acquire has gone through some level of editorial control and gatekeeping; the professional can be reasonably confident of its quality if the gatekeeper's reputation is high.

HUMAN CONTACTS FOR TRADITIONAL PROFESSIONAL LEARNING

Traditionally, a professional learns much from his or her peers and mentors. Illich (1971) noted that outside of formal educational settings, much of the individual learning that occurs in a professional's life-time results from informal group interactions and the help and support provided by peers and colleagues, what Illich termed one's "learning webs".

"Learning webs" (Illich, 1971)

For professional learning, these personal "webs" or "networks" are critical. They serve not only as trusted filters, but also as intelligent agents, able to supply information relevant to the requester's complex situation, without much description of that situation. Each person in one's professional-contact circle is also involved in other circles, thus bringing a way to increase one's own personal contacts as well as information sources.

Also, a human network can be turned to for requests for help, for clarification, for collaborators, for partners in short-term learning tasks.

The phrase "learning web" is interesting, in that Illich's use of it in 1971 long predated distributed hyperlinking of resources, such as is now so commonly available with World Wide Web technology in 1995. The concept of Learning Web is being re-expressed in terms of these distributed cross-linkage possibilities (see Norrie and Gaines, 1995, and see later in this chapter) but the basic concept of a Learning Web as a synergistic social-collective mechanism for acquiring and deepening one's knowledge and professionalism remains as Illich saw it: a critical aspect of professional learning.

Intangible benefits of a human network

And the human network is important for the intangible aspects of professional learning, as well as the specific.

A human network can provide the necessary communication partners for argument, debate, brainstorming, and discussion, critical to the social construction of knowledge (Kaye, 1992b). And, even more personally, one's human network is a group with whom one has a common language, a common frame of reference, and with whom one can express one's doubts and frustrations as well as one's learning contribution, confident that the companions in the network understand the implications of the situation.

Also, the synergy that can come from human networking is important to one's own levels of motivation. The positive experiences of one's peers can be models and sources of stimulation. The negative experiences of one's peers can also be sources of learning.

Constraints on human networking

Accidents of geography have been a major constraint on human networking. The professional learner, defined as he is by his workplace, has been largely surrounded by his physical colleagues. Occasionally the professional learner is able to go to a conference or serve on a committee or in some other way expand his or her range of human contacts. But traditionally, these expansions have been constrained by finances and geographic circumstance; the professional in a small town in a rural area with limited budget to travel would be much less likely to be able to increase his or her human-contact network than the professional fortunate enough to be in a large organization with many opportunities to work with others from outside the organization and to attend professional conferences.

■ 4.1.5 WHAT ARE CRITERIA FOR THE SUCCESS OF PROFESSIONAL LEARNING?

It is easier to define criteria of success for professional learning than for informal learning and perhaps even for formal learning. The professional him- or herself decides on the relevance and on the payoff, unlike formal learning where a teacher or institution makes this decision. ("Why do we have to learn this?" is such a familiar comment to the secondary-school teacher and even, alas, to the university instructor.)

With professional learning, the professional him- or herself can use local indicators to decide if a type of information or a human source of information is useful. Can I use this tomorrow? Is this going to help me with my report or my project? Does this apply to my problem? Will it be perceived as useful in my workplace if I have these new skills or insights? The individual professional can, and does, make these decisions on an on-going basis, and probably more accurately than anyone else could make them.

The risk of this self-determinism is short-term relevance at the expense of long-term development, a problem every professional confronts. Another risk is the isolarity of self-decision making: without a critical lens and broad input, the professional may drift into a line of development that comes to suit his interests rather than his growth within his professional community.

■ 4.1.6 WHAT IS PROFESSIONAL TELE-LEARNING?

In each of the above paragraphs, limitations on the efficiency and effectiveness of traditional professional learning were indicated. I took the time and space to highlight them deliberately as barriers to traditional forms of professional learning, because every one of the limitations can be addressed by some aspect of professional tele-learning with its expanded possibilities for information access, exchange, construction, and networking. And in addition, the strengths of professional learning, including particularly the strengths associated with the Learning Web concept, can be amplified by professional tele-learning.

The last sentence is the thesis of this chapter. To argue this thesis more effectively, let us now define professional tele-learning for purposes of this chapter.

PROFESSIONAL TELE-LEARNING: A DEFINITION

Framed by the elaboration of professional learning in the previous paragraphs, we define professional tele-learning in terms of 1995 tele-learning technology as *the subset of professional learning that involves making use of networked information and communication opportunities.*

Mainly the Internet...

While the networking in professional tele-learning does not have to be through the Internet as its transmission channel, the international spread of professional communities and resources available through the Internet and the synergy possible from being able to selectively make use of this, means that the Internet and its major tools of e-mail, file transfer, distribution lists, LISTSERVs (in a few cases, newsgroups), and the WWW are the major focuses in this chapter. Of course, there are other networks that are important to professional tele-learning, such as closed networks within an organization or network services organized for a certain group of professionals making use of a non-Internet connected network. And there are occasional, technologically fortunate, professionals who can learn from each other via video-conferencing, shared-workspace or "whiteboard", or desktop multi-media conferencing sessions (see Chapters 2, 8, and 10; also see popular summaries such as Boroughs, 1995).

However, in terms of 1995 tele-learning technologies, the major target audience for professional tele-learning are those professionals with desktop (and thus, not time-restricted) access to the Internet. Thus this is the focus in this chapter.

PRIME CANDIDATES FOR PROFESSIONAL TELE-LEARNING

Not every professional with a connection to the Internet will proceed at the same rate and depth of use of this connectivity for professional tele-learning. Professionals need the technological connectivity but they also have different levels of incentives associated with their own work and their own views of what it means to develop professionally. Curran (1993) for example has identified the following categories of professionals as most likely to be significantly involved in tele-learning at the time of his analysis because of: (a) their likelihood of having widespread access to the Internet as a communication channel, and (b) some particular features of their professional-learning needs:

- Professionals in areas of rapidly developing technologies such as engineers and medical personnel
- Professionals whose level of expertise is such that collaboration with other experts for mutual professional development tends to be at a distance
- Professionals in higher education, and increasingly in training and schools
- Researchers

- Professionals involved in the design, production and delivery of educational materials (educational technologists) (Curran, 1993, p. 26)

These groups generally meet what McCreary and Brochet (1990) call "essential elements for CMC implementation":

- The need and desire to communicate
- Commitment from senior management
- Access to equipment
- Time to learn
- Access to basic training or support for using the equipment
- Critical mass of users and messages

Some professionals have it easier than others...

As we will see, these general requirements are met in a wide variety of ways and in a wide range of adequacy, among different professionals and even whole groups of professionals. For example, teachers as a group of professionals have minimal levels of adequacy in most of these elements; professional educational technologists working as faculty members in universities, are much more fortunate. (These differences will show up in the examples discussed in Chapters 5, 6, and 9.) Because teachers and educational technologists are two professional groups that are important to this book, they will often be used as examples in this chapter on professional tele-learning.

Now, let's get to specifics: Tele-learning and the two general categories of professional learning—acquiring useful stored (usually printed) information and interacting with one's human contacts. An important first aspect of professional tele-learning is that these two categories are becoming fused, in new and powerful ways.

■ 4.2 New ways of information dissemination and exchange: traditional information providers

We noted earlier that professionals have typically obtained stored information from professional sources, such as libraries and other professional information depositories, book and journal publishers, conferences, professional associations and from human contacts. We will call the first four of these "traditional information suppliers" and in this section will see how they are changing through the use of networking technologies primarily via the Internet. These changes have an important impact on professional tele-learning.

■ 4.2.1 LIBRARIES

We indicated some aspects of the metamorphosis of the library in Chapter 3, relative to the development of networked access to library resources accessible to the family. Here we will focus on some implications of the increasing digitization of academic libraries and their services for professional tele-learning. "Digital libraries" is a phrase that represents both a concept and a trend. The trend is seen in the steady movement in libraries toward new ways to deal with information by digitizing it, and thus new ways to "manipulate it, find it, link it, visualize it, use it, publish it, manage it, store it, protect it, and, oh yes, share it with the rest of the world" (Crawford, 1995, p. 5). The concept, made possible because of digitization and hyperlinking, is of digital libraries as "the space in which people communicate, share, and produce new knowledge and knowledge products, ... as support for learning, whether informal or formal"(Fox, Akscyn, Furutu and Leggett, 1995, p. 25). Professional tele-learners are prime candidates for occupancy of this space.

ADVANCES IN INFORMATION RETRIEVAL

Libraries throughout the world are active in research to make distributed information request and retrieval more efficient and powerful, which is of course relevant for professional tele-learning. Box 4.3 indicates some ways in which this is happening.

Each of these advances are relevant for professional tele-learning, in that these

---

Box 4.3

Advances in information retrieval in libraries

Advances in retrieval engines

Advances in indexing coupled with more sophisticated natural-language processing

More effective filtering and routing of information directly to subscribers, based on the subscriber's "profile"

Enhancement of subscriber profiles through more sophisticated use of user statistics

Access by browsing as well as query, and when query is used, interative query refinement

Provide tools to support visualization of search spaces (Croft, 1995; Rao *et al.*, 1995)

services will be increasingly available via computer networks to distributed clients. Development work is underway at many libraries on various aspects of support for remote information retrieval. WWW search engines and robots (see Chapter 3) represent the class of hyperlinked information-retrieval tools based on different kinds of mark-up coding which are being developed for digital collections of information in professional libraries.

Digitizing information

For tele-learning, information provided by libraries needs to be increasingly in digital form, to begin with via digital indices and abstracts, later full digitization of text and images. Many libraries are busy now in this sort of conversion process, partly in anticipation of the needs of professional tele-learners. An example is that of a group of libraries in New Zealand and Australia, where a data-compression system has been developed, and is freely available over the Internet, that allows searching of compressed text and images (Bell, Moffat, Witten and Zobel, 1995). This compression technique not only allows full-text searching of compressed material but also of compressed indices of the materials. Searching compressed indices accelerates the time needed for full-text retrieval. (A single CD-ROM can hold, compressed, a 1.5 gigabyte database, in which inquiries can be processed by a personal computer in seconds.) This compression system is freely available via the Internet by:

Anonymous ftp from `munnari.oz.au` [128.250.1.21] in the directory `/pub/mg`

This sort of speed and compression is critical for serious professional tele-learning involving network queries of extensive data sets, particularly when this must occur in a situation where connect and search time must be minimized.

Other examples of information compression for high-speed availability

Many other libraries are compressing information and making it available via the Internet. For example, the University of California has put the equivalent of 260,000 books onto 270 CD-ROMs, a portion of which can accessed via ordinary WWW connectivity, and the rest through other Internet methods such as ftp (Merrill, Parker, Gey and Stuber, 1995). For more information go to:

`http://cedr.lbl.gov/cdrom/doc/cdrom.html`

where the current status of the CD-ROMs is updated three times daily, usage data as to look-ups are provided, and frequently-asked questions about installing these data sources at local sites are answered.

As another example of making information digitally available via electronic networks, the Electronic Beowulf Project at the British Library is particularly interesting. A full-colour electronic version of the medieval document "Beowulf" will be available to on-line as the enormous job of properly photographing and digitizing its priceless pages proceeds. The entire process is discussed and explained, as well as illustrated with rich visual examples, on the WWW site:

The Electronic Beowulf:

```
http://service/uky/edu/ArtsSciences/English/Beowulf/
```

This site also includes an extensive discussion of the digital preservation, restoration, and dissemination of medieval manuscripts, as well as the latest developments in the Electronic Beowulf Project itself (Kiernan, 1995).

More generally, hundreds of academic libraries now offer Internet access to both public and restricted groups of users. Box 4.4 shows a sampling of just a few of the publicly open sites.

Box 4.4

Sample of academic libraries with Internet access

Library of Congress (US)
URL http://marvel.loc.gov

Colorado Alliance of Research Libraries (CARL)
Telnet to: csi.carl.org
.... *Access to large number of databases, academic and public library catalogues, and many other indexes*

Washington and Lee Library
URL: http://honor.uc.wlu.edu:1020
... *Approximately 3,000 libraries are linked to this site*

Indiana University School of Law Library
URL: http://www.law.indiana.edu
... *Typical of subject-specific library, this one with more than 1,000 links*

National Library of Medicine (US)
URL: http://www.medinfo.rochester.edu/pub/MedicineIb.html
...*Example of library with rich amounts of digitally available visual materials*

The Library of Congress homepage is typical of WWW library services in 1995, with choices for:

- What's new for the current month on the server
- Usage statistics
- General archival information about the Library
- Detailed information about special exhibits and events, services and publications
- Tools to search and view items from digitized collections
- Search tools with specialized forms
- Links to other libraries and information collections

COPYRIGHT ISSUES AND DOWNLOADING BOOKS

A particular issue facing libraries as they make more and more of their materials available digitally and via network to learners is copyright and associated concerns about plagiarism. Samuelson (1995) after examining a range of issues related to copyright and digitalization from a legal perspective, concludes that "as long as leaks do not become hemorrhages, tolerating some leakage [in copyright protection] may be in the long run of interest to publishers" and that libraries must work together with publishers, authors and users to find new systems appropriate to networks "that ensure that public access is available on fair, reasonable, and nondiscriminatory terms" (pp. 21, 110).

Technical constraints on prodigious downloading

However, on-line contact with libraries is more likely to focus on the location of resources than for their immediate downloading for a number of years in the future. Network bandwidth limitations and the disinclination of subscribers to print out prodigious quantities of (often unformatted) text will limit the attractiveness of downloading books. Nonetheless, there are already locations available via the Internet where electronic versions of books are available for ftp retrieval (see Sanchez, 1995a, for a listing and discussion). Probably the best-known of these locations circa 1995 is that of the Gutenberg Project, with a goal of having 10,000 "e-books", generally classic literature with no copyright restrictions, available by the year 2001. This project has been underway since 1971(!). For information about the Gutenberg Project see:

Gutenberg Project
```
URL http://jg.cso.uiuc.edu/pg/pg_home.html
```

The texts themselves are available by ftp (the WWW page is the best source of information about these addresses and directories).

IN SUMMARY: CHANGES RELATED MORE TO SCALE THAN TO CONCEPT

My general impression with regard to library services and the professional tele-learner is that the changes which are occurring in those services are more related to scale than to concept. For libraries, accommodating the growing demands of professional tele-learning for distributed access to searchable collections appears to be a substantial task, but one in line with the general evolution of libraries toward digitalization for their own internal procedures. The new aspects of making collections of library materials available via electronic networks have in fact been under systematic development for many years. Thus the needs of the professional tele-learner seem to be more related to increases in the scale of what is available and changes related to increasing convenience in distributed searching rather than a new conceptual dimension for library services.

However, while libraries may not appear to the professional tele-learner to have conceptually changed their function, the professional journal is undergoing a number of revolutionary developments. We look at these in the next section.

■ 4.2.2 THE PROFESSIONAL JOURNAL

For many professionals, especially university-based academics and researchers, the scientific journal is not only a main way of getting new information, but also a main way in which the individual professional can communicate to his or her peers. This form of communication, one-way through refereed text-based publication, has also become the index of productivity for many academics. Thus academic journals are important channels for professionals, both as sources of new information and insights, and as the way to communicate one's self to one's broad academic community.

A key aspect in this dynamic is the assurance of quality control, of a review process which validates the work before it is accepted for publication. This review process thus serves a gatekeeper mechanism. This gatekeeper mechanism is felt to be critical, both to the eventual reader, who should be able to feel assured that a quality-control process has been at work, and to those who evaluate the productivity of the authors, who use the referee process as an baseline for validation of the authors' intellectual work.

Electronic networking is bringing revolutionary changes into these aspects of professional journals and professional tele-learners will be the key group involved in the changes. We discuss three important ways in the next subsections: Bringing two-way communication into scholarly publication, adding links to publications, and blurring the conventions for quality control and the power of scholarly gatekeepers.

ELECTRONICALLY AUGMENTED FORMS OF PRINTED JOURNALS

Academic journals are moving to on-line availability in a number of different ways. One way is to maintain traditional print-format publication, but augment this by having the indexes or tables of contents included in on-line repositories. Another way is to make abstracts available via the Internet. Still another form is to allow pre-prints to be available on-line to subscribers. A major UK publisher, for example, will move by 1996 to a method of offering subscribers (who are mostly institutional libraries) the option of the standard print subscription, or an augmented subscription. In the augmented subscription, libraries will pay an additional fee and for this fee can issue a password to any of their subscribers which will allow all those persons to go to the WWW page associated with the journal, and obtain the full-text of pre-prints of the material in the printed journals (Chapman & Hall, 1995). None of these variations involve a conceptual change from the current forms of journals. In the Chapman & Hall example, the institution still pays the standard shelf subscription price but access to and readership of the journal is likely to be enhanced because of the convenience of desktop or remote browsing of the contents via the WWW page and immediate downloading, rather than photocopying of pages of articles useful for the reader.

PARALLEL BUT ALTERNATIVE FORMS

Another variation for professional journals is to produce a parallel but different version of the print journal for on-line access and distribution. The journal "Chronicle of Higher Education", for example, produces a "complimentary information service" called *Academe This Week* that is related to each of its print editions by putting on the network at 12:00 Tuesday of each week:

- The table of contents of the associated print issue
- All of the "positions available" information (situations where the time aspect is important, so that all potential candidates have the same temporal starting point in terms of information about new positions)
- A calendar of events and list of important deadlines

This parallel publication can be accessed at location:

Academe This Week
```
URL http://chronicle.merit.edu
```

In these cases, the electronic version is not a new version of the journal itself, but an enhancer (and advertisement) of the journal.

Another variation is to group subscribers via a listserv and notify them when an article is "published", i.e., available for ftp, or more, commonly, to send the on-line version of the journal directly to those subscribing to the listserv.

Box 4.5 includes a number of sources of information about parallel forms of electronic and print-based professional journals.

Box 4.5

Sources for examples of electronic and print combinations of professional journals

Electronic Journals, Newsletters and Texts
URL: `http://www.lib.ncsu.edu/stacks/index.html`

Information Sources: The Internet and Computer-Mediated Communication (December, 1993)
URL `http://www.december.com/net/tools/index.html`

Preprints and Electronic Journals from Around the World
URL: `http://www.geom.umn.edu/external/`

WWW in Scholarly Publishing
URL: `http://muse.mse.jhu.edu`

Electronic Tests, Journal, Newletters, Magazines and Collections
URL `http://dewey.lib.ncsu.edu/stacks/index.html`

CICNet Electronic Journals
URL: `gopher://gopher.cic.net`

ELECTRONIC-ONLY FORMS

As long as a traditional print form of a professional journal exists, the quality-control and validation processes that we mentioned earlier that are currently critical to academic recognition of a publication are not challenged. The major problem is for the publisher and/or copyright holder who see the easy dissemination of electronic material not so much as a convenience to readers but as a wholesale reproduction (and re-manipulation) of their works without further control or financial compensation.

However, the basic assumptions of quality control and gatekeepers begin to get cloudier when the only form of a professional journal is its network form. Box 4.6 gives a sample.

Box 4.6

Professional journals available only in network form

The Computer-Mediated Communication Magazine
URL: `http://www.rpi.edu/~decemj/cmc/mag/current/toc.html`

DEOSNEWS
Send Subscribe request to `LISTSERV@PSUVM.PSU.EDU`
...In its fifth year in 1995, this copyrighted, refereed and list-based journal has 3,376 subscribers in 60 countries and is published by the American Center for Distance Education. The ISSN is 1062-9416.

Journal of Computer-Mediated Communication
URL: `http://www.huji.ac.il/www_jcmc/jcmc.html` [for information]
for Volume 1, Issue 1 itself goto
URL `http://cwis.usc.edu:80/dept/annenberg/vol1/issue1/`

CONCERNS ABOUT ELECTRONIC-ONLY JOURNALS

In concept, a network-only academic journal can be exactly the same as a print journal in terms of editorial board, review and referee process, and other familiar mechanisms of quality control. What is missing is interesting on two levels.

This doesn't look like a journal...?

The first thing missing about a network-only version of a professional journal are its external attributes such as the look and physical appearance of the journal, the place it fills on the shelf. Professionals determining the legitimacy of publications have a long-developed sense of recognition of various indicators of professional quality which can be quickly communicated simply through the look and feel of an issue in one's hand. While these in themselves are superficial, their absence causes a sense of distrust. Are pages coming out from one's printer along with e-mail and uncontrolled LISTSERV sendings, believable as a scientific publication? How does one reference a citation, when there are no page numbers?

Perhaps these are trivial issues, and a function of the novelty of the new publication form. However, I see another set of issues that are more substantial and less likely to recede with familiarity.

What happened to what I said??

A traditional print journal fixes a "quality" version of an article, quality both in the totality of its substance and in its presentation. Even if subscribers can also print out and digitally manipulate an electronic form of the article, the print version is there, as a consistent reference anchor. With all-electronic publications, any reader along the way can become a "second author", removing, adding, rearranging text, and forwarding the new version to others. Without a commonly referable fixed version, readers and those making citations of the article in different parts of the world and at different times may be in fact referring to critically different documents. The confidence that the author has that her words are communicating her thoughts is seriously eroded. The confidence that the reader has that what s/he reads is what was intended by the author and the original reviewers is also eroded.

IMPACT ON ELECTRONIC FORMS OF JOURNALS

I feel these issues are fundamental, and will limit the quality of what is available in electronic-only form for professionals, for many years to come. For certain types of information, I am glad as a professional that I and any of my colleagues can put material out for broadscale distribution, even with the risks of distortion that I described above. But for other types of careful, serious writing, I am not yet willing to take these risks. And as long as professionals have this distrust, the professional information available via public networks, such as WWW pages is likely to be in three categories: (a) information meant to be more of the nature of an announcement of activities, work in progress, and other time-sensitive material; (b) information that is an added-value channel for quality-controlled print materials; or (c) information whose level of quality is dubious.

Negative? No, because of the added value...

But, does that mean that I am negative about electronic professional publication? No, partly because Category (a) is valuable for reasons related more to human contact and overviews of the field, but mostly because of very interesting new dimensions to professional publication that I see occurring as "added value" to print forms (Category (b) above). Two of these which are particularly important to professional tele-learning are the capacity to add communication and feedback to publication, and the capacity to add links to additional information. I see these as major new dimensions for professional exchange and they are part of what I call professional tele-learning.

Change 1: Bringing communication into publication

An article is in its very nature a form of communication, but a one-to-many form, a broadcast message, frozen in time through its encasement in words stored on a medium which many different people can read. In the Journal of Computer-

Mediated Communication, whose URL is given in Box 4.5, features can be found that illustrate the addition of other forms of communication to that of broadcasting, communication by those receiving the communication. Not only can responses be sent immediately and directly to the authors of an article and to the editors but also to other readers of the article.

ADDING DISCUSSION

While it has always been possible to write a letter to the editor or author of an article that one has read, the time lag involved in making one's comment known has precluded anything approaching discussion. Now, particularly with WWW technology the reader can communicate as s/he reads (if forms have been provided by the author), can read the reactions left by other readers, and can also comment on those comments (if the page is coded for this). Something like the face-to-face interchanges that happen at professional conferences when an author presents a paper to an audience can now happen on-line, but free of the restrictions of time and space that limit conference participation (and that limit the opportunity to express ones' self, even if at the conference).

GETTING FEEDBACK WHILE WRITING

For the author, the chance to get immediate feedback from readers and to participate in critical discussion about one's work is bringing a new phase of activity (and perhaps discomfort) into the life cycle of writing and publishing an article. This process can change the sense of an article being finished, to one that is continually under peer review. With a broader audience than one's own circle, there is more chance of new perspectives and critical feedback. The article may never be "finished" until there is no longer interest in it.

ADDING FOLLOW-UP MODERATED DISCUSSIONS

The editors of the JCMC journal noted above also plan to hold and moderate "online miniconferences" around issues, to add extra structure to the communication process. This idea is catching on as an added-value dimension of many different print and/or electronic journals. For example, the listserv *ITForum* has carried this idea forward, outside the framework of a "journal". During the year 1994–1995, a series of authors were recruited and articles were solicited. These articles were reviewed and if accepted, where then posted to the list on pre-announced days. Following the day of posting, the author of the article agreed to be available for interaction for a one-week period following the appearance of the article. Anyone subscribing to the list was encouraged to contribute comments and to participate in any discussion that developed.

For the archive of the *ITForum* articles and for subscription to the list itself (a list for professional educational technologists, see Chapter 8), go to location:

ITForum
URL: `http://129.8.48.23/InTRO/InTRO.html`
or
Subscribe to `LISTSERV@UGA.CC.UGA.EDU`

Change 2: Adding links

We mentioned earlier that many journal publishers are integrating supplementary electronic services with their print-based journals. The Chapman & Hall example can be mentioned again, but this time to illustrate another added-value feature of electronic journals that has particular value to professional tele-learners. This is the ability to add links within a document. In a WWW environment, this means that fugitive and grey-literature sources could be added as linked material, making them really accessible to the reader. It means that links can be made within an article, or between articles in an edition. It means that links can be added to other resources that the author is willing to make available. Chapman & Hall are planning to phase in various types of links in their electronic-subscription journals beginning in 1996, and many other publishers are also working in this direction.

NEW TASKS, NEW LEARNING ...

This puts a new load on the author, to make available what s/he cites as a reference when possible (copyright remains a limitation) and to think herself in terms of cross referencing. It puts a new load on editors, who must check the availability of linked material as well as its citation forms. It gives a new learning opportunity to the reader however, and lets him better share the frame of reference of the author. It also allows the reader to better judge the interpretation of the author about cited materials.

OTHER ADDED-VALUE LINKS FOR PROFESSIONAL TELE-LEARNING

As another added-value of linkage, an electronic journal (or journal supplement) can also be organized with embedded search tools, so that the reader can quickly see if what he is interested in is available in the journal. Links can be embedded within the article to multi-media supplements (see Welz, 1995, or any number of WWW sites, for up-to-date information about multi-media documents on the WWW; also see **Interface 3**). Links in the form of clickable images can be used to give a visual overview, a concept map, of the relationship of terms within an article or articles within a special issue.

As a very nice example of this, the August 1995 issue of the print journal, *Communications of the ACM*, not only focused on issues relating to hyperlinked information systems (see Bieber and Isakowitz, 1995), but also supplemented this issue with a WWW site that placed the Special Issue's opening statements, six articles, and ten sidebars on the WWW; featured over 150 links added among the articles to show their cross-relationships; provided for various sorts of links such as those for more in-depth information and definitions; and used links in different formats relative to their user-interface aspects. Overall to the Special Issue, the WWW site includes a visual outline of the issue, showing the relationships among the variable features and articles in graphic form, which also provides clickable entry to the articles. To see these very nice features, which add considerably to the learning value of reading the articles themselves, see:

ACM, August 1995 Overview
URL `http://irss.njit.edu:5080/papers/overview.html`

These different types of links expand the informational value of an article considerably. The links can provide more context for the article, particularly links that relate to the authors themselves and their associated publications. And, as we noted before, links can be to people as well as stored materials; thus links can also improve communication about an article.

Change 3: Blurring the gatekeepers

The *JCMC* journal mentioned in Box 4.6 indicates clearly in its editorial policy that it is a refereed journal, with an editorial board. However, many of the other electronic journals now available are less formally edited, and even encourage reader contribution to the extent that the boundary between "real" articles and open contributions is hard to distinguish. As the *ITForum example* shows, scholarly writing and electronic publication, accompanied by structured communication, can be initiated via a listserv and the listserv's moderators rather than by editors. And what the author says in follow-up discussion to his article may be of considerably greater length and even depth than the original article, with no editorial control whatsoever.

And what is going to happen to the gatekeepers who traditionally maintain the academic quality of a journal, and its reputation? I predict an important change.

In the current world of professional publishing, the final decision makers are editors and editorial boards, most often making a decision many months after an article is submitted, most often communicating through a single editor some feedback as to the fate of the article. The author may be given the opportunity to rewrite, if he follows the editor's suggestions; the likelihood of dialogue either between the reviewers or between the author and reviewers is remote. The gatekeepers thus have a profound filtering effect on what appears in print.

The gatekeeper process has another important effect: the measurement of quality occurs before an article is published. The indicator of success that is asked for by faculty committees is number of publications. The sense of evaluating the reaction to the publication from its larger group of intended readers is not part of this process (other than in very broad terms; one's reputation grows slowly in either positive or negative directions).

TURNING THE PROCESS AROUND

What I see happening slowly but surely with electronic forms of publication are changes in both these gatekeeper-related aspects. First the necessity to go through a gatekeeper, i.e., the editor of a traditional journal, will gradually diminish as more-and-more forms of alternative network publications gradually find their identities and quality-control procedures. The ITForum example above showed a publication process outside the framework of an established journal which could mature into a process recognized as "scholarly publication" of the same credibility as a print journal. (The concern I raised earlier about distortions of one's work resulting from the lack of a shared, fixed reference document is removed in the ITForum model, in that the moderator/editor has this fixed document and sends it en masse on an announced day to all members of the list. Even if the article is subsequently massaged by other readers, there is a fixed reference version).

Bypassing the gatekeepers...

And as the functionalities of an electronic journal can be also made available without the framework of a journal, the importance of journals as ways to tell about one's work to the scientific community will recede. Receding at the same time will be the gate-keeper network of senior academics who now serve as editors of journals. Most importantly, the validation of an contribution will more and more be accessed after the publication fact, based on the comments it generates and the follow-up links requested, than before, based on the opinions of a small number of editors.

Judged by reaction from the field...

I see this as a fascinating turn for professional writers, to be judged on the reaction of our real audience to our work; not on the reaction *a priori* to publication of a few persons in editorial positions. Our ideas will have to fight harder for their testing. We must become more responsive to criticism, less surprised by critical comments, more aware of the many people who do not see the world as we do. Thus: better writers, better professionals, even better people.

But, among the barriers...

As I see it, the major barrier in this evolution will be the willingness of decision makers in the professional's own home institution to legitimatize such contributions as "scholarly output". Resistance and skepticism toward change are particularly strong in institutional structures whose members have reached success in the old ways, as is often true of faculty committees making decisions on the weighting and legitimization of indicators of scholarly productivity.

INTERACTION WITH ONE'S PEERS

But regardless of the resistance to change with respect to publications on the part of traditional gatekeepers, many changes in professional information exchange have already occurred and are continuing to occur, because of the functionalities available through networks and particularly the Internet. Most important, if we turn back to the professional tele-learner herself, is the sense of adding interaction with one's peers to information exchange. For the professional tele-learner, reading an article will change from a passive event (perhaps enlivened by the act of photocopying the article for one's reference files) to an interactive event, from being a subscriber to a broadcast event to a participant in a discussion. For the author, publication also becomes an experience in professional tele-learning, changing the author from being the expert in a non-interrupted broadcast to a partner in a discussion which may move out from his control.

Until recently, the major way that professionals experienced such interactivity/information exchanges among the broader community of their colleagues was to be members of professional associations and attend the yearly meetings of those associations. How is this aspect of professional learning being effected by networks and the potential of tele-learning?

▨ 4.2.3 PROFESSIONAL ASSOCIATIONS

Professional associations have long been an important source of information for those in their target groups, not only because such societies frequently are associated with a (print form) journal and because they organize professional conferences (with the accompanying refereed and printed proceedings) but also because they provide a range of other information services for their members. Not surprisingly, professional organizations are now developing electronic communication and information services to complement their traditional activities.

Box 4.7

Examples of professional societies with services for professional tele-learning

ISTE (International Society for Technology in Education)
URL http://iste-gopher.uoregon.edu:80
...*Maintains various LISTSERVs and distribution lists for up-to-date information to its members*

ACM (Association of Computing Machinery)
URL http://info.acm.org
...*Provides in addition to a range of information browsing and dissemination services, features such as "Technology Outreach Program" where experts provide personalized services to particular groups through all-electornic means such as adding sound bites to comments and to the experts' homepages*

Organizations and Conferences
URL http://matia.stanford.edu
...*For an overall collection of links to the WWW sites of professional organizations*

Some typical examples are noted in Box 4.7:

EXTENDING THE RANGE OF TRADITIONAL SERVICES

The ACM site is a typical example. If offers predictable information—on membership, publications, programs, by-laws, and its constitution. However, more innovatively, it also offers a way to extend its existing "Technology Outreach Program" in which the association serves as a sort of brokerage between those who would like the services of ACM members and ACM members willing to offer those services. The extension is that not only is all communication handled electronically, mediated by the central ACM server, but also text- and graphic presentations from lectures occurring in this framework can be previewed over the Internet. Sound bites have been added to the proposed lecturer's home pages as well.

A continual concern of professional associations is how to bring their services to their members in as equitable a way as possible. In particular, many professional communities are particularly concerned about how to bring the benefits of conference attendance to those of their members who cannot afford the time and travel to physically attend the conferences. This is a major problem for

■ 4.2.4 PROFESSIONAL CONFERENCES AUGMENTED BY TELE-LEARNING

A major form of professional learning is via attendance at conferences. Not only is the event a systematic form of information exchange, but the opportunity exists to communicate in varying degrees of formality, and to extend one's personal networking channels.

But, do the rich get richer?

The constraints on attendance, and thus on learning value, for a conference are the time and cost involved in attendance (limiting the professional to perhaps only one per year and perhaps rarely to the conference that would be most valuable to her as a learning experience). And in addition, even for the fortunate who make it to the conference they wish to attend, the physical constraints while at the conference in terms of only being able to attend one parallel session at a time and the cognitive constraints of information overload also limit the learning value.

ELECTRONIC ADDED-VALUE

Professionals traditionally accommodate themselves to these time, distance and overload problems associated with conferences by voraciously accumulating handouts and print materials from the conference for study at a later date and by possession of the proceedings of the conference. (There are other strategies, too, such as sending one's graduate students to the conference and asking them to do the voracious accumulation of papers and handouts!)

Extension of learning value, before the conference

Electronic support for professional conferences is able to circumvent these sorts of time and information-overload problems and thus is substantially extending the learning value of the conferences for both those who can attend and those who cannot. Such support can involve the use of listservs and other distributions lists to disseminate information about the conference and to stimulate discussion about the conference prior to the conference; the maintenance of a WWW site for information and communication about the conference, thus widely increasing the traditional subscription base for the conference; and the use of the WWW site for access to abstracts of papers at the conference (sometimes the entire papers are available, usually via a gopher site, but this is less likely, given time constraints and issues relating to competition with the sales potential of the print proceedings of the conference).

Pre-conference WWW sites

Increasingly during 1995, conferences added the provision of a pre-conference WWW site to their organizational activities (see also Chapter 9). Prospective authors are increasingly being told to submit their papers in HTML and PostScript formats, thus anticipating WWW-based accessibility. The minimal pre-conference WWW site has information about paper submission and about the conference itself, but the learning value increases with the extra features that are being added to these minimal aspects. For example, announcements of real-time discussions with featured speakers at the conference, via MOO or IRC formats, are starting to appear. Hyperlinked overviews of the previous year's conference also are become a regular feature, allowing the tele-learner to not only make a better decision about the fit of the conference for his or her own needs, but also to browse and otherwise utilize the older proceedings for a number of learning goals. For example, those planning to attend the upcoming conference can look at papers submitted by certain speakers at the previous conference, both to check on the personal interest, and also to get a better base for understanding the progress that will be reported at the new meeting.

These sites may come and go with conferences; for those that are stable over time, it is most likely that they are supported by a professional association, and thus can be accessed through the association's WWW pages.

OTHER WAYS TO AUGMENT CONFERENCES VIA TELE-LEARNING

While the services illustrated above increase the subscriber range of a conference as well as the range of dissemination of its information, electronic on-line services can also bring other dimensions of learning value to the conference, if a subscriber is in physical presence or not.

Moderated discussions

The addition of a moderated on-line discussion around a featured speaker at a conference, prior to or after the conference, is now becoming common. Some times this discussion is via a listserv but other times experimentation is occurring with various real-time events, such as MOOs (as we have mentioned); via some form of audio/video conferencing (on the Internet, CU-SeeMe software allows limited-quality real-time video-conferencing over ordinary Internet network connections, if the various sites involved have multimedia computers with video cameras and microphones; or possibly some combined use of local broadcast and video-conferencing resources.

Making the conference virtual

And, when synchronous and asynchronous conferencing can be used to extend interaction and communication exchange before and after a conference, why not during the conference itself? This is increasingly happening, either by extending some portions of the face-to-face conference, via video-conferencing, to remote sites, or even more radical, replacing the face-to-face locus altogether.

Being there, by asynchronous communication

There are interesting examples of both asynchronous and synchronous conferencing being used to replace the face-to-face professional conference. Long, Pence, and Zielinski (1995) describe an "On-line Conference on Applications of Technology in Teaching Chemistry" that was held over the period of 12 June and 20 August 1995 using the Internet. In this conference, there was a traditional-type call for papers and registration procedure, but then the pattern of conference participation differed from traditional forms. Fifteen papers were selected for the conference and edited for e-mail distribution. A LISTSERV was set up for paper distribution and also conference organization information. During each of the three 3-week portions of the conference, participants discussed five of the conference papers. During the first of these three weeks, interaction was limited to participants sending short questions to the authors or other participants, but during the second and third weeks there were intense, moderated discussions. Four-hundred and fifty participants from 33 countries took part. All original papers, the full transcript of the discussions, summary papers that were developed after the conference and even post-conference discussion logs are available at

Anonymous ftp:
`inform.umd.edu`
Path:/Educational Resources/Faculty Resources and Support/Chenistry Conference (CHEMCONF)

The benefits of different forms of information provision can be seen in comparing the concise summary of Long, Pence and Zielinski (1995) from a scholarly journal with the original data available at the ftp site. Sometimes it is much desirable to have a scholarly reduction process!

Being there, by synchronous communication

For information about real-time multi-media communication and its use of professional discussions see Welz (1995), or go to sites such as the following:

Multimedia Integrated Conferencing for European Researchers
URL: http://www.cs.ucl.ac.uk/mice/

This European-based site offers full information about how to technically participate in real-time multi-media conferencing via the Internet (and also via higher-speed networks such as Mbone) and about seminars using multimedia conferencing open for participation in 1995. Of particular interest for those waiting to implement such conferencing alternatives are documents available relating to:

- Specifications for video compression
- Codec user manuals
- Descriptions and user information for the video-conferencing system used by the partners in the consortium represented by the WWW site
- Documentation on the internetworking of the Internet and ISDN networks for multi-media conferencing (see Chapter 2 for more discussion of these topics)

Maintaining contact

And, if you were at the conference face-to-face or virtually, it is still valuable to be able to follow up contacts with persons at a later date. Such personal networking is important to professional tele-learning, as we discuss in Section 4.5. Distribution lists can be maintained after a conference for follow-up information and contact among participants as a key way to maintain connections.

Thus the addition of discussion and communication possibilities that transcend location and time is a powerful way to extend the learning value of a conference to the tele-learner, and to allow the tele-learner to participate in many more conferences, in a targeted and non-costly way, than is possible with physical attendance.

■ 4.2.5 OTHER TRADITIONAL INFORMATION SERVICES

Already designed for on-line access, information services such as ERIC (the Educational Resources Information Service) are also providing powerful and popular services via the Internet for tele-learners. The ERIC site is located at

ERIC
http://ericir.sun-site.syr.edu

There are very interesting data about this ERIC site, relevant for professional tele-learning. First, the WWW-based component of the site provides more than 140,000 users a day with not only professional information about education, but also software and multi-media materials. In addition, the site provides integrated human-electronic assistance, via its AskERIC service with over 15,000 direct-access questions per week in 1994. In addition, the sale of CD-ROMs with complete data-bases of information is also increasing steadily.

To send an individual question to AskERIC, an e-mail message, in the inquirer's own natural language rather than as a combination of search terms or Boolean expressions, can be sent to:

AskERIC
```
askeric@ericir.syr.edu
```

A personal reply, sent by a trained staff member, is guaranteed by return e-mail within two business days.

I do not find this mutual increase of service provision to be forms in competition with each other, but forms in integration. Each form has its strengths, professional tele-learners are able to choose the media and information-provision service best suited for their questions. I discuss this new kind of integrated support environment as part of the tele-learning environment from the perspective of the educational technologist in Chapter 9.

■ 4.2.6 BLURRING THE BOUNDARIES BETWEEN TRADITIONAL AND NON-TRADITIONAL INFORMATION PROVIDERS

Thus professional information services are adapting to the needs of tele-learners via expansions of their traditional services, and in some cases, qualitatively new dimensions, particularly involving the incorporation of communication forms into information sources.

However, as we noted while discussing electronic journals, a new and parallel form of information provision is developing via networks that allows new suppliers of information to present themselves in the same way and environment as traditional suppliers. What are some examples of non-traditional information suppliers and are they competing or complementing traditional information suppliers for professional tele-learning?

■ 4.3 NEW SUPPLIERS OF PROFESSIONAL INFORMATION FOR TELE-LEARNING

It is in this category that the most vibrant growth in information provision for professional tele-learning is occurring. Universities, graduate students, professionals as individuals, and new forms of commercial services are now offering, via networks and particularly via the Internet, information sources of a similar form and nature to those supplied by traditional professional information providers. Because any one can publish on the Internet, a floodgate of creative potential has been unleashed; this is the good news. The problematical side of this good news is the predictable range in quality which must accompany the flood.

OUTSIDE OF THE TRADITIONAL GATEKEEPERS

Without the gate-keeper function of traditional information suppliers to validate information before it is made public, the information-overload phenomenon is especially strong for professional tele-learners who as a broad group have better and more flexible access to computers and networks than home learners or instructors and students taking courses in educational institutions and thus are in a more-conducive situation for disseminating their work on-line.

Leveling the playing field..

This phenomenon brings an opportunity for equitable dissemination of professional materials and ideas of both a scale and dimension that have never happened before. The home page of a novice and of a senior professor are equal in terms of being WWW entities, they can have an equal position in the search possibilities of the tele-learner, and in fact, those of the novices may often be more initially engaging. The senior professional may not have the inclination to disseminate his work and ideas via transmission channels such as WWW, while the comparative beginner in a field may be more likely to set up his WWW page and put up his undergraduate essays along with his homepage about his hobbies.

And drowning in the flood...

From the perspective of the professional tele-learner, the emergence of non-traditional information suppliers offering information resources parallel to those of traditional suppliers means vastly more choice, and less confidence about the adequacy of a choice. A search tool with some sort of "intelligence" is necessary to shift through the consequences of non-gatekeeper publication. Or, the professional must turn more and more to the filtering services of her professional society

■ 4.3 New suppliers of professional information for tele-learning

It is in this category that the most vibrant growth in information provision for professional tele-learning is occurring. Universities, graduate students, professionals as individuals, and new forms of commercial services are now offering, via networks and particularly via the Internet, information sources of a similar form and nature to those supplied by traditional professional information providers. Because any one can publish on the Internet, a floodgate of creative potential has been unleashed; this is the good news. The problematical side of this good news is the predictable range in quality which must accompany the flood.

Box 4.8

Sample of types of non-traditional information providers for professional tele-learning

Provider	URL
1. University department: a faculty of education uses a WWW site to provide information about on-going learning projects for k-12 and to facilitate participation in those projects	`http://ics.soe.umich.edu/`
a medical school maintains an multi-media site, with links "primarily for healthcare providers" and links "primarily for patients:	`http://indy.radiology.` `VirtualHospital.html`
2. Educational Technology support centres at universities: TECFA centre at the University of Geneva	`http://tecfa.unige.ch/` `info-edu-comp.html#www` `_intro`
3. Professionals as Individuals: An atlas of pathology images from the personal collection of a physician, indexed for learning purposes	`http://www.med.uiuc.edu/`
4. Project groups: The IBM Writing Project, for support of undergraduate writing	`http://www.ucet.ufl.edu:80/` `writing/`

5. Media Support Centres:
   A district office for community colleges offers materials for innovations in community-college teaching

   `http: //hakatai.mcli.dist.mariopa.edu`

6. Teachers:
   Schools sets up a site with links to other schools on the WWW, projects, and resources; useful for teachers in other schools

   `http://www.prs.k12.nj.us`

7. Other groups:
   NASA, making large amounts of multi-media information available relating to space travel

   `http://www.nasa.gov`

Such addresses will come and go; a source of vibrancy and frustration to the professional. However the use of a WWW search engine with search terms appropriate to one's field will bring a large sample to the professional tele-learner's screen.

MOTIVATIONS FOR NON-TRADITIONAL PROVIDERS

What motivates the creation of all these sites? Partly it is a genuine urge to share: to make available, to tell the world or at least anyone who might locate the page, resources that are judged to be important and interesting. Partly it is a genuine creative urge. Probably for many of these sites maintained by non-traditional service providers, the major audience for the sharing was intended to be persons in the host institution of the creator of the page, but making the site available via the Internet adds a new dimension to how the professional thinks about his or her resources.

And the motivation is not completely generous, of course. By 1995 it has become expected of higher educational institutions that they will offer a WWW site as an entry point to information and communications about their operations and intellectual activities. In February 1995 there were over 1,000 universities (half outside the US) with such sites. By September of 1995, this number had nearly doubled and 62 countries are represented (Mello, 1995).

WWW sites have become the commonplace "entry points" to academic entities, for public relations value as well as information and communication sources. What each site offers is distinct to the imagination and priorities of those who maintain it and increasingly are environments for a wide range of learning resources and activities as well as more-traditional information and communication services (see Chapter 9).

NETWORK SERVICES

To add to the complexity of non-traditional information providers now also providing information to professional tele-learners, school districts and ministries of education around the world (as well as other organizations, both educational and commercial) are supporting what might be generically called "educational network services" (see Chapter 9). Such services usually involve:

- Subsidized provision to schools and perhaps individuals of access to an electronic network, and increasingly of access to the Internet
- Technical support for the infrastructure and for access to the infrastructure
- An electronic entry point for access to the electronic network, which to the user appears as a user interface of a computer-software package through which interaction with the environment occurs
- Managed and moderated local resources relevant for education, available through the user interface as "one-stop shopping". The local resources are of both print and discussion-forum variety.
- Human contact and support for use of the network, including teacher training

Different inventories of these integrated network services are available; comprehensive examples are Schrum (1994), and Kurshan, Harrington, and Milbury (1994), both focusing on the US; and Veen, Collis, De Vries, and Vogelzang (1994), for examples from European countries.

It is complicated to categorize such services. Some are commercial, some are offered as part of a nationally-supported initiative, some are self-supporting, some operate out of the computer of one person in a resource centre or curriculum agency or many other varieties of physical locations, some are "bulletin boards" some of which have now matured in user interface and gateway possibilities far beyond others. In Chapters 7 and 9 we look more closely at network services relating to education from the perspectives of educational decision makers, who must decide to support them or at least support access to them, and of educational technologists who increasingly are the ones designing, maintaining, and supporting their use.

But there are network services for a wide variety of professions, not just those associated with education (Ellsworth, 1994). Services for lawyers, doctors, managers, artists, and many others are being called "the key to survival in a changing profession" ("Networking...", 1995, p. 29). Part of the reason for this sort of reaction is the fact that network services move beyond filtered information provision to include peer communication, and also the creation of new information from that communication. We call this professional information creation and discuss it next.

■ 4.4 PROFESSIONAL INFORMATION CREATION

Professional information creation allows the tele-learner to move beyond gate-keepers and the formalisms of documents and articles to the extraction of insights and information directly from communication among and/or with her colleagues. Thus another, vibrant, source of information for the tele-learning professional are the many discussion forums, listservs and newsgroups available via local networks and/or the Internet in which participants can enter their own information and talk to each other about such information. Some of these environments are closely moderated and access is restricted; these tend to have high-standard information. Others are open to the public and non-moderated; with more human bandwidth comes more diversity in quality of information. Ellsworth (1994) supplies listings to hundreds of such professional environments, particularly for professionals in computing science, business, library science, medical fields, journalism, and the arts. And, fortunately, newsgroup readers typically provide search tools for the user to locate seemingly-relevant groups. Experience or advice, however, is needed to determine if the discussion in the groups is professionally useful.

Various sites on the Internet provide listings of listserv resources pertinent to various subject areas. One such meta-list of lists is:

List of Lists
```
URL http//galaxy.einet.net/GJ/lists.html
```

Lists differ in general intent from newsgroups in that lists are more likely to be oriented toward information dissemination among peers, with occasional comments, while newsgroups are more likely to be oriented to discussions and comments with occasional more-systematic information dissemination.

COMMUNICATING FOR INFORMATION VS COMMUNICATING FOR PROFESSIONAL NETWORKING

We look more specifically at professional activities that are of the communication-dominant sort in Section 4.5. As we will see there, the intention of that type of interaction is more often not so much the communication itself but the creation and nurturing of community membership in which such communication takes place. With the sorts of information provision we have been considering in this chapter so far, the dominant motive is still information: access and dissemination.

We conclude Sections 4.2–4.4 on information provision for professional tele-learning with a summary of what we see as key points.

■ 4.4.1 POSITIVE ASPECTS OF NEW FORMS OF INFORMATION ACCESS FOR PROFESSIONAL TELE-LEARNING

- Enormous dynamism, up-to-date, opportunities for publication, not limited by traditional gatekeepers and their (perhaps conservative) orientations
- New ways to bring added value to print materials, such as traditional journals, particularly through links and communication possibilities
- Immediate opportunities to follow-up and contribute to information providers, if one wishes
- New environments and tools in which the professional can not only seek information but can ask for help, for additional information, for partners, for ideas; and can get immediate, human responses from peers, experts, and perhaps, critical, outsiders
- Distributed multi-media archives which can be searched like standard text material
- New ways to organize communication among peers so that flows of professionally relevant information result
- New opportunities to transcend the face-to-face conference experience

■ 4.4.2 NEGATIVE ASPECTS

- Overload of information, extreme variability in usefulness, too much time needed to search for what might be helpful to a particular professional need
- Even when found and judged to be useful, awareness that the reliability of the information may not have been validated
- Tools and procedures to help separate irrelevant material from relevant are still only emerging (see Chapter 3 and **Interface 2**)

Thus, reflecting on all the above, the major implications of new forms of information access for the (information-hungry) professional tele-learner appear to be those summarized in Box 4.9.

> **Box 4.9**
>
> **Key aspects, new forms of network-based information and professional tele-learning**
>
> Enormous increase in information available through one's personal computer, at a time and place convenient to the professional
>
> Enormous increase in ways of dealing with information, from following-up links to multi-media representation
>
> Addition of communication possibilities to stored information, for immediate clarification, follow-up, discussion and questioning
>
> Opportunity to find vast amounts of information through the contributions of non-traditional information providers
>
> Opportunity one's self to be a non-traditional information provider without negotiation of traditional review-board mechanisms
>
> Challenges to traditional gatekeepers of quality-controlled information
>
> Validation through personal assessment of the value of information rather than depending on professional filtering

Perhaps it is because I am a professional using these information-rich forms of tele-learning on an on-going basis that I know their vibrancy and their frustrations so well. It is my observation that it is the large and somewhat vaguely defined group of professional tele-learners which is providing a major stimulus for and source of the proliferation of resources on the Internet circa 1995.

So, when we are not busy looking for and collecting and asking each other about information, what else are we as professional tele-learners doing with our network access?

We are networking.

I will explain this apparent redundancy in Section 4.5.

■ 4.5 NEW FORMS OF PROFESSIONAL NETWORKING

Although in many cases interpersonal communication was occurring in the examples in Sections 4.2–4.4, the emphasis was on getting information. Interpersonal communication that occurs is more often in the framework of embellishing information, clarifying it, reacting to it, even contributing it. But in general the identities of the participants, as persons, were not of central importance, or even known.

But as we noted in Section 4.1, professional learning is not only about information, it is also about human networking, of being part of different human groups ranging from those specifically involved with one's learning task (Illich's "learning web", 1971) to those who share the awareness of one's professional situation and can be sources of inspiration, ideas and help in professionally-relating tasks. In this section, we will look at networking for professional tele-learning, where the emphasis is on these human-community aspects of networking.

First I anticipate some confusion about the use of the word "network" because it can be a noun or a verb, a technical system or a metaphor.

■ 4.5.1 WHAT IS NETWORKING?

The word network can be, and is used in a wide variety of ways in the tele-learning context. Variously, the word is used as a noun and a verb by different authors (and even the same author) in at least the ways summarized in Box 4.10.

Box 4.10

Uses of the word "networking" in the tele-learning context

- The technological infrastructure, the transmission channels themselves

- The technology that determines the way that signals are sent through the transmission channels (i.e., an ISDN network)

- The hardware and software involved with the use of the technological infrastructure

- A self-contained system, involving computers and wires or cables that connect them and software that allows them to share resources and pass data (i.e., the school network)

- A set of networks interconnected via gateways and sharing the same basic protocols (i.e., such as the Internet system)

- A non-specific term meant to indicate the applications and data available via any of the above kinds of networks (i.e., "network-based resources")

- A combination of technical infrastructure, some number of local-area networks, and a human organizational framework through which services and resources are maintained for its subscribers (i.e., a regional educational network service). These networks may be short-term and finite, based on a particular project initiative, or on-going, such as many of the state educational networks in the US (i.e., TENET)

- A human organizational framework through which services and resources are maintained for the subscribers but which is not responsible for the technical side of the access to the network (i.e., the European Schools Project, Sligte and Meijer, 1993). These organizational frameworks may be short-term, the length of a certain project initiative, or continuing

- A group of persons with which one feels a professional and personal contact, which may or may not involve the use of electronic networks or electronic network services and which may or may not be mediated by any external organization (i.e., persons with whom I network, my network of friends)

- A metaphor used quasi-romantically to describe the experiences of those who "live in the global community", joined in a "global matrix of minds", "sailing through cyberspace together" (chapter titles from Harasim, 1993)

- A verb, to network, to describe the act of personal interaction described above, and its associated action term, "networking" (i.e., to "reduce professional isolation by networking")

NOT JUST A MATTER OF WORDS...

This semantic problem is important to note, in that I have often observed that phrases such as "set up a network", "collaborate over the network", and "networking" are used in group settings where the participants seem to have different representatives of the interpretations in Box 4.10 in their use of the word "network". Usually, they do not realize the others in their group have such widely varying interpretations of the word, and so all go on, making plans about "setting up a network" which will inevitably bump into each other. Thus from the perspective of the professional tele-learner, a first concern is to "get on the network" in a technical sense but at the same time to connect to the network services that provide a (user) interface to the information and contacts he wants to access. (This whole business can be even more confusing if a "network service provider", typically someone selling Internet interconnectivity, must be involved in the step between one's computer and the connection to the network to which the subscriber wants to connect.) Once the tele-learner is connected to "the network" (and the desired network service) then at least three kinds of human networking can occur: Personal networking, Project- or structured networking, and open networking within an organized structure.

Confused? That is quite predictable.

The words network and networking are ambiguous and the assumption that others share your use of the word networking will probably lead to misunderstandings. The terms should always be defined when used in a tele-learning context, used carefully rather than metaphorically.

TYPES OF HUMAN NETWORKING

Given this warning, let us look at three forms of human networking, each of which has applications in professional tele-learning. We introduce them here as generic categories and discuss them in more detail in Sections 4.5.2–4.5.4.

Personal networking

Personal networking is contact among peers, usually without direct intervention or support of a mediating person. This can occur through a personally maintained distribution list on the professional's computer which is analogous to his or her paper-wallet address book. Through this the professional makes contact with some subset of his or her human-network colleagues, using an electronic network as transmission channel. Via this variety of networking, she asks her colleagues (her "network") for help or for resources, or sends a message relating to a mutual interest.

Project- or structured networking

Project- or structured networking occurs within the organizational framework of a project or with an on-going well-defined group. One's networking companions are other persons in the project or other members of the group. There is a moderator associated with the project or group management who provides the structure and support for the networking activities.

Open networking, within an organized structure

Open networking within an organized structure occurs when, through some sort of organized structure, one can look for human contacts and interact with them in various ways.

■ 4.5.2 PERSONAL NETWORKING

For many professional tele-learners, particularly those with more experience in using networked resources and tools, the major way in which networking occurs is through one's own initiative or within the framework of a task which a team of tele-learners are organizing themselves.

On my own computer, for example, I have many (20, at the moment) distribution lists set up of categories of persons whom I may wish to contact communally or individually for various reasons. I also have electronic address books organized around other categories of persons, so that I can choose my own target group for a particular learning-related need. At the same time I have a number of listserv lists and computer-conferences set up in relation to tasks or specific research or teaching activities in which I am involved.

These electronic lists and addresses are critical to my efficiency as well as my professional tele-learning. The management trick is to have all that you need on your system, but to keep cleaning them up. Otherwise finding the addresses you want and entering them on messages becomes too tedious. The annoying "Returned mail from Postmaster" messages that come back with failed email each time I use my distribution lists are a regular part of my day.

CHARACTERISTICS OF PERSONAL NETWORKING

While my comments about address books and returned messages may seem trivial, they relate to a very important way that I work and learn: my capacity to interact with targeted colleagues whose advice or help or input is valuable to me at a given moment. Personally, I never participate in newsgroups where I do not know the participants; I don't have time or patience for the sifting through the noise and validation problems. But the addresses in my personal lists are colleagues I do know, and value. Maintaining this network is at the heart of how I work and learn.

Speaking more generally, the main purposes of these networks is for work-related communication, about which either the individual maintaining the distribution lists makes the initiating decision (via sending a message to a distribution list) or anyone in the group can make an initiating decision (by sending a message to a listserv list or a conference). The participants know either other well, they do not use the communication channels for casual information exchange. They use there personal networks for professional work, as efficiently as possible. No one moderates this kind of tele-learnerning, it is a self-selective and self-regulated process.

Tools are critical for personal networking

While the approach to the maintenance and use of personal networks of colleagues may differ, one aspect of personal networking is always present: our electronic tools are critical and can help or interfere with communication. If I am using a mail-package environment, I must have convenient ways for file attachment and for sending and reading files with different formats and with graphics; otherwise I send an attachment and many of my respondents answer back that they can't read it. Time is wasted for me and them, sorting this out. Some functionality is necessary on one's desktop for archiving messages in various large-capacity directories, for sorting and retrieving particular messages efficiently, for editing directly on a message and forwarding it to others. I also must be able to cut-and-paste and easily move text and formatted material between personal files and the communication environment. I need split-screen capabilities, so that I can maintain one message for reference while I prepare a new message.

If I am using computer-conferencing software, I need all the functionalities mentioned above, but in addition I must have a way to personally mark particular messages for later reference, and to easily move between sending messages and replies to the conference and to individuals (in order to not flood a common conference environment with messages that are of practical value to only a subset of the conference subscribers).

Without these sorts of tools, I am less efficient, less effective in professional tele-learning. My current environment offers me some but not all of the tools I need, and I sometimes feel acutely how limitations in my tools affect my professional tele-learning management.

Human actions

And in addition to software tools, networking tele-learners working personally with each other need to decide among themselves as to the human-protocols they will use for their work. How often will they communicate? Who should take the lead in calling for decisions or setting timelines? Who sends what to whom? Who saves what? How are different versions of documents harmonized? How do we handle all of this in a professional but friendly way?

In all this, I need technical support; I do not want to be the one to maintain the server for the conferencing and mailing environment I use; I want someone to ask in my building when I have technical problems. But I do not want interference from a content- or procedural side, nor do I want the "outside world" to contribute to my personal-networking discussions. This is a difference in this sort of networking and the next two categories we will discuss.

WORK AND LEARNING INTERTWINED

For many professionals, much of our tele-learning is intertwined with experiences and activities in which we are working collaboratively with distributed colleagues, on the organization or execution or analysis or report-generation with respect to professional projects. The increasing value of such distributive collaboration is important in both our work and collective learning.

> ...Collaboration, greatly facilitated by advanced telecommunications networks, has become a dominant mode of conducting academic work...For at least ten years, co-authored articles have dominated journal table of contents, and a growing percentage of federal (US) research funding is awarded to consortia of investigators rather than to individuals...New ways of collaborative learning are central to today's academic vision. (Acker, p. 2)

And this emphasis on professional collaboration is especially strong in multi-culture countries such as Canada and Belgium and throughout the European Community; research projects of any substance in terms of funding require consortia of distributed partners, working collaboratively with each other. Increasingly, this collaboration is carried out via the Internet, interspersed with occasional face-to-face meetings. Parallel to these collaborative projects, a considerable amount of research is occurring around tools for facilitating distributed collaboration (see Chapter 8 and **Interface 8**). As one example, the VMDL Project ("Virtual Mobility and Distributed Laboratories", Lewis and Collis, 1995) involves researchers from the UK, The Netherlands, Norway, Switzerland, and France working apart–together on the investigating of tools and procedures for collaborative networking among professionals.

■ 4.5.3 PROJECT OR STRUCTURED NETWORKING

As extensive as personal networking is among professionals, there are many other situations where professional networking takes place under the framework of a more-structured project or task, typically with a moderator steering discussions and facilitating the development of professional contacts among the participants. It is typically hoped that the interaction among the participants will move to personal networking after the project period is over.

EXAMPLES FROM TEACHER NETWORKING

There are a number of examples of this kind of project-structured networking involving teachers. The LabNet Project involves a "community of over 1,000 US primary and secondary school science and math teachers...and has been carefully engineered to provide an accessible, fertile, and friendly environment for supporting conversations about teaching" (Spitzer and Wedding, 1995, pp. 247–248). The importance of the cadre of teacher moderators trained for working with the LabNet teachers as well as other carefully thought-through aspects of the project are its "ingredients for success".

In The Netherlands, a current project to stimulate groups of teachers to support and stimulate each other with respect to computer use in the classroom is making use of the strategy of project-structured networking among the teachers, closely steered and organized by curriculum-area specialists working with each networking-group. This initiative, called the PIT Project, has involved more than a thousand teachers in 1993–1995, and over 30 of these networks, and has proved to be very successful in stimulating teachers to not only exchange experiences with one another, but to translate this exchange into more use of computers in their classrooms (Collis and Moonen, 1995a, b).

CHARACTERISTICS OF THE STRUCTURED NETWORKING ENVIRONMENT

Many other examples can be cited of this type of structured, project-based networking. Most critical to the success of a structured networking experience as a learning experience among professionals are aspects such as the following:

- Planning a communication strategy and procedures
- Attention to the communication styles of others
- Effective leadership in fulfilling the moderator's role
- Easy-to-use software
- Face-to-face meetings in addition to the electronic networking (McCreary and Brochet, 1990)

Similarly, McCreary and Brochet note factors most likely to inhibit effective networking:

- Long start-up phase
- Poorly-defined costs
- Unreliable communication connections
- Lack of basic training for participants
- Support that is overwhelmingly technical
- Infrequent users and insufficient number in the on-line group
- Lack of commitment to share ideas
- Duplication of messages
- Large number of participants who have never met in person (p. 83)

IMPORTANCE OF MODERATOR AND SUPPORT

This list in its general aspects has been effectively paralleled many times (see for example, *How to Design a Successful Project*, Andres and Rogers, 1995), from those with experience in structured networking projects for professional tele-learning. When well handled (i.e., provision of the points on the first of McCreary and Brochet's lists and avoidance of those on the second list), then the sense of human contact that develops is described as "enormously rewarding" as well as being a profitable learning experience.

For teachers, overcoming the chronic problem of isolation from professional interaction is a particularly important result of structured networking for professional tele-learning (McMillan, 1993; Parker, 1994). Similar benefits are also reported for other professional groups in many different situations; for example, for medical doctors for whom structured-project support was used for organizing and archiving information contributed by the professionals during their electronic conversations (Gardiol, Boder and Peraya, 1993).

As another observation, Kurshan, Harrington, and Milbury (1994) underscore the importance of a variety of different roles in the maintenance of structured forms of networking:

- A facilitator, to initiate, promote and channel discussion, and provide help
- An integrator, to help participants integrate network activities into their working situations, both technical and contentwise
- A librarian, to maintain and communicate an overview of what resources are available to support communication, and how to access those resources
- A project or community coordinator, to manage the overall flow of obligations within the network, and relate network activity to both obligations and goals
- A system operator, for technical assistance to participants
- A trainer, to help participants use the environment, both technically and contentwise (p. 22)

For financial reasons, such requirements will often have to be met by the same one or two persons in structured networking situations, but to a probable decrement in support.

■ 4.5.4 OPEN NETWORKING, WITHIN AN ORGANIZED STRUCTURE

Another variation of professional tele-learning involving networking occurs when a large-scale conferencing environment is made available to a group of professionals, perhaps in a multi-site corporation or more loosely-defined project, and a general structure is provided for use of the environment. As an illustration, the discussion conferences available to all the teachers in a state-wide or national educational network service could be seen as this sort of networking.

CHARACTERISTICS

Such environments have as a characteristic that they are relatively stable, so users can develop the habit to come to them for discipline-specific communication. One such example is SCIENCEnet, which provides network support for research oceanographers using the Internet as transmission channel. SCIENCEnet had 4,000 subscribers in 1993 and "provides value-added services for access to scientific resources" (Hesse, Sproull, Kiesler and Walsh, 1993). The added-value services include not only access to appropriate data bases but also maintenance of various special-purpose bulletin boards and project-specific distribution lists. The service also supports access to mailboxes via satellite for oceanographers out at sea. In an interesting and careful study of the relationship between research usage of this network organization and scientific outcomes, Hesse and his colleagues found network usage to be positively associated with number of articles published, professional recognition, and extent of social integration into the professional community of international oceanographers. While correlation cannot be taken as causation (the oceanographers making extensive use of the network organization may have other qualities likely to be associated with professional development), at least the active use of the network was clearly associated with professional productivity and learning.

There are many examples of such network organizations. Box 4.11 shows three example, for teachers.

Box 4.11

Examples of network organizations, in support of teacher networking

The GENII Project
Contact: `kwallet@vdoe386.vak12ed.edu`
...For teachers in Australia, to support their use of the Internet

PreSTO listserv,
Contact: `listproc@ra.msstate.edu`
Message in body: subscribe presto Yourfirstname Your last name
...Organized to support discussion and communication among beginning teachers around the world

Global SchoolNet
Contact: `arogers@bonita.cerf.fred.org`
...An organization that connects educational professionals to more than 150 local BBSs for teachers, for exchange of ideas and experiences

---

An organization with a very different target group is the Ki Net in Scotland (Wolff, 1995b). The organization focuses on offering support to small-to-medium sized businesses involved in engineering and architectural design through various distinct services:

- A database of actual or potential partners

- A global list of contracts and projects suitable for teams formed from among the participants
- General technical support to the distributed teams including provision of computer-conferencing software and groupware tools
- Internet connectivity support
- Brokerage and managerial support for the creation of "virtual teams" to work collaboratively on contracts and projects

This sort of organizational-network support is especially important for professionals working in small companies with limited access to networks and limited in-house support for making connections to a network. Teachers working in professional isolation are also good candidates.

■ 4.5.5 OTHER FACTORS THAT INFLUENCE NETWORKING SUCCESS

While networking interactions such as described in all three of the categories personal networking, structured networking, and organized networks may not lead into personally satisfying professional tele-learning for the individual, they may and frequently do. In a survey of approximately 500 US teachers responding to a questionnaire made available through various lists and sites on the Internet, Honey and Henríquez (1993a, b) noted that teachers valued very much the networking that they were able to obtain through organized network environments, with the most valuable aspects being:

- Opportunities to communicate with other professionals and share ideas
- Access to information that would be otherwise diffiicult to obtain
- Help in combating the professional isolation often felt in the workplace

MORE NEEDS TO BE KNOWN...

Electronic support of human networking among professionals is a new area, of both practice and research. Many different aspects of how better to support networking among professionals are being investigated (such as the VMDL Project, mentioned earlier). Most of these studies are at the descriptive and interpretive level. Rueda (1990), for example studied what use the employees of a large multi-national company made of network conferencing made available to them at their desktop computers. He made observations such as the following:

- In 62% percent of the dialogues, communications began with questions relating to real and specific problems.

- Typically there was a fast response to an individual's question, with most responses coming within the first day of posting the question
- Sometimes a debate followed a question for a few days, but usually only among a few persons, the one who proposed a solution and a few others who subsequently commented on the proposed solution. Those persons who do get involved in a network discussion often made serious and extensive comments.
- Participants made a conscientious effort to maintain the efficiency of the conference, referring back in detail to previous points. However, software tools for fast indexing are required

As another example of descriptive insight, Kiesler (1990) also analysed networking practices among professional employees in another multi-site organization. She noted a predominance of "Does anybody know...?" questions. She also noted that the large majority of the persons who responded via the network to such questions were not personally acquainted with the question asker.

BUT THE NEXT STEP?

So participation in various forms of networking can be a powerful source of organization strengthening, as well as personal learning. But moving from "Does anybody know...?" questions to questions requiring more reflection is not such an easy step. Kraut, Edigo, and Galegher (1990) note that extended contact is necessary before more abstract issues and personal views are shared within human networks. They also remark that "real intellectual teamwork" over a network is a process that requires partner selections "in many ways analogous to the process of choosing a mate" (p. 155), combined with regular, intense interaction. They urge something like "electronic hallways" to encourage informal incidental contact among potential collaborators who do not work in physical proximity with each other to compensate for the lack of physical cues in text-based networking environments.

▨ 4.6 CONCLUSIONS: TELE-LEARNING AND THE PROFESSIONAL

All of these examples and experiences with networking and with new forms of information engagement raise many questions for professional tele-learning but also professional work as well. I conclude this chapter with just a few of these. I have no definite answers, but in Chapter 10 I make some predictions.

Tools...

What sort of network tools and organization would best help me in my needs for knowledge access, collaboration support with distributed colleagues, and targeted contacts with new colleagues? Are there generic tools that every professional will have in the Year 2005, similar to the fact that most professionals in 1995 have a computer with word processing software, a fax in their workplace, and increasingly an Internet address? Will these tools let me switch back and forth among information access, document-sharing with remote colleagues, and video- and audio discussions with colleagues at multiple sites?

Information sources...

This one is easier, as I imagine we will continually find ways to make it easier to digitize information and compress it if necessary, to access and contribute video as well as text, voice as well as typing....But how will this information be best organized for professional tele-learning? I imagine in a hyperlinked system, the evolving generations of the WWW, but who will dominate the organization of the information and linkage of these systems for my profession? No one, or one party?...

Value

As a professional I gradually build up skill in quick selectivity, in filtering information sources, and yes, even people, via minute cues as to their contribution to my own learning needs. Certainly, my scan system is not perfect, but it does suit me. Is there any way technology can adapt itself to my skills and needs with regard to helping me find what is "out there" in terms of valuable information of which I am not aware? Of wonderful colleagues I am never meeting? Will any "agent" really help me, or only provide a baseline filter?

Meaningfulness

To what extent will my distributed network of colleagues replace my colleagues in my corridor in terms of their meaningfulness to me in my professional life and my tele-learning? And what is the relationship between the ability to connect with increasing amounts of information and people, and wisdom?

Necessity

Could I continue my work as a professional without the sorts of tele-learning indicated in this chapter? Well, yes, in the same way I would have to adjust if I were suddenly blind...or otherwise cut off from some on-going source of sensory (read: cognitive) input.

Validation

Does the world call what I am doing, at my computer each day—searching and reading, and communicating—learning? Do my colleagues? Do I get recognition for it, in terms of salary increase or promotion?

The answer to this last set of questions will vary for every professional.

But will I go on doing it?

Yes.

Because learning and making connections to ideas, to people, to the excitement of experience in my field, is just part of who I am. Fortunately for me, tele-learning technologies make it possible through my fingers...

NEW ROLES FOR THE PUBLISHER AND CLIENT

Almost a decade ago, Nicholas Negroponte at the Media Lab at MIT spoke of a future convergence of the realms of publishing, electronic media and computing[1]. He predicted not only a technological convergence but a fundamental shift in roles. The traditional receiver of broadcast information and print newspapers and magazines can gradually become the "broadcatcher", taking over some of the roles of the programmers, editors and even producers.

This shift does seem to be emerging, although co-existence might be a more accurate term. Broadcasters and editors still abound, but are increasingly aware of the need to offer a range of choices and services beyond their traditional procedures and media. New forms of publication, predominately making use of the WWW environment, are growing in presence. The major question is: Will they be seen as bringing added value to existing channels and media, or will they come to phase "the old ways" out?

ADDED VALUE OR ALTERNATIVES?

There are a range of new forms of publication emerging, that form a kind of continuum in terms of the likelihood that they would come to replace existing forms of publications over time.

Simplest conceptually is to use the WWW for, in effect, advertising of print media. This can be done through sites being maintained by publishers that show table of contents and perhaps abstracts of existing print items. There are also sites with rather extensive lists of tables of contents and brief summaries of articles. This runs parallel to an old idea (relatively) of providing on-line access to title and abstracts of articles and documents along with an ordering mechanism, so that a click of the keyboard (plus your credit card number already verified) is all that is needed to send a copy of the chosen article to you. This is a fee-per-unit approach and of no conceptual novelty; it does not appear to have become a threat to library subscriptions or book purchases.

A step further are WWW sites maintained by book publishers who may offer sample chapters of new books via WWW pages as well as titles and abstracts. And even further is the idea of allowing purchasers to select a portion of a book from an on-line overview and order only that portion. This puts new strains on the author, who may not have thought of his book as being modular but instead incremental. However, it does give the purchaser more flexibility, and the opportunity to pay for what she wishes rather than material she may not wish.

---

[1] Brand, S. (1987). *The Media Lab: Inventing the Future at MIT*. New York: Penguin Books.

Moving up in terms of variety, if not conceptually in any competition with its core broadcasting product, some news broadcasters such as CNN are offering WWW pages of updated news in a multi-media format—text, photos, sound, and even video clips.

Moving up in terms of added value are the parallel on-line forms of many commercial magazines, particularly computer magazines, that are now appearing. Often these on-line forms are available both on the WWW and, in another version, on a entry-controlled commercial on-line service. The added value of these on-line extensions of the print magazines are:

- Well organised retrieval of comparative data such as benchmark tests and test results of computer products from previous issues
- Opportunities to scan the schedule of upcoming product testing and on occasion get information about the testing process as it occurs
- Opportunities to download demo versions of software products reviewed in the print magazines. Also opportunities to immediately access WWW page URLs appearing in the journal via the WWW-based extension of the journal
- Opportunities to conveniently ask questions and get time-sensitive updates ("new bugs", etc.), faster than could occur via the printed magazine.
- Opportunities to hear and see clips of multi-media packages; an added value not possible in the print form of the journal.

Also moving toward the "broadcatcher"

position, a number of newspapers are now developing various forms of WWW-based versions, some of which allow the consumer to tailor in different ways the news he receives, both in terms of topic and depth of information.

For example, a multi-media version of the cross-European weekly newspaper, *The European,* is to begin to offer its interactive version via modem and telephone line. The downloading is supposed to take no more than ten minutes. Clicking on icons can call up extra information, in text or audio form. Even advertisements will be interactive, and include options to find out names of local dealers of products. Interactive chess and bridge games will be available. While not directly tailored to the wishes of the consumer, the consumer can indeed broaden her involvement with items of her choice.

NEW APPROACHES TO SCIENTIFIC PUBLISHING

Publishers of academic journals are particularly challenged by electronic publishing and Internet distribution possibilities. Typically there are transitional patterns, such as on-line scanning of abstracts. A variant of this is for the journal to sell an electronic subscription as well as or instead of a traditional print subscription to a academic library (the major subscribers to scientific journals). The electronic subscription allows persons authorised by the library to obtain a password and not only read an interactive abstract but to download whole copies of articles of interest directly to the desktop of the authorised person.

Electronic versions will also obtain added-value features not available in print form, such as hypertext links between related articles, and access to information not in the print form, such as additional reports or citation literature. In addition, on-line forms will offer speedier publication and better index and search tools.

Home pages will allow authors to post information about new work, as well as typical overviews of information from the publisher itself. E-mail lists are being maintained to periodically send contents lists of new journals to all individuals whose institutions have paid the electronic subscription fee.

The roles of editors and editorial boards are not changing, nor is the review process. From the publishers' perspective, two major issues—how to manage revenue generation and how to thwart copyright infringement—are coming better under control due to network security developments on the Internet.

AN ELECTRONIC PUBLISHING PLAN

The *Association for Computing Machinery* (ACM) has perhaps one of the most extensive plans for electronic publication. ACM publishes 17 periodicals, and its 79,000 members hold 55,000 subscriptions to these magazines. Special Interest Groups publish their own newsletters and conference proceedings (17,000 pages a year).

ACM sees many breakdowns and frustrations in the traditional publishing pattern and has set a publication policy with features such as the following:

- Journals will become streams into a database and retain their identities as database categories; articles will be entries into the database. Separate issues of journals will disappear.
- Individuals will cease to purchase journal subscriptions but instead will purchase right of access to a database. They will post interest profiles and be automatically notified via e-mail when an article matching their interest profile appears in the database.
- Copyright fees will be nominal and collected by automatic meters when copies of documents are extracted from a database.
- Multi-media effects will enhance print materials in the database.
- New kinds of services such as search, extract, print on demand, and repackaging will become available. Publishers will distribute notices of availability and consumers will decide what they want.
- "Move aggressively toward the entire ACM literature in an on-line digital library...Phase out print versions and phase in electronic distributions... Access from home, work or school desktops from the around the world will become a primary mode of acquiring knowledge."[2]

[2] Denning, P. J., & Rous, B. (1995). The ACM Electronic Publishing Plan. *Communications of the ACM*, 38(4), 97–103.

5 Tele-learning in the K-12 classroom: The teacher's view

In this chapter we move into a more well-defined domain than was the case with our two categories relating to individual learning. This domain is the classroom in the K-12 school. Within this setting, we look through the eyes of the classroom teacher: How do classroom teachers encounter tele-learning?

We consider four categories: (1) as a way for teachers to get new lesson ideas and resources, (2) as a way to enrich their on-going classroom teaching through tele-learning activities, (3) through opportunities to participate in special collaborative tele-learning projects, and (4) by teaching students who are in another physical location via video technologies.

The chapter is filled with examples, many to do with television and other video technologies, but most of them relating to new possibilities in networking and in particular with the World Wide Web. And, to tell the end of the story first, what will be the conclusions of this chapter, after we discuss all these possibilities? The conclusions are: There are many exciting and feasible tele-learning activities that can be done in the ordinary school and classroom, the teacher is the key factor in what happens with tele-learning in the classroom, and the teacher is faced with many challenges to exploit the potential of tele-learning in the current school setting.

Objectives

After this chapter you should be able to:

- Identify major ways in which the classroom teacher can have access to new lesson ideas and resources through tele-learning sources

- Compare and contrast the services offered by different types of lesson-idea providers, particularly via the WWW: traditional information providers such as national curriculum agencies; institutional providers such as faculties of education; and non-traditional providers such as computer magazines, all of whom are offering teachers lesson resources via the WWW

- Contrast North America and Europe in terms of approaches to the provision of network services to teachers

- Be aware of the pervasive use of classroom television as a form of tele-learning, and see how network services are now being integrated with television programming for multi-faceted tele-learning

- Cite examples of a variety of ways that the classroom teacher can augment on-going classroom instruction with tele-learning, including:
  Opportunities for motivating students and for up-to-date infusions of new ideas, in a variety of representational forms
  New forms of peer interaction both in and outside the classroom, particularly with a focus on cross-cultural- and communication skills
  Opportunities to bring students into contact with outside experts
  New ways to work with science data and investigation
  New forms of field trips and excursions, and
  New opportunities for creative expression

- Indicate major ("first-level" and "second-level") problems and concerns confronting the classroom teacher with respect to tele-learning

- Be aware of new forms of collaboration for the classroom teacher, as a member of a tele-learning project team

- Identify guidelines for the teacher involved with teaching students not in the same face-to-face location, using tele-learning technologies. Note in particular the challenges involved in teaching distant students via audio-graphics and via two-way interactive video.

■ 5.1 SETTING THE SCENE FOR TELE-LEARNING: THE K-12 CLASSROOM AND TEACHER

In this chapter we move to a familiar educational setting—the classroom in the traditional school—and from within this classroom look at tele-learning through the eyes of the classroom teacher. And because the teacher is busy and is so much constrained by the realities of the school and classroom and task, this chapter will be as realistic as possible: exciting ideas, yes, but also feasible. It can be difficult to integrate technology into a lesson; this integration generally brings demands on the teacher's time and energy, no matter how much s/he wants to innovate and enrich. In particular, there are many difficulties and challenges teachers face with computer-network tele-learning in school settings (For example, I myself have studied these implementation problems for the secondary-school teacher in many countries and settings; Collis, 1992a,b; Collis, 1993b; Collis and De Vries, 1991; Collis, Veen and De Vries, 1994).

Thus ideas for tele-learning in the school setting must be practical as well as motivating, and should begin where the teacher is at in terms of experience, interest, teaching style and time. That is why we begin the examples in this chapter with a set relating directly to helping the teacher obtain new resources before we move into examples of new types of lesson activities that are emerging with tele-learning. Obtaining lesson materials from distributed collections of resources can save the teacher time and energy and is a good way for the teacher to become familiar with the use of tele-learning technologies, particularly the World Wide Web, before trying to manage the use of those technologies in the instructional setting.

But before we begin the examples, it is good to clarify the context. This section sets the scene by giving a brief sketch of the typical situation that we envisage as the background for this chapter. What is the reality frame of the classroom teacher? How will this affect tele-learning possibilities?

■ 5.1.1 THE TEACHER'S SITUATION

In this chapter, we are picturing the teacher in a classroom in a traditional school. By a traditional school, we mean either an elementary or secondary school with its usual rooms and schedules and equipment and budgetary constraints. The teacher works with a class full of students, which makes the management of individualized activities at computers difficult. If it is elementary school, it is probably a class that the teacher is with for some or all of the day, a class he or she teaches for a number of different curriculum areas. If it is a secondary school, the teacher is with a series of different groups of students, together as an entity for a relatively short time each day when the particular class meets. These time constraints frustrate innovation of any sort, not only tele-learning. In both the elementary and secondary school situations, the teacher is responsible for covering a certain amount of content, using some standard textbooks, and expected to bring the students to displayable levels of competency by pre-set dates. This display of competency is highly related to student performance on tests, the more so as the age of the student increases. Again, these conditions are constraints on innovation and exploration in the classroom.

TEACHERS AS INDIVIDUALS

This, then, is a typical setting. What about the teachers themselves? Some may be male, some female; (gender doesn't matter for tele-learning; to reflect this I will sometimes call the teacher "he", other times "she"). Although some of the teachers may be young and new, and thus the products of fresh training experiences, many of the teachers cannot be described this way.

Established patterns, limited exposure to new models

The longer they teach, the more likely that they have developed patterns and styles of teaching and student interaction that fit their own circumstances and the more they will need convincing that they should change what they see as appropriate pedagogy for themselves and their subject area (Veen, 1993). And the longer they have been teaching, the less likely that they have encountered tele-learning as part of their own formal preparation, although, as members of families they may be getting involved with tele-learning on an individual basis in their homes (see Chapter 3). Because they are often relatively isolated, having contact mainly with a handful of teachers in their own department or corridor, teachers are not likely to be exposed to examples and models of tele-learning in the classroom. And above all of this, teachers are as different as their personalities.

TEACHERS AND THEIR ACCESS TO TECHNOLOGY

Most teachers teach in a classroom with no computer technologies available on an on-going basis. However, many of them will have an overhead projector in their classrooms. Typically, there are computers available in the school, but usually clustered in a computer room and probably not yet attached to a network that goes outside the school. In contrast, many schools and classrooms are wired or cabled and equipped for receiving broadcast and/or digitized video programming (see Chapter 7 for a focus on decision making concerning the school's technology infrastructure). The innovations in tele-learning technology we discussed in Chapter 2 in terms of high-speed networks and desktop multi-media computers are a long way from the reality frame of the classroom. In this chapter we reflect what is most likely to be available to the teacher: a classroom television and occasional access to computers connected to a network outside the school. In some cases, broadcast or cable television reception is supplemented or replaced by some form of two-way video; in some cases, the network access is to the Internet.

Access to technology for lesson preparation?

It is not only the technologies from which the teacher can choose for instructional purposes that are important for tele-learning; the access the teacher himself has for exploration and preparation is also critical. And this access is very poor for the majority of teachers. When the teacher wants to prepare, or to learn something new, he probably either has to do it at home, on his own time and phone bill, or he will have to go to the teacher's staff room, a not-very conducive area for reflection as it typically also serves as a communal area for lunch and relaxing. The teacher doesn't have the luxury of his own desk with its own computer where he can work without interruption. Wherever it is in the school that he prepares for his lessons, he will probably not have access to a computer for extended periods of time for his own use. Also, he probably will not have convenient access to a computer networked to a server outside the school, although such a computer may be available in the school library or in the central administration or in the workplace of the computer specialist (in the secondary school). Unlike the professional in Chapter 4, sitting at her desk doing all sorts of innovative information creation and networking activities for professional tele-learning, the teacher does not have privacy or time during the school day for personal (tele-)learning.

THE TEACHER'S LOAD

Too much to do: the teacher is always very busy. There is little time during the day that is not scheduled in direct contact with students. There is much time that must be spent in evenings preparing for the next day of work. There are meetings, and considerable time and attention must be given to student evaluation and reporting of evaluation. When does the teacher find time to browse the WWW or have newsgroup discussions with distributed peers? And it is not only lack of personal time that is a problem: there is also a lack of flexibility with respect to time.

Limited flexibility in time

The teacher not only has little time in general to be innovative, but is further constrained by having virtually no flexibility in instructional timing: decisions are made and announced centrally as to when major school events, such as reports and examinations, will occur as well as the daily timing of classes and activities. Classes change at preset times throughout the school and throughout the day, lunch happens at precisely a certain time, the school day ends (and school buses depart) at precisely a certain time.

Limited flexibility in the curriculum

And just as there is little flexibility in time, there is often little flexibility available to the teacher with respect to what is taught: in many countries the curriculum is centrally set at least in terms of topics and general expectations for attainment. It is not the teacher who makes the majority of decisions about content or pace of moving through the curriculum. Frequently the teacher has very little choice over the textbooks that are used and little variety in educational media may be conveniently available. Finally, the teacher cannot very often make an independent decision about anything that has financial implications. If the teacher wants to have her students use the Internet, for example, much decision making at the school or even regional level must have first occurred to put the infrastructure or budget into place to make this possible (see Chapter 7).

■ 5.1.2 REALITY FRAME FOR CLASSROOM TELE-LEARNING

This, then, is the reality frame for tele-learning in the K-12 classroom. The main aspects relative to tele-learning are: the teacher has limited flexibility, limited contact with other teachers outside of her school or even her smaller group, little time for exploration, and limited personal access to a networked computer, particularly one connected to the Internet. In the home, it is largely the family's financial position which will set a reality frame around tele-learning opportunities (see Chapter 3); in the school it is a larger combination of factors that have this influence, many of which the teacher can do little to change, unless the teacher moves into a position of decision-making influence in the school.

OPPORTUNITIES NONETHELESS...

But despite the constraints, there any many exciting possibilities for the classroom teacher and tele-learning. We are optimistic! Teachers around the world are increasing their awareness of different forms of tele-learning, and their experience with these forms. That is the good news of this chapter. There are good opportunities, even in mid-1990s conditions, for some of the potential of tele-learning to be realized in traditional K-12 classrooms. This chapter gives but a taste.

Fortunately, the teacher does not stand alone in his or her desire to make use of tele-learning; with the informed support of decision makers and the support and contribution of specialists such as district educational technologists and media professionals, much can be done. This is also part of the story of Chapters 7 and 9.

A side note: keeping an international perspective

In this chapter, as throughout the book, we try to keep an international perspective. Thus when we generalize in this chapter about classrooms and circumstances we realize that in a particular country or region there maybe a very different technical infrastructure and approach for tele-learning. Some teachers think of tele-learning as classroom television, others as classroom access to the Internet and particular the WWW, others as access to e-mail. In a recent study, my colleagues and I examined the overall strategies for support of tele-learning in secondary schools in 17 European countries, and certainly found this diversity (Veen, Collis, De Vries and Vogelzang, 1994).

Also, for purposes of space, this chapter is restricted to schools where the circumstances are good enough so that it is feasible to think in terms of television or networking in the school, and now and then in the classroom itself. In Interface 7 we look briefly at the application of tele-learning in schools in less-developed countries and countries in unstable circumstances or in rapid transition. Looking at tele-learning from the perspective of teachers in these sorts of countries could easily be the subject of another book. (In fact, it already is; see Collis, Nikolova and Martcheva, 1995.)

WELCOME TO THE TELE-LEARNING CLASSROOM...!

Now that the context for the classroom teacher has been sketched, let's begin. The chapter is structured around four categories through which the classroom teacher can encounter tele-learning. The first is as a source of lesson ideas and resources (Section 5.2), the second is through the possibility of many new sorts of projects and activities for students (Section 5.3). The third relates to new opportunities for collaborative projects for the teacher herself (Section 5.5), and the fourth to new skills that the teacher may have to learn in terms of teaching students who are at a distance (Section 5.6). Between the second and third categories we consolidate some of the major problems and issues facing the teacher working with tele-learning in the traditional classroom (Section 5.4).

■ 5.2 ACCESS TO NEW LESSON IDEAS AND RESOURCES

The first of our categories of ways that teachers can encounter tele-learning is one that might be metaphorically called a Pandora's box—tele-learning environments used to bring new and different resources to the teacher without her having to leave the school.

Teachers are usually on the alert for new lesson ideas and resources. Where do they usually look? This question is a good start for thinking about tele-learning through the eyes of the classroom teacher, because a prime application of tele-learning for the teacher relates to the Pandora's box idea. Perhaps we should use a more-modern metaphor: particularly through computer networks, we can think of tele-learning environments as shopping malls for teachers. And what is in the metaphorical shops? Lesson resources and lesson ideas...

In this section we begin by noting the traditional ways in which teachers "shop" for ideas and resources, and some of the limitations of those approaches. Then we canvass a variety of ways that computer networks can be used to overcome some of those limitations and bring the teacher into a very large shopping mall indeed. As one particular example, we look at using networks to get lesson ideas about television in the classroom. We also give a birds' eye view of other application areas besides classroom television for which teachers can find large amounts of lesson ideas and resources via network services or the Internet itself.

Some "ifs"...

If teachers have access to a network service or the Internet, then the good news is that most of these "lesson-idea shops" have no extra cost for what the teacher wants to sample and take away—beyond the general cost of being connected. The ifs that condition this good news relate to having access and the affordability of the general cost of this access.

And there is a second "if" that is also important to note: the "network shopping mall" is a wonderful metaphor, but it also carries with it a cultural bias. The portability of lesson ideas and resources from one country and culture to another is a complex business. Because teachers suddenly have access to lesson ideas from teachers in other countries and cultures does not mean that those ideas will transfer well to new settings. The question of the portability of educational resources has been long studied, particularly with respect to educational software (see Collis, 1996, for a summary) and is encountering a new iteration with respect to tele-learning resources available through the Internet.

The teacher from two perspectives: looking at herself as a professional, looking at her class in terms of lesson preparation

We can also distinguish the teacher activities in this section from the teacher-networking examples that we discussed in Chapter 4. The emphasis in the examples in Chapter 4 was teachers communicating with each other as professional colleagues, where a wide range of topics and focuses may be under consideration. In this chapter, the teacher is thinking directly of her students and her up-coming lessons. She is asking herself questions such as: Can I use this idea in my next lesson? Is it feasible in my circumstances? Does it relate to the learning priorities I and others have for my students? Will the students like it? Can I manage it?

Of course these two perspectives may overlap, and both perspectives fuel each other.

Thus, as we go shopping in our hypothetical lesson-resource mall, let's begin, as we stroll in, with a few general thoughts on teachers and lesson ideas.

■ 5.2.1 EXPANDING THE TEACHER'S RANGE OF IDEAS AND RESOURCES

Getting new and relevant lesson ideas and resources is an on-going task of core importance to the classroom teacher. What do teachers look for in these resources? What chain of events may occur before the teacher gets access to resources for evaluation or use?

TEACHERS APPRECIATE RELEVANT RESOURCES

How do teachers usually get lesson ideas? There are many ways.

Teachers traditionally get ideas for their lessons from talking to their colleagues, from reading suggestions in curriculum materials or professional magazines, from occasional teacher inservice sessions or conferences, from their own children, from the mass media, and from each other. Although a major filter between exposure to an idea and translation of it into classroom practice is the teacher's own imagination, teachers nonetheless appreciate very much hearing about and getting new lesson ideas, especially those that other teachers have found useful. And what makes a lesson resource seem relevant? Lesson ideas seem most contagious if:

- They have been tried out, successfully, in practice by other teachers
- The teacher can see the fit of the ideas to his own curriculum and teaching style
- The teacher feels that she can make use of the resources in a relatively direct manner, without too much time and effort for preparation and set up
- The teacher feels that his students can carry out work with the lesson materials, and
- The resources are not costly, in financial terms or in the time and energy needed for use. (Collis & Moonen, 1995a; Veen, 1993)

So, these are the relevance criteria we will keep in mind in our tele-learning shopping-mall metaphor.

GETTING RESOURCES TO TEACHERS FOR A DECISION

Teachers can't shop unless they can get to a store, or unless the store is brought to them. Many professionals are in the business of developing lesson ideas and materials for teachers in the hope that teachers will find them attractive and useful enough to put to use. But there is a major problem: How do teachers find out about these resources, how do teachers get in contact with them to look them over? Where is such a lesson-idea shopping mall?

Time and access problems

Teachers often do not have the time or opportunity to travel to resource centres and examine a wide range of materials themselves. And even harder: what can the teacher do about ideas and resources he reads about in a magazine or hears about from other teachers? For example, how can the teacher try out a CD-ROM about which he has just read? What are the steps needed to get an example copy into his computer at his school so he can preview it? How much time will this all take? Where can he get the reactions of other teachers to the resource? And, how does the teacher find the time himself for all the steps needed for efficient resource selection?

Durham, a resource specialist working at one of the teachers' centers operated by NASA (a national agency in the US for aerospace research and development) noted that teachers, even when they could get time from work to travel to a NASA resource center, were overwhelmed by the resource possibilities to choose from once they got there (Durham, 1995). There are thousands of videotapes, thousands of printed collections of lesson materials, thousands of photographs of space—all in theory available for the teacher, but in fact drowning the teacher in their volume. (Durham's response to this problem has been to create an electronic "performance support" resource for teachers, whereby they can use a computer to search for locally stored NASA lesson materials and also through the same interface can go onto the Internet to access NASA materials elsewhere. We discuss this sort of integrated support environment again in this section, and also in Chapters 8 and 9).

Through a chain of specialists

In general, lesson-idea browsing for the teacher is the last link in a chain of specialist filters. For many teachers this browsing process takes place via a district resource centre or the facilities of some other central support body whose task it is to bring learning resources to teachers' attention in a variety of ways (we look at this from the other side of the counter in Chapter 9, from the perspective of the educational technologist who works in such a resource centre). Sometimes lesson materials are evaluated by a specialist in the resource centre and then a sample of them is selected and sent on to the schools. Within the school, ideas get further filtered as they are passed on to a particular teacher (a media specialist or a content-area specialist) who makes a further decision about relevance before disseminating the remaining resource information to her colleagues, the other teachers in the school.

Weak links in the chain

But there are problems with this typical chain, with all its links. The ordinary teacher is many steps away from the original, large pool of potential lesson ideas. Each step acts as a filter, which may select out some materials that in fact a particular teacher would have appreciated if she had had the chance to see them herself. But of course, the chain also is in operation for the teacher's help: because of time and access problems, the teacher can't often can't do this previewing and selecting herself. Looking for something in large shopping malls can be exhausting.

Most-common strategy: disseminate ideas by print

Because of the time and access problems in bringing the teacher to the point of hands-on contact with potential lesson ideas and resources, print information about the availability of lesson resources is widely disseminated. The most typical information-dissemination method is some combination of direct mailing to schools and other kinds of distribution of print materials announcing available and future materials. These print materials range from flyers distributed by the thousands as inserts in trade magazines, as direct mailings to schools, as piles of give-aways at teachers' meetings and conferences, to notices in teachers' magazines. When an agency is involved, the print materials often include an overall reference booklet with previews, overviews, and lists of still-available older materials, sent in mass to schools before the start of the school year.

Strengths and weaknesses of print dissemination

Disseminating information to the teacher via print has a mixed-level of effectiveness. The hit-rate of an idea reaching a teacher who would find it useful is frequently low. Print materials sent to schools often do not trickle down into the hands of the individual teacher in an efficient or time-sensitive manner. Materials piled on the staffroom table or pinned to the staffroom bulletin board may get attention from some teachers, but more likely get lost or overlooked or are otherwise poorly maintained. How can the teacher find what might be available when she plans her lessons, if the original printed information material has been floating by and around in an unsystematic manner and is not accumulated and searchable in an efficient way? Of course, some schools may be well-organized and put all pertinent flyers and print material in a date-sequenced binder, but even in this happy situation, the teacher may have no quick and efficient search mechanism. This need is particularly great if many flyers and announcements and brochures which are not integrated with each other have accumulated.

Additional strategies: Disseminate ideas by other media

Meyer's (1992) survey of European agencies involved in school television showed that most of the agencies offered lesson-idea dissemination about their broadcasting by more than print means alone. As a typical example, a series of television programs about science developed for 11–14 year olds in the UK was accompanied by a parallel television series for teachers on how to use the first set of programs for the teaching of science, as well as extensive print materials for the teachers (and other support materials for the students, computer simulations as well as a book and worksheets; Jelley, 1992).

Clearly this kind of dissemination strategy is a high-budget and long-term plan. The results of this plan, when they finally reach the teacher, should be useful and stimulating. But the more complicated the plan, the farther away the teacher is from herself initiating the content focus of lesson resources. She becomes a receiver, receiving when the agencies involved have all these complex and sophisticated materials ready for her. If she wants them, or wants them at the time they are offered, is another question.

With these difficulties in mind, we now turn to tele-learning to see how the time, access, and weak-link problems in bringing teachers in contact with lesson ideas and resources may be lessened. More positively, we will see some examples of how teachers can have efficient access to more personally-appropriate lesson ideas and resources than ever before. To me, this is one of the main benefits tele-learning for the classroom teacher: not directly in terms of what her students will do with tele-learning, but what the teacher can do with it, partially via the metaphor of a lesson-idea shopping mall (Collis, Veen and De Vries, 1994).

Most likely, teachers go lesson-idea shopping with a certain subject and topic in mind and a clear picture of their students. You could say that teachers know their students' measurements, to keep going with the shopping-mall metaphor.

In the next section, let's assume that the teacher, with measurements in hand, is ready to shop, and as an example that shows how two kinds of tele-learning technologies can complement each other, to shop for ideas that relate to lesson enrichment via classroom television.

■ 5.2.2 LESSON IDEAS INVOLVING TELEVISION, FOR CLASSROOM ENRICHMENT

Teachers can easily picture their students making use of the learning experiences that can come via well-designed instructional television, but how does the teacher make those lesson decisions that involve television in the first place? The important step is getting information to the teacher ahead of time about possibilities that will be made available via television. The simplest form of this process is sending the teacher's school a broadcast schedule, but other ways of getting those ideas to the teacher are now available.

In this section, we first detour a bit by making a very brief overview of television as a form of tele-learning in schools. Then we turn our focus on the teacher looking for lesson ideas involving television. In particular, we see some interesting ways in which computer networks are being used as channels for lesson ideas about television.

One comment is important before we begin: There are two main ways in which television is used in schools. One way is as a delivery method for entire courses, typically to compensate for a school not having adequate in-house resources to provide a certain course itself to its students. In these cases, it is not usually the classroom teacher who makes the decision about the use of television. We discuss this aspect of television for tele-learning in other places in this book (including later in this chapter, in Section 5.6, and from the decision-maker's perspective in Chapter 7). The second way that television is used in schools is not to "bring a teacher in" but to provide enrichment resources for the teacher who is already there. It is this second type of television use that we are considering in this section.

A BRIEF OVERVIEW: TELEVISION IN SCHOOLS

Three main points about television in schools are: that it is a familiar form of tele-learning that is widespread and well-established throughout the world, that advances in transmission and video-processing technology are bringing many more possibilities for the use of television in schools, and that classroom television needs to be integrated with other learning activities and with careful preparation by the teacher in order to exploit its educational value. These three points are elaborated in the next paragraphs.

Television in schools: widespread and long established

Throughout the world, many schools, particularly secondary schools, have provision for receiving broadcast television resources. In the US, nearly every school has at least one TV set for use in the instructional program and as long ago as 1991 the average number of television sets per school was 12 (US Congress Office of Technology Assessment, 1995). As another example, classroom television use is also well established in the UK. Moses and Croll (1992) document the widespread and frequent use that British teachers make of classroom television with a book full of data such as the following:

> *...Over 90 per cent of the primary teachers and just under 80 per cent of secondary heads of departments use school television...for the most, as part of a regular pattern of viewing. Over 85% of the programmes viewed were part of a series which the teacher used regularly. Television usage also has a wider impact on classroom life and 86% of the programmes used were follow-up in some way in the classroom. (p. 18)*

Similar sorts of data are available from agencies and reports around the world. Meyer (1992) for example is an excellent source for the scope and coverage of educational television throughout Europe and some countries of the Middle East and North Africa.

Developments in television technology

There are two major developments relating to television as a technology that are of direct importance to teachers and to their use of television as a tele-learning resource. One of these technological developments relates to the increase in ways of getting programming into the classroom and the corresponding increase in quantity of selection. The second development is the VCR or videorecorder. (A third development, the integration of video technology with computer technology, is still in the future for most classroom teachers in 1995 at least, and thus will not be discussed here in this chapter. It is discussed in Chapter 2 and Chapter 10).

More choice...

In the least-flexible form of classroom television, a teacher would only be able to select from the range of programming available on standard television stations if she wanted to use television in the classroom. However, the proportion of schools with direct cable connections is rapidly increasing, as is the number of schools and districts with satellite dishes enabling them to directly access a broad range of broadcasting. The data that describe these proportions vary from country to country, depending on the extent to which cable service is already widespread in a country or region as well as many other issues that relate to the decision to put a satellite dish on one's school and capture direct-broadcast signals (see Chapter 7 and also Meyer, 1992, and US Congress Office of Technology Assessment, 1995). In this chapter, looking at tele-learning from the classroom teacher's perspective, the major impact comes down to: more choice of programming and more flexibility in time and place of accessing the programming.

More flexibility in time and place...

Perhaps even more important for the teacher than having many channels from which to choose for lesson resources are developments in technology that allow her flexibility in time for the use of television programming. The VCR (video cassette recorder) is a critical piece of tele-learning technology: the teacher needs it to be able to pre-view broadcast materials and make instructional decisions about them, and to be able to use broadcast programming when her class is ready for it, which is usually not when the broadcaster transmitted it. Most schools or regions now maintain a library of pre-recorded video cassettes, some recorded at home by individual teachers, others handled professionally by district and regional staff (see Chapters 7 and 9; also many of the national case studies in Meyer's European overview (1992) stress the pedagogical importance of taping broadcasts for later use).

But still constraints...

But even with these technological advances, there are still constraints on teachers' use of classroom television. Even though schools have VCRs and television monitors, teachers still feel they have inadequate access to facilities for viewing and previewing broadcasts (see, for example, Moses and Croll, 1992). While many classrooms have television hookups, not all do, and not all children can see a single monitor well when they watch it as a group in the classroom. More fundamental is time: teachers need considerable time to sample a broadcast, to preview it, to study it well in order to use it well in instruction. How and where do they find this time? And at the beginning of the chain is information: Teachers need to know the broadcast or taped materials are available before they can consider using them.

THE NEED FOR INSTRUCTIONAL SUPPORT MATERIALS

Here is where specialists come in, often educational technologists working for agencies involved the support of educational television for schools (see Chapter 9). Such specialists, with differing job titles, can be found throughout the world, working on the development of support materials for television programming, lesson materials and ideas for the teacher that can not only save her time in terms of sampling and previewing a broadcast, but also go many steps forward to suggest to her ways to integrate the programming into instructional practice.

The support materials and advance information are important...

It is well established that these sorts of support and lesson-idea materials are very helpful to teachers, even necessary, for effective television use (see Chapter 8; see also, among many possible references, Wetzel, Radtke and Stern (1994), for an extensive review of research about school television; Tiene (1993), for observations relative to the US; and Forsslund (1992), for Europe).

But, how do teachers get this material?

Prior information and support materials are important for teachers if they are to make effective use of television. But even if these are available, a problem still remains: How do teachers find about and get THIS material? How do they get it in time to make a planning decision about television? How do they access information they want, efficiently and in a targeted way?

TELE-LEARNING FOR IDEA DISSEMINATION

To respond to these questions, let us re-examine the traditional ways for getting information about resources that we introduced earlier in Section 5.2, and then, in particular at ways that make use of network tele-learning for idea dissemination about classroom television.

Print and other-media dissemination of information about classroom television

Traditionally, those who produce broadcasting for school use also have well-developed systems for disseminating information about the programming, and also lesson ideas and support materials relating to the programming. These dissemination systems vary from country to country and region to region. All make use of various forms of print as information dissemination (see Meyer, 1992; Moses & Croll, 1992). Often, other media are involved as well, as we saw in the example from the UK of a parallel television series made to help teachers learn new pedagogies to make use of the target television series in the classroom.

Networks for lesson-idea dissemination about classroom television

A very interesting new development is occurring in the ways that teachers are accessing information about lesson ideas and lesson resources for classroom television, and this development relates not to the use of television but to computer networks and network services. Many examples are accumulating of how computer networks are being used as information and lesson-plan dissemination sources for school television. These range from WWW pages maintained regionally or on the Internet by the broadcast agency to bring information to the browsing teacher, to elaborate integrations of network organization and broadcast resources. We illustrate this by looking in some detail at a particular example that demonstrates the power of using networking for lesson-preparation for classroom television.

"CNN CLASSROOM": INTEGRATING NETWORKS AND TELEVISION

A particularly interesting example of integrating the strengths of television with the strengths of computer networks and network organizations is the *CNN Classroom*, an educationally oriented subsidy of the internationally known Cable News Network (CNN; Turner Educational Services, Inc.). Those involved with CNN Classroom have developed supplementary educational materials to be integrated with a wide range of excerpts and re-edited segments of CNN News' archive of broadcast programming. In particular schools are offered a service whereby those which subscribe receive, generally by satellite, a 15-minute television broadcast each school day that synthesizes the top news stories of that day and combines them with segments of "student interest".

By subscribing to this service, the school also receives teacher-oriented support materials each day, providing teachers with a detailed summary of the daily broadcast, definitions of key terms, suggested discussion topics and learning activities, and other resource materials. The school must pay a subscription cost per year.

And how are these lesson ideas and materials made available? They can be disseminated to the school in a number of ways, but most powerful and versatile is the use of a commercial network service in the US ("America On-Line") through which an area for CNN Classroom is available. (See **Interface 5** for more about network organizations providing services for tele-learning.)

Added value of the network service

For schools who also subscribe to the network service, the resources and lesson ideas and support materials for the teacher related to the CNN Classroom television programming are very impressive. Let's look at some of the added-value aspects.

Teacher control of print materials...

By downloading print materials from this network service, teachers can not only receive a wide range of lesson resources correlated with the broadcasts, but that they can do this themselves, in an efficient way. The information is there at the teacher's fingertips. She can find it when she wants it. As an additional added value, it is up-to-date.

And because they are in digital form she can manipulate the print materials that she selects to adapt them further to her own purposes. She can download them, look at them on her own word processor, decide if she wants to use them, and if so, what parts she wants to use. She can edit the materials directly on her computer if she wants, retaining and printing out only these portions which are useful to her teaching. She can even add questions or materials of her own, for more direct relevance as study materials for her own situation.

Moderated discussions

But for our focus in this section—teachers making decisions about lesson ideas—another added-value of network integration with television programming is that asynchronous or even synchronous discussions can be organized by the network service provider to accompany the television programming. For CNN Classroom, these on-line discussions are sometimes planned for student participation; the network service provides a way that the teacher can find out more about the moderated discussions, even sending e-mail inquiries directly from the keyboard as she reads about the possibilities. She can also register her class for participation, if she makes this decision, again through her own fingertips.

But it is most interesting that on-line discussions are also organized for teachers themselves, to discuss with each other lesson strategies to accompany broadcasting or to discussion with the designers of the lesson materials themselves what some of the implications and follow-up of the broadcasting might be.

Network capabilities for communication make this additional source of personal interaction about television programming accessible to the individual teacher; she is no longer the last link at the end of a chain, waiting for others to move information down to her. She can search for what interests her, ask questions about it, and discuss it with other teachers. This individual interactivity is one of the main strengths of network tele-learning; now it is available to teachers in support of their potential use of television-type tele-learning. It frees the teacher to move from being a passive receiver to an active questioner.

Adding more media: the field trip

In addition to lesson ideas relating to specific broadcasts, the CNN network organization makes available to teachers information about a series of "Electronic Field Trips" professionally organized each year by the CNN service and integrated with broadcast programming. These field trips are described well in advance, both in content and in the range of learning resource material that will be involved. The learning materials for these field trips include a professionally integrated mixture of broadcast, networked and live-broadcast events. To participate, a school must pay an additional fee. What is needed is the same equipment that is involved in finding out about the field trips and participating in the daily newsroom: a subscription to the commercial network service, a cable hookup or satellite-receive equipment, and a television monitor. Teachers can plan to make such an instructional unit a major educational experience for their students, and can even plan for a face-to-face excursion associated with the unit. This planning is done by the teacher via networking.

Access to multi-media support materials

As yet another added-value of the network organization associated with CNN Newsroom broadcasting, teachers can choose from an extensive library of other educational resources, again through the same computer connection. They can browse, and order, educational resources of a wide variety of types but all of a professional quality, including video tapes. They can download for no additional cost a large variety of digitized resources: text, graphic, even audio. The user interface of the software through which teachers interact with the CNN network service is particularly well designed and user friendly and the downloading of these supplementary resources is a good example of this user-friendliness. Teachers are warned in advance about how long it will take to download each resource, in that for visual and audio resources the time may be considerable, and also how much disk space they will need, so that they can decide ahead of time if they wish to carry out the task. They can even choose to have the materials downloaded at another time, perhaps when transmission costs are lower.

And the price of added value?

Choosing the time in which downloading of resources will occur is an important point, not only a convenience. There are two sets of connect costs involved in this example of networking used in support of broadcasting: connect costs to the commercial service provider, and connect costs to the telephone company. If the teacher is subsidized in such costs through her school or district or country, she is fortunate (see Chapter 7). Many times, however, in many countries, she must do her "lesson-idea shopping" on her own time, at her own cost. This means the teacher must be convinced the network shopping will pay off in good lesson ideas, and that the costs be as low as possible.

USING THE WWW FOR LESSON IDEAS RELATING TO TV

The CNN example shows the exciting possibilities of the professional combination of a network organization and quality television materials, and in particular the benefits of a network organization for teachers as a source of lesson ideas and resource materials related to eventual television use in the classroom. However, it has the disadvantage of being an added-cost service, and also the disadvantage of not generally being available to teachers outside of the US because it is not available via the Internet but via a commercial network-service provider in the US.

There are many other examples of how networking can be used as a source of television-related lesson ideas for teachers, examples that have the benefit of being openly available via the Internet and the WWW. Box 5.1 highlights a few of these.

Box 5.1

Using the WWW for lesson ideas involving television

Public Broadcasting Company (PBS, US)
URL http://www.pbs.org/learning/k12/resources/ptvresources.html
...This attractive site contains an "Online Newshour" and extensive information about PBS television programming, including lesson ideas such as the "Cybersurfari '95", the "PBS Store", an area of "Learning Services" and the section "Frontline Cyberspace". A particular feature are the pages for PBS MATHLINE, the first discipline-specific service of the PBS, which offers a broad range of resources for mathematics.

The BBC Educational Pages (British Broadcasting Corporation, UK)
URL http://www.bbcnc.org.uk/education.index.html
...Support for all the educational broadcasting of the BBC, with details of programming and back-up materials.

Discovery Learning Community (US)
URL `http://ericir.syr.edu/Discovery/`
...Supporting the "Discovery Channel", a US broadcasting company, this WWW site includes an educator's guide, an entry point to subscribe to a moderated LISTSERV discussion about focus issues, and other interesting material to help the teacher make lesson decisions about The Discovery Channel's broadcast programming

Live from Antarctica (Tanski, Riel, & Hodas, 1995)
URL `http://quest.arc.nasa.gov/livefrom/livefrom.html`
...This WWW site is used as integrated entry point to the "Live from Antarctica" Project, which involves a combination of television programming, teachers' and students multi-medial resources, and e-mail communication with a real research team in Antarctica. The WWW site brings together a wide range of learning resources, ranging from weekly newsletters, photographs, journal entries from the scientists themselves, and links to many relevant lesson resources and also shows how these relate to the television programming. The four television broadcasts include interactive telephone connections with selected schools whereby the students in those schools could ask questions of experts relating to the broadcasts.

Now this is really tele-learning! And this is how the strengths of a network environment can help teachers enormously with respect to accessing timely, relevant lesson-idea materials that can bring television use in the classroom to a new dimension. The network environments, as "lesson-idea shopping malls" for teachers, not only let teachers shop for themselves among a vast range of possibilities but make their own decisions as to whether they want to browse further or sample or discuss the possibilities with other teachers.

A SPECIAL CASE: "CHANNEL ONE"

Before we leave this section on lesson ideas for television use in schools, it is interesting to comment on one extraordinary strategy for the stimulation of classroom television that has been made available in the US. This is an initiative called *Channel One* that does not involve networking for lesson-idea dissemination but instead a different kind of incentive.

In the period since 1990 approximately 40% of all secondary schools in the US have been equipped with a television network through their participation in the *Channel One Project* (Tiene, 1993; Tiene and Whitmore, 1995; US Congress Office of Technology Assessment, 1995). This innovative and controversial project involved a donation to each participating school of a schoolwide television network, including a satellite dish to receive downloaded signals, several videocassette recorders, a head-end unit to send television signals to classrooms, wiring throughout the school building, and television monitors in every classroom with seating capacity of 25 or more (Whittle Communication Corporation, 1992).

Commercials in the classroom?

And what are the conditions on the part of the school for this technological bonanza? To agree by contract to broadcast to all students in the school a daily 12-minute newscast made specifically for students. Why should this be controversial? Because...each broadcast contains approximately two minutes of paid, corporate advertising.

Mass exposure

Despite this advertising and the strong feelings of aversion to commercial advertising in the classroom expressed by a variety of groups, over 12,000 US secondary schools by the spring of 1993 had accepted the conditions, and according to a recent survey (Tiene and Whitmore, 1995) 87% of these schools claim to be presenting the daily broadcast to their students. Thus by 1994 data, 18 million teenagers, almost 40% of all 12–18 year-olds enrolled in school in the US, are supposedly watching these daily news broadcasts as classroom tele-learning (US Congress, Office of Technology Assessment, 1995).

Learning results?

As part of this detour from our discussion of how to bring lesson ideas about classroom television to the teacher, it is interesting to stop for a moment to ask what learning effects are emerging from this massive US experience. Teachers want information about learning results, as much as they want lesson ideas. Are these 18 million teenagers better informed about world news because of daily tele-learning via the Channel One broadcasts? Are they better world citizens? (Or are they being corrupted by the advertisements for jeans and hamburgers?)

Tiene (1993) compared a control group of non-Channel One students with Channel One students on a multiple-choice test carefully designed to reflect basic world events covered by the Channel One newscasts over a particular two-week period. Yes, the Channel One students did significantly better on this test than the non-Channel One students, but the difference was very small (60% correct compared to 52% correct). And subsequent examination of the data showed that these differences were mainly related to questions on "feature items", segments on topics of interest to teenagers, presented incrementally over a five-day week, rather than on the major news items themselves. On questions relating to world awareness, particularly about the major news story of the particular two-week period, there was no meaningful difference among the students with and without Channel One and its daily tele-learning broadcasts.

Why?

Why, given all the technological resources in the Channel One package—TV in the classroom, satellite on the roof, tailor-made programming—was no learning difference found? Among the possibilities: students are watching without paying attention, the time of the broadcasts is too brief, the vocabulary and pacing cannot be just right for all of these 18 million teenagers, and teacher follow-up discussion of the broadcasting was not part of the contract and thus rarely occurred. In a separate study (Supovitz, 1991) it was found that students whose teachers did take the effort to follow-up the broadcasts by integrating the material into classroom lessons did do significantly better on the general-knowledge test compared to non-Channel students.

It appears that the teacher is the critical variable...

Spin-off tele-learning activities

But other things besides the daily newscast are occurring in schools with the Channel One network and its TV sets in every classroom. The broadcast network also gives access to the "Classroom Channel" in which broadcasting programming previously aired on the US Public Broadcasting Service (PBS) is re-transmitted. Also, some educational programming for teachers themselves is broadcast on the so-called "Educator Channel".

The respondents in Tiene and Whitmore's (1995) survey indicated that they were taking advantage of the programming on the Classroom Channel, as well as presenting the contractually required daily newscast. More than half of the teachers were utilizing the Classroom Channel programming five or more times per week and only 5% never took advantage of it. The programming on the "Classroom Channel" that is most popular relates to what North Americans call "social studies", a mixture of world events, history, geography, and other related topics, with science following in interest. In contrast, teachers made very little use of the Educator Channel, with half the responding schools indicating they never selected it.

The Channel One experience is fascinating because it supports yet again what so many have found before: that with any technology in the classroom, it is still the teacher who makes the critical difference. In addition, the top-down efficiencies of Channel One may not relate to what teachers themselves want in terms of choosing their own programming and choosing their own ways of using programming.

Let's move now from the specific focus on helping the teacher have better access to lesson ideas about television use in the classroom, to helping the teacher browse in general about lesson ideas. Coming back to our shopping-mall metaphor, we could say that we are leaving shops relating to classroom television lesson ideas, and browsing more generally in terms of content areas.

■ 5.2.3 GETTING GENERAL LESSON IDEAS VIA A NETWORK

As we saw in Chapters 3 and 4, network services and particularly the Internet have as one of their main functions the provision of information. It is not surprising that there are many, many locations available via specific network organizations for teachers or via the Internet in general in which teachers can look for lesson ideas and examples. In this section all we can do is indicate different categories of the providers of this information. In Chapter 9 we take the perspective of some of these providers themselves and in **Interface 5** we zoom in on some network organizations in particular, but here in Chapter 5 our focus stays on the teacher and her quest for lesson ideas. Once teachers have access to a specific network organization or even directly to the Internet and know how to search for what they want, then a strength of networking is that the teachers can take control: the teacher is not passive, waiting to be told about possibilities. The teacher can "go shopping", look for what s/he wants, see if it fit her students' measurements, and take it home!

Now, for a sampling of such sources of lesson-idea information. The providers of such information include Ministries and regional educational bodies; agencies, institutions and faculties of education; and a great variety of others, with varying types of background and degrees of professional recognition. As we saw with professional tele-learning, a strength of open network organizations and particularly the Internet is that anyone can participate. But this is also a weakness: If anyone can contribute lesson ideas and lesson resources, then the teacher himself has more of a task in terms of judging the quality and relevance of what is offered.

The main forms of tele-learning environments for lesson ideas and lesson-resource collections are: closed collections of professionally made materials (as will usually be the case if a Ministry of Education, for example, maintains an on-line information collection); collections in publicly available WWW sites; and information and ideas that are generated from communication among teachers themselves via conferencing or newsgroup or LISTSERV environments.

OFFICIAL COLLECTIONS

In many countries and regions, the central educational authority will be a sponsor of a network-based depository of lesson materials and resources for teachers (see Schrum, 1994, and Kurshan, Harrington, and Milbury, 1994, for US summaries; and Veen, Collis, De Vries, and Vogelzang, 1994 for a European overview. Also see Chapter 9). In terms of their technological environments, these depositories are evolving from restricted-access BBS-type systems (see Chapter 3); through local, restricted-access environments offering teachers various options for reading and downloading lesson materials; to WWW-based environments with both local and external hyperlinked information sets and communication possibilities.

European examples

In Europe, examples of these various stages of evolution are given in Box 5.2.

Box 5.2

Examples of European ministry of education-subsidized network-based collections of lesson materials

Switzerland (Canton of Geneva; Morel, 1995):
...All resource materials produced by Ministry of Education are in electronic form and supplied to all schools via a comprehensive network service; lesson materials are in French, German, Italian and Romans; an extensive collection of "success stories" is maintained concerning teachers' uses of information technology in teaching; the collection has been available to teachers as well as others in the region via a closed videotext-based network. These services are moving toward a WWW-based network environment that allows access to the Internet.

Spain (Catalonia; Vergés, Castells and Ruiz, 1994)
...Extensive database of successful lessons involving tele-learning experiences, contributed by teachers and maintained as a teaching resource by the central educational-network service. The resources are accessible by dial-in connections to a central server.

Ireland (McKenna, 1994):
...The NITEC Network has evolved over a number of years to connect schools and other educational authorities, offering a range of services including many data bases of lesson materials and repositories of downloadable software.

Denmark (Weidemann, 1994)
...The Schools Database Service (SDBS) provides access to a range of databases with "a reasonable degree of educational value", either through the recommendation of teachers or of specialists in the Ministry of Education. There is continual updating of the databases. The schools pay a yearly subscription fee, but then have unlimited access for both students and teachers. This unlimited access is also for a range of moderated conferences and for Internet access. Every user, student and teacher, has an Internet address.

The Netherlands (Collis, Van Holstein, Rikkerink and Woerts, 1994):
...A large collection of downloaded lesson materials is accessible to teachers via a BBS run by the national curriculum institute; over 25 moderated discussions, organized around curriculum areas, are also maintained, and teachers are subsidized in their costs of accessing the network by the national PTT (telephone company). The service is changing platforms so that Internet access can also be offered.

(For other examples from European countries, see Samways and Davies, 1993; Collis and De Vries, 1994; and Veen, Collis, De Vries and Vogelzang, 1994)

European trends

The European situation with regard to network-accessible collections of lesson ideas for teachers has generally been characterized by a careful and professional initiative, usually centrally subsidized, with a high priority given to quality control and relevance of lesson materials. Relevance is in terms of curriculum, but also in terms of language and culture. Another aspect of European network services is that Internet access has not been viable for teachers, and is only gradually becoming viable in 1995. Connections to the network service must be done via modem, over costly telephone lines. Thus considerable effort goes into making information collections as well-organized as possible for the teacher, so he can get on, download the files he wishes, and log-off quickly. This is a different frame of reference than "browsing the WWW" and picking and choosing among what one finds.

Throughout Europe, system after system is slowing moving to WWW dissemination of lesson ideas and materials to teachers and away from closed (often videotext) BBSs. The general model is one of evolution to a closed-access WWW environment but with Internet gateways. This is a slow process, however, and not only technologically.

In Europe, the Ministries of Education and also teachers expect well-organized, mother-tongue materials, professional in quality and relevant to the curriculum. The evolution toward WWW sites for teachers in many European countries reflects this sort of expectation: browsing the WWW (in English) and shopping around in sites that may have been set up by organizations or by individuals with no particular professional background is often not felt to be a very good use of the teacher's time (let alone money). But this orientation is broadening quickly in Europe in 1995, and many of those in Ministries of Education who were extremely skeptical about the Internet having any value to teachers (or to anyone) in 1993 have put up their own WWW sites, "on an experimental basis" in 1995. While the sites are mostly repositories of local curriculum materials as well as newsletter-type information, there is a steady increase in external links.

North American examples

Many different US states and Canadian provinces also have lesson-idea examples available to teachers via a network service. As with Europe, there has been considerable evolution in North America, yielding a great many models of network organization (see Kurshan, Harrington and Milbury, 1994, for five categories). The state- or district-wide collections may be part of an extensive range of professionally managed teacher-support services (as is the case in US states such as Florida, California, and Texas as well-established examples) to

WWW sites largely reflecting the extra-time efforts of one or two persons working in a district office. The FIRN (Florida Information Resource Network (Baumbach, Eason, Bird and Brewer, 1995) is a good example of an extensive professionally managed service at the state level (we describe this particular example in **Interface 5**). As an example of a site maintained by an individual working in a school-district office, see Matusevich (1995).

One of the most efficient ways to get an overview of WWW servers now being maintained by the US Department of Education, school districts and state departments of education throughout the US is to access a site maintained by TENET, the Texas Educational Network (TENET, 1995) which lists all of the US states as well as a sampling of Canadian provinces and sites from outside North America. From each of these links, another list of sites occurs, including official sites of ministries or departments of education, of districts or regions, of educational institutions such as universities, and other providers. This site is located at:

WWW Sites for K-12, Listing maintained by the Texas Educational
Network (TENET, 1995)
URL: http://www.tenet.edu/education/main.html

Trends in North American sites maintained by educational authorities

North American trends are more difficult to summarize than the European experience, partly because of cultural differences between the two parts of the world in terms of how central educational organizations provide services. For one difference, in North America local school districts have considerable autonomy, and thus the cultural inclination for grassroots, individual approaches in North America is different from the way educational enterprises such as an on-line information networks develop in Europe. In Europe, there is much more likely to have been high-level decisions, provision for subsidies to teachers, involvement of the national telephone companies, and many years' worth of high-level discussion before an "official" service is launched. In North America, the pattern is more diffuse. It is my opinion, knowing both parts of the world, that individual initiatives, just "getting started", characterizes more of the North America sites than is the case in Europe.

As an example, in 1993 I was involved in a conference on telecommunications in education in the US, primarily for US teachers and other educational professionals, and then I returned to Europe and soon after was involved in two European conferences with the same theme. I was very much struck by a particular contrast: In the US conference, a dominant discussion point (plea?) was the individual teacher asking "How do we get on the Internet?" As a generalization, there seemed to be a feeling that what teachers needed was to be able to "get on" and then....well, teachers would and could do wonderful things. In the European conferences the dominant discussion point was quite different. Instead of questions suggesting the teacher herself should be "getting on", questions were more of the nature of "Why isn't the European Community (or the Council of Europe—those were the sponsors of the two meetings) providing a subsidy to stimulate consortia of Ministry and corporate partners to develop and maintain a quality trans-European service?" There was little sense of expectation that teachers would want to "get on" until much serious and professional work had been done to provide a high-quality environment, both in technical aspects and in the materials offered through it. (The proceedings of these meetings also reflect these different orientations; see Foster and Jolley, 1993, and Commission of the European Community, 1994.)

Agencies, institutes and faculties of education

In addition to department or ministries of education, many agencies, institutes and particularly faculties of education having information of potential interest to teachers are maintaining Web sites or other forms of Internet collections of lesson ideas. Hundreds of examples could be given, and new sites are appearing daily in 1995. A teacher is most likely to be aware through other channels (print materials, word of mouth, e-mail messages) of sites which have resource collections likely to be relevant to the local curriculum and situation. Only a few examples representing these categories of lesson-idea providers are given here: representatives are noted in Box 5.3 and also in Chapter 9.

Non-traditional information providers

As we saw in Chapter 4, part of the vibrancy of the Internet at the current time is the inclination of non-traditional information providers to also maintain their own Web pages (or gopher site or files available by ftp) with information they wish to share. We will only indicate a few interesting sites circa 1995 to give an idea of the range of ideas now available to teachers via non-traditional providers via the Internet (see Box 5.4).

The sites mentioned in Box 5.4 (and many others described in magazines and newspapers and books, see Sanchez, 1995b, and Ellsworth, 1994) are suddenly just there, parallel to those maintained by established educational agencies. We do not know, generally, about the educational backgrounds of these new non-traditional providers or what qualifies them to select and provide lesson ideas. This vibrancy is both the strength and danger of lesson-idea shopping on the Internet. Let the consumer beware...

Box 5.3

Examples of institutional providers of WWW sites with lesson ideas for K-12 teachers

The Explorer Data Base (University of Kansas and the Great Lakes Collaborative)
URL http://unite.ukans.edu/
...*Curriculum materials for mathematics and science, supported with the purpose of "engaging educators and students in creating and using multimedia resources for active learning and 'on-time' delivery".*

Franklin Institute Educational Hotspots and Virtual Science Museum (US)
URL http://sln.fi.edu/tfi/
...*Links to many resources for science education as well as multi-media presentations about Benjamin Franklin and the heart as well as other exhibits in the Franklin Institute.*

Northwest Fisheries Science Center (US)
URL http://listeria.nwfsc.noaa.gov
...*Extensive information on oceans and links to other sites with educationally relevant lesson ideas.*

Canada's SchoolNet
URL http://schoolnet2.carleton.ca/
...*This site is supported by a variety of educational organizations across Canada and is attractively laid out in two columns, one side French, one side English. Its purpose is to "facilitate excellence in learning through electronic networking across Canada" and it offers many services, including contests for children and on-line educational resources and activities.*

The Virtual Schoolhouse (US)
URL http://sunsite.unc.edu/cisco/cisco-home.html
...*The site includes a comprehensive list of schools and universities on the Internet, curriculum-related links, library and book-related sites, links to museums and on-line exhibits for classroom exploration. The site is a cooperative venture of the University of North Carolina-Chapel Hill and Cisco Systems Incorporated.*

AskERIC Virtual Library
URL http://ericir.syr.edu/
...*ERIC is the Educational Resources Information Center in the US, and offers not only a vast collection of lesson ideas (accessible via various kinds of forms and search tools) but also a service whereby teachers can send a personal question relative to their lesson-idea interests (or any other educational topic) and receive a personal answer, via e-mail.*

University of Michigan Clearinghouse for Subject-Oriented Internet Resource Guides
URL http://www.lib.umich.edu/chhome.html
...*Over 140 guides, many for curriculum topics relevant to K-12 teachers, indexed for full-text searching.*

Instructional Uses of the WWW (University of Texas at Austin, US)
URL http://wwwhost.cc.utexas.edu/world/instruction/index.html
...*Extensive collection of lesson ideas and links.*

Operation Success Stories (Centre Informatique Pédagogique, Geneva, Switzerland; Morel, 1995)

URL http://tecfa.unige.ch/edu-comp/success-stories/

...Hundreds of lesson ideas, from 12 countries (Japan, Israel, Austria, Belgium, Portugal, Denmark, France, US, Italy, UK, The Netherlands, and Switzerland), organized in a common format that describes pedagogical, cultural, social, technical, logistic, and institutional aspects of each lesson idea. Teachers can search in a variety of ways, and in four languages (French, German, Italian, and English).

EdWeb (Corporation for Public Broadcasting, US)

URL http://k12.cnidr.org:90/resource.cntnts.html

...In addition to links to a number of pages related to educational television broadcasting, this site includes links to articles of interest such as "Computers and Kids: Life on the Front Lines" and "The Role of the WWW in Education", a listserv discussion group with 1,400 subscribers, and a resource section with links to extensive collections of lesson resources.

NASA (US)

URL http://hypatia.gsfc.nasa.gov/NASA_homepage.html

...A site with a vast collection of images, educational materials and links to other countries' space agencies. As an example, within a few days after a lift-off of the space shuttle Endeavor more than 350,000 requests came into the Web site for images and taped conversations of the astronauts as well as other materials, all retrievable over the Internet. (see also Durham, 1995).

Box 5.4

Sample of WWW sites, circa 1995, with lesson ideas for K-12 teachers from non-traditional information providers

The SchoolHouse

URL http://www.webcom.com/velan/

...An electronic magazine "designed for the educationally minded Web Surfer" with articles and lesson ideas, discussion groups for teachers, and extensive links to lesson-relevant sites.

Janice's K-12 Outpost

URL http://k12.cnidr.org/janice_k12/k12menu.html

...Described as "a new place for people (teachers, administrators and parents) interested in K-12. The Outpost is a collection of what's out there on the WWW".

Educational Sites

URL http://www.iw.com/v6n10/extra/

...Maintained by the magazine "Internet World", a hotlist of educational sites.

Mighty Media

URL http://www.mightymedia.com/index.html

...Maintained by commercial providers, the site includes lesson resources for teachers and a "teacher talk" area.

Teacher listservs and conferences for lesson ideas

Teachers themselves may be the suppliers of lesson ideas accessible via network organizations or the Internet. They may do this by contributing comments about their lesson experiences and even by sharing their lesson materials during LISTSERV or newsgroup-type discussions, most likely on their own local educational networks, but also even on the Internet. Listservs in general are a better place for lesson materials than newsgroup discussions, in that the access to the materials is likely to be more directly controlled by the list supervisor. Ellsworth (1994, pp. 166–167) lists 27 Internet-available listservs of particular value to K-12 teachers as sources of lesson ideas (rather than for interpersonal networking). These include lists such as the sample shown in Box 5.5.

Box 5.5

Sample of LISTSERVS with lesson ideas for teachers

SUSIG, teachers discussing ideas about teaching mathematics in secondary schools
Address: `listserv@miamiu.bitnet`

T321-L, teachers discussing ideas about teaching science in elementary schools
Address: `listserv@mizzou1.bintet`

Tesl-L, teachers discussing experiences with teaching English as a second language in secondary schools
Address: `listserv@cunyvm.bitnet`

Thus tele-learning by access to network resources, particularly through the combination of a WWW interface to organized local collections of network resources with links to external sites via the Internet, can now bring a wealth of new ideas to the teacher in the school. Because of the needs teachers have for new ideas and resources, and because of the weak links in the traditional idea-dissemination chain that may filter out information that the teacher himself would find valuable, I feel that the "lesson-idea shopping mall" is a particularly important aspect of tele-learning for K-12 teachers.

The next step...? Ideas into action

It is one big step forward to have better access to lesson ideas and to resources, but still another step to carry them out via an activity in the teacher's own classroom and situation. In Sections 5.3 and 5.4 we look at this translation aspect from two sides: What types of lesson activities might the teacher actually try?

What considerations and problems will confront the attempt to implement tele-learning activities in the classroom?

■ 5.3 A CATEGORIZATION OF TELE-LEARNING ACTIVITIES FOR THE CLASSROOM

Probably, for a number of teachers, this is the section they will turn to first in this chapter, because teachers are practical and oriented toward thinking first of their students. This section directly addresses the question: What can I do in my lesson with tele-learning? We will divide our answers to this question into six main categories and give examples of each in this section. But first, how do we choose these categories?

■ 5.3.1 GENERAL PERSPECTIVES ON CATEGORIZING TELE-LEARNING ACTIVITIES IN FOR THE CLASSROOM

There are many ways to categorize tele-learning activities for the classroom. One approach is to categorize analytically, such as in terms of various forms of student-student interaction. Another way is to begin with a list of popular motivations for tele-learning in the classroom. Examples of these two approaches follow.

CATEGORIZING BY STUDENT INTERACTIONS

One way to categorize tele-learning activities for the K-12 classroom is to think in terms of different combinations of student interaction. Squires (1990) for example categorizes peer interaction possibilities when a computer is involved in the ways shown in Box 5.6.

Arav (1995a) presents a different framework for an analysis of student-interaction possibilities for the use of tele-learning in the regular classroom setting. He considers two dimensions: the purpose of tele-learning and the way that learners communicate during tele-learning. For the purposes of tele-learning, he identifies three possibilities:

- Increasing access to education
- Enriching learning through new forms of instructional activities
- Lessening the feeling of interpersonal isolation of teachers

For forms of communication, he describes six cases:

- Communication outside class time among students involved in groupwork

- Communication between teacher or student and the computer that maintains external sources of information
- Communication between the teacher and an external expert
- Communication between the class and an external expert
- Communication among those involved in a project involving a number of classrooms
- Communication between a learner studying from home and her school

For each of the 18 combinations of these purposes and forms of communication, different case studies can be found in the literature. In his synthesis of these cases, Arav concludes with the observation that "the distinction between traditional education and distance education is now blurred because of these various tele-learning activities". Educational resources and experiences do not have to be found inside the school. The interaction approach that the teacher is most likely to prefer with her class for tele-learning, such as a orientation toward group work or more-individual activity, depends very much on her general preferences for class organization (Veen, 1993) and also what is possible logistically. If only one computer is available to a class and it is not in the classroom but in a location such as the library, the sort of student activities the teacher will choose are likely to be different than those she would select if the class will work, all students at the same time, in a networked computer room. We discuss these sorts of constraints on teacher decision making about organizing students for tele-learning later in this chapter.

Box 5.6:

Tele-learning activities in terms of student interaction

Multiple stand-alone use:
...Here each student in the classroom uses the same resource but individually and without any specific communication with each other. This is possible for a tele-learning resource such as a WWW site but not for a tele-learning resource involving television.

Independent work in a common workspace or on a shared task:
...With computer-based tele-learning an example of this would be students as individuals contributing new data in a scientific project or written contributions to a project involving a cross-cultural exchange with another school in another country.

Group work with similar or shared tasks:
...With group work, each participant has a certain role and responsibility and these must be coordinated and combined for the overall task to be successful. Role playing as an extension of a television broadcast about an historic event or cooperative work involving an electronic simulation of preparation for travel on a space shuttle are examples.

Analyses such as Arav's and Squires' are valuable for those thinking at an overview level, but in general teachers are not so likely to use analytical categories as ways of choosing tele-learning activities for their own classrooms. It seems more likely that teachers may think in terms of a general educational motivation for a tele-learning activity. What are some of these?

Categorizing tele-learning activities by general educational motivation

A number of surveys have been carried out among teachers identifying their perceptions of motivations for classroom tele-learning activities. Harasim (1993) summarizes two large-scale surveys from the US by noting the following motivations:

- Tele-learning experiences will "open up the world for students, globally and culturally"
- Tele-learning experiences let students get information they otherwise could not get in any school library or from any one teacher, no matter how informed the teacher or well-stocked the library
- Tele-learning activities can enhance thinking skills, such as those needed for inquiry and analysis of multiple forms of information, and be a stimulus for problem-solving activities
- Tele-learning activities involving computers give students experience in up-to-date forms of information-technology use, a generally desirable type of functional literacy to develop in students (see also Collis and Anderson, 1994)
- Students like tele-learning activities and find them motivating; a feeling of accomplishment is relatively easy to achieve
- Tele-learning activities let students experience a range of opinions and ideas beyond those of the teacher and textbook, and can give the students possibilities to communicate with persons outside the classroom (Harasim, 1993, p. 24)

Non-mother tongue communication as a motivation

In European surveys, similar motivations for tele-learning are also being expressed by teachers, but with one notable addition: the opportunity to practice multiple-language skills is also a high motivation for classroom tele-learning activities (Collis and De Vries, 1991). (Just as an example of the centrality of languages in many European curricula, in The Netherlands every student is required to study not only the Dutch language, but also English, French, and German until the age of about 15 or 16. And they not only study the languages, they can and do use them and at a competent level.)

Also, in many countries cross-cultural interaction is not just a choice of a pleasant experience for students (what Harasim extracts from the US surveys as a somewhat vague desire to "open up the world for the student"), but a necessity in the lives and futures of the students. Thus deepening cross-cultural awareness particularly as it affects communications that the students will be actually engaging in "in their real lives" and having additional practice for multiple-language skills are major motivations for tele-learning outside the US. Sligte and Meijer (1993), long involved with the European Schools Project, are a good source for more information about this. In this Project, in operation since 1987 and now involving approximately 200 secondary schools from 20 countries, teachers themselves network via e-mail to choose tele-learning topics for their classes, and most frequently focus on ideas that provide a context for practicing non-mother tongue communication.

MOVING FROM MOTIVATIONS TO ACTIVITIES

Even when the teacher is clear on a motivation for a tele-learning activity, there is still a major translation step needed for the shaping of an actual learning activity so that it is manageable in the classroom. What does an idea look like in operation with my class?

From US surveys, the major types of classroom tele-learning activities (in the pre-WWW days of tele-learning) that teachers actually carry out are: viewing of broadcast materials for enrichment and different points of view; participating in e-mail projects with students outside one's class, and participating in a scientific data-collection activity with students in other regions and countries (Harasim, 1993; Honey & Henríquez, 1993). Combining European (Veen, Collis, De Vries and Vogelzang, 1994) and North American experiences with classroom tele-learning, and adding 1995 WWW-use ideas, the following categories of tele-learning activities seem most representative for K-12 classrooms:

- new possibilities for presentation and demonstration during lessons
- new forms of peer interaction both in and outside the classroom, particularly with respect to cultural and communication-focused experiences
- new opportunities to bring students into contact with outside experts
- new ways to work with science data and investigation
- new forms of field trips and excursions, and
- new opportunities for creative expression

We look at some examples of these in Sections 5.3.2–5.3.7. (For other sources of examples, a favorite source of many teachers is Harris (1994b).)

■ 5.3.2 NEW POSSIBILITIES FOR DEMONSTRATION DURING LESSONS

A substantial part of classroom time is spent in teacher presentation—the teacher, in front of the class, explaining certain concepts to the students, motivating them to want to study the concepts, and helping them see the practical application of the concepts. Networked-based resources, particularly visually rich resources available from networked multi-media collections and WWW sites on the Internet, can be a powerful source of lesson-support materials for the teacher to use during class presentations.

THE TEACHER RATHER THAN THE STUDENTS SELECTS THE RESOURCES...

The wealth of audio-visual materials becoming available via network organizations and the Internet itself can be searched ahead of time by the teacher in order to select examples that are valuable to use for demonstration purposes during whole-class presentation.

A main characteristic: a wealth of visual materials...

Many times these collections of audio-visual materials are not specifically presented for educational purposes, but the imaginative teacher can see how they can be used to explain and motivate concepts. Examples are WWW sites with collections of weather charts, of views of the solar system, or of historical paintings. Once the teacher is familiar with the use of a WWW search tool, for example, he can routinely look for visual resources to accompany a lesson presentation that he is developing for his class.

And not only are a wealth of audio-visual resources available via the Internet, there are also increasing numbers of resources specifically developed for educational purposes available via the Internet and other network services which could be used by the teacher during whole-class presentation, perhaps as an advanced organizer to the later use of the resources by the students themselves as well as just being valuable for the illustration of ideas during a lesson presentation. Box 5.7 includes a few examples of WWW sites with potential valuable lesson-presentation resources.

Teacher selection of resources: good sense both practically and pedagogically

On first glance, it may seem inappropriate that the teacher and not the students be the one doing the network searching, especially in terms of the idea that the value of a resource collection is that students can access it to develop their inquiry skills, but in reality very few school situations allow students to individually browse network resources in any extensive way. Thus, in many settings, teacher

---

Box 5.7

Examples of tele-learning resources useful for class presentation

---

Materials not specifically organized for education:

University of California, Berkeley, Paleontology Museum
URL `http://ucmp1.berkeley.edu/exhibittext/`
...Visually rich collection of materials relating to the ancestry and descent among animals and the history of life for organisms on earth.

Climate: The NOAA/TMAP Data Library
URL `http://ferrret.wrc.noaa.gov/bin/climate_server`
...Extensive data relating to world climate over 40 years which can be displayed in a wide variety of visually effective graphs.

Smithsonian Computer History Pages
URL `http://www.si.edu/perspect/comphist/computer.htm`
...Includes the "Information Age Tour" with images and sound clips from Samuel Morse's telegraph to a robot factory.

Earth Viewer
URL `http://www.fourmilab.ch/earthview/vplanet.html`
...User can specify images relating to the earth from space, showing day and night regions at a given moment; views from the sun or the moon; the earth from any location specified by longitude, latitiude and altitude; and weather-satellite imagery, among others.

Canada Hall, Canadian Museum of Civilization
URL `http://www.cmcc.muse.digital.ca/cmc/cmceng/canp1eng.html`
...Many pictures relating to Canadian social history, such as typical farm life in 17th New France along the St. Lawrence River.

Materials specifically organized for learning:

Educational Space Simulations Project
URL `http://chico.rice.edu/armadillo/Simulations`
...In addition to lesson plans and suggestions for experiments and activities, this site offers software for space simulations which in turn can be used in a teacher-led demonstration followed by student use of the simulations.

Mega-Math
URL `http://www.c3.lanl.gov/mega-math`
...Includes material specifically organized for teacher presentation, such as "colorful mathematics" and "the hotel infinity". Various mathematics games and exercises are available through the site, which the teacher should first demonstrate in a whole-class setting before students use them in pairs or individually.

Virtual Frog Dissection Kit:
URL `http://george.lbl.gov/ITG.hm.pg.docs/dissect/info.html`
...This site allows students (and the teacher) to make choices as to which body parts of the frog they wish to focus upon in a simulated dissection of a frog, and offers a variety of subsequent decisions such as if the skin is to be left on or off in the dissection. Based on the choices, the WWW server for the site then responds by showing a graphic of the dissected frog.

selection of visual resources for lesson presentation may be one of the only feasible ways to bring tele-learning directly into the classroom. The students can be doubly motivated by the downloaded materials, not only for their learning value which the teacher makes clear through their use in the lesson, but also by knowing that these materials were found by the teacher in a variety of far-reaching sites. Also, when a teacher is developing a lesson to introduce a concept or motivate students for subsequent study, his stress is generally on an effective and orderly presentation carried out by himself at the front of the class. This is not a time for student hands-on interaction, but for student attention to a well-prepared demonstration.

But, there is a critical step here. Once the teacher finds excellent lesson resources on a network, how does he bring them from his computer screen to the eyes and minds of his students during a class presentation? The teacher needs some technological tricks, such as the following.

Print out a WWW page and use as overhead transparency or as handout

One trick is convert images from a network site to a more convenient form for use in the classroom, such as an overhead transparency sheet or a handout.

- To do this, use the edit functions in the WWW browser to print the page.
- From this printout, make a transparency for the overhead projector to show the students and/or make photocopies of the page or portions of the page and distribute this to the students as a handout to refer to during the lesson presentation

In this way the teacher can cut-and-paste (using real scissors) a page printout to suit her own lesson purposes, and also have an example of information and ideas about a certain topic coming from another part of the world to share with the students.

Screen-capture of WWW pages

Another way of building network resources into lesson presentation is for the teacher to capture an electronic version of a WWW page or image and further manipulate this electronic version in a word-processing program.

- Use a *screen-capture utility* (or simply the PRT SCR key or other key combination, whatever it is on the computer that places a copy of the screen or page in the computer's clipboard) to grab a screen dump of interesting material found on a network. (Some WWW browsers allow you to capture an image separately from the rest of a page, simply by

holding down the mouse button while the cursor is on top of an image in a WWW page)
- Then, by moving (toggling) from the WWW browser to a word processor program, paste the screen dump into the word-processing environment
- Type in questions or explanatory comments next to the screen dump and print out the file as an ordinary word-processed handout making sure that a reference is given to the source of the adapted material.

This technique makes it easy to add text to the screen dump so that the teacher can make the relevance of the captured visual clear to the students. As the final step, the teacher can either print copies of the word-processing file as a handout for each student, or can make an overhead-projector transparency, or both. The WWW images can thus be a powerful and personally tailored lesson resource.

Using other computer tools

Another way for the teacher to make use of WWW resources for lesson presentation is to have a *presentation program* open when browsing the WWW site, capturing screens from the site, and then immediately pasting the screen dumps into a series of frames in the presentation program. Then, after exiting from the WWW site, the teacher can work off-line with the presentation program, adding explanatory text to the frames, editing the captured materials and otherwise preparing a good handout (if printed) or set of sheets for the overhead projector.

These techniques are strategies that I use extensively, in my own teaching, for the development of custom-made learning-support materials to use during lessons, and for students to refer to as follow-up after the lesson. It takes a little while to get handy with the business of capturing screens into the clipboard, and later on the teacher can include the use of an image-editing utility as a step between the clipboard and the lesson handout so that only the portions of the screen display that are desired for the lesson are shown. (Even better, ask some students to help with this. I find that my students are much handier with image editing and drawing programs than I am and asking for their help in lesson lesson-preparation materials is a good way to interact with them on a collegial basis.) It is also a good opportunity to teach the students about proper referencing of the work of others.

Once these techniques are part of the teacher's repertoire, then she has a powerful new way of using tele-learning to extend teaching and classroom presentation.

ADVANTAGES OF A TEACHER-PRESENTATION APPROACH

There are a number of valuable aspects to this teacher-presentation approach to the use of network resources as a type of tele-learning for the classroom. Box 5.8 lists some of these.

Box 5.8

Benefits of teachers using screen dumps of networked resources during lesson presentation

1. The use of screen dumps fits with the teacher's familiar approach to lesson presentation:
...Teachers generally spend a certain amount of time presenting a lesson and leading discussion in a whole-class setting; using network-acquired resources as a way to add motivation or examples to those presentations and discussions is a natural extension and strengthening of the teacher's familiar lesson-presentation skills.

2. Screen dumps fit with logistic realities of the classroom:
...This approach relieves the teacher of needing a network connection in the classroom or, if lucky enough to have one, of distracting the students during the non-productive time that occurs as a desired resource is being brought up. It also avoids the possibility of the network connection not being successful, which frustrates the flow of the lesson.

...Also, classrooms are much less likely to have a networked computer with a projection device so the whole class can see what the teacher wants to show during her lesson presentation, than they are to have an overhead projector. And any class can be given photocopied handouts, without the need for any display technology in the classroom at all.

3. Screen-dump handouts fit with teacher's need for, and skill in, selecting appropriate illustration material for her students:
...The teacher can carefully choose the information from various network sources that best fits the objectives of the lesson and can organize these, through cutting and pasting, in a targeted way. This also avoids the problem of students encountering inappropriate materials on a network which can occur if they are searching themselves.

4. Screen-dump handouts fit with the teacher's desire to develop lesson materials ahead of time:
...There is often just no time or opportunity available for students themselves to look around on a network for illustration material, especially in anticipation of a lesson presentation when a topic or issue is going to be first introduced. The teacher needs to pre-select the network materials the same way as any other material is pre-selected for a lesson presentation.

Teachers don't often think of this approach, despite its advantages...

Given all these benefits, it is surprising that few teachers seem to think of this screen-dump approach for the use of network resources. From my own experience, it seems that often teachers automatically assume that a tele-learning activity that makes use of a network or particularly the WWW must involve all students using the network, even all at the same time. The logistic problems (not to mention other sorts of control and cost-related problems) of some or all students accessing a network, particularly the Internet, are enormous in many schools, but the teacher should not conclude that nothing valuable is then possible with tele-learning in the classroom. The use of network resources as illustrations in teacher presentation is an important way to enrich lesson delivery while avoiding student network-access problems. With this approach, the teacher is using network resources as she uses videotaped broadcast resources, as illustration material that she has pre-screened and filtered and that is shown to the whole class at an appropriate moment in a lesson.

■ 5.3.3 NEW FORMS OF PEER COMMUNICATION BOTH IN AND OUTSIDE THE CLASSROOM

The second of our categories of tele-learning activities for the K-12 classroom is the oldest and most familiar (see, for example, Steinberg, (1992), and Collis, (1992a), where a number of studies of CMC use by secondary-school students in the 1980s are summarized). Some call this category "electronic penpals", sometimes in a disparaging way; more appropriately the category can be called "CMC projects", where CMC refers to computer-mediated communication.

CATEGORIES OF CMC PROJECTS

There are many examples that could be cited of students communicating with each other, via e-mail, for educational purposes. Early writing about CMC, by pioneers such as Margaret Riel and her colleagues (Cohen and Riel, 1989; Riel and Levin, 1990; Riel, Levin and Miller-Souviney, 1987) as well as more-recent work such as Harris (1994b); Waugh, Levin and Smith (1994); and Sligte and Meijer (1993) highlight examples of classroom CMC projects, the educational benefits of these projects, and problems and issues confronting the projects. In Box 5.9 we summarize these different sources by identifying five general types of CMC projects for the classroom.

Box 5.9:

Types of CMC projects for the classroom

- Students practice functional writing, by writing to a real audience
- Students practice writing in a language other than their mother tongues as part of studying a second language
- Students prepare for a field trip by communicating with their future host-class classmates
- Students become more culturally sensitive by finding out about different customs and lifestyles from their distant writing partners
- Students discuss a current news topic with students in other cultures, to get different points of view

And these are examples from projects only involving CMC; there are many other examples of CMC used as part of a larger tele-learning project, and therefore as a way to discuss and analyze whatever it is that is happening in the larger project (for example, collection of acid-rain levels from a variety of countries). Another example of CMC as a part of a broader tele-learning experience is the growing presence of forums, discussion groups or newsgroups that accompany some external event, such as the moderated conferences that accompany CNN Newsroom broadcasts and are intended for students.

A nice and typical example of a CMC project that represents the first and the fourth of the categories in Box 5.9 is the "Letters to Santa Project" (Cowick, 1995). This project, which has been operating each year since 1984, has as its goal the improvement of writing skills in primary and upper-grade students. Teachers register their classes in the project and are then sent detailed instructions of the project procedures. And what are these procedures?

- Teachers register by November 3, with details about their classes, schools, and the setting of their schools (geographic area, cultural and social aspects, etc.). Teachers can register either a primary class (Grades K-2) or a secondary-school class (Grades 7–12). To register, teachers first send an e-mail to the project management, and then fill in the registration form which is sent back to them via e-mail. The registration form is carefully structured with regard to the information to be provided.
- The project management pairs primary and secundary classes and teachers, and sends each pair of teachers names and information about each other on November 8
- Teachers send greetings to their partner teachers on November 13.
- Between November 14–17 the paired teachers practice sending word-processed files to each other.
- Between 13–22 November the primary students, with the help of their teachers, compose their "letters to Santa Claus" using a word processor.
- Between November 27 and December 1 the teachers of the primary classes send the letters as files to their partner teachers in the secondary classes.
- Between December 4–8, the secondary students compose responses to the letters, replying as "Santa".
- On December 11, the secondary students send their responses back as e-mail to their primary-class partners.
- Between 12–15 December, the primary teachers send a summary of the reaction of their students to the Santa letters to the secondary class and teachers. During the same time, the secondary students compose a sum-

mary of their experiences and send it both to the project management and to the primary teacher (Cowick, 1995).

BENEFITS OF CMC PROJECTS

The general conclusion from these many different CMC projects in the classroom? It seems to be that, when the CMC project is well managed both practically and educationally, then students find it motivating, they are willing to spent more time on task than the teacher describes as usual for these students, and the teacher perceives that learning value has occurred (Collis, 1992a, 1993b; Riel, 1992; Waugh, Levin and Smith, 1994).

Actually measuring this learning value is more elusive (Collis, 1993b); anecdotal samples of students' written work seems the most frequent source of data, as well as observations of student engagement and enjoyment and results from short questionnaires distributed to participants.

WELL-MANAGED IS THE KEY...

But what about the condition that the "CMC project must be well managed both practically and educationally"? There is considerable evidence to suggest that, to be successful, a CMC project must well managed by the teacher, and this in turn entails many tasks and considerations. The example of the planning and organization that is used for the successful "Santa Letters Project" (Cowick, 1995) that we gave above shows the sort of management that is desirable for a CMC classroom project. Box 5.10 summarizes some of these considerations.

Thus it is clear that the deceptively simple CMC project is indeed not at all simple. Of course, it is relatively easy to have a first flurry of pen-pal type communications, and students are predictably pleased to receive some mail from e-mail correspondents, but to do something educationally relevant with a CMC project in the K-12 classroom is much more challenging.

Help for the teacher

Fortunately, many different structures are available to help the CMC Project process. The references cited in Box 5.10 are examples of carefully explained guidelines. Also, the "Santa Letters" project is an example of a carefully pre-structured project. Another noteworthy example of such well-structured projects was the AT&T Learning Network, which functioned as a pioneer in CMC for the classroom in the late 1980s and the first part of the 1990s. This was a prime example of a professionally structured framework for CMC projects, led by well-trained Learning Circle "mentor-coordinators" who helped steer and support each step of communication (Riel, 1992).

Because there is so much literature on the e-mail type of CMC project for the

Box 5.10

A successful CMC project is:

- Based on clear and careful pre-planning among the teachers involved, relating to learning intentions, communication procedures and timelines, and closure
- Involves teachers who somehow found each other in the first place and agreed upon a common learning goal for the CMC project and a common sense of how the goal can be reached
- Involves teachers who stick to these agreements, particularly with respect to timelines
- Includes accommodation for events that do not happen at the same time in participating classes, such as vacations, examination periods, and other school priorities
- Has agreements for the mechanics of communication among the students: for example, will the teacher print out and circulate a response from a class to a class, for example, or will individuals also communicate? If a class makes a response, how is this organized?
- Has a common agreement about issues such as spelling and grammar; for example, Who checks these? Should the classroom teacher? If so, should all communications go to her first? Should she check revised versions as well before they are sent?
- Has contingency planning to handle things not going as anticipated; for example, when responses do not come, or are of a disappointing level?
- Has had mutual agreement among the teachers about the extent of expected communication; for example, Should all students communicate a certain amount? (at least one message, etc.)? What about those who like to do it compared to those who don't? And how can all students have computer time to prepare messages, even if the teacher sends the messages as a batch (single message)?
- Has had mutual agreement among the teachers as to how to distinguish short, informational communications from more substantive writing submissions; for example, Who handles the "routine communication" (organizational aspects) of the CMC activity? When are some messages simply responded to in a memo-type way, and others taken as the basis of class discussion and writing?
- Has had discussion among the teachers involved as to how assessment will be conducted on students' performance in the different sites

(See sources such as Andres and Rogers, 1995; Collis, 1992b; Harris, 1994b; Kimeldorf, 1995; and Riel, 1992 for elaboration on these considerations.)

classroom, we will not dwell further on it here, but move on to new forms of CMC projects utilizing WWW environments that are starting to emerge.

CMC PROJECTS ON THE WWW

A new variation of a CMC Project is for learners to contribute writing for publication on a WWW site. Sometimes the major motive of this contribution is the experience of creative writing; we will discuss examples of this later, in Section 5.3.7. Other times, however, the WWW site serves as an integrative environment for student communication about a particular topic. Box 5.11 gives some examples.

Box 5.11

Examples of CMC projects in WWW environments

The Berlin Wall
URL http://192.253.114.31/Berlin/Berlin/Introduction/Berlin.html
...*This collaborative-writing project occurred in 1995 around the topic of the Berlin Wall. Students from 30 schools around the world contributed writing as well as archival visual material (photographs) relating to the Berlin Wall. Students are using the project to create a "virtual museum" about the Berlin Wall, available to all over the Internet.*

Women's History Collaborative Page:
URL http://www.teleport.com/megaines/women.html
...*This site is maintained by a third-grade and fourth-grade class and the technology coordinator at their school as a collection of resources for Women's History Month. Students in grades K-12 are invited to send either creative writing pieces or encyclopedic-style biographic entries about famous women. These entries are then added to the WWW site.*

Trees of the World
URL http://www.hipark.austin.isd.tenet.edu/home/trees/main.html
...*A fourth-grade class in Texas has set up a WWW site that includes a questionnaire for submitting data about trees indigenous in various areas of the world. To respond to the questionnaire, a paragraph of information about such a type of tree must be sent in and a scanned photo of the tree if possible. When the data comes in, the teacher of the fourth-grade class adds it to the WWW site. Within a few months after setting up the site, entries have been submitted by children from six states and three other countries.*

These new forms of CMC Projects, based on the publishing potential of the WWW, bring a new face to CMC possibilities in the classroom (Carvin, 1995). Typically the WWW-sited projects not only provide the structure, both technical and organizational, needed for educational CMC activities, but also an attractive dissemination medium (generally not true for e-mail based CMC output). Writing becomes an extended hypertext and a collaborative activity involving distant partners. A concern is that the writing may loose focus, if the audience to which one writes is "any reader on the Internet". However, the examples in Box 5.11 show that an educationally valuable CMC project, both in terms of process and product, can be mounted in a WWW environment, with its added benefits of hyperlinking text, and including graphics (and even sound) with textual communication.

OTHER POSSIBILITIES FOR CMC TELE-LEARNING

In addition to the projects we have been discussing, it is also possible to use network resources for language-practice tele-learning outside of the project framework. For example, the teacher can use text downloaded from listservs or even newsgroups on the Internet as data for language practice. Rézeau (1994), a teacher of English to seecondary students in France, uses news items from network sources, downloads them as ASCII, and deletes various words (leaving underlined blanks) so that the remaining "Close-type" text can be used by students for language practice. Rézeau notes three advantages to this source of practice text compared to textbook exercises:

- The language for the exercise is authentic
- The contents are topical, and if the student does not understand the English content, he can make inferences about it from knowing about the topic of discussion through knowing what French people are saying about the topic
- This type of downloading and adaptation of text is not difficult or time-consuming for the teacher, allows the teacher to edit away all inappropriate materials, and thus is feasible for busy language teachers

■ 5.3.4 OPPORTUNITIES TO BRING STUDENTS INTO CONTACT WITH OUTSIDE EXPERTS

A variation of the peer-to-peer CMC project is the CMC project involving student communication with an outside expert. There are many examples of this, particularly for secondary-school learners.

ASK AN EXPERT...

The communication between class and expert can be asynchronous, via e-mail, or even synchronous, via chat or video-conferencing via the Internet or other two-way compressed video networks.

ASYNCHRONOUS CONTACT

As one example, Garcia and Ribera (1994), teachers in Spain, worked extensively with their secondary-school literature students, studying the works of a prominent contemporary Spanish author. The students then, under their teachers' supervision, sent messages to the author at a pre-determined time, asking him various questions about the meaning and context of his work. The author responded to the students via e-mail, and the classroom teachers used the response as basis for class discussions and for a subsequent e-mail communication to the author.

Another example of the "ask-an-expert" type of CMC project, from Canada, shows further variations. This example involved organizing a conference among a set of "local experts", persons from the community in a Canadian school district who offered to respond to students' submissions about various topics related to school content. At the end of the one-year period, students had sent 768 messages, including 75 to a local expert on whales and 44 to someone in the community who had considerable information about bears (who was only identified to the children as "Mr. Bearman"; Teles and Duxbury, 1991).

Real-time chat

As another example, Matusevich (1995), a teacher in the US, describes how she, in the context of an instructional unit on the country Wales with her fourth-grade students, arranged for CMC communication with a teacher in Wales. This Welsh teacher agreed to participate in a real-time chat session with the class. The technique for this session was that the students indicated what they wanted to ask the Welsh teacher, and Matusevich typed in their questions during the chat session. In this way, the problem of students' lack of typing skills was not a barrier to the communication with the distant expert. A real-time communication session by chat as a technique for an "ask-the-expert" tele-learning activity is particularly useful in that it focuses the communication, assures that a remote communication partner will be present, and puts a finite timeframe around the "ask-an-expert" activity.

Real-time video communication

Real-time communication can also be done now, via the Internet, with both video and audio connection through the CU-SeeMe software if both parties have computers with camera and microphones and can run the CU-SeeMe software; see Chapter 2 for an introduction to the technology, and Andres (1995a,b) and Vacca (1995) for examples of how this technology is being used in the *Global Schoolhouse* and *Scientist on Tap* Projects. In the Scientist on Tap example, a team of expert volunteers has gradually emerged, willing to interact with students both via e-mail but also via CU-SeeMe video-conferencing. These "scientists on tap" are described by a teacher whose class has communicated with a rocket scientist via the project as having:

> *...opened our students' cognitive window by creating a new "virtual schoolhouse" only made possible through worldwide electronic networking. As*

budgets shrink and resources within the school building diminish, the Internet can connect students to the expanding resources of a "global schoolhouse" limited only by bandwidth and populated with fellow students, teachers, scientists, astronauts, and other experts around the world (Andres, 1995b).

Ask an expert via the WWW

It is not surprising that "ask an expert" projects are increasingly making use of WWW sites to integrate contact with collections of learning materials relevant to the expert's interests. One such example is:

UT Science Bytes
URL `http://loki.ur.utk.edu/ut2kids/science.html`

In this example, scientists at the University of Tennessee describe their research in a way appropriate for elementary and secondary-school students and their teachers, and make it easy for students to submit questions directly to the researchers through forms in the WWW page. Examples of some of these descriptions made available by the researchers are "Mad about Marmosets", "On the Wings of a Dragonfly", "Rhinos and Tigers and Bears—Oh My!", and "The Future is Yours".

Another example is a WWW site maintained by Michigan State University:

Multi-Media Detectives
URL `http://www.mitn.msu.edu/mmd/mmd.htm`

through which students in schools in the surrounding community can participate in various on-line text-based chats organized with experts from a variety of fields. Students must submit questions prior to the real-time session, the expert sends some comments based on these questions, and then real-time interaction occurs.

A final example is the interesting project "Where on the Globe is Roger?" (Pasos, 1995). In this project, a person called Roger is traveling around the world in his truck and sending back regular reports to the project manager, who places these in a WWW site as well as posting them directly via e-mail to the over 300 schools registered in the project. Students are encouraged to send Roger questions and comments. Roger makes a special point to visit schools and teachers during his travels and send back information about these visits. The goal of the project is to "foster better understanding between countries and cultures...for students to look with new eyes at distant lands...to learn more about their geography, customs, way of life" (Pasos, 1995). Keeping all the reports available on the WWW site makes it easy for students to look at the entire collection and also is bringing in many more participants than would be possible in a e-mail only project.

ASK-AN-EXPERT...WHERE THE STUDENTS ARE THE EXPERTS

Avery interesting variation on the "ask the expert" type of CMC project was described by Traw (1994) and involved preservice teachers who were preparing to go out into a local elementary school to teach an instructional unit relating to children's literature. Such practice-teaching experiences are important, but "had suffered from a lack of knowledge of how real kids in elementary schools would respond to the units" (p. 28).

The solution to this was to use e-mail and have the preservice teachers communicate their ideas for the teaching unit to the students themselves, asking the students to give feedback on the ideas. Students and preservice teachers communicated back and forth for two weeks (because only one computer was available in the classroom, the classroom teachers solicited the students' ideas and typed them in as messages to the preservice teachers.

The project was a "great success" according to its supervisor because:

● The preservice-teacher groups developed a better instructional unit than they would have without the students' input
● The preservice teachers learned much about the developmental levels of the children, their reading tastes and levels of understanding as well as their responses to literature, before they went to the school to teach their units
● Everyone learned to use e-mail
● The children received a great boost to their confidence and self-esteem; they were the experts whose suggestions were treated with great respect (Traw, p. 30)

Thus, the "expert" can be a young child, in this sort of CMC project!

(For other examples of CMC projects and preservice teacher education, see Chapter 9.)

CAREFUL PREPARATION NEEDED...

The "ask an expert" model of CMC project needs careful organization; for example, in addition to all the considerations for a successful CMC project summarized in Box 5.10, someone has to contact and negotiate agreement with the participating experts. For this purpose Harris (1995b) is offering a "matching service" called the Electronic Emissary to help teachers with access to the Internet locate other Internet account holders who are experts in different disciplines, to set up curriculum-based, electronic exchanges among the teachers, their students, and the experts. The on-line discussions associated with various educational broadcasters in the US such as CNN Newsroom are another example of how a professional staff can be engaged in contacting an expert and set up the conditions for the "ask an expert" interaction. Or the classroom teacher may wish to make the contacts herself, as did Garcia and Ribera (1994) in Spain. But in any case, "ask-an-expert" tele-learning can be a valuable use of networking in the classroom.

■ 5.3.5 NEW WAYS TO WORK WITH DATA COLLECTION AND COLLABORATIVE INVESTIGATION

Projects involving data collection and collaborative investigation among students in different locations are a third general type of tele-learning project for the K-12 classroom. All the conditions stated as necessary for the success of CMC projects (see, again, Box 5.10) are also necessary for tele-learning projects involving data-collection and collaborative investigation. However, even more organization is necessary than with CMC projects, in that standard formats for collecting and reporting data must also be agreed upon, and some sort of central repository for the communal data must be maintained. This can be technically and conceptually more complicated than all participants saving copies of their e-mail messages.

EXAMPLES OF DATA-COLLECTION PROJECTS

Data collection in the framework of science investigations is probably the most common form of K-12 project involving joint data collection (Harasim, 1993), although students can also collaborate on survey data collection for social-science purposes, including "social action projects" (Harris, 1995a). A social-action project is one motivated by a humanitarian goal such as "save the beaches". Harris describes the SAFER Project (Student Ambassadors for Environmental Reform), focusing on water-run offs and involving classrooms in three US states and in the UK, with CU-SeeME video-conferencing organized for discussions with expert guests. CU-SeeMe software allows live, multipoint video at 12–15 frames per second over the Internet using phone lines. The data collection focused on problems associated with water runoff in the respective communities of the students involved in the projects.

Another example of a data-collection project is "Math Pen Pals Communication through Numbers", whose goal is to encourage students to compare and contrast numbers while learning more about other communities (Winrich, 1995). A number of possibilities for shared data collection are extended to participating classes, including those with weekly data input such as for high and low local temperatures or amount of precipitation, or monthly data input such as average hours of

TV watched or prices of common items in grocery stores. Important to the project is that students must find common ways to create visual and numerical summaries of the overall data collected. The focus is on communication, but around and through numbers.

Many more examples of "pooled data analysis" projects are available in Harris (1994a, 1995a), and at an anonymous ftp site that Harris maintains at:

Data-collection Project Ideas (Harris, 1994b)
`ftp://tcet.unt.edu`
directory path: `pub/telecomputing-info/ed-infusions`

STRUCTURED SCIENCE PROJECTS

Data-collection projects relating to science topics such as acid-rain measurement collection and comparison have been well established for a number of years. Usually these are managed by a central network organization, such as the National Geographic Kids' Network in the US (TERC, 1993), to which schools can subscribe and in turn receive a kit with equipment for the data-collection activities, extensive teacher-support materials, and a detailed timeline and set of responsibilities for participation. Special software allows the students to see the accumulated data in various ways such as graphs and tables, as well as a map indicating the locations of participating schools (see Waugh, Levin and Smith, 1994, for a description and comparison of this and other tele-learning project structures.)

Another notable example of collaborative science projects for the classroom was the LabNet project, also managed by TERC in the US. LabNet was a major initiative involving many hundreds of science teachers and their classes (Ruopp, Gal, Drayton and Pfister, 1993). LabNet was just as much focused on promoting teacher networking (see Chapter 4) as it was on structuring collaborative data-collection projects among the classes of the participating teachers.

WWW SITES FOR COLLABORATIVE DATA-COLLECTION PROJECTS

And, not surprisingly, schools are beginning to use WWW sites as integrating environments for data collected in collaborative projects. One such example is:

The River Rouge Virtual Tour
URL `http://www.nceet.snre.umich.edu/`

This site was used as part of an instructional project relating to the environment. Students went in small groups to different locations near a local river and took photographs of the sites as well as samples of different sorts of relevant data.

Once back, their data were added to a WWW site, linked to a map of the river region.

Going out into the field, collecting data, and then later using the computer as a tool to share and communicate the data is a form of tele-learning project that involves an excursion into the "real-world". Many examples can be found of students participating in such field trips but without leaving the classroom, via tele-learning. We look at a few of these in the next section.

■ 5.3.6 NEW FORMS OF FIELD TRIPS AND EXCURSIONS

As we noted in Chapter 3 while referring to the family, a major benefit of tele-learning is to allow the learner to have at least some of the benefits of being in a certain place without actually having to go there. A good video documentary, accompanied by a variety of other learning resources, can provide this feeling of being there while still in the classroom, and is one of the major motivations for classroom television (Wetzel, Radtke and Stern, 1994). In addition, the interactivity and mixture of text, visuals, and sound available via WWW sites on the Internet also can be used by the teacher to develop a remote-excursion tele-learning experience for students.

VARIATIONS OF ELECTRONIC EXCURSIONS

What is called an electronic field trip or excursion has different meanings to different persons. Sligte and Meijer, for example (1993), uses the phrase to describe collaborative projects among participating schools, of the sort that we have called CMC projects or data-collecting projects in this section. But an excursion can also focus more on the place being visited and what it has to offer than on the process of collaborative data collection.

TELE-FIELDTRIPS: BEING THERE... (IN ONE WAY OR ANOTHER)

The Global Schoolhouse Project (Andres, 1995a) uses the phrase "tele-fieldtrips" to describe what happens when teachers and students share their observations and experiences made during local (real) fieldtrips to museums, historical sites, parks and zoos in their own area. The project maintains information both about local fieldtrips that have already been taken and fieldtrips that participants plan to take. In the latter case, others can send questions that they would like the real field-trippers to try to answer while on their outing. Harris (1994a) describes a similar project in which a group of students actually went along with oceanographers during a research expedition on the Mediterranean Sea and sent back their daily logs to students around the world who were participating in the fieldtrip remotely, via the Internet. Variations of this follow-the-participants model have already occurred many times, in contexts of space and world travel.

Virtual hands-on exhibits

We saw in Chapter 3 that there are literally hundreds of museums and other real-world locations which now offer WWW-based opportunities for visitors to interact with material and exhibits from the locations without actually being there. The teacher can canvass these sites regularly for examples that offer "hands-on" activities for a virtual excursion complementing what the class is studying in their classroom. Extensive lists of such "educational exhibits" can be found at locations such as:

Educational Hotspots
```
http://sln.fi.edu/tfi/jump.html
```

and

The Virtual Schoolhouse
```
http://sunsite.unc.edu/cisco/cisco-home.html
```

Among the many different sorts of tele-learning activities available at such virtual-excursion sites are opportunities to learn about the fossilized remains of a blue whale found in the mountains of Vermont (far from any current ocean); "visit" the planets in the solar system; listen to the sounds of Australian birds in their native habitat; and play a melody on an large organ in a certain auditorium.

The teacher must find and manage the excursion possibilities...

As we saw in the case of the family, the teacher with Internet access has a wealth of new types of interactive learning experiences available for use as supplements to a learning unit. However, the teacher needs to know how to find them, and to see how to manage their use in the reality frame of the classroom. The individual use of a WWW search tool can be mastered relatively quickly, but classroom management of interactive uses of a WWW site is considerably more challenging, for all the reality-frame reasons identified in Section 5.2 of this chapter. The techniques of screen capture and handout creation discussed earlier can be very helpful when there is no way to let a whole group of learners interact individually and extensively with a rich WWW site. However, virtual-excursion sites on the WWW are most valuable when the learner can make her own choices in the hyperlinked environment. For this reason, virtual-excursion sites are an example of tele-learning that may be more feasible for the home setting than the classroom, given the current limitations on student-computer access in schools.

■ 5.3.7 NEW OPPORTUNITIES FOR CREATIVE EXPRESSION

Finally, the last of our categories of tele-learning projects for the K-12 classroom is one relating to new opportunities for creative expression. A major way this is now occurring is related to WWW sites, through the design and creation of Web pages themselves, and through contributing to sites already set up to motivate creative expression.

MAKING YOUR OWN WEB PAGES

As we have already discussed in Chapter 3 and will zoom in on in **Interface 6**, a new form of computer-based self-expression has appeared, and has exploded in popularity during 1995 among schools and classes of young students throughout the world (Carvin, 1995). This form relates to creating one's own pages for access in World Wide Web sites. Such sites may be local, residing only on a local-area network, or may be linked to the WWW system on the Internet. We discuss the technical aspects of how to make WWW pages in more detail elsewhere in the book; the main point here, from the perspective of the K-12 teacher, is that students around the world are setting up their own Web pages similar to the way they develop school newspapers, as communal learning projects.

Many different locations on the Internet provide lists of K-12 schools with student-developed Web sites. None of the lists are complete, as the number of schools and classes adding pages to the WWW escalates daily. For a typical example, the first elementary school to construct WWW home pages in The Netherlands can be found at:

Basisschool De Ranonkel, Someren, The Netherlands
URL `http://www.dse.nl/ranonkel/index2.html`

The scanned-in class photographs at sites such as these are delightful ways to see groups of children in different cultures and settings. For good summaries of K-12 WWW sites developed with the objective of being vehicles for students' creative expression, see Box 5.12.

Such sites, like their parallel form, the school newspaper, are a delightful mixture of student self-expression and public information. As we noted in Chapter 3, these sites are a valuable way for parents and the community more generally to be better informed about what is going on in local schools. They also

> **Box 5.12**
>
> **Collections of WWW sites developed by students in elementary and secondary schools**
>
> K-12 WWW sites
> URL `http://toons.cc.ndsu.edu/sackmann/totalstat.html`
>
> WWW Schools Registry
> URL `http://hillside.coled.umn.edu/others.html`
>
> Classroom Web
> URL `http://www.wentworth.com/classweb/default.html`
>
> Schools!
> URL `http://k12.cnidr.org/janice_k12/schools.html`
>
> K-12 Schools with WWW sites (TENET, 1995)
> URL `http://www.tenet.edu/education/main.html`

provide a publication forum for student projects, student writing, student drawing, student surveys, and student biographical information. Baker and Davis (1995), provide a useful description of how an elementary school can proceed with setting up its own WWW server, or can make use of a server located elsewhere for mounting their students' pages. The ease with which a scanned photograph or drawing can be linked into a Web page stimulates children to submit their artwork and their graphical representation of information. Box 5.13 gives just a few examples circa 1995, to show the creative outpouring taking place within student-oriented WWW pages.

The learning value in students designing and creating a Web site is more than the satisfaction of having a forum for self-expression that can be responded to by persons from throughout the world. There are also benefits such as the following:

- Students must organize information flow among themselves, and experience working as a coordinated team
- Students must work out how to share and distribute tasks
- Students must harmonize their writing styles and take great care with the presentation of their writing, for the overall look and quality of the site
- Students have to discuss face-to-face and also sometimes with remote contributors at each step of the planning, design, implementation, and maintenance phases of the project

---

Box 5.13

Examples of school-based WWW sites for creative expression

Arleta Elementary School, Portland OR.
URL: http://buckman.pps.k12.or.us/arleta/globe.html
...This site includes student reports, with photographs, of their work in the "ESL Globe Project" where children in an English-as-a-second-language course used paper mache and balloons to create globes and then painted the continents and oceans on these globes. The reports include student-written descriptions of how they did this activity, as well as photographs of themselves with their globes.

Atlantic View Elementary School, Lawrencetown, Nova Scotia, Canada
URL: http://fox.nstn.ca/nbarkhou/avshome.html
... This site is more like a typical school newsletter, with a variety of hyperlinked reports on student activities and school happenings, and including student autobiographies and links contributed by students and teachers to other interesting Web sites outside the school, some from other local schools, some with a Canadian focus, some pointing to outside Canada.

Patch American High School
URL http://192.253.114.31/
...The first secondary school WWW server in Europe, located at a school in a US military base in Germany, has featured projects about events such as the fall of the Berlin wall and the 50th anniversary of the end of WW II. The latter project was visited by more than 77,000 persons from 39 countries in four months via the WWW.

- Students receive a valuable experience in an up-to-date aspect of computer literacy, equivalent to many of the skills and awarenesses which formerly were argued as being a justification for teaching programming as part of introduction-to-the-computer courses
- Students work in a real-world environment collaborative environment

(See Schneider and Block (1995), for a number of other references relating to these sorts of learning benefits.)

If the technical process of actually making WWW pages or linking them to a server is not appropriate for a class, alternative arrangements are developing. Dígnazio (1995a), for example, describes the "Multimedia Detectives Project" in which students use editors with which they are already familiar—word processing, paint programs, sound editors, tools to work with clip art, etc.—and design their own electronic multi-media materials. They then give their various multi-media documents to the project staff at the Michigan Information and Technology Network, who in turn translate the documents into WWW documents, link them coherently, and make them available through:

Multimedia Detectives Home Page
URL `http://www.mitn.msu.edu/mmd/mmd.htm`

Prestructured WWW sites for creative expression

In addition to student-created WWW sites, there are an increasing number of Web sites in which an external agency has already created the structure within which students can submit their writing or artwork or other creative entries. We mentioned some examples of these in Table 3.4 in Chapter 3. The teacher can take advantage of these as creative-expression opportunities for her students, without needing to focus on the technical aspects involved in designing and maintaining a WWW page itself. A good example circa 1995 are the pages of this sort maintained by the Global Schoolhouse Project:

The Global Schoolhouse Project
`http://k12.gsh.org/`

which offers a service for publication of student's contributions. Another example is the "CyberFair" project (Cisco Systems, 1995) in which participating schools are conducting a research project involving their communities and will see their results published on a WWW site that will be called "The Internet 1996 World Exposition". This site is described as being modeled after "the great world's fairs at the turn of the 20th century" and is based on the belief that such projects enable students to "explore their technical and creative capabilities through the use of networked multimedia resources such as the World Wide Web".

There are many such sites springing up in 1995, even sites of this sort developed by children themselves. This is the excitement of tele-learning for creative expression that has been amplified by the attributes of WWW environments. If such environments lead to better writing than text-only CMC projects focused on creative expression cannot yet be said; but they do offer linking and much easier insertion of visuals, which together may stimulate more-creative expression than text-only environments. Such sites also offer a broad audience, all who visit the site as opposed to only those to whom the class sends its messages: this can be motivating for many children.

■ 5.3.8 CONCLUSION: TELE-LEARNING AS PART OF ON-GOING LEARNING IN THE K-12 CLASSROOM

Looking back at this long section, it is clear that there is a broad range of possibilities for tele-learning activities as enrichment in the regular K-12 class-room. In fact, there are so many good and feasible ideas that it can be argued that all teachers need training experiences in "tele-learning pedagogy" in the same way as they need training experiences in other forms of educational delivery (see Chapter 9).

However, given all these rich and exciting ideas, why isn't every K-12 teacher busily adding new forms of tele-learning to his or her daily practice? The reality frame described in Section 5.2 rears its ugly head! Tele-learning is still a challenge for the teacher to implement in the circa-1995 classroom for many reasons. Section 5.4 brings some of these together through the perspective of first-level and second-level problems.

■ 5.4 TELE-LEARNING: PROBLEMS CONFRONTING THE CLASSROOM TEACHER

Unfortunately, the teacher trying to implement tele-learning in the classroom is typically confronted by many challenges and obstacles. Many of these are the same as the problems that have been long-recognized as barriers to any technological innovation into educational practice. Fullan, Miles, and Anderson, (1988) summarize these sorts of obstacles in the framework of theory relating to the diffusion of an innovation in educational practice. We look at this theory and its implications from the perspective of the educational decision maker in Chapter 7 and the educational technologist in Chapter 8. Here we will focus more directly on the problems the classroom teacher is likely to meet when trying to implement tele-learning in the classroom.

■ 5.4.1 FIRST- AND SECOND-LEVEL PROBLEMS

Based on a literature analysis as well as practical experience in a number of countries, we have identified "first-level problems" and "second-level problems" confronting tele-learning in the K-12 classroom (Collis and De Vries, 1991; Collis, 1992a,b). It is our observation that the first-level problems will be easier to solve than their second-level brothers. These two levels of problems are summarized in Box 5.14.

We made this categorization of problems in 1991 and some progress has been made since then, but the list still appears pertinent in 1996. This book is intended as a contribution to the second-level problems. Let's look more closely at a selection of the problems in Box 5.14 and relate them to the teachers' reality frame that we described in Section 5.2. How much will this frame constrain the possibilities of the tele-learning lesson activities that we just extolled in Section 5.3?

> **Box 5.14**
>
> **First- and second-level problems confronting tele-learning in the K-12 classroom**

First-level problems

- Unavailable or unusable equipment
- Unknown or too-costly or too-difficult network connections
- Inability of teachers and students to have access to network connections
- Inability of teachers to have adequate access to network connections for lesson preparation and personal exploration
- Not enough time within the curriculum or the school timetable for trying out tele-learning in lessons
- Not enough time for the teacher for exploration or for the development of new types of tele-learning lessons
- Limited technical familiarity of teachers with equipment and tools for tele-learning
- Too-high costs, in terms of time and money, to make use of tele-learning
- Not enough in-school support and technical help
- Limited awareness by teachers of educational possibilities

Second-level problems

- Teachers lack ideas with regard to how to bring tele-learning into a traditional classroom, even one where there is a computer or a television available
- Teachers are not convinced of the educational relevance of tele-learning
- Teachers lack experience and models for the management of tele-learning in the classroom
- Teachers lack pedagogical strategies for dealing with new forms of communication and information handling in their lessons
- Teacher training and support is not well organized with respect to tele-learning
- The software and electronic tools for computer-based tele-learning have not been designed for learning and classroom purposes

■ 5.4.2 SPECIFIC FIRST-LEVEL PROBLEMS

The simple summary of many tele-learning experiences in classrooms around the world is: Until the first-level problems are adequately managed for the classroom teacher, little or no sustained tele-learning occurs beyond what is done by highly motivated pioneers. Two of these major first-level problems are access and costs.

ACCESS TO FACILITIES FOR TELE-LEARNING

With regard to access, there is currently a powerful advantage for the broadcast video and (in some cases, two-way video) category of tele-learning compared to network-based categories. Schools are much more likely to have worked out a way to bring television into the classroom and to have a monitor for displaying television programming to students available in the classroom, than they are likely to have worked out ways for students and teachers to access network-based resources in the classroom.

This is particularly so for the Internet, in that very few classrooms at yet, in any country, have convenient access for both students and teachers in the regular classroom setting. The difficulties involved in trying to access an external network from one's classroom are insurmountable for most teachers; if network-type tele-learning is to occur, student experiences must often take place outside the regular classroom. Alternatively the teacher may have to conduct them through her own tele-learning access point (often via a home modem, at her personal expense) and then bring the results to the students, such as during lesson-presentation (see Section 5.3.2). For example, Cervantes (1993) in his case study of implementation issues facing teachers trying to bring tele-learning into their lessons, found that tele-learning projects where only the teacher used the tele-learning hardware were much better candidates for successful implementation than projects where students were expected to use the hardware. For many tele-learning projects, the "task of logging on, downloading messages, and printing them out can be perceived as a chore that must be performed in order to gain access to the network's prime resource: ideas" (p. 16), a chore that is time consuming and often logistically frustrating. Removing the need to have students involved in these chores when the chores are not an objective of the learning activity itself can greatly increase the range of tele-learning experiences available for the classroom.

Home access to tele-learning resources for the teacher has been found again and again to be important to the teacher's eventual use of those resources with his or her students (see for example, Gallo and Horton, 1994). Thus it is frequently recommended that such home access for teachers is desirable. In Chapter 7 we consider the implications of this recommendation for the school decision maker: Who pays for what?

COSTS

In some jurisdictions, teachers have free or highly subsidized access to the complex and expensive components of tele-learning. As we noted earlier, initiatives such as *Channel One* in the US have stimulated wiring of schools for television and video reception, but it is still much less common to find similar initiatives to subsidize classrooms for network access. (We discuss emerging trends in Chapter 7.) One of the main reasons for this is cost.

There is still serious concern among teachers, and with justification, about the costs of accessing network resources, particularly the Internet. In many countries, such as those in most European countries, such access is metered by the telephone company in ways prohibitively expensive to teachers. The problem is confounded by schools not knowing how to plan for network tele-learning expenses in their budgets; ironically the more successful a school's involvement in network tele-learning, the higher the costs. We discuss this problem more specifically in Chapter 7. For the classroom teacher, however, cost implications generally mean that on-line browsing is not possible, that on-line time must be carefully controlled and limited, and that lesson preparation is frequently a matter of personal expense for the teacher.

What evidence do we have for this conclusion? The most-frequent time for teachers to access the Internet or national educational networks appears to be evenings, late evenings, and thus at home (Honey and Henríquez, 1993, Collis, Van Holstein, Rikkerink and Woerts, 1994). Very few teachers seem to be the beneficiaries of fully subsidized costs for their tele-learning preparations done from home. These costs involve not only equipment—a modem, a computer—but also logistical issues such as sharing the family telephone line. And then the connect charges and the line charges come on top. We ask a great deal of dedication from the teacher who wishes to use tele-learning when we expect him or her to cover these financial aspects personally. In many situations, this is what is happening.

■ 5.4.3 SECOND-LEVEL PROBLEMS, EVEN MORE CHALLENGING

But sooner or later, schools are gradually getting organized for the technical and organizational aspects of tele-learning. This are first thresholds to cross for efficient tele-learning in the classroom, but an even-more challenging second level of challenges still will remain. We called these "second-level problems" in Box 5.14. The recommendations for successful CMC projects that were summarized in Box 5.10 are an example of what is needed to be done to respond to second-level problems. The problems are responsibility- and priority-related as well as personal, and are directly associated with the teacher.

RESPONSIBILITIES

Somekh (1989) points out that the coordination needed among teachers for successful cooperative tele-learning projects is not just a matter of good planning, "in effect being team teaching at a distance" (p. 245). It is also highly vulnerable to a range of other differences in the classes and teachers involved, such as the ways that each classroom tolerates "noise" or "exchanges grades for compliance". These are subtle understandings that develop between a teacher and his students, often much more pervasive than can be explained to a collaboration partner at a distance. What it means in practice is that collaborative activities involving other classrooms are always vulnerable:

> ...no teacher can put a responsibility to other students and another teacher in a remote classroom before the interests of those for whom s/he has a specific responsibility. It will never be worth risking violation to the fragile balance of the negotiated curriculum. (Somekh, 1990, p. 246)

PRIORITIES

The latter relates to the question of the teacher's priorities. As long as tele-learning activities are optional enrichments in the regular classroom, they are highly vulnerable to having a low level of priority in terms of the "real business" of the teacher. Particularly in the secondary school, this real business is often related to student performance on standardized tests reflecting a textbook- and fact-based curriculum. In many countries, "league tables" of school performance on standardized tests are published in the newspapers or made public in other ways. In contrast, most of the tele-learning activities described in this chapter are probably not the most efficient and effective ways for a teacher to cover "the material on the test" for which s/he is publicly accountable. The argument that profound and important new types of learning are going on via tele-learning possibilities needs to be translated into "improvement in test scores" before it is objectively defensible in many school jurisdictions.

IMAGINATION AND EXPECTATIONS

Another complex factor limiting the impact of tele-learning in schools is that much of its benefit must come through the imagination of the teacher, to see how a resource, such as for example, weather-service data from around the world, can be turned into a valuable learning activity. Ross (1995) provides a example with respect to weather-service data that shows how rich lessons can be generated from material in a general-purpose WWW site, but only with imagination on the part of the teacher. Hettinga, (1995), as another example, had to spend consider-able time and creative attention to develop lessons on the environment for her secondary-school students that made use of WWW resources. The many sources of lesson ideas we mentioned earlier in this section provide similar potential for translation, but unless someone else makes the detailed lessons for teachers in a way that relates closely to the local curriculum and situation, the teacher himself must make a last jump of imagination. How can this idea turn into something that can really happen in my classroom?

Given teachers' lack of personal experiences with tele-learning in their own training and backgrounds, this "jumping" process is heavily influenced by the imagination of the teacher, the flair that the teacher needs to create a new type of lesson. Some teachers have more creative flair than others.

Cervantes (1993) notes that experience helps:

...The pattern of involvement among the teachers [in this case study] leads me to conclude that network use widens for participants as they acquire more experience. There is an expertise that is acquired that includes not only technical skills, but an understanding of the network community and resources...[and] what types of projects are useful. The attempts made by [teachers in his cases] to initiate their own network activities indicate that it is a trial-and-error process, that often begins with limited success. (p. 16)

The willingness of teachers to be part of activities with "limited success" is very much related to the personality of the teacher but also, quite sensibly, to the teacher's perception of how s/he is rated in terms of competency by the school administration, parents, peers, and the students themselves. Is she rewarded for students showing gains on district-wide standardized tests and for managing a smoothly running, well organized classroom? Or is she rewarded for taking some risks, for innovation, particularly when this may requires extra technical support and costs? Although the two sets of rewards do not have to be mutually exclusive, in the current classroom reality frame for many teachers, they often are.

Thus, although there is much to gain with classroom tele-learning in K-12, there is also a cost and a risk. Helping to minimize these latter aspects is the goal of many of the special collaborative projects for tele-learning that occur throughout the world. Without special projects to lubricate a district's first experiences with new forms of tele-learning, a long time might have to elapse before any structural decisions within the district could be made to support tele-learning on any continuing basis. Another goal of these projects is to push the boundaries of classroom tele-learning, such as through new combinations of video technologies and broadband, highspeed networks as we discussed in Chapter 2. We look at a few of these special projects from the perspective of the teacher as a member of the project in the next section.

■ 5.5 THE TEACHER AS A MEMBER OF A SPECIAL COLLABORATIVE PROJECT

The discussion so far in this chapter has been focused on what the classroom teacher can do to introduce tele-learning activities into the classroom, based primarily on the teacher's own initiative and on-going opportunities. However, for many teachers the way they first encounter tele-learning is in the framework of participating in a special project. For some teachers, the special project is a way to experience the cutting-edge of tele-learning possibilities, such as combining the benefits of instructional use of digital compressed video with those of networking. In this section, we look at a sample of some special projects, circa 1995. Then we reflect on some major implications of participating in such projects for the classroom teacher.

■ 5.5.1 EXAMPLES OF SPECIAL PROJECTS FOR TELE-LEARNING

Although getting going with instructional use of e-mail may require a special-project framework for many teachers, the examples we mention in this section would be seen as innovative in most settings. In some cases, the project first organizes itself and then offers its benefits to a wide range of teachers who may wish to participate. In other cases, a small group of teachers may be much more closely involved in the conceptual design of the project and/or its first trials of its new technologies.

SPECIAL PROJECTS OFFERED TO A BROAD GROUP OF TEACHERS

For almost a decade, there have been special tele-learning projects organized by pioneers and visionaries with various degrees of formality and financial support. Teachers hear about the projects and some are able to find a way to participate. The European Schools Project (Sligte and Meijer, 1993); the "Computer Pals Around the World" initiative (Beazley, 1988); the FredMail service (now available through the Global SchoolNet Project, Andres, 1995a); and the AT&T Learning Circles (Riel, 1992) are among many examples. These sorts of initiatives have been and continue to be important to the growth of tele-learning in educational settings. They provide the initiative, expertise, enthusiasm and organization necessary for many teachers to get started with innovative teaching ideas. A few of the special projects evolve to the level of institutional practice and support, but most remain special projects, vulnerable to financing changes and volunteer participation on the part of teachers. We look at a few examples, the first of which is closest to reaching institutionalized status.

Kidscience TV: broadcast integrated with hands-on activities

An interesting example is Kidscience TV, sponsored by the Hawaii State Department of Education. This series is a live interactive distance learning science program for fifth-and sixth-grade students throughout the state of Hawaii (Barker, Bannon and Miller, 1994). Television broadcasts through a microwave communications network among the Hawaiian chain of islands send the programming to the different islands, where it is further distributed via local cable television public-access channels. Thus the programming can be viewed in homes on cable as well as in schools. However, a toll-free telephone for student call-in questioning during the broadcasts (this enabling "interactivity" in the broadcasting) is only available to schools which formally are participating in the project.

To participate, a school agrees to make a direct-access telephone line available to students to call in questions if they wish, to provide either a videotext terminal or computer and modem so that text messages can be exchanged, and a television set in the classroom. Teachers also agree to collect and organize the materials needed to carry out the science activities demonstrated on the television broadcasts (they do this during the time intervals between successive broadcasts) and to assist the students in carrying out the activities and in communicating with the central experts for the project.

Topics for the activities and the broadcasts are chosen to correspond to the science textbooks being used throughout the state. In addition, guest speakers participate in the broadcasts.

Approximately 50% of all the fifth- and sixth-grade students in Hawaii participated in these lessons in 1994. Teachers do not see them as a replacement for their own teaching, but as a well-organized form of supplement for the existing curriculum (Barker, Bannon and Miller, 1994). The teacher is not part of the project team, but is nonetheless critical to the success of the project in the classroom.

"Live from Jupiter" : (interactive) television and computer networks

This is an example of a project involving a consortium of partners who are presenting the opportunity to teachers to participate in some or all of the tele-learning activities the consortium offers with regard to the topic "Exploring Jupiter and the Stars" (Riel, 1995). In this case, the consortium is a partnership of contributors in the US, including NASA (National Association of School Administraters), NSF (National Science Foundation), government research agencies, public television stations, foundations, corporate sponsors, science educators and individual schools. Classes who participate can be involved via "television and telecomputing" in a wide range of activities relating to the Kuiper Airborne Observatory, a scientific project in which special telescopes are mounted on a jet that flies beyond the distortion caused by the earth's atmosphere and sends back digitized infrared data about Jupiter and the stars. The activities involved in this project include those in Box 5.15.

Box 5.15

Live from Jupiter (Riel, 1995)

Television broadcasts throughout the US by satellite, with arrangements for certain schools to be involved in interactive television sessions via satellite two-way links; other schools can watch the broadcasts without two-way interactivity

Provision of lesson materials, including extensive collections of visual materials, classroom project materials, and a database of associated information, via a professionally managed network organization

Opportunities for classes to communicate with each other about the project and to communicate with the members of the Kuiper Airborne Observatory team via e-mail, WWW chats and CU-SeeMe videoconferences

Access to an integrative WWW site, where all these different aspects of the project are coordinated: URL http://quest.arc.nasa.gov/interactive.html

Opportunities to be included on a regular electronic mailing list for the project, to receive updates on new activities; also the opportunity for teachers to join a discussion-oriented listserv about managing the project in their classrooms

---

The Wetlands Project: (interactive) television and networking

The partners in this US-based project include an educational advisory group, the Satellite Educational Resources Consortium (for the satellite uplink network), the University of Nebraska Educational Television Agency for broadcast programming, the Global SchoolNet organization for network-management expertise and resources for data sharing, and the Technical Education Research Center (TERC) in Boston for curriculum support and collaborative data-handling software. Twenty-six schools from 16 different US states participated (Collins and Pawloski, 1995).

The project offered participants the activities shown in Box 5.16.

Box 5.16

The Wetlands Project: (interactive) television, CMC and data-sharing activities via a network

Broadcast television via satellite uplink of programs illustrating wetlands issues via interviews and with demonstrations of how to gather data for the local field trips involved in the projects

Use of the satellite uplink to show local sites new information about the project, such as how to handle revisions in the software, and also to broadcast a teacher-training video made for the project

Some opportunity for two-way television interaction during a "national forum" that concluded the project

Use of fax for submission of students' journal samples and experts' comments

Sharing via a network of data collected during local field trips to wetlands in the regions of each participating school. Data were submitted by e-mail using a special template and could be requested for downloading by the participating schools. Students could also communicate with the project staff and other schools via e-mail.

SPECIAL PROJECTS INVOLVING A CLOSED GROUP OF PARTICIPANTS

In contrast to the above projects which were set up by a professional team and then offered to a wide range of teachers, another important type of tele-learning experience is the special project that involves a closely interacting closed group of participants, including some selected schools and teachers. This group typically works together for a specific length of time and is often focused on the exploration of the instructional potential of some innovative technology. Four examples follow.

ISDN desktop tutoring between school and university

Exeter University in the UK, in partnership with British Telecom, a regional teacher-support centre, and local schools, is involved in a series of projects exploring the potential of desktop multi-media communications between the University and the schools via ISDN network technology (N. Davis, 1995a)

In one of the explorations, students in their school setting interacted with a university-based expert in order to learn to use a complex software package for mathematical expression. The partners in this tele-tutoring session simultaneously shared the use of the same software package while talking to each other through their computer-based microphones. In another exploration, teachers received personal tutoring from a distant expert on the use of a new software package through the application-sharing capabilities of the desktop conferencing system. The expert can talk with the teacher as together they share the same software package. This kind of support for software familiarization is even better than could be provided in a traditional face-to-face inservice session between teachers and a specialist, and brought the added value that the teachers did not have to leave their school for the experience.

Educational telematics in Australia

In Australia, there is extensive use of audio-graphics technology for tele-learning (Oliver and Reeves, 1995). Australians call this educational telematics. It involves three forms of technology:

- Telephone, an audio-conferencing link using hands-free telephone systems, for interactive voice contact between teachers and students
- Fax, to enable instructional materials and student work to be transferred among teachers and students in real time
- Computer, networked and using special software that allows the computers to function as "interactive blackboards" that can be viewed and used by all

These three forms of technology respectively provide an audio link, a document link, and a visual link among the participating classes and teachers. Later in this chapter we look at some of the implications for the teacher working in this kind of environment. But here we mention just one of the special projects that have recently occurred in Australia using these technologies.

The Pilbara Project involved six secondary schools in remote areas in Western Australia where students wished to study Japanese. There was only one teacher available; she worked face-to-face with one class and at a distance with other classes. A support teacher was appointed at the remote schools to coordinate the technical aspects of the instruction and to liaison with the delivery teacher. Audial activities such as singing and role playing were used extensively. The project was judged to be a "total success by all stakeholders" (Oliver and Reeves, 1995, p. 51).

CoVis (multimedia network resources)

The third of these closed-group, special-project examples is CoVis Project (Learning Through Collaborative Visualization), a US initiative whose partners are the NSF, two universities in the midwestern US, the Exploratorium Science Center in San Francisco, and two secondary schools. CoVis heavily emphasizes its conceptual framework: authentic scientific inquiry through collaborative visualization.

The collaborative visualization is made possible through special software written by the project. This software is summarized in Box 5.17.

Box 5.17

Special software developed for the CoVis Project (O'Neill & Gomez, 1995)

The Collaboratory Notebook
URL http://www.covis.nwu.edu/Geosciences/index.html
...Educationally oriented groupware faciliating student journals for private note- taking, shared information for group projects, and support for public discussions.

Visualizer software
URL http://www.covis.nwu.edu/ CoVis_Visualization.html
...Software to support collaborative visualization of data relating to the greenhouse effect, climate and weather.

The CoVis Web Server
URL http://www.covis.nwu.edu
...Home page for the Project, this site is maintained with up-to-date project information; a biography of papers and presentations, learning materials and full information about the software tools produced for the project; links to other servers related to the project; and video clips from the project.

KIE Project

The "Knowledge Integration Environment" is a special project based at the University of California at Berkeley (Bell, Davis and Linn, 1995). Its purpose is to "combine network resources and software with sound pedagogical principles to improve science teaching...With the KIE, students use evidence from the Net and tools such as an electronic notebook and on-line discussion tools to make collaborative decisions" (p. 14). The software used in the project includes a regularly available WWW browser, HTML editor, and e-mail package, and also special software developed for the project:

- KIE Tool Palette, an interface for navigation of all other components
- Netbook, groupware for students to organize, analyze, and author "evidence" from the Internet
- Networked Evidence Databases, organized collections of scientific evidence both from the Internet and created by students

- SpeakEasy, a multi-media real-time discussion tool
- Student Knowledge Integration Planner and Profiler, a tool for the teacher to organize and design Internet-oriented activities
- Knowledge Integration Coach, an on-line guidance system to support and prompt the students

We discuss this kind of special project, involving the development of new software, in more detail in Chapter 8, from the perspective of the educational technologists involved in the software design and development. For further information about KIE, see:

KIE
URL http://www.clp.berkeley.edu/KIE.html

HOW CAN THE TEACHER GET INVOLVED IN SPECIAL PROJECTS?

This is only a taste of hundreds of special collaborative projects involving innovative applications of tele-learning into schools. Perhaps the first reaction of the teacher is to ask: " How can I get involved in such innovative projects? Or even in smaller-scale projects?" Fortunately, there are also projects to help the teacher make connections with special projects. Some examples are noted in Box 5.18.

Box 5.18

Helping teachers to get involved in special projects

Intercultural E-Mail Classroom Connections
URL: http://www.stolaf.edu/network/iecc/
...Mailing lists where teachers may announce or request help with specific classroom projects. In June 1995 there were 2,545 teachers subscribed to these lists, from 36 different countries including Egypt, India, Argentina, Saudi Arabia and South Africa. The majority of teachers are from the US, Australia, and Canada.

Center for Networked Information Discovery and Retrieval: K-12 Opportunities and Resources
URL http://k12.cnidr.org/k-12_lists/lists.html
...Large collection of projects as well as lesson resources.

Internet Projects Registry Archive Services
URL http://gsn.org/gsn/projects.registry.html
...A clearinghouse for project information, a central location to find and plan for on-line projects ahead of time. A standard format is used for all project descriptions, including month and year the project will begin, how long the project will last, and e-mail address of the contact person.

So, there are many projects, and many ways to get involved in special collaborative projects. What can the teacher expect if the chance occurs to participate in such a project? Will this be a gateway to making tele-learning a regular state of affairs for the teachers involved?

■ 5.5.2 BENEFITS OF SPECIAL PROJECTS

The experience of being part of a special project in contrast to the on-going use of available tele-learning resources typically includes the following benefits:

The special project involves a collection of partners that are not usually part of the teacher's day. This collection may involve a television provider, a telecommunications network provider, an industrial partner, university researchers and other contributors such as technical personnel, and other partners in the district or region with whom the teacher may not normally have contact. Thus part of the learning experience (and time involvement) of a special project is the development and maintenance of the project team itself.

The special project brings resources, both technical and human, to the classroom that are not available ordinarily to the teacher.

The special project often provides the teacher with some released time to try out new things, with the special resources mentioned above at his or her disposal.

The special project can be professionally stimulating, motivating some teachers to return to university for graduate study or to take the initiative to sustain some aspect of the project activity in the school after the project and its temporary resources are gone.

■ 5.5.3 DISADVANTAGES OF SPECIAL PROJECTS

But special projects have their costs as well as benefits for the teacher.

Projects take time and can disrupt regular teaching. The teacher must give time to project meetings, not all of which are directly relevant to the classroom. The teacher will probably have to fit into the planning and framework of the project with regard to the timing and types of tele-learning activity that will occur; this will often not be a natural fit with the on-going reality of the classroom. The teacher and students must contribute to data-collection procedures and disruptions to their classroom routine because of visits from the project team for various reasons, including someone in the team bringing visitors around. The teacher and class may have to tolerate disruption and frustration when new technologies do not work and a lesson cannot go forward as planned.

The Project may never really become cohesive or productive. Despite their good intentions, the different members of the collaborative teams may never really find a common ground of communication, and teachers may never really come to have much interest in the sorts of research perspectives focused upon by the university personnel (and written about in their scientific reports). Also teachers can come to resent the feeling that they are "being used as guinea pigs" for what they sometimes perceive as the promotional interests of some of the sponsoring partners. In most projects, a long time elapses between the initial "opening of the project", and the time when anything really involving classroom use of the innovation actually begins. The project may open with a "media event", involving a certain amount of publicity, visits by corporate vice-presidents, etc., and widely publicized broadscale intentions of the project (sometimes using incautious words such as "revolutionize..."). In contrast, because of technical problems and a myriad of other unforeseen events, the classroom use of the innovation may be slow in starting or, even worse, never really happen. Perhaps only a portion of some of the expected activities actually get tried out, and then in a very artificial manner relative to actual classroom learning.

Leadership may be lacking, or goals mixed and unclear. Sometimes disappointments happen in tele-learning projects because the projects are formed without a clear leadership structure (the leader may be more of a figurehead, bringing in support for the project prior to its start but not interested in the day-to-day management of the project), or with each of the participants wanting its own group represented in the leadership of the project. There is often no sharp consideration of goals. Doing the project for the "experience" and the presumed benefits of "being part of the future" or some similarly lofty goal is agreed upon by all, but after that the different agendas of the various partners are often not in harmony. The teacher's agenda—to enrich her class without disrupting it—is often the least realized. In many projects teachers understand the reasons for the delays and problems and still appreciate the learning opportunities that do arise (Collis and Carleer, 1993).

The projects mentioned in Section 5.5.1 are not examples of any of these problems, but many other projects could have been mentioned that are.

Thus, patience, realistic expectations, good communication with the project management, and a shrewd sense of how to get benefits for one's class out of the experience are recommendations to the teacher involved in an innovative tele-learning project. Despite the problems, special projects are generally encouraged by schools, as learning experiences, and as ways to get resources and experience that would not otherwise occur.

A main aspect of these special projects, and most of the tele-learning activities that we have discussed so far in this chapter, is that they are voluntary for the individual teacher, and likely to be chosen as an enrichment activity to supplement normal classroom teaching. In the final section of this chapter, we turn our focus to one other way that some teachers encounter tele-learning—as teachers to students at a distance when the decision has been made by their school or district or region that such a teaching-delivery variant will be implemented. In contrast to the individual and voluntary aspects of "classroom-enrichment tele-learning", teachers do not get involved in lesson delivery to students at remote locations without many other persons being involved in the process.

■ 5.6 TELE-TEACHING: TEACHING STUDENTS NOT IN THE SAME FACE-TO-FACE LOCATION

So far, we have considered the classroom teacher to be operating in his or her familiar setting: the classroom, with a class of students in face-to-face contact as the tele-learning activities occur. But there is a very different aspect of tele-learning that confronts a number of teachers: having to teach a class of students who are not in the same room or location. We will call this, for convenience, "tele-teaching", as in some countries this term is often used for this kind of delivery. (In some cases, however, this term tele-teaching is more broadly used to describe what the teacher does when s/he is teaching with tele-learning resources in the regular classroom. In other cases, particularly in the US, what we are here calling tele-teaching is what others call distance education or distance learning. Our use of the term "tele-learning" in this book includes all these variations.)

Unlike tele-learning in the regular classroom, where the teacher's motivations are generally to enrich existing practice, tele-teaching as we are discussing it in this section is more likely to be externally motivated. The educational decision makers in a region decide that compensation is needed for specialist courses of different sorts which cannot be offered in a region due to lack of resources, and/or because of changes and shifts in school-age demographics (We discuss this from the decision makers' perspective in Chapter 7; see also Kitchen and Hughes, 1992). Populations are increasing or decreasing, in either case bringing the consequence that existing schools and teaching staffs are unable to offer a full range of instruction. Rural areas have the greatest difficulties offering a range of educational offerings to their small numbers of students, and have the greatest difficulty recruiting or paying for specialist teachers in specialist areas. The National Association of School Administrators in the US estimates that "tele-teaching" will be needed to fill up a void of up to one million educators by the year 2000 because of these conditions in the US alone.

To respond to this challenge, small school districts and other forms of organizational consortia are working together to offer tele-teaching, primarily as compensation for lack of specialist teachers for secondary-school instruction in remote areas. This phenomena is certainly not only happening in the US; it is well established in Australia (Oliver and Reeves, 1994); in the Nordic countries, and in many other countries, including new initiatives in Brazil. The technology combinations involved in these implementations differ, as do the funding approaches and management strategies, but for the teacher involved, new skills and didactics are involved.

■ 5.6.1 TELE-TEACHING TECHNOLOGIES, FROM THE TEACHER'S PERSPECTIVE

The first skill the tele-teaching teacher must deal with is how to handle the particular technology that is used in his or her situation.

WHAT EQUIPMENT DO I HAVE TO HANDLE?

Tele-teaching most typically occurs using broadcast or interactive video technologies. The broadcast technologies are often analog television but may also be radio. They may also involve combinations of broadcasting and networking. Sometimes the teacher's technical facilities are the same as those in the remote sites but other times the teacher is in charge of a more complex technical configuration. Sometimes, the teacher works simultaneously with a face-to-face class and one or more distant classes. She sees the distant classes through a television monitor, as they see her.

Sachs (1995b) describes a typical room-sized compressed video system for tele-teaching as requiring:

- Electrical connections for all cameras and monitors
- At least two or three cameras, one aimed at the teacher, one aimed at documents, one aimed at a face-to-face class if it is present
- One or more television monitors, at least one to show each remote site. If face-to-face students are present, they and the teacher will need separate monitors
- One or more microphones for the teacher and the face-to-face class
- A switching panel, remote control or computer keyboard for selecting cameras and operating special effects

- A codec to process the video and audio signals for transmission
- A telephone to call remote sites or to call for technical assistance
- Connections to the transmission channel
- Optional additional equipment, such as a VCR, an audio mixer, a computer and printer, a graphics tablet, a fax, a separate speaker system, and others
- Special seating arrangements in the room to accommodate the equipment

Sometimes compressed video facilities are designed to be portable or "roll-about", housed in special wheeled cabinets. However, the system must still be connected to phone lines, transmission lines, and electricity, as well as to video cameras, microphones and monitors. Audio readjustments may have to be done if a system is used in different physical environments. Thus the apparent benefits of a more-flexible roll-about unit may well be outweighed by the difficulties of relocation.

There are many variations in the technologies used in tele-teaching. For example, audio-graphics technologies may be used instead of compressed video for tele-teaching (see the Australian example in Section 5.5.1). In audio-graphics, teacher and students communication orally via an audio conference set-up, while at the same time, through a different network connection, can see the same displays on their computer screens. A few examples are beginning to occur of computer networks need for school-level tele-teaching (see Chapter 7).

Clearly all this technology is a challenge for the teacher: How can she concentrate on teaching, when she first has to handle and adjust to this highly unnatural equipment?

CLASSROOM CONTROL SYSTEMS

One approach is to invest in still more technology: particularly in tools to help the teacher control the cameras and microphones. One way to control the camera involved in tele-teaching is for the teacher to do it all himself; usually meaning he stays stationery in front of one camera and occasionally uses a fixed-position document camera. At the other end of the spectrum a technical person may be present with full camera-control options, comparable to professional television production. Many different technologies are becoming available to give the teacher better control options without the need for a physically present technical specialist. These include:

- Automatic tracking equipment relating the teacher's camera to some sort of sensor worn by the teacher; as the teacher moves, the camera follows him or her

- Commands allowing the teacher to pre-program various zoom locations so that he has only to select a number from his hand-held remote control device during the actual broadcast
- Wireless audio for the teacher so he is not encumbered by microphone wires
- Student-camera positions automatically called up when students indicate they wish to speak (usually via pressing a button)
- Options for the instructor to override student-control features (Sachs, 1995a)

New skills and a need for training

Thus it is clear that handling tele-teaching technologies involves the tele-teacher mastering a major set of new skills. Only a few get formal training, other than on-the-spot tips, when they start tele-teaching. Some initiatives are in place in various jurisdictions to provide formal teacher training for tele-teaching. As an example, the US Department of Defense Satellite Education Network, which has been in operation since 1985, offers an 80-hour course through various media, to train teachers who are to be themselves teaching using the one-way video, two-way audio technology provided by the Network. Occasional courses are also available through some faculties of education or other support agencies (see Chapters 7 and 9, and also Hakes, Cochenour, Rezabek and Sachs, 1995, for profiles of such courses).

Given this arsenal of equipment and the skills to handle it technically, what might the teacher actually be doing from an educational perspective when she is tele-teaching? We give a variety of examples in the next section.

■ 5.6.2 SOME EXAMPLES OF TELE-TEACHING FOR SECONDARY EDUCATION

There are many examples of different organizational and technological configurations that may be involved when the classroom teacher begins to teach distant groups of students as well as, or instead of, his or her face-to-face class. The examples that will be discussed subsequently in this section are summarized in Table 5.1

BROADCAST EXAMPLES

Broadcast video delivery may be by satellite or by cable systems or a combination. A national survey in the US recently studied 130 rural K-12 schools in 32 of the US states (Barker & Hall, 1993). Each of these schools comprised an entire school

Table 5.1 Tele-teaching scenarios for teaching at a distance in secondary education

Tele-teaching scenario	Example
One-way broadcast (via satellite)	The Star Schools Project (US; Jordahl, 1991)
One-way broadcast, with return audio or fax for immediate questioning	Canadian examples, including radio tele-teaching (McGreal, 1993)
Two-way audio with real-time computer exchanges (audiographics; in Australia, "telematics education")	Australian examples, (Gray and O'Grady, 1993; Oliver and Reeves, 1995)
Two-way compressed digitized video	PATH Project (US; Chavkin, Kennedy and Carter, 1994); Other US examples (Hakes, Cochenour, Rezebek and Sachs, 1995)

district and enrolled 300 students or less. Half of these schools received tele-teaching courses via broadcast video, with secondary students the predominant target audience. Greatest programming needs were indicated to be in the areas of foreign-language instruction, mathematics and science.

Many particular consortia can be identified that provide the infrastructure for such broadcast tele-teaching, (in the US, see Jordahl, 1991; and Kitchen & Hughes, 1992, for inventories). One particular national project in the US was both extensive and well-known: The Star Schools Project. Beginning in 1988 consortia were funded to develop programming for tele-teaching to be delivered to isolated, small, and disadvantaged schools in the US. This initiative, called the Star School Project, has since grown so that courses have been delivered to nearly 3,000 schools as of 1991 (Jordahl, 1991).

There are interesting examples from many countries, not only the US. Canadian examples are particularly diverse, including some which involve radio tele-teaching.

One of these radio tele-teaching projects has been carried out under the direction of the Chiefs of 23 First Nations in northwestern Ontario. This project reaches over 200,000 sq. km of bush and semi-tundra to extend tele-teaching to the small, isolated First Nation communities that are not connected to any road system, and mostly only have one telephone line. Tele-teachers broadcast radio lessons from a central location, and students listen to the broadcasts on their personal radios and then organize their questions so that they can be consolidated efficiently on a central technical device, by which only one telephone line is needed to send the questions back to the distant teacher. The teacher listens to the transmitted questions, and answers via the radio. This is all possible through the support of a Native-owned radio station which has placed small transmitters in each community. Each of these small communities, if it has a school or not, has a learning centre where there is a small library, study desks, a radio and the transmission device to send back questions, a fax machine, a photocopier, and a VCR unit with TV.

AUDIO-GRAPHICS EXAMPLES

Radio or audio-graphics tele-teaching requires different skills on the part of the teacher than does video-broadcast tele-teaching, in that the teacher can no longer be seen, or see the students. Thus, the use of the audio aspect of communication, as in the Canadian Native radio example, becomes much more important. But unlike the Canadian radio example, audio-graphics tele-teaching does give everyone a common visual to look at: whatever appears on the computer screens (or, in some cases, on the whiteboard unit, but this rarely is available to K-12 situations). What then becomes critical in audio-graphic tele-teaching is learning how to prepare materials for display via the audio-graphics software needed to coordinate the distributed computers (Gray and O'Grady, 1993).

Although the teacher in a video-based tele-teaching situation should also make careful use of well-prepared graphics for the document camera, much of his delivery can still be animated through "seeing him in action". (While this may not be ideal, it is also the predominant mode of traditional face-to-face lesson delivery in the classroom, with small gestures toward visualization through occasional use of a chalkboard, or of an overhead projector). The teacher working in an audio-graphics situation, however, must learn:

- To handle the software involved
- To give considerable time to preparing and organizing the slides to be used in the lesson
- To send these slides ahead of time to the receive site so that they can be downloaded and available in the remote site's local computer for immediate access during the tele-lesson

- To coordinate her speaking with her handling of the slides, including how to display slides out of their original order when students ask questions
- To avoid the tendency to fill an entire teaching period with teacher talk and questioning, and instead to give more time to independent student activities
- To manage a procedure for students to indicate they have a question and for transfer of the cursor control while using the software
- To involve the supervising teacher at the remote site as a partner with the delivery teacher
- To plan carefully for the support materials that students will be using alongside the audio-graphic equipment, such as charts and pictures around the computer (Gray and O'Grady, 1993; Oliver and Reeves, 1995; Stacy, 1995).

All of these are complex activities. A whole new pedagogical repertoire of skills and competencies needs to be developed. In Australia, hundreds of schools and teachers are involved in these "bi-directional lessons involving voice and computer screen" (Nicholson, 1993). Oliver and Reeves (1995), after working closely with many teachers, found that teachers not only needed strong technical and communication skills, but also tended to overemphasize teacher–student interactivity and underemphasize independent student activity. Perhaps this is a natural reaction to not being present with a remote class—to feel that one has to compensate by talking to them all the time and continually urging them to answer back. But good pedagogy also requires a mix of instructional methods, including students working individually or in small groups with only occasional teacher intervention (see Chapter 6). How to bring a mix of instructional strategies into tele-teaching remains a pedagogical issue. Considerable time and practice are needed to handle the technologies even before the pedagogical focus can begin.

EXAMPLES WITH TWO-WAY VIDEO
There are many examples of tele-teaching with two-way interactive video. Falten (1994) lists "hot" examples, and Hakes and her colleagues (1995) give seven user profiles, each involving school consortia. As one example, the PATH Project (Chavkin, Kennedy and Carter, 1994) shows how a fiber-optics network is being used not only for the delivery of interactive tele-teaching but also for instructional interaction among teachers and specialists.

PATH Project
The PATH Project in Mathematics (Partnership for Access To Higher Mathematics) is a project carried out by a consortium of partners—a university, a school

district, a telephone company, and the local community—to improve the mathematical skills of "underserved" students in five secondary schools. Each of these schools is linked by fiber optics to the other project-partner sites and all sites are fully equipped for two-way video interactivity, including separate document cameras (Chavkin, Kennedy and Carter, 1994). Although the project is primarily aimed at the development of new curriculum and methods for this target group, the students are involved in all the testing of the materials and methods. Positive results are reported, particularly for the students who would not otherwise have been participating in higher-mathematics courses.

■ 5.6.3 ISSUES FOR TELE-TEACHING

The two major issues that dominate tele-teaching pedagogy, after skill development for handling the technical environment, appear to be facilitating effective interaction and communication, and winning student and community acceptance for the validity of the courses taught by a distant teacher (Rezabek, Cochenour, Bruce and Shade, 1995). The first of these is directly the teacher's problem, while the second is more of a strategic issue involving many players including the teacher. (We discuss the latter in Chapter 7.)

INTERACTION: HOW MUCH IS BEST?

How much interaction is important when students are at a distance from their teacher and watching her through a television screen or listening to her through an audio receiver? How often should the tele-teaching teacher call on distant students for a response? How can s/he try to stimulate them to ask questions and contribute to discussions? These are questions that are keenly studied by distance-education professionals serving adults (see Chapter 8) and are equally pertinent for tele-teaching for K-12 students.

THE EVIDENCE?

A general belief among tele-teaching participants, particularly in the US, is that real-time interactivity is critical. However, the evidence for this is mixed. Often students do not offer any questions, just as they do not offer questions in the face-to-face class. There is even some research to imply that actual interactivity is not as important as knowing that there is an opportunity for interactivity (Van Haalen and Miller, 1994). If students know they can ask a question if they wish and that this hypothetical question would get a good and quick response, they are often satisfied.

Even more, it may be better for students to be content that they could ask questions if necessary but to resist asking them too often. Van Haalen and Miller found an "inverted U relationship" between the amount of questioning by distant secondary students and their success in various tele-taught courses. Students who never used the telephone to call in a question, and students who used it a great deal relative to the class norm were equally likely to be less successful in the tele-courses compared to students who used the call-in facilities in a limited way. The more succesful students only called in when they really had a question and needed teacher help. "Moderation in student telephone interaction appeared to coincide more directly with student success....Instructors cannot assume that a high level of student audio interactivity indicates a high level of student performance gain" (p. 4).

VALIDITY

A major issue in tele-teaching is the acceptance by those involved that this is "real teaching", with as good results as in face-to-face instruction. A special aspect of this is how to handle student management and testing, if the teacher cannot be present with "eyes in the back of her head". Many different sorts of strategies are suggested for these credibility issues, such as putting the tele-teaching receive classroom in a glassed-in area so that someone in the local setting can "keep an eye on" the students and monitor them when they take a test. However, the general consensus seems to be that, if handled well (again a responsibility for the teacher!!) students and their school communities are satisfied with tele-teaching as a legitimate form of learning (Fyock and Sutphin, 1995).

And as a final aspect of tele-teaching, Rezabek and her colleagues (1995) offer one additional observation to the participating teacher: "Prepare to be tired".

...Many instructors report that distance teaching not only requires additional preparation and planning, but is physically and mentally more demanding than teaching in a face-to-face setting. (p. 140)

■ 5.7 CONCLUSIONS: BACK TO THE TEACHER

The main point to be made in this long chapter is, after all, a familiar one: the teacher is central, the key, in whatever happens in K-12 classrooms, with tele-learning as well as everything else. The teacher may be using new ways to get lesson ideas and inspiration, may be trying out new activities in his or her regular classroom setting, may be experiencing new partnership possibilities as a member of special tele-learning project teams, or may be performing him or herself as a teacher-at-a-distance, in all of these ways encountering tele-learning. But nevertheless, no matter how sophisticated the technology, the teacher remains the critical filter through which tele-learning opportunities are realized in K-12 classrooms. The major tasks of the classroom teacher:

- To stimulate motivation
- To nurture a productive learning climate
- To respond to cues from student reactions and adapt lessons accordingly
- To effectively use supporting media
- To effectively handle learner questioning
- To make available appropriate learning materials to students
- To consolidate learning

remain his or her major tasks, especially when teaching at a distance through tele-learning technologies. All of these teacher tasks can be augmented and enriched through tele-learning. But it probably won't be easy.

GETTING ON: WHERE IS THE ON-RAMP?

You have read about the Internet and you are convinced: you want to get on. Perhaps you are a teacher, and would like to have home access for practice and familiarisation, and you also would like to have access in your classroom. How do you proceed? A few of you will be fortunate: your school or school district or region will have arranged it for you, at least the school connection. You will probably not have a connection in your classroom even if the school itself does have a connection. Others of you might have to try to convince your school administrator to subscribe to some sort of service. And others of you must deal with it yourselves, particularly with respect to home access.

What are examples of these alternatives for the teacher?

SYSTEMWIDE SYSTEM FOR SCHOOLS

The state of Florida in the US provides an example of a region offering two sorts of network services to schools, one apparently older, one being being phased in via a special project.

FIRN is the Florida Information Resource Network, a **wide-area network** created by the combined efforts of the Florida educational community and the Florida Legislature to link all levels of the public education system. FIRN allows dial-in log in to a central computer. Access can also be provided to schools via a host site at a university or some other organisation. FIRN provides access to a statewide e-mail system, limited access to services on the Internet, and a BBS for both teachers and students. Teachers can receive lesson-materials from CNN Newsroom, the Discovery Channel, and others, as well as information about educational television for distance learning available in the state. Some local databases are also available for teachers to access.

Parallel to this, the Florida Department of Education has announced purchase of seven Internet servers as part of its "Schoolyear 2000 Project". These servers handle full Internet server functions and will be installed in Sun workstations in each of seven county locations, serving 35 schools. The organisation providing the servers will also provide training for the county staff, staff from FIRN, and others associated with the Project. The servers have special user software to help staff to customise and administer the servers without having to learn the underlying UNIX operating systems on the servers.

CAMPUSWORLD, A UK EXAMPLE

A broad-scale version of service offer to schools in occurring in the UK, called *CampusWorld*. British Telecom has for many years offered an on-line service to

UK schools and teachers, something like FIRN but with many more organised lesson ideas and activities. This service ran as a closed, dial in service. Now (1995) the service is revising itself to update its technology and offer Internet access.

Based on its long experience, the CampusWorld staff know that teachers wish Internet access, but also want to control and restrict it in terms of their students. In addition, teachers want well-structured lesson activities, relating to their own curriculums and schools. Finally, teachers also want access to the *French Minitel* system, as a valuable resource for teaching French.

Thus CampusWorld is offering a variety of subscription plans: to its "Walled Garden" area for information carefully checked for its suitability for schools, "or to venture out by special password onto the full Internet". Subscriptions can be to single users or to LANs, and can be to the "Walled Garden" only, or to the Walled Garden and full Internet access. Schools or individuals must supply their own computers, modems or ISDN connections. A starter pack of access software must be purchased. Charges are at a fixed rate, monthly, regardless of how much or little use is made. There are no additional charges for storage or volume. A helpline is available and support personnel give both technical help and curriculum advice. Special projects will be regularly launched, training can be arranged, and the staff will work closely with schools and staff. Current tele-learning projects include:

- Worldwide survey of TV viewing habits; analyse data using spreadsheets

- Computer conference for senior students on 20th-century history and the United Nations. Guidance from university staff.
- Cinema 200, a collaborative project between France and the UK, where schools pair up to research and then plan a short film.
- Poetry On-Line, in which samples of poems are sent to primary students via e-mail and children are encouraged to try their own versions. These are subsequently sent to other schools for reading. Final products are printed and distributed.
- Special projects for younger children "Ask the Police", "Living in Space", "Masquerade", "Newspaper Day", and "Science Net".

INTERNET SERVICE PROVIDER

The CampusWorld example shows the power that can come when a professional organisation with good educational experience and support offers an on-line service to teachers and schools. But many teachers will have to make their own connection to the Internet if they wish to make use of tele-learning. During 1995 **"Internet service providers"** proliferated in communities throughout the world, offering individuals access to the Internet, for a fee.

Service providers generally compete with one another, so their services are client oriented. They can differentiate themselves according to:

- Connection speed and number of access points and if direct TCP/IP connections are available
- Software provided for the user interface

- Rates and methods of charging (time, tick, fixed price)
- The Internet search tools and Web services offered, including serving as a host server for WWW pages
- The quality of human technical support offered.

But once on, the subscriber is on her own in terms of teaching support. She must find where she wants to go on the Internet and make her own contacts for lesson ideas and communication.

COMMERCIAL ON-LINE SERVICES

In some countries, commercial on-line services are competing vigorously with each other for customers, including teachers and tele-learners of all kinds. This is particularly so in the US, where a number of these services already have long histories. There were estimated to be 11.8 million people with subscriptions to major US on-line services in October 1995.

Like the Internet service providers, the commercial services compete heavily on cost, service, and access variations. They also compete on the range and quality of the information and communication services they offer in their own enclosed areas. As with the "Walled Garden" example from the UK, the commercial services promise safe and filtered information for families and students. Internet access is often filtered as well.

Various well-published legal problems relating to what certain subscribers said or did while using a commercial service have heightened awareness of issues relating to libel, copyright infringement, and moral problems.

Offering Internet access has become part of the packet for all the commercial on-line service providers. How do they differentiate themselves? Besides the points listed for Internet service providers, are:

- Innovative guided tours
- Monitored discussions
- Internet access integrated via icons in the user interface
- Special user interfaces for both the closed area and the Internet browser
- Interactive guided tours
- Real-time chat
- Access to thousands of newsgroups including downloading of newsgroup text for off-line reading.

DECISIONS...

In regions or countries with competitive network service providers, or in countries with a highly professional educational service offered at a competitive price to schools, the teacher has good alternatives to choose from in terms of making connections for tele-learning. However, commercial services are not free (except perhaps for some promotional episodes), and decision making must occur as to the cost of services vs the quality of support.

6 Tele-learning and the post-secondary instructor

Teaching courses for adults—this is the profession of many persons. Sometimes these post-secondary instructors work in educational institutions, such as universities and higher vocational colleges. Sometimes they work in training centers or workplace-based groups supporting professional education in corporations. Sometimes they teach courses to relatively young adults with unclear views of what they want as a career; at other times they work with persons who are fully established in a career setting and who know very clearly why they want some additional, targeted training. In this chapter we look at some of the possibilities and implications of tele-learning from the perspective of the post-secondary instructor of courses, in this range of settings. Our major focuses are post-secondary instructors in universities and colleges who work with traditional face-to-face groups, and post-secondary instructors whose students are not generally in the same place as the instructor—the traditional distance education or tele-course model. Our thesis is that tele-learning has considerable potential for both sets of post-secondary instructors.

▓ **6.1 Being a post-secondary instructor**

▓ **6.2 Adding tele-learning to face-to-face courses**

▓ **6.3 Tele-teaching: issues from the perspective of the post-secondary instructor**

▓ **6.4 Problems for the post-secondary instructor teaching students at a distance**

▓ **6.5 Convergences: the post-secondary instructor and tele-learning in new combinations**

▓ **6.6 Tele-learning: shifts for the post-secondary instructor**

Objectives

After this chapter you should be able to:

- Consider differences and similarities in the roles of the instructor who works with adults in face-to-face course settings, and the instructor who works with adults taking courses at a distance

- Identify six general ways that the post-secondary instructor working face-to-face with students can incorporate tele-learning in his or her course delivery

- Contrast tele-learning used to alter the balance of instructional components in a course with tele-learning used to enrich a particular component; relate each of these to "pedagogical re-engineering"

- Identify major problems confronting the instructor of post-secondary face-to-face courses wishing to expand or enrich his or her teaching with tele-learning

- Cite major reasons for adults to take courses at a distance instead of face-to-face

- Identify and give examples of common technology combinations used to support the delivery of courses to adults at a distance

- Indicate key issues involved in organizing post-secondary tele-learning courses

- Examine ways the instructor can increase communication, interactivity and collaboration in post-secondary tele-learning courses

- Identify challenges facing the instructor adapting courses and his face-to-face teaching style to teaching at a distance

- Be aware of new combinations of face-to-face and at-a-distance tele-teaching for the post-secondary instructor

■ 6.1 BEING A POST-SECONDARY INSTRUCTOR

We begin this chapter by setting the scene: Who are post-secondary instructors? What are their characteristics? How do they normally design the courses that they teach? What are the major implications of tele-learning for this large group of instructors?

■ 6.1.1 WHAT DISTINGUISHES POST-SECONDARY INSTRUCTORS FROM K-12 TEACHERS?

Post-secondary instructors can be distinguished from teachers in the K-12 sector in three major ways: the characteristics of their students, the backgrounds of the instructors themselves, and the relative role of teaching in their overall work situation.

CHARACTERISTICS OF THEIR STUDENTS

No matter the setting, training center or university, vocational school or workplace, post-secondary instructors share some basic similarities in their work. A first, critical point is that they work with adults, not children. Adults, more so than students in K-12 education, tend to be goal-oriented, are critical if courses do not meet their requirements, can often make their own selection as to which institution they attend and what courses they take, are more self-reliant, and expect more control in decision making about their work and study requirements.

BACKGROUNDS OF THE INSTRUCTORS

Just as there are differences between their students, there are also some critical differences between the post-secondary instructor and the teacher in K-12. One major difference is background: most post-secondary instructors have never had any pedagogical training. They are instructors without ever having studied any theory about how to instruct. They are content specialists, or researchers, or both, who have come to be teaching courses as part of their professional work. They have probably worked in their profession in some way before they became an instructor. They probably did not start their careers planning to be instructors, and many of them do not see being an instructor as the major part of their professional identity.

RELATIVE IMPORTANCE OF BEING AN INSTRUCTOR

The last sentence reveals the second major difference between post-secondary instructors and teachers in K-12: post-secondary instructors usually do many other things in their work that define their professional identity besides being instructors. They may be researchers and supervisors of specialist students and responsible for the organization or management of projects and day-to-day work units. They may be authors and members of commissions and curriculum-development teams. They are involved in committee work and grant applications and paper preparation and other responsibilities to both their work organizations and their professions. They are also expected to be involved in the sort of life-long learning we discussed in Chapter 4; continually expanding or upgrading themselves as well as teaching others.

Thus, the post-secondary instructor is typically rewarded not so much for his work as an instructor but more for other sorts of output, such as research papers or grant-winning or institutional administration. All these factors affect the time and attention the post-secondary instructor will give to teaching innovation, and thus affect the perspective of the post-secondary instructor with respect to integrating tele-learning possibilities into instruction. Making teaching more efficient and meeting student needs more effectively are more likely to be direct motivations for voluntary changes in one's instructional practice in post-secondary education than were the motivations that we saw for K-12 teachers in Chapter 5.

OTHER POINTS OF DIFFERENCE BETWEEN K-12 TEACHERS AND POST-SECONDARY INSTRUCTORS

Thus the teaching practice of post-secondary instructors is different from that of K-12 teachers in a number of fundamental ways, all of which will relate to the implications of tele-learning that we will focus upon in this chapter. Sometimes these differences make teaching more difficult for the post-secondary instructor than her K-12 counterpart, while in other cases the post-secondary instructor has some definite advantages.

Aspects of teaching that can be more difficult for the post-secondary instructor

Because adults take courses as conscious decisions, and often are paying for the opportunity, the post-secondary instructor is potentially more vulnerable to the wishes of his students and sensitive to their criticisms than the K-12 teacher needs to be. The post-secondary instructor must deal with clients who can and will express themselves and their dissatisfaction in a way that K-12 students cannot (although in some cases their parents may do it for them). And conversely, the post-secondary instructor is much less likely to get overt signs of appreciation and positive affective reaction from his students than the K-12 teacher, sometimes not even getting to know his or her students beyond brief and formal encounters. Thus the task of teaching, being less personal, can also be less personally rewarding.

Aspects of teaching that can be less difficult for the post-secondary instructor

Conversely, the post-secondary instructor generally has more flexibility and self-determination in his own day-to-day working patterns than does the K-12 teacher, with relatively fewer student-contact hours and more opportunity for making his own decisions about content and instructional organization of courses.

Finally, and very important to the development of tele-learning strategies for his teaching, the post-secondary instructor probably has his own office and desk and computer, and can set his own times for using these. In an university, he is likely to have non-restricted access to the Internet. In his institution he is more likely than the K-12 teacher to have an in-house service group of professional support staff (often professional educational technologists; see Chapter 9) to help him with his tele-learning requirements.

There are exceptions, but...

There are exceptions, of course, to these generalizations about post-secondary instructors and K-12 teachers. Sometimes a post-secondary instructor may be as tightly scheduled into courses and contact hours as a secondary-school teacher. Sometimes a post-secondary instructor may not be expected to do other professional tasks besides teaching. Many times a post-secondary instructor is part-time or works in more than one institution, and thus does not have a personal home-base desk nor institutionally supported network access. But in general, the post-secondary instructor, be she a university or college faculty member, someone who delivers courses for inservice or professional development, or a member of a professional training centre or other educational institution, has more flexibility in her teaching practice, more responsibilities outside of teaching, and more support services at her disposal than K-12 teachers.

All of these aspects have implications for the role that tele-learning can have for the post-secondary instructor. We will identify these implications throughout this chapter.

■ 6.1.2 DESIGNING CLASSES AND COURSES

But there is one critical job characteristic that most post-secondary instructors and K-12 teachers share: responsibility for designing and delivering the classes and courses that they teach. Here, again, the amount of independence a teacher or instructor has for course design will vary, depending on institutional circumstances, but in general there are two basic decisions that the professional makes during instructional planning. These are: What balance to give to different aspects of the course? and within the chosen balance, how to implement each aspect? Let us look at these two basic decision areas in course design, before turning our specific attention to tele-learning and its implications for this balance.

Instructional components and their balance

From an instructional-design perspective, a course can be thought of as some combination of instructional components in a balance with each other relative to their weight within the entire course. How important are lectures compared to practical activities? How much emphasis is given to students studying on their own, primarily by reading, compared to students working together on a group task? We look at instructional components and their balance more systematically in the next paragraphs and use this to introduce the idea of "pedagogical re-engineering".

A post-secondary instructor generally plans for some combination of the following in any course for which she is responsible:

1. Presentation/lecture, with differing amounts of student questioning and student interaction
2. Communication opportunities between the instructor and students outside of the class-presentation setting
3. Discussion opportunities among the students
4. Assignment of student reading

5. Assignment of individual student practice and production activities, usually with feedback from the instructor
6. Assignment of group projects or other group activities, with feedback from instructor
7. Formal assessment and evaluation of student performance

Variations in balance

Of course, the balance among these components, in terms of emphasis by the instructor, or in time proportion spent on the component by the students, will vary in every course. Some instructors will make no provision for discussions, others considerable. Some will make no provision for group activities, others extensive. Table 6.1 contrasts the balance of instructional components in five typical types of post-secondary courses: The large-lecture course in university; the skill-development course in vocational education; the traditional "distance education" course built around a correspondence model; the "tele-teaching" course using video technologies to deliver instruction in real-time to remote sites; and the seminar-type course.

The percentages in Table 6.1 are only meant as general examples of what is meant by the balance of instructional components within a course. In general, students in post-secondary institutions expect to spend time in a course studying reading material and working on an individual assignment. After this, the other five instructional components may or may not be present, and if present, will have different weights in the course experience, from the perspective of how the student is meant to spend his time during the course.

DECISIONS ABOUT BALANCE, AND TELE-LEARNING

We will argue in this chapter that a major way that tele-learning can impact upon the work of the post-secondary instructor is to force or stimulate him to change the instructional balance within his courses. For the instructor working with students in a lecture-type course model, such as the first row in Table 6.1, a realignment of instructional balance may come through using tele-learning to bring opportunities for communication and discussion into a course which were not much possible without tele-learning. For the instructor working with students in the correspondence-type model of distance education, tele-learning technologies make it feasible for him to add group discussions and more personal communication to the instructional balance. We could call these

Table 6.1 Balance of instructional components in five models of post-secondary courses, from perspective of percentage of student time engaged in each component

Instructional Components \ Type of course	1. Attend Lecture	2. Personal contact with instructor	3. Discussion among students	4. Self-study, reading	5. Do an assignment, individually	6. Do an assignment, as a group	7. Take an examination
Lecture-type course	20%	5%		35%	30%		10%
Skill-development course	5%	25%		10%	40%	20%	
Correspondence-type distance education				55%	45%		
"Tele-teaching-type" distance education	35%		5%	30%	30%		
Seminar type		20%	40%	20%	20%		

changes in balance in the instructional composition of a course "pedagogical re-engineering" to indicate that more than just a change in percentages is involved.

Tele-learning and the re-engineering of course-component balance

By adding components such as group work and discussion to a course via tele-learning there is an effect on each of the other components of the course as well, not only in quantity of importance, but also in characteristics. For example, as an instructor comes to place emphasis on group discussions via asynchronous computer conferencing as part of overall course composition, then this should affect what the students do in assignments, the content on which they are examined (or graded), and the topics they feel are relevant for personal communication with the instructor.

Thus one of the perspectives we will use in this chapter about tele-learning and the post-secondary instructor is to ask what tele-learning can contribute to change the overall instructional balance of courses for which the instructor is responsible.

TELE-LEARNING AND CHANGE WITHIN COMPONENTS

Another way that tele-learning can affect the teaching of the post-secondary instructor is to allow or motivate her to qualitatively alter what happens within any one (or more) of the seven types of course components we identified in Table 6.1. For example, the instructor may have always had "reading" as an expectation for her students in a course, but with tele-learning may be able to ask students to discriminate among a wider range of possible readings than was possible before, by expecting students to seek relevant study materials from sites on the Internet or even to choose their own readings rather than be told what to read from a textbook. Or, an instructor may have always expected students to carry out some form of assignment on which they will be given feedback, but with tele-learning these sorts of assignments may involve resources and contacts with persons that could never have taken place in the traditional course setting.

Implications for tele-learning

Thus, a second point we will make throughout this chapter is that tele-learning can change not only the balance among instructional components within a course, but can also affect each of those components in a qualitative way. When this change within a component brings a substantial change to the overall course experience, we can also think of this as pedagogical re-engineering.

■ 6.1.3 DELIMITING THIS CHAPTER

A few additional comments are useful before we begin the substance of the chapter, concerning the target group for the chapter, terminology used in the chapter, and the structure of the chapter.

TARGET GROUP

In this chapter, we speak through the perspective of the post-secondary instructor. Thus we will not directly address issues that are the domain of the decision makers in the instructor's organization. These issues include institutional-level decisions about the form of tele-learning to be supported, and the support provided for this form. For example, it is not the instructor but others in his institution who decide if the institution will commit itself to compressed interactive video-delivery of courses to distant groups. It is not the instructor but others in his organization who will decide if all students have a network account with Internet access and if they can access this account from home or their workplaces. It is not the instructor who decides the basic relationship between his institution and its students, such as how much flexibility is possible in their course requirements or how much time is to be spent in the field for practical work. The relationship of tele-learning to these sorts of structural considerations is discussed in Chapter 7. In this chapter, we will assume the instructor works within the institutional decisions made by others.

Also, we do not focus in this chapter on those professionals whose work it is to support the post-secondary instructor, either technologically or pedagogically. These, often educational technologists, are the focus of Chapter 9.

Finally, in this chapter, we do not look at innovations in teaching with respect to tele-learning through the perspective of the relatively few specialists for whom tele-learning is their research area as well as a tool for instructional delivery. These sorts of specialists are given attention in Chapters 8 and 9.

TERMINOLOGY

Finally, with respect to convenience of terminology, we will use the term "instructor" throughout, instead of "trainer" or "faculty member". We will use the term "student" throughout instead of alternatives such as learner, trainee, client, or PhD candidate. We will use the term "institution" to include a broad range of post-secondary settings, such as universities, colleges, training centres, professional-development centres, or adult-education centres. And we will interchangeably use the pronouns "she" or "he".

STRUCTURE OF THE CHAPTER

For the structure of the chapter we divide its domain relative to the sort of instructional organization in which the instructor is primarily involved: face-to-face classes (Section 6.2), students at a distance from the institution (Sections 6.3 and 6.4), and new combinations of these two delivery modes (Section 6.5).

■ 6.2 ADDING TELE-LEARNING TO FACE-TO-FACE COURSES

Every instructor who works in an educational institution in which the students converge, at set times in a classroom or lecture hall with the instructor, and have various forms of face-to-face interaction with the instructor is in this category. Of course, students only experience a portion of a course in a face-to-face situation in the presence of the instructor. Most of the time in a post-secondary course, students typically are engaged in self study, reading or working on an assignment. Normally besides regularly scheduled class sessions, there will also be some period when the instructor is available for personal contact ("office hours") and there may be some scheduled time when the students work in a practical situation or work as a group on an activity. There may also be a certain amount of time when the students are being examined.

The instructor, in return, in addition to her office hours and lectures, is committed to the time it takes to give feedback on the assignment(s) and assessments and to determine the final grade for the course.

OPPORTUNITIES FOR TELE-LEARNING

Given this familiar construction for the face-to-face post-secondary course, we can identify six general ways in which tele-learning can be used to extend and enrich such a course. All of these are feasible within the constraints affecting the post-secondary instructor that we noted in Section 6.1. Although tele-learning may be utilized in a relatively modest way by the instructor, it may also become a tool and stimulus for pedagogical re-engineering, as the examples in this section will show. The six general categories for tele-learning as an integral part of a face-to-face course that we will discuss are:

- Making information about the overall organization of the course and its resources more organized and accessible to students (Section 6.2.1)

- Improving the effectiveness of the lesson-presentation session, during and after the class session (Section 6.2.2)
- Improving communication between the instructor and students (Section 6.2.3)
- Improving discussion among the students (Section 6.2.4)
- Improving the range and quality of resources available to the students and shifting the responsibility to the student for the selection of appropriate resources (Section 6.2.5)
- Improving the range and quality of learning activities available to the students, particularly in terms of collaborative learning (section 6.2.6)

Mapping these categories onto the seven instructional components in Table 6.1, we see that Section 6.2.1 reflects a sort of meta-level, while the other five sections map fairly directly onto each of the instructional components, with the exception of the component relating to assessment and being examined. It is not much yet the case that tele-learning is changing methods of examination in face-to-face teaching institutions, either qualitatively or in terms of the examination's place in the overall instructional balance of a course. While there are exceptions, there are not enough of them to warrant a section in this chapter, not yet at least.

■ 6.2.1 MAKING COURSE MATERIALS MORE ORGANIZED AND MORE ACCESSIBLE TO STUDENTS

A first use of tele-learning for course instructors relates to using some form of integrated environment accessible via a computer network to bring a collection of course materials together in an efficient way for the student, a way that she can access when ever she wishes and from wherever she has a network connection. This collection of materials can include any combination of course syllabi, lecture notes, sample examination questions, additional reading materials, information about the assignments, course calendars, and multi-media learning resources for the course. As a general term, we can call this a "course materials site".

This integrated provision may be done using any one of a variety of software systems. Instructors can use an existing campus-wide information system, a set of WWW pages, some sort of local bulletin board system, a computer conferencing system, or some other form of CMC to provide this kind of integrated, always-assessable central point for course information and resources. During 1995 the most vibrant growth area for this integrated provision of course materials has been through WWW pages.

WWW PAGES

During 1995 it has become common for universities and colleges in countries throughout the world to maintain a site on the WWW. For example, "It is now *de rigeur* for an American college to have a presence on the World Wide Web, the interlinked digital archive for thousands of Internet users" (Hafner, 1995, p. 44). And there are sites that provide listings of sites:

Colleges and Universities Home Page (US)
URL http://www.mit.edu:8001/people/cdemello/univ.html
Global Campus (International)
URL http://www.wvu.edu/~instadv/tour/int.htm
Good and Poor Higher Education Sites
URL http://www.ilt.Columbia.edu/academic/classes/
TU5020/projects/he/b&w_sites.html

The last of the above URLs is that of the Institute for Learning Technologies at Columbia University in the US, which carried out an evaluation of 450 college and university WWW sites in September 1995. In this evaluation, institutional sites were distinguished in terms of 11 categories of information, most of the categories factual or intended for public relations. (The survey also notes what it judges as being "good" and "poor" examples in each of these categories.) Within these institutional WWW sites, instructors are rapidly adding links to integrated collections of course materials.

There are now hundreds of such examples of course materials being made available to students via a central, hyperlinked WWW environment, and an increasing number of instructors who are writing about their approaches to making use of these environments (see for example, Windley, 1995). A major (circa 1995) source of links to WWW-based course-materials sites can be found at:

The World Lecture Hall (University of Texas-Austin)
URL http://www.utexas.edu/world/lecture/index.html
...48 categories of courses, from Accounting to Zoology, within each of which is a list of links to sets of class materials, syllabi, assignments, lecture notes, sample examination questions, course calendars, and an increasing variety of interactive multi-media learning materials

Variations in site design

Just as there are variations in instructors' approaches to presenting course outlines and syllabi in traditional form, there are many variations possible in the design of course-syllabus sites. A quick scan of some of the hundred of links in the World Lecture Hall site makes this variety clear. Some of the approaches to site design can be as simple as the transcription of a few pages of text, giving procedural data about the course. Others can be sites through which some of all of the course reading materials are made available, either as flat or hyperlinked text. The more innovative sites can include a wide range of links to dynamically available resources that could never be included in a print syllabus There are hypertexts, MOOs (areas organized for real-time textual discussion), interactive materials, links to a wide range of external sources, student work, multi-media resources such as audio clips for language courses, extensive sets of images, quizzes, and integrated forms for communication with the instructor and others. The World Lecture Hall contains a wealth of examples, showing the explosion of creativity that is occurring with relation to the decision of individual instructors, mostly at universities, to develop a dynamic course environment within a WWW site. Windley (1995) for example, now writes all his lecture notes directly in HTML and to keep them as dynamic as possible, only makes them available in his course's WWW site up through the current lecture.

The sites can also function as working and communication areas for the course itself, as we will illustrate in examples throughout this section.

BENEFITS OF A WWW SITE FOR COURSE ORGANIZATION

There are many benefits accruing from the decision to maintain a WWW site as a central integrative environment for a course. Some of these are generic to any central electronic site but are made particularly flexible through the WWW's hyperlinked organization:

- Students can access the environment at any time, from a variety of locations. (This is useful not only for students already enrolled in a course but also those considering taking the course, to help them in decision making about the course). For example, there is no need for either the instructor or students to be inconvenienced if students did not get a copy of a particular handout; they can simply download it or print it out from the WWW site
- The material can be continually updated, although some procedure to help students identify what has been changed or added is important. Updating relates not only to procedural aspects of a course, but also to lecture notes (see Section 6.2.2), to new resources that the instructor, and the students, identify as useful to the course and to student work itself
- The instructor has an efficient way to communicate and disseminate information and resources to the students, avoiding the need to have to bring photocopied piles of handouts to class. The instructor can offer a

broad range of course-resource possibilities to students, which the students in turn can choose to retain or not.

Mueller (1994) has found that use of the WWW as an information system can reduce average study time by better and more efficient information provision, as well as relieve the instructor of some administrative burdens. And, as further examples will show in this section (and in Chapter 9 and Interface 9), an electronic course-organizer site, especially a hyperlinked site, can be much more than a source of information; it can become a learning environment for the course itself.

Sites can remain local

It is useful to note that a WWW site for a course does not have to be automatically available to the world via the Internet. It can be maintained for local access only, which can be an important consideration for instructors for a range of reasons, including not wishing to have certain personal resources made available to the outside world and not wishing to have one's "workspace" accessible to the public without a context for the work in progress. The instructor can keep a site local while it is in use during a course, and then "clean it up" and make it a publicly available archive after the course is over. This can be described as a difference between "intranetworking" and "internetworking".

With regard to this sense of personal control, Turoff (1995) notes that:

> ...Essentially an instructor needs an ability to maintain and offer his "courseware" as a personal database that becomes a server to students. This view is also very consistent with the long standing tradition that the course notes and other learning materials (e.g. workbooks, textbooks) that an instructor develops are his or her property. The instructor's server is a combination of a bulletin board, printing press, and publishing/distribution system. (p. 8)

The WWW is not the only sort of electronic system that is useful for provision of course materials to students. BBSs as part of CWISs (campus-wide information systems), distribution lists and computer-conferencing also are being widely used.

CWISs and distribution lists

Bulletin-board type environments are sometimes all that is available to an instructor and can be used as one-to-many information sources, less dynamic than WWW sites but still efficient. The continuum from BBSs to CWISs (campus-wide information systems) to WWW sites has many overlaps.

Another approach, if students all have electronic addresses, is for the instructor to set up an e-mail distribution list prior to the start of a course for students on the enrollment list for the course, and through this mechanism send a flat-text copy of course materials, starting with the course outline, to the students as e-mail. This is a useful way to target information to specific students especially before a course starts when the students do not yet have any pattern of going to a WWW page or other central source of information for the course. The information is sent to the student, rather than the student coming to the information.

A distribution list is also a useful way to make sure students get critical information, such as changes in lecture times or clarifications of assignments. Distribution-list functionalities within e-mail systems send a copy of the message from the instructor directly into the electronic mailbox of each student; there is no excuse for the student to miss a sensitive piece of information (if he reads his mail, at least). The e-mail message may be used as a pointer or an alert for something new that has been added to the integrated WWW source, drawing the students' attention to the need to check out the new information. This is helpful to the students the more a central environment becomes a work area for the course, and thus can get flooded with (too much) information as the course continues.

COMPUTER CONFERENCING ENVIRONMENTS

Computer conferencing systems, if supported by the instructor's institution, can also be used as dynamic course-organization environments (thus serving a larger function than discussion support). A number of examples of this use of computer-conferencing systems are included in the final report of "The CoSy Project" (Stockton State College, 1990). (CoSy is the name of a computer conferencing software environment; other internationally used computer conferencing environments are the older Caucus[2] and the currently very popular FirstClass[3] packages; these packages and their generic features will be discussed in more detail in Chapter 8; see also De Vries, 1994, and Mason, 1994.)

The Stockton Report describes how 20 different courses at the college, spanning the curriculum from social sciences to technical subjects, began using CoSy, and

---

[1] CoSy is the licensed trademark of a package available through Softwords Research International, Victoria, BC, Canada.

[2] Caucus is available through Camber-Roth, 3588 Plymouth Road, #223, Ann Arbor, MI 48105-2603, USA.

[3] FirstClass is the licensed trademark of a package available from SoftArc Inc., 100 Allstate Parkway, Markham, Ontario L3M 6H3, Canada. A FirstClass server can be maintained as a local environment, and can also be accessible remotely through the Internet.

as is also the case with WWW pages, each instructor made use of the environment in a different way for course organization. Emmons (1990), for example, notes that for his political science course, he set up five conferences in the CoSy environment with the themes, "Rolecall", "Evidence", Jury Box", "Most Wanted", and "Shoot". The first of these contained the course syllabus, announcements, course updates, and assignments. The others were used more dynamically in the course, as areas where students built a collective data base, had discussions, and reacted to statements or questions presented by the instructor.

Benefits of computer conferencing environments for course organization

In a computer conferencing environment, files or messages are not hyperlinked to each other, as they are in a WWW environment, but they are grouped by topic ("conference"), and within a conference, can be ordered and grouped in different ways, including by "threading", following a particular chain of responses from a certain starter message. Conference environments offer the benefit of letting the instructor see the "history" of a message, a specific list of who has read the message. They also offer the instructor the immediate choice of responding to a message either to the class as a whole, a subset of the class subscribed to a particular conference (useful for group work, where each group has its own conference), or to individuals. This sort of flexibility in communication is only just becoming conveniently available in WWW environments.

More than the integration of information...

Emmons (1990) notes that "the act of common use of CoSy binds students...Their engagement in the process of using CoSy—getting literate, comfortable, expert— apart from the contents of comments and mail unites them to a degree. They are like a platoon at the front in wartime" (p. 4). While such a metaphor may not be what the average instructor hopes to engender from maintaining an electronic course-materials environment, the point about its value as an integrating agent, not only for information about the course, but also for the persons participating in the course, is important.

The subtle value of building a sense of human community through the shared on-going use of a common organizational environment is perhaps a major benefit of this application of tele-learning, especially for university courses where a sense of human community is often lacking.

COURSE-ORGANIZER MATERIALS AS SOURCES OF IDEAS FOR INSTRUCTORS

It is not only students who benefit from making course materials electronically available in some sort of integrated environment. This availability can also be useful to post-secondary instructors themselves, as sources of ideas for their own teaching. Spencer, Nibert, and Sgro (1994) for example maintain a WWW site for their course in Molecular Biology that is intended not only for their students but also for their colleagues. The site includes computer-generated images, animations of virus structures, topographical maps of virus surfaces, digitized electron micrographs, reports, and tutorials. Other virology instructors are encouraged to announce themselves and to ask or answer questions via a newsgroup available within the WWW site. These other instructors are invited to submit their own course syllabi to the site and to customize the server for their own students via a fill-in form interface that allows the remote instructor to create a "hypersyllabus" embedded with hyperlinks to documents on the Virology course server or elsewhere. A similar approach, but dealing with a course in genetics is the WWW site "MendelWeb". This site was built to be a resource for both students and other instructors and is described by Blumberg (1994).

Another way that a tele-learning tool can be used as a way for post-secondary instructors to share instructional ideas is through e-mail and listservs and, to some extent, newsgroups. E-mail messages sent over distribution lists to students can be also made available to other instructors active in teaching courses with similar content. Listservs to which instructors may be subscribed for their own professional interests (see Chapter 4) are also convenient ways for them to share their own course materials with each other, as well as the URLs for the full support environments if available as WWW sites through the Internet.

As a typical example of this professional exchange, the listserv ITFORUM (contact: ITFORUM@uga.cc.uga.edu), a lively discussion list for professional educational technologists (see Chapter 4), sometimes will include a request from a subscriber for information or ideas about some aspect of content or organization relative to a course that she teaches. Such a recent informal request from someone in the US brought an immediate response from a subscriber in Australia who provided a copy of his course outline and study guide for a similar course (Zariski, 1995). These materials were of interest to other list subscribers not because of the content of the course itself, but for the ideas they included about how Zariski organizes group work for e-mail-based problem-solving activity in his teaching.

As post-secondary instructors have little or no formal pedagogic training, and little professional opportunity to focus on pedagogical innovation, such electronic sharing of experiences among peers is very important.

Although listservs can lead to valuable ideas, their noise:value ratio is high. The public availability of Internet-accessible WWW pages can become particularly important here; the isolated instructor does not have to first be subscribed to a list in order to find ideas. As long as she knows how to search WWW sites or has a convenient starting place such as the *World Lecture Hall*, she can determine for herself how far and how much she wishes to look for teaching ideas. And she can avoid a mailbox overflowing with messages from lists which she may not have time or interest to read.

In any case, through these sorts of electronic sharing, the instructor now has access to a broad range of ideas for course organization, content and activities, as well as a convenient way to communicate with other instructors about their experiences in managing certain forms of instructional activities. This is valuable for pedagogical re-engineering.

▓ 6.2.2 IMPROVING LESSON-PRESENTATION EFFECTIVENESS, DURING AND AFTER THE LESSON

One thing most post-secondary instructors working with face-to-face classes do is organize and deliver lesson presentations. These presentations may be relatively short, as in a training session which is intended to introduce a hands-on activity, or they may be lectures that fill an entire class period. The most typical technology that instructors use to support lesson presentation is probably an overhead projector. (A recent study of 250 four-year colleges and universities in the US found that less than 25% of faculty use any sort of technology for instruction, "Survey results...", 1995). However, more and more instructors are preparing their overhead sheets using computer tools, either word processing software or presentation packages, such as PowerPoint[4] (Wiggins, 1995a). With these tools, instructors can not only prepare legible and professional-looking overhead sheets but they can also include screen captures as graphics for the sheets (see Chapter 5). In addition, they can make hardcopy versions of the sheets available as handouts.

Tele-learning can add to this current lesson-presentation repertoire of the instructor in at least three ways: by allowing her to conveniently make her lecture notes and sheets available before and after the lesson presentation via a network environment; by making it possible for her to use tele-learning resources as multi-media demonstration materials during the lesson presentation; and by giving her to the tools to "bring in", via tele-learning channels, a guest lecturer to the presentation.

MAKING LECTURE NOTES AND SHEETS AVAILABLE

When instructors maintain an electronic organization environment for a course, they typically place lecture notes and the electronic versions of sheets within the

---

[4] PowerPoint is the registered trademark ©1995 of the Microsoft Corporation, Redmond, Washington, US.

environments, so that students can access these before and after the class for reference. There are many variations possible on this:

- The students may be expected to study the lecture notes before the lecture, as an *advanced organizer* or after the lecture, as a *consolidator*. The instructor can embed comments and questions in the lecture notes to facilitate this
- The students may be asked to bring a *printout of the overhead sheets along to the presentation* so that they do not have to spend time copying down what is written on the sheets for their notes. And because these sheets are electronically available to the whole class, students do not have to come to the instructor asking for copies of the overheads
- The instructor may develop his *lecture notes in HTML* originally, so that he can use the hyperlinked environment himself during the lecture (this requires having a computer with large-screen presentation device in the lecture hall. It is advisable to have the WWW site ready loaded and cached in the browser so load-up delays or breakdowns do not occur during access of the pages during the lecture)
- The instructor can add a *reflective comment* to the lecture notes, giving a deeper view on her motivations for a certain point in the lecture, which might be disruptive or difficult to do during the lecture itself. Or the thoughts may be stimulated by questions that were asked during the presentation or more generally by the reactions of the students to materials in the lectures. In any case, the instructor can add comments to the lecture notes themselves or make the comments available as a separate, associated file

Rebelsky (1994), for example, in his WWW site for an Introductory Computer Science course, not only includes the sheets, transcriptions and notes from each lecture, but requires the students to add more in-depth notes as well as questions and comments following a lecture. In this way, the students add to the web of resources for each lecture.

BENEFITS AND ISSUES...

Major benefits of electronically available lesson-presentation materials thus include the extra learning value that can come to the lecture if students have studied an advanced organizer of the presentation, with embedded questions and other study guides; if students can make notes on copies of the instructor's presentation materials during the lesson; if students can follow-up the lecture by reading further annotated comments from the instructor or delve into extra resource materials that may help to clarify points in the lesson; and if the instructor can make all this available without much extra work besides that of his ordinary presentation preparation. It is also useful to have a permanent record of a lecture or lesson always available. Having students contribute notes on the lecture as part of the course expectation and having those notes publicly available for other students is another benefit.

Permanent record

In particular, students appreciate having a "permanent record" of the lecture, especially if they were not in attendance. Shepherd and Bowser (1992) have found that students value tele-learning technologies that allow such an archive to be made available more than tele-learning technologies lacking permanent records, which are "least preferred". Students want a "permanent record which they can peruse at choice for further elucidation and/or revision" (p. 6). In particular, respondents in Shepherd and Bowser's study indicate they value such a flexible-access permanent record more than they value interactive tele-learning technologies such as audio-conferencing, or video-conferencing or interactive television with their provision for real-time interaction.

Video-on-demand

However, this does not have to disqualify multi-media and video resources from the permanent-record aspect of lesson-presentation support. Carnegie Mellon University in the US is among a number of universities experimenting with what "just-in-time" lectures, video recordings of lectures retained on videotape and available on demand to students in environments served by adequate network capacity and having a video server (Hafner, 1995). The Dean of the Faculty of Engineering at Carnegie Mellon is quoted as saying "This could completely break down the structure of students sitting in classrooms in front of lecturers" (Hafner, p. 46). We discuss this further in Chapter 10, when we look into the future.

Printing implications

An interesting side-issue of making materials available from a common electronic environment is the practical problem that can occur when the instructor expects or suggests that the individual students regularly print out lecture materials and other resources. If these files contain graphics, printing can be a slow process. (This is why it is advisable to use only the outline form of presentations for the electronic version supplied to students if a presentation package is used to prepare course materials, rather than copies of the full sheets themselves).

But graphics or not, the load on campus printing facilities can be considerable if all the students in a large class are printing out sizable amounts of information from a WWW site or other environment. Furthermore, in many universities students have a ceiling on how much they can print; an enthusiastic instructor, in her zeal to make so much available to students, may inadvertently make them use up their printing allotment (and their disk-space allotment on a shared server). Finally, an advantage of electronic lecture-support materials is that they can be made up-to-date at the last minute; this is also a disadvantage, in terms of large numbers of students needing to access the materials and print them out just before the lecture.

One other advantage: develops the habit of going to the network

Putting lecture notes in an electronic environment has another additional benefit: it can be an incentive to get students in the habit of going onto the network and going to the course site, especially if lecture notes also contain comments about assignments. As is frequently noted, students need an incentive, a definite need or some motivation related to earning points in the course, to stimulate them to develop the habit of checking and interacting with central electronic information sources (Posner, Danielson and Schmidt-Posner, 1992–93). Putting high-value materials such as lecture and assignment notes onto a course server is such an incentive.

BRINGING MULTI-MEDIA RESOURCES INTO THE PRESENTATION

Another valuable way that tele-learning can enhance the face-to-face lecture is through its capacity to provide the instructor with extraordinary visual materials that can be projected during the lecture to illustrate points as well as to improve the motivational quality of the presentation. These visual materials may be portions of broadcasts, saved on videotape and displayed on a video-playback unit with large monitor or monitors in the classroom. Or they may be multi-media resources located by the instructor from an network collection, captured electronically, and worked into his lecture presentation materials.

Using broadcast segments as illustration

The instructor may be fortunate enough to lecture in a room equipped with appropriate wiring or cabling, enabling him to be able to call for such video segments from a storage center somewhere in the institution; in working with adults in limited-time class situations it is highly unlikely that the instructor would want to use real-time broadcast materials. It is more likely he would want to pre-select an appropriate small segment of a previously stored broadcast that illustrates a lecture point. (Note: we identify an interesting exception to this comment about the use of live video later in this section.)

Using networked resources for illustration

A particularly useful benefit of the information collections being made available via the Internet is that the instructor can extract screen dumps of outstanding visual materials, and work these electronically into lecture notes, overhead sheets and computer-based presentations, giving proper reference to the original source. The techniques we described in Chapter 5 for the K-12 teacher are much more likely to be used by the post-secondary teacher, because of the latter's more convenient access to both network resources and a personal computer to construct such support materials. Also, because the post-secondary instructor teaches less often in clock hours than his K-12 counterpart and more often in terms of a lecture rather than on-going interaction with a class, she has more time and focus to develop specific lecture materials.

Highly visual sites, such as many relating to medical education or to art history education or geography and cartography, can be located ahead of time by the instructor (who sometimes must wait patiently while they download, even with fast network connections) and used as valuable lesson-illustration materials. This sort of sites is legion already in 1995, but a few examples are given in Box 6.1.

And increasingly, interactive WWW sites are available that can be useful for lecture presentations. For example, the site with location:

Population Projections
```
URL  http://geosim.cs.vt.edu/index.html
```

includes access to a program that allows input of different parameters relative to population projections, and then shows the projection in terms of a graph. Such a graph can be screen-captured and used as part of an appropriate lecture. Students could be then asked to use the simulation themselves interactively, as a learning activity, after its demonstration in the lecture.

BRINGING GUEST LECTURERS INTO THE PRESENTATION

A third way in which the post-secondary instructor can use tele-learning opportunities to enrich lesson presentation is through the live-interview approach. This currently can be done via the Internet, using CU-SeeMe software (see Chapter 2); as an example, the technique was recently used at the University of Amsterdam, to include a guest contribution from an American colleague as part of a lecture to a large lecturehall-full of students in Amsterdam. The Amsterdam site used a large-screen projector to beam the image of the distant guest speaker so that it could be seen by all those in the hall. Audio was similarly amplified.

Box 6.1

Examples of WWW sites with visual materials useful for lecture support

The Virtual Hospital
URL http://indy.radiology.uiowa.edu/VirtualHospital.html
...*Particularly useful for lecture support are the Multimedia Teaching Files, and the Patient Simulations*

Chemistry Hypermedia Project (Virginia Polytechnic Institute)
URL http://www.chem.vt.edu/chem-ed/vt-chem-ed.html
...*More than 120 hypermedia presentations for chemistry students, ranging from the absortion of light to X-ray spectroscopy. Included in the exhibits are video segments and the texts are linked to other references.*

The Nanoworld Home Page
URL http://www.uq.oz.au/nanoworld/nanohome.html
...*A large collection of microscopic images of atomic, molecular, cellular, and macromolecular scales.*

The Urbana Atlas of Pathology
URL http://www.med.uiuc.edu/PathAtlasf/titlePage.html
...*Extensive collection of images of cells and tissues*

OnLine Images from the History of Medicine
URL http://www.nlm.nih.gov
...*Site with 60,000 photographs and other images.*

The Visible Human Body (National Library of Medicine)
URL http://www.nlm.nih.gov/research/visible
...*Thousands of pre-computed three-dimensional representations of the male and female human body.*

American Memory Collection (Library of Congress)
URL http://rs6.loc.gov/ammem/amtitle.new.html
...*Images and sounds relevant to American history, including timelines and extensive visuals from the Civil War period.*

ArtServe
URL http://rubens.anu.edu.au/
... *Access to 10,200 images relating to art history and architectural history, through a database interface*

This sort of enhancement requires nothing more than an Internet connection at both ends, appropriately set-up computers (this means that each has a video camera and microphone attached to the appropriate card inside their computers, and that each site has downloaded and installed the free CUSeeMe software). It also requires that the instructor take the initiative to contact a colleague and organize the interaction. Scheduling the colleague for this live-interview is often the major logistical problem, especially when different time zones are involved and lecture times are inflexible. However, the benefits of expanding and enriching lecture presentations through real-time guest visits from remote experts coupled with the extra range of learning value already brought to the lecture through the use of a WWW environment have the potential to make lectures in post-secondary education radically different in the future. The tools are already here; now it is up to the instructor to make use of them (Koch, 1995).

Via ISDN or other broadband connection

The guest speaker idea, however, can be incorporated, and with much better quality video, through appropriate high-speed networks (such as ISDN) in sites that can operate as two points of an interactive video connection (for a lecture situation, this would be most likely to be through some sort of fiber optic or ISDN connectivity. In training centers, it will be more likely that a two-way digital video connection is available than in universities, while an Mbone connection may be available to a university but unlikely to be available elsewhere.)

As an example, in a recent series of lessons for students in a vocational college in The Netherlands, students in their own classroom via an ISDN connection were able to have a presentation from a professional in the sort of work for which the students were training (Arav, 1995b). But this guest speaker was more than a talking head; the same ISDN connectivity enabled application sharing as well as the real-time audio-visual connection. The remote expert was able to show the students some complicated software he uses in his work and the output from the software when different parameters were entered. As their assignment, the students then were able to download a set of actual data from the company, work off-line with these data on their own computers, and send their formatted results back to the professional for his inspection. On a later day, the students had another guest-speaker session with the remote expert, in which he gave them feedback on their projects and answered their questions. All this could occur without the students leaving their classroom.

This example shows the overlap between presentation support and innovative learning activities that can be made possible via tele-learning. Of course, considerable organizational effort and some creative imagination must be present.

Television and networking

As a final example, Heller and Kearsley (1995) describe their experiences using a combination of instructional television and a BBS to teach graduate students. The television component was used as a supplement to lectures, for guest interviews, and for software demonstration. The BBS was used to stimulated interaction among students and the instructors.

This last example leads into a more general category of how to support course delivery with tele-learning: the category probably most familiar to the widest range of people. This is tele-learning to improve the quantity and quality of communication between students and the instructor. We look next at this category.

◼ 6.2.3 IMPROVING COMMUNICATION BETWEEN THE INSTRUCTOR AND STUDENTS

Simply stated, communication between the instructor and students can occur through one-to-one messages initiated by either instructor or student, or through one-to-many messages from the instructor to some or all of the students. However, there are many variations, and many educational reasons why a variation can be valuable. Different functionalities can be utilized depending on what software is available to the instructor and her students for their communication. Major current categories of communication environments are e-mail, WWW-site forms, and computer conferencing systems.

E-MAIL ENVIRONMENTS

Any electronic communication environment offers a basic improvement on one aspect of ordinary instructor-student contact: flexibility. Students can send a question or comment when they wish, instructors can answer when convenient, and vice versa. Much of the need for office hours is removed when e-mail contact is available.

Other benefits of simple e-mail

And, as a further improvement over face-to-face meetings during office hours at least for certain sorts of student questions, e-mail messages can be handled in various ways:

- The instructor can print a series of student messages out, and consider a joint response rather than individual ones, if the same question appears from a number of students. If the point at issue seems sufficiently important, the instructor can send the response to the whole class, and thus prevent further repetitions of the same question. Electronic copies of both questions and responses can be saved in a directory for the course or kept available in a folder in the e-mail environment, in case it is handy to re-use an earlier response, by readdressing and revising it and then forwarding it

- The instructor can answer directly on the message, or on an edited version of the message, and return it. This is handy when a student asks a complicated set of questions
- The instructor can keep copies, electronically or in printout form, of what she receives and what she sends. This is easier and more efficient than making notes after a face-to-face meeting and can serve as a reminder of points that need attention later in the course, or in the next round of the course
- The style of e-mail messages encourages friendly and informal contact between instructor and students, a type of contact sometimes lacking in post-secondary situations
- Messages can become extra lectures or tutorials, if the instructor reflects in a lengthy fashion about an issue. They allow reflective follow-up to a lecture by both instructor and students

Concerns with e-mail communication

But there are frustrations as well as improvements in instructor–student communication via an e-mail environment. Sharples (1993) describes them as breakdowns: mismatches between the instructor's intentions and the users' practice. We mention three sets of frustrations and potential breakdowns.

Technical problems can frustrate students and require considerable time and energy to solve. First is the issue of getting on the mail system itself, well-supported in some institutions but not at all supported in others. Once connected, students can have other problems. For example, file attachments for the handling of graphics or formatted text cause many students and instructors difficulties, especially if working with a variety of computers and e-mail systems. This can be not only time-consuming and frustrating, but also some communication looses its interpretability (such as tables) if formatting is lost.

Management problems can also become distracting and frustrating. E-mail typically provides no way for the receiver to discriminate among messages, other than by putting them in alphabetical order, or arranged by date or sender. When the instructor receives 50 or 100 messages a day (which easily happens, once a large class is encouraged to communicate with the instructor, and the instructor receives considerable other e-mail as well), the organizational work in handling the communications efficiently and effectively is very time consuming. Although e-mail messages have room in their subject line for a brief indication of their content and its urgency, in general the instructor has no way to differentiate messages other than reading them, one by one. Each act of reading involves a series of steps in terms of handling the e-mail software. Unless the student explains the context of his question, the instructor may be forced to return a message asking for more clarification, thus increasing the managerial work.

Communication-overload problems can frustrate both students and the instructor as all become the victims of the success of e-mail communication. Replying to student messages in a timely way becomes very difficult when there are so many of them, but to the individual student this translates into a new complaint: "You haven't answered my message". Rather than saving his question until a scheduled office-hours session (and perhaps finding a solution to it himself), the student develops the habit of just sending the instructor a message. For the instructor, this means her course-management and student-interaction time seems never to end, difficult when teaching is not her only or even main professional responsibility.

And students have overload problems as well; the enthusiastic instructor can forward and reflect and send comments to a degree beyond what the students wish or can handle, either in terms of time or mail buffer or disk storage or print limits. Students as well as instructors may want to plan their time and attention, and thus not have daily interactions with respect to a particular course.

COMPUTER CONFERENCING

Computer conferencing offers all the benefits of e-mail, but with some additional advantages and some additional difficulties from the instructor's perspective. Among the added advantages are:

- Messages are automatically sorted into conference areas and can be furthered followed as threads
- The grouping of messages around a topic can facilitate communication visually as well as organizationally
- Conferencing software often includes history options, to allow the instructor to see who has read a certain message
- Conferencing environments generally support real-time chat, which may have some educational value and often has social value

But, still, disadvantages: In addition to those for e-mail the following regularly frustrate instructors and students using computer conferencing for communication:

- Conferencing software may be separate, and have a separate cost from the ordinary e-mail in an institution, having implications relative to support and access, and also meaning that instructors and students must move between two, incompatible systems in their overall communication tasks
- Pre-selection of categories for messages often does not fit new themes as they evolve, or messages with multi-theme content
- Having to check within a variety of conferences for new messages, and not knowing if there is a temporal or logical relationship among the messages in the different conferences can distort communication rather than enhance it

Computer conferencing as a support environment for post-secondary instruction has become an active research area, with streams of input from traditional distance-education specialists who focus on the pedagogical and managerial aspects of the communication (see, for example, Mason, 1994) as well as from software-design specialists who focus on the functionalities and user interface of the instrumentation and how these affect communication and learning (such as Turoff, 1995). We give considerable attention to this research in Chapter 8.

NEW DEVELOPMENTS IN COMMUNICATION ENVIRONMENTS

Besides the familiar CMC tools, such as e-mail and computer conferencing, there are new developments in communication environments that will have implications for at least some post-secondary instructors. We look briefly at groupware, real-time conferencing, and communicating via WWW environments.

Groupware

Groupware products are similar to computer conferencing environments in that they include e-mail and various shared data bases. These products are continuously evolving and improving commercially, adding functionalities such as decision-support tools, search and retrieval tools, and tools for collaborative work (Klemm and Snell, 1994). We discuss these further in Chapter 8 in terms of their being objects of research. Their eventual implications for the post-secondary instructor? All the management and overload problems of e-mail and conferencing combined!

Real-time communication

Also, the increasing availability of various tools for real-time communication involving voice and video images of the communicators is also suggestive of new possibilities for communicative exchanges between instructors and students, such as improved remote tutoring as we saw in Arav's (1995b) example of the remote expert. However, even when real-time communication becomes more readily available to instructor and students, it will probably not replace most of the use of e-mail and computer conferencing, as the benefits of these are based on their asynchronous and flexible nature and on their functionalities such as the ability to save and manage one's messages and responses in different ways. (See Chapter 8 for more on these considerations.) There is always the telephone, of course...

Communication through WWW pages

It is possible to embed the option for users of an WWW page to send a message to the maintainer of the page, simply by clicking on an indicator (often the name of the maintainer). Then a message window automatically opens, addressed to the maintainer. This messaging has the benefit of adding a context to communication as the message is identifiable as coming from the WWW site. (At present, circa 1995, messages can generally only be sent out from WWW pages but not received by the pages. However, depending on the server, newsgroup functionalities can be embedded in WWW pages, thus allowing a broad range of conferencing options).

WWW pages also allow "forms", interactive structured areas where specific replies can be solicited and sent directly to the instructor, so that a gauge can be obtained of student understanding (or interest) as the students make use of the WWW site. Mayes and Neilsen (1995) describe their WWW site which includes an "answer web" component, in which student questions and responses to those questions from the instructor are used as the base for extending a WWW site as a course goes on. These sorts of creative developments are adding new pedagogical value to communication between the instructor and student.

■ 6.2.4 Improving discussion among students

One step beyond communicating is discussing. Discussions are frequently difficult to incorporate in post-secondary courses because of the size of the classes, the lecture-like presentation style often used by the instructors, the reluctance of students themselves to contribute, and the logistics of conducting a discussion (a large lecture hall where students sit in tiers of seats facing the front, is not conducive to discussions, but at best to a few comments from those willing to shout to be heard across a large room).

TRADITIONAL CMC TOOLS FOR DISCUSSION

The e-mail and computer-conferencing tools we have examined in Section 6.2.3 for instructor–student communication can also be used for asynchronous class discussions. In theory, this seems straightforward: every one can enter his or her contributions to the conference discussion at a convenient time, after reflection, and with time to prepare the contribution in advance. No one need be excluded. Students already may know one another; they all know the instructor, which helps communication. The discussion topic can be presented in a face-to-face setting and also followed-up in such a setting. (Mason, 1994, is a good summary; see also Chapter 8).

Challenges in effective conferencing

But these theoretical benefits are difficult to realize in practice for at least the following reasons:

- Discussion is confusing, because the group, responding at different times, ends up discussing several themes at once (the "multi-level effect")
- Discussion can be disjointed because the discussion may have moved on before an individual can enter his carefully prepared reflective comment
- The time demands on the instructor that come from the handling of e-mail and personal communication are multiplied when she tries to effectively moderate a discussion. One reason is sheer volume. Harasim (1993) notes active discussions can generate thousands of messages, typically five to ten per person per week
- Another reason is the skill needed to effectively chair an asynchronous discussion. Such moderator skills are still outside the experience range of most post-secondary instructors

Because moderating is such an important part of the success of any use of asynchronous discussion within a course, and because the instructor typically must be responsible for this moderating, we look at this activity more closely in the following paragraph, and return to it as a research focus for educational technologists in Chapter 8.

MODERATOR SKILLS

Just as a face-to-face discussion needs alert guidance from the instructor, an asynchronous discussion also requires this skill and attention. Kaye (1992b) and others (for example, De Vries, 1994) have noted pedagogical aspects of these moderating skills:

- To steer the discussion
- To "pre-moderate" messages to prevent duplicated or irrelevant items
- To set the objective for the discussion
- To set the tone of the discussion and procedures for contributing
- To set expectations for contributing—Must everyone contribute in order to gain some marks? How can contributions be distinguished in terms of quality?
- To review and pick up important points
- To keep the discussion on track
- To restrain those who tend to dominant the discussion and elicit contributions from the reticent
- To conclude the discussion

Friedman and his colleagues (1995) summarize their experiences with moderating listserv discussions among 20 classes and demonstrate activities requiring each of the above skills. They emphasize the importance of the instructor maintaining a well-structured discussion, and determining before the start of the class what role he intends to play in the discussion in terms of intervention and tone. They suggest the instructor participate "as much as an individual student would", encouraging both formal and information discourse and public and private communication among the students. They also urge the instructor not to close down communication too quickly if it seems as if it is idle chat, as such conversations often give rise to useful insights.

Thus among the constraints affecting the success of an asynchronous discussion are: the number of students involved, the time that the instructor can give to moderating, the skill the instructor has in moderating, the skill with which the instructor integrates the discussion into the learning objectives of the course, and at another level, the software tools available to the participants. As most who write about the pedagogical aspects of computer conferencing indicate, these are not easy conditions to meet (Harasim, 1993a, c; Lowry, Koneman, Osman-Jouchoux and Wilson, 1994).

MOTIVATING PARTICIPATION IN DISCUSSIONS

It is also clear from experience and the literature that students expect a structure for asynchronous discussions, and expect to earn some course points for their time and effort. Everett and Ahern (1994) for example, found inconsistent and sometimes critical reactions to discussion suggestions among students for whom conferencing was an optional activity. However, once participation in conferencing was indicated as a course requirement, worth a certain number of points, a different reaction occurred:

*When the [conferencing] was presented as part of the requirements of the
courses, there were no dissenting reactions, no comments either positive or
negative, and no questions... (p. 344)*

Posner, Danielson, and Schmidt-Posner (1992–93) note a similar phenomenon;
I have also found it in my own experiences with attempting to re-engineer
face-to-face courses at university by adding an asynchronous discussion component. Adult students are busy and practical; many of them are not likely to take
the time to contribute to a discussion (and participation in a conference does take
time and effort) if it is not part of a course requirement. It can be a small number
of points, but some sort of official recognition is important for a critical mass of
comments to develop.

Both as a way to motivate student contribution and as a survival strategy for
the instructor when the students do start to contribute, the strategy of giving
students tasks in terms of the conferencing, including having turns at being
responsible for moderating and summarizing it as a course requirement, has
much to recommend it. Harasim, 1993, mentions the strategy of "weaving",
students working in small groups to review the discussion transcript and synthesize the main themes and issues that emerge. However, the instructor then
has the task of evaluating the work of the weavers, a double-level interpretative
task, because first she must be closely aware of the raw materials that the weavers
have summarized.

Thus asynchronous communication systems as tele-learning tools can bring an
instructional component into face-to-face courses that is not often part of the
balance of those courses—real discussions. But the price for the instructor is high,
not only in time and skill demands, but also in terms of strategies for manageable
evaluation of student contributions.

■ 6.2.5 IMPROVING RESOURCES AVAILABLE TO THE STUDENTS

Although students may be able to access taped versions of video material on their
own as study materials (and in the future will undoubtedly be able to access
previously given lectures as video-on-demand, see Chapter 10), currently it is
most likely that students will be able to make use of additional learning resources
via access to networks, either via collections of materials that the instructor has
organized for their course (see Section 6.2.1) or materials they can access via the
WWW.

WWW RESOURCES: QUANTITY AND QUALITY

The same wealth of subject-specific information available to post-secondary instructors via the Internet is also available to their students. Thus sites such as the Virtual Hospital and ArtServe that we mentioned in Box 6.1 as valuable resources for lecture support can also be valuable resources for students, as an extended, multimedia, up-to-date library to accompany a course. Every subject area can be associated with sites of information (easily located with WWW search tools, see Chapter 3); the student, the same as the instructor or the professional (Chapter 4) must learn to search and select in an effective and discriminating manner. Students can no longer say "I couldn't find any information about...." if they have access to the Internet. The information may not be, eventually, relevant, but the process of making that determination is a learning experience in itself.

Typical examples of student-useful reference sites include those in Box 6.2.

INTERACTIVE LEARNING VIA THE WWW

But more than collections of information, the instructor can find an increasingly wide range of interactive learning resources available via WWW sites.

Simulations

Popular among these are WWW-based educational simulations, software programs which can be accessed remotely—the student sends in parameters to the simulation software on a central server and gets in return a display showing the reaction of the simulated system to his parameters. Smeaton and Slater (1994) have developed a toolkit whereby simulations can be encapsulated within a hypermedia shell through the use of a tool that allows messages to be passed from a WWW browser to another application—the running simulation. An example of this is:

> Environmental Engineering Laboratory:
> URL
> http://www-interact.eng.cam.ac.uk/TLTP_EXHIB/DEMOS/index.
> html/labintro.html
> *...Simulation to understand the transport processes of contaminants in groundwater systems*

This site not only gives access to the distant simulation package (at Cambridge University in the UK) but also structures that access in such a way that the student is helped in his reporting and interpreting of the results.

Box 6.2

Examples of tele-learning resources for post-secondary students

Division of Economics, Graduate School, University of Tokyo
URL http://e.u-tokyo.ac.jp/
...Site with links to economics resources at many different universities and up-to-date financial indexes and graphs.

The Daily Planet (University of Illinois at Urbana-Champaign)
URL http://www.atmos.uiuc.edu/
...Maintained by the Department of Atmospheric Sciences, satellite images and weather data, local and global climatic data, and hypermedia instructional modules.

The Internet Poetry Archive (University of North Carolina Press)
URL http://sunsite.unc.edu/dykki/poetry/home.html
...Selected poems from contemporary poets, accompanied by audio clips of each poet reading his or her work, as well as photographs and other illustrations. The poems are presented in their original languages, with English translations, if necessary.

Labyrinth
URL http://www.georgetown.edu/labyrinth/labyrinth-home.html
...Large collection of resource materials related to medieval history, including bibliographies, music and manuscripts.

Indiana University School of Law
URL http://www.law.indiana.edu/
...Site with links to legal journals, legal information servers worldwide, large collections of environmental law documents, LawTalk (a real time radio-type broadcast), and reports from meetings and conferences posted at the same time as the events occur.

Digital Video in Medicine
URL http://zax.radiology.arizona.edu/
...Site with medical video segments retrievable and playable using tools also available for downloading from the site.

HEASARC: Astrophysics in Cyberspace
URL http://guinan.gsfc.nasa.gov/
...Site maintained by NASA's High Energy Astrophysics Science Archive Research Center with a large collection of articles and references, and links to many other astrophysics sites.

Chemical Engineering
URL http://www.che.ufl.edu./WWW-CHE/academic/
...An extensive collection of chemical engineering resources available on the WWW.

Einstein and Relativity
URL http://sac.uky.edu/~msunde00/hon202/Einstein.html
...Collection of resources related to the field of General Relativity, supplemented by software tools and related links.

Biochemistry, Biophysics and Molecular Biology
URL http://golgi.harvard.edu/biopages/biochem.html
...Part of the World Wide Web Virtual Library, this set of pages contains a large collection of resources and links relating to the biosciences.

Gateway to World History
URL http://www.sfsu.edu/~history/www.htm
...A document repository and collection of resource links relating to world history.

Another example is:

The Open University Virtual Microscope
URL http://met.open.ac.uk/vms/vms.html#top1

With this "virtual instrumentation" the students rotate and view thin sections of simulated rock, rotated by three different methods. The views of the rock that are generated would not be possible with a conventional microscope.

Other examples are budget- and stock market-simulations, giving the user feedback on the effect of changes in the parameters involved in the simulation (Berlin, 1995). Some examples are:

University of California Center for Community Economic Research
URL http://garnet.berkeley.edu:3333/budget/budget.html

Institut für Betriebswirtschaftliche Geldwirtschafte
URL http://www.wiso.gwdg.de/ifbg/stock4.htm
(large collections of stock market simulators)

Many researchers are working on ways to improve the functionality of WWW environments with respect to the use of simulations, such as to provide instructors with the ability to record their inputs to a simulation, edit and eliminate interactions that are not of central instructional value, document their reasons for their choice of inputs, and link all of this to a WWW site that also allows students access to the simulation (Turoff, 1995).

Simulations as case studies

Another way to take advantage of tele-learning simulation material is for students to retrieve simulation material as case studies. The Virtual Hospital site identified in Box 6.1 has an outstanding collection of "Virtual Patients", or patient simulation materials, complete with extensive graphic resources such as X-rays and even audio resources when appropriate (i.e., the sound of a patient's cough).

Other innovative learning materials via WWW sites

Many other innovative tele-learning resources are becoming available via WWW environments, such as "WILT", a WWW based interactive language-teaching tool which can be used to dynamically generate exercises based on the type or types of grammatical structures in which they are interested (Lieberman and DiVito, 1994). WWW forms are used for exercise creation, and immediate feedback is given. The WWW site includes links to a collection of nearly 2,000 classic French texts.

The capacity to move in an interconnected way between a CD-ROM or a software program on the student's hard-drive or local network and an Internet-sited WWW page is beginning to be discovered as a source of tele-learning resources. (This was the technique used for the Open University Virtual Microscope noted earlier.) As another example, if a student is using the software package *Mathcad 6.0* (MathSoft, 1995), and is connected to the Internet, a Mathcad menu command will link her directly to MathSoft's home page. From there, an assortment of Mathcad documents can be moved directly into the program. This means that MathSoft can make available a greater variety of functions and services available than would be possible with a disk-only version of the program, including a guided tour of the software and a large assortment of solved and unsolved mathematical problems. The link "Quicksheets" for example includes more than 120 worked-out examples that can be directly imported into the student's current Mathcad worksheet. The location of MathSoft's WWW site is:

MathSoft: Mathcad Documents
```
URL http://www.mathsoft.com/
```

This capacity to link to a WWW site from a CD-ROM or other locally stored software could well become important educationally, as it allows the updating and personalizing of software in a new and powerful way. It can also bring a communication layer to locally available software, allowing discussion and dialogue among the program's users.

What is important about such innovations in the use of WWW sites for this chapter is that the instructor of face-to-face post-secondary courses, where students are likely to have convenient access to computers with WWW access, can anticipate that students will be able to find and use a broad array of learning and study materials from the WWW. While making use of this new range of study materials may not change the overall instructional balance of a course, it can certainly add new depth and stimulation to at least two of the components of that balance: reading new types of study materials, and carry out new types of individual study activities.

■ 6.2.6 IMPROVING THE RANGE AND QUALITY OF LEARNING ACTIVITIES FOR THE STUDENTS

As the previous examples show, providing new resources and facilitating students' engagement in new kinds of learning activities often overlap in the tele-learning context. In this section we list a sampling of new types of learning activities that the post-secondary instructor can incorporate into the face-to-face course via tele-learning.

EXAMPLES WITH AN EMPHASIS ON COMMUNICATION

Asynchronous communication among students can be utilized for more than discussion purposes. Among the many ways that communication can become a learning activity in itself are:

- Students place drafts of their written work in a conferencing environment, and as an assignment critique each other's work
- Students select appropriate articles from the network about an assigned topic, download them and print them, and submit analyses or reflections about them to the instructor (giving the instructor a copy of the printout so that she has it as a reference for her evaluation of the students' analyses)
- Student contribute sample test questions and answers to a conferencing environment relating to course objectives, and then answer and critique each other's questions and answers (Hiltz, 1995)
- Students put examples of their work on the Internet (within a Web site or as submissions to a listserv or newsgroup), ask for critical comment from the "outer world", and then evaluate their work based on this outside comment (Bos, Kikstra and Morgen, 1996)

EMPHASIS ON PROBLEM SOLVING AND GROUP COLLABORATION

The example just referred to by Bos, Kikstra and Morgen involved students working collaboratively on the construction of WWW pages as a design activity. Use of the WWW as a learning tool in this way is just beginning to emerge in post-secondary education Wray and his colleagues (1994) note that there have been "few explicit efforts to incorporate hypermedia authoring in the class-room"...allowing students to design and build hypermedia documents as part of the normal curriculum is a relatively unexplored area". (We describe the example referred to by Bos and her fellow students in **Interface 9**.)

Authoring collaboratively in HTML is of course only one example of new types of collaborative learning experiences becoming available to post-secondary students because of tele-learning tools and environments. Whenever students work together on a problem-solving task, the instructor can structure the activity as a collaborative-learning experience. There is considerable enthusiasm for collaborative learning as a strategy to increase instructional effectiveness (Heeren, 1995; Jonassen, 1995). Collaborative activities among students in face-to-face settings can be enhanced by tele-learning in a number of ways, such as the following:

- Students participate in an on-line simulation involving role play about management issues or marketing or other complex activities (see Wild and Winniford (1993) for an example involving two face-to-face classes in different locations working together on such a project)
- Students are paired by the instructor with remote experts (i.e., colleagues of the instructor who agree to participate) and get on-going critical comments on their development of course-project materials
- Students collaborate through shared annotation (marginal notes) on a set of documents using WWW forms (Davis and Huttenlocher, 1995)

EMPHASIS ON VIDEO-CONFERENCING

For many post-secondary students, skill development in interpersonal communications is important. This is especially so for students in subjects such as management or law, where cross-boundary communication may be critical for negotiation success. Tele-learning environments can be used in a variety of ways to support practice in authentic communication settings. As an example focused on language learning, video-conferencing can be used for language-practice sessions (Enkvist, 1992). Other examples, for development of management skills in solving a business case, make use of two-way video, either broadcast television with ISDN used for return video (Garito, Parisi, Hediard and Natali, 1995), or video-conferencing (Wheeler, Valacich, Alavi and Vogel, 1995) for realistic interactions. For skills in cross-cultural negotiation, interactive television is being used for role playing of negotiations among groups in different countries (Reif, 1995). However, these sorts of real-time collaborative activities are still generally in the experimental stage in traditional post-secondary institutions, and thus not likely to part of the contemporary tele-learning experience for the instructor working with face-to-face classes. Thus we will not discuss them further here.

AND MANY MORE POSSIBILITIES...

Thus there are many ways the post-secondary instructor can enhance learning activities or implement some sort of pedagogical re-engineering through the addition of collaborative activities in courses using tele-learning tools or resources. Paulsen, Barros, Bush, Compostela and Quesnel (1994) list 32 pedagogical techniques for CMC of which several relate to collaborative activities.

They also list 15 ways in which the post-secondary instructor can become a "pedagogical role model" for CMC learning for her peers. These include being a: goal-setter, discriminator, host, pace setter, explainer, lecturer, tutor, facilitator, mediator, mentor, assistant, provocateur, observer, and participant (p. 18).

Clearly, the post-secondary instructor has many possibilities for tele-learning, even when she works with face-to-face classes. But what limits these, besides the facilities available to the instructor in her face-to-face institution and the instructor's own imagination and energy?

■ 6.2.7 LIMITATIONS ON TELE-LEARNING FOR THE INSTRUCTOR OF FACE-TO-FACE POST-SECONDARY COURSES

Given all these possibilities described in Sections 6.2.1–6.2.6, why isn't every instructor in a traditional post-secondary institution already engaging in some form of pedagogical re-engineering with the help of tele-learning? Like all innovations, there are many barriers and inhibitors. For the post-secondary instructor, we deliberately anticipated many of these constraints in the opening section of this chapter when we looked at aspects of the reality frame around teaching at the post-secondary level. In particular, we suggest the following are the major limitations on the deployment of tele-learning by the instructor working with face-to-face post-secondary courses at the current time:

1. Institutional constraints

First are the constraints relating to what technical infrastructure and support for tele-learning are available to the instructor and to the students (we discuss this more in Chapter 7, from the institution's perspective). If students do not have convenient access to computers, to the Internet, to printers, and do not have skills in handling these, then clearly the instructor is constrained in her ideas for new learning activities.

2. Time and innovation constraints

All of the innovative teaching ideas in Section 6.2 will take time for the instructor to implement, sometimes considerable time. There is usually no real reward from the institution for this time expenditure; one's other work must go on. In fact, there may be criticism for attempting innovation: from the administration, if this involves non-budgeted expenses; from the students themselves, if new ideas turn out to be difficult to execute or evaluate in a traditional way ("We can see that innovation is good, but do we have to be the guinea pigs?"); from the technical-support persons in the institution who did not anticipate these new demands in their own work planning.

3. Communication- and information-management demands

Not only is communication and information-handling often time consuming, it also requires new technical skills in being able to use the environment and tools available. For example, the instructor who is now enthusiastic about the idea of a WWW page as an integrative course environment, may find that she has to learn how to make Web pages herself in order to have such an environment for her courses (luckily there seem to be students around to help...). Students will be confused or annoyed if communication seems disorganized or is not timely or if integrated sources of information are not functioning properly.

4. Pedagogical and imagination demands

And all of this innovation usually occurs without any pedagogical training or instructional support for the instructor. Just as the post-secondary instructor is meant to have good pedagogic skills without pedagogic training, she must develop good tele-learning skills on her own initiative and through her own imagination.

Sigh..., especially as there is often no official recognition for teaching innovation in terms of the career ladders of post-secondary faculty.

This state-of-affairs with respect to support for tele-learning has been discussed in terms of the post-secondary instructor working with students in a face-to-face institution. Perhaps the situation is considerably better for the instructors in our second category: instructors who work with courses where there has already been an institutional decision to serve students at a distance? We discuss this category of post-secondary instructors and why things may be easier for them with respect to tele-learning in the next section of this chapter.

■ 6.3 Tele-teaching: issues from the perspective of the post-secondary instructor

In this section, we focus on the instructor whose job includes teaching groups of students at a distance. As we did in Chapter 5, we will call this form of tele-learning "tele-teaching" to indicate the instructor is institutionally committed to teaching students he does not see in a face-to-face capacity, or does not see very often. This form of tele-learning may be in a post-secondary institution completely focused on such an approach, such as the 16 distance-teaching universities in Europe (see EADTU, 1994a) and the Open Universities in the UK and The Netherlands. This category also includes many different organizations providing training and professional education via courses offered to clients at a distance, sometimes within a multi-site company itself, or sometimes via a consortium or corporation that sells course delivery to companies. This category may also include persons working for a traditional face-to-face institution, university or training center, which also offers some of its courses at a distance (see Chapter 7 for a discussion of the infrastructure and support implications of this kind of tele-teaching offer within a traditional university or college).

By "tele-teaching at a distance" we mean the most familiar meaning of the term distance: that the instructor and students are at physically different locations from one another during the (major part of the) execution of a course.

■ 6.3.1 How is using tele-learning for teaching at a distance similar or different than using tele-learning in the face-to-face course?

Having spent so much time in Section 6.2 focusing on the post-secondary instructor working with face-to-face classes and making use of tele-learning for pedagogical re-engineering of those classes, it is useful to make some contrasts between the "face-to-face" instructor and the "at a distance" instructor in terms of their work conditions. As we will see later in this section, the uses that both of these categories of post-secondary instructors can make of tele-learning often are the same or similar. However, the surrounding context is quite different in a number of aspects.

While the instructor in the face-to-face situation probably introduces tele-learning into his teaching out of his own initiative, to improve instruction or to innovate, a considerably different situation exists for the instructor whose institution has made an organizational decision to support "distance education", the delivery of courses to students who are not in the same location as the instructor. Why is this situation different? Looking at each of the four categories of constraints on the face-to-face instructor for the implementation of tele-learning from Section 6.2.7, we can make the following comparisons:

1. Institutional support

For the "tele-teaching" instructor, it is the institution, not the instructor herself that has made the choice for this form of tele-learning (see Chapter 7 for more on this decision process). It is the institution which has made a commitment to supply a certain sort of technical infrastructure to support the tele-learning. It is usually not for the instructor to decide if tele-learning will take place via, for example, a compressed video system or the Internet; these are institutional decisions into which the instructor must fit. But to compensate for this lack of freedom of choice, the instructor has targeted institutional and technical support not only for herself but also, generally, for the remote sites from which the students will participate in the course.

2. Time-and-innovation constraints

While, as we will see, time is still a problem for the post-secondary instructor teaching courses to students at a distance, the basic idea of tele-learning is not an innovation that he must pioneer for himself in his institutional setting. Also, students who enroll in distance-education situations involving tele-learning know from the beginning that course delivery will take place at a distance; this changes some of the necessity to motivate and justify the use of tele-learning opportunities for the students that confronts the face-to-face instructor.

3. Communication-management demands

The same problems arise in this category for the instructor teaching courses to students at a distance as come to the face-to-face instructor, only potentially worse, as students in the face-to-face setting know that they will and can see the instructor on a regular basis, in class sessions, in her office, in informal ways. And when the face-to-face instructor communicates with students during lectures and lesson presentations, she can use her familiar instructional strategies in a familiar environment; tele-learning is an add-on to a familiar communication setting, not a total immersion into a new communication setting. For instructors working with students at a distance, the latter may be the case.

4. Pedagogical and imagination demands

Here things are both more difficult and perhaps more easy for the instructor working in a distance-education setting compared to the instructor working with face-to-face courses. More difficult, in that many things are different in terms of the pedagogy of teaching at a distance, when no face-to-face sessions form the core of the course. As we saw in Chapter 5 for the K-12 teacher involved in teaching students at a distance, not only are complicated technologies involved, but many different insights and skills need to be developed to handle the new teaching situation.

But the pedagogical demands may, perhaps, be less difficult for the tele-teaching instructor compared to the face-to-face instructor making use of tele-learning, for two important reasons:

- There is a long history of systematic efforts to study and support teaching-at-a-distance which has been accumulating for more than a century among distance-education professionals (see for example, Evans and Nation, 1989; Schlosser and Anderson, 1994; and Wagner, 1990). Through this long tradition of research and experience, (the International Council for Distance Education has been active professionally for a number of decades) the post-secondary teacher working in an institution organized around the delivery of courses at a distance has considerable information and models and guidelines of how to proceed.
- For some kinds of tele-teaching, particularly the two-way video sorts based on a philosophy of replicating the traditional classroom situation as closely as possible, there may be relatively little attempt at pedagogical re-engineering. If the ideal is that the instructor do what she would with a face-to-face class, with tele-learning technologies being used to make distant participants "feel" that they, too, are in that classroom, this may not involve any conceptual rethinking of one's instructional balance. As Gray and O'Grady (1994) observe

> ...the presence of the visual link per se does not necessarily improve the lesson's educational effectiveness. Often, it simply served to demonstrate that old practices which are ineffective in a mainstream classroom can be just as ineffective using this technology. ..this style of teaching only served to simulate a classroom environment in which the technology generated a safety net for producing 'comfortable' mirror images of mediocre classroom practices. (p. 668)

Soloway (1995) makes similar hard comments:

...Why wire up [a remote site] so they can pipe in lectures? We know that when instruction is centered around a lecturing, talking head, students don't learn. Why, then, should we believe that it will work any better when students view the talking head on a TV set? And, adding an audio backchannel so that students can ask the talking head questions does not profoundly change the pedagogy. (p. 20).

Of course, all the distance-education literature relating to lesson delivery at a distance emphasises the importance of good pedagogy, rather than mediocre talking-head approaches (see for example, Cyrs and Smith, 1990). It is just a risk that needs to be mentioned. Tele-teaching may seem easier than pedagogical re-engineering in the face-to-face situation, because it will be easier if no comparable pedagogical engineering takes place in the distance situation.

Given these reflections, let us backtrack and better clarify what is included in the category of teaching courses to students at a distance. We look first at the motivation for such courses and the various sorts of technology combinations that characterize them.

■ 6.3.2 MOTIVATIONS FOR COURSES AT A DISTANCE

The history of giving courses at a distance is more than 100 years old. The strongest motivations have always been to overcome the time- and place-bound aspects of taking courses, particularly for adults (see Kaye's overview, 1989, for many of the classic references).

MOTIVATIONS RELATING TO DISTANCE AND TIME

Sometimes the student is not able to come to the physical setting of an educational institution, for a range of reasons that include health and family circumstances. Another set of reasons can occur when the student is also employed. Then the time away from work and the cost to the employer of supporting travel to a distant site are major reasons for taking courses at a distance. For example, it has been estimated the single largest cost component in training and upgrading among employed adults is the working time lost to the employers when the employee goes away for courses, and that this can be up to 85% of the total training cost (BIS Mackintosh, 1990)

MOTIVATIONS RELATING TO MORE TARGETED LEARNING

There are further reasons for taking a course at a distance beyond those of direct financial consequence. We mention three:

Increase transfer likelihood

One reason relates to the evidence that transfer of learning may be more likely to occur the closer in time and circumstance the training is to the workplace (Schoenmaker, 1993). Going away to attend a course may not lead to as good a payoff on the job as being able to take the course closer in time and place to needs as they occur in the workplace setting. This idea relates to the "just-in-time" learning approach, gaining popularity in both theory and practice (Lewis, 1995).

Increasing instructional flexibility

Overlapping motivations for time-and-place flexibility are also motivations for a variety of other types of flexibility. We can identify more than 20 "dimensions of flexibility" relating to giving the student more choice in instructional method, in pace and sequence of learning, in media used for learning, and even in method and timing of evaluation (Collis, Vingerhoets and Moonen, 1995). We discuss these types of flexibility in Chapter 8, from the course-designer's perspective; each of these types of flexibility has good reasons to recommend it, for certain students.

Trying to support different aspects of flexibility for different students in the same face-to-face course is obviously very difficult. Thus, gradually, courses being taken at a distance have sometimes become testbeds for other sorts of instructional flexibility as well as time and place flexibility. Sometimes distance education, open learning, and more-flexible learning are assumed to be so much overlapping as to be synonymous. This assumption is generally not correct.

"OPEN AND FLEXIBLE LEARNING"

Openness involves the willingness to make a course open to all who wish to take it, a motivation that has social and political as well as generous impulses. The conviction that individuals should not be disenfranchised from taking a course which they feel is important for them because of the lack of background qualifications or opportunities is also part of the growing development of "non-traditional" forms of course delivery. Tele-learning and tele-teaching in this context would have to be related to the relaxation of entry requirements for a course, not to openness in terms of instructional flexibility once within the course.

Openness is especially important as a strategic mechanism to stimulate better equality of educational opportunity throughout Europe as well as in other countries. Many different publications summarize these aspirations; in Europe, see the location:

CORDIS
URL http://www.cordis.lu/
...Information about European Community initiatives, including those relating to "open, distance, and flexible learning"

It is interesting to look briefly at these European initiatives, as representative of a strategic motivation for certain types of tele-learning. In Chapter 8 we look at the initiatives from their scientific value.

European initiatives for "open and flexible learning"

In Europe there is considerable commitment to the concept "open and flexible learning" (OFL), which is sometimes also called "open and distance learning" (ODL). Large multi-national projects supported by the Commission of the European Community (see Van den Brande, 1993; P. Bates, 1995), support and stimulate many different manifestations of more-flexible ways to follow courses through the use of tele-learning and its subset, tele-teaching. (See for example, the various reports coming out of the "TeleScopia Project" which involves distance delivery of courses throughout Europe: Collis, Parisi and Ligorio, 1995; Collis, 1995d.)

However, despite many different projects and initiatives throughout Europe for more than a decade, there is still no consistently used definition of open, flexible and distance learning. In the literature, terms such as the following may have something to do with what we are calling "tele-teaching" and tele-learning:

> *...Correspondence education; correspondence study; home study; independent study; directed private study; open learning; extension education; external studies; distance education; distance teaching; teaching from a distance (in French, télé-enseignement); distance learning; distance study (in German; Fernstudium for the higher-educational level, and Fernunterricht, for the "further" education level); open universities, flexible learning, open and distance learning (ODL), self-study courses, on-line courses, ...*

Given this diversity, "it is perhaps best to describe [open learning] as forms of education and training which have sought to become more open by responding to the specific needs (e.g., for materials, support or assessment) and aspirations of individual learners" (Rumble, 1993, p. 3).

IMPLICATIONS FOR THE INSTRUCTOR

These sorts of distinctions matter very much to the instructor of courses whose students are at a distance. They relate to the choices he can make with respect to content focus in the course and the sorts of learning activities that will be perceived by the students as acceptable.

One final point is important to note from the instructor's perspective: more and more, institutions are making the decision to offer courses at a distance for competitive and financial reasons as well as educational and philosophical (see Chapter 7). Thus the instructor may also have to be aware that he must work hard to satisfy the customers of a course, in order to build the market for his institution's expansion. This also has many implications for the instructor.

■ 6.3.3 TELE-LEARNING AND DISTANCE EDUCATION

Distance education does not have to involve tele-learning or its subset tele-teaching, and in fact "correspondence education" involving text-based course material sent through the ordinary mail to the student is still the major means of communication and teaching in distance education. Postal delivery of instructional materials was part of most distance-education courses throughout the world in 1993 and the only transmission channel for a majority of the courses (Van den Brande, 1993, p. 97).

However, we can identify three main streams of distance education that involve tele-learning and each has very different implications for the instructor involved (Dunning, Van Kekerix and Zaborowski, 1993; and Taylor, 1992). These streams are: (a) one evolving out of the traditional print-based correspondence form of distance education; (b) one evolving out of the idea of "bringing the classroom to the student" via two-way video and broadcasting; and (c) one, newer form, evolving from the idea of using computer networking for course delivery.

In the first of these, tele-learning has developed as a supplement, a way to add or enhance communication; in the second and third, tele-learning is part of the basic approach. The second, involving real-time two-way video or interactive television, is what is commonly called "tele-teaching" because it preserves the instructor's familiar ways of teaching, in real-time, in front of a group of learners, as much as possible. In the remainder of Section 6.3 we look at each of these three categories of course delivery at a distance from the perspective of the post-secondary instructor involved in that delivery.

▨ 6.3.4 PRINT-BASED DISTANCE-EDUCATION COURSES, WITH TELE-LEARNING USED FOR COMMUNICATION

In this stream of distance education, tele-learning is most typically used to support communication. This communication takes place in the framework of the study of carefully designed print materials. In traditional print-based distance education, the identity of the instructor can become blurred. The instructor, in fact, speaks not through lectures or live presentations but through the design of the print materials, so in one sense the "instructor" is the author of the print materials. However, these authors may have no interaction with their eventual students. Those who do interact with the students studying the print materials, as contact persons or to give feedback and assessment on the students' written work, are probably not the same persons as those who wrote the materials. Yet for the students, these persons, sometimes called tutors, fulfill many of the expected functions of an instructor.

TELE-LEARNING FOR COMMUNICATION

Tele-learning emerged as a component of print-based correspondence education as the use of the telephone for communication purposes evolved. More and more, distant students could use the telephone (or as recent variants, fax and e-mail) to contact their tutor/instructors for purposes ranging from information to intensive one-to-one tutoring. Thus one of the weaknesses of print-based distance education, the slow turnaround in instructor/tutor feedback, has been long addressed by forms of what we are calling tele-learning technologies in this book.

With the addition of audio-conferencing and then later, computer conferencing, other important omissions in print-based distance education were addressed: the lack of student interaction, the lack of discussion, the lack of learning from (oral) communication with others.

We have already discussed the implications for the instructor of having to manage and deal with the additional communication made possible by e-mail and computer conferencing; these managerial and pedagogical issues are similar regardless of if the instructor is working with a class that occasionally meets face-to-face or one that meets at a distance, so we will not discuss them again here. Instead we will give attention to one form of conferencing that is not likely to be used with students in a face-to-face institution but has a considerable history in traditional, print-based distance education. This is audio-conferencing.

AUDIO-CONFERENCING

During an audio conference, the skilled instructor/tutor/moderator can lead the distributed class members through a valuable learning experience. Conversely, the unskilled instructor can witness a poor or negative educational experience (Cookson, 1995). The instructor leading an audio-conference as part of a distance-learning course must use all the skills that a face-to-face instructor uses for a successful group discussion, but with the additional need to compensate for:

- the lack of visual cues
- the lack of a sense of community among the participants
- the lack of visual reference points
- the lack of ways to "see" if all members how the group are responding
- the lack of most of the usual ways of knowing that individuals wish to contribute (see for example, Mason, 1994)

Cookson (1995) suggests strategies such as the following that the instructor can use to minimize the above lacks:

- Reduce the feeling of sensory awareness by devices such as a role call; ask the students to identify themselves in the order in which they are sitting and make a seating chart so that the instructor can picture the group; use examples and anecdotes that conjure mental pictures; have all student preface their comments by giving their names and seating location; select a student to be a visualizer at each remote site, to paint word pictures of what is going on; send supplemental visuals ahead of time so there is a common reference point to look at; encourage everyone to circulate photographs of themselves
- Manage the communication by being consistent in the way you respond and give feedback; discourage off-mike conversation; suggest some informal communication prior to the start of the lesson or discussion; try to form small discussion groups with students from different sites; make sure all participants speak slowly and with frequent pauses

And there is another major difficulty: the instructor leading the audio conference may not be (and probably is not) the same person as the one who designed and developed the course materials. This can bring inconsistencies in message and emphasis for the students.

Advantages of audio-conferencing

Nonetheless, audio-conferencing is seen as bringing important enough benefits into print-based distance learning that it is a form of tele-learning that is widely practiced. The US Congress Office of Technology Assessment (1990), for example, estimates that 9% of training in the US makes use of audio-conferencing, because it involves relatively simple technological provision or skill training (a room with speaker phone if more than one person at a site is involved, one's own telephone at work or home is adequate otherwise); can be participated in at the workplace so that the trainee's time off work is minimized; and along with these benefits, brings some level of social interaction, as well as time- and task structure, to the course at little expense.

Disadvantages of audio-conferencing

The first disadvantage is the loss of flexibility of time, and perhaps of place, both of which are valued so highly for the correspondence-stream of distance education. Audio-conferencing is a real-time, or synchronous, event which in turn pushes participants into needing to be at similar points in the learning material in order to benefit educationally from the discussion. This in turn further reduces the flexibility-of-time aspect of distance education. Furthermore, any real-time cooperative event requires scheduling and organization among all the participants, which again can be difficult to manage and in contradiction with the on-the-job situations of many distant learners.

Thus the instructor utilizing audio-conferencing for discussions in print-based distance education courses may be dealing only with some of the potential students, who may or may not be at the same point in their study of the learning materials, and who may or may not know anything about each other as individuals. A picture could be worth a thousand words in this situation....

Technical issues

Audio-conferencing, if using one's own telephone, requires only that the instructor or his institute organize via a telephone company an audiobridge connection by which different speakers can hear and talk to each other at the same time. Usually this means that a telephone operator must call each participant one by one and add them to the multi-point call. Clearly this in turn means that participation must be well-organized in advance, another task for the instructor. If there is a group at a remote site, then issues relating to movement of the microphone and minimizing noise while maintaining consistent volume have to be addressed.

New aspects to communication

From the instructor's perspective, a major issue in audio-conferencing is how to make sure everyone is heard. This may involve physical distancing from respective microphones and it also involves techniques in speaking clearly, in agreeing on procedures for identifying one's self as the speaker, and on procedures for interruption and turn-taking (see for example, Heeren (1995) for a literature review about these strategies in audio-conferencing, and Mason (1994) for practical suggestions).

FURTHER EVOLUTION OF THE CORRESPONDENCE STREAM

The difficulties of getting participants together at the same time, of making sure audio connections are working properly, and of moderating an effective audio discussion are such that there is an increasing interest is replacing or supplementing audio-conferencing with computer conferencing in traditional distance education. Partly this is because of the asynchronous nature of computer conferencing and partly because computer conferencing reduces some of the management issues associated with audio-conferencing, such as procedures for turn taking, or for making sure that all who want to, have the opportunity to contribute. This evolution is occurring relatively slowly in training, because of the technical problems of providing students with computer access and network connections. However, many of the large distance-teaching institutions are experimenting with computer-conferencing components instead of audio-conferencing for some of their courses (the Open University in the UK is a major example; see Chapter 8 and also see their home page at location URL `http://www.open.ac.uk/`).

Despite this evolution from audio, real-time conferencing to computer, asynchronous conferencing, many of the traditional distance-education course providers still see printed materials as the core form of lesson presentation. In contrast, the second stream of distance education we are considering in this chapter comes from a different basic premise. The difference relates to the importance of the instructor as the central focus of instruction. In traditional distance education, the instructor was hidden within the pages of a book or between the lines of well-designed text material; in "tele-teaching" type distance education, the instructor is visible and hear-able and central to the momentum of course delivery.

■ 6.3.5 TELE-TEACHING WITH INTERACTIVE TELEVISION OR COMPRESSED VIDEO: EXTENDING THE CLASS SESSION TO STUDENTS AT A DISTANCE

While the core of the correspondence-stream of distance education is the assumption that the lesson-presentation skills of the teacher can be re-presented through well-designed print materials, the core of the "video" stream of distance education is to use technologies and pedagogical techniques to make it seem as much as possible that the distant student is sitting in the face-to-face classroom of the teacher. This can be called "tele-presence": "Being there while being here" or "being there without having to" (Frenkel, 1995, p. 73). Thus "teaching" in the familiar ways of lesson presentation by the instructor, questioning, and feedback-giving exchanges with students during the lesson, is to be maintained. Interactive television and two-way video make this most directly possible, providing some immediate opportunity for the questioning and student-instructor interaction to occur. As we have seen in Chapter 2, there are many technological combinations possible to facilitate this form of tele-teaching; what matters to the instructor is if she can see her remote-site students or not. Common in all the combinations is that her students can see her, as she teaches, and can ask a question in real-time if they wish.

EXAMPLES OF VIDEO/TV "TELE-TEACHING"

This form of real-time tele-learning, what we are calling "tele-teaching" for convenience, is well established in both training settings and in traditional higher-education institutions which decide to broaden their delivery options by serving students at a distance. In both cases, those involved in basic decision making are most familiar with the face-to-face classroom or lecture-hall type of course delivery, and believe that this type should be retained and duplicated as much as possible for students at a distance. (This is in contrast with the traditional distance-education institutions, who very early decided to replace the centrality of the live teacher with the centrality of well-designed instructional materials.) We next look at a few examples of real-time video "tele-teaching" from both training and university settings.

Tele-teaching: training examples

In training settings, the form of tele-learning that appears to be most typically chosen is the real-time tele-teaching approach, using interactive television or two-way video-conferencing. This is consistent with the fact that real-time tele-teaching is most like traditional lecture-type classrooms, and so is an expansion of the student base rather than a form of pedagogical re-engineering. For example, in the US, 88% of "large companies" utilize a lecture approach for training and 90% utilize television-delivered courses and increasingly two-way compressed video for at least some portion of their training needs (US Office of Technology Assessment, 1990). In the US, there are over 140 privately-owned business television networks and in the UK a number of commercial business television networks are now offering services to distributed companies (Murray, 1994). Business-television networks programmed specifically for certain occupational groups (financial executives, automobile dealers, lawyers, engineers, law enforcement officers, fire fighters, hospital administrators, among many) provide services and business television training networks owned and operated by corporations are increasing in the US as well (Rush, 1991).

As an example of a private broadcast network for corporate training, the Ford Motor Company is spending $100 million US to link all 6000 dealers in the US and Canada to its Fordstar Network to receive eight channels of live, full-color video broadcast from a central station in Michigan. Since the mid 1980s, this direct-satellite broadcasting has been providing one hour of training per day to 200 management offices in the two countries, but "advances in compression technology have now created economies of scale that make the Fordstar network [to dealerships] possible" ("Ford links...", 1994).

The number of instructors providing courses via real-time tele-teaching to students at a distance in the training and corporate-education context is considerable. It is interesting to note that very little information about these courses can be found on the WWW and very little use of networking at all has yet become part of these courses.

Examples from traditional universities

When traditional universities decide to offer some of their courses at a distance, their choice has been predominately through television delivery and more recently through two-way video delivery through a variety of transmission channels. As with the training situation, many examples can be given, particularly from the US. In the US, over half of the higher-education institutes offer some form of what they call "distance learning" and of this, nearly 80% involves television or two-way video in various forms (Cotton, 1995). It is further estimated that 15 % of the enrollment in traditional higher-education institutions in the US is involved in these forms of tele-learning. We discuss this more in Chapter 7. Box 6.3 provides some other examples.

IMPLICATIONS FOR THE INSTRUCTOR

The instructor involved in this kind of extended-classroom teaching may not be re-engineering her approach to instruction, but certainly has at least three major areas of concern that the face-to-face instructor does not encounter. These include (interactive) television delivery skills, problems with audio, and issues involved with managing interactivity among distributed participants.

- The Stanford Instructional Television Network (since the early 1970s) provides hundreds of credit courses in graduate-level engineering and computer science broadcast to the workplaces of its students (SITN, 1995)

- California State University, Chico, has offered 672 courses taught by 216 of its faculty through its microwave-based interactive television system, and 163 courses taught by 22 of its faculty through its satellite-based interactive television system (Chico State University, 1995).

- In Australia video-conferencing via satellite is being used for specialized courses for practicing nurses in remote areas (Latchem and Rapley, 1992).

Television-delivery skills

A major challenge in video-based tele-learning for the instructor involved is how to perform on camera. The instructor must learn how to be more than a talking-head, which is both a matter of television-handling skill and pedagogical insight, as we already discussed in Chapter 5. Bruce and Shade (1994, 95), Cyrs and Smith (1990) and Sorenson (1995) are among many who provide guidance to the instructor for these types of skills and insights. A particular comment is often made as to the importance of appropriately designed visual aids. Tykwinski and Poulin (1995), for example, have prepared a handbook for compressed video instructors which includes design and layout criteria for visual aids. Aspects to consider include balance, placement, size, quantity, resolution, contrast and color of the elements used in the visual aid. Of course, illegible visuals are a concern in face-to-face settings as well as instructional television and two-way video settings.

Problems with audio

Audio problems are not usually an issue in face-to-face delivery, but certainly are in real-time video-based distance delivery. Certain technical problems relating to the audio-aspects of video-based course delivery frequently confront the instructor. For example, Pugh, Parchman and Simpson (1992), in a study done for the US Navy regarding video telecommunications (VTC) for training of its distributed personnel, indicate that

> ...the most consistently reported problem with VTC systems is poor quality audio...there are too few microphones to pick up all participants in group

discussions. More importantly, the person speaking often hears a very distracting echo effect. Most of the sites surveyed reported problems with static on telephones, audio feedback, fluctuations in volume, insufficient microphones and echo. (p. 60)

Echo in particular is still a problem in ISDN-networked situations (see Chapter 2 and Arav, 1995).

Managing interactivity

There are special challenges in managing student interactivity when students are at a distance, challenges that escalate when multiple sites are involved or when the instructor is working with both a face-to-face group and remote groups. How to manage student interactivity has emerged as a question of interest not only to instructors as those who must integrate interactivity into their tele-teaching sessions, but also to researchers looking for generalizable principles relating to frequency and form of interactivity (see for example, Zhang and Fulford, 1994). We discuss this in more detail, from the researcher's perspective, in Chapter 8. What matters to the instructor is how to smoothly integrate questions and student responses during a lesson, a problem by the way that most face-to-face lecturers in large lecture halls have not successfully solved.

EVOLUTION OF TELEVISION-TYPE TELE-LEARNING

From the instructor's perspective there has not been too radical a change in pedagogy in the subset of tele-learning that we are calling real-time tele-teaching over the last decade. Instructors still, in general, try to reproduce a good face-to-face class presentation, where the presentation is delivered in traditional ways. The transmission channels and technologies involved in this delivery are rapidly changing, but in general, what the instructor is doing is not. There is not much evidence of pedagogical re-engineering in terms of either new combinations and balances of instructional approaches or in new, enriched approaches within a particular aspect of instruction. What is different from traditional face-to-face classes is that some of the students are physically somewhere else. Most of the efforts involved with technology and pedagogy in real-time tele-teaching are aimed at making these students feel they are actually in the instructor's face-to-face class. If that face-to-face class would be better taught if re-engineered is not generally a focus of attention.

In particular, and very interesting when universities and university instructors are involved, there seems to be very little use of networking in the many ways associated with pedagogical re-engineering that we described in terms of the post-secondary instructor in traditional settings described in Section 6.2 of this chapter, or in terms of the substantial efforts being made to integrate communication within correspondence-type distance education that we discussed in Section 6.3.3. There are notable exceptions: for example, courses offered by the University of Central Florida involve one-way video with multi-point audio-conferencing, but also e-mail via the Internet for between-session discussions, group project planning, and submission of some assignments (for information, contact `Cornell@Pegasus.cc.UCF.edu`)

However, an integration of real-time video-based technologies with asynchronous use of network technologies appears to be still unusual in practice. We will discuss this further at various points in the book, particularly in Chapter 10.

■ 6.3.6 COURSES VIA COMPUTER

A third, and relatively new, approach to distance delivery of courses is to offer the courses via a computer network. We can identify three categories of such courses, each of which brings particular challenges to the instructors involved. One category is courses offered entirely through a computer network (usually the Internet). The second is courses offered via audio-graphics conferencing, a real-time combination of audio-conferencing and some form of shared computer workspace. The third category is through specialized computer-based systems in physical locations such as regional centres where students go to access the special technologies and the support persons and technologies that are all part of the overall delivery-setup. What are major characteristics of these sorts of distance-delivered courses and what are some implications for the instructors of such courses?

"ON-LINE COURSES"
Instructors involved in the delivery of entire courses over a network in 1995 are typically pioneers or entrepreneurs in new sorts of start-up ventures looking to revolutionize educational delivery in various ways. The consortium called GNA, Globewide Network Academy, which is attempting to act as a sort of broker or coordinator for such courses is one such example:

GNA (Global Network Academy)
URL http:// uu-gna.mit.edu:8001/uu-gna/

University instructor involvement
However, not only pioneers and entrepreneurs are involved in networked-delivered courses: a number of universities are deciding at the institutional level to support network-based "on-line" courses in addition to their face-to-face

offerings. The number of such universities is still small (certainly compared to those who for many years have been committed to instructional television and video delivery) but growing. A recent report indicates 70 universities offering "on-line" courses ("Virtual colleges...", 1995). Often these are traditional universities, offering one or two of their normal courses, in an adapted way, to remote participants. Broker organizations are starting to coordinate the dissemination of information about the courses, and stimulate a stream of students to register in the courses.

Examples of networked-based courses

Certainly a pioneer example in the delivery of courses over a network is the New Jersey Institute of Technology (NJIT), US, where for more than a decade a mixture of research and institutional-delivery innovation has occurred. This innovation involves the integration of specialized software and a particular pedagogical approach that are together called "The Virtual Classroom" (Hiltz, 1990, 1995). The work was so pioneering at its start that the term "virtual classroom" was copyrighted. Many different courses at NJIT have been taught via the virtual-classroom environment, generally showing the results to be as good as those for students taking parallel versions of the courses at the same institution via face-to-face methods. (We discuss the software used in The Virtual Classroom in more detail in Chapter 8.)

As another example, the University of Paisley in Scotland, in collaboration with others, is supporting the "Electronic University", a networked-based infrastructure for taking courses at a distance, which includes the integrated use of e-mail, closed and open computer-based discussions, occasional live tele-conferencing events, access privileges to both university library facilities and resources available via the Internet, tutors assigned to each ten students for close interaction, and the optional provision for some face-to-face get-togethers, primarily for social purposes, if students wish. Courses are given academic credit by the University of Paisley, and the entire service is run in a formal and professional way.

For information about these courses, see location:

OnLine Education: The Electronic University

```
URL http://www.online.edu/index.htm
or contact: info@hka.online.edu
```

There are many other examples of networked-delivered courses, each with innovative aspects. Box 6.4 lists a sample.

Box 6.4

Examples of courses offered via the Internet or other networks by traditional educational institutions

---

"Problems and Principles in the Use of Computer Networks for Course Delivery", London University, UK
...Students use the CoSy computer-conferencing environment for all course activities except for self-study of reading materials and preparation of essays.

"Environmental Management", UETP-EEE (a consortia of European universities and industrial partners providing specialized education for engineers involved in environmental issues, managed in Helsinki, Finland; Taukojärvi and Jarvilehto, 1995).
URL http://www.dipoli.hut.fi/TechNet/org/ (Note: the course itself requires a password to enter, in recognition of the fee-paying status of its students)
...This course is offered via a WWW site which incorporates extensive reading materials, links to external sites, and newsgroup functionalities for moderated discussions of each module of the course. In addition, students participate in three video-conferences, in order to get to know their fellow students and their distant instructor. More personal support is supplied by local tutors.

"Introduction to Philosophy", Oregon State University
URL: http://www.cs.orst.edu:80/department/instruction/phil201/

"Commentary on Art", Pennsylvania State University (Maddox, 1995)
URL http://salazar.aa.psu.edu/courses/art122w/122WHome.htm
...This course is taught via a combination of WWW sources, scheduled real-time chat periods, newsgroup discussions, and e-mail.

Convergences and their implications

The latter example, Maddox's "Commentary on Art" course, is an interesting example of the coming-together of face-to-face courses and distance courses via networking at traditional universities. This coming-together is well established with respect to television-type or instructional video courses, where frequently a face-to-face group with the instructor present and a remote group participate in the same course at the same time. However, the discovery of these possibilities for course delivery via computer networks is newer for post-secondary institutions, and brings new issues to the instructor as well as the institution.

One issue relates to the potential increase in number of students that can be served by an Internet course. What are the implications for the instructor if many, many students want to participate in her course?

This is not a fanciful question, as the following example demonstrates:

- A course on Internet navigation was developed at the University of Pittsburgh and taught in face-to-face settings. Its instructor then decided to offer it to the public, via the Internet (R. Smith, 1995). Within a short period, 864 people from more than 20 countries registered for this Internet-delivered course. A second round of the course drew more than 15,000 participants from more than 50 countries. The course was run through a listserv where assignments involve retrieving information efficiently and effectively from locations accessible via the Internet.

The Finnish example noted in Box 6.4 (the course on "Environmental Management") offered via a WWW environment on the Internet, is probably an organizational model for network-based course development; the Internet and its tools are used because of their range and sophistication, but the institution retains control (and financial interest) via a password and firewall system. For the instructor, this means he can know who his students are; a major issue in instructing at a distance, regardless of the modality. Also, the closed environment allows the instructor to work on the development of group cohesiveness and collaborative activities among the distributed participants, not possible if network lurkers can drop into the environment. During 1995 software developments for access control to WWW sites, mainly motivated by commercial interests, are becoming commonplace (Wiggins, 1995b).

AUDIO-GRAPHICS SYSTEMS

The extensive Australian experience with audio-graphics teaching also has many examples involving the post-secondary level (Ellis, Debreceny and Crago, 1995). We discussed the pedagogical and logistical challenges facing the secondary-school teacher in an audio-graphics teaching situation in Chapter 6 (see also Oliver and Reeves, 1994). These same issues and challenges pertain to the instructor in a post-secondary institution teaching via audio-graphics so we will not repeat them here.

COMPUTER-BASED SYSTEMS IN SPECIALIZED PHYSICAL LOCATIONS

The third type of course-delivery configuration involving networks for distance delivery of courses to students is hard to describe in a few words. This is the type of system in which computer-delivered instruction is the core aspect, but in which this instruction is supported and delivered through an integrated series of regional and local centres, usually connected by ISDN networking, so that a sophisticated client-server infrastructure is made available for the students. The regional centres not only are the locations with the computers and network connections able to access the centrally stored multi-media learning resources, but also include a broad variety of support features for the students, including meeting rooms for local groups, print-based and software resources of various sorts, and trained personnel to offer support as local tutors or counselors.

European examples

In Europe, there are various examples of this sort of composite environment. In France, for example, the CNAM Remote Teaching Network is aimed at working and unemployed persons and involves more than 100 local centres (CNAM, 1995). The local centres make it easy for students to come together, communicate with each other and with on-site "motivaters" and use collective general resources such as computers, access to ISDN networks, and audio-visual materials. From these centres the students study at a distance from remote instructors, via combinations of real-time communication (text-based chat and sometimes video-conferencing), e-mail, and access to educational software and study materials from the "pedagogical data base" located on a central server. Special software has been developed to support these various possibilities. Because of the ISDN interconnectivity between the regional sites and the central server, the student can access video resources as easily as text resources.

A similar large-scale system operates in Germany via the "Funline" network (Deutsche Telekom, 1994). This network is described as an application platform whereby approximately 140 local-area networks involving more than 4,000 local PCs in various training centres for Deutsche Telekom throughout the country are connected via ISDN to central servers. These servers offer software for more than 30 courses each composed of a series of modules, as well as supporting tutor–student communication possibilities via asynchronous e-mail. The central software automatically records each learning session for each learner. The educational software available from the central server is developed with a standard user interface and utilizes a common database of course materials. Learners download about 1.5 million training hours per year, and learning sessions can be chosen by modules rather than complete courses, meaning that "the user no longer has to purchase and pay the entire course but only the parts he really needs" (Hammerschmidt, 1994)

The role of the "instructor" in these environments is hard to define, as many persons are involved in the course-delivery process. (see also Chapters 7 and 8). The instructor may no longer be involved in the design of the course or its instructional balance, but be primarily focused on the roles of communicator and motivater of the distributed students as they work in a more-or-less self-study arrangement. The converse may also be the case, as well as combinations of both design and delivery aspects. Whatever the combination, the instructor is operating in ways quite different from her counterpart in a traditional post-secondary face-to-face institution.

In Section 6.3, we have looked at some of the extensive developments in different forms of distance education with tele-learning applications. Some of these forms are conceptually and experientially familiar to many post-secondary instructors, such as "tele-teaching" via television or two-way video to distributed groups of students. Other forms involve pedagogical as well as technological innovations, such as the courses being offered via the WWW or other specialized network environments such as CNAM and FUNLINE. But in all cases, the post-secondary instructor teaching students who she is not working with in a face-to-face, traditional course setting is faced with some challenges and special issues. In Section 6.4 we bring together some of the general problems confronting the post-secondary instructor whose students are at a physical distance from the instructor regardless of what combination of technology is being employed.

■ 6.4 PROBLEMS FOR THE POST-SECONDARY INSTRUCTOR TEACHING STUDENTS AT A DISTANCE

Regardless of the modality of delivery, there are certain common problems and issues confronting the instructor who delivers courses to distant, adult students. In this section, we look at some of these common problems and how they can be addressed by the instructor in the different delivery modes. We also look at problems that are unique to certain of the modes.

In this section, we discuss the instructor's perspective on:

- Problems with course organization and management
- Problems with lesson presentation and interactivity
- Problems with student communication and enrichment activities
- Other problems, such as coordination with local support and assessment

when she works with students at a distance. In many cases, the problems are similar to those described in Section 6.2, from the perspective of the instructor of face-to-face courses making use of tele-learning, in that tele-learning is making physical proximity with the instructor an increasingly arbitrary construct in course delivery at the post-secondary level (Mason, 1994).

■ 6.4.1 PROBLEMS WITH COURSE ORGANIZATION AND MANAGEMENT

The instructor is not alone in organizing and managing the course with which he is involved in most of the examples in Section 6.3. Usually the institution offering the course is responsible for many aspects of information and communication about the course, the instructor perhaps not at all. It is also important that the institution provides instruction and support to students with respect to the technical requirements of their participation in the course. The institution, or perhaps the innovative instructor, may also set up some form of electronic course organization such as a WWW site (see Section 6.2).

But regardless of the amount of institutional support, the instructor is central in setting up or at least carrying out the course procedures with the students, and in helping to develop a sense of dynamism and group chemistry for the course. The need to develop a feeling of community among course participants is seen as a key task of the instructor, if this occurs via asynchronous computer conferencing (Kaye, 1992a), or two-way instructional video (Cyrs and Smith, 1990). This demands new pedagogical skills on the part of the instructor.

■ 6.4.2 PROBLEMS WITH LESSON PRESENTATION

Here the differences between the different modalities of delivery (print with audio or computer communication, television/video, and computer delivered) critically affect lesson-presentation effectiveness for instructors involved with distant students.

In the variants of distance education predominately based on print materials, "lesson presentation" is generally done not by a live instructor, but by the wisdom of a live instructor translated into the lesson materials which the student will read and study on her own. There are many skills needed for the design of such self-standing print materials (see Burge and Frewin, 1989). The time and skill needed for the development of quality learning materials intended to teach without an instructor being present is considerable.

TEACHING VIA TELEVISION OR TWO-WAY VIDEO

From the instructor's perspective with regard to delivery of courses to distant students, perhaps the most attention has been given to helping the instructor present lessons effectively in a television/video environment. Cyrs and Smith (1990) note that the major deficiencies in television-type courses are likely to be the following:

- Poor course adaptation, thinking that a traditionally taught course can be directly replicated in front of a camera
- A "talking-head" delivery approach by the instructor, with poor use of visual aides
- Poor and uncorrelated handouts to accompany the live class session
- Poor audio-presentation skills, often barely audible and at times inarticulate
- Boring and uninspired didactic approaches (Cyrs and Smith, 1990, p. 3)

In other words, the same weaknesses as face-to-face post-secondary instructors often show in the lecture hall!

Issues and recommendations

The instructor teaching via television- or two-way video has a variety of sets of guidelines to choose from to help her improve her instructional delivery (for example, Cyrs and Smith, 1990; Rezabek, Cochenour, Bruce and Shade 1995; Lewis, 1994; Willis, 1993). Most of these guidelines contain suggestions which are also sensible for face-to-face teaching (this is not surprising as simulating the face-to-face lesson-presentation experience is what television-type and two-way video tele-learning is trying to achieve). Some of these guidelines include those in Box 6.5.

Given an environment that may involve two or more cameras, hanging microphones, a bank of monitors and even a control station to integrate all the technology involved, the "relax and have fun" recommendation is perhaps the most demanding of all these guidelines for instructors working live with groups of students at a distance.

Finally, when discussing effective pedagogy and management techniques for instructors teaching via television- and two-way video, the point is often made that "old practices which are ineffective in the mainstream classroom can be just as ineffective using video technology" (Gray and O'Grady, 1994). Having video does not necessary mean better teaching than not having video; it all depends on the instructor.

■ 6.4.3 PROBLEMS WITH COMMUNICATION AND ENRICHMENT

Communication between the instructor and her distant students can take place during a lesson presentation, as is regularly the case with interactive television or two-way video forms of tele-learning. It can also take place outside the lesson presentation, as is so when computer, audio or video-conferencing is used for discussions or other sorts of learning activities outside the instructor's lesson

Box 6.5

Typical guidelines for the instructor delivering lessons via television or two-way video

- Make sure you are fully competent with the use of the technology through practice sessions
- Keep your lesson presentation short, with checkpoints of different sorts after about each ten minutes and a break after at least 50 minutes (Lewis, 1994; Bruce and Shade, 1994)
- Use visual aids because television and video are visual media, not something to listen to. Consider incorporating demonstrations as these make good use of the capabilities of the media (Kendall and Oaks, 1992)
- Make sure graphics are readable (use computer-made overhead sheets with 18-point bold font or larger; see Cirtin, 1995), but do not read your sheets aloud. Try to provide copies of your overhead or graphic material for students in print form (by mail, fax, or e-mail) before the lesson
- Be consistent in your presentation style, especially in the way you communicate with your students and the procedures you develop for calling on students or responding to their questions
- Use interactivity carefully; more interaction is not necessarily better or more appreciated by students (Zhang and Fulford, 1994)
- When requesting that students break among themselves at a remote site for a brief discussion or activity, make sure that the task is very clear to them, and give regular indications of how much time remains
- Work out procedures to handle students "chiming in" or talking among themselves at a distant site; Will you tolerate it? encourage it? How will you handle it in a multi-site course? (Bruce and Shade, 1994)
- Be alert to cues from the students; make "eyeball-to-eyeball" contact via the camera and monitor (Ward, 1990)
- Include deliberate "processing" time during the presentation, as well as planning for instructor-talk and student-comment (Bruce and Shade, 1994)
- And finally, "relax", "enjoy yourself", "have fun"! (Lewis, 1994, Willis, 1993).

presentation. As soon as asynchronous communication is involved, as for example, computer conferencing, all the points of attention and benefits identified earlier in this chapter for the face-to-face instructor (Section 6.2) are also relevant for the instructor of remote classes. Moderator skills are necessary, software features have a major impact, discussions must be structured and relevant, students need incentives to contribute to discussions (Farnes, 1993; Harasim, 1993c).

EXTRA TASKS FOR THE INSTRUCTOR

However, there are some substantial differences for the instructor in managing asynchronous communication when the students in a course never or rarely meet together physically. Students participating in a course fully at a distance have little or no opportunity for face-to-face informal discussions among themselves or with the instructor compared to face-to-face students who can say hello to each other over the coffee machine. Also, distance students may be more heterogeneous in their personal situations than a group of face-to-face students within an institution; the distance students may be working full time and fitting in their course participation as a side-event in their lives, compared to students at a face-to-face institution. The fact that students may not know each other thus requires special communication skills on the part of the instructor. Even more challenging for the instructor may be the case where different groups of students are involved in a single course.

Blending different student groups

Spenciner and Squibb (1994), for example, discuss a course in early-childhood special-needs offered through a statewide interactive television system (ITV) in the US where the students were a face-to-face group of undergraduate education majors with no practical experience while the four remote sites involved students who were all working in the field, some with many years' experience. As instructors, Spenciner and Squibb note the concern they felt that these two groups would find the course equally effective. They were relieved to note that "an unexpected benefit to this course was the blending of the preservice and inservice participants. On-campus students working towards their degrees received important exposure to their future peer groups..." (p. 9). However, the benefits to the practicing professionals of interacting with the inexperienced students were not mentioned.

The more heterogeneous the student group, the more strain on the instructor in the way she leads and moderates communication during the course.

Collaborative learning activities

Organizing collaborative learning activities for distributed students is especially challenging. A large body of research coming not only out of distance education but also out of the area of CSCW (computer-supported cooperative work) and CSCL (computer-supported collaborative learning) relates to the role appropriately designed software can play to help in the collaboration process (as one example, from the Open University in the UK, see Alexander, Lefrere and Matheson, 1994). However, regardless of software tools, collaborative learning activities among distributed adults are primarily a function of the instructional skill of the instructor. The "Virtual Classroom" at the New Jersey Institute of Technology (Hiltz, 1995) is an example of the interrelationship between software tools and the instructor's pedagogical strategies for successful collaborative activities among students involved in courses at a distance.

■ 6.4.4 OTHER PROBLEMS

Two other problems confronting the instructor teaching students at a distance should be mentioned here. One is the interaction between the instructor and local support persons; the other is the problem of student assessment.

INTERACTING WITH LOCAL SUPPORT PERSONS

Local facilitators or support personnel at remote sites are often arranged by the host institution for institutionally organized distance education (see Chapter 7). Many times these are persons whom the instructor does not know at all, and perhaps persons knowing little about the course itself. Communicating and harmonizing instructional expectations with these persons is important for the instructor; however little provision is typically made for this. In situations where the different parties do not have an easy way to communicate with each other, such as e-mail, it is even more difficult for the instructor to work as a team with local support staff. Local support may turn out to be unhelpful or even counter-productive without such communication (Flaskerud, 1994).

ASSESSMENT

Handling student assessment at a distance is one example of where a local facilitator is valuable, to monitor the administration of a test and the submission of test papers to the instructor. In situations where students do not finish a course at a common time, or where there is no local facilitator, assessment may be based on submitted assignments rather than testing. The mechanics of the process of submitting of assignments depends very much on the institutional arrangements; the instructor may or may not find it a personal burden.

■ 6.5 CONVERGENCES: THE POST-SECONDARY INSTRUCTOR AND TELE-LEARNING IN NEW COMBINATIONS

So far in this chapter, we have looked at post-secondary instructors as working in one of two settings: with face-to-face classes or with classes at a distance. However, as with the technology of tele-learning in general, many convergences are occurring in the ways in which the post-secondary instructor may come to be also a tele-learning instructor and these ways are blurring the distinction between being a "distance-education instructor" or a "traditional" instructor. We conclude this chapter by noting a few of these examples; in Chapter 10 (about the future) we will consider them more carefully.

■ 6.5.1 EXAMPLES OF NEW MODELS FOR TELE-LEARNING AND COURSES FOR ADULTS

New models can be seen in a variety of convergences, not only of technology and pedagogy, but also of imagination. Following are five examples, each involving post-secondary instructors in new combinations of face-to-face and distance delivery.

AT A DISTANCE, BUT WITH INTENSE COLLABORATIVE INTERACTION

The cognitive psychology "virtual summer school"
The Open University in the UK operates in all the technology combinations described in this chapter, with the exception of students coming to the campus as "traditional" face-to-face classes. However, provision is made and for some courses required, for students to assemble face-to-face for certain portions of courses (often a one-week period in the summer). In order to help compensate students who cannot attend these face-to-face course portions the OU is developing a "virtual summer school" and tried it out in the summer of 1994 with students enrolled in the otherwise-at-a-distance course, D309 Cognitive Psychology (Eisenstadt, 1995).

Seventeen persons at the OU were involved in supporting the virtual summer institute for the (approximately) equal number of students. Computers and software were provided to the students and the instructors so that they could interact together in the ways shown in Box 6.6:

The course designers and instructors thus needed a considerable amount of technology to try to optimize the feeling of "being there" for the 17 distributed students.

This example shows one convergence possibility for post-secondary instruction: moving from a correspondence model to a model with virtual face-to-face interaction, via multi-media and mixed real-time/asynchronous computer networking. Implications for the instructor? First of all, significant technical interest and skill. Secondly, more intense interaction, in time and effort, than one would expect in a face-to-face teaching situation.

Box 6.6

Moving distance education to virtual face-to-face participation via computers

- Use e-mail, newsgroups, live chat lines, and computer conferencing for continual communication, both moderated and informal
- Have access to the Internet via a WWW browser for access to course resources
- Use the CUSeeMe technology for Internet video-conferencing
- Use a presentation package to allow synchronized slide and movie presentations across the student sites
- Provide separate, mobile-telephone support, if help was needed while the student's home phone line was busy with the networking
- Provide audio conferencing to support the CUSeeMe video conferencing.
- Provide students with a variety of tool-type software, such as word processing and statistical analysis packages
- Organize social events for the students, such as a "Virtual Disco" via a WWW page through which music is available. (Eisenstadt, 1995)

FACE-TO-FACE WITHOUT EVER MEETING FACE-TO-FACE

"Commentary on art"

Ironically, while many such as those in the Virtual Summer School example, are busy using tele-learning technologies to bring the advantages of face-to-face instruction to those "not fortunate enough" to be face-to-face, others are seeing tele-learning as a way to liberate the face-to-face student from the time- and place-demands of face-to-face course sessions. The example of the art course taught at Pennsylvania State University described earlier in Box 6.4 (Maddox, 1995) is an illustration of this. Maddox has replaced face-to-face sessions altogether for a rich mix of real-time and asynchronous interactions via networking which in fact makes the participation in his course a distance-teaching experience for his on-campus students.

Implications for the instructor? All the problems besetting the teacher of distant classes.

JUST-IN-TIME TELE-LEARNING

Distance apprenticeship in Norway

In Norway, video-conferencing via ISDN is being used extensively to provide courses to remote professionals who cannot otherwise travel to distant cities, and more positively, want to stay at their workplaces and study specialized courses tailored to their own needs. In various initiatives sponsored by Norwegian Telecom and different Norwegian universities, these sorts of specialized courses are being given (Flyndal, 1995).

As an example, physiotherapists often desire advanced training. A physiotherapist in a central location can demonstrate different exercises on a doll, using video-conferencing, and then the physiotherapist-students practice the same exercises, under the supervision of the distant instructor, on real patients at their sides of the camera. Discussion and critical evaluation follow these practical sessions, also via video-conferencing.

Implications for the instructor? Developing a tailored and highly responsive course, and being able to see and hear adequately to monitor practical activities at a distance.

COMBINING VIDEO-CONFERENCING AND THE INTERNET

International MBA in management

As an example of a variety of technological and organizational convergences the MIT Sloan School of Management in the US is working together with partners in Singapore and the People's Republic of China to offer a masters degree in management to Asian-based students, from the Sloan site (Feller, 1995). The technologies used are satellite-based video-conferencing projected onto large screens in the Asian receiving classrooms for lectures and other real-time activities; and the Internet, for various WWW pages for different groups of students and for access to course materials, database libraries, and for communication among the students and the MIT faculty.

Implications for instructors? Now they will have to handle both the problems of television-type instructional delivery and the new techniques needed for use of CMC and WWW pages as instructional tools.

INTERACTIVE LECTURES AND REMOTE-SITE DELIVERY

"ENIC" (Ecole Nouvelle d'Ingénieurs en Communication)

ENIC is an institute for the continuing education of engineers in France (Keskinen, 1995). It is organized as a set of 20 centres, in different French cities. The sites, called Visiocentres, are connected by ISDN and a multi-point bridge for video-conferencing and form a nationwide distance-learning network. A Visiocentre has four distinct rooms: the instructor's studio, a video-cabled "Interactive Room" for students, a video-cabled room for extra students, and a self-training room for personal use of computers (Lafon, 1995).

The interactive room can accommodate up to 32 learners who participate in live sessions, not quite face-to-face with the instructor, because he is sitting in his next-door studio. The instructor's studio is equipped with a document camera, an instructor's camera, monitors that show the classrooms in which students are present, a computer, and a videotape player.

The instructor selects a video source to transmit via the computer. The video source may be the camera shot of himself, teaching; the image coming from the document camera; a view of any of the remote classrooms; a view of the learners present in the classroom adjacent to the instructor; or a video segment from a tape in the videoplayer. These tapes are especially made for each course and contain an important part of the lesson presentation.

The selected video source is digitized, compressed, and transmitted to all the connected sites via ISDN.

Each interactive room has a movable camera with remote control and tables with microphones equipped with request buttons at which the students sit. When any student has a question, the student presses a request button. This request signal is sent to the instructor's computer and an icon representing the location of the student will flash on the instructor's computer monitor. The instructor validates the question by clicking on the flashing icon. This validation by the instructor moves the remote camera to the student who requested a question, and zooms in on the student. The video-cabled rooms for extra students do not have the microphones or question buttons.

Between the live-presentation sessions, the instructor uses e-mail, fax and telephone for communication with the students. The students send approximately ten e-mail messages per day to the instructor during each module. Students can reserve a telephone tutoring session. Also, at each of the sites, there is a local tutor to supply personal support to the learners at that site. A typical class consists of 50 students, ten at each of five sites. Occasionally a one-day face-to-face session is organized at each of the sites, with the students working with their local tutor as they do practical exercises.

Each module is 40 hours of work and consists of 12 live sessions, two face-to-face sessions for practical work, 30 minutes of personal telephone tutoring, and individual study by the students of the videotapes used in the live presentation and associated text material. The instructional components are carefully balanced with each other based on a pedagogical approach called "Tuttelvisio" in which the relation between the self-study periods, the "meeting sessions" and the asynchronous contact with the instructor and tutors is carefully worked out (Lafon, 1995). This is truly an example of pedagogical re-engineering in which tele-learning plays a number of key roles.

Implications for the instructor? The technical and cognitive challenge of attending to multiple monitors during the live presentations, synchronizing the cameras, handling the question-asking routine, preparing his lessons in detail around the videotapes and text material for the course so that the students can re-use the materials for their independent study, and close interaction with the local tutors at the remote sites.

■ 6.5.2 POST-SECONDARY INSTRUCTORS SHARING EXPERIENCES

These examples have shown just a few of many innovative situations in which post-secondary instructors are now encountering tele-learning. We discuss more of these in Chapters 7, 8, and 9 and also in **Interface 9**. Interesting in all of these examples is the changing meaning or lack of meaning of the words "distant" and "face-to-face" for the instructor in terms of how she prepares the instructional balance of her teaching.

One consequence of this is that post-secondary instructors in face-to-face teaching situations are gradually becoming aware of the considerable experience that has already accumulated in distance-education institutions. This experience not only relates to handling the various technologies that may be involved in tele-learning, but also, and more importantly, focusing on the pedagogy of teaching. As Taylor (1992) has observed, the "tyranny of proximity" may have lulled post-secondary instructors in face-to-face institutions to think they need to give little attention to pedagogy or technology in their teaching. Instructors working at a distance from their students, in contrast, take instructional delivery and pedagogy very seriously, in both practice and research. Box 6.7 lists a sample of the many well-organized informational sites about distance education that are now present on the WWW with pedagogical information of interest not only to post-secondary instructors working in traditional distance-teaching institutions, but also for post-secondary instructors working in traditional face-to-face institutions.

It may well be that one of the major benefits in the long run of tele-learning for post-secondary education is the cross-fertilization that is occurring among the different categories of post-secondary instructors, with as a result increased attention to pedagogy and to making connections that is now occurring. We conclude with some thoughts about these changes.

Box 6.7

Sites with distance education resources of interest to post-secondary instructors

---

Distance Education
URL `http://www.nova.edu/Inter-Links/education/distance.html`

Distance Education Resources from OISE, Canada
URL `gopher://porpoise.oise.on.ca/11/resources/IRes4Ed/`
`resources/distance`

International Centre for Distance Learning , UK
URL `http://acacia.open.ac.uk/`
...Contains a database with over 7,500 items of literature on all aspects of distance education.

Distance Education: Electronic Sources for Information and Discussion
URL `http://www.iat.unc.edu/guides/irg-06.html`
...Contains information about a number of listservs, Internet journals, and newsgroups related to distance education, as well as WWW sites.

Faculty of Extension, University of Alberta
URL `http://www.extension.ualberta.ca`
Nicely designed site for life-long learning opportunities at the University of Alberta.

Distance Education Related Web Links
URL `http://www.access.digex.net/~nuance/disted1.html`

ANDREA moderated listserv
Subscribe: Send message to `listserv@nki.nl` with following: subscribe andrea your name
...Moderated list hosted by the NKI Distance Education Norway.

▓ 6.6 TELE-LEARNING: SHIFTS FOR THE POST-SECONDARY INSTRUCTOR

In this long chapter, we began by sketching some common aspects of the role of the post-secondary instructor, as well as sketching some very different situations in which he may find himself working. We looked in some detail at the idea of instructional balance, of the choices that the instructor makes in terms of the blend of learning activities that comprise a course. We saw many examples of how the instructor working in the traditional face-to-face educational institution can accomplish a pedagogical re-engineering of his instructional delivery through tele-learning applications. We also looked at another large group of post-secondary instructors, those who work involves their use of tele-learning in some form by definition, as the students they work with are frequently or entirely at a physical distance from the instructor.

The main message of this chapter? Perhaps it can be captured in the word "shifts".

More and more, instructors working with course delivery to adults will find themselves involved in shifts and changes: shifts in the balance of instructional components within their courses, shifts in the sorts of activities they are involved in within these components, shifts in the ways they interact with students because of the filter and facilitation of technologies, shifts in the way they lecture, shifts in the persons with whom they interact for course-delivery support, shifts in the persons with whom they share experiences.

And the consequences of these shifts, and the time and effort and strain they may cause? Certainly, much more expenditure of time than if the instructors just taught "as usual". Certainly, new skills to be handled.

But what is the payoff, besides the innate desire to do one's job well? This has much to do with how the institution which employs the instructor values all these shifts. We discuss this in the next chapter.

PAGE DESIGN: ART AND SCIENCE

Effective design of WWW environments is both art and science, both creativity and sober application of existing guidelines for user interfaces. There are considerations related to the user interface in general, and to the user interface of a hyperlinked system. These considerations must be adapted to the WWW circumstances. Then there are particular issues relating to WWW page design itself, in terms of its unique characteristics. Finally there are issues that relate to the application of the WWW page and its intended users. Some design decisions are based on considerable research, others on vision and creativity.

GENERAL DESIGN GUIDELINES FOR USER INTERFACES

Many researchers study and write about design guidelines for user interfaces of computer software. Some guidelines appear repeatedly:

- Design to fit the user's conceptual model of the system; help users visualise the system
- Be consistent without being boring; particularly, be consistent in terms of commands used, and in procedures for user control and movement
- Provide shortcuts for experienced

users and more-detailed prompts for new users
- Give feedback to user actions, do not leave the user looking at a blank screen
- Make screen layout understandable and economical
- Use positive terms, simple action terms; avoid jargon, contractions, and abbreviations
- Do not right justify, separate paragraphs by blank lines, use paging not scrolling
- Prevent errors and when they occur, make error correction simple

(from: K. Cox & D. Walker, *User-Interface Design*, Prentice-Hall, New York, 1993.)

Although these and other such guidelines are well-established in the software-design literature they are frequently ignored in the design of WWW documents.

SPECIAL CONSIDERATIONS FOR WWW DESIGN
INTERFACE DESIGN

Frequent violations appear to each of the previous guidelines. Keeping layouts economical and consistent and anticipating and supporting the user's conceptual model of the environment appear to be particularly important to mention, as they are so often apparently not considered in WWW page design. Also, the hyperlinked and distributed aspects of WWW environments complicate design further, because of the lack of linearity in the way the user interacts with a page, and the fact that external links will put the user in an environment sure to be different from and inconsistent with the environment in which he started.

In particular, WWW design involves site structure, page design, and efficient use of the WWW environments.

DESIGN ISSUES RELATING TO STRUCTURE AND NAVIGATION

Site structure includes helping the user navigate the site, keeping a clear view on where she is in the site, where she can go, and how she can get back. Some WWW-specific design guidelines include:

- **Design** your site in advance; set your **goals**
- Decide on **basic structure** of the site. Make a template. How do the pages relate to each other? Is the general approach to have "menu" pages in a tree-sort of structure until reaching the end of a branch of the tree, where some substantial information will be found? Or is the general approach to treat each page as a chapter in a book, or as a self-contained topic?
- Be **consistent on the structure**; **visualise it** for the user, not only from the home page of the site but also from all pages of the site
- If using **links within a page**, make sure the user is aware that this navigation is occurring. Jumping somewhere on the same page and later, scrolling to the same point is confusing without an overview of the navigation plan
- In using links external to the page, incorporate the text that **anchors** the link into the text of the page. Give textual **indications** of what will occur if an external link is chosen so the user can decide if this step will be productive or not for her
- Have **good reasons for using links**; test external links regularly to avoid dangling or otherwise non-functioning links
- Provide clear and consistent **links back** to the home page and to other significant pages
- **Avoid long pages**; break material up if more than a few screens' worth, unless it is clear that the material is an informational file (which may be better downloaded and read in a paper or off-line setting)
- **Group related materials** visually and semantically

GUIDELINES FOR WWW PAGE DESIGN

Design guidelines for user-interface page design are also relevant for WWW page design, but with extensions for the unique WWW circumstances:

Guidelines for the individual page

- Use images for a purpose. Pay attention to text layout, font size and choice, and use of space
- Pages should be treated as independent documents, as readers will enter them and re-enter them in many different combinations
- Do not overuse or underuse emphasis devices. Help readers to scan quickly to see if they are interested in the contents of a page

- Provide an informative footer at the base of each page, with author's name and e-mail contact, revision date, and navigation choices
- Provide a device to let the reader know the length of each page and an overview of its content
- Provide a link to a separate file that contains the full-length text of the entire site, all in a single file, which the user can conveniently download or print if she wishes
- Don't use an icon that looks like a clickable image but isn't. Make it clear to the user where she can click as well as what the results will be
- Update often, giving the date of last updating on each page, as well as the URL

Guidelines for the pages as a set

- Be consistent among the pages; visually they should be a whole. This relates to buttons and links, to use of colour, to tone and style of language, and to overall layout
- Be consistent in the way pages are introduced and completed, in the way links relate to page titles, and in the way headings and lists are used through the site

DESIGN GUIDELINES FOR EFFICIENT USE OF A WWW ENVIRONMENT

Finally, design for efficient and effective use of the WWW environment:

- Keep **images small**, in actual physical dimensions or in the number of colours, to keep downloading time to a minimal. A rule-of-thumb is to keep in-line images under 20K
- Use images effectively, considering the implications of the images, given different browsers and access speeds of page visitors. Provide alternatives to images for users who prefer text-only browsing or printing
- Provide links between **text-only** or **thumbnail** and **full-graphics** versions of a page, and indicate the size of the full-graphics link before it is chosen
- Design for **differences:** different screen dimension, resolutions, even colour or no colour, as well as different fonts and browsers
- **Update** often
- Keep a **"rule of three":** users won't find content buried more than three links from the initial screen
- Use the **same graphics** with the same file names if you repeat an image; users will not have to contact the server separately for each image
- Do not have **too few or too many pages**
- Advantages of *large pages:* Easier to maintain, better for mirror real-world document structure if the page is be printed and distributed. BUT long structures are rigid, and scrolling and scanning to find desired information is not good from the screen
- Advantages of *smaller pages:* Pages load quickly. The entire page may be on one screen, so information can be scanned quickly by the reader. BUT jumps can be jarring and break continuity
- Consider the use of **different types of links**: explicit links that move to main units of structure within a site, definition links, footnote links
- Provide **non-electronic versions** of content
- Remember: Three important **motivation features** of the WWW are its hyperlinks, its potential for attractive use of images and layout, and its consistency and easy learnability. Make good use of these features in your pages

7 The planning and management of tele-learning in educational institutions

In this chapter, we take a different perspective from that of the teacher or instructor. The perspective is that of the person who makes the institutional or jurisdictional decisions that set the policy for tele-learning and that determine the infrastructure for tele-learning within a school, district, region, or post-secondary institution. We know that such policy and infrastructure are not the product of a single decision by a single person, and that teachers and instructors and sometimes even students can be involved in the decision making. But however the decision making is embodied, there are persons who at a certain time make decisions for the school, district or region, university or training organization that facilitate some aspects of tele-learning and constrain others. Cost and cost-payoff perspectives underlie these decisions. We look at important aspects of these decisions in this chapter.

Objectives

After this chapter you should be able to:

- Be aware of basic approaches and issues in anticipating the costs of tele-learning

- Identify alternatives for networking in the school, and considerations for decision making concerning those alternatives

- Assuming the technological infrastructure is in place for tele-learning in the school, apply principles relating to the diffusion of an innovation to decisions about teacher stimulation and support for tele-learning

- Compare different models for the systematic planning of tele-learning in the school district or region, with particular consideration to the balance among telephone, television/video and computer networking solutions

- Give examples of how the school district or region can contribute to teacher training and support through tele-learning

- At the post-secondary level, consider the implications of adopting tele-learning as a way to increase student numbers

- Give an indication of the minimal and "competitive" levels of on-campus tele-learning infrastructure and support expected of the post-secondary educational institution

▓ 7.1 EDUCATIONAL DECISION MAKERS AND THEIR PERSPECTIVES

Tele-learning is an innovation that does not come casually into an educational jurisdiction. For tele-learning to be supported in a school, district or region, university or training organization, substantial decisions must be made at various junctures, decisions that involve not only critical issues relating to fiscal concerns and staffing, but also to the vision and philosophy of education in the jurisdiction. Even "doing nothing" to support a certain form of tele-learning is a decision that has profound implications for the teacher/instructor and student as well as the jurisdiction as a whole.

An underlying perspective for these decisions is that of cost. What will tele-learning cost? Is it worth the cost? How can it be budgeted for and paid for? How can alternatives be compared in terms of short- and long-term cost/payoff perspectives? We will look briefly at this underlying perspective (Chapter 7.2) before we look more specifically at decision making in the school (Chapter 7.3), the school district or region (Chapter 7.4), and the post-secondary institution (Chapter 7.5).

▓ 7.2 COST IMPLICATIONS OF TELE-LEARNING

Tele-learning is expensive for the jurisdiction, both in start-up costs and in on-going support and provision. The following general categories of concerns apply at every jurisdictional level. (For a fuller discussion, see Duning, Van Kekerix and Zaborowski, 1993; and Eidgahy and Shearman, 1994.)

CATEGORIES OF BUDGETING

To begin with, budgeting for tele-learning may be approached from the perspective of:

Program, line-item expenditures and revenues for a self-supporting activity, typically under one manager and for a specific time period

Supported service, line-item expenditures that are dependent on the allocation of limited resources during a budget period

Subsidy, allocations from a reserve or development fund for a specific purpose

Capital equipment, the generation and expenditure of funds for capital items that could return value to the system (Eidgahy and Shearman, 1994).

Particularly important to tele-learning planning and management is the distinction between self-supporting program and supported service, the distinction between re-occurring budget components and one-time subsidy allocations, and the interpretation of "bring value to the system" that can motivate capital-equipment expenditures. Being self-supporting and thus having to produce enough revenue in some way to cover operating costs puts a different frame around tele-learning services compared to what is the case if the service is supported as a budget line item. Often tele-learning decisions are taken with the expectation that eventually capital expenses will be repaid from income and, even more, that the tele-learning enterprise will result in some cost saving or payoff increase. If these can be quantified, the tele-learning activity will usually be expected to move from being a supported budget item to being a self-supporting program.

PERSONNEL AND EXPENSES

Within any of these budget categories are further categories, including personnel and operating expenses such as facility maintenance, travel, mail, print materials, contract services, PR, supplies, transmission costs, computers, and overhead. Operating expenses are estimated by Eidgahy and Shearman to involve 30–55% of a tele-learning budget, depending on signal-transmission costs.

Transmission costs

Under transmission costs, Eidgahy and Shearman include the cost of transmitting tele-learning data from one point to another, where cost is proportional to bandwidth, from computers (narrow bandwidth) to compressed video (moderate width) to full-motion television (broad bandwidth).

As an example of how variable transport costs can be even within one jurisdictional area, Kugemann (1993) has calculated the delivery costs for a megabyte of digitized information via various sorts of transport channels in Germany, and, among a variety of observations, found that the costs of sending video material on cassette videotapes (before digitization) through the mail to be substantially less than sending the same material via satellite (a factor however which varies according to the number of receivers; for sending to one receive site it is a ratio of 1:100).

In contrast, Kugemann calculates that sending 1 MG of textual information (approximately 200 A4 pages) by ordinary mail can be 30 times more expensive than if sent via modem-transfer through ordinary telephone lines. The scaling of these costs in terms of number of receive sites must be calculated differently than in the case of satellite receive sites, but the main point of Kugemann's analysis is, that the decision to add real-time interactivity to video transmission vastly increases the cost of delivery, whereas for text, where asynchronous access is expected, network technology can substantially decrease the cost of delivery as well as increase the speed.

Human costs

Another major fiscal component of tele-learning is the staffing necessary to support it. In addition to whatever allocation is needed to cover the costs of preparing and delivering instruction for a tele-learning episode, there must be persons responsible for technical support, persons responsible for handling participant needs (training, contacts from remote-site students, general clerical staffing), and a managerial staff. Tele-learning, if taken seriously in a jurisdiction, will need teams of persons in each of these categories. We will look at this comment in more detail relative to different sector focuses in this chapter.

COMPARING COSTS

A. Bates (1995) is one of a number of specialists who make projections on the relative costs over time and number of students for the operating expenses of different forms of transmission technologies. A first issue in any comparison is what to use as the unit. Bates uses "costs per study hour" and "costs per student contact hour". These are not the same, and very much depend on the instructional design of the course rather than some intrinsic cost-aspect of a transmission technology itself. For example, it cannot be assumed that one could substitute one hour of video-conferencing for one hour of computer conferencing.

As another consideration, variable costs that depend on the number of students are different than fixed costs. And there are many other factors that make cost calculation and comparison very difficult: Moonen (1994) points out that so many variables affect cost calculation that only generalities emerge after any careful attempt at analysis. His major conclusion, after a number of years of research and practical work in this area? To reduce costs in the long run, some costs must be shifted to the student. Students must take more responsibility for learning themselves, and expect less personal contact from instructors.

In one way, tele-learning resources such as interactive learning materials made available via WWW sites, can help this to occur. On the other hand, the desire for communication that tele-learning resources stimulate—through e-mail and different forms of conferencing—can increase the amount of time that students expect to have from their instructors.

So it is complicated to make a decision about costs. It becomes even more difficult when effectiveness or benefit is added to the consideration.

COMPARING BENEFITS...

The decision maker must think about payoff on a broadscale basis, strategically with relation to the many goals and needs of her jurisdiction. The advantage to the jurisdiction of some tele-learning decisions may be immediate and concrete, such as being able to provide students in small and geographically remote secondary schools with access to specialist courses in which they would not otherwise be able to participate. The advantage may also be a projected one: that a tele-learning provision will bring more student enrollment and thus, after costs, be revenue-generating.

Intangible benefits

However, the hoped-for advantage of a tele-learning decision may also be more intangible and hard-to-measure, such as is often the case with initiatives that are based on a desire to "enrich" education or "prepare students for the future" or "improve motivation". Most of the examples we have given of tele-learning in traditional classrooms and face-to-face post-secondary courses in Chapters 5 and 6 are in this category: they enrich and "re-engineer" education, but cannot be shown in objective ways to be making instruction more efficient. Marchioni (1995) indicates a number of examples of intangible benefits, such as "changing how learners think and behave" that can be argued to have eventual payoff and also, in the course of time, even a global impact. But these are predictions, not the sorts of throughput data at which decision makers must look.

DECISION MAKING...

Despite their complexity in calculation, the decision maker is grounded by cost-effectiveness considerations when she makes plans and commits institutional resources for tele-learning. Budget considerations must be estimated and weighed against projected benefits in her jurisdiction. How much a decision maker will commit financial support to intangibles as payoff for tele-learning will vary from circumstance to circumstance.

Awareness of overall picture

And no decision about tele-learning is made in isolation in an educational jurisdiction. There are many competing demands on resources and priorities, and many different voices. In addition, decisions may seem self-evident at one level: that tele-learning will "improve education", for example, or "will prepare our students for the future", but the translation of these global beliefs into operational items, as well as the collision of the cost implications of that translation with other expenditures in the jurisdiction, is a different story. It is the story of this chapter.

In this chapter we will see a number of examples of issues and approaches involved in this translation-of-vision-into-practice process with regard to tele-learning.

Cost constraints

And, of course, the decision maker is bounded by cost realities. In any jurisdiction, there are many fixed costs and there is a ceiling on operational revenue that is available unless a special project or external grant is obtained. Often tele-learning initiatives must be based on the premise of subsidy funding, particularly through external infusions of funding support for projects and special consortia. The step between short-term funding for a special tele-learning initiative and sustained support service for tele-learning within the institution is a major one. Often this sustained support is based on the implicit or explicit expectation of tele-learning covering its costs or even generating income for the jurisdiction.

Given this basic framework for decision making about tele-learning in educational institutions, we turn now to three different role focuses: the decision maker in the elementary or secondary school; those who make decisions about schools in a region (this may be a district, state, or country, depending on the way educational decision making is organized); and decision makers relating to support and infrastructure in post-secondary institutions.

■ 7.3 DECISION MAKING ABOUT TELE-LEARNING IN THE SCHOOL

Many issues face the decision maker in the elementary or secondary school with respect to tele-learning. Some of these issues, such as whether to wire a school with coaxial cable or with fiber, are very much related to district or regional policies and practice with respect to television/video-type tele-learning. The school is not apt to make a decision in isolation of district decisions. Thus we will not further discuss the television/video-type of tele-learning in this section.

However, there are at least two major categories of decisions that a school administrator does seem to be personally confronted with in the management of his or her school:

- One set of issues relates to the way, if any, that the school will connect itself to the outside world via networking and how the school will monitor access to a network connection among the students and teachers in the school
- The other set of issues relates to the effective administrator's on-going

quest to stimulate educational quality in her school, through nurturing the engagement and support of the teachers, through providing leadership with respect to professional development among the teachers, and by supporting constructive change and innovation in the school program. How does the school decision maker stimulate and support teachers in their encounters with tele-learning as an innovation, for their own growth in accepting the innovation, and for the good of the school?

A note about terminology is in order. In different countries the person or persons in a leadership position within a school are called by different titles: administrator, principal, school director, headmaster, chief teacher, etc. We will use the terms school administrator and school decision maker interchangeably. The school administrator is the person most consistently involved in school decision making about computer use and networking access (Bruder, 1993), and ultimately most responsible for effective implementation of innovations within the school (Fullan, Miles and Anderson, 1988). Bruder describes the school administrator as the "gatekeeper for technology" in 96% of the US schools responding to a national survey. Furthermore, the general tendency in a number of countries is to shift purchasing decisions for curriculum materials to schools ("site-based management") while retaining decision making about larger purchases, such as rewiring in fibre, at the central level.

■ 7.3.1 Decisions about wide-area and (inter)networking in the school

Most elementary and secondary schools in non-disadvantaged countries and regions have computers for both administrative and instructional purposes. Even in disadvantaged regions, computers in schools are now established, and there is no longer much debate on if a school should "get computers" or not (Pelgrum, Janssen Reinen and Plomp, 1993). (However, the debate still continues on how to use those computers.)

Schools have generally evolved an organizational scheme for their instructional computers. The organizational scheme relates to where the computers are located and how access to them is regulated. The scheme also often includes the assignment of responsibility for the computers to a person or persons, most likely teachers who may or may not have any official title, time allotment or training for their efforts.

Given this context of a relatively well established computer organization in schools, we look at four particular aspects of decision making about connecting school computers to the "outside world". These aspects are:

- How should the connection occur relative to the already existing physical organizations of computers in the school, such as existing LAN networking?
- How should the networking occur relative to the already existing computer organization in the school?
- Once a technical connection to the outside is organized, to what does the school allow connection?
- How is access for students and teachers facilitated and paid?

Each of these issues is ultimately the responsibility of the school decision maker, although she is often supported in these decisions by a technology committee of some kind.

CONNECTING SCHOOL COMPUTERS TO THE OUTSIDE

In schools, computers are either stand-alone or connected in a local-area network (LAN). They are either distributed throughout the school or concentrated in one or a few areas. In any of the combinations of the above, there are substantial difficulties in connecting any of these computers to a computer or network outside of the school.

In two US inventories, (Newman, Bernstein and Reese, 1992; US Congress Office of Technology Assessment, 1995), it was found that:

- WAN (wide-area networking) connectivity often begins in a school "with a pioneering individual teacher making personal connection to a network through a dial-up modem" (US Congress, p. 110)
- The networks to which individual teachers connect are regional-level educational services, special dial-up services such as BBSs, commercial services, or directly (via an access provider) to the Internet. In addition, many of the regional-level services and the commercial services offer Internet gateways of various sorts
- Of schools that had LANs in 1992, only 10% also had connections to the outside, and of these only a relatively few made that connection from the LAN itself. These percentages do not seem much changed in 1995, although comparable data were not directly available
- Of those that did make connections to the outside, the large majority of them did this through stand-alone computer and modem through a telephone line
- A lack of telephone lines in schools and classrooms remains a substantial barrier. "Many of the telephones that do exist in schools often serve administrative purposes and are not available to teachers for classroom

use or for making outside calls to networks...For example, there are 84,683 phone jacks in Texas school districts, ...but only 2% of the classrooms had access to a phone line" (US Congress, 1995, p. 111)

What are the main problems and issues here?

Connecting from a school to a WAN

Newman, Bernstein and Reese (1992) paid particular attention to the schools in the California sample who had both a LAN within the school and were making network connections outside the school. They studied 43 such schools, and found different scenarios based on two dimensions of distinction. One of these dimensions relates to if the school connection functions simply as a remote terminal to a specific, centralized host, or if the school computer could function as part of a distributed system with its own address and able to send and receive messages. The other dimension relates to if the school computers are stand-alone or in a LAN. Each school considering tele-learning with networking must choose for one of these options. The distinctions are as shown in Box 7.1.

ISSUES...

Decision making about one of these alternatives for a school is usually a function of technology, access policy, cost issues, and control issues. We look briefly at these aspects here.

Technical and access issues

Technical complexity. Networking is technically complex, and connecting a network to a network is another level of complexity, as well as requiring additional hardware and software. A school computer will probably need to be upgraded not only in RAM but also in hard-disk capacity in order to serve as a local server. School networking itself may need to be upgraded.

A piece of hardware called a router is needed to send packets of data from the local site to where they are going. Also, a "gateway" may be needed to connect a networks within a school to the interface of an Internet router.

Given all these technical demands, and the skills and time needed to handle them, it is unlikely that many schools have internal personnel who can handle the task.

Stand-alone computer access. Accessing an external network through a stand-alone computer eliminates some of the technical issues involved with linking a LAN, but introduces its own set of problems. These include the familiar stumbling block of no telephone outlet anywhere near the computer

---

Box 7.1

Types of school connectivity to outside networks

Type 1: A *stand-alone computer with a modem* and a connection to a telephone jack, making contact with a district BBS or a remote network service, which may be commercial or may be provided by the larger educational jurisdiction to which the school relates.

Type 2: A so-called SLIP *connection to a Internet provider* through a stand-alone computer with modem and ordinary phone line access (although the higher-speed the line and the faster the modem the better, especially if any attempt will be made to access graphics). Vendors offering SLIP connections to individuals, be they in a school or at home, became a highly competitive business in 1995, with the technical complexity of connecting to the Internet rapidly decreasing.

Type 3: "*Network modems*" occur when there is a LAN in the school, connected as a terminal through a phone line and modem to an external host. The difference between this and Type 1 is that any of the computers on the LAN can be used as the local terminal. However, only one can function at a time, and only one address is available for the local site.

Type 4: Connecting a LAN via a *leased line to a local university* where the school will be given one or more addresses and accounts

Type 5: "*Portage*" category where schools make an outside connection through one computer (or LAN) but do not physically connect the data received from this outside connection to the mainstream LAN in the school. Called the "portage" approach, this strategy means someone in the school transfers mail or files received from outside to mail accounts or other locations on the LAN.

Type 6: The "*ultimate model*" where through its own server, any computer on the entire school LAN can function as a network computer, and the school server connects directly to an external network, including the Internet. Although Newman and his colleagues only describe two schools in their 1992 analysis as having this "ultimate" connectivity, the fact of hundreds if not thousands of schools now, in 1995, having their own Internet address and making their own WWW pages suggests that probably many schools now have a local network-to-outside network connection

(from Newman, Bernstein and Reese, 1992).

---

with a modem, coupled with the associated problem that when a telephone outlet, computer, and modem can be brought together in a usable way, this is usually not where the teacher teaches or the students have access. Honey and McMillan (1994) report that teachers consistently ask for a phone line into their classrooms, a computer and modem in the classroom to connect to this phone line, and a personal Internet account to which they can connect from their classroom. Only with this do the teachers feel they can really make strides to "go online as a regular part of instruction" (p. 15).

And even in the happy event that the connection is feasible, modems and telecommunications software are often still difficult to install and to use for the average teacher.

Cost-related

Here we look at three layers of cost problems:

Budget uncertainties. Schools have difficulty with budgeting for external networking. A main reason for this is the difficulty of predicting in advance what connect costs and telephone line charges will be built up. A successful tele-learning project in terms of generating activity will likely become more and more expensive, because more use of the connectivity potential is being made.

Unlike programming that can be paid for upfront, such as many varieties of television/video-type tele-learning, at least some of the costs of network tele-learning are time sensitive. Thus wonderful new possibilities such as searching for resources on World Wide Web pages are increasingly expensive the more they are used. (WWW sites are doubly costly, in that, with slower connections and modems unless the learner works in a non-graphic mode, the time to move a page to a client can be very long and graphics may not be possible, US Congress, 1995, p. 111.)

Accounting difficulties. And compounding the complexity, many schools do not have a convenient way to separate out networking costs from other telephone-line charges, unless a separate telephone line is available. This is desirable, in that traffic from networking is guaranteed to conflict with school voice traffic, but it is another cost.

Layers of costs. Finally, once it is possible to make external connections, whatever service it is that is connected to may include its own costs, particularly if it is a commercial service provider. And there may be telephone changes as well (if not subsidized by the central authority). More and more, a network service is being provided by districts or states or national educational bodies (see **Interface 5**, Section 7.4.2, and Chapter 9), but these too may have subscription costs and line costs.

However, with networking, it is not so much the cost but the lack of way to comfortably budget for the costs in advance, as well as the lack of confidence that costs will stay "at a reasonable" level, that are main problems influencing the school administrator as he considers school policy for connecting to outside networks for tele-learning.

Control

Control of who can access what through networking outside the school is partially a cost-related concern, but also is very much related to security of sensitive data, and to restricting student access to potentially obscene or otherwise inappropriate data.

Security for existing sensitive data. Many schools are already involved in networking, but for administrative data rather than tele-learning. In addition, when districts or regions support a wide-area network, they frequently wish to use it for efficient interchange of sensitive data. No one wants to risk the leakage or lack of security of these data. This fear prevents many schools from direct connection of a school network to uncontrolled outside sources such as the Internet.

Inappropriate data. And, of course, a school is highly sensitive to its responsibility to protect students from inappropriate data or communications. There are two basic ways to do this: only allow networking to "safe" external sources, such as a district electronic service, or restrict access to selected students and under direct surveillance of a teacher.

To deal with these problems and others relating to appropriate and inappropriate use of networks, many schools are drawing up policy with regard to computer-network access. As one example, Fluck (1995) reports at his school in Australia, students are required to sign a "Computer Use Agreement" promising not to use network resources illegally or in ways that may annoy or offend other users. The different problems relating to ethics and morals of network use, including flaming and spamming in e-mail messages, became the basis for a series of lessons with the students about privacy issues and computer ethics.

These problems relate to what we described in Chapter 5 as First-Level problems confronting network tele-learning in schools. The next set of problems for the school decision maker to confront with respect to networked tele-learning are partly First-Level, but partly more subtle and difficult.

CONFLICTS WITH EXISTING COMPUTER-USE PATTERNS IN THE SCHOOL

Another, perhaps not so immediately obvious, problem that can occur with networked tele-learning in the school is the collision that this may involve with the established pattern of use of computers in the school. We look at this from four different angles.

Conflicts in scheduling

In many schools, the computers are continually booked and busy; busy with scheduled classes using them as computers for computer literacy, for word processing, and for instructional integration. When a teacher wishes to develop a tele-learning activity with his or her students, the class may not be able to schedule access to a computer with an external connection at times appropriate to the class. As the teacher cannot send students to work independently with networking in most cases (see above, "cost and security issues"), tele-learning ideas often become limited to what the teacher can do herself, outside of class time.

School procedures

Here, again, there are problems with networked tele-learning in schools. School computers may be locked up after class time, for security reasons. Or, the computers, for insurance and security purposes, may be literally bolted to tables, making their relocation to somewhere near a telephone jack physically and procedurally impossible. The sort of time and access needed for quality tele-learning browsing or "virtual excursions" or creating one's own WWW page may not be available even to the teacher, because of the way school computers are positioned in the school. The school administrator must be alert to these frustrations and deal with the policy adaptations that may have to occur.

Human issues

But policy adaptations may have to involve human issues as well as logistical ones. The computer specialist in a school, usually a secondary school, is likely to have built up his (here, the "his" is used advisedly) expertise and position in the school over a number of years and perhaps outside of any experience with tele-learning. He may not be informed about what needs to be done to technically facilitate tele-learning for a teacher who has a particular wish, for example to create WWW sites or try a new search tool. More than this, he may be skeptical of the wish, thinking of it as somewhat frivolous ("electronic pen pals?" "Internet hype?") compared to the well established curriculum of, say, school computer science courses of which he is well informed.

In contrast, the teacher becoming interested in tele-learning may not be a long-time computer user and may not know the appropriate terminology to phrase his or her questions. She may not know how to install downloaded browsers under Windows or unzip ftp-ed files. In fact, she may not even know how to do those activities away from tele-learning. She may not have been particularly interested in computers in school until becoming aware of the communication or hyperlinked information aspects of the Internet. She may feel uncomfortable among the established and self-confident computer people in the school.

Culture clashes

Ironically, we have seen a number of times that it is this "culture" clash between the computer establishment in the school and the teacher getting interested in tele-learning which is a major source of difficulty confronting the diffusion of tele-learning in the school. The school decision maker, who is probably, after a decade, well established in his relationship with the teachers in the school who represent its computer culture, may find himself disinclined to favour the explorative urges of teachers just coming to discover tele-learning, especially if these urges seem disruptive and potentially a problem to the overall computer-use organization in the school.

We return to culture considerations in Section 7.3.2 in the framework of the more general issue of how the school administrator can best support and nurture the diffusion of an innovation in her school.

TO WHAT DOES A SCHOOL CONNECT?

Assuming the formidable obstacles described above have been overcome and a teacher has a way to connect via a school computer to the outside world for tele-learning, to what can she connect? How does she find and get on the fabled "information highway" once she finally gets the car started, to use a metaphor?

This is a matter of policy within the school, policy relating to the costs and security issues discussed earlier. Typically the alternatives are: allow connections to a controlled local environment, probably maintained by the regional educational jurisdiction; allow connection to this same environment but also allow some or full Internet access through the controlled service; allow dial-in access to a special project; or allow connection to a commercial service (most of which now offer some or full Internet access).

The benefits of restricting access to controlled local educational environments are:

- Most efficient for the teacher, in his or her own language and related to his or her own curriculum
- Best controlled in quality and topical relevance of information
- Best controlled in terms of costs and support

However, the disadvantages are the reverse side of these advantages. It can be that the local or regional service never develops the critical mass of ideas, information, and different points of view which infuse networked-based tele-learning with so much of its educational potential. It can also mean that new technical developments that occur so rapidly on the Internet (such as developments in WWW browsers and tools) will not be available on the controlled service, in that regional sites may take longer to discover and implement these developments. In addition, the local service may not really wish to implement them, as this might cause instability to their established services.

Thus the controlled services may end up, as they have in many places, as underutilized, technically limited BBSs, serving more as file-exchange conduits for a relative few heavy users than as vehicles for tele-learning in schools. (We studied this, in The Netherlands, in terms of a subsidized BBS available for teachers; while the teachers valued the local resources and control of discussions, they also wanted Internet access for the other things they would like to do with tele-learning; Collis, Van Holstein, Rikkerink and Woerts, 1994.)

A final set of policy issues for the school administrator to handle with respect to networked tele-learning have already been anticipated in many of the previous comments. These are issues relating to access policy, from the point of who monitors access and who pays for access.

A final set of policy issues for the school administrator to handle with respect to networked tele-learning have already been anticipated in many of the previous comments. These are issues relating to access policy, from the perspectives of who monitors access and who pays for access.

MONITORING ACCESS

Student-access issues

We have already mentioned reasons why students may not have direct access to external networks, or if they do, why this access may be highly limited and supervised. "The ideal situation is a classroom-based terminal with close teacher supervision" says a recent bulletin on how to manage the Internet in a school (Sturm, 1995). This same set of guidelines also makes suggestions about "off limit areas", "supervision". "acceptable use" and "student accounts", all mirroring critical decision points about student access to tele-learning environments.

But who does this supervision? How much will it cost? Who will be in charge of student accounts and responding to student questions? The school computer coordinator? He often is overworked now and undercompensated. And, as we noticed before, he may really not be interested in doing it. But whoever is obtained will cost the school extra...

Teacher-access issues

And what about teachers? We already mentioned the difficulties teachers have getting access to a network connection in school for practice, exploration and lesson preparation. Teachers are beginning to ask for their own Internet accounts and their own phone line connections in their classrooms (Honey and McMillan, 1994). Teachers also are beginning to argue that the costs of home connectivity for lesson preparation should be compensated for in some way (Collis, Veen and De Vries, 1994). And teachers want and need time, to browse ideas, discover and plan. Is that time to be compensated?

These, too, are decisions for the policy maker in the school. Usually the decisions results in an answer of "no" or in no answer at all. The reason for such a response is probably not insensitivity to the wishes of the teacher. It more likely is a mixture of cost considerations such as we discussed in Chapter 7.2, and overall priorities for planning, as we discuss in the next section, Chapter 7.3.2.

■ 7.3.2 DECISIONS RELATING TO THE DIFFUSION OF AN INNOVATION

While the decision maker in the school must make some new decisions about networking, he or she does have considerable experience with a broader phenomenon: how teachers relate to an innovation in schools. Based on theoretical frameworks well developed for many years (see for example, Rogers, 1983; Fullan, 1982; Fullan, Miles and Anderson, 1988; and Goodlad, 1983), there is much to guide a school decision maker with regard to anticipating the steps through which teachers predictably go when confronted with an innovation. And it is not only a matter of anticipation; the school administrator is a key figure:

> *...in short, innovation implementation is more likely to succeed in schools where principals have already established a high priority on improvement in student learning, where resources such as external innovations are seen as opportunities and used to further this goal, and where norms of active peer collaboration in school improvement are in place.* (Fullan, Miles, & Anderson, 1988, p. 3.88)

PHASES IN THE DIFFUSION PROCESS

It helps that the diffusion process is comparatively well understood. Diffusion of an innovation through a social system is shaped by characteristics of the adopters, particularly the early adopters, and the perceived value of the innovation.

Importance of early adopters

Although the different theorists use somewhat different terminology, certain aspects of their messages are similar: innovations face a difficult path becoming diffused, or accepted, by teachers. Without careful and wise nurturing by the administration in a school, an innovation is not likely to move beyond what Rogers (1983) calls the "early adopter phase".

Early adopters are those first responsive to an innovation, in this case, to tele-learning in the school. Such teachers typically are fueled by their own enthusiasm, their own vision of what tele-learning could bring to their students. Early adopters can be filters and models for the innovation in the school by influencing their colleagues about the value of the innovation.

Early adopters need support

But without support from the administration, the diffusion impact of early adopters is slowed down or even lost. If the not-yet adopters in the school do not feel the innovation, and those who were early to adopt it, are valued by the administration and supported in some critical ways, the likelihood of the innovation diffusing to the larger group of teachers is reduced.

Why does diffusion matter?

Diffusion matters in a school for a number of reasons. Teachers influence each other very much; the more teachers in a school gaining experience with tele-learning, the more likely experiences will be shared and amplified. Also, the more experience in the school, the lower the threshold of start-up difficulties for the next wave of teachers new to tele-learning: there will be more people to turn to for help, more of the technical issues will have been solved, and more procedures will be in place for access and activities.

HOW TO STIMULATE DIFFUSION?

As initial steps, the administrator should look to help and support the early adopters (Fullan, 1982; Rogers, 1983) in at least the ways listed in Box 7.2.

These seem reasonable. Where might the school decision maker encounter difficulties in realizing these recommendations with respect to tele-learning? A major problem relates to the cost and scale of establishing a tele-learning infrastructure in the school.

INVOLVE THE TEACHERS...

A general conclusion about successful diffusion, and successful leadership more generally in the school, is to build teacher involvement and ownership in decision

Box 7.2

Facilitating acceptance of an innovation in the school

Show conviction about the relative advantage of the innovation: Help communicate the idea that the innovation is better than the situation without the innovation

Reduce fears about incompatibility: Emphasize ways in which the innovation is compatible with existing values and needs of the teachers

Facilitate try-ability: Look for ways in which teachers can gain some initial first-hand experience of the innovation is as safe and simple a way as possible

Reduce complexity: Help find ways to simplify communication and understandings about the innovation

Communicate observability: Help find ways to communicate and disseminate the success stories of early experiences with an innovation

Involve teachers in all phases of decision making about the innovation

Make the goals of the innovation clear

making. Teachers need to have experienced the practical value of an innovation such as tele-learning before they will be committed to it (Williams, 1994). But because of the cost and complexity of tele-learning infrastructures, major decisions about such infrastructures and their support are frequently not made at the school level, but at the district or state or national level. For example,

- A decision is made centrally to buy into a consortium supplying broadcast programming
- A decision is made to set up a districtwide network and through it carry out both administrative and instructional functions throughout the district.
- A decision is made at the regional level to develop a network service for education

We will look at some decisions such as these in Section 7.4. These are decisions that for various reasons are made outside of the school. The risk is high that teachers will not feel personally involved in these decisions and will not engage themselves with them. What should the administrator do?

Internet as a current case

The example in which this is most clear at the current time is access to the Internet. In general, this sort of tele-learning is a bottom-up phenomenon in schools, stimulated by early adopters willing to give substantial time and effort to its investigation. In contrast, the district definition of tele-learning may be broadcast programming, where much money and effort has been invested to set up and support a central distribution facility. Networking is seen by the central administration as a method for the efficient and secure transfer of administrative data, not for children doing things with the WWW.

If schools want to proceed with Internet access, they may have to do it on their own, without the benefit of district support. Should the school administrator take this decision, to nurture the bottom-up enthusiasm of some of his or her teachers?

CHANGE AND ITS OWNERSHIP...

Thus decision making about tele-learning in the school has an important philosophical note: How far does the administrator want to stimulate deep-seated change in educational practice in his or her school? How far is the decision maker willing to go to bring the more explorative and creative aspects of tele-learning into the school? Is he willing to find a way to pay for it, if it is not subsidized centrally?

Does the decision maker in the school have the belief, the energy, and the strategic skills to take leadership in stimulating tele-learning as an innovation in the school?

■ 7.4 CHOOSING AND SUPPORTING A TELE-LEARNING MODEL: DECISIONS FOR THE SCHOOL DISTRICT OR REGION

Schools are generally coordinated and supported with regard to technology by an administrative level over the schools. The range and name of this level varies in different countries and settings. In the US it is both the district and state, in different combinations of pervasiveness depending upon the location. In Canada, it is a combination of district and province, while in Australia is more likely the state level. In other countries it may be the national level that supports broadscale technology initiatives in schools, as is the case in many European countries as well as Asian countries.

In this section we will focus on this level, whatever it is called in a particular jurisdiction. For convenience we will call it the regional level. First, what are some of the characteristics of this level that relate to tele-learning decisions?

CHARACTERISTICS OF REGIONAL TELE-LEARNING INVOLVEMENT

Characteristics of regional-level involvement in tele-learning decisions include:

- Budget and mandate from the ministry or department of education to assume leadership in central decision making about tele-learning
- Funds available to extend to schools for tele-learning, based on the regional-level planning
- A specialist staff with contacts throughout the schools and also with universities, vendors, and politically influential groups
- Funding for special projects, evaluations, conferences, and occasionally research

CHARACTERISTICS OF SPECIALIST STAFF

Specialist staff at the regional level are not in direct daily contact with teachers, as are decision makers in schools. They have more time and scope to look at larger trends and issues with regard to tele-learning. They also have the opportunity to set up major region-wide initiatives, either on a project basis or intended as long-term structures. They sometimes have teacher-inservice responsibilities, particularly with respect to any innovation they set up. They can compete for external funding and often aggressively look for new partnerships and consortia in the region, perhaps involving industrial partners. They may be related to as few as one school or as many as thousands.

MULTIPLE ROLES

On one hand, regional decision makers are responsible for innovation, particularly with respect to stimulating consortia and new partnerships which bring funding and a range of new possibilities into the region for exploratory projects. On another hand, they are responsible for setting and implementing a model for region-wide planning. On yet another hand, they are responsible for on-going regionwide support services, such as regional technology centres and continuing services relating to school support. Thus there may be inherent conflicts within the same administrative group, between those seeking innovative partnerships for projects (and as a way to get some extra equipment and expertise into the schools), and those responsible for the day-to-day support of on-going, more-routine activities in schools.

Given these characteristics, what are major issues confronting decision makers at the regional level concerning tele-learning in schools? We have selected two clusters: (1) Finding an effective model for the systematic planning of tele-learning in the school district or region, with particular consideration to the balance among telephone, television/video and computer networking; and (2) making decisions about teacher-support strategies.

We discuss each of these in this section.

■ 7.4.1 EFFECTIVE PLANNING MODELS

There are many different planning blueprints that can be developed at the regional level for tele-learning support. Perhaps the most consistent aspect of successful planning relates to process, rather than product. Involvement of as many stakeholder groups as possible during as many aspects of the planning as possible is seen as key. In this section we look at a selection of examples of plans judged successful by their stakeholders, in both process and outcome.

There are many different planning blueprints that can be developed at the regional level for tele-learning support. Perhaps the most consistent aspect of successful planning relates to process, rather than product. Involvement of as many stakeholder groups as possible during as many aspects of the planning as possible is seen as key. In this section we look at a selection of examples of plans judged successful by their stakeholders, in both process and outcome.

INFLUENCES ON PLANNING DIRECTIONS

Just as in schools, administrators at the regional level do not make decisions about tele-learning solely on theoretical considerations. Each decision has a complicated context, past and present.

History and current context

Planning may be dominated by many issues, such as the history of tele-learning in a region, the extent to which tele-learning is a "hot" issue from broadscale social and political perspectives, and the personal convictions of key persons influencing decision making at the regional level. The history of tele-learning is particularly important, because a region may have previously set a general direction (i.e., interactive television for bringing classroom-like courses to areas with deficiencies in their own resources) which will not be likely to fundamentally change while capital investment is relatively new. Also previous experiences at the project level may have left a strong positive or negative feeling in the region, at least among its decision makers, shaping their (dis)inclination to embark on more systematic planning for the particular tele-learning innovation that was involved in the previous experience. Wagner (1992) notes that these perceptions can be historically biased ("We've seen this before, and we know how it's going to end") even though conditions may well have changed since the earlier experience. She also notes that such collective memory may be "great lies", "inaccurate assumptions which have been repeated so often that they have come to represent current thinking regarding distance education, as we know it today" (p. 42).

Current context

In addition being influenced by history and perceptions of history, tele-learning like many technological innovations before it, is sensitive to public energies. The idea of the "information highway" has literally swept the world in 1995, capturing the imagination of the public, and of politicians making educational decisions. Whatever the information highway might be, we are reading about it and how important it is to get on it, in the popular press in countries around the world. "Getting on" is even being called a "fundamental right" for schools and students (see, for example, "Internet ABCs...", 1994), equivalent to the need for "computer literacy" a decade earlier (Collis, 1995c).

Just as getting computers in the schools became a universal motivation in the 1980s (see Hawkridge, 1991, for six categories of reasons for this motivation), getting on the Internet is starting to have this sort of pressure on regional planning for tele-learning in schools in many countries.

However, that certainly does not mean that every region is planning for Internet access. There are many different models of planning for tele-learning; we will look at a range of examples, all of which are built on more-stable approaches to planning than "the information highway" and its on-ramps. After the examples, we will comment on some of their similarities and differences.

EXAMPLE 1: VIDEO STEERS THE DECISIONS

Broken Arrow Public Schools, Oklahoma

In a number of regions, bringing "immediate and unlimited amounts of data, audio and video" (and multimedia) into each classroom is a major emphasis in long-term planning. In addition, regional goals often involve the possibility for the classroom teacher to call up "video on demand". These plans are a mixture of how (through air, wires, cable or fiber) the video signal travels from a central resource centre to schools, how the school is wired so that the signal gets into the classrooms, and how the teacher selects and controls the various signals that come into her classroom.

As an example, the Broken Arrow Public School District in Oklahoma, with the goal of increasing educational opportunities for its 14,000 students, and having "an outstanding staff, a budget (as well as a mainframe computer in the district office used for administrative purposes) strained to the limit, and a hefty portion of vision, perseverance, and teamwork" has recently connected all its facilities by a fiber-optic network (Hill and Judd, 1995, p. 37). The district is spread over 114 square miles, outside a major city (Tulsa).

Decision-making process

A strategic planning team of 100 persons, representing the parent, business and educational communities of the region, and guided by a statement of philosophy from the School Board, met many times to consider solutions. They finally determined that computerizing the district administrative staff would lead to a dismantling of the some of the staff, and a cost savings from not refilling positions as staff members left. Thus a district-wide information system based on networking came first.

Following this, the decision to, eventually, provide students with immediate access to memory-intensive graphics, sound files, and digitized video as well as text, led to the decision to tap into the existing fiber optic system in the region. This system went, in many cases, close to the doors of the schools.

Choice of fiber

Fiber was chosen because:

> ...It provided immunity from interference from radio and electrical frequencies, allowed connectivity over great distances, and had the potential for adding more users over a long period. Furthermore, fiber was the only carrier we felt was capable of the bandwidth needed to transmit video across the district. (Hill & Judd, 1995, p. 38)

(For other, less-convinced, positions on fiber compared to coaxial cable in a school, see Galbreath (1993) and Kovacs (1993); neither of them are as convinced as the Broken Arrow decision makers about the superiority of fiber to coaxial cable, but they do agree that it depends on the circumstances, such as the distances involved.)

Financing

Quotes were taken for a 10 MB fiber-optic network, and the successful bidder arranged a lease-purchasing plan with the district over a five-year period for the cost of installing the fiber optic lines from the streets to the school buildings. Funding was obtained at the district level from an "early retirement incentive plan" and a change that was negotiated in the number of sick days for which the teacher got a financial compensation. A student management package was purchased to link administrative functions among all schools. Twelve fibers were installed, although only two were in initial use.

Next?

Now, the district is "Committed to training staff and improving the overall use of the network, as well as developing creative partnerships with other institutions to expand funds available for technology" (p. 38).

Another, similar example of a commitment to two-way interactive video can be found in the US state of Iowa (Simonson and Schlosser, 1995). The state, through its Iowa Distance Education Alliance, has even adopted a definition of distance education that fits their commitment:

> *...Distance education implies formal, institutionally based educational activities where the teacher and learner are normally separated from each other in location but not normally separated in time, and where two-way interactive telecommunication systems are used for the sharing of video, data, and voice instruction."* (p. 13).

This definition in turn has lead to a statewide two-way full motion interactive fiber optic communications network with at least one point of presence in each of Iowa's 99 counties, with about 120 secondary-school classrooms connected. Being connected means having a fully equipped distance education classroom, consisting of approximately four monitors, two or more cameras, and microphones at every seat. In the next phase of the plan, an additional 400 schools, libraries, armories, education agencies, and hospitals will be connected.

EXAMPLE 2 COMBINATION OF VIDEO AND DATA NETWORKS, WITH AN EQUITY ORIENTATION

North Dakota: goals for tele-learning

North Dakota began its planning for a "statewide distance learning" facility in the context of substantial budget cuts at the local school district level. "Since part of the perceived strength of North Dakota is its predominantly rural way of life, ways and means had to be found, even within a reduced budget, to strengthen the rural educational system and bring it, in terms of opportunity, to parity with urban school systems" (Shapiro, Heck and Freedenberg, 1992). Some rural districts had started their own consortia for broadcast programming delivery, but the different systems used were incompatible with each other, and inefficiencies and duplications in programming offer were occurring.

Creation of a council

Thus the state government created an Educational Telecommunications Council to create a statewide, efficient system, to overcome the possibility of "an inefficient conglomerate of incompatible systems" (p. 28).

Equity-oriented goals

A set of 12 wide-ranging goals were developed, where eight of the goals emphasize issues relating to equity of access to education. Four of these goals are:

- To provide the same ancillary services to all K-12 students as now exist in the largest districts
- To address the educational problems of Native Americans
- To address the literacy problems of those who do not possess a high school education
- To continually upgrade the technical and business skills of the labor force

Video network

A major orientation for the state network came to be the provision of courses, for credit and non-credit. This occurs through an interactive video network connecting schools within different regions of the state using a compressed video system and TI telephone lines. Programming is provided by state colleges, and many colleges set up studios for this provision. A Network Operations Center is the overall technical and managerial focal point. Video-conferencing rooms in schools are used for K-12 instruction during the day, teacher inservice training in the late afternoon, and adult education at other times.

Computer network

A statewide computer network was also established to connect (as terminals) all schools and universities and regional offices, for access to remote bulletin boards, library searches, mail and to provide access to centrally maintained, downloadable collections of educational software.

EXAMPLE 3: COMBINING IT ALL FOR SCHOOLS-COMMUNITY CONNECTIONS

St. Louis Park School District, Minnesota

In St. Louis Park School District there was also a motivation to involve the community with the schools through a tele-learning network, but with a focus on distributing information to the community. Holte (1995a) describes the choices made to connect schools with their communities via computer and telephone (including IVR, "integrated voice response") access, fax, and cable TV and radio, all through an integrated approach. The goal is not only to bring information to the community, but also to "provide community members with communications technology as a remote learning tool", and to have efficient ways for two-way communication between school-district staff and the community (p. 44).

Holte lists 23 types of information now available to the community, ranging from information on student assessment via fax to call-in shows on cable television. IVR, or computer-controlled voice mail, is an alternative in 19 of the 23 types. Also, students display their work on WWW pages, with again an emphasis on information provision.

Major criteria

The major criteria for decision making about the sort of tele-learning infrastructure to meet these goals were: provide equity of access; reduce costs by sharing facilities between the instructional needs and community use; development of a community and staff culture for use of the environment; and control of security, privacy, and inappropriate access.

Technical provision

To handle all this, a combination of telephone, video and computer network reaches every classroom. Each classroom has the equipment listed in Box 7.3.

EXAMPLE 4: REGIONAL COMPUTER NETWORK WITH AN EMPHASIS ON TEACHER SUPPORT

The Barcelona XTEC Network

Some regions have not given video and audio networking priority, but have focused on enriching the services available to schools through a computer network service. The XTEC Network in Catalonia, a region in Spain, is one of the European examples of this type (for others, see Veen, Collis, De Vries and Vogelzang, 1994).

In the Catalonian example, the emphasis is on teacher support, for lesson ideas and materials, and for inservice. The XTEC Network links all secondary schools in Catalonia, many of the elementary schools, and the educational institutions. It is a terminal–host system, with the host located in the district central offices. The host supports software for conferencing, for data base management and retrieval, e-mail, file transfer, a news service, and file transfer of any type of software (Vergés, Castells and Ruiz, 1994). The central server is a UNIX environment. A subsidy is provided for teachers to access the environment via ordinary phone lines and a modem.

Services

A major service provided for teachers accessing the system is a database of educational resources and teaching ideas, all in the Catalan language and indexed

---

Box 7.3

Classroom technology provision in a community-communication oriented district

---

Each teacher has his or her own phone, voicemail connection and personal telephone number. Teachers can have access to the voicemail from their classrooms and get and leave messages from parents and the community.

Each school has a fax machine, accessible to staff and students.

There are two video connectors in each classroom attached to coaxial cables. One connector is for regular-subscriber cable channels and is used for CNN Newsroom (see Chapter 5) and others. The other connector is for the district's interactive video system. Classrooms can broadcast out to the community. There is also provision for two-or three-way video-conferencing among classrooms or the community.

The district has a satellite dish to bring in broadcast programming. Teachers can, from their classrooms, request a program by e-mail, and it is delivered by cable directly into their classrooms.

Every classroom has a computer connected to a school LAN with ethernet networking, fast enough to access a CD-ROM in another part of the building.

All school LANS are connected, with data sent between buildings via the video cable. In addition, every computer can be used as a network connection to the Internet, and every student and teacher has an individual e-mail address for Internet communication.

Modems in the district office can be dialed into, from home or the classroom, so that any student and all staff can dial into the network from home.

(Holte, 1995a,b; also location `http://www.stlpark.k12.mn.us`, or contact: `Jeff_Holte@stlpark.k12.mn.us`)

---

for the Catalan curriculum. Over 12,000 educational resources are available for the teacher to search in many different ways and download.

Tailored tele-learning activities for students

Another service available via the system is the provision of carefully developed tele-learning experiences for teachers to consider using with their classes. As one example, a novel written by a contemporary Catalan author which is regularly assigned as required reading in secondary school literature courses was used as the basis for a tele-learning event, in which 22 selected classes, based on the prior preparation of their teachers, participated in various structured discussions and debates about the novel, discussions which included the author of the novel.

Inservice courses

Other services available via the network are inservice courses for teachers, completely or partially offered via the network, with an emphasis on collaborative activities among the distant teacher-participants.

EXAMPLE 5: STATEWIDE LEARNING-SUPPORT SYSTEM

Florida Learning Support Systems

In the state of Florida, the idea of a centrally available database of exemplary lesson materials, as was part of the Catalonia example, is carried forward and magnified within the *Florida Schoolyear 2000 Initiative*. This initiative describes itself as "supporting a new model of schooling for public schools in the next century" (Gaede, 1995, p. 235) and involves, among other aspects, the investment of state funds for the development of distributed "performance-support systems". These systems are to provide for students, teachers, and staff "the tools and information [they] need in the performance of their work at the moment of need" (Gaede, p. 236).

Components of the system

In the planned FLSS environment, the log-in identification of the user identifies if s/he is a student, teacher, or parent. A different user interface then appears, in which some of the overall tools and information routes in the system are available and others are not (and are not visible). In this way, a tailored access to e-mail, learning materials, databases with learning resources, and student-assessment databases maintained at the district level is provided. In addition, some classes of users will also have access to the Internet.

EXAMPLE 6: PROVIDING COURSES VIA EMAIL

Ulster County New York and advanced-placement calculus via e-mail

As a final example of a regional tele-learning initiative, five school districts in the state of New York identified the need for an advanced-placement calculus course for a total of 15 secondary-students from those five districts (Amodeo and Bullowa, 1995). In the US, the response to this sort of compensation situation is generally to assume that a televised/video form of tele-learning should occur, with an expert teacher teaching remotely, providing real-time questioning opportunities for the students while being seen and heard.

"Virtual face-to-face" is not the only way

However, it should not be assumed that video-based instruction, simulating the experience of being in a face-to-face class, must the way that courses-at-a-distance are provided to distributed secondary-school students. In Australia, for example, there is extensive use of audio-graphics teaching at a distance, even with young children. Gray and O'Grady (1993), for example, describe how one specialist teacher in Japanese is providing Japanese instruction to children in 80 elementary schools in a widespread region, via audio-graphics.

Collaborative learning via CMC

Back to the New York example. The remote teacher and the 15 students were supplied with computers and modems to use at home, and a file server was set up to handle different aspects of computer-based interaction. Telephone and fax contact were also available. A collaborative approach to learning was emphasized for the students, as all were encouraged to make their work commonly available on the network, and to help each other in their content-related solutions and problems.

Results? Comparable, and better

The results of the New York approach, in terms of the number of students who successfully completed the common advanced-placement examination, was similar to the level of success of students in face-to-face settings.

More than this result, however, was the finding that the CMC students had evolved from a teacher-led, content-centered way of thinking to a more self-directed, student-centered mentality, "gaining self-confidence in the process of critiquing each other's work" (p. 13). The teacher became a facilitator and mentor as well as an instructor. And the cost was considerably lower than a television/video-type delivery approach would have been in this situation.

There are other examples of Internet-delivered courses now being offered to secondary-school students, with careful attention to the instructional design of the course and the interaction and communication possibilities within the course.

For example, through the "CyberSchool", associated with a school district in Oregon, courses are offered in Russian literature, statistics, geography, culture of the deaf, history, and others (Layton, 1995). Box 7.4 shows some aspects of one of these courses:

COMPARING THE EXAMPLES

In these examples, selected out of many possibilities, we see the way district decision making can shape what becomes feasible as tele-learning in the schools

> **Box 7.4**
>
> **Russian literature: an Internet course for secondary school students**
>
> Course is the equivalent of a one-semester senior secondary course.
>
> Prerequisites are access to the WWW and an Internet e-mail account, the ability to purchase at least four textbooks; completion of US Grade 8; and a serious interest in Russian literature. Students will be selected on the basis of preliminary essays.
>
> The reading list for the course is extensive, including Gogol, Lermontov, Chekhov, Tolstoy, and Dostoevsky
>
> The course will involve finding partners among the course participants and having regular e-mail discussions with those partners as well as the instructor (a practicing secondary school teacher) for each of three sets of reading materials. Essays will also be submitted over the Internet and discussed with the instructor.
>
> see **CyberSchool**, `http://CyberSchool.4j.lanc.edu/CyberSchool.html`

of the district. The orientation chosen, be it future-oriented delivery of multimedia learning materials, course delivery for equity purposes, community communication, or teacher support, lead to different decisions about the technical infrastructure supported for the region.

Effect of regional decisions on outcomes

It is interesting to compare the educational results likely to occur from the different regional decisions in the examples:

- Students expecting to access multi-media resources may be a main outcome of Example 1; the challenge to the district will be to find and stock those resources so there is something to access, and then for the teacher to determine how to manage instructional activities for classes of students making use of the resources A similar problem has confronted the use of computers in education for a decade. Assuming resources are available, the school and teacher have much flexibility in how this network will be used

- A major result of Example 2 will be members of the community making use of school resources for educational video delivery. The individual school and teacher does not appear to have much input into this system, but can access a network-based bulletin board and other resources. What the teacher does have is familiarity in how to make use of what is offered; if there are students in the rural school who qualify for a certain course and the course is available via the video network, then the teacher has little more to do than make sure the student is present

- Example 3 is heavily dependent on the teacher and school and students communicating, telling, disseminating, informing, talking to the outside community. What they are talking about, and if it is worthwhile saying, will have to shaped and monitored by the teacher, as well as the students' skills in doing the communication

- In Example 4 a technology was chosen that could be available to all teachers with existing resources, as long as they can connect a computer via a modem to a telephone line. The material available on the network is of high relevance and quality, but of limited quantity. The teacher's choice is limited to what is offered, but what is offered is very important, for his or her inservice, for usable lessons for students, and for lesson resources. No video or audio is possible, nor does it seem particularly necessary

- In Example 5, a centralized decision was made to stimulate and support a networked-based resource and learning environment. For students, there will be a systematic way to receive traditional computer-based instruction materials, managed by the teacher and a system to pace the student through mastery-type learning. However, at the same time, the student will also systematically gain access to more information-handling tools and perhaps even access to the Internet to use those tools

- Example 6 shows that providing a compensatory course at a distance does not have to happen through students watching a remote teacher via a television monitor. The technology chosen by the region and the support it gave (providing teacher and students with computers to use at home, so that access and time were not restricted) also facilitated a new approach to student-centered tele-learning emphasizing peer-to-peer communication and discussion

The message?

There is no one way to plan for tele-learning at the regional level, but if well planned, each route that is chosen will have very different implications for the teacher and students in the schools affected by the plan.

■ 7.4.2 REGIONAL TEACHER TRAINING AND SUPPORT THROUGH TELE-LEARNING

It is well established that if teachers are to make effective use of a technology they need training and support. "Training must be written into and funded by the district networking plan" (Schuster, 1995). How this training and support is organized and offered varies from jurisdiction to jurisdiction.

TEACHER INSERVICE AND TELE-LEARNING

In some countries there are ministry-supported institutions specifically for teacher support and inservice. In other countries inservice is primarily offered by universities. In many countries there is a mix of possibilities, often with special rounds of inservice available for a certain initiative running parallel with the normal inservice program.

With respect to the region, tele-learning and teacher education, we can identify three main categories:

- Regional initiatives, using traditional methods, to provide teacher education about some form of tele-learning
- Regional initiatives, using tele-learning, to provide teacher education about tele-learning
- Regional initiatives, using tele-learning, to provide on-going professional support to teachers

A major decision that a region must take is what it is going to do about teacher education for whatever tele-learning form is supported by the region. In this section we give examples of the categories above, as a sample of some of the more innovative choices available to the district. (We discuss teacher inservice and support in more detail in Chapter 9).

FACE-TO-FACE TEACHER EDUCATION FOR TELE-LEARNING

We assume the first category mentioned above—face-to-face teacher education for tele-learning—is already familiar; each region has its own on-going organization for "traditional" teacher education, in the form of face-to-face sessions, where teachers come together to a location and are taught or led by a specialist, and then disperse and go back to their classrooms. Probably many of these organizations are now offering courses about the Internet, as a new interest area for inservice.

Weaknesses in the traditional approach

The evidence is that this traditional model of teacher education is comparatively weak (see, for example, LeBaron and Bragg, 1994). It is on one hand costly and complicated, in that teachers must leave their classrooms to someone else or take the training on weekends or during vacations. Sometimes they must incur travel costs. And on the other hand, it is weak as an approach, in that the likelihood of transfer and consolidation in the classroom is poor unless there is follow-up and reinforcement as close to the teacher's experiences as possible, when she tries to put ideas from the inservice into practice (Ross and Regan, 1993).

An additional weakness in the traditional inservice approach specific to tele-learning is that the traditional approach may not provide the opportunity for teachers to actually experience tele-learning as a learning environment for themselves. They may hear about it, and have some "interface-interaction introduction" (Hillman, Willis and Gunawardena, 1994), but are not likely to gain deeper insight of what it feels like, at both the content level and the subjective level, to teach and learn via monitors and networked computers.

Of course, innovative ideas can still occur in face-to-face settings; in a district in the state of Washington, for example, students are trained to be network managers and consultants and THEY in turn train the teachers (Schuster, 1995).

But instead we will here note some ideas for regionally sponsored teacher education *via* tele-learning which not only address the weaknesses of traditional teacher inservice but also illustrate where tele-learning brings clear added value to the inservice experience.

ABOUT TELE-LEARNING, VIA TELE-LEARNING

Nordic Schools Network

The five Nordic countries—Denmark, Iceland, Finland, Norway, and Sweden—often collaborate together on issues relating to learning-resource development. Recently, this collaboration has extended to the development of a network and network service to link Nordic schools with each other, and with the outer world via the Internet (Rannebo, 1994). This Nordic School Network is not only a coordinated technical venture, including for example, the development of software tools to allow students and teachers to handle characters in the Nordic languages that do not typically appear in ASCII-based computer communication, but also a coordinated venture in terms of teacher education.

Coordinated teacher practice via tele-learning

Particularly interesting in the Nordic Schools Network is the careful planning that has gone into the inservice component of network introduction. Coordinated centrally, inservice takes place using a two-day model. Each two-day model begins on a pre-set day. Teachers in all five Nordic countries come together locally for the first day of the two days, and in their own environment and language have a familiar face-to-face session that partially provides an "interface introduction" to the Network but also focuses on instructional applications.

Learning partners

On Day 2, each group of teachers is paired with another group meeting in another country, and activities take place allowing them to practice on-line with each other the sorts of learning activities in which they may choose to engage their students. Because of the centrally organized approach, all the teachers have had a common orientation on the previous day and are thinking in terms of a common set of initial collaborative-learning projects. Also because of the centralized approach, teachers can be authentic practice-partners with each other, and learn about tele-learning via tele-learning.

LEARNING VIA TEACHER NETWORKING

The PIT Project: teacher networking as inservice component

Another innovative approach to teacher inservice that can be organized at the regional level is to use tele-learning via a regional network as a way to extend traditional face-to-face inservice. In The Netherlands, an initiative has been in place since 1993 in which secondary-school teachers and curriculum specialists, in groups of about 25 teachers each, form specialist network groups around different content-related issues, such as helping immigrant students with the Dutch language or teaching physics using a data-modeling approach (Collis, 1994; Collis and Moonen, 1995b). Each of these groups meets six times a year in a face-to-face session, coordinated by a ministry-level management team.

But between the face-to-face sessions, teachers continue to work together on sharing their experiences and developing lesson materials, via free access to a national BBS for teachers. During the 1995–1996 school year, a WWW environment with Internet access will be also used. The teacher networking between face-to-face sessions has emerged as an effective model for teacher support, providing the teachers with a moderated and useful reason to keep interacting with each other and thus to learn from each other.

Thus electronic networking is an extension and facilitator of human networking, convenient to all teachers and schools because of the nationally subsidized (by the Ministry, the National Curriculum Institute, and the Dutch telephone company) electronic network service already available.

As before, many other examples could be presented of how regions are coming to use tele-learning as a method of teacher education, either about tele-learning, or for teacher networking for professional development. Regional decision makers have an increasing range of models and possibilities for the use of tele-learning for teacher education. Available technology is one of the boundary conditions; imagination is another.

■ 7.5 DECISION MAKING ABOUT TELE-LEARNING IN POST-SECONDARY INSTITUTIONS

Institutions of higher education are in the on-going practice of providing more and better support to their students with respect to learning. There are fewer overt decision points with regard to the extension of this support to tele-learning than may be the case in a school district; there are technology-service agencies and network-support staff in every post-secondary education institution, many of whom become involved in tele-learning support as part of the natural evolution of their jobs. We discuss this more specifically in Chapter 9, where we focus on the work of the educational technologist.

As in Chapter 6, when we use the term post-secondary institutions in this chapter, we intend a full range of possibilities, including universities, colleges, and continuing-education institutions. These institutions share the characteristics that adults take courses from them, on a voluntary basis; that they obtain some portion of their operating revenue based on the number of students they register; and that increasingly, they are competing among themselves to be the choice of these adults. We focus in this chapter on decision making about support for tele-learning; not the actual teaching of or design of courses.

Simply stated, a post-secondary institution expects to be serving its students on-campus or at a distance from the home institution or in both forms. A few institutions are created with the intention of only serving off campus students. These may be called distance-teaching institutions (or distance education institutions or distance-delivery open universities). Others may have no provision for students who are not on-site. However an increasing number of post-secondary institutions operate on some sort of a dual-mode basis: serving some proportion (usually the large majority) of their students on campus, but also providing for some off-site delivery of courses. When this off-site delivery involves communication technologies (primarily television, interactive video, or computer connections), the institutional decision makers are confronted with many issues. Why make this expansion of services? How can they be implemented? How can these off-campus students be adequately supported?

For many post-secondary institutions, the decision to expand their services to off-campus students is developed through the idea of offering their on-campus courses to groups at a distance. The television/video delivery of an existing course has seemed a most-natural model for doing this. Thus in Section 7.5.1 we focus on issues confronting the decision-maker in a post-secondary institution responsible for planning and maintaining courses offered via broadcasting or two-way video to off-campus students. In Section 7.5.2 we look instead to the post-secondary institutions organized from the start for off-site delivery: what issues or innovations relating to tele-learning are important to decision makers at those institutions? Finally, in Section 7.5.3 we turn to the on-campus support of tele-learning for post-secondary institutions: What are some of the main issues and trends for decision makers with respect to campus networks?

■ 7.5.1 PLANNING AND MANAGING EXTENSION SERVICES FOR STUDENTS AT A DISTANCE

What motivates a post-secondary institution to extend its services to off-campus students? When broadcast television or two-way video are chosen as the delivery means, what are the implications for the home institution? What are different strategies for supporting students at a distance?

MOTIVATIONS FOR EXTENDING SERVICES OFF-CAMPUS

Why should a post-secondary institution want to extend its delivery and services to off-campus students? Basically there seem to be social or political motivations, or economic incentives.

Social and political motivations

A post-secondary institution may have a moral or practical sense of obligation to serve those who cannot come to its campus physically, for reasons of geography or personal circumstances. This is common in many countries such as Canada, Australia, and China. The obligation may have evolved for socio-political reasons; those who for various reasons cannot come to the university have the right to be able to obtain the same level of instructional opportunity as their more-fortunate peers. This means students in remote areas, handicapped students, students whose work or family obligations prevent them from on-campus attendance: all should have the right to the same quality and range of educational opportunity as those who do not have these characteristics. This can become politically sensitive in some jurisdictions.

Financial incentives

However, post-secondary institutions have limited resources and cannot make decisions only on humanitarian motivations. Many institutions move into delivery provision to off-campus groups more directly on the basis of (partial) financial considerations: off-campus students form a new enrollment group and funding based on enrollment makes this group important. However, there is an "if"— if it does not, in the long run, cost more to serve them than the increased revenues they will generate.

ONE-WAY/TWO-WAY VIDEO DELIVERY

Many post-secondary institutions have responded to the motivations to serve off-campus students by making a commitment to broadcast-type or two-way video delivery of courses. Television broadcasting is used extensively.

Telecourses

In the US, such courses are sometimes called "telecourses", defined as "a full sequence of lessons offered over closed circuit or broadcast television for credit or auditing purposes" (Tremblay, 1991, p. 192). Many telecourses are offered as one-way video, two-way audio, and some may be delivered via two-way video, particularly compressed-video systems. Hakes, Cochenour, Rezabek, and Sachs (1995) profile compressed-video applications at 26 post-secondary institutions or combinations of institutions. Tremblay notes that telecourses with one-way video are widespread in the US, with about 25% of post-secondary institutions offering them. Interestingly, Tremblay's inventory found that about 80% of "telecourse" delivery is offered by what in the US is called the community college sector, and 90% are employed for introductory courses. However, universities are also active in telecourse delivery. Tremblay indicates that nearly two-thirds of "research universities" in the US have some telecourse provision, predominately in engineering, education, and business. As a more-recent indicator in the US of telecourse popularity, the Public Broadcasting Service is providing "a nationwide effort to coordinate adult telecourse offerings...and has signed up 49 colleges to participate. The colleges will list their courses in PBS's catalogue, and assign faculty to be responsible for answering students' questions and grading assignments" ("Going the distance..", 1995).

Some post-secondary institutions have made telecourse delivery a highly professional (and perhaps profitable) business. Chico State University in California is an example. Box 7.5 shows some of its range of services for "distance education" in 1994.

Support and professional staffing

As the Chico State example shows, this sort of delivery strategy can require a large and professional support staff as well as a significant investment in equipment and a formal commitment of the institution. Although it may be conceptually non-complex to think of course provision at a distance as "beaming out" in some way what the instructor is already doing in the lecture hall or classroom, in fact, it is a complex support operation. To offer one-way or two-way video delivery to off-campus sites can involve considerable personnel implications, as shown in Box 7.6.

Box 7.5

Distance education offered by Chico State University

- BS and MS in Computer Science, delivered live via satellite to corporate sites throughout the US
- 615 hours per year of live broadcasts of courses on the Satellite Education Network
- 2,752 enrollments at corporate sites
- 109 Computer Science classes broadcast live via satellite since Fall 1984
- 650 courses in 40 disciplines and involving 213 faculty involved in interactive classes (one-way video, two-way audio)
- Self-paced core courses on videotape—packaged complete with text, study guide and academic support—"for maximum student convenience"
- Access to faculty and staff
- Academic advising available, sometimes at the work site (Center for Regional and Continuing Education, Chico State University, 1994)

Box 7.6

Personnel and their roles in the delivery of one- or two-way video courses for off-campus students

Marketing personnel. ("Telecourses are expensive. The costs of production are recovered by the sale of the telecourses. ...Marketing must be a purposeful activity and one must not make the assumption that it is self-sustaining" ; Cyrs & Smith, 1990, p. 294)

Personnel for instructor training, including how to organize the course, and how to make effective use of the television environment (Cyrs and Smith suggest this usually involves 4-6 hours or training and 3-4 hours of practice before program production)

Production personnel, including all technicians and operators in the areas of television, graphics, photography, desktop publishing and audio; all of these must work under the direction of the instructional developer of the course

Site facilitator, who handles a variety of tasks relating to being the liaison between send and receive sites, including tasks such as scheduling, archiving, and being the first-line contact with the receive sites and the students

Engineering staff, to ensure the equipment runs properly at both send and receive sites

Instructors (usually faculty members from the home institution)

Remote-site staff, persons responsible for remote-site organization. This can involve different groups of remote-site staff—technical staff, local tutors, and local counselors

Course administrator, in charge of managing and integrating all of the above

(from: Boaz and Hardy, 1993; Cyrs and Smith, 1990; Kitchen and Hughes, 1992; and Davis and Elliot, 1992)

Yet more tasks...

And many more tasks could be added to those explicitly mentioned in Box 7.6, such as responsibility for distribution of lesson materials to support the course, responsibility for procedures for testing, responsibility for timely delivery of handouts and timely handling of assignments, contacts with off-campus students prior to the course or during the course with general information about meeting times and other logistic aspects of being in the course, and packaging and distribution of multiple-media course materials before and after a broadcast including videotape libraries of the televised sessions. The institutional decision maker can be confronted with extensive personnel requirements if a commitment is made to provide competitive course delivery of the television/video type to remote students.

Instructor engagement: A particular issue

In Chapters 5 and 6 we noted the many challenges and demands placed on the instructor teaching this sort of remote-class course via television or two-way video. From the decision maker's perspective, a particular issue is how to provide the incentive for faculty to make the effort to contribute to extension services. Boaz and Hardy (1993) describe the substantial faculty orientation and training that is being provided at a number of post-secondary institutions to better prepare instructors. Such training requires staff and budget decisions. Even with staff support provision, faculty may still not wish to participate. Blanch (1994) identifies barriers to faculty participation in televised courses and notes that faculty feel little status or incentive for such participation, unless the administration takes the initiative in some way (perhaps financial, perhaps through providing released time from other duties) to convince faculty to take on the extra burdens of teaching to remote groups.

Supporting off-course students

A particular issue for the decision maker is the form of involvement and support to be given to off-campus personnel engaged in supporting students in their remote participation. The farther the geographic range of delivery, the more complex and expensive it can become to have appropriate remote-site support. Finding qualified persons for off-campus support, and finding a way to engage them professionally, differs from institution to institution. These persons may be called local tutors or site facilitators, or many other names. They may or may not be well informed about the course that a student with problems is following, or they may only be engaged as a general contact person for the home institution. They may operate only in a responsive way, available for practical questions if the student contacts them, or they may work in a much more proactive role, stimulating various face-to-face interactions among the members of local groups or offering one-to-one tutoring. Who finds these local support persons, who actually employs them and pays them and who monitors them are other important issues for the decision maker.

Alternatives for support for students at a distance

Not only personnel must be considered in the support of off-campus students; there are a variety of ways that technologies can be used to supply some or all of this support, and in addition to circumvent the problems of quality control and cost of remote-site human staff. Voice mail is being used by a number of post-secondary institutions to provide an efficient way for call distribution as well as information and materials updating. In a typical voice-mail system, students can dial in, via ordinary telephone and receive services such as those listed in Box 7.7:

Box 7.7

Use of voice mail and fax for support of off-campus students

Students can call in via telephone and:

Listen to information on any particular course

Order automatically by push-button or voice telephone printed material for a specific course, which is either faxed automatically to the student if the student has a fax number or mailed locally to him

Answer certain types of homework questions by directly entering the code of the answer (from a multiple-choice format) and hearing immediate, pre-recorded feedback

Order by the telephone a variety of support materials, such as answers to practice exercises, or hints

Request a personal call from the instructor
(From: Jussila, 1994)

The services listed in Box 7.7 are being supplied in a number of countries such as Japan and Finland to remote students. They show that this kind of voice-mail can in fact become a tele-learning environment.

BBSs and other electronic information services

As another example of support for remote students which bridges information and tele-learning, Edith Cowan University in Australia is one of many post-secondary institutions to offer an electronic information service of the BBS type. The Edith Cowan BBS service provides all distant students with e-mail facilities, informational menus, chat and real-time talk facilities, Internet access, access to university libraries, and file transfer. Students are provided with modems and their communication costs are covered. Work is underway to provide some students with access to multi-media resources such as videotapes via higher-speed and higher-bandwidth networks (Ring, Watson, & Ring, 1994). This kind of support provision is a substantial institutional decision; in Edith Cowan's case particularly because the remote students being provided with subsidized call-in access are located throughout a wide area in Western Australia as well as in South East Asia.

Combining two-way video course delivery with WWW and CMC support

Afew examples are emerging of "telecourse" delivery of courses being supplemented by asynchronous support of the courses via a WWW site or e-mail or computer conferencing. Greenbowe and Burke (1995) for example indicate how this is being done for introductory chemistry courses in the state of Iowa, facilitated greatly by the fact that Iowa has a statewide fibre-optic communication network to which both universities and remote sites can connect. However, the Iowa example appears to be exceptional; as we will discuss later, there is a considerable gap in contact and awareness in post-secondary institutions between those who are involved in the delivery of courses via television or interactive video, and those who are involved in the use of data networks such as the Internet for tele-learning.

Fragmented expertise

And as if all these considerations are not enough, the planning and management of extension-type courses is further complicated by the large variety of locations and administrative units in post-secondary institutions which may become engaged in course delivery. Sometimes specialists are working under the direction of library services; under some ad-hoc unit under the direction of a variety of persons such as the academic vice-president or education dean; in specific units such as extension services or media centres; or associated with faculties or departments (Johnson, 1994). In many cases, media service professionals are not the persons at their institution who are involved in television-type program origination or distribution. For example, Di Paolo, an engineering dean and the director of *The Stanford Interactive Television Network*, an enterprise extensively involved in engineering-related course delivery via interactive television and video-conferencing to industrial subscribers, notes (personal correspondence, November 1994) that there is no input to this operation from the Stanford University School of Education (with their worldwide reputation as specialists in research relating to learning and teaching).

NO SIMPLE DECISION

Thus, it is clear the decision to offer television/video-type courses to off-campus students is no casual decision. If the motivation is "a way to facilitate enrollment growth without concomitant capital outlay for new facilities" (Blanch, 1994), then the cost implications must be carefully compared to the projected revenues that can come from the enrollment growth before a decision is made. If the motivation is social or political, then the institution or government or some other social agency must be convinced to subsidize the costs.

▩ 7.5.2 DISTANCE-TEACHING INSTITUTIONS: WHAT ARE NEW ALTERNATIVES FOR DELIVERY AND SUPPORT?

While traditional post-secondary institutions may generally have the choice of how much they wish to be involved in the off-campus delivery of courses and the corresponding support of off-campus students, some institutions or institutional units are set up from the start to serve students at a distance. As we noted in Chapter 6, most of these institutions have evolved out of the correspondence-course model, where a prime motivation is that students can take a course at their own choice of time and place. There are, for example, distance-teaching universities throughout the world. Australia has "distance education centres" associated with universities throughout the country. In The Netherlands and the UK, there are "Open Universities" offering an extensive range of courses to students who prize being able to study at their own rate and from their own homes. Thus these sorts of institutions have extensive provisions for course delivery and support already in place. What are new alternatives, relating to tele-learning, that are possible for the distance-teaching institution?

NETWORKED STUDY CENTRES

One way to handle the student-support problem is for the distance-teaching institution to set up study centres of various sorts in local communities. In these centres, local personnel can be supplied with appropriate equipment to be in contact both with the students and the central institution. They may not know much or anything about the specific content of a course, but they know the host institution, what it expects, who to contact there, and what its procedures are. They may also be equipped with computers and a network connection to the host institution, making various forms of tele-learning possible for students who could not afford or wish to handle computer-based tele-learning on their own from home computers.

EuroStudy Centres

In Europe, a prime example of this sort of local support is the collection of "EuroStudy Centres", 48 different local centres that have grouped together as integrated contact points for students enrolled in universities associated with the EADTU (European Association of Distance Universities). EADTU includes not only full-scale distance-teaching universities (offering only courses at a distance) but also 150 traditional European universities who now offer some courses at a distance. Fifteen countries are involved in EADTU, and 600,000 students attend the member post-secondary institutions. Thus there is a large market for the study centres. There are currently (1995) 45 designated EuroStudy Centres in 13 European countries, categorized as offering one of three levels of support (Basic, Standard, and Advanced). Some aspects of this support are indicated in Box 7.8:

Box 7.8

Support services offered by EuroStudy centres

Basic Level:
Equipment to support "open and distance learning", such as computers and printers, audio-visual equipment, television monitors, fax and telephones, and general learning resources
Staff "trained in European issues"

Standard Level: All of the Basic Level services, plus
Software for computer-based learning, applications software, CD-ROM players and CD-ROM software; satellite receive facilities for terrestrial broadcasting
Staff trained to offer tutoring and counseling and to offer special support to non-national students

Advanced Level: All of the Standard Level services, plus
Local- and wide-area network connections; software for e-mail and computer conferencing; equipment for audio and video-conferencing; broadcasting (uplink) facilities for radio and television
Staff encouraged to be involved in trans-national course delivery and projects
(EADTU, 1994b, 1995 see also http://www.ouh.ml/eadtu/separator.html)

What is perhaps most interesting about the EuroStudy Centre initiative (which has received support in various ways from the Commission of the European Communities) is that Centres offering services at the Advanced Level are all interconnected with each other as well as with their national institutions. Increasingly, this means being connected to the Internet as well. The interconnectivity of the Centres is done to facilitate student mobility across Europe (thus a social and political motivation more than a learning motivation); students can subscribe to a distance-offered course from any of the EADTU member organizations even if it is in a different country, and get local, informed support in his or her own country and mother tongue.

A similar sort of network of study centres is emerging in Australia, through its Community TeleService Centres and the newly-formed Open Learning Technology Corporation, set up by the Ministers of Education and Training to facilitate a national collaborative approach to the use of communications technologies in education and training (Horton, 1994).

ELECTRONIC SUPPORT SYSTEMS

Providing human support through study centres is an excellent idea, but with limitations. The study centre may not be at a location convenient to the student, the personnel at the study centre may not be available when the student wishes, the student may prefer to ask his or her questions from his or her desktop computer or home telephone rather than go to a centre or try to make a real-time call to centre personnel. For these and other reasons, a number of distance-teaching universities are supporting their students by providing them with asynchronous network services.

Supporting remote students with networked communication services: Institutional implications

By far the most familiar of these are communication services such as e-mail and computer conferencing; we have discussed these services already from the instructor's perspective in Chapter 6 and will discuss them again from the educational technologist's perspective in Chapter 8. From the decision-maker's perspective issues relate to both staff and students. From a staff perspective, what training is needed to handle tele-learning via CMC as part of the instructional balance of a course? How will courses have to re-designed and what will be the cost implications? What are the implications of scale? (Distance-teaching institutions operate on economy-of-scale considerations; the high costs of preparing well-designed materials are defrayed by large student registrations, but large student registrations will require more staff if e-mail and computer conferencing are to be used for tele-learning).

Supporting remote students with networked communication services: Student implications

A particular issue relating to offering students support via networking is what to do about remote students who do not have a computer, and/or access to a network, and/or support for their communication costs? With small groups of students, computers and modems may be loaned out and communication costs paid. With larger groups, this is not feasible.

Sometimes the solution is to simply to require that student have a computer and network access. With a target student group such as practicing engineers, it is highly likely they have access to a computer at their home or workplace, or if not, can arrange it. Other times, however, this expectation of personal access to a computer is more problematic. Then the solution may be to make computer access available via a local resource centre, or allow it to be optional, with other ways of communicating also supported. Each of these has equity dimensions to which the decision maker must be sensitive. The Open University in the UK is gaining considerable experience with suggesting or requesting that students have access to their own computers for network connection during the course (see Jones, Kirkup and Kirkwood, 1994, and Kaye, 1993, for summaries of the experience at the OU-UK and also the OU's plans for the future with regard to requiring students to have computers and to make networked connections as part of course participation).

Integrated software and human support

As another example of innovations that distance-teaching universities are implementing for better support of their students, The Open University in The Netherlands has developed a way of using a type of groupware (and now, other environments) as a common support environment for students in specific courses (Ellermann, Huisman, Schellekens, Zwaneveld, & Berns, 1992). This groupware environment, called StudieNet, allows the student to call into the server and access a variety of sample study materials, such as worked-out examples of homework assignments, for each unit of the course, to get additional reading material or information about the course, and to directly post assignments or questions to his tutor.

The StudieNet example is representative of a number of innovative approaches to the support of remote students that are emerging from traditional distance-teaching universities (we discuss more of these in Chapter 8, from the perspective of those who design them and research their effectiveness). From the institutional decision-maker's perspective, such innovations are being stimulated by the increased competition that traditional distance-teaching institutions are encountering from traditional institutions because of tele-learning.

■ 7.5.3 Tele-learning infrastructure and support for on-campus universities

While not every campus-based post-secondary institution is committing itself to the delivery of courses to off-campus students and thus competing with the traditional distance-teaching institutions, most campus-based institutions are committed to supporting the computing needs of their on-campus students. Universities in particular now provide networking, both local and wide-area, as routine infrastructure. As we have seen in Chapter 6, a networked infrastructure with Internet access is the basis for extensive tele-learning activities. In this section we look at some issues involved with the infrastructure and support of tele-learning on the typical university and college campus. We identify the types of tele-learning support which are becoming a minimal expectation for campus provision. We also identify some more advanced aspects of support which decision makers increasingly are considering for their institutions.

To begin, we start with some "advanced" examples.

EXAMPLES OF ADVANCED SUPPORT

George Mason University, US
George Mason University, serving the Washington DC area, has three campuses which are being comprehensively linked by a multi-media communications infrastructure "to allow the university to reach its goal of becoming the intellectual and cultural center for the entire Northern Virginia area" ("Bell Atlantic..", 1995). Instructors and students will be able to communicate and access information through voice, data, and interactive multimedia networks and via cable TV from George Mason campuses dormitories as well as off-campus locations around the Washington DC area. The link will also extend to local companies and governmental agencies.

The infrastructure consists of three major networks. One is an on-campus data network employing a pilot asynchronous transfer mode (ATM) so that multi-media applications will be available, an on-campus switched Ethernet network connecting more than 100 buildings at one of its campuses, and a "multimegabit" WAN connecting all of the universities' locations. The second of the major networks being laid is an interactive video and multimedia network. The third is an integrated cable and wiring infrastructure by which the campuses will be rewired with fibre optic cable, fast-switched Ethernet, and new video and data systems.

Also provided will be specially equipped video-conferencing facilities at two of the campuses, an interactive classroom with 25 high-performance student workstations linked to those of the instructors, a presentation classroom with the instructor station linked to the university library, 10 campus cable channels and 30 commercial cable channels, and direct links to student dorms. Up to 15 "electronic classrooms" are to be added.

University of Twente, The Netherlands

At the University of Twente, no particular massive rewiring project such as at George Mason University is going on nor is there any single initiative to describe; however, the University of Twente is a good example of how a university can incrementally develop its tele-learning infrastructure for on-campus staff and students.

Networked (often multi-media) computers for student use are copious around the campus, and there is no difficulty in assigning students to construct WWW pages, participate in both real-time and asynchronous computer conferencing, and work collaboratively over the networks. Internet access is available without restriction to everyone, students and staff. Every staff member has a desktop computer linked to the full network. The University of Twente has the highest percentage of use of the national academic network (SurfNet) in The Netherlands which in turn is the Internet gateway, with 96% of faculty and 86% of students being users. Support staff with networking skills are part of each faculty and in addition an institution-wide centre for education support and another for networking and computer support provide both baseline and innovative service. Presentation platforms are available in many of the lecture halls, as well as some provision for ISDN video-conferencing and desktop multi-media conferencing (including some limited provision of course delivery to distant students via video-conferencing, and also via regular Internet). Some courses are entirely mounted on the Internet in WWW environments (see Interface 9), and all first-year students in the Faculty of Educational Science and Technology begin their study by constructing WWW sites as a first design and production exercise.

A recent step has been to link every student room in the dormitories, and soon in the local urban area, not only to the university network but to the Internet. Both the telephone company and the regional cable company are involved.

New initiatives are continually occurring, based on a combination of project and consortium funds and on-going internal provision. ATM networking technology is now being used to connect certain students to a "distributed graduate school" involving two other universities, and applications such as document sharing and real-time conferencing are regularly used.

The institution actively supports all of these initiatives, recently funding a multi-million gulden (similar to a multi-million US dollar) special "educational innovation project" which a member of the Faculty of Educational Science and Technology is project leader, to study ways to increase the effectiveness and efficiency of on-campus teaching via networked tele-learning. Tele-learning is already being shown as being associated with higher success rates and faster completion rates in various courses compared to traditional approaches. A cross-faculty "tele-learning" committee has been in place for a number of years which also includes outside partners, such as representatives of the cable television company in the area and the telephone company. This committee is managing a list of projects, all involved with maximizing the use of the campus-wide network for on-campus instructional purposes. In addition, an institute has been set up involving seven of the ten faculties in the university to bring together innovative research and practice with regard to communication technologies: tele-learning has been chosen as a main application area for this institute. This institute works closely with a national centre for telelcommunications research, supported by the government and industry, which is also housed on the campus.

As part of its goal, to be a center of telecommunications expertise to its students, its region, and its country, the University of Twente is involved in a wide range of collaborations, including European projects and initiatives such as the "Telematica-Stad-Twente" (Telecommunications-Region-Twente), bringing together leaders of municipal governments in the surrounding area, business representatives, representatives of other educational institutions, with specialists from the university to work together on various initiatives, many of which relate to tele-learning.

This is the environment in which this book has been written.

And there are many, many more examples that can be given of innovative institutional decision making to support tele-learning infrastructure and delivery to on-campus students at universities. A sampling is given in Box 7.9:

BASIC CONSIDERATIONS

Moving from advanced settings to minimal provision, what should universities be considering with respect to minimal tele-learning support? The following seem more and more to be expected:

> **Box 7.9**
>
> **Examples of innovation on university campuses to support tele-learning**
>
> - Stanford University is testing methods to digitally store video, audio, text, and graphics, and deliver these materials via high-speed networks, the Internet, and standard telephone lines to students both on and off campus.
> - The Helsinki University of Technology is experimenting with supplying lectures on demand via ATM technology so students can call up a lecture from a video server and watch it at their convenience. In addition, student computer laboratories are networked both for the Internet and for ISDN desktop multi-media conferencing.
> - The Institute of System Sciences at the National University of Singapore is working on projects that integrate multimedia with artificial intelligence, multimedia applications in real time, and software for distributed collaborative work for students.
> - The College of Gjøvik in Norway makes extensive use of ISDN networking to connect lecture halls, student workstations, and instructors' workstations for multimedia applications and both real-time and asynchronous communication.

Student accounts to a network with Internet access

Every student should have an account which gives him or her direct access to local resources and the Internet. The access, at least if on campus, is through a high-speed Ethernet LAN, so that via computers available throughout the university students can access graphic resources with little problem with time delays. Students can access WWW sites and make frequent use of e-mail for communication with their instructors and each other.

Other student provision

Students routinely check their e-mail every day and have convenient ways to use their e-mail environment for group projects. Printing is also convenient, with both line printers and laser printers near every cluster of computers. Students have a printing account and a certain amount of space on a network-based drive; they can purchase more of either when they need. Access to computers is virtually around the clock, although support when problems occur may only be available during more normal workday times.

Help and orientation

A helpdesk for network and computer needs is staffed and available, and trouble-shooting information is also available on-line. All students, at the beginning of their university career, have an orientation to the network and to common tools on the network, such as word processing, graphics and drawing tools, Internet-access tools, presentation-software tools, and basics of the operating system supported as the in-house standard.

Thus, for students, networked computing is becoming more and more ubiquitous. Institutional decisions must evolve continuously to keep up with these "routine expectations" (Bull, 1993; Hafner, 1995). Its use in tele-learning is, however, two steps further along, after access and infrastructure are in place.

Individual use of tele-learning for learning activities

The first of these steps is for the student to gradually grow in sophistication in her independent use of the networked tools available, so she can see for herself where and how she can incorporate tele-learning into her studying, without always needing formal indication about it from an instructor. As we described in Chapter 4 and 6, the contemporary learner, both in and outside of an educational institution, is more and more coming to expect to go to the Internet for resources, both through the use of WWW search tools, but also through becoming aware of addresses of lists and newsgroups where a question can be asked and helpful responses likely to be found. Checking networked entry points to library resources is becoming second-nature. Communicating and working together by passing files back and forth and other sorts of CMC activities with classmates via the network are increasingly part of the way students organize their study and learning activities.

Students are also experiencing a culture change with respect to communicating with their instructors. They are coming to expect to send an e-mail to an instructor with questions or requests or information ("I won't be in class tomorrow because....Sorry; perhaps you could send me the lecture notes?"), and to expect a personal answer. They are expecting to be informed, via a network, in a timely and efficient way, if there is a change in rostering or some other change in organization of classes. Students are coming to feel that it is unexcusable to arrive at a classroom with a locked door and no sign of the instructor, and not have had a message about the course cancellation ahead of time via a network. When students go home for the weekend, they expect to be able to log into their campus computer accounts from home, via a dial-up account.

Thus these activities are increasingly part of the study life of the university student, a growth into independent use of tele-learning tools and resources for support of her course work. This is a change not only in skills and actions, but also in mentality and culture for many students; institutional decision makers need to anticipate it and support it. This is sometimes difficult to orchestrate, in that the network access and tools needed are not explicitly requested as part of a course requisition; students just expect them to be available.

TELE-LEARNING STEP TWO: SUPPORT FOR THE INSTRUCTOR

The next step in minimal provision for tele-learning is to support the instructor to make use of tele-learning during her courses.

E-mail support

As a minimal, this means that the instructor has a networked desktop computer with (apparently) unlimited disk space and mail-storage space, and e-mail software that makes it easy for her to create distribution lists, manage large amounts of mail from students, and print and respond to it conveniently. She also has unlimited access to internal and external mail, through local and Internet systems, in a way which is transparent to her. All the mail is just there, as are software tools to sort and manipulate it. The institutional decision maker must make provision for all of this.

Support for using a central communication and information server

In addition, increasingly, the instructor should have an easy way to pass course information to the persons in her organization who manage the information system or WWW pages for the faculty or institution, so that she can forward through the network what she wants disseminated to students via these systems, with a few instructions, and find the material mounted and maintained. She needs to be able to easily send updates or ask for information to be removed or made secure, and the service should be turn-around and pleasant. If she wants to handle her own WWW site as an organizing environment for her classes, or would like her students to create WWW sites for her or as learning experiences (see Bos, Kikstra, & Morgen, 1995, for a student account of the educational value of doing this), she can ask for technical support if necessary and has no financial or institutional problem in putting the material up. The creative ideas for tele-learning that we discussed in Chapter 6 for the post-secondary instructor require imagination on the part of the instructor to be sure, but also can only develop with supportive and facilitative institutional support. Here, again, is the contribution of the institutional decision maker.

Support for tele-learning demonstration during lectures

In addition, the innovative instructor may wish to be able to demonstrate tele-learning activities or resources to his students during lecture or seminar times, so that the students can then work further with those resources on their own. This means that he needs to have access to a teaching room or lecture hall with a networked computer (running the same tools and system as in his office, so he is not distracted by trying to work a different system during teaching), a projection device connected to that computer, and a way to semi-darken the room so that students can see what he is demonstrating as he discusses it. All of these support provisions are the result of decisions made not by the instructor but by institutional mangers and decision makers.

Giving assignments involving tele-learning

Because of the networked infrastructure she knows is available to her students, and the convenience with which she can communicate with the students over the network and receive electronic material from them, the post-secondary instructor is increasingly including aspects of tele-learning in the way she manages student course assignments. She may want students to work together, collaborating on an assignment to read, analyze and synthesize a series of materials, using tele-learning tools. She may require students to look for examples and counter examples over the Internet and circulate critiques among themselves and the instructor. She may wish to engage in pedagogical re-engineering of her courses (see Chapter 6), but she cannot do this on her own. The institution, via its decision makers, must anticipate what is going to be needed to support innovative learning.

Eliminate roadblocks

To realize this level of service, much has yet to be done at many universities, in turns of equipment, support personnel, and transmission channels. However, for decision makers, perhaps most importantly, policy roadblocks that thwart tele-learning must be removed. These roadblocks include those listed in Box 7.10:

Box 7.10

Institutional roadblocks to tele-learning

Only allowing students access to minimal-level network tools and a restricted amount of time they can use a network

Not allowing students to download and save files (presumably to prevent illegal copying of software)

Not allowing students to have full Internet access, (out of the fear that they might abuse it, or because they are only given access to limited-capacity, old, computers unable to handle graphic user interfaces or the speed and memory requirements of many tele-learning applications)

Closing students' log-in privileges for a range of sins such as overdue library books or late payment of fees

Making it a tedious or confusing task to find the person who assigns log-in ID s in order to arrange to have one's account made active or reactivated or to get help with network problems

Limiting students to computers with a non-graphic work environment (ancient DOS instead of Windows, for example)

Not allowing students access to computers "after hours" or via modem

Not accommodating file transfer in the mail system available to the students

All of these roadblocks are in common practice in post-secondary institutions. Most are the result of policy reasons relating to "control" and "security" that are reasonable to understand but that have serious limiting effects on tele-learning. Decision makers must be bold enough to take some risks if the environment is to be adequate for innovative tele-learning applications in their institutions.

AND THE FUTURE?

The totally wired campus with convenient student access to networked resources will come to be an expectation on many post-secondary campuses in the not-too-distant future (Rowland, 1994; see also Chapter 10). At the current time, many campuses are reasonably on the way to this in many aspects. Box 7.11 shows some forward-looking applications about which institutional decisions are being made at the current time:

Box 7.11

Next-step decisions for campus support for tele-learning

Expect faculties and courses to maintain WWW pages with accurate and up-to-date information for access from within and outside the institution (no more students calling in for information about a course...)

Work toward a "one port per pillow" standard by wiring residence halls, eventually with at least three jacks by each pillow; a cable TV line for video of lectures and demonstration on demand, a 10-megabit Ethernet connection to the data network, and a phone line

Subsidize low-cost personal computers for students with easy connectivity to the Ethernet network

Wire lecture halls for network access and projection and have computer systems available and set up to take advantage of that access

Channel all administrative contact with students thought the network, including registration

Digitize library resources, and support access of multi-media library resources

Provide convenient tools for students and faculty to conference, have real-time communication and make multi-media links to other contact points for guest lectures and collaborative work

---

MOTIVATION?

Institutional motivations for all this activity are complex, partly stirred by the research interests of the university, partly by national upgrades in the high-speed backbone to which the campus computer centre may connect, partly by the professional interests of key decision makers.

But another reason is competition:

What's driving the rush to get wired? Competition among schools is one thing. There are fewer students, rising costs and changes in government funding for research...'We would not be comfortable if prospective students and parents noticed that the dorms at [x, y, and z] are wired and we are not.' (Hafner, 1995, p. 46)

And also,

...Our students are going to graduate in a wired world...They're going to have to collect and analyze information and do their business in an environment in which we have instantaneous multimedia access. (Hafner, p. 46)

HELP FOR THE DECISION MAKERS

Thus for decision makers at universities, planning for tele-learning is a major, and high-exposure, task. With continuing changes in technology, and generally different requirements from different faculties, this decision making requires much information. One of the major sources of technology-related information for university decision makers is the professional society, EDUCOM, which sponsors a large conference in the US each year as well as printed information and Internet resources such as the bi-weekly technology update through the listserv EDUPAGE (subscribe via listproc@educom.edu; archives are available via ftp from educom.edu); see also:

EDUCOM
```
URL http://educom.edu/index.html
```

A comment about EDUCOM is an appropriate way to end this chapter. Decision makers at all levels of education must confront both the potential of tele-learning and its complications and costs. This in turn means that it is highly desirable that they experience various forms of tele-learning themselves, as professionals (see Chapter 4). EDUCOM and its extensive range of on-line, print, and face-to-face services is an excellent base location for that experience.

INTERNET ACCESS IN LESS-DEVELOPED COUNTRIES

While the Internet system does allow global interconnectivity and over 100 countries have Internet domains, the system in still predominately one being used by North Americans, Western Europeans, and Australasians. The continuing problem of inequities between more-developed and less-developed countries of the world could on one hand be further escalated by the Internet, or on the other hand, have a significant opportunity for improvement because of the Internet.

In terms of being an opportunity for reduction of inequities, the Internet brings the same opportunities to those connected, where ever they are. Thus for the first in history, there is a mechanism in place to provide at the same time the same "playing field" to those who can access it. While making connections is not in itself a sufficient step for change and social improvement, it can be a valuable part of the process.

But potential is not the same as realisation. In 1995 even the first step of making connections is impossible for many of the world's peoples. The African continent and China are two useful cases.

INTERNET ACCESS IN AFRICA AND CHINA

In 1995, there are about 600 million users of the Internet worldwide. Africa, with a population of 650 million, has less than one percent of its population with access to the Internet (and less than one percent of the world's computers). China, with between 20 and 25% of the world people, has about 500,000 PCs in operation, but extremely limited Internet connectivity. In some ways the reasons for these ratios are similar between the continent of Africa and the country of China, but in other ways they are different.

Africa

Some indicators of the African situation are:

- Africa has 54 countries but only seven (as of November 1995) have full Internet access.[1] Of these seven (Egypt, Ghana, Kenya, Tunisia, Zambia, Zimbabwe, and South Africa), only South Africa can be said to be following the robust pattern of Internet use that is typical of major-user countries. For example, in South Africa, there is considerable

[1] Jegede, O.J. (1995). From talking drums to electronic networking: Africa's snailmobile through the cyberspace. *FID News Bulletin, 45*(7/8), 218–224. (FID is the Federation for Information and Documentation). Founded in 1885, it is the leading international organisation in the information sector.

public response to newsgroups and WWW sites focused on the process of approving a new national constitution; 27 of South African universities and approximately 20 local service providers provide Internet connections to an estimated 200,000 persons; approximately 200 WWW servers are registered; school districts are beginning to set up Internet servers to connect their schools; and an international commercial network service is establishing points of presence throughout the country.

- However, in the rest of the continent, connectivity is much more problematic. Forty of the 54 countries have some form of electronic connectivity and 30 have some form of e-mail access to the Internet, but in almost all cases this interconnectivity is generally through fragmented initiatives developed and maintained by an external donor agency and involving connection through some limited form of batch processing of text data to a server agency server outside of the continent.

- Recently (April 1995) a Symposium on "Telematics for Development" was held in Addis Ababa. This symposium was sponsored by four international donor agencies. Thirty projects involving African networking were discussed. According to an evaluation of the seminar[2], most projects are sponsored by external donor agencies, most only enable a few participants to send and receive e-mail, few involve using networking for purposes which may influence or enhance either the donor or receiver's organisation, little cooperation or coordination or even mutual awareness exists among the

[2]Odedra-Straub, M. (1995). Contemporary issues in electronic communications in Africa: A summary of the Addis Ababa Symposium. *FID News Bulletin, 45*(7/8), 225–227.

projects, and very few projects are ever evaluated. Also, "representatives of the international donor organisations...dictated and directed issues, prepared the action plans and recommendations without input from others, least of all the Africans..." (p. 227).

- Telephone infrastructure, particularly within and between African countries is extremely poor and 75% of the population is rural without basic facilities of electricity or telephone.

- Because of their history of colonisation, no African country uses its native languages or even one of them as both an official and instructional language. Also, there is no common language of communication among the countries (as their official languages are a mixture of English, French, Portuguese, Spanish and Arabic).

Thus, in Africa, the problem is one of lack of infrastructure, of money, of trained personnel, but more pernicious, of a mentality "that the world has made Africa believe that development has to be initiated from outside the continent, must be technology laden and has to be handed down by consultants and experts from the North armed with aid money which instantly turns African nations to beggar nations" (Jegede, p. 221).

How to move forward? Jegede and Odedra-Straub, as well as other well-informed Africans, suggest: (a) African nations should turn more to South Africa for expertise and assistance than to international donor agencies; (b) the human capital of African background now productively working in countries throughout the world should be more systematically engaged in assisting

African internal human-capital development; and (c) university libraries and computing science departments are a particular target for professional upgrading, and a target that can be feasibly helped by Internet access. And another recommendation could be added: (d) look to satellite provision of data communications rather than wait for internal telephone line capacity to develop.

China

China shares with Africa the characteristics of a vast rural population with little or no telephone connections, and a poor telephone infrastructure even in its major cities. Only about two percent of the population have telephones. After this, however, the Chinese situation with telecommunications potential is different from Africa in a number of important ways:

- China already has a well-established system for satellite delivery of broadcast television and a well developed infrastructure for use of the broadcasting for educational delivery throughout the country, particularly for teacher education. In 50 regional areas there is a high-capacity satellite receiving station and 50,000 teacher-training centres have a smaller-capacity receiving dish. Over two million teachers have completed teacher training through this well-organised operation.
- Internet access has been possible in universities for a number of years, but in an extremely limited fashion. One reason is the Chinese language and the relatively low level of confidence with written English even among researchers. More significantly,

however, is a mixture of politics and culture. According to the supposed words of Deng Xiaoping, "when the door opens, some flies are bound to come in". Thus an internationally oriented networking culture is still treated with distrust and access to it is apportioned with great restraint. Coupled with a culture that is not yet at least oriented toward an information mindset, the potential of Internet for tele-learning remains very low in China.

The realisation of satellite-delivered broadcast television for education is already well-developed and being effectively realised in China. Individual homes may not have telephones, but they are much more likely to have a television and to be served by a regional television station. These stations, cooperating with the national educational broadcasting agencies operating out of Shanghai and with high-quality educational programming, could provide a model for at least some of the African countries.

FITTING TECHNOLOGY TO LOCAL CULTURE

The Chinese have one great advantage over the Africans in terms of developing a cost-effective approach to tele-learning infrastructure and deployment: a shared language and culture. Nationwide educational broadcasting can among most of its population thus fit with local culture and circumstances in China. Given the fragmentation of language, culture and circumstance in Africa, the situation is more difficult. Development of human capital and library resources in universities seems a most-productive African focus at the current time.

8 Tele-learning and the educational technologist: designing and developing

In the previous chapters we have looked at tele-learning from the perspective of users, in the family, on the job, in the classroom, or decision makers in the organization. In this chapter, we turn our focus to those responsible for tele-learning's design and for research on that design. These are, often, educational technologists; professionals whose work it is to study, design, develop, and support tele-learning and translate its potential into lesson materials, programs, courses, software, Web pages, and support services. Although not always labeled "educational technologists" they are a broad international professional community. What sorts of tasks are they carrying out with respect to tele-learning? What are they considering when they design courses that involve tele-learning? What are their major challenges? In what areas is innovative design activity occurring?

Objectives

After this chapter you should be able to:

- Be aware of major categories of tasks for educational technologists with respect to tele-learning

- Cite general influences on the design of courses for a tele-learning context

- Indicate how flexibility and pedagogical re-engineering relate to the design process of courses involving tele-learning

- Give some specific examples of guidelines for the design of courses involving television, video-conferencing, and computer conferencing particularly in support of collaborative learning

- Be aware of innovative developments in the design of courses for network delivery

- Know about new developments in the design of innovative tools and environments for tele-learning, including computer conferencing software, desktop multi-media packages, integrated software systems, WWW sites, and integrated hardware and software environments

■ 8.1 EDUCATIONAL TECHNOLOGISTS AND TELE-LEARNING

Who are educational technologists? What are their major domains of activity? How do these relate to tele-learning? In this section we give a general answer to these questions; the remainder of this chapter and of Chapter 9 are expansions of the answers.

■ 8.1.1 WHO ARE EDUCATIONAL TECHNOLOGISTS?

The issue of how to define and delimit educational technology as a profession is a periodic activity among those active in it. Seels and Richey (1994), note that "for at least forty years the field...periodically has pursued processes of collective self-examination, resulting in statements which describe itself professionally" (p. 1).

WHAT'S IN A NAME?

Speaking on behalf of an American-based committee, they suggest the term "instructional technology" instead of educational technology, on the basis that the adjective "educational" sounds too much like being only focused on educational institutions and thus does not take in training and other out-of-school learning. (In Europe, this is generally just the opposite.) They do note that the connotation of the adjective is culturally variable, and that educational technology and instructional technology could be considered synonymous terms.

What matters to us in these chapters is a common functional definition: we will follow Seels' and Richey's definition, but use the term "educational technologists". We define educational technologists as those involved with:

> ...the theory and practice of design, development, utilization, management and evaluation of processes and resources for learning (Seels & Richey, 1994, p. 1)

NO SINGLE DEFINITION

Such semantic discussions are important because they indicate a larger fact: that there is no clear-cut label, no standard training process or job definition for educational technologists. Those doing the work of educational technologists may be called by many different titles, even in English-speaking settings. The titles in Box 8.1 are names of graduate-degree programmes relevant to educational technologists in 167 US and 33 non-US higher-education institutions replying to a 1995 survey of the Association for Educational Communications and Technology (AECT; Johnson, 1995a, b):

Box 8.1

Sampling of titles for educational technologists

Educational media specialists
Educational communications specialists
Educational communication and technology specialists
Educational materials developers
Educational software designers
Computers in education specialists
Educational library media specialists
Educational information technology specialists
Education and training systems designers
Learning technologists
Educational media and technology specialists
Educational media services specialists
Instructional technologies
Instructional media specialists
Instructional systems design specialists
Instructional resources specialists
Instructional developers
Instructional systems designers
Instruction and performance technologists
Instructional designers

And there are others... For this chapter, we will not concern ourselves with the history and philosophy behind one term compared to another, but just use the designation "educational technologist" as a generic term. (As some justification for this we can note that in an inventory of all the titles of graduate programmes listed in the AECT survey, "educational technology" was the term used most often, in 22 of the 210 titles. Also, the term "educational technology" is the most common term outside of the US.)

■ 8.1.2 WHAT DO EDUCATIONAL TECHNOLOGISTS DO?

As well as reflecting on what to call themselves, Seels' and Richey's committee (like many before them) also focused on major categories of task definition for educational technologists. In their analysis, they see five main "domains" of application.

DOMAINS OF APPLICATION
- Design
- Development

- Utilization
- Management
- Evaluation

and within these they make the further distinctions shown in Box 8.2.

Box 8.2

Jobs of educational technologists

Orientation
Researcher, Practitioner

Settings
K-12 education, Post-secondary education, Business/industry,
Health, Government, International

Products
Lesson, Module, Unit, Workshop, Course, Curriculum, Environment
(Adapted from Seels and Richey, 1994, p. 102)

We include these here to give a sense of the range of interests of educational technologists. In all permutations of the three categories in Box 8.2 there are tele-learning activities in which educational technologists are involved and examples that we will show in this chapter and in Chapter 9.

APPLICATIONS TO TELE-LEARNING

As with any list, a different person, approaching the question through a different filter of experience, will be likely to prefer a different categorization (especially when the field in question is not specifically defined, and continually evolving). Thus for this chapter, we will consider the work of educational technologists relating to tele-learning through categories that are expressed somewhat differently than those of Seels and Richey. We will consider educational technologists professionals doing work as shown in Box 8.3.

These categories, from our experience, provide a reasonably good match of the activities of educational technologists involved with tele-learning at the present time. The first three of categories are the focus of this chapter, the next three of Chapter 9. The category of reflective thinking should overlay both chapters.

More specifically, in the remainder of Chapter 8 we look at three general issues involved in designing courses for tele-learning (Section 8.2), some specific aspects

Box 8.3

Educational technologists are:

- Designers, developers and adaptors of courses or episodes for tele-learning
- Professionals involved in the delivery of tele-learning courses or episodes
- Specialists in the design, development or adaptation of specific materials and environments for tele-learning
- Professionals involved in the support of tele-learning in the field
- Teachers of those who will be or who are already tele-learning professionals
- Learners themselves in a rapidly changing field
- Reflective thinkers about tele-learning

of course design related to transmission channels (television/video or computer network, Section 8.3), and designing innovative tools and environments for tele-learning (Section 8.4). These innovative tools and environments include: instrumentation for computer conferencing (Section 8.4.2), instrumentation for desk-top multi-media conferencing (Section 8.4.3), integrated on-line systems for learning support (Section 8.4.4), innovations in the design of the WWW as a learning environment (Section 8.4.5), and integrated hardware–software environments for tele-learning (Section 8.4.6).

■ 8.2 DESIGNING COURSES FOR TELE-LEARNING: GENERAL CONSIDERATIONS

In this section we introduce an important word in education technology—design—and apply it to the planning of courses where tele-learning plays a role. We begin, in Section 8.2.1, with some general aspects of the course-design context. Then we move to two major issues in course design involving tele-learning: Media and technology choice (Section 8.2.2) and designing for pedagogical re-engineering (Section 8.2.3).

■ 8.2.1 GENERAL ASPECTS OF THE COURSE-DESIGN CONTEXT

What is design? What are educational technologists designing? In what ways are educational technologists involved in course design for tele-learning? These are contextual questions that give a frame to the course-design process we highlight in this section. Before we focus in on course design issues for tele-learning, it is useful to look briefly at the design framework itself.

WHAT IS DESIGN?

There are entire books and long-standing debates about the meaning of the word "design". Having shown some of the complexity behind the term educational technology in Section 8.1.1, we will not also go into the "design" debate here. Instead we will use a simple definition of design as the "process of specifying conditions".

The boundary between design and development is also often unclear, as the design process itself is more and more being seen as one of "rapid prototyping" (J. Moonen, 1995) in which iterative loops of (re)design, (partial) development and evaluation occur. Adding the variable of adaptation of existing entities compared to designing new materials complicates the design process further.

Similarly, the object of the design process can also be seen on a continuum rather than as discrete categories. We can make the distinction between (a) designing learning events, such as courses, workshops, modules, lessons, or field trips, all of which imply a sequence of activities in which learning resources are employed in various ways; and (b) designing the materials and resources themselves which are used in those events. Again, the overlap may often be fuzzy.

In particular, we will look at educational technologists as course designers

---

Box 8.4

Ways in which educational technologists are involved in course design

Being specifically employed to develop courses for a distance-education institution such as the Open University in the UK

Being specifically employed to develop courses for subsequent self-study

Being specifically employed to develop courses for a large training centre, where the same course materials will subsequently used by a number of tutors or instructors

Being employed to develop courses for a course-provider agency, often an agency specializing in broadcast-type course delivery

Being employed as part of a curriculum team to develop courses that support a new curriculum or a new didactic approach (such "courses" may be more like a series of lessons)

Designing one's own courses (educational technologists are often post-secondary instructors themselves)

Being part of a project or experimental activity in which course or course materials are developed within the framework of the special project, usually involving a consortium of partners and some forms of new technologies where tele-learning in some way is included in the design of the course (Sections 8.2 and 8.3), with a focus on current issues and decisions that occur in this design process. After this, we turn our focus to a more micro level: not a whole course but a tool or new environment to use within courses.

EDUCATIONAL TECHNOLOGISTS AND COURSE DESIGN

How are educational technologists involved in course design? This can happen in a variety of ways, including those listed in Box 8.4:

WHAT IS THE CONTEXT FOR COURSE DESIGN AND TELE-LEARNING?

A basic starting point in course design relative to tele-learning is the core delivery framework for the course. The key dimensions of this framework relate to the nature of the organization which offers the course. Table 8.1 gives an overview of such organizations and the corresponding position of tele-learning in new course development. (See also Chapter 7 for more about this organizational perspective.)

KEY DECISIONS ABOUT TELE-LEARNING

As Table 8.1 shows, in some cases, decisions about tele-learning will have already been made before the educational technologist enters the course-design process. For example, an institution may have decided to deliver courses by two-way compressed video to remote sites, and so the course designer must work within this framework. However, at other times the issue of technology choice is an important task in the course-design process.

Other issues are more pervasive to the course-design process. We list some of these in Box 8.5.

These and many other issues are of major concern to course providers considering the design or adaptation of courses for various combinations of tele-learning delivery. Books, meetings, and research projects abound on this issue, engaging many educational technologists both in theory and in practice. We will focus on two aspects: media/technology choice, and designing for pedagogical re-engineering.

■ 8.2.2 MEDIA CHOICE FOR TELE-LEARNING

Among the many types of design decisions faced by educational technologists working on course or event design, perhaps the one which has most attention in both literature and practice is "media" choice. Media choice has long been an issue before there were tele-learning aspects (see, for example, Reisner and Gagné (1982); with tele-learning possibilities the complexity of media choice is

Table 8.1 Organizational framework for decisions about course design and tele-learning

Organizational context for the course design	Main implications relating to tele-learning for the educational technologist as course designer
1. Traditional face-to-face teaching institution, offering face-to-face courses	Courses are typically designed by the teachers or instructors themselves, so a professional educational technologist is not involved
2. Traditional face-to-face teaching institution, having made a decision to expand its delivery range by offering courses at a distance	The institution will probably have decided on the basic delivery strategy, such as compressed video, interactive broadcasting, or computer networking; the educational technologist must work within that decision and seek to maximize its possibilities
3. Traditional face-to-face teaching institution, wondering if it should commit itself to some form of tele-learning	The course designer must focus on the cost-effectiveness of tele-learning versions of an existing course compared to traditional delivery or compared to each other; initial versions of courses may be used to collect such comparative data
4. Institution already organized around non-face-to-face instruction competing for new clients	The course designer considers tele-learning in terms of increasing the competitive attractiveness of the course as a product to be sold, and thus must balance cost and innovation in terms of changes in course design
5. Course provider is part of a consortium for a special project, testing the feasibility of some form of tele-learning (usually that supplied by the vendors who are also a partner in the special project)	The course designer must harmonize the special-project course with traditional courses within his or her institution in order to convince skeptics that the possibly disruptive special project involving tele-learning is legitimate and meaningful to the institution (beyond the benefits of being in a project)
6. The course to be designed involves some aspect of tele-learning as a funded research project	The educational technologist works with the researcher who has funding for some sort of research, such as "concept mapping as a cognitive tool in distributed learning groups"; the course to be designed must reflect the experimental needs of the researcher

---

Box 8.5

Some key issues in course design for tele-learning

- The incidence and forms of tele-learning in a course; the balance between face-to-face and distant contact and between real-time and asynchronous contact among course participants
- Decisions about the "core medium" in a course: the instructor? written materials? broadcast or video programming?
- Decisions about the combination of learning materials to use within a course and the relationship of those learning materials with the transmission channels through which a course will be delivered
- The relative importance of being able to feel part of a "real classroom" particularly in terms of seeing and interacting with one's instructor and classmates
- The importance of getting immediate feedback to one's questions
- The importance of various aspects of flexibility in course design, such as time, place, pace, sequence, media, instructional approach, assessment methods, support opportunities, study methods, and others
- The extent to which a course should be designed according to an established plan, and the extent to which a course can be "pedagogically re-engineered"

---

componded to a media/instructional method/delivery technology triad which is presenting a considerable challenge to educational technologists. Media choice can be seen as selection (a) from an overall pallette where many different factors influence the decision, or selection (b) based on explicit empirical comparison between specific media alternatives, or (c) both.

The terms media and technology are defined differently by different authors. For example, is a computer a medium or a technology? Is computer conferencing a medium or a technology? What is a Web page? We will not make a detour into further definitions here but proceed somewhat intuitively, using terms the ways that various authors use them. The general sense of the words as used in the course-design context for tele-learning is that "technology" most often implies the technologies involved with transmission over a distance, while "media" relate more often to the carriers of messages in a more static sense. A message is printed on paper or saved on computer disk or recorded on tape. The tools we use to manipulate messages, such as computers and computer-conferencing software thus have something to do with both technology and media.

MEDIA CHOICES FOR TELE-LEARNING

A first place where this confusion in the terms media and technologies becomes apparent is in the copious literature about "media selection in course design".

When tele-learning will be part of a course, many different sets of decision-making criteria can be applied to the media/delivery-technology choices. Table 8.2 shows a sample of the many studies carried out by educational technologists which involve media/delivery-technology choices in the context of tele-learning.

A particularly good current resource is A. Bates (1995) in which a sophisticated cost-effectiveness approach is applied to educational television broadcasting, print, one- and two-way audio, and computer-based learning and communications.

WHICH IS BETTER? X OR Y?

While researchers such as Bates attempt to survey the overall range of possibilities for media selection in tele-learning, there are many studies that look more specifically at one delivery approach compared to another, to answer the (apparently) straight-forward question: Is it better to deliver this course using technology X or technology Y? While such a question seems reasonable, particularly for institutional decision makers (see Chapter 7), such comparison studies are always limited in how much of a direct answer they can provide. We will look at one example in some detail to illustrate some of the problems confronting educational technologists asked to do "Which technology is better?" research.

AN EXAMPLE: TV VS NO TV?

Hutchinson and Koplin (1995), evaluated a pilot program in Australia called the TV Open Learning Project Pilot Scheme (TVOL), in which a consortium of universities offered through national television a series of broadcasts for tertiary study of the French language. The series used was purchased from outside Australia. The focus of the evaluation was to compare the TV-delivered variation of the course with other delivery options.

Research design

Three groups of students were studied: (a) adults following the course on television and with print materials sent through the mail, and carrying out communication about their assignments with tutors at the university by ordinary mail or telephone; (b) adults studying comparable print materials at home, with no TV component, also carrying out communication about their assignments with their university tutors by ordinary mail or telephone, but also participating in two four-day face-to-face residental periods at the university; and (c) students in the traditional university setting, using the same materials as Group (b) but also attending regular face-to-face classes and having full use of a language laboratory for practice.

Table 8.2 Sample of studies relating to media/delivery-technology choices for tele-learning

Study	Media/Delivery-Technologies	Major Focus
Stahmler, Bourdeau and Zuckernick (1992)	Print-, audio-, video-, computer-based technologies, multi-media	Strengths and weaknesses relative to implementation issues, including costs
Bates (1984b)	Audio cassettes, audiographic systems, video cassettes (from TV broadcasts), computer conferencing	Experiences from the Open University (UK), orientation to practical issues related to teacher and student use
Jones and Knezek (1995)	Comparison of traditional classroom instruction and 12 other delivery systems (from mail to videoconferencing)	Matrix of issues related to costs and access and modality; instructor and student variables
Watabe, Hamalainen and Whinston, (1995)	Audio, audiographics and computer conferencing; shared network applications	Relating student learning activities to "off-line" and "on-line" learning
Eijkelenburg, Heeren and Vermeulen (1992)	Systems for communication, resource-sharing, group-activity support, and presentation-support	Relation to same- and different time, same- and different place for learning
Mason, (1994)	Computer and video conferencing, audiographics	Choice based on variables related to learning style, course design, and context
Bork (1995)	Print, audio, video, teleconferencing, computers (low and high interaction, with or without multi-media)	Relative benefits of quality of learning, number of students, and cost per student
Charp (1994)	Print, radio, television, video, computers, audiographics, interactive television, satellite conferencing, computer communications	Comparison of use in countries and regions, including Africa, Japan, Thailand, Turkey, US, UK, Canada, and others
Romiszowski (1993)	Telephone, multi-media workstation and networks, audio-, video- and computer conferencing, audiographics, fax, email, CSCW environments, "virtual classroom"	Technical developments and costs related to phases in distance education
Pohjonen (1994)	Comparison of models of media selection	Relationship of media-selection models to learning models and to efficiency comparisons

The three groups were tested on comparable material, through written assignments and tests which shared many items in common.

Results: In favour of television

And the results? After allowing for potential differences among the students themselves, the following results were found:

The TVOL students (Group (a)) did significantly better than the other two groups on all written assignments and tests, and both groups of distance-studying students (Groups (a) and (b)) did better than the on-campus group (Group (c)).

But the differences were not only in the television...

Interpreting the results, the researchers felt that being able to re-view the television broadcasts, at home, when convenient to the students, was an major reason for the relative success of the TVOL group. However, they acknowledge that the method used in the TV broadcasts was "dynamic, fun and intriguing, as well as being rigourous and well-structured" while the method used in the print materials studied by Groups (b) and (c) "lacks the light-hearted dimension that makes [the TVOL] materials such as enjoyable and engrossing method of study" (Hutchinson and Koplin, 1995, p. 10).

In addition, the researchers noted that the university-based tutors made more effort to contact the TVOL students than they did with the other groups of students, believing that the TVOL group would be strongly disadvantaged by their isolation.

FRUSTRATIONS IN METHOD-COMPARISON STUDIES

Hutchinson and Koplin's study, although a carefully done example of its type, points out a major problem confronting the educational technologist in making decisions about variables in course delivery: the impossibility of determining the effects of a particular aspect of course delivery, considered in isolation. We cannot say from the TVOL study if "television" was better, or if the television mattered at all, compared to the effects of the different method and the more-frequent personal contact from tutors that were also present in the Group (a) approach.

Similarly, Sholdt, Zhang and Fulford (1995) reviewed the findings about the difficulty of natural interaction in interactive television settings and showed in their study, that with a skilled instructor distant students found interaction easier than did face-to-face students. Hackman and Walker (1995) found that when the instructor used good teaching techniques, such as addressing students by their first names, probing students' feelings about assignments, and displaying, when appropriate, a sense of humour, that students in a remote setting were as satisfied with the educational experience and performed as well as students in a face-to-face setting.

Too many variables, all interacting...

There are just too many variables, interacting and affecting each other, to carry out "Is media X better than media Y?" research in a straight-forward way. Increasingly, researchers are recognizing the weaknesses in such comparative assessments, and trying to refine their design methodologies (see Salomon, 1990); or to ask different types of questions (Reeves, 1995); or just to postpone the comparison.

Effort invested in a major variable

An important example of "asking better questions" when comparing media, is Salomon's work with the concept "AIME" (1983). Salomon's concept of "AIME" is that the "amount of invested mental effort" the learners expend while learning with a medium is not only directly proportional to the learning that occurs but is also strongly related to the perception the learner has of the difficulty of the medium. Saga (1993) further supported the AIME hypothesis by noting that in Japan children's learning from one medium compared to another was strongly effected by their perception of how important their teachers felt the various media to be.

No simple answer...

Thus, the question "Is television better than no television?" cannot be uniformly answered; so many variables, such as the amount of mental effort learners invest in watching broadcast television, are culturally influenced, and so much is influenced by the instructional strategies used by either the television teacher or the local teacher (see also, Forsslund, 1992; and Sholdt, Zhang and Fulford, 1995). Saga concludes:

> *...effective learning from media still depends on how teachers characterize and use them for instruction.* (p. 158)

This was also the main point of Chapters 5 and 6 of this book...

OVERALL SUMMARY OF THE MEDIA/DELIVERY TECHNOLOGY RESEARCH?

Given the difficultly of summarizing studies such as the above, there do seem to two major conclusions with regard to the technology/media chosen for courses involving tele-learning. We summarize them in Box 8.6.

> **Box 8.6**
>
> **Major conclusions from media/delivery technology research**
>
> - Most content can be effectively conveyed through most media; there is more variance within categories of media-delivery applications than between them (Stahmer, Bourdeau and Zuckernick, 1992; Oliver and Reeves, 1995)
> - It is not the technology alone that determines whether or not tele-learning is successful, but the way in which the technology is used (Kristiansen, 1993; Schramm, 1977)

Also, much of media/delivery-technology choice is determined by the context, particularly the history of such choices in an institution. A post-secondary institution committed to one-way broadcast, two-way audio, for example, for course delivery (see Chapter 7) will probably expect courses to be designed for that setting. A more fundamental question is: how willing is the institution to fundamentally reconsider its general choices of technology and media? Are the video broadcasts going to change to WWW pages because of an objective analysis of their various attributes? Probably not.

■ 8.2.3 DESIGNING FOR PEDAGOGICAL RE-ENGINEERING

The last question is a fundamental one to course delivery: to what extent do course providers expect to follow an established pattern and to what extent do they want to be or can they be innovative? We noted in Chapter 6 that the post-secondary instructor working with face-to-face classes in traditional settings, has two major ways to engage in "pedagogical re-engineering". One is to change the balance among instructional components in a course, the other is to deepen, enrich or change an individual component. Both of these considerations are involved when we think about designing a course so that there is more flexibility for the learner. In the following we look briefly at overall issues in designing for more-flexible courses, and then look at an example of a particular focus for pedagogical re-engineering in a tele-learning context. The particular focus is that of re-engineering course design through the integration of computer conferencing.

DESIGNING FOR FLEXIBILITY

Flexibility and tele-learning are often assumed to have a direct relationship with each other. Figure 8.1 shows a series of flexibility dimensions, each of which can be affected by tele-learning within the design of a course.

Each dimension is represented by:

Fixed   Flexible

←——→

1. Flexibility related to time:

Time (for starting and finishing a course)

Time (for moments of studying within the course)

Tempo/pace of studying

Moments of assessment

2. Flexibility related to content:

Topics of the course

Sequence of different parts of a course

Size of the course

Level of the course

Assessment standards

3. Flexibility related to entry requirements:

Conditions for participation

4. Flexibility related to instructional approach and resources:

Social organisation of learning

Language to be used during the course

Learning Resources

Instructional organisation of learning

5. Flexibility related to delivery and logistics:

Time & place where support is available

Method of obtaining support

Types of support available

Place for studying

Delivery Channels

From: Collis, Vingerhoets and Moonen, 1995, p. 12

Figure 8.1 Flexibility dimensions in course design

Flexibilities and their restraints

The most immediate impact of tele-learning on course design is often considered to be its contribution to an increase in flexibility of place or location: because of tele-learning, learners can be at a distance from resources, from their instructors, from their classmates. However, this aspect of flexibility has its limits: if learners have to come to a remote-classroom site to participate in an interactive television session or have to go to their post-secondary institution to use certain computers in order to access the WWW, then we note that the idea of "flexibility in place" may be not really accurate.

Flexibility in time is also closely associated with tele-learning; however flexibility in time, being able to study and learn when the learner wishes, may also be constrained even with tele-learning options. Tele-learning may allow the learner to interact with her instructor via e-mail at whatever hour of the night she comes to her computer, but the learner probably doesn't have the flexibility to decide to postpone this communication until the following month.

Thus each type of flexibility has its constraints. mostly because of the overall design decisions taken for a course. Sometimes the constraints are inherent to the natures of the dimensions involved: For example, If the course designer chooses to emphasize giving the learner freedom of choice about time with regard to course participation, then the designer foregoes the opportunity to plan for group projects or group discussions with peers as integral parts of a course.

Designing more-flexible learning into courses

But tele-learning does allow more-flexible options relative to a number of dimensions in course design, not only time and place, that are important for the course designer to consider. Among the most important considerations seems to be:

- What is the relative importance to a particular learner of flexibility in time compared to opportunities for group participation and discussion?

If time flexibility is most important to a target group, then asynchronous tele-learning resources such as WWW sites are useful to consider during course design. If group interaction is important to a target group, then real-time and asynchronous conferencing experiences are useful to emphasize and should be integrated in the overall design of the course.

Carried further, this approach to course design could result in the case of not designing a course at all: To give the learner maximal flexibility in pace, content, approach, amount of communication, etc., perhaps the designer should not be thinking in terms of "courses" at all, but in terms of tools and resources for individual learning (see Chapters 3 and 4)?

The TeleScopia Project: flexibility in course design

As an example of educational technologists busy with the consideration of tele-learning and flexibility in course design, the "TeleScopia Project" was in operation in Europe during 1994 and 1995, and involves course designers from six countries being given the chance to "re-engineer" a selection of their courses for trans-European tele-learning. Each of the courses was already organized for some form of distance delivery. TeleScopia provided the opportunity to extend and enrich the course organization while at the same time bringing each of the courses to a wider range of learners. The results of the TeleScopia Project (see Collis, 1995d) show that:

- Adult professional learners appreciate being able to stay at or near their workplaces for a learning episode rather than having the disruption of travelling to a course at a different location
- In addition, they appreciate flexibility of time more than having real-time video interaction, (as the two are in conflict with each other)
- But they appreciate the opportunity to hear of their fellow learners' experiences through asynchronous computer conferencing and especially appreciated having classmates from different countries and cultures
- The TeleScopia course designers in general did not change the instructional balance of their courses when given the chance for re-engineering. Instead they mainly used the tele-learning possibilities to increase communication possibilities within the courses while maintaining the same overall instructional approach and balance
- Only one course provider took advantage of the Internet and the WWW for tele-learning purposes other than adding communication
- In general the course providers still maintained all decision making about the readings for the courses and learning materials used in the courses as well as about the content, pacing, and instructional activities of the courses

What is interesting about the TeleScopia example is the limited amount of pedagogical re-engineering that occurred even when course designers were given the choice of extensive options for tele-learning (interactive television, ISDN networking, desktop multi-media conferencing, Internet access, etc). In general, course designers used the tele-learning technologies to add more communication to their courses, but did little to re-conceptualize, or pedagogically re-engineer their overall approach to instructional organization.

DESIGNING FOR DISCUSSIONS AND COMPUTER CONFERENCING

While in the above section we thought about course design from a global perspective, we can also zoom in on a particular component of course organization, and see how tele-learning can affect that component. The facilitation of communication is one such component. Many educational technologists are involved in the particular study of computer conferencing, either as a way to improve the communication already in a course or to change the instructional balance of a course by making discussion a more-central feature.

Table 8.3 summarizes some of the considerable literature about computer conferencing as an aspect of course design. (In Section 8.4.2 the design of the user interface through which computer conferencing takes place is considered.)

Thus the educational technologist has much to consider when s/he designs a course and wants to plans for the integration of computer conferencing. The extent to which the conferencing is successful depends on many variables (notice Hiltz and Turoff's 349 factors!), but it appears that the meaningfulness of the conferencing to the overall course design, the skill of the instructor or moderator in implementing the conferencing, and the characteristics of the software through which the conferencing takes place are particularly powerful variables (Pincas, 1995).

In this section we have looked at some of the general considerations relating to course design and tele-learning that confront educational technologists. There are also many specific issues related to the choice of real-time video-based tele-learning or asynchronous network-based tele-learning. We highlight a few in Section 8.3.

■ 8.3 SPECIFIC DESIGN CONSIDERATIONS RELATED TO TELEVISION/VIDEO-BASED COURSES AND NETWORK-BASED COURSES

There is a much longer history in both research and practice of how to design courses around a model involving real-time audio–visual interaction among its participants than there is for designing courses to be delivered asynchronously over a computer network. We will look briefly at some of the specific design issues for these two approaches for course design. We start with broadcast television, as it has the longest history.

■ 8.3.1 DESIGN CONSIDERATIONS FOR BROADCAST TELEVISION

Broadcast television for schools is an old technology, and has a long body of research associated with it. Many of these insights are as applicable to broadcast

Table 8.3 Selected research on computer conferencing as an element of course design

Study	Major Insight for Course Designers
Thorpe (1989)	Computer conferencing adds substantially to the time load on the instructor
Florini (1989)	Students need time to respond, but specific deadlines must also be set
Mason (1989)	Computer conferencing is an interesting but marginal activity for the majority of students; for a minority it becomes exciting and satisfying
Søby (1992)	The potential application to collaborative learning is high but students have difficulty in formuating good questions and to structure and adhere to planning when using computer conferencing
Henri (1991)	The content of computer conferences can be analyzed using a particular coding method around five dimensions: participation, interaction, social, cognitive, and metacognitive
Hardy, McConnell, Hodgson and Reynolds (1991)	If well executed, computer conferencing can (partially) replace face-to-face seminars, tutorial sessions, and groupwork sessions
Goldman and Newman (1992)	There are important differences in communication via computer conferencing and face-to-face interaction, particularly with respect to initiation and response patterns, turn taking, and distinguishing between public and private communications
Wood (1993)	Computer conferencing is appropriate for "high solidarity" course settings, such as graduate courses and colloquia
Gunawardena and Heeren (1993)	Students may prefer to reflect rather than contribute; is this a problem in computer conferencing, and if yes, how should it be addressed?

Hiltz & Turoff (1993)	There are 329 (!) factors identified that can influence the success of computer conferencing; the various combinations of these are enormous. These factors are in four major groups: contextual, intervention related, group-adaptation related, and outcome related
Mason (1994)	Computer conferencing supports humanistic aims in education in that it uniquely combines reflection and written communication with human intimacy and personal openness
De Vries (1994)	The moderator and the way s/he carries out eight different categories of roles are critical to the educational value of computer conferencing
Berge (1995)	54 recommendations are offered for integrating computer conferencing into course design, grouped according to moderator's role, pedagogical design, social issues, managerial aspects and technical aspects
Pincas (1995)	Consider a pedagogical approach where students are given a task, and use computer conferencing to comment on their discoveries (instead of teacher input → student activity, student activity → teacher input)

television for adults as they are for school-age learners. Some of the insights deal with pedagogical scenarios, others on the combination of broadcast television with other media, and others on increasing learner interactivity or mental effort.

PEDAGOGICAL SCENARIOS

Foley (1995) summarizes experience in Ireland with educational television by identifying five scenarios particularly appropriate for educational television. These are summarized in Box 8.7.

Each of these scenarios requires didactical skill on the part of the educational technologist designing the television episode. Part of the didactical skill is knowing how and when to mix the televised episode with other pedagogical scenarios. This can happen within a broadcast, or around a broadcast.

Box 8.7

Pedagogical scenarios for broadcast television

- Studio discussion, where several persons are brought together for a discussion
- Virtual classroom, where the television teacher tries to simulate the face-to-face classroom experience as much as possible (a technology for learner response is needed)
- Mediated presentation, where a presenter interviews an expert and draws out an explanation of a topic for the benefit of the students
- Documentary, in the same sense as regular television documentaries
- Virtual workshop, where the students watch a broadcast, then carry out some tasks explained in the broadcast, and then rejoin the broadcast, interactively if possible, for review and discussion

---

Combining broadcast television with other media

One way to combine pedagogical scenarios involving broadcast television is to mix them within a broadcast, for example, combining a mediated presentation with short, informative video segments, or integrating a discussion into a documentary. Another way is to combine broadcast television with other media, particularly print media (see Meyer, 1992, for a wide range of examples from European school television). In a research study done by educational technologists in the UK, adults with experience in various forms of distance education were asked to rank order 12 media in terms of effectiveness. Television, by itself, was ranked last. However, when television was combined with print material and tutor support, it was ranked third (behind written materials combined with personal tutor support, and written materials and videotapes combined with personal tutor support; Bentley, Bentley, Drobinski and Watts, 1992).

Increasing learner interactivity and mental effort with instructional television

One of the major research focuses with respect to broadcast television is the issue of interactivity. There is controversy over the degree to which interactivity should occur for different learners, and also the form that it should take. The most typical view is that "without interactivity, students who are already physically distant from an instructor will become mentally distant, and little learning will occur" (Phelan, 1995). However, comparative cross-cultural research shows that the "amount of invested mental effort" (AIME) (Salomon, 1983) that learners expend on watching broadcast television is a critical variable relative to the meaningfulness of interaction during television broadcasts. Interacting in itself is not necessarily better learning and providing a way for immediate questioning of the television presentor does not have to occur in order for quality interaction, particularly in the AIME sense, to occur. When a local teacher is available, as is often the case with broadcast television, it may be that the interaction within the local class, after and even during the broadcast, is more beneficial than a two-way interactive link to the television presentor. This in-class interactivity can be further improved if the classroom teacher has viewed a videotape of the broadcast earlier and is prepared to stop the tape at various moments for emphasis and discussion (Meyer, 1992). This strategy however, makes it even less likely that the learners can have a real-time question-and-answer interaction with the distant presenter.

When students are learning entirely at a distance and without tele-communication possibilities, interactivity must be stimulated by the design of the learning materials; as was seen earlier in the TVOL research (Hutchinson and Koplin, 1995), this is the task of the educational technologist designing the course.

■ 8.3.2 Designing for small-group work and video-conferencing

While educational television is often used for pre-structured instructional sequences, compressed video and other video technologies (see Chapter 2) also make it possible for learners in remote settings to interact with each other in group activities, rather than only responding to teacher-led discussions or presentations.

The pedagogies of group work are however challenging, even in face-to-face groups and more so for distributed participants. Box 8.8 indicates some of the design techniques that educational technologists involved in the design of video-conferencing for real-time interaction among distributed learners engaging in a group learning activity need to consider.

Box 8.8

Techniques and guidelines for designing video-conferencing sessions for tele-learning

- Make sure speakers are identified, and a procedure is developed for turn taking
- Techniques for the use of microphones when more than three persons are involved at a site must be carefully worked out
- If windows are involved on the monitor, the upper-right corner is considered good for self-views; the number of windows used should be held low
- Cameras must be carefully placed to minimize parallax error, whereby participants do not make eye contact (ISSUE Consortium, 1994)

As the last point in Box 8.8 illustrates, the technology of video-conferencing has a language and a set of techniques that educational technologists will have to master if they become involved with course design involving video-conferencing.

■ 8.3.3 DESIGNING COURSES FOR NETWORK DELIVERY

While there is considerable experience with the design of courses involving television-type tele-learning and video-conferencing, and more and more experience developing for the design of courses involving computer conferencing as an instructional component, a relatively new design area is that of courses to be entirely conducted via a computer network, primarily the Internet. In this section we indicate three such examples of this sort of course design.

EXAMPLES

"The Virtual Classroom"

Among the pioneers of course design for network delivery are the team involved in the "The Virtual Classroom" initiative at the New Jersey Institute of Technology (Hiltz, 1990, 1993; Turoff, 1995). In over a decade's worth of development, the groupware system with the copyrighted name "The Virtual Classroom" has evolved as the delivery environment for their courses. This system involves a number of software tools such as features for computer conferencing, for private messaging, for individual and group notebooks, instructor gradebook tools, and other features, including now the integration of multi-media courseware and a World Wide Web interface (Turoff, 1995). A number of courses have been designed specifically for this environment, and have been taught and evaluated (Hiltz, 1993). Course design is based on principles of collaborative learning and active participation, as well as the sharing of thoughts and problem-solving processes among instructors and students. Particular use is made of simulations and gaming as instructional strategies integrated in the course design.

CNAM and "TéléSITE"

Other interesting examples of courses being designed for network delivery can be seen in France and Canada. In France, the CNAM (Conservatoire National des Arts et Métiers) has installed a "remote teaching network" to connect over 100 local training centres, serving both working and unemployed persons (see Chapter 7). Centres are connected to a regional centre through ISDN and other special networks. Learners coming to the local centres can "tele-load" course materials from the regional server into their local-centre computers, can use these same computers for asynchronous interaction with the distant tutor, and can also send their practice exercises and tests via the network to the regional centre computer, where the tutor provides rapid feedback.

Important to the courses is "TéléSITE", a multi-media software environment through which the learners can download not only text-type tutorial software but also a large variety of video lessons (Rolland, 1995). "TéléSITE" runs under Windows and is an interface that integrates a number of standard products available on the market. Remote sites are connected with ISDN routers, and thus multi-media documents can be handled. The courses that are designed for "TéléSITE" reflect the strategy of providing access to many different multi-media resources to the learner through this networked environment.

Télé-université and the "Virtual Campus"

The "Télé-université" in Quebec is a Canadian example of an institution where educational technologists are designing courses via a special methodology that makes use of the so-called "Virtual Campus Environment". This environment includes a video-codec and an ATM platform that together allow multi-point multi-media communication (Paquette, Ricciardi-Rigault, Bourdeau, Paquin and Liégeois, 1995). The Télé-université also designs courses to make use of an earlier version of the Virtual Campus environment (Paquette, Bergeron and Bourdeau, 1993).

Thus software-environment design and course design complement each other at the Télé-université; the courses emphasize collaboration and access to shared resources while the software environment makes this possible to learners at a distance from each other and from the resources.

DESIGN OF WWW-BASED COURSES

As we have seen in a number of examples in Chapters 5, 6 and 7 an increasing number of courses are now being offered completely over the Internet, and more specifically, completely through a WWW site. Because there are so many examples in other locations in this book (see also **Interface 9**) we will only indicate some key design issues and illustrative sites here, in Box 8.9.

AND IT COSTS TIME AND MONEY...

A valuable resource for those who are considering the design of courses for the Internet, both for non-WWW and WWW settings, is a report from the University of Wisconsin, Engineering Professional Development Section (Oscheske, Klus, Stremikis and Hoyman, 1995); see:

Design of Internet Courses
`http://epdwww.engr.wisc.edu)`

In this comprehensive report, experiences with the conversion of 13 already-existing independent-studies courses for delivery over the Internet were carefully analyzed. In particular, the tasks and the time the conversion process required were analyzed for the content author, the editor, the technical-support team, and the manager of the overall design process.

The conclusion of the analysis was that conversion of a course for gopher presentation took an average of 704 hours (or 17,6 hours per page) and for a WWW presentation took 940 hours (or 23,5 hours per page). Thus the costs of the WWW presentation were nearly double that of the gopher presentation.

These sorts of estimates are collaborated by Novick and Fickas (1995) who

---

Box 8.9

Examples of some key design decisions in WWW-based courses

What should be the balance between links and references to external sources and locally available study materials?
See URL `http://enuxsa.eas.asu.edu/cse471/`
as an example of a course which is predominately an organizational framework for locally available study materials

To what extent should communication and information be integrated with the course site?
See URL `http://www.dipoli.hut/fi:8080/org/TechNet/org/EEE/`
as an example of a course with a newsgroup environment integrated within the course (note: a password is needed to participate)

Should the WWW site be designed as an interactive learning site, for example, where the learner can interact with simulations or other computer-based learning materials through links in the site?
See URL `http://lenti.med.umn.edu/anatomy/heartblo.html`
for an example of a course organized around the "Clickable Heart Anatomy Tutor" in the WWW site.

Should the learning materials in the course site be structured in the way that the student proceeds through them, or hyperlinked so that the student is encouraged to search and move about as she wishes?
See URL `http://www.ch.ic.as.uk/GIC/`
for an example of a course with a searchable index to take the learner to wherever she wishes to go in the course environment.

(adapted from Rikkerink, 1995)

describe a course built around a WWW site in which the course designers collaborated from three different institutions. The conclusion was that the preparation of this course involved "significant extra effort as compared with televised courses or traditional CAI...we judge the effort...comparable to the effort involved in writing a textbook"(p. 160).

Thus, course design for delivery via networks is a complex business. More generally, course (re)design for tele-learning is a challenging task in which many educational technologists in countries around the world are engaged.

FROM COURSES TO TOOLS AND ENVIRONMENTS

In this section we have focused on the design of entire courses. We have seen that course design is both art and science, and when tele-learning is involved is also technique and creativity. However, many educational technologists are involved not with course design, but with research into the design of innovative tools and environments that can play a pivotal role in tele-learning, within many different courses. Thus in Section 8.4 we look more specifically at innovative tools and environments in themselves, not necessarily designed for immediate use in a particular course.

■ 8.4 DESIGNING INNOVATIVE TOOLS AND ENVIRONMENTS

Courses are made up of instructional sequences involving learning materials, carried out in various educational environments. In Section 8.2 and 8.3 we considered overall courses that involve tele-learning in some way, and same of the roles that educational technologists are playing in the design of such courses. Course designers must keep their focus on the eventual implementation of their courses, with specific learners and within specific institutional contexts. What about those educational technologists who focus not on complete courses, but on designing tools and environments for tele-learning that can be used within courses? Their work is the focus of Section 8.4.

■ 8.4.1 DESIGNING INNOVATIVE TOOLS

Many educational technologists are involved in tele-learning, not in the context of the client-satisfaction demands of course delivery but through a more research-oriented perspective that focuses on new developments in tools and environments to support tele-learning.

RESEARCH FOR COURSE IMPROVEMENT

Sometimes this research and development focus is directly coupled to a course-delivery situation, where the designer produces a new tool or environment that is put to the test by his or her colleagues in an actual course-delivery setting. Other educational technologists may be involved in the evaluation of the new tool or environment, providing formative feedback to the design team for their further development work.

RESEARCH FOR MORE ABSTRACT MOTIVATIONS

Other times however the design activity is more related to conceptual research motivations, where the educational technologists begin with a theoretical interest, design to a prototype level a new tool or environment based on the concept, and observe the responses of a small group of subjects (often their own students) making some limited use of the prototype. From these experiences, educational technologists can explore the implications of the new design ideas for future tele-learning applications, or more abstractly, can obtain new insights into some aspects of learning, such as "distributed cognitions" (Salomon, 1993).

An entire book could be written around the sorts of work highlighted in Section 8.4; we can give only a taste of the extensive activity that is going on among educational technologists in this area relating to research in the instrumentation of specific materials, tools and environments for tele-learning. Some of the research and design work highlighted in this section relate to questions such as the following:

- What about the software environments that support asynchronous computer conferencing? How might they be better designed to support the specific needs of tele-learning (Section 8.4.2)?
- What are design guidelines for the software that supports currently available desktop multimedia conferencing? How should it be designed for tele-learning use (Section 8.4.3)?
- What about integrated network environments that combine a number of different sorts of tele-learning tools? What sorts of design and research work are educational technologists doing with these more-complex environments (Section 8.4.4)?
- What about the fastest-growing new environment for tele-learning, the Wide World Web? What are educational technologists doing with regard to the design and development of the tele-learning potential of WWW systems (Section 8.4.5)?
- What happens when a tele-learning system involves an entity as complex as a collection of buildings, networks, pedagogical approaches, and a

particular form of institutional organization such as we saw in the examples in Section 8.3.3? What are design issues for educational technologists working in these integrated settings (Section 8.4.6)?

■ 8.4.2 THE DESIGN OF COMPUTER CONFERENCING SOFTWARE TO SUPPORT TELE-LEARNING

Computer-conferencing software has in general not been specifically developed for tele-learning applications, but is more generically targeted toward support of asynchronous group communication in a variety of settings, such as distributed work groups in companies. However, many educational technologists have been involved in the process of mapping the specific needs of asynchronous communication in tele-learning situations to the functionalities provided in computer-conferencing software. Sometimes this mapping is to better take advantage of functionalities already provided in the software by seeing how they can be conceptualized and applied in a tele-learning context. From this mapping, and experience with existing computer-conferencing packages, educational technologists often are coming forward with suggestions for improvements in existing features and functionalities in computer-conferencing software and also with suggestions for augmenting existing features with new functionalities specifically of value to tele-learning. The user interface of computer-conferencing software receives particular attention in much of this research.

In the five components of Section 8.4.2 we highlight these various types of research activities.

WHAT IS COMPUTER-CONFERENCING SOFTWARE?

Before computer-conferencing software can be used in tele-learning, its typical functionalities must be understood. Among those educational technologists producing inventories of the functionalities of computer-conferencing packages are De Vries, 1994; Palme, 1992; Turoff, 1991; and Hardy, McConnell, Hodgson and Reynolds, 1991. Core aspects are summarized in Box 8.10.

All such functionalities must be integrated into the computer-conferencing software, both in terms of their basic functionalities, and in terms of the way they are presented to the user through the user interface of the client software. There are considerable variations among computer-conferencing software with respect to functionality inclusion and user-interface design, variations which have a strong influence on their eventual use in tele-learning. (See De Vries (1994) and Hardy *et al.*, (1991) for several examples of comparative evaluations of the usability of computer-conferencing software.)

Box 8.10

Computer-conferencing software design components

1. Architecture, the way in which the software handles the presentation and manipulation of comments:
—*Branching design, where users can attach responses to previous entries at any point after reading the entry, and are not forced to read all the entries or to add their entry at the end of the set of items*
—*Book design, where users must read through all items associated with a starter item and can only append their responses to the end of the responses already attached to the starter item*

2. Facilities for connection between client and host: to help the user connect her client computer to the distant host, such as compatibilty with different types of modems, scaleable architecture for user expansion, interface to different platforms (particularly Mac and PC), capabilities to work with any ANSI terminal emulator, automatic character translation, low server memory requirements, and other performance-specific features

3. Support for a complete electronic mail facility, including attachments (text, graphics, and sound), various addressing facilities, support for use of fonts and different text styles, support for searching one's mailbox, tracking of messages, and support for gateways to other mail systems

4. Support for different conference types: Open, closed, restricted, protected, write-protected, each with searching facilities

5. Support for operations on conferences (by conference manager, operating through the host): Create conference operation, membership lists, announcements, directories, archives; handle membership and withdrawal applications and suspensions; assign privileges to moderators and participants; designate statistics collection and user limits

6. Support for handling of contributions to conferences by participants: Submitting to a conference, submitting to multiple conferences; individual, group, or conference reply; forwarding of conversations to additional recipients; deleting contributions; scanning contributions and history of contributions

7. Metaphors and user-interface support for user roles and system facilities: Cohesive vocabulary and integrative framework for: those with different roles in the system; for messages and conferences; and for other facilities such as forms, lists, directories, attachments, and notifications; on-line help; display of folders and items by name or icon; cut, paste, and print support; windowing support

MAPPING COMPUTER-CONFERENCING FUNCTIONALITIES TO TELE-LEARNING

While a first step in using computer-conferencing software in tele-learning is knowing what functions are available and anticipating what difficulties the learner will have in using those functions, a next step is making the connection between available functionalities and their application in tele-learning situations.

This step occurs less often. Paulsen (1995), for example, summarizes a variety of "pedagogical CMC techniques", all of which could be implemented via computer-conferencing software, but gives no specific indication of which combination of functionalities in the software and which user-interface characteristics would be appropriate for the various techniques. Turoff (1991) is one of the few who explicitly map tele-learning needs onto computer-conferencing functionalities. He also indicates how, within a system which he and others have designed, these functionalities are being realized. Kaye (1992b) summarizes some key

---

Box 8.11

Examples of design suggestions for computer-conferencing software based on tele-learning experiences

- Design the software so that learner is not shown the same message as new more than once, to discourage the sending of messages to more than one conference
- Allow the sender, particularly the tutor, to see who has read a message
- Allow flexibility in terms of who has privileges to start conferences (including instructor and learners)
- Include features that support group consensus, such as polling or voting tools
- Add options in the user interface for the learner to see various "views" of the environment: the system as a whole, from the metaphor of an "electronic campus" or cafe; of each conference, relative to each member's status and new items; of each item, including its history; and of each participant, to see his or her roles and contributions to the group task. (From Kaye, 1992b, pp. 19–20)

---

insights in this mapping process (see Box 8.11).

In addition to Turoff and Kaye, other educational technologists, from their experiences with the use of computer-conferencing software in tele-learning situations, have also made recommendations for further enhancements of such software. We will mention some suggestions relative to the user interface itself, and some relative to the addition of new functionalities.

ENHANCEMENTS IN TERMS OF IMPROVING THE USER INTERFACE

System learnability through simple, menu-driven screens

There is a considerable literature about user-interface design from software-engineering perspectives and from the domain of human–computer interaction (see for example, Preece *et al.*, 1994). Such literature often identifies areas of design decisions, such as the choice of menu-driven vs command-driven interfaces.

Saiedian (1992–93) refers to such criteria in his defense of the user interface designed for a computer-conferencing system at his university. The interface for this conferencing environment was designed on the basis of the concept of "stepwise learnability"—where the amount of information the user must assimilate "is decomposed into a set of unintimidating steps" (p. 111). For this reason, the interface was designed in terms of sequences of simple, menu-driven screens.

GUI conferencing interface designed for tele-learning

Collins and Bostock (1993) through their research noted that difficulties which prevent students gaining the full benefits of computer conferencing are often "due to the human interface provided by conferencing software"(p. 334). In particular they observed difficulties caused by the combination of a potentially complex conference structure and the interface provided by the remote host computer, where "students often get lost in the structure [of the conferences] and are unsure of the options available to them regarding navigation (p. 337)

To respond to the difficulties they noted in their research, Collins and Bostock designed "FICS", a "Friendly Interface to Conferencing System" and are using it with their students in a UK university. FICS is a front-end to an existing conferencing system, designed to handle all interactions with the conferencing system itself so they are hidden from the user. Particular features of the FICS front-end interface include those described in Box 8.12.

Many other such initiatives relating to user-interface design for computer-conferencing software for tele-learning can be described, for example, Alexander's

---

Box 8.12

Components of the FICS interface for computer conferencing software used for tele-learning

- Runs under Windows, thus allowing features such as resizable windows and multi-tasking integration with other tools such as the clipboard and word processor
- Command options are provided as point-and-click icon buttons
- Local copies of conferences can be made for the student's own editing and annotation
- Navigation is aided by a map window which displays the hierarchy of responses within a current item as a collection of selectable objects
- Conferences with many responses can be seen by scrolling the map in the map window
- Levels are represented by vertical lists, while depth of response to an item is represented by horizontal scrolling to the right
  (see Collins and Bostock, 1993, pp. 338–341 for various screen dumps).

(1992) work on an interface design to stimulate collaborative learning during computer conferencing. In Alexander's design, "personalized face icons" are available to help develop the sense of belonging to a group; those involved in a conference discussion have their face icons visible on the screen, outlined if they have contributed to the discussion; and personal comments are added to specific messages, not only in text, but with the personal icon of the commenter also displayed. In addition, "thumbs-up" and "thumbs-down" icons are available as the basis of a simple group polling system, and an icon with the image of a paper clip on it can be used to indicate that an individual has attached a personal message to a given item.

NEW FEATURES FOR TELE-LEARNING

In addition to user-interface design aspects, there is creative work going on with respect to the addition of specific features to computer-conferencing software in order to improve collaborative knowledge construction.

Navigation and discussion maps

Collins and Bostock are among many who have noted the confusion that tele-learners have with navigation within the structure of complex conference discussions. Some educational technologists, as researchers, have designed and tested prototype computer-conferencing systems that focus on the visualization of conference structure through various tools provided to the tele-learners. Ahern (1993) and Ahern and Repman (1994) designed the "Idea Web" as a tool to mediate group discussion. A major innovation with this environment is its graphics-based discussion map. When a learner wishes to add a comment to a topic under discussion, he or she must click the "Comments" button, which then presents a new icon labelled with the learner's name and the date, as well as an attached message form in which the learner enters his or her comments. The key step then follows: the learner goes to a "discussion map" screen where his or her icon is placed, and indicates to which of the previous icons in the discussion the new icon is to be linked. This linkage is then shown in a graphical way, as an interconnected network of icons. Browsing can occur by selecting any of the icons, and then following the sequence of icons linked to the particular icon.

In a test of the system by which it was compared to a text-only system without the graphic linking tools, Ahern and Repman note that using the graphic organizer took considerably more time than the text-only system, but that time was partly a function of learners being "more committed" to participation, perhaps because the visual cues concerning the state of the interaction "motivated students to contribute to the ongoing discussion because they could quickly see if anyone had responded to them" (p. 545), and because they will "respond more often if they perceive their comments have value, which they define as someone attending to what they say in an interaction". When a learner notices that his previous comment was left unlinked, "he felt uncomfortable, ...and pleaded with the other group members to create a link with him"(p. 546). Ahern and Repman conclude their analysis by noting that while the "interface had no effect on the level of participation, achievement, or satisfaction for computer-mediated small-group discussion, ...the interface does have an impact on the number of messages and the audience for whom the message was intended" (p. 546).

Tools for case-study discussions

As another example of tools being added to computer-conferencing software in order to better accommodate tele-learning, Romiszowski and Chang (1995) have developed the "Response Matrix". This tool presents a variety of comments that may or may not be pertinent to the case study on which learners are working. Each learner constructs a response for the particular case by choosing some combination of these responses. Another tool then provides some feedback relative to the responses which were chosen, and gives the learner the opportunity to enter his or her own comments. These comments are moved into a "discussion log" for the case that can be studied by other learners.

FUTURE DIRECTIONS FOR COMPUTER-CONFERENCING SOFTWARE

Thus a major area of activity for many educational technologists is the design of enhanced tools for computer conferencing for better support of tele-learning. Important directions are in the area of "group graphs" (Ahern and Repman's is one such example) but where members of a group can make modifications in each others' diagrams (Turoff, 1991) or where members of the group can create their own icon sets to use as part of the visualization process. Particular attention is being paid to the "multi-media issue", whereby communication is not only in text (Derycke, 1992). Sometimes, non-textual communication is important to the nature of what is being discussed; San Chee (1995), for example describes a computer-conferencing system where learners can append not only text attachments, but also video, sound, and complex graphics files.

Other times the importance of multi-media is more focused on the needs of the discussants themselves and their feeling of being part of a group. While the personalized icons described by Alexander and the name-labelled buttons visualized into a graphic map described by Ahern and Repman can help this sense of identity, they cannot replace the information richness that can come from actually hearing and seeing persons as they comment. We discuss systems that extend computer conferencing to multi-media conferencing in the next section.

■ 8.4.3 THE DESIGN OF SOFTWARE FOR MULTI-MEDIA DESKTOP CONFERENCING TO SUPPORT TELE-LEARNING

In order to improve the richness and realism of computer conferencing, one area of development is to augment its text-only aspects with other modalities of communication, particularly audio, and audio combined with video. Increasingly, the single desktop computer, running appropriate software, outfitted with a video camera, microphone and videocard, and connected to a appropriate network (relative to both bandwidth and speed), is moving into use for tele-learning. Such systems are often called multi-media desktop conference systems (see Chapter 2). In this section, we first describe such systems and particularly their instrumentation in some more detail; then identify examples of software and user-interface design relating to use of the systems for distance tutoring, for collaborative learning, and for teaching, all aspects of tele-learning. We also examine some software environments that support both synchronous and asynchronous conferencing, and consider some major design issues for such systems.

DESKTOP MULTI-MEDIA CONFERENCING

Desktop multi-media conferencing systems are only now (1995) evolving, technically and in the marketplace. Standard terminology for such systems and standard functionalities have not yet stabilized. However, a general set of characteristics is emerging, whereby participants can simultaneously do the activities noted in Box 8.13.

Various analyses of currently available desktop conferencing systems appear in the computer literature, contrasting the functionalities offered by such systems as well as the hardware, software, and network requirements of the systems. For example, in comparing 12 "desktop videoconferencing systems" Labriola (1995) found the software features listed in Box 8.14 to be present in most of the systems.

There are many differences in the user interfaces of currently available desktop-conferencing systems, and the systems themselves are not yet compatible with each other. However, they do share the characteristics that they offer participation through the user's desktop computer; real-time communication occurs in at least two modalities and usually three; they offer various tools for collaborative work

---

Box 8.13

With a desktop multi-media conferencing system learners can...

- Talk with and see each other while communicating, as well as communicate via text
- Not only see one's communication partner but also his or her surroundings
- Exchange and view full-motion video, voice, images, and data, while in audio and/or video contact for communication
- Share and conjointly edit files, reports, charts, and diagrams through shared workspace tools, and work conjointly within the same application software through application-sharing tools; all while being in audio and/or video contact for communication and coordination.

---

and coordination of communication; and they offer some forms of information handling, both in real time and using stored (multi-media) resources. Clearly such functionalities are most suited for real-time communication and particularly for collaborative learning activities or activities involving close interaction, such as tutoring. How are educational technologists involved in the design of instrumentation for these sorts of tele-learning settings?

RELATING FUNCTIONALITIES TO TELE-LEARNING NEEDS

One contribution educational technologists can make to the design of desktop conferencing software for tele-learning is to analyze needs relating to learning at a distance through computers, and communicate those needs to the commercial developers of desktop multi-media conferencing software. In a recent review of

---

Box 8.14

Functionalities in desktop multi-media conferencing software (circa 1995)

- Videoconferencing software
- Document-conferencing software, by which 2 to12 participants can work together on the same pages or document, while talking to and even seeing each other
- Annotation tools, including tools for selecting text and objects, for making and moving annotations, for increasing the number of annotation colours as well as colours of markers and pens so that each user has his or her own colour
- Real-time application sharing (in 9 of the 12 systems)
- Address book facilities
- Real-time text chat facilities
- Facilities to capture and transmit still images and do file transfers in the background as conferencing occurs

the literature, Collis and Smith (1995) synthesized the following user needs for one broad category of tele-learning applications involving collaborative learning and further evaluated a particular software environment for desktop multi-media conferencing to see how well it served the needs. The purpose of the evaluation was to provide formative feedback to the software developers. Box 8.15 itemizes these user needs.

Desktop multi-media conferencing is better able to support these needs than other types of conferencing (computer, audio, video, or audio-graphics; see the analysis in Collis & Smith, 1995, p. 32). Even so, the design of software for desktop environments to support all of these needs is a challenging task, as the examples in Table 8.4 indicate.

The projects mentioned in Table 8.4 have been selected as representative of activities going on in many different countries around the world; all at an experimental or special-project level, all hoping to bring not only new tools but new insights into the support of tele-learning with desktop multi-media tools and environments.

SPECIAL ISSUES FOR REAL-TIME TOOLS

Out of the extensive CSCW and CSCL literature (computer-supported cooperative work and computer-supported collaborative learning; see for example

---

Box 8.15

Needs for distributed collaborative learning

Needs relating to communication:
    to provide feedback to the speaker
    to support turn taking
    to support both private and group communication

Needs relating to information handling:
    to support efficient storage, retrieval, and sharing of information
    to define and make available the "group memory" to the participants
    to support the flow of information among the group
    to provide a common workarea to develop new ideas and documents
    to prevent information overload and incomplete use of information

Needs relating to participant coordination:
    to provide meeting- and time-management support tools
    to provide tools that support group decision making
    to provide features that stimulate a sense of group awareness (from Collis & Smith, 1995)

Table 8.4 Examples of design projects for desktop multi-media tele-learning

Project	Main Features	Current Status
MITS (Multimedia Interactive Tutoring System; Ng, Chan & Tsang, 1993)	Shared screen (to load in and manipulate text and graphics), but also private windows Concurrent access to shared data, but only the person with floor control (usually the instructor) can modify the data Voice transmission important, but only the person with floor control can speak	Being tested in Hong Kong with two applications, an image viewer and text editor Floor control mechanism is useful when there are more than two participants, but awkward with only two Learner requesting connection to the tutor does not know how long he will have to wait
"University without Boundaries" (Milner, 1995)	–Support of off-campus learners in the course "Microcomputer Skills", (in the UK) using both ISDN-videoconferencing and desktop conferencing with audio and document sharing	For the learning of computing, learners preferred audio-graphics to video-conferencing, in that they felt it most valuable to show their tutors their work and discuss it with their tutors while it was displayed on the screen and could be changed by either party. Seeing each other at the same time might only be distracting
"ECOLE" (Pals, Mulder, Nelissen, Wolswijk and Bruining, 1995)	ISDN-based integrated services, computer conferencing, email, screen sharing, address book, and file transfer, used for support of course in Cross-Cultural Communication (with Swiss and Dutch participants)	Problems with lack of ISDN compatibility across borders Important to have a practice period with the software before the start of a course Learners did not use the help functions despite many technical problems Learners performed as well as in face-to-face versions of the course, but at lower costs (because of eliminating international travel and time away from work)
"ImagineDesk" (Pozzi, Tancredi and Tisato, 1994)	Real-time interaction via a shared workspace and video-audio communication	Still at the prototype level (in Italy) Focus is on special tools and services for the planning and organization of the cooperative activity

"VIEW" (Harasim and Teles, 1994)	System to deliver distance education courses, based on tutoring Offers "designer's toolkit" for combinations of computer conferencing, videoconferencing, video-on-demand, Internet connectivity and tools, and other workgroup tools	Under development in Canada Special focus on group interaction in multi-media conferencing environments
"EDUBA" (Pastor, Sanchez and Alvarez, 1994)	Tools to hold real-time (ISDN) conversations and share information through video, audio, and multi-media documents Different interfaces and tools for teachers and learners	Under development in Spain, a multidisciplinary team is necessary Openness, reliability and easy integration are of major importance, but hard to realize technically
"CODILESS" (Watabe, Hamalainen and Whinston, 1995)	Distributed, many-to-many multi-media communication via the Internet with both off-line and on-line components; on-line components are both synchronous and asynchronous	In experimental phase, (Japan, Finland, US) Examining strategies for relating information from course materials to information retrieved from the Internet
"COVIS" (Edelsen & O'Neill, 1994)	Special application called the "Collaboratory Notebook", a communal database into which students record their thoughts and actions; supports both synchronous and asynchronous use ISDN linkage between schools and a science museum for collaborative activities	Large-scale collaborative project (in the US) Project tries to serve as a "technological lever" to overcome "the general tendency in science education of product over process" (p. 147)

Schnase & Cunnius, 1995), we highlight a few of the many design issues under exploration.

"Fly on the wall"

Tools to support real-time desktop tele-learning frequently are built upon careful analyses of what is needed to make the learner feel part of a group and learn productively with his or her fellow-learners. Sometimes this analysis is rooted in psychological principles, as with the COVIS project (Edelson & O'Neill, 1994); sometimes the orientation comes more from computer science and the CSCW literature (see for example, Li and Mantei, 1992; Gutwin and Greenberg, 1995). Li and Mantei have studied the ways that people interact with each other face-to-face, and have extended this to guidelines for the user interface of software for distributed interacting. Their 12 major observations include the need to be able to:

- implicitly establish a colleague's level of accessibility
- enforce reciprocity in information exchange
- trivially make verbal and visual contact
- filter out unwanted noise

and other capacities, all of which they translate into functionalities available through the user interface of their "virtual open office" environment at the University of Toronto. They call the environment VOODOO; it supports an open video channel between points, shared screens, telepointing, a 3D sound system, and various other features, including a "fly on the wall" camera to take informal shots of the overall environment.

Group awareness

Gutwin and Greenberg (1995) approach the problem of improving group awareness in real-time desktop conferences through a categorization of "task and view proximity". They argue that individuals involved with the same task and the same view are in high-interaction situations and thus need detailed information about their shared task and also about each other, such as facial expressions and gestures. Thus the tools needed for this situation should be multi-medial and "WYSIWIS" (what you see is what I see).

In contrast, learners in working on different sorts of tasks may need only "coarse indicators of presence and location, a global understanding of other peoples' goals, and knowledge of long-range side effects" (p. 6). Based on these sorts of analyses, Gutwin and Greenberg describe a tool environment "GroupKit" which they are developing, with many different tools (such as a multi-user scrollbar, a gestalt viewer, WYSIWID tools (what you see is what I am doing), a "viewport" history mechanism to trace the view of different participants of the shared workspace over time, etc.) to fit different awareness needs.

SMALL-GROUP TUTORING

Another application of desktop multi-media conferencing is to support intensive tutoring among distributed participants. There are many examples, particularly in Europe where ISDN networking is more aggressively marketed than in many

Table 8.5 Desktop-conferencing for small-group tutoring

Setting	Didactic emphasis	Technology components
14-year old students at their school and student teacher at his university, UK (N. Davis, 1995a)	"Teaching by successive refinement"; students taught a technical-drawing package to their student teacher, while the student teacher taught the students how to apply principles of design to the drawing they were collaboratively developing	ISDN connection between two sites Each site had software for application sharing as well as speaker phones
Teacher in school and support-centre specialist at local resource centre, UK (N. Davis, 1995a)	One-to-one tutoring on use of a complex new software package without each party having to leave their workplace	ISDN connection between two sites Each site had software for application sharing as well as desktop audio
Tutor in training centre in Germany and clients in other countries participating in trans-European tele-learning course in accounting methods; Germany, Poland, UK (Collis, 1995d)	Scheduled periods of walk-through feedback between tutor and inidividual learners, involving the application of accounting principles during the use of a complex software package	ISDN connections (via satellite transmission, to connect Germany and Poland) Each site has multimedia desktop conferencing software allowing application sharing, video windows, and voice transmission directly through the computer
"Virtual Summer School" for replication of entire face-to-face course in cognitive psychology with 12 adults at their homes throughout the UK, (Eisenstadt, 1995)	Replicate the benefits of face-to-face interaction and course participation as much as possible but without the participants having to leave home; thus supporting real-time group discussions, setting up and conducting experiments as learning activities, obtaining one-to-one tuition, working in teams, having full access to resources, giving group presentations, attending lectures, and "socialize and chit-chat"	Provision of multi-media computers loaded with a large variety of software to each participant, as well as a cellular phone so that calls for help could be made while using the main phone lines for modem-network connectivity Provision of dial-up access to the university and to the Internet Software included a specialized "virtual campus" interface, computer-conferencing software, CU-SeeMe videoconferencing via the Internet, remote presentation software, mobile telephone support and audio

		conferencing, screen-sharing software, software to run desktop video demonstration programs, and other bundled software to use during the course
Three groups of engineering students, in different locations on their campus, work collaboratively on a design problem, US; (Gay and Lentini, 1995)	Focus on how and when the availability of multiple channels of communication were useful to the learners: when they needed to increase the depth of communication for understanding, the breadth of their communication for complex visualizations, and when they had technical difficulties with one channel	Three-way, closed-circuit video conferencing system Chat function (text) Shared drawing tool Access to a shared multimedia database of engineering information Common access to scanned resource materials Multi-media spreadsheet research tool for subsequent analysis of all video records
Common real-time and asynchronous resources for students at various campuses of the University of Oslo, Norway (Dybvik and Lie, 1995)	Integration of videoconferencing for real-time lectures with a hypertext archive for access of lecture materials outside the lectures	High-capacity network infrastructure can support real-time video conferences as well as standard networking and Internet access Classrooms equipped with large-screen projection surface, two cameras (one on instructor, one on class), and a document camera Specialized software that "massages" presentation materials into HTML so that they are available asynchronously as a WWW page
Expert in his office shares complex data and software with vocational students in their school in another city, Netherlands (Arav, 1995a)	Replace the "excursion" to a company setting for trainees and also give the trainees the chance to work, under direct guidance, with the software and data in the expert's computer	ISDN connection between company and school, with one channel connecting two computers, and another channel connecting two videoconferencing units (desktop multimedia conferencing software could have been used, but projection equipment was not available in the school that could handle both video and computer data so that a class of students could see a wall-sized projection of what was on the computer screen)

other areas, of the use of point-to-point desktop multi-media conferencing for small-group tutoring. Among the examples are those mentioned in Table 8.5.

Table 8.5 gives just a taste of the new possibilities challenging educational technologists in many university settings. The conclusions from Eisenstadt's (1995) report summarizing the "Virtual Summer School" experience of the Open University in the UK are typical of conclusions from such summary reports (circa 1995; see Box 8.16).

Box 8.16

Help! for desktop conferencing

- We must lobby for ever-increasing bandwidth.
- We must radically improve both (i) the user interfaces and (ii) the underlying layers of communication tools
- We must obtain a better understanding of the nature of remote groupwork.
- We need to improve 'tutor leverage'(their ability to reach and influence more people), so that ...less fanatical tutors can deal with larger numbers of students in a comfortable fashion...('don't give me an eighth student or I'll collapse...') (Eisenstadt, 1995pp. 2–3)

BUT ALSO BENEFITS...

Arav's report (1995a) gives a detailed look at the pedagogical and organizational problems that occurred during his remote-classroom experience. Noteworthy aspects of his experience were that (a) many months were needed to set up the two live sessions, (b) organizational problems frustrated the planning, particularly in trying to fit the working time of the expert to the rostered time of the students in their secondary school, and (c) the educational technologist spent many long evenings of his own time when the classroom was not in use to work on the technical preparation for the lessons. These frustrations map onto the conclusions of Eisenstadt (1995) in Box 8.16.

But in Arav's case, as in most of the others reported in Table 8.5, balanced against these demands on the educational technologist were two clear, positive educational results: (d) the students were very enthusiastic, and (e) the students were able to have a relevant, real-world experience that they would not otherwise have had, and without leaving their classrooms.

Although desktop multi-media conferencing is complicated, it does have the simplicity of being accessible through one interface to the user. In the following section we look at a further sampling of environments for tele-learning which also integrate a variety of different components.

■ 8.4.4 THE DESIGN OF INTEGRATED ENVIRONMENTS FOR TELE-LEARNING

In Section 8.3.2 we identified different examples (*The Virtual Classroom, The Virtual Campus,* and *Télésité*) of network-based environments designed to support tele-learning. Educational technologists are involved in many such design activities. In this section we look at a sampling of network-based environments in more detail.

A practical way to differentiate research-and-design activities, such as we discuss in this section, from the service-oriented activities involving integrated on-line environments for tele-learning that are grouped in Chapter 9 relates to funding. If the funding of the activity has been incorporated into the on-going budget of the host organization then we see it as institutionalized support and discuss it in Chapter 9. If the funding is transitory, based on special-project or research-grant sources, we include it in this section. We group our examples here under the general headings of "support systems" and "specialized learning environments".

SUPPORT SYSTEMS

"Electronic performance support systems" (EPPSs) are emerging as a new type of software environment in business as well as learning contexts (see, for example the Special Issue of the journal *Innovations in Education and Training Internation*, Barker and Banerji, 1995; and also Collis and Verwijs, 1995). A number of educational technologists are involved in research and development in this area. For example, at the University of Twente we are visualizing EPPSs in terms of a "champagne-glass metaphor" (Collis and Verwijs, 1995), where support of the user's on-going learning needs occurs globally in three basic ways:

- Support for the user when s/he needs to browse for new ideas, the "bowl" of the champagne glass
- Support for the user when s/he needs to find specific tools and information for working out a particular solution, the stem of the champagne glass
- Support for the user when s/he can benefit from informed feedback with respect to his or her proposed solution, the base of the champagne glass.

When wide-area networking, particularly access to the Internet, is involved in these support aspects, EPPSs can be seen as environments for tele-learning. Many different examples of EPPSs to support tele-learning are now under development.

Internet interfaces as EPSSs

In a number of regions and countries, educational technologists are involved in the design of interfaces to collections of resources and services, many of which are accessible via the Internet while others may be accessible only through local bulletin boards. We have called these types of systems "CISOs" which stand for the Dutch words for "Communication and Information Systems for Education" and have participated in a number of research studies relating to their design and development. Some of these studies focus on the software by which teachers make contact to the on-line service (De Vries and Collis, 1993); others focus on teachers' reactions to the user interface of current versions of such on-line systems (for example, Collis, Van Holstein, Rikkerink and Woerts, 1994); and still others relate to design considerations for the user interfaces of such systems themselves (Collis, De Diana and Sterk, 1993). Table 8.6 summarizes some other examples of design projects for on-line learning-support environments in which educational technologists are involved.

In Table 8.6 we see just a sampling of the many innovative projects going on in 1995 relating to the design of an integrated on-line support environment relating to some form of learning need or setting. Most of these environments involve a combination of secure local resources and access to the Internet for a broader range of contacts and resources (only the *"StudieNet"* example in Table 8.6 is a totally closed environment with no Internet connectivity, but as its underlying commercial groupware system is now available via Internet access, environments such as StudieNet will soon not have to work through separate network connections).

Increasing opportunities for development of integrated on-line resources

As Internet access and environments to combine different forms of on-line services become easier to handle, we see an increasing volume of activity among educational technologists with respect to the design and investigation of environments such as those in Table 8.6. Tools are commercially available to support the development of client-server systems by which one can create an "on-line service" with features such as e-mail, discussion areas, file libraries, computer-conferencing tools, survey tools, multi-media file exchange, real-time chat and shared-workspace tools, and full Internet access (see http://www.gcomm.com for an example). These tools will allow more and more educational technologists to move into support-environment design and research, as the complexity of development of integrated on-line environments is rapidly being reduced through the commercial marketplace.

Table 8.6 A sample of projects for the development of on-line support environments for tele-learning

Project	Target group and type of tele-learning needs	Features
"The Houston Consortium of Urban Professional Development and Technology Schools" (US; Robin and Miller, 1995)	Teachers, faculty members and staff from a consortium of universities, schools, and educational-service agencies Remote access to multi-media resources for professional development	In addition to bundling access to a number of Internet tools through a user interface that is convenient to use via a variety of modems and connection possibilities, special focus on an "electronic filing cabinet" for local and project-specific information
"Teacher Education Internet Server" (US and UK, Bull, Cooper and Davis, 1994)	Teacher educators and student teachers Remote access to services to facilitate collaboration among teacher-education programs	Integrated tools for shared documents and files; for shared instructional materials, exemplary papers, and demonstration materials in multi-media formats; and support for moderated discussions
"Knowledge Integration Environment" (US, Bell, Davis and Linn, 1995)	Secondary-school students, exploring various scientific ideas Allow students access to remote experts as part of their learning process	Integrated tools, such as "Evidence Databases" in which students enter information both from the Internet and created by themselves; the "Discussion Tool" helping students to conduct structured, on-line discussions about their scientific ideas; and the "Student Notebook". helping students to organize their obtained evidence
"StudieNet" (NL, Schellekens, 1995)	Students enrolled in the Open University in The Netherlands, a distance-education institution offering more than 260 courses Support for learners whose only contact with the institution is via telephone lines	Through a common interface, based on a client-server workgroup environment, access to a wide variety of types of information, including detailed examples and exercise explanations for particular courses; also direct access to communication with one's tutor

"CURIE" (US, Meisner and Hoffman, 1995)	Teachers Inservice training related to a particular professional-development program	Through a specially designed user interface, access to a locally developed instructional-materials database, Internet search engines services, and contact to technical-support persons
"Teachers Curriculum Assistant" (US, Stahl, Sumner and Owen, 1995)	Teachers Professional development	Through a common user interface, access to a database of information about selected educational resources on the Internet, a "design workspace" where teachers can organize retrieved ideas into a lesson-plan format, and tools for discussion about the ideas
"Florida Learning Support Systems" (US, Gaede, 1995)	Teachers, students, parents, professional staff, "external clients" involved with education throughout Florida On-going learning and information needs	Through a specially designed frontend, users are routed to services and databases open to them; databases are local, statewide, and global

DESIGN OF SPECIALIZED TOOLS FOR TELE-LEARNING

In addition to projects that are focusing on the design of front-ends to integrated communication and information services for tele-learning, there are many other projects focused on more specific tools or environments. We noted some of these, such as tools for visualizing the interconnectiveness of contributions in an asynchronous discussion, in our discussion of research and development with respect to computer-conferencing software in Section 8.4.2, and the "Discussion" and "Notebook" tools in the *Knowledge Integration Environment*" (Bell, Davis and Linn, 1995) example in Table 8.6.

Other examples

Another such example is the *"NetSem"* environment developed at the University of Glasgow as part of the UK-wide TLTP Project for the stimulation of innovative uses of technology in higher-education teaching (Duffy, Arnold and Henderson, 1995). NetSem allows the integrated use of materials stored from seminar presentations, of contributions made to discussions via computer conferencing, and of various tools for communication and writing. This environment is being used to augment face-to-face instruction at the University of Glasgow, not to replace it.

A final example is *"NetFace"*, an on-line system with its associated user interface characteristics being used for support of distance students at the Monash University in Australia (Wood, 1995). *NetFace* is described as a teaching, learning, and assessment system; as an integrated CMC system; as an information-management system; and as tailorable groupware. By tailorable groupware is meant giving instructors the options to establish read, write, and create access for their classes, through the naming and creating of directories that will hold their class activities.

But examples that do not make some use of the World Wide Web as part of the design and research environment for innovative tele-learning support are becoming proportionally fewer in number compared to those that are based in a WWW environment. We turn next to an overview of WWW-related developments.

■ 8.4.5 INNOVATIVE DESIGN OF WWW SITES FOR TELE-LEARNING

During 1995 the amazing phenonmena of interest in the WWW also became important to many educational technologists involved in research into the design of innovative learning environments. In **Interface Sections 2, 3, 6 and 9** we give various overviews of some basic information about the World Wide Web as a tele-learning environment, and also some more specific insight into basic aspects of designing and constructing WWW pages. Throughout this book we have been showing examples of WWW sites already in use for tele-learning. In this section we give an overview of some of the explosion of innovative design and research relating to the World Wide Web occurring in 1995 among educational technologists.

INNOVATIONS IN LEARNING-SUPPORT FEATURES IN WWW ENVIRONMENTS

During 1995 the WWW has been extensively studied by educational technologists in terms of stretching its learning-support possibilities beyond that of offering a "home page", offering the capacity to add hyperlinks to a document, or serving as an organized reference resource for a collection of learning-support materials. All of the above features are educationally useful, but appear so routinely now (within one year!, see Interface 3) that educational technologists wishing to do innovative research and development with the WWW have to stretch beyond these "standard-practice" aspects. Some examples of this "stretching" that occurred during 1995 are summarized in Table 8.7.

Table 8.7 Innovations with regard to WWW functionality for tele-learning

Innovation	Source and location
Integrating educational simulations into WWW sites	Smeaton and Slater, 1995, UK http://www-interact.eng.cam.ac.uk/TLTP_EXHIB/DEMOS/index.html Ambach, Perrone and Repenning, 1995, US http://www.cs.colorado.edu/corrina/agent_remexp.html
Integrating newsgroup functionality into WWW sites for learning-related communications	*Environmental Management*, Finland (Taukojärvi and Jarvilehto, 1995) http://www.dipoli.hut.fi/TechNet/org/EEE/
Integration of educational games and demonstrations into WWW sites	*MegaMath* site, 1995, US http://www.c3.lanl.gov/mega-math
Integration of tutorial courseware into WWW sites	Maricopa Regional Education Center site, 1995, US http://www.mcli.dist.maricopa.edu/aaim/linear/L3.html (see also Marshall, 1995, UK, for a discussion of an authoring environment for such courseware)
Integration of different types of test items, as well as features such as user-selected hints and responses dependent on answer	Carleton University, Canada, 1995 http://www.civeng.carleton.ca:80/~holtz/tut/doc/doc.html
Integrating case scenarios in WWW sites	Ward, 1995, UK (contact: r.d.ward@hud.ac.uk)
Integration of "thought paths" to reinforce linkages in a WWW site relative to learning goals	Whalley, 1995, UK (contact: b.whalley@qub.ac.uk)
Using the WWW to support lectures, with handouts, complementary slide packs, and course-evaluation questionnaires	Browning and Williams, 1995, UK http://www.gly.bris.ac.uk/www/comp/network/tasks.html
Learner-oriented agent tools for ("intelligent") searching and monitoring of learners as they search	Kirby, McAndres, Kilgour, Taylor and Mayes, 1995, UK (contact: icbl@heriot-watt.ac.uk)
Adding "virtual instrumentation" to a WWW site, such as "The Virtual Microscope"	Open University, 1995, UK http://kmi.open.ac.uk/
Presenting a "hyper-book" using the metaphor of a question-answer conversation	Institute for Learning Sciences, 1995, US http://www.ils.nwu.ehu/e_for_e
Integrating an intelligent tutoring system into a WWW site	Nakabayshi et al, 1995, Japan (contact: naka@nttaip.min.ntt.jp)

EXAMPLES OF NEW DIRECTIONS FOR WWW ENVIRONMENTS

While Table 8.7 indicates many innovative functionalities being added to WWW sites specifically in support of tele-learning, there are even more broadscale development projects in which educational technologists are involved that further stretch the (1995) limits, both technically and of the imagination, of WWW applicability in learning. Three such examples will be mentioned here: EDEC for courseware distribution; Answer Web for utilization of learners'questions as learning resources; and Hyper-G, a new network-information system seen by some as the "next generation" of the 1995 WWW.

Courseware distribution via the WWW

The "EDEC Distribution System" is being designed as a WWW-based environment to distribute courseware across eight universities in the UK for evaluation and to control the review and revision process evolving from this evaluation. Members of the eight-university consortium will be able not only to have protected access to a collection of courseware and associated documentation, but also to the common set of development tools that have been used for developing the courseware. In addition, members have access to a common set of tools for evaluating the courseware and for distributing their evaluative comments. All of this is integrated via a WWW system, where a public-domain browser has been modified with a customized helper application and run-time versions of development tools using a customized installer. For more information, contact A. Hartley-Smith at: `hartley@fs5.ee.umist.ac.uk` or see:

EDEC Distribution System
`http://edec.ee.umist.ac.uk`

Parallel in some ways to the EDEC Distribution System is the WEST site (for Web Educational Support Tools), a multi-media learning environment designed to support the delivery of course materials over the Internet using the WWW. The system provides tools for course providers, tutors, and students including built-in messaging, electronic submission and processing of student exercises, course material that can be tailored to various student characteristics, and support for video conferencing. Information about this WWW site and its tools can be found at:

Web Educational Support Tools
`http://www.west.ie/home.html`

Learning from the questions of others

At Herriot-Watt University in Scotland interesting work is in progress on the "Answer Web" application for WWW environments (Mayes and Neilson, 1995). In this application, the WWW environment is used to support a database of "frequently asked questions" in a course, a database that "grows" organically as the course continues. This happens through the organization of questions in a hierarchically branching "tree structure" through which a learner moves when she, too, has a question. If she traverses a branch of the tree without finding a question similar to her own, she can leave the new question as an e-mail message that is then sent to an "expert" assigned to the corresponding portion of the course. If the expert believes the question to be relevant to others in the course, he posts it in the appropriate place in the "answer web". Otherwise the expert can send a private message to the questioner, to deal with the answer either by sending the questioner to another location in the "answer web" or just supplying an isolated answer.

Hyper-G

Hyper-G is a new (1995) "multi-user, multi-protocol, structured, hypermedia information system which runs as a client-server application on the Internet" (Andres, Kappe and Maurer, 1995, p. 3). Under development by a team of computer scientists and educational technologists in Austria, the system is compatible with current-generation WWW protocols, but adds many new aspects such as being designed specifically for multi-lingual use and new sorts of visualized navigation tools as well as support for three-dimensional visualizations of collections of information. The educational implications of this new system are under study at a number of educational-technology centres, and the system received a high degree of attention at the *1995 Educational Multimedia and Hypermedia Conference* in Graz, Austria (Maurer and Schneider, 1995). For more information, see:

Hyper-G
http://info.iicm.tu-graz.ac.at

OTHER EXAMPLES OF WWW INNOVATION

The examples are accumulating by the day in 1995 of innovative research and design work in which educational researchers are opening up the WWW for new forms of tele-learning. Box 8.17 shows some examples.

Box 8.17

Other examples of WWW innovation for tele-learning, circa 1995

WWW-based "open-learning environments" are being constructed and tested–
see, for example, Wolf, 1995, Germany
`http://www.abw.uni-giessen.de/solew3.html`

LISTSERVs are becoming available for open discussion of issues in WWW courseware development
contact one such list, maintained in Canada, at:
`LISTSERV@UNB.CA`,
Subscribe WWWDEV your-first-name your-last-name

Careful analyses are being made of the time and talents needed to convert existing courses to WWW delivery
see Oscheske, Klus, Stremikis and Hoyman, 1995, US
`http://epdwww.engr.wisc.edu`

Continuously adapted student models are being built into WWW sites so that "adaptive sequencing" can occur
see Brusilovsky, 1995, Russia (contact: `plb@plb.icsti.su`)

But, of course, not all innovation in tele-learning environments is WWW based; we complete this section on innovative design activities for tele-learning by considering a sample of complex environments involving a combination of various hardware and software components and even the rooms and buildings to contain them, that are now being researched by teams that include educational technologists.

■ 8.4.6 DESIGNING COMPLEX HARDWARE/SOFTWARE ENVIRONMENTS FOR TELE-LEARNING

A number of educational technologists are engaged in the design and implementation of complex hardware/software environments for tele-learning. In this section we look at some examples, including systems that involve the integration of existing equipment and systems which have grown to include rooms and facilities and institutional organizations as well as tele-learning technologies.

SOFTWARE-HARDWARE INTEGRATION

Increasingly, educational technologists are attempting to integrate existing resources to support tele-learning in their institutions. One set of applications relates to support of real-time instructor–learner interaction, not through the scenario of remote groups interacting with the instructor through television-type technologies, videoconferencing, or desktop multi-media conferencing, but rather, through other sorts of hardware–software combinations. In some cases, these combinations can be used to enhance instruction in face-to-face institutions as well as distributed settings.

Tools to improve real-time lecturing

In one such example, Pilon, Raymond, and Raymond (1995) describe a computer-aided classroom "lecturing and attending software package" which involves a set of tools to improve communication between an instructor and students, such as to enable them to interact more effectively during lectures and to help students to take more-relevant notes. In this (Canadian) example, the computers of the learners and of the instructor are all connected through an Ethernet LAN with the possibility of connection to distant sites through a router. The instructor's computer is attached to a large-screen projection system, allowing video clips to be projected or the instructor to make some particular points in a whole-class, lecture-type format.

Innovative in Pilon, Raymond, and Raymond's work are six software tools that run simultaneously on the learners' and instructor's computers. These tools are: the note-taking tool, the question tool, the fill-the-slide tool, the quiz tool, the monitoring tool, and the head-to-head tool. The function of each of these tools is explained in Box 8.18.

These tools can do much to address familiar concerns in television-type tele-learning with regard to learner engagement and the handling of learner questions. The fact that they are also powerful tools for the face-to-face classroom where learners are sitting at computers is a good example of how tele-learning innovation can transcend application settings.

Other real-time lecture support

There are many other examples. Baloian, Hoppe and Kling (1995), in Germany, describe their "COSOFT" environment, in which the contents of a live-board presentation can be connected to learners' computers, and a variety of tools, similar in some respects to those of Pilon, Raymond and Raymond in Box 8.18, can be employed. They refer to their system as "teachware". Eschelbeck (1995), in Austria, describes an "interactive multi-media communication system", again with similar

---

Box 8.18

Tele-learning tools for improvement of the lecture situation

Note-taking tool—The instructor's notes or slides (perhaps in the form of a computer-based presentation) appear on one side of the computer screens with a notepad on the other side. Learners can make real-time notes directly on the notepad. These can be studied later, in association with the instructor's slides, and can also be shared with learners who were not present.

Question tool— Rather than learners raising their hands to ask a question (either in the face-to-face setting or distant setting), the learner enters a question into the Question Tool. The question, labelled with the name of the learner who sent it, is relayed immediately to the instructor, who can decide when to answer it, during the lecture or personally after the lecture.

Fill-the-slide tool—Learners receive partly filled in versions of the instructor's slides at the time the instructor is discussing the slide. The instructor asks the learners to fill in blanks on the slide, as a way of testing their comprehension.

Quiz tool—The instructor can offer multiple-choice questions during the lecture, and get immediate feedback from the learners' answers as to how well the learners understand what is being discussed.

Monitoring tool—The instructor can switch to the screen of any learner in the group to monitor directly what the learner is doing, perhaps during the use of the Quiz Tool or the Fill-the-Slide Tool.

Head-to-head tool—The instructor can decide to send the contents of his or her own screen to an individual learner's screen, or can send one learner's screen to all other learner's screens.
(Pilon, Raymond, & Raymond, 1995)

---

functionalities, although with different tools available through the instructor's and learners' user interfaces. Maly, Overstreet, Abdel-Wahab, and Gupta (1994) extend this sort of approach to include an integration of television-type lectures to groups at a distance, but with those groups all having access to computers in order to send and receive their interactive exchanges with the distant instructor.

Interesting in all of these is that tele-learning support for lecturing is as relevant in the face-to-face setting as in the distributed setting.

INTEGRATION INCLUDING ROOMS AND FACILITIES

There are also examples of educational technologists being involved in the design of environments to support tele-learning where the environments involve not only hardware and software but also innovative physical settings as well. One example of this is the "IBM Writing Project" at the University of Florida, in which five classrooms have been created, each holding 30 learners, so that the integration of the use of computers, hypermedia, in-class electronic conferencing, cooperative writing and revision tools, and access to the Internet and remote libraries can all be facilitated within the teaching areas. For more information, see:

IBM Writing Project
URL http://www.ucet.ufl.edu:80/writing/

The "learning theaters" at the University of Maryland are similar examples (Shneiderman, Alavi, Norman and Borkowski, 1995), see information at:

Learning Theaters, at the University of Maryland, US
URL http://www.cs.umd.edu/projects/hci/

and

URL http://www.umcp.umd.edu/TeachTech/ Welcome.html

Another example is the TEA³M Consortium Project in Texas (Hirumi, Harmon and Palumbo, 1994), through which a "Teacher Technology Exploration Center" has been established. The Center includes a model "classroom of the future" in which full (inter)networking capabilities are available, not only for Internet access but for asynchronous and synchronous conferencing. Teacher-training sessions, university graduate seminars, and workshops are held in the room. A "showcase arena" room allows teachers to try out various tele-learning environments. A resource library has on-line connections. A video production studio serves as a receiving point and distribution site for video-conferencing sessions, television-type tele-learning via satellite or microwave, and closed-circuit television. An on-line information service will allow the outside community to be informed about events in the Center.

■ 8.5 CONCLUSION: A DESIGN EXPLOSION

The intention of this chapter is that the reader feels overwhelmed, because that is a good word to describe the vibrant area of innovative design for tele-learning and the exciting work being done by educational technologists throughout the world in this area. In this chapter we have represented some of the range of "behind the scenes" work in which educational technologists are involved relating to tele-learning. In this chapter, educational technologists have been engaged as course designers and as designers of innovative tele-learning tools and environments. In the next chapter we bring the educational technologist more in direct contact with the field. Sometimes this contact is through the provision of support and services; other times it is through being in a teaching situation him- or herself, teaching others, particularly other educational technologists, about tele-learning.

COLLABORATIVE LEARNING AND DISTRIBUTED GROUPS

Interest in **collaborative work and learning** among people who are not always in face-to-face contact with each other is coming from many directions:

- As a step in the progression of interest in cooperative learning activities that has been well established in K-12 education for many decades, first with **small groups** in the classroom, then with small groups still in the classroom but using a computer in a cooperative way, and now with groups of children still in the classroom but collaborating with partners at a distance, via tele-learning technologies
- As a **learning strategy** in higher-education, especially for students in disciplines where working in small groups will be part of their professional experience. These students are likely to be at the same campus but wish to make use of tele-learning technologies to work together asynchronously between opportunities to work together face-to-face
- As a **workplace-learning** strategy in companies and offices: employees distributed around different locations work with each other on problem-solving tasks via tele-learning technologies
- As professionals **networking** together to learn from each other and occasionally to collaborate on a problem or project, while at a distance
- As people who have in some way found each other as a "**virtual community**" through interest in a common theme

CONVERGENCE OF INTERESTS

There are rich lines of research relating to each of these perspectives, often based in different disciplines and too often unknown outside their own disciplines, even though parallel issues are under investigation.

In school settings and (less frequently) in higher education collaborative learning or cooperative learning are developing into a loosely defined area called "**CSCL**" (computer-supported collaborative learning). In businesses and companies, a long history of study of group decision support and group meeting support is developing into a focus on groupware and distributed groups. In human-computer interaction studies a multi-disciplinary interest has developed around "**CSCW**" (computer-supported cooperative work) and its group tools and interfaces.

Tele-learning technologies and applications are in the intersection area of these interests. This can be in the context of the small, well-defined group with a distinct learning task, or in the context of the larger, less-well defined group involved as a virtual community with one another. In both broad categories we can speak of **"tele-collaboration"** and its **support tools**.

DIMENSIONS OF TELE-COLLABORATION SUPPORT TOOLS

A number of dimensions are being studied with respect to tele-collaboration support tools, including:

- Same-time or different-time interaction?
- Same-place or different-place interaction?
- Structured or free interaction (constrained or unconstrained input)?
- Tools for structured interactions, such as voting systems?
- Tools for free interaction such as shared work spaces?
- Group-structure issues: Who initiates, who waits, how is turn-taking handled, who talks to who? who concludes?
- Distributed or centrally stored shared resources?
- Persistent or ephemeral discussions, captured, stored and re-addressed or the opposite?
- Private vs group vs private interactions and decisions?
- Privileges for control of group resources, during production or when stored: What procedures are there for determining who can revise a common document?

And in addition to this list (representing projects underway related to each of the issues), there are more global categories of support needs:

- Support for the task itself: **Shared resources**, access to appropriate remote resources and specialists; tools for drafting documents while at a difference from one another
- Support for the **social maintenance** of the group, to support a sense of "being there while I am still here", of **"tele-presence"**, and to support the development of group rapport and the minimalization of group discord and disruption
- Support for the project **management** of the group, such as maintenance of a group calendar, of common archives, of common agenda materials for distributed or face-to-face meetings

All these are being studied, from many perspectives: improving work efficiency, improving cross-cultural communication, strengthening the organization as a "learning community".

TOOLS FOR TELE-COLLABORATION

Which tele-learning tools and environments can be employed for tele-collaboration support? At least the following:

At the technologies level
Audio-conferencing
Audio-graphics conferencing with
  whiteboard-type graphics
Audio-conferencing with a shared
  workspace
Video-conferencing
Desktop multi-media conferencing
Desktop multi-media conferencing with
  application sharing
Computer-conferencing
E-mail

At the instrumentation level: For real-time collaboration

With audio-graphics conferencing and a shared workplace, or with desktop multi-media conferencing with application sharing:

- Tools to indicate and manage turn-taking (to avoid cursor wars)
- Tools to provide either freehand (pixel based) or object-based drawing capacity
- Specialized tools such as **concept-mapping** tools or outlining tools

Tools to improve the realism of video and audio transmission, such as "fly-on-the-wall" cameras
Tools for **collaborative visualization** of discussion streams and topics

At the instrumentation level: For asynchronous collaboration

Tools for **shared annotation** of documents

Tools for entry and retrieval of items from a **shared data base**

Groupware tools to improve management of incoming messages, of shared planning, of common access to spreadsheet and graphics tools

Tools for full-text searching of stored messages and for reorganization of the messages from computer conferencing in one's personal workspace.

BEING A VIRTUAL COMMUNITY

While the CSCW/CSCL research is typically focused on small groups who know each other in a professional capacity and are working on a specific task while at a distance, there is a parallel stream of interest in more loosely defined groups who could be called **"virtual communities"**. Virtual communities are rooted more in freedom and spontaneity of expression than in task performance, and tend to focus more on socio-psychological aspects of communication and group bonding, such as:

- The global community as a **metaphor**; tele-collaboration leading to a new definition of community based on mutual interests rather than geography or circumstance. We can "customize our social contacts from fragmented communities"[1]
- Tele-collaboration as an **engine of social relations** and the space in which the relations occur, occurring in a socially produced space in which people move and live.
- **Mobility** in terms of moving within the social space without moving physically; Mobility in terms of terms of new definitions of "meet" and "face" that can liberate those who meet from barriers related to status, age, or personal circumstance.
- **Sharing of information** as the currency of tele-collaborative social relations....

Tele-learning intersects these worlds as well.

[1] Jones, S. G. (1995). Understanding community in the information age. In S. G. Jones (Ed.) *Cybersociety: Computer mediated communication and community* (pp. 10–35). Thousand Oaks, CA: Sage Publications.

9 Tele-learning and the educational technologist: providing service and leadership

In Chapter 8 we observed educational technologists "behind the scenes" with tele-learning—designing and developing the courses, materials, tools, and environments that others will use. In this chapter, we see the educational technologist involved more directly with his or her public: as an advisor, someone who can systematically be a source of information and experience, someone who serves and supports those involved in tele-learning in a direct and personal way. Sometimes this support is very practical, other times it takes place through being able to work together with practitioners to translate research findings and theory so that they are closely applied to a particular practical situation. Educational technologists are fulfilling all these roles with respect to tele-learning, but they are also visible in two other broad ways: as educators themselves, teaching others about tele-learning, and as visionaries and reflectors, interpreting experience and predicting the future to their audiences. We look at all these roles in this chapter.

▪ **9.1 Serving the field: providing direct support and information**

▪ **9.2 Serving the field: supporting practice through implementation research**

▪ **9.3 Teaching teachers about tele-learning**

▪ **9.4 Educational technologists as teachers of educational technologists**

Objectives

After this chapter you should be able to:

- Be aware of a variety of ways in which educational technologists supply direct support to those involved in tele-learning: decision makers, suppliers of products and equipment, local technical-support persons, instructors, and learners

- Identify a variety of ways in which educational technologists bring information about tele-learning to the field:
  Counseling and supporting individuals
  Working in media and computing service centres
  Through professional organizations

- Describe some key ways in which educational technologists are translating research results into practical application with respect to the implementation of tele-learning

- Give examples of how educational technologists are involved with applying tele-learning to enrich and expand the pre-service and inservice education of teachers

- Identify the current level of training about tele-learning that educational technologists themselves receive, and that they are providing for their own students

- Be aware of some innovations in the education of educational technologists with respect to tele-learning and consider their broad-scale applicability

■ 9.1 SERVING THE FIELD: PROVIDING DIRECT SUPPORT AND INFORMATION

Many educational technologists are occupied in the direct support of those involved in tele-learning, responding to their needs, and anticipating those needs through the provision of services in a variety of ways. In Sections 9.1.1–9.1.4 we look at various categories of such service provision, ranging from personal and specific, to field-wide and general.

■ 9.1.1 SUPPORTING INDIVIDUALS ENCOUNTERING TELE-LEARNING

Educational technologists are frequently involved in consulting and advising roles with respect to tele-learning. Such roles require not only that the educational technologist be up-to-date and well informed about technical developments relating to tele-learning, but also can supply specific examples that are relevant to the local situation. We look briefly at some examples of educational technologists as support to decision makers, to product suppliers, to local technical personnel, to instructors, and to learners as they personally encounter tele-learning.

SUPPORTING DECISION MAKERS

Decision makers often consult the educational technologist for practical advice, for example, in preparation for visits from competing technology service providers. Hakes (1995) gives a good overview of how educational technologists were involved in pilot testing of competing point-to-point compressed video systems being considered by a college of education for implementation of compressed interactive video tele-learning to remote sites.

From this pilot testing, the educational technologists were able to advise the decision makers that certain frequently held assumptions about the compressed-video systems were largely incorrect: for example, that classrooms must be refigured as television studios with special lighting and that special technicians will be required to operate the equipment. More positively, the specialists were able to provide the decision makers with specific questions and categories of selection criteria to apply when meeting with candidate vendors. Such categories of selection criteria, plus samples of the sorts of questions and language to use with vendors, include those shown in Box 9.1.

Box 9.1

Points of consideration when making a decision about a compressed video system

- Multi-point capabilities: *Can you cascade (hook together) multipoint control units to handle larger conferences?*
- Upgrades: *Are a certain number of upgrades guaranteed or will you have to purchase them? Are they software, firmware or hardware upgrades?*
- Peripherals: *Can you interface a computer with the system to interactively work with the software or conduct software training? Can you use a lavaliere microphone?*
- Audio: *Does the product provide good echo cancellation and support diagnostics which may be activated each time the system is moved to a new location?*
- Training: *Is training a hidden cost or can it be provided at no charge as part of the contract negotiations? If it is provided, must the purchaser pay travel costs to attend training sessions at the vendor's headquarters?* (from, or adapted from, Hakes, 1995, pp. 104–107)

There are many other examples of how educational technologists can help the organizational decision maker with respect to decisions about video-conferencing and compressed video for instruction, see for example, Box 9.2.

Box 9.2

Helping the decision maker with choices about video-conferencing and compressed video for instruction

- In Finland, educational technologists at the Centre for Educational Technology at the University of Oulu have pilot tested basic equipment for two-way compressed video-conferencing using satellite channels and from their experiences have delivered observations and recommendations to their institutional decision makers (Hiltunen, Sjöman and Martinmäki, 1994; contact Jukka Hiltunen at hiltunen@oyt.oulu.fi)
- In the US, Sachs (1995a, b) consolidated his experiences at North Virginia Community College and with the Virginia Distance Education Network Task Force to identify critical factors in compressed-video use
- In Europe, the ISSUE Consortium, representing national telecommunications organizations in the UK, Italy, The Netherlands, Finland, Spain, and France, has issued a detailed set of guidelines for user organizations about the selection of video-conferencing systems and services for tele-learning (ISSUE, 1995). They itemize advantages and disadvantages of a series of decision alternatives, such as the choice of public or private equipment and networking; built-in, roll-around, or desktop options; bandwidth and codec choices; and choices between point-to-point or multi-point.

The educational technologist, with practical and technical experience, can provide a valuable service by helping the local decision maker anticipate such questions, and have the correct vocabulary when discussing the questions with competing vendors. But, as the above examples illustrate, this service must be delivered in an efficient way, with well-organized points, and with an awareness of the information needs of the decision maker, as well as the appropriate language to use with those involved in the decision (see also Chapter 7). With such a rapidly changing field, this is a challenge.

LIAISON BETWEEN PROVIDERS AND THE FIELD

Another way in which educational technologists are directly engaged in support of parties involved in tele-learning is to work in a liaison capacity between parties providing services or products for tele-learning, and those in the field who may use those products. As an example, The ISSUE Consortium guidelines (1995) mentioned in Box 9.2 also contain detailed advice to video-conferencing service providers as they prepare to interact with decision makers in educational settings. This advance ranges from how to portray video-conferencing, how to help organizations prepare for video-conferencing, what sort of options to offer to organizations, what ergonomic considerations are important in field settings, and what levels and types of user support should be offered.

There are similar examples for every variety of tele-learning technology. For example, we saw in Chapter 7 how Newman, Bernstein, and Reese (1992) provided carefully organized guidelines for school decision makers with respect to network configurations and connecting to external networks such as the Internet. Lee (1992) gives a detailed view of the liaison services of two major UK broadcasting authorities with respect to educational decision makers but also for teachers, learners, and parents with respect to educational-broadcasting offerings. He notes that although this liaison is increasingly occurring through fax and e-mail, "more effective communication and accurate reporting (of field reaction) through intermeshing forms of information technology" (p. 195) are needed. Lee's concluding comments, although made in connection with television-video instruction, are equally applicable to other forms of tele-learning:

> ...*Good and effective liaison will need to continue at every level to maintain the knowledge and insights that have contributed to the excellence and relevance of the product. The work of liaison is essential to quality and to progress, its assessments and its contact networks varying from phase to phase, subject to subject and region to region provide a vital flow of information...* (p. 195).

DIRECT SUPPORT TO THE TELE-LEARNER: STUDY CENTRES

As well as supporting decision makers and suppliers, many educational technologists are occupied with direct support of tele-learners themselves. Sometimes this occurs in the framework of a broader set of support activities that are offered through a regional or national service agency; we discuss these in the Section 9.1.2. Other times, however, the educational technologist is specifically employed in the support of tele-learners, not as a tutor but more generally concerned with their study and learning needs.

The traditional distance-teaching institutions have long recognized the value of local, human support for learner needs. One way that this is organized is through the establishment of local "study centres" to which learners enrolled in distance-education courses can go for general support, and in the case of tele-learning, for access to specialized equipment that would not be otherwise available to them at home or in the workplace.

A major organization of such centres has occurred in Europe under the name of the EuroStudy Centres. Over 875 study centres operating in Europe to support students involved in distance-teaching universities were inventoried (EADTU, 1994b). Based on this, a plan was developed whereby a subset of these study centres would be uniformly equipped and connected to one another as "EuroStudy Centres". The goal of this network is to facilitate learner mobility throughout Europe and also to stimulate standardization of technical equipment and support expectations among the centres (we have discussed this in Chapter 7).

How to provide such personal service to tele-learners is the task of a number of educational technologists.

■ 9.1.2 SUPPORTING TELE-LEARNING FROM WITHIN A REGIONAL OR NATIONAL SERVICE CENTRE

In the examples in Section 9.1.1, the educational technologists involved were specifically focused on tele-learning support. In practice, however, what more often happens is that an existing support agency, in which educational technologists are employed in a variety of service functions, finds itself expanding its service range to accommodate emerging needs relating to tele-learning. We look at a few such examples in this section. First, however, it is useful to review some general aspects of "media centres" (as one common name) in terms of working places for educational technologists.

MEDIA CENTRES

"Media centres" have long been established at post-secondary educational institutions and also to support the school sector at either a regional or national level. Johnson (1994) in a review of media centres in the US, noted that diversity was the norm rather than the exception for such centres: diversity in name; in institutional placement (in 1990, most often to the Director of the Library; see also McConeghy and McConeghy, 1990); and in role designations for its staff. In general, school-district media centres focus on service to the classroom teacher, post-secondary non-university media centres typically share facilities with the library staff, and in universities media centres tend to be separate operations reporting generally to an academic administrator.

Television-video tele-learning ⇔ media-centre staff

Particularly relevant to tele-learning are the findings that, in media centres in US colleges or universities at least, 64% provided satellite and/or tele-conference reception for "distance education", and 34% were involved in program origination and distribution, either by themselves or in collaboration with another campus department. At the same time, however, there is little attention being reported to networking, which is seen as the domain of computing services. Media centres in general and particularly in North America seem to have developed out of audio-visual roots separate from those from which campus-wide network services have developed.

Computer-based tele-learning ⇔ computer centre staff

Albright (1994) supports this dichotomy between television-background media centres and computer-background computing services centres in his observation that in 1992 only about 20% of the members of the (US) Consortium of College and University Media Centers even had e-mail addresses.

⇒ Different support centres for tele-learning

This division of responsibility between more-traditional media centres, with an educational technology background, and computing-service centres, with a computer-science background, occurs in many countries. The phenomenon is important to the support and growth of tele-learning within educational institutions; traditional educational media centres in many countries tend to equate tele-learning with television-type instruction and provide good leadership in this direction. But when tele-learning involves computer networking, leadership is coming more from computer-services groups, often without a professional base in educational technology.

Convergence in support?

With the growing convergence of video- and computer technologies, in theory it should be that the two streams of expertise come together to offer a range of integrated support for tele-learning, but in general this has not yet occurred. Even when the technology is converging, such as with desktop multi-media conferencing, the computer aspects of desktop multi-media systems frequently are dominant, with support coming from computing services rather than from media centres.

But times will change. While Albright, in 1994, still needs to explain e-mail and basic Internet tools to instructional media-centre managers, he also notes that many media centres are now establishing their own LANs and WAN connectivity. And the rapid appearance of World Wide Web pages coming out of "media centres" during 1995 shows that the educational technologists in those centres are more and more representing both aspects of tele-learning.

ON-LINE SUPPORT SERVICES IN HIGHER EDUCATION

Given this background, let us look at a sampling of examples of how support-service groups with an instructional-media background or in which educational technologists are involved in various higher-education settings are expanding their services to include support for computer-based forms of tele-learning. Table 9.1 gives some examples.

As Table 9.1 shows, the most visible way in which educational technologists involved in university-centered learning-support services are extending themselves into tele-learning appears to be via the WWW, either through its use as an information and communication channel through which the distinct voice and service orientation of the support service can be visible, or as an object of service-support in itself.

The Maricopa Center for Learning and Instruction example, noted in Table 9.1, is an excellent example. Faculty at the community colleges served by the Maricopa Center, through the services of the Center, have produced many interesting and innovative examples of WWW-based instructional environments. Some of these can themselves be visited from the Maricopa home page.

Maricopa Center for Learning and Instruction, AZ
```
URL http://www.mcli.dist.maricopa.edu/TL/other.html.
```

Cooperation in support

Gradually, partnerships are starting to emerge among computing-services specialists and instructional media-centre specialists in terms of the support of tele-learning in their institutions. Often, such partnerships emerge through the

Table 9.1 Examples of media-center support related to network-based tele-learning in higher-education

Institution	Type of support activity	Further information
University of Wales, UK	Use of WWW for a variety of instructional needs	Holyfield & Liber, 1995 (contact: iss038@bangor.ac.uk)
MITN, University of Michigan, US	Maintenance of a WWW-based directory of network resources, satellite-broadcast resources, and desktop video tools for tele-learning	http://www.mitn.msu.edu/distance.html
TECFA, University of Geneva, Switzerland	Maintenance of multi-media, multi-national WWW-based directories of services and software; special attention to AI, multi-media, computer-related developments and projects for tele-learning; also a MUD page	http://tecfa.unige.ch/info-edu-comp.html#www_intro
Educational Technology Services, University of Pennsylvania, US	Maintenance of WWW page with self-study learning material about using the WWW; also support of on-line seminars and projects ("The Virtual Language Lab", etc.)	http://ccat.sas.upenn.edu/ETS_home.html
CNAM, France	Maintenance of WWW page with multi-media cultural and technical resources ("virtual museums"), offered in French and English	http://www.cnam.fr/ (note: the site offers an overview of visitor activity; thousands of persons enter per day and the sites containing collections of art in the virtual museums are most popular)
EduTech Institute, Georgia Tech University, US	Laboratory for investigating new software and types of learning, focus on multi-media, networking, and intelligent systems Maintenance of WWW site with links to projects and events in the Institute	http://www.cc.gatech.edu/cogsci/edutech/edutech.html

Centre for Interactive Computer Based Learning, Herriot-Watt University, Scotland	Support of a variety of innovative projects for the innovation of university teaching Maintenance of WWW sites for general information, on-line journal and newsletter, and dissemination point for information about the more than 70 projects in the UK in the TLTP Initiative	`http://www.icbl.hw.ac.uk/` For the newsletter and journal, `http://www.icbl.hw.ac.uk/ray/alt.html` For the UK-wide dissemination: `http://www.icbl.hw.ac.uk/ltdi`
Maricopa Center for Learning and Instruction, Arizona, US	Maintenance of WWW site, support of "think-tanks", tutorials and support for faculty creation of their own WWW pages for instructional support, on-line publication about educational technology	`http://www.mcli.dist.maricopa.edu/homePage.html`

framework of a special project or initiative, with fixed-term funding outside the normal budgets of the individual support groups involved. Box 9.3 shows two such examples. The transition of such projects into integrated, regular-budget support provision is, however, still not often seen.

OTHER SUPPORT CENTRES

It is not only post-secondary institutions that are extending their range of support services to involve new forms of tele-learning, but also agencies focused at regional training needs, and at national, and international service levels.

Box 9.3

Partnerships for tele-learning support

"Project Tele-Learning", University of Twente, The Netherlands. Partnership of computing services, the Faculty of Informatics, different educational support services and inter-faculty institutes and the Faculty of Educational Science and Technology for stimulation of tele-learning in university teaching
URL `http://www.nic.utwente.nl/oc/oc.htm`

"Colorado Education Online", US. A collaboration between the School of Education and the Computing Services Department, supporting a network using an adaptation of the FirstClass computer conferencing software which links education professionals, students, and parents within and outside the university
URL `http://www.cudenver.edu/lsherry/edschool/CEO.html`

Clearinghouses and brokers

A number of agencies or organizations are now appearing that could be described as clearinghouses or brokers, to help bring together tele-learning partners or services and clients. One such example is the Academy for Curriculum Leadership and Technology (ACLT; Mollgaard and Sides-Gonzales, 1995). ACLT was founded by a grant by a private foundation and is housed at the University of Montana's Faculty of Education. The principle user of ACLT's broker services is the "Achievement Television Network" (ATV) in California. ATV describes itself as producing satellite-delivered broadcasting and video-conferencing for students at 30,000 sites in the US. ACLT's role in this partnership is to write lesson materials to accompany this programming. ACLT organizes phone-in questions from schools, and also maintains a location on a commercial network service provider in the US through which students subscribed to this network can send e-mail questions.

Regional training needs

The support of the training needs of small and medium-sized companies is an important challenge for many regional authorities. In the Valencian region of Spain, for example, IMPIVA, the Institute of Small and Medium-Sized Enterprises of the Valencian Community, is responsible for coordinating the training needs of companies in its region with the training initiatives of 13 technological training institutions and four business and innovation centres in which training-resource centres are also located. Abel (1995) describes the strategies being used to harmonize this training situation, with WAN-connectivity of the training-resource centres as a core infrastructure.

National and international support agencies

Many countries have national support agencies focused on some aspect of technology that can be used for tele-learning. The extension of these services to include tele-learning can be regularly seen. As two examples, the NISS (National Information Services and Systems) has been in operation since 1988 in the UK as a gateway to a broad range of worldwide information services relevant to education (Lafford, 1994). It also supports, through a network service and via a common user interface, discussion-groups, different search and retrieval tools customized for Internet access, and electronic publishing services. Thus, reflecting its information-services background, NISS is moving in the same way that integrated communication and information services are developing in support of many other educational sectors.

In contrast, the NIAM (a national agency for audio-visual media in The Netherlands), with a 50-year-old background of instructional television, films, filmstrips, audiotapes, videotapes, and radio broadcasting, only began to formally support the exploration of "new media" in 1990. It has defined new media as interactive video, CD-ROM, and on-line information bases. However, beyond a pilot project involving school access of on-line (tele-text) databases, the NIAM remains strongly rooted in the television-type of tele-learning and has had no real contact with the many computer-based initiatives for tele-learning in The Netherlands. The NIAM is the representative of The Netherlands in the International Council for Educational Media, in which 30 lands participate. This situation is an example of how the traditional conception of educational technologists as "media people" who think of tele-learning as television-type instruction can be slow to change, despite the mushrooming of WWW pages out of media centres in 1995.

OTHER EXAMPLES OF INNOVATIVE SUPPORT

There are many other examples of innovative support strategies coming out of service agencies in response to new forms of tele-learning. Many of these services are being provided by educational technologists. A final set of examples is given in Box 9.4.

WORKING ON THE FRONT LINES...

And, not only are educational technologists busy in service agencies with the support of tele-learning, an increasing number are directly employed in the delivery of tele-learning, and in user support to accompany this delivery. Some of these agencies are directly involved in network-access provision (see Chapter 7), now spreading to provision through broadband cable (projects in The Netherlands and the UK are supplying Internet to homes and schools via already existing cabling). Others are involved in the support of multi-site training networks, such as Funline in Germany, that connects 140 regional training centres via ISDN networks to a central server which trainees can access for downloading of appropriate multi-media courseware. Other national delivery and support agencies include those noted in Chapter 6 and the sample shown in Box 9.5.

Thus, just as educational technologists involved in the "behind the scenes" design of courses and environments for tele-learning are busy being innovative (as we saw in Chapter 8), educational technologists "on the front lines" of service provision are also exploring new possibilities for providing support for tele-learn-

Box 9.4

Further examples of innovative support for tele-learning by educational technologists working in service and support capacities

The *European Children's Television Centre*, located in Athens, Greece, sponsors a variety of projects under its overall orientation: "The Electronic Media in the Hands of Children".

The TERC in Boston, US, supports an online communication- and information service to support its work in innovating science and mathematics teaching (see US Congress, Office of Technology Assessment, 1995, p. 118).

The Commission of the European Communities maintains a multi-lingual WWW site with information about tele-learning initiatives throughout Europe
URL http://www.echo.lu/

A consortium of partners from US universities have set up the InTRO, an "electronic forum dedicated to providing professionals in the field of Instructional Technology with an electronic forum to quickly disseminate, discuss, and advance research in instructructional technology and related fields"
URL http://129.8.48.23/InTRO/InTRO.html

Purdue University offers an on-line "writing lab" through a WWW site that supplements a face-to-face writing-support service with access to Internet resources as well as local resources appropriate for writing-skill development.
URL http://owl.trc.purdue.edu

A consortium of European universities have developed a WWW site to support "virtual student mobility" among the European countries. The site is evolving to support the delivery of multi-media courseware and training programs as well as more culturally and socially oriented services, so that students unable to physically travel to another country for part of their university experience will be able to participate in trans- European learning experiences while not leaving their home institutions. (see Hutchinson, 1995)
URL http://infosys.kingston.ac.uk/Erasmus/home.html

The INDIOS Consortium, representing educational technologists from eight European universities and agencies, is offering tools to support the collaborative design and production of multi-media courseware, where the collaborators in such projects are distributed among different countries. This work goes on through satellite-delivered data communication. (contact: H. Vedelaar, at henri@ktechno.be)

ing. In the next section we discuss another category of service provision—service to the field through a professional organization—and illustrate several of these organizations in which educational technologists are involved that are active in support of tele-learning.

Box 9.5

National delivery and support agencies

In Europe (see Held and Kugemann, 1995)

ETSIT, for network connection via satellite to universities in Spain

The CNAM Remote Teaching Network connecting 50 regional centres and 100,000 students in France

SOLnet, the Swedish Opening Learning Network, serving municipalities, schools, and learning centres throughout sparsely populated areas of Sweden.

In the US

For compressed video, see Hakes, Cochenour, Rezabek, & Sachs (1995), for a listing of 64 state and regional delivery agencies for support of compressed video for instruction in US settings.

For networks, see Kurshan, Harrington, and Milbury, 1994, for a discussion of major state-based service agencies supporting tele-learning via networks.

In Mexico

ITESM, for compressed video services for Masters Degree programmes provided to 26 receive-site campuses in 25 Mexican cities

---

■ 9.1.3 SUPPORT OF TELE-LEARNING THROUGH PROFESSIONAL ORGANIZATIONS

Professional organizations are important sources of individual development for educational technologists (see Chapter 4). It is not surprising that these organizations are implementing tele-learning services for their members. In this section we look briefly at services relating to the non face-to-face dissemination of information and at services relating to the traditional professional conference.

ORGANIZATIONS AS DISSEMINATORS

Many educational technologists are involved with professional organizations, some of them donating time and energy to the dissemination and stimulation-oriented services of the organizations. Some of these organizations were established to support some aspect of tele-learning from their inception; others have come to expand toward some aspects of tele-learning, as tele-learning in itself has grown in importance in the educational community.

Such organizations are important vehicles for the exchange of ideas and experiences about tele-learning among educational technologists, particularly at the international level. In Table 9.2 we list some representative organizations, and events relating to tele-learning that they are sponsoring in 1995 or early 1996. The purpose of Table 9.2 is to show the diverse and extensive interest in tele-learning among educational technologists through their professional organizations at the time of writing in 1995; the list is by no means meant to be exhaustive.

And this is only a small sampling. As one of its services, ISTE (the International Society for Technology in Education) distributes through a LISTSERV on the Internet a "Conference Calendar" for educational technology, with usually about 40 different conferences listed, mostly in the US, and many with explicit themes relating to tele-learning. (for information, contact: iste@ccmail.uoregon.edu).

Another good source of information is "EDUCOM Update", available via the Internet as a service of the professional organization EDUCOM. EDUCOM represents persons in higher-educational institutions, predominantly in the US, responsible for technology decisions (see Ubois, 1995 for an interview with its director). EDUCOM Update is a regularly appearing on-line (Internet) distribution-list newsletter, with updated conference listings. Among the tele-learning oriented conferences indicated in the EDUCOM Update in 1995 were those in Box 9.6.

To subscribe to the EDUCOM Update and receive regular conference updates via e-mail, send a message to conf@educom.edu or visit:

URL http://www.educom.edu

INNOVATIONS IN CONFERENCE-INFORMATION DELIVERY

It is interesting is that almost all professional conferences relevant to educational technologists maintain a WWW site with further information about their conferences as well as other interaction possibilities. Often, associations are offering not only materials from their conferences via the Internet but also alternative forms of their printed publications (see Chapter 4 and **Interface 4**). For example, the proceedings of the 3rd WWW Conference are available at:

URL http://www.elsevier.nl

Sometimes conference registration is required to obtain a password that then allows full access to downloadable versions of the conference papers, while those who do not register for the conference obtain only abstracts or selected papers.

There is considerable interest among educational technology community as to how to improve dissemination of conference results via tele-learning

---

Box 9.6

Sample of conferences with a focus on tele-learning, with calls for participation via the Internet (1995)

"Educational Technology and Telecommunications Markets Conference", San Diego, CA (US)

"Winning the Networking Game", St. Louis, MO (US)

"Western Cooperative for Educational Telecommunications Annual Meeting", Spokane, WA, (US)

"Technology and Distance Education: Sharing Experiences Around the World", Costa Rica

"NetMedia '95", London, UK

"INET '95", Fifth Annual Conference of the Internet Society, Honolulu, US

"Exploring the VideoClass Alternative", Raleigh, NC (US)

"Third International WWW Conference", Darmstadt, Germany

"TeleCon Europe: Videoconferencing and its use in Distance Learning", London, UK

"The Learning Superhighway: Third International Interactive Multimedia Symposium", Perth, Australia

"European Workshop on Interactive Distributed Multimedia Systems and Services", Berlin, Germany

"Breaking the Boundaries of Time and Space: A Focus on Distance Education", University of Maine at Augusta, US

"Best Practices of Computer Conferencing in Distance Education", American Center for the Study of Distance Education, University Park, PA, US

"Online Educa", Berlin, Germany and Seoul, Korea

"Tele-Working, Tele-Learning: Working and Learning on the Electronic Highway", Amsterdam, The Netherlands

"TeleCon XV: Teleconferencing in the Mainstream", Anaheim, CA, US

---

technologies. Maurer and Schneider (1995), for example, note the variety of ways in which conferences are now expanding the range of professional-development services associated with conferences by using tele-learning tools for information dissemination and participant discussion through the Internet. Some examples are:

- Invitations to participation via mailing lists and LISTSERVs
- Submission of contributions via the Internet
- Review process handled on-line
- Registration processes handled on-line
- Capture of scientific presentations at the conference itself for later distribution via the Internet and/or CD-ROM
- Scientific exchanges before and after the conference, including via real-

Table 9.2 Sampling of professional organizations involving educational technologists with activities involving tele-learning in 1995

Organization	Target group	Sample activity relating to tele-learning
SATURN (European)	Companies and institutions interested in flexible learning and training in Europe	Newsletters, reports, database of contacts
EADTU (European)	Higher-education institutions in Europe offering distance teaching	Projects, cooperative activities, conferences, workshops
Norwegian Association for Distance Education (as a typical example of national associations throughout the world)	Institutions engaged in distance education	Representation of interests of distance-education nationally and internationally; cooperation with Ministry of Education on quality assessment and statistics collection; sponsor projects and conferences; liaison with industrial partners
Association for the Advancement of Computing in Education, US (international membership)	Tele-learning aspects oriented toward designers and researchers	Journal, *International Journal of Educational Telecommunications*; ED-TELECOM 96, World Conference on Educational Telecommunications, June 96, Boston contact: `http:/aace.virginia.edu/`
SEAMEO INNOTECH (Southeast Asian Ministers of Education Regional Center for Educational Innovation and Technology)	Educational decision and policy makers	Conference, The Philippines, Dec. 1995, where three of the five the conference themes are: Classroom technologies of the next generation, open and flexible delivery systems for the future, and multi-channel learning
EDUCOM (representing over 600 higher-education institutions in the US); for an interview with the director of EDUCOM, see Ubois, 1995	Decision makers with respect to information technology in higher-education institutions	Internet newsletter, special task forces and studies related to tele-learning and networking infrastructures (`http://www.educom.edu`)

IFIP- Technical Committee 3, Information Technology and Education (international)	Professionals in the application of information technology to education	Books, meetings, conferences such as "Teleteaching 1996", Australia http://www.dit.upm.es/~cdk/ifip.htm
ISTE (International Society for Technology in Education), US (international members)	Teachers, teacher educators	Special Interest Group on Telecommunications in Education with newsletter and listserv; next tele-learning focused conference: "Tel-Ed '95", Fort Lauderdale, FL (contact: iste@oregon.uoregon.edu)
National School Boards Association, US	School administrators and decision makers, including a "Technology Leadership Network"	Next tele-learning event: Conference "Learning Together: A Changing Environment" (October 1995, near Vancouver, Canada)
International Council for Distance Education (ICDE)	Institutions and professionals in distance education	Next event: (cosponsored with UNESCO); Conference on "Networking into the 21st Century: Prospects for the 21st Century", Indonesia, November 1995

time sessions in MUD environments
- Support for asynchronous communication during the conference
- Dissemination of multi-media conference materials after the conference

Maurer and Schneider (1995) further note how the *Hyper-G environment* (see Chapter 8) can support all of the above functions in a fuller way than can current WWW and Internet environments.

These services relate to major ways for an educational technologist to stay up-to-date: to read professional literature, access professional resources via the Internet, attend occasional professional meetings, and examine conference topics. The latter is especially interesting as an indicator of trends, and as an accuracy-tester of the predictions, after a few years have elapsed.

Thus these innovations associated with professional conferences are important. They are the way that educational technologists teach each other, and up-date their own learning (as we examined in Chapter 4). They are important opportunities for educational technologists to practice what they preach.

■ 9.1.4 SUPPORTING THROUGH REPORTING AND SUMMARIZING

A final way in which educational technologists are regularly involved in serving and supporting those involved with tele-learning is by being good sources of information. While conferences are important ways in which educational technologists themselves get informed: educational technologists are in turn frequently called upon to summarize trends and experiences in the field with respect to tele-learning, as a service to practitioners and decision makers.

We have already described one example of how being well-informed allows one to make good suggestions to decision makers, in Box 9.1, with relation to guidelines for decision making about compressed-video systems (Hakes, 1995). Table 9.3 shows a sampling of other recent, good examples of summaries of trends and experience with various aspects of tele-learning. All are based on extensive collections of facts and experiences; what determines their quality is (a) how up-to-date and relevant those facts and experiences are for the intended audience, (b) how well the author organizes and presents the materials, and (c) the way in which the author interprets insights and trends from the materials. The entries in Table 9.3 are arranged in an approximately increasing order of author interpretation, from less to more interpretive.

Each of the above incorporates many different sources and attempts to make a contribution to practice through the compilation and interpretation of these sources. To the extent to which the authors move toward a critical framework that adds another level of analysis to the sources, it could be said that their work moves from "information provision" to "research". In the next section, we look at another set of examples of research relating to tele-learning being carried out by educational technologists with clear practical value to the practice of tele-learning. This set relates to improving the likelihood of the implementation of tele-learning in practice.

■ 9.2 SERVING THE FIELD: SUPPORTING PRACTICE THROUGH IMPLEMENTATION RESEARCH

The lines for an educational technologist that separate "research", "design" and "practice" are often hard to define, particularly with tele-learning. So much of what we do is new and exploratory, yet at the same time insights that we have obtained throughout the years about people and learning and technology are still valid. For example, one insight from many decades of research in educational technology is that new technologies can change educational practice, but slowly.

Table 9.3 Sample of summary and synthesis reports relating to tele-learning

Source	Description and interpretation
Bacsich, 1994; Jacobs, 1994	Issues with respect to ISDN for tele-learning
Hakes, Cochenour, Rezabek, & Sachs, 1995	Core of the book consists of survey responses from 64 US institutions using compressed video for instruction; no synthesis of the survey responses, which limits the value of all the survey entries to the practitioner—which of the 64 should s/he read?
Van den Brande, 1993	Overview of technologies for distance learning, European initiatives for distance learning, and reports from 16 European countries and a number of non-European countries with respect to experiences with distance learning; only a brief synthesis is given
Wetzel, Radtke and Stern, 1994	Literature-review type summary of many hundreds of research studies relating to the educational use of television, video, and film. The last chapter is a "discussion and conclusions" which in itself is a good synthesis, but is not written in a way that is convenient for practitioners
US Congress Office of Technology Assessment, 1995	Extensive overview of US teachers' use of technology circa 1995; each of the chapters includes a summary of key findings and also there is an overall summary, with some careful conclusions drawn

Messages such as this must also be communicated to the emerging tele-learning field, particularly to the newcomers to this field.

In this section we look at a line of research in educational technology that has a long history and consider its application to tele-learning. The line of research relates to factors that influence the implementation of technological innovation in an educational setting.

▓ 9.2.1 GAINING INSIGHTS INTO IMPLEMENTATION

In Section 9.1 we saw many examples of educational technologists active in support of the implementation of tele-learning in different educational settings. There is a long research history relating to the implementation of innovative technologies in education that provides an important theoretical framework for such service activities. This framework precedes tele-learning, but also applies directly to it.

First, however, what is meant by "implementation"?

Sippel (1994) calls implementation "the art to deal seriously with a new application within a certain living organization" (p. 81). By implementation, we mean moving a learning event from the "special-project" or "experimental" category, to some level of incorporation into the regular instructional routine of an instructor or institution.

Such transitions are not automatic. Many barriers must be confronted, or better, anticipated and preventing from occurring. These sorts of barriers have been inventoried and categorized many times by educational technologists. Also, the evolution through which practitioners move in their acceptance of a technological innovation into their instructional practice has also been extensively studied, and regular sequences have been observed (see Chapter 7.2).

As tele-learning specialists, what can the educational technologist learn from the research about the implementation of other innovations such as computers into mainstream educational practice? We review some of the research relating to the implementation of computer-related technologies in education in this next section and apply this to tele-learning implementation.

IMPLEMENTATION AS A CHALLENGE AND GOAL

That the implementation of technology into regular instructional practice is difficult is repeatedly seen by survey results such as the following:

> ...there is much support for the use of computers in education. Strong evidence for this is the increasing number of computers available per student—the microintensity level...Yet, teachers have not overwhelmingly adopted computer technology for teaching. According to a national survey [in the USA], only one teacher per school, on average, integrates computer technology into his or her teaching. (Marcinkiewicz and Wittman, 1995, p. 400)

Although the quotation is based on data from a particular country and the ratio indicated will vary in different countries and in different surveys, the general problem being expressed is acknowledged throughout the world: implementation of computers and computer-related technology into the secondary-school classroom is difficult (see Pelgrum, Janssen Reinen and Plomp, 1993, for a comprehensive international overview; see also Chapter 7.2).

Implementation research perspectives

Many analyses have been conducted, not only of the reasons for the implementation difficulties but also of strategies to help overcome the difficulties (see Moonen and Kommers, 1995, for a recent analysis for the European context). Sometimes these strategies are derived from the more-general study of how persons respond to an innovation (Rogers, 1983); others from the more-specific study of the educational-change process (Fullan, 1991; Khan, 1995). Still others focus more closely on individual teachers and their response to computers (Veen, Van der Neut, Spoon and Vogelzang, 1991).

The teacher is the key

Regardless of the perspective, the conclusions of implementation research with respect to computer-related technology in education are usually similar: the teacher or instructor is central in any implementation of computers in the classroom, and the educational institution as well as the teacher must be involved in the changes that accompany integrating computers into instruction.

Studying the teacher's acceptance of technology

Many researchers have looked more carefully at the process of acceptance of a technological innovation into instructional practice, and have observed a predictability to this process with respect to the individual instructor. Collis, Veen and De Vries (1994) for example, predict the likelihood of implementation success to represented as the "vector sum" of three other vectors—perceived or expected advantage, problems associated with accessibility, and pleasure in usage attractiveness. Figure 9.1 shows these "3-As". If the vector sum does not reach a hypothetical "acceptance level" *or* if any of the vectors goes below a hypothetical "rejection" level, the model predicts that implementation will not occur.

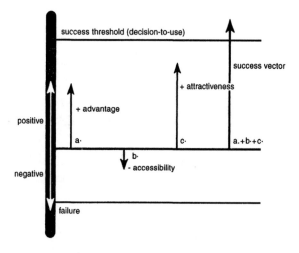

Figure 9.1 The "3 P" Model to predict implementation of an innovation in instructional practice

The CBAM Model and a modification

Hall, Loucke and Rutherford (1977), developed a different predictive framework relating to the diffusion of an innovation in schools nearly two decades ago that is still regularly being applied, including now to implementation of tele-learning. This framework is based on the "CBAM Model" for measuring teachers' changes in involvement with an innovation in their instructional practice.

According to the CBAM model, which has been adapted and applied in many countries and settings, teachers move through a series of "stages of concern" or "involvement" as they mature in their relationship with an innovation. The original CBAM model consisted of seven of these stages, ranging from no awareness of the innovation to two levels of leadership with respect to use of the innovation. Table 9.4 shows a modification of this model, to stages of involvement with computers in instruction, that has been recently used as a criterion measure for changes in teacher involvement with computer technology in Dutch schools as a result of a two-year national implementation initiative carried out by the Ministry of Education (Collis and Moonen, 1995a, b).

One conclusion from the implementation research is clear, and is repeated

Table 9.4 Modified CBAM Levels, to measure teachers' changes in level of involvement with computer-related technologies in instruction

Level of the adapted CBAM Model	Type of concern	Action toward the innovation
1. Minimal awareness level	1. "Should I know something about this?"	
2. Some knowledge	2. "How does this work?" "Can I figure it out and handle it?	2. Interest in browsing and exploring
3. Some use of one or two types	3. "Is there a manageable way I can use these in practice?"	3. Tries some things in practice
4. Regular use	4. "How can I make this part of my day-to-day practice?"	4. Makes some uses of IT routine in his/her instructional setting
5. Regular use and leadership role	5. "How might I stimulate my colleagues to see the educational potential of this?"	5. Makes regular use of IT in instructional practice and also works in various ways to stimulate his/her colleagues to also make use of IT

Adapted (Collis and Moonen, 1995a, b) from Hall, Loucke and Rutherford (1977)

again and again: the implementation of technological innovations into practice, outside the framework of the special project or the influence of champions or pioneer enthusiasts, is difficult and requires insight and strategy. It is not surprising that this conclusion is also relevant to tele-learning.

IMPLEMENTATION RESEARCH APPLIED TO TELE-LEARNING

Implementation or "utilization" or "acceptance" research (as other ways of describing implementation research) have been extensively carried out with respect to many different forms of tele-learning. Box 9.7 notes some examples.

Box 9.7

Examples of implementation research applied to tele-learning

- School television utilization in Germany, (Hasebrink, 1992; Hauke, 1992)
- Wide-area networking in K-12 schools in the US (Eurich-Fulcher and Schofield, 1995)
- Home learners enrolled in the Open University in the UK in courses where computer use is required (Kirkwood, 1993)
- Trainers in large multi-national organizations attempting to bring tele-learning via interactive television into the organization (Reif, 1995)

The MTS Project: an example of implementation research

A typical example of such implementation research is Sippel's (1994) evaluation of the *Multimedia TeleSchool Project* (MTS), sponsored by the Commission of the European Community, and in operation from 1992 through 1994. MTS involved the design or adaptation of five courses ("English for Banking," "English for Telecommunications Workers," "Environmental Issues," "Agrofood," and "Telecommunications Principles for Engineers"). These courses were offered by a number of course providers, using tele-learning technologies, to professionals in 12 European countries. Self-study learning using print materials was combined with a variety of forms of interactive television (direct broadcasting by satellite) accompanied by two-way interaction via real-time ISDN technology and by telephone, fax, e-mail, and computer conferencing. More than 1,000 clients were involved.

Based on an extensive evaluation throughout the Project by a multinational team, Sippel concluded that

> ...the introduction of tele-training in corporate environments is a complex socio-technical process substantially challenging the traditional training practice

*and involving many motivational, organizational and technical restrictions....
Offering telecommunication mediated training...is an implementation challenge
which should not be underestimated. (p. IV)*

But the contribution of the educational technologist to the field must go further
than analysis. There must also be help and suggestions. We look at some of these
in the next section.

▨ 9.2.2 RESEARCH-BASED RECOMMENDATIONS FOR IMPROVING THE IMPLEMENTATION OF TELE-LEARNING

As is typical in implementation-research studies, Sippel offers an extensive list
of "critical success factors" for the implementation of tele-training, some of which
are summarized in Box 9.8.

Box 9.8

**Success factors for the implementation of tele-training, from the MTS
evaluation**

- Bring more flexibility and responsiveness to the courses; tailor them, including their technology mixes, to the organizational needs and situation of the clients
- Negotiate clear understandings with personnel departments in client organizations as to the number of clients, their participation conditions, and the local support and study facilities available to them
- Locate the appropriate decision makers in the organization concerning training, and gain their support through personal contacts and through professionally prepared preview materials about the tele-training courses
- Liaison closely with those responsible for technology and support at local sites, as well as those responsible for on-going training. (Sippel, 1994; see also Fries, 1995)

OTHER IMPLEMENTATION RECOMMENDATIONS

Sippel's list of implementation recommendations was aimed at corporate training. Similar lists can be found for implementation of tele-learning in other sectors,
for example, those in Box 9.9.

In addition to the studies noted in above, there are many more examples of
implementation research relating to tele-learning. Table 9.5 summarizes a selection
of other studies done by educational technologists relating to the implementation
of tele-learning and indicates highlights of the recommendations from those studies.

Box 9.9

Recommendations for implementation of tele-learning

- Sixteen obstacles to the use of a two-way full motion fiber-optics telecommunications system for teacher educators involved with agricultural teachers in Iowa were identified; recommendations to improve the status of teachers in the adaptation process, perhaps through the collaborative development of curriculum materials in areas where the teachers perceived a need for new materials (i.e., agricultural economics) were offered (Miller and Doerfert, 1995)
- Sixteen rural secondary schools in Australia were involved in a project to bring specialized instruction via audiographics conferencing into the schools; 25 "assertions and recommendations" were given relating to instructional effectiveness, effectiveness management, and school organization (for example, "telematics delivery and receival requires the use of a special purpose room") (Oliver and Reeves, 1995, pp. 79, 105)
- Staff at the seven campuses of the University of Maine needed to be stimulated and supported to participate in a television-type tele-learning initiative to "open the college" to at least 2,500 new students; 39 skills were identified as relevant to implementation success and subsequent staff-support initiatives focused on those skills in which faculty indicated a high level of interest (LeBlanc, 1993)

And these studies are only a small sampling. In a review of the international research literature about computer-related tele-learning in schools in 1993, for example, it was found that the majority of studies were focused on improving the *implementation likelihood* of tele-learning, compared to only a relatively few that focused on results following actual implementation into practice (Collis, 1993b).

CRITICAL LINK BETWEEN RESEARCH AND PRACTICE

Whenever the educational technologist deals with the reality of implementation, s/he must think much more broadly than the potential benefits of tele-learning or the attractions of a particular course or episode involving tele-learning. Although many of the recommendations coming from implementation research (i.e., the "micro-politics" described by Reif, 1995) may not sound like the domain of educational technologists, they are—if the educational technologist wants to see his or her ideas and designs move from the special-project to the implementation level.

Thus an implementation focus requires that the educational technologist get into the field and listen and observe. The "cutting edge" of one's ideas about

Table 9.5 Recommendations from research for the implementation of tele-learning

Study	Implementation focus	Implementation insights
McCreary and Brochet (1990)	CMC as part of tele-learning	There must be a need and desire to communicate, and a critical mass of users and messages
Lampikoski (1993)	CMC as part of tele-learning	Decentralized decision making, short-term finances and strict budgets lead decision makers to say "no" to CMC for financial concerns; find arguments for CMC relating to the image of the institution or the long-term publicity value
Marriott, Currie and Smith (1995)	Conferencing as part of tele-learning	If at all possible, bring participants together face-to-face at least one time
Schrum (1995)	CMC, WWW access as part of tele-learning	Participants do not have adequate time for participation; stimulate funded, released time from their employers
Smith (1995)	Tele-learning with innovative technologies	Projects often suffer from under-informed designs; Bring users via formative evaluation into each step of the design and development process
Tiffin (1989)	Broadcast television	Lack of integration with existing educational structures; Do not invest in equipment before a needs analysis involving existing educational structures

tele-learning can quickly be blunted by the dulling impact of implementation realities, but without an awareness of such realities tele-learning cannot diffuse into mainstream practice. The effective educational technologist must work to locate the points of best fit between feasibility and innovation.

■ 9.3 TEACHING TEACHERS ABOUT TELE-LEARNING

Who do educational technologists teach? How is tele-learning affecting their teaching? In this section we look at one particular target group with whom educational technologists are closely involved—teachers—and consider a variety of ways that tele-learning is now being used by educational technologists as a method of instruction and delivery in teacher education. In Section 9.4 we turn our focus to the target group of educational technologists themselves.

Many educational technologists are involved in teacher education. Those who are members of faculties of education or teacher-education institutes are often involved in the initial preparation of teachers (called pre-service teacher education in many countries), teaching a required course about "media" or "computers". As another task, many educational technologists are involved in the in-service training of teachers, in courses or workshops relating to some aspect of technology, or in support of less-structured professional development. We look at these two focuses of activity in Sections 9.3.1 and 9.3.2.

■ 9.3.1 EXAMPLES OF TELE-LEARNING IN INITIAL TEACHER EDUCATION

Initial teacher education generally occurs in an institutional setting, with the student teacher dividing his or her time between formal courses in the higher-education institution and practical experiences in a school setting. Tele-learning is bringing new experiences and possibilities into both aspects of initial teacher education. In this section, we briefly discuss these new possibilities under three general headings: (a) extending and enriching the traditional course environment in the initial teacher-education institute; (b) extending and enriching the communication and contact between student teacher, supervisor, and sponsoring teacher in the school; and (c) and bringing new sorts of partnerships in the initial teacher-education situation.

EXTENDING AND ENRICHING THE TRADITIONAL SETTING

It is now becoming typical to install a local-area network which can be used for tele-learning support within any higher-education institution, including teacher-education institutions. An example, in Box 9.10, from the Liverpool Polytechnic (Stanley, 1991) is a typical account of some of the benefits.

Another example of the use of tele-learning in initial teacher education is that of the institutional BBS (bulletin-board system), facilitating student and

---

Box 9.10

Networks in teacher education institutions: an example from the UK

- Libraries of exercise files available at all times on the network
- Educational software for various learning activities is available at any of the 26 computers located at different places in the institution
- A specially designed user interface provides a common and familiar entry to the many different services and packages accessible through it
- Collaborative working can be facilitated, through students being able to individually contribute to a common task
- Joint and cooperative production of reports and projects is facilitated
- Opportunities to leave and receive messages can be among students or between faculty and students (Stanley, 1991)

---

instructor interaction through the sending and reading of messages. One such system is that of the School of Education at California State University (Slovacek and Doyle-Nichols, 1992). A BBS was set up, a users' guide was created, modems were given on loan to the student teachers, and a fax board was installed in a computer on a cart for classroom demonstrations. Students could obtain a variety of types of information about their courses, could upload files and assignments, could connect to the Internet, and could communicate with each other and their instructors. Usage increased steadily, with students becoming more and more likely to send messages to their instructors with regard to their assignments. This was seen to be important, not only to improve course performance, but also to "breaking down the barriers" between students and faculty.

Comes and Kirkwood (1992) give a similar example, also from the US. They note how students in initial teacher education can make use of the integrated information and communication resources at their institution (Ball State University) to access each other, the instructor, electronically stored library resources, external data bases and discussion groups, all from their dormitory rooms. The same communication system connects all the 200 classrooms at the University, so that transfer of text, voice, and/or video data can occur as it is wanted during class instruction.

This example can be extended to connect the multiple sites of an institution or to allow a pre-service student, via a modem, to access the network from a remote location without always having to come into the institution. Hedberg and Harper (1993) give examples of this in Australia.

Www sites for pre-service enrichment

Many examples are emerging of educational technologists being involved in the development of a WWW site for the enrichment of course experiences during pre-service teacher education. One example is the "Dewey" site from the School of Education at the University of Michigan in the US, located at:

The Dewey Site
URL `http://ics.soe.umich.edu/`

The Dewey site is described as an "experiment in global education" whereby pre-service teachers can not only find out about a variety of learning activities that could be used in their future classroom activities, but can participate themselves in those activities, through the WWW, as part of their pre-service education. Among the projects on the Dewey Web in March 1995 were those in Box 9.11.

Box 9.11

WWW-site projects for pre-service teachers at The University of Michigan

"The World Forum", where students experience the didactics of role playing in a simulated trip to an exotic part of the world

"The Journey North", where students experience how the classroom experience can be expanded with reports from scientists and explorers, via the Internet

"The Arab–Israeli Conflict Simulation", where students participate in a role-playing simulation exercise with other groups of student-teachers from around the world

"The International Poetry Guild", where student teachers exchange examples of their own writing in order to anticipate the benefits that such critical exchange can bring to their own future teaching in secondary schools

"Earth Odysseys", where student teachers interact with a person actually traveling on the Trans-Siberian Railway, in order to see how this sort of interaction can be valuable for a variety of learning goals in secondary school, such as environmental issues and cross-cultural appreciation

(for more information, contact Roger Espinosa, at `roger@trillium.soe.umich.edu`)

Reaching new groups of students

There are many examples of tele-learning being used to bring initial teacher-education experiences to groups of students who find it difficult or unattractive to come to traditional institutional settings (see Collis, 1995a). One such initiative is going on the UK, where the Open University is hoping to attract university graduates into a distance-delivered programme of initial teacher education. The programme will be part-time over 18 months, entirely offered by distance methods, with every student receiving a computer and modem as part of the programme. In this way, regular communication can occur between the student and the OU tutor, both while the student studies at home and when s/he does his or her required practice teaching in a school. The teacher-mentor in the school is also included in the computer conferencing (for information, contact F.Banks@Open.Ac.UK).

The LOTE Project in Australia is another example of the use of tele-learning to reach new groups of clients for initial teacher education. In the LOTE Project, the emphasis is on the development of modern-language teachers, especially in remote areas. The same materials used for pre-service education are also being used for teacher in-service in the same remote areas (Hedberg and Harper, 1993).

Providing new types of course assignments

In many initial teacher-education institutions tele-learning is being used to provide new types of course activities and assignments during regular face-to-face instruction. The examples in Box 9.12 are illustrations.

These are just a few of the many examples of the use of tele-learning to enrich coursework in initial teacher education. The UK-based "Journal of Information Technology for Teacher Education" is an excellent source. Volume 4, Number 2 was entirely focused on tele-learning for teacher education (Davis, 1995b).

Using tele-learning to enrich the practice-teaching aspect of initial teacher education is also proving to be a powerful application.

Tele-learning during the practice-teaching experience

It is now becoming common in many regions for tele-learning to be used to link students, instructors, and supervising teachers in regular communication during the practice-teaching component of initial teacher education. Such electronic linkage eliminates the frequently long stretches of time between visits of the faculty instructor to the school setting because of difficulties in time and organization to plan a visit to the school. Such a problem becomes critical in remote areas. Box 9.13 gives an illustration.

Box 9.12

Using introducing pre-service teachers to the pedagogy of interactive television and computer-based communication projects

Preservice secondary-education teachers at the University of Sydney (Australia) communicated with other teacher-trainees and educators around the world via the Internet on ideas for the instructional use of computer-based communication in curriculum areas

Student teachers then visited schools in which teachers and learners were participating in such international CMC projects

Students also learned to use computer-conferencing and e-mail systems, and "listened" to the classroom teachers in their preparations and discussions with others concerning the CMC lessons

Student teachers participated themselves, via CMC, in various learning activities involving learners and their teachers in schools around the world (Horsley and Beazley, 1993)

Preservice secondary-teachers used case studies and collaborative computer-assisted communication to support conceptual learning in a methods course on critical reading (Pugh, 1993)

Teacher education majors learned to use two multi-media software packages to make interactive-television presentations to fellow students at two other colleges all linked by fiber-optic networking (Herring, Smaldino and Thompson, 1995)

Box 9.13

Using tele-learning for "teleapprenticeships"

- At the University of Illinois (US) faculty, student teachers, and teacher-mentors make use of regular three-way computer conferencing
- Sometimes both student teachers and teacher-mentors enter reflective comments on their own teaching
- Wide-ranging e-mail discussions are held concerning classroom experiences and their relation to theory; this occurs on a daily basis while student teachers are in the practical situation, through the loan of laptop computers and modems
- Student teachers share their lesson plans and experiences with each other on a daily basis and get quick feedback and comment from both their teacher-mentor and faculty supervisor, who could enter their observations at times convenient to all involved but within a short time after the practice lesson
- Student teachers very much appreciate the rapid feedback, the on-line discussion among themselves and their supervisors, and the chance to keep in touch with each other when "in the field" (Levin, Waugh, Brown and Clift, 1994)

NEW PARTNERSHIPS

A particularly powerful application of tele-learning in initial teacher education is in the facilitation of new sorts of partnerships in learning experiences for the student teachers.

The PLUTO Project

The PLUTO Project (Libotton, 1994) is a major European example. This project, with industrial support, links approximately 19 initial teacher-training institutions in 14 European countries with each other and with schools in their regions for various on-line collaborative projects, so that the student teachers can get a feeling of what such projects can offer to education and also a beginning sense of a didactic for such projects.

Other examples

In another example, of a smaller scale than PLUTO, 31 fifth- and sixth-grade children in Canada participated in an on-line project with 17 student teachers in California. The student teachers not only got to experience the management of an on-line activity while still on their own campus, but also had to develop strategies for tasks such as evaluating children's writing, and tailoring their language to be appropriate for discussion with a child. The on-line setting made it possible that this be done under the supervision and comment of the faculty instructor, something much harder to replicate in the full-scale practice-teaching situation (Zinck, 1989).

The last example, deliberately selected as one from some years ago, give some indication of how long this type of innovation has been occurring in teacher education. It continues to the present, as for example, the case we noted in Chapter 5 where children became reviewers and "experts" to help preservice teachers prepare for their upcoming practice teaching (Traw, 1994).

■ 9.3.2 TELE-LEARNING IN INSERVICE TEACHER EDUCATION

As was the case with initial teacher education, there are many new possibilities emerging in in-service teacher education through tele-learning. In this section we give some examples relative to tele-learning in in-service education. Tele-learning can augment an in-service course which meets occasionally in a face-to-face manner, or it can be the major vehicle through which the teachers involved participate in the course.

TELE-LEARNING FOR INSERVICE COURSES

There are many examples of inservice courses which relieve a part of the logistical burden of in-service education on teachers by replacing some or all of the time to be spent in the course in a face-to-face basis with study done at a distance, using tele-learning. Box 9.14 gives an illustration.

Multiple-technology examples

Other examples similar in various ways to the Catalonian illustration in Box 9.14 can be found in many countries. In the US, for example, the "Mathematics Learning Forums Project" involves a particular institution (the Bank Street Center for Children and Technology and Graduate School of Education) leading a series of 24 on-line seminars in which teachers across the country can take part. Each on-line seminar lasts about two months. Participating teachers are first sent videotapes to give them "a vivid picture of the aspects of teaching about which they are learning", as well as various print materials. In the on-line conversations that go on throughout each seminar, faculty at the Bank Street institution guide their teacher-students as they try new teaching strategies in their classrooms. The teacher-students discuss with each other, via computer conferencing, their experiences with the new teaching strategies. Approximately 750 teachers are participating in the on-line seminars (Honey, 1993).

As another example, an innovative inservice course called (perhaps unofficially?) the "One-Minute Guru Course" offered by the University of Central Florida and the Florida Department of Education, has enrolled up to 2,000 teachers at a time (D'Ignazio, 1995b). The course is based on the philosophy that teachers need a network of "one-minute gurus" as instant electronic partners to turn to when the teacher needs help or support in working with innovative technologies in the classroom. The course is taught with a combination of video programming broadcast by satellite, a live interactive broadcast, a set of instructional ideas and resources organized via a gopher server, a "human gopher" (an educational technologist serving as the key on-line contact person for questions and overall course organization), and e-mail communication with the instructor responsible for the television broadcasts. To do their assignments, teachers search through (on-line) information about the other teachers who are participating in the course and find a partner teacher (and class) to work with on collaborative projects.

EXTENDING THE FACE-TO-FACE INSERVICE COURSE WITH TELE-LEARNING

One very powerful application of tele-learning to inservice teacher education is to extend the contacts and interaction that have been made in a face-to-face

Box 9.14

Examples of tele-learning for in-service teacher education in Europe

Catalonia

Teachers in eastern Spain want to participate in various in-service programs, but find it difficult to move from their homes and working centres to the major city of Barcelona and to pay for their travel and expenses. Thus tele-learning became not only a topic to teach about in some of these courses, but also a training and communication channel.

The regional educational-support centre set up a network and its associated on-line services, with on-line data bases of educational resources for teachers to use in their lessons. The network also supported a computer conferencing system called AGORA.

Teachers received a variety of materials: text materials, a computer-based tutorial on how to use the on-line system, complementary readings and software on disk, and a user handbook

Face-to-face meetings were also held, to give the teachers instruction in how to use the different media and particularly the conferencing and e-mail options (Simón, 1992)

LEARN, based in Denmark

LEARN is a Network Service offered in cooperation with the Royal Danish School of Educational Studies and Computer Resources International. LEARN provides a number of facilities which make it easy for inservice teachers and teacher educators to be involved in tele-learning.

From the inservice teacher's point of view, LEARN is seen as a software package which makes it easy for the teacher to get and send mail, assignments, and other course materials; which includes an integrated text editor for editing responses, notes, and e-mail; which offers menu-driven access to various file-handling tasks; and which supports a BBS and various communication options. Students study off-line.

From the inservice educator's point of view, LEARN is an environment in which it is easy to add and take away materials and edit the BBS.

From an administrator's point of view, LEARN offers facilities to register students, teachers, courses, enrollments, available materials, etc., on the host.

The general model for LEARN is: inservice teachers retrieve material on-line, logoff and work off line on the materials, and go back on-line to send materials back or discuss the materials.

A variety of inservice courses are currently taught with LEARN support, not only to Danish teachers but to teachers in a number of other countries (through multiple-language interfaces for the LEARN software; Larsen and Malmberg, 1991).

inservice course after the course is over. There are many examples of this model. Two examples are shown in Box 9.15.

Box 9.15

Extending an in-service course with outside-course networking

PIT (Collis and Moonen, 1995a, b)

In The Netherlands, over 1,000 teachers have been participating in a network-oriented form of in-service. Teachers meet occasionally in face-to-face sessions with a curriculum specialist, but between the face-to-face sessions, exchange experiences with each other and work together with each other on various lesson activities, via networking.

CAWP (Fine, 1993)

The CAWP is a method for improving the teaching of writing which involves a Summer Institute or a site-based course. The method has been delivered to over 3,100 teachers in the US.

A major intention of the method is that the participants become expert teachers of teachers themselves after they finish the course, but this expectation means that there is much contact and follow-up needed

Thus a computer conference was established, called CAWP On-Line, specifically for the teachers who had finished the leadership training.

The on-line service offers e-mail, 45 "general discussion centres" (conference topic areas), file transfer, and access to an on-line information resource that provides access in turn to data bases and other resources

Approximately half the potential users do in fact become high users of the on-line service, predominately the e-mail aspects

---

These examples lead into an additional category of tele-learning for teacher education: that of support for on-going professional development. We introduced this category earlier, in Chapters 4 and 5. Here we refer to it again, from the perspective of educational technologists who support and lead such support.

■ 9.3.3 TELE-LEARNING AND SUPPORT FOR PROFESSIONAL DEVELOPMENT

By on-going professional development we mean a variety of activities with a common characteristic that the teacher chooses a particular learning activity him or herself, not because it is part of a course assignment, but because the teacher finds it helpful and/or stimulating at a given moment. Sometimes these activities may be directly focused on a particular problem or task; other times they will be more diffuse, a response to a feeling of general interest, or more theoretical, such as the desire to reflect over one's professional practice. In this range of activities, tele-learning also can play an important role.

SUPPORTING THE TEACHER'S PROFESSIONAL DEVELOPMENT

Teachers more and more often are turning to on-line network services for their specific information needs. Sometimes information comes from stored collections of materials, other times from specific persons. But in either case, an on-line service, or access to the Internet itself and to WWW pages, is increasingly popular among teachers.

Honey and Henríquez (1993a, b) in their survey of US teachers using telecommunications found that the responding teachers valued very highly the on-going sorts of professional support that they could acquire through Internet tele-learning activities. Teachers indicated they appreciated accessing educational research, downloading curriculum materials, accessing libraries, and researching subject-specific data bases. In particular, the many innovative uses of the WWW are also presenting new learning experiences for teachers. One example is the collection of multimedia teaching cases relating to education in modern South Africa, located at:

```
http://curry.edschool.Virginia.edu:80/redcases/
```

These cases, designed to encourage reflective practice among teachers, are maintained by the Faculty of Education at the University of Virginia. They involve multi-media, including video segments and sound, and can be accessed by any teacher with an appropriate Internet connection.

On-line services

As we have seen in Chapter 5 and 7 and Interface 5, there are now many different educational network services available, some through the Internet and others on local or commercial networks, which are designed to offer flexible professional-development resources to teachers. As we have given so many examples already, we indicate just one more here, in Box 9.16.

Sometimes such educationally oriented on-line services emphasize the support of information searching, as is the general case with the OTAN example above. Other times the focus in more on communication (see, for example, a Norwegian example, Braatane, 1993). In many cases, the service offers both, and teachers react enthusiastically (Collis, Veen and De Vries, 1994).

Box 9.16

A network service for teacher education and support

- In the state of California in the US a network service called OTAN has been established. OTAN stands for Outreach and Technical Assistance Network. The Service is focused on support for teachers working with students have special needs
- OTAN combines a computerized communications system with regional resource libraries that disseminate commercial and teacher-made materials, including training packets with accompanying videotapes, resource documents, and public-domain software
- OTAN is both an electronic archive and a distribution source for materials, reports, and studies
- Options to choose from in OTAN include: The Master Calendar, Who's Who, Department of Education Information, Resource Centres, Current Articles, Course Outlines, Curricula Resources, Lesson Plans, Public Domain Software, Demo Software, Legislative Information, Reference Materials, Educational Funding Sources, Job Opportunities, On-Line Discussions, and an Upload Area (US Congress, Office of Technology Assessment, 1993)

EPSSs

The illustration in Box 9.16 involved a service organized to serve a broad public, via access through public telephone lines. There are many other sorts of "electronic performance support systems" being used by teachers for both the support of their work and also their on-going professional growth, that usually are based in one computer system but allow connectivity to external networks. We saw a number in Chapter 8; Box 9.17 shows one additional example.

Such performance-support environments are becoming very popular, and have many variations. They may even include access to video resources, for example of video clips of different sorts of lesson activities in actual classroom settings, depending on the capacity of the network available. The boundary between getting information and life-long learning overlaps when a teacher uses such a resource.

ON-GOING TEACHER PROFESSIONAL DEVELOPMENT THROUGH NETWORKING

By networking in this sense we mean the teacher becoming part of a supportive and interacting group of colleagues who interact with each other, giving each other support and ideas (see Chapter 4 for a more general discussion). In the PIT example earlier from The Netherlands in Box 9.15, teachers interspersed face-to-face in-service sessions with interpersonal networking. However, network-based

Box 9.17

A teacher toolkit: performance support for teachers involving tele-learning

- In British Columbia, Canada, a software environment has been created for teachers to help them in their work. This integrated environment continues many different sorts of aids useful to them in categories such as: Accessing and developing lesson strategies; Recording, evaluating, and reporting student progress; Planning and scheduling; and Accessing and developing resources
- Options often involve automatic use of tele-learning to connect the teacher to collections of information or resources available not in the computer itself but in district or regional centres
- Teachers can add material themselves to the regional collection. They can also use the Toolkit to make contact (simply through the click of an icon that looks like a telephone) to a specialist in a regional centre or to colleagues in other schools (Hoebel & Mussio, 1990)

tele-learning technologies can enlarge the range and composition of the groups with which a teacher can network and support interaction among those groups, even without face-to-face in-service. The example in Box 9.18 shows this kind of networking:

Box 9.18

Labnet: a network to develop a professional community of practice among science teachers

- The LabNet Project in the US was a three-year, multi-part project whose overall goal was to improve classroom science teaching. But building a "professional community of practice" among teachers involved in the project was seen as a major aspect
- The 562 teachers involved were from 37 US states. They interacted with each other occasionally in face-to-face small groups in their own regions but most generally through computer conferencing
- The goal of the conferencing was to increase the teachers' self-reflection about their classroom practice, but they also used the computer conferencing to exchange ideas about classroom activities and to interact with professional scientists who were also part of the Network community
- Occasionally teachers would be sent new sets of software and learning materials and then would use the computer conference to receive instructional help from Project Leaders and to support each other in their problems and experiences in trying new computer-based activities in the science classroom (Ruopp, Gal, Drayton and Pfister, 1993)

This illustration shows a network for professional development being guided by a professional project-leadership team and integrated with a range of other types of in-service activities. There are many examples of teacher-related network communities, with varying degrees of formality and of associated in-service activity. We saw the CWAP example in Box 9.15, relative to the teaching of writing; there are examples in many disciplines and in many countries.

Often a special feature of such a network community is the presence of persons whom the teacher in his or her ordinary practice would never have the opportunity to meet. For example, physics teachers in California involved in such a network were able to electronically interact with the authors of the textbook they used in their teaching, with on-going questions about the text and its support activities. In this way, "telementoring" relationships are developing of a type not likely to occur in the teacher's ordinary range of contacts (Wighton, 1993).

Such use of computer conferencing for networking among teachers is being seen as a major stimulus for teachers' professional development, since:

> ...teachers, like students, [who participate in cooperative on-line communities] acquire knowledge, develop teaching/learning strategies, increase self-esteem, and develop meaningful relationships with their peers" (Riel, 1990, p. 452)

Such good results do not happen automatically (see, for example, Schrum (1995) for a close examination of the implementation and motivational problems faced by teachers who are involved with professional development through networking). The educational technologist is increasingly busy with the new forms of teacher in-service and support that are emerging. Many of these forms parallel the also-emerging opportunities for individual professional development via tele-learning that we considered in Chapter 4.

■ 9.4 EDUCATIONAL TECHNOLOGISTS AS TEACHERS OF EDUCATIONAL TECHNOLOGISTS

Many educational technologists are employed as faculty members in a university or college in which preparation programs or advanced-degree programs are offered in the domain of educational technology itself. Thus, another way in which educational technologists are becoming involved with tele-learning is through teaching about it to their own students, or supervising graduate work that relates to it. What are some trends here?

We look first at an overview: How much are educational technologists teaching their own students about tele-learning? Then we close the chapter by looking at some innovative examples of how they are doing it.

■ 9.4.1 TELE-LEARNING AS A TOPIC OF STUDY

Tele-learning can be a topic of study in specialist courses for educational technologists, taught by educational technologists, in three broad ways. One of these is through being integrated in some way within a course with a relevant, more-general theme, such as "Integrating Computers in the Curriculum" or "Designing Learning Resources". A second way is to develop a specialist course itself around some topic relating to tele-learning. Usually these courses are at the graduate level. A third way is to emphasize some aspect of tele-learning in the theme of a graduate program, so that not only specialist instruction but other graduate-student activities and research are focused on the domain. We look at an overview of the extent to which tele-learning is being integrated into regular and specialist courses and programs in this section.

COURSES INVOLVING TELE-LEARNING

A useful source of information about courses in educational technology in general is the descriptive directory of "Degree Curricula in Educational Communications and Technology", published regularly by the Association for Educational Communications and Technology. Its Fifth Edition (Johnson, 1995a) appeared in February 1995 and contains listings of 167 graduate programs in the US and 33 outside the US in the domain of "educational communications and technology" (see also Johnson, 1995b, for a summary).

The AECT Inventory

Just as the term "educational technology" can be translated in many ways in different institutions and cultures (see Box 8.1), what is included in a graduate program in "educational communications and technology" can also vary widely. Also, like any survey, the AECT inventory is not exhaustive (those included must somehow or other know of the AECT initiative and fill in its survey form) and cannot remain perfectly up-to-date, it is a good representative overview of at least its own sampling base.

For each graduate program represented in its inventory, the AECT database lists the course titles of all courses in the program along with their number of clock hours per week. Also, among other information, the respondent from each institution responding to the inventory was asked to estimate the areas of emphasis within the curriculum, by apportionment of credit hours, given to the following topics:

- Media Management
- Telecommunications

- Instructional Development
- Learning Theory
- Instructional Design
- Materials Production
- Information Systems
- Librarianship
- Computer Technologies
- Other

"Telecommunications" was given as an area of emphasis in the graduate curricula of 117 of the 167 US institutions and 21 of the 33 non-US institutions responding to the survey.

What the institutions define as "telecommunications" may of course vary, but it is clear that tele-learning in its various forms is being stressed and is an object of study.

Courses about tele-learning

In what courses is tele-learning the general topic of study? The AECT Inventory gives some interesting insights. We scanned every course title listed in the Inventory for the 200 surveyed institutions and found 119 whose titles reflected aspects of tele-learning as we are defining it in this book. Box 9.19 lists a sampling of these.

And there are quite a few others. Reflecting the different backgrounds of tele-learning that we have been noting during this book, there are a number of institutions that offer three distinct courses called "Telecommunications in Education", "Educational Television", and "Distance Education". Given the convergence in technologies and the blurring of the meaning of "distance" which we note throughout this book, an overlap in such courses will be inevitable.

A needs analysis for tele-learning courses?

Interestingly, not much appears in the literature about rethinking the content of educational-technology curricula to reflect the many changes in technology that now are becoming so well established in practice, and in society in general. The whole process of changing curricula in a faculty program is slow and complicated. Educational technology curricula do not seem to be an exception. More often, courses are added on to the curriculum, due to the advocacy of an instructor who is especially interested in a topic, rather than because of an objective needs analysis of the field. (This was the result found in an analysis of 42 of the 43 faculties of education in Canada in the early 1980s with respect to the rationale

---

Box 9.19

Sampling of titles of graduate courses in educational technology focused on some aspect of tele-learning

Distance education (listed many times)
Educational or instructional television or broadcasting (different combinations of these
   two pairs of words were listed many times)
Telecommunications and networking in education
Educational telecommunications
Utilization and evaluation of instructional television
Telecommunication for instruction
Interactive television
Distance learning resources and telecommunication
TV in training and in business
Electronic networks for education
Telecommunications systems management
Instructional television and the school media center
School applications of portable TV
Cable communications
Instructional TV and modern media
On-line searching
Distance learning delivery systems
Telecommunications, distance learning, and collaborative interchange
Communicating with computer-based interactive technology
Contemporary trends in telecommunications
Introduction to the Internet
Design and management of distance learning systems
Interactive TV studio production
Technology and distance education
Basics of communication technology
Media pedagogy in the information age
On-line and distance learning
Telematics (from Johnson, 1995a)

---

and process by which courses relating to computers in education were added to their programs, Collis and Muir, 1986.) There is not much to suggest, from looking at the titles of courses in the AECT 1995 inventory, that this "adding on" process is not still occurring, and that "tele-something" is a new candidate for being added-on.

Of course, exceptions do exist, and some educational technologists are involved in the systematic assessment of the needs of those involved in tele-learning delivery in order to suggest priorities for the content of tele-learning "training courses" (Sherry and Morse, 1995). Thach and Murphy (1995) for example have done a careful analyses of competencies needed in distance education and identified different lists of competencies needed for the instructor, the instructional designer, the technology expert, the technician, the administrator, the site facilitator, the support staff, the editor of print materials, the librarian, the evaluation specialist, and the graphic designer. The top five competencies used most frequently by all roles are:

- Interpersonal communication skills
- English proficiency (they had only Canadian and US respondents)
- Collaboration/teamwork skills
- Writing skills
- Planning skills

How these can be translated into curriculum is not discussed. But the work of Thach and Murphy is a valuable contribution: not much overall analysis of the emerging roles of educational technologists in tele-learning seems to have occurred, and how these roles should be anticipated in curriculum revision in educational-technology faculties does not much seem to have been much discussed.

This book itself is meant to be a contribution to such an analysis.

■ 9.4.2 TEACHING ABOUT TELE-LEARNING, VIA TELE-LEARNING

There are a number of interesting and innovative examples of how educational technologists are teaching specialist courses about tele-learning, via the use of tele-learning. We look at a few examples here.

EXAMPLES

The course "Problems and Principles in the use of the Internet for Course Delivery", offered by the London University Institute of Education (UK) as part of its degree program in Online Education and Training, is taken by students throughout the world, as it is offered via e-mail and computer conferencing through the Internet. During the 100 hours of the time that students will spend on the course, they study:

- The role of computer-mediated communication in education and training
- The effectiveness of online education and collaborative learning
- Online services and their application to education

The faculty have extensive experience in the design and delivery of on-line courses. The philosophy of the course is that students learn about the topic by the experience of participating in the topic as on-line learners themselves.

The same philosophy can be seem in operation in a number of other courses, such as those listed in Table 9.6.

Table 9.6 Sample of courses about tele-learning, taught via tele-learning

Institution and Course	Description
EHRD 689 (graduate course in distance education), Texas A&M University	Students used video, audio, and computer conferencing for content-specific discussions that included graduate classes at five other universities (Yakimovicz and Murphy, 1995)
ResCMC, "Research Issues in Computer-Mediated Communication", Ontario Institute for Studies in Education	Course is taught entirely through e-mail functionalities available in LISTSERV (for information and syllabus, send a message to: Comserve@Rpitsvm.bitnet with the commands: Send ResCMC Material and Send ResCMC Syllabus in the body of the message
EME 6809, "Information Retrieval Systems/Distance Education", and EVT 4368 "Advanced Teaching Techniques in Vocational Education", University of Central Florida College of Education	Both courses focus on the application of technologies for distance education, and utilize various technologies including one-way video via microwave or satellite with audio-conferencing for live sessions, and e-mail via the Internet between sessions for further discussion, group-project planning, and submission of assignments (contact: Dr. Richard Cornell at Cornell@Pegasus.cc.UCF.edu)
ITL07 "Open/Distance and Student Centred Learning", Lancaster University (UK)	In addition to occasional face-to-face sessions, students and faculty interact and carry out course activities via computer conferencing (Goodyear, 1994; contact P.Goodyear@cent1.lanc.ac.uk)
"On-Line Learning and Distance Education", University of Twente, The Netherlands	In a mixture of face-to-face, computer conferencing, e-mail-functionality usage, and the WWW, students learn about the design of tele-learning environments and also tele-learning pedagogy through designing their own learning materials (see **Interface 9** for more information).

The last entry in Table 9.6 is an example of how senior students in educational technology can learn about tele-learning not only through the use of tele-learning technologies but also through the design and construction of tele-learning resources in a course approach based upon social constructivism (Bos, Kikstra and Morgen, 1995). To see the course environments for "On-Line and Distance Learning", created together as a collaborative learning activity by the instructor and 30 students, visit or contact:

On-Line Learning
URL
```
http://www.to.utwente.nl/ism/online95/campus/campus.html
http://www.to.utwente.nl/ism/online96/campus.htm
collis@edte.utwente.nl,
```
because they are my classes!

GRADUATE PROGRAMS IN TELE-LEARNING VIA TELE-LEARNING

Finally, just as there are courses about tele-learning taught via tele-learning, there are an increasing number of graduate-degree programs about tele-learning offered via tele-learning emerging for educational-technology specialists. Some of these evolve out of an academic background in distance education, others out of backgrounds in computer-based education, or other possibilities. Some examples of complete graduate-degree programs offered via tele-learning and relating to tele-learning as a topic are shown in Table 9.7.

GRADUATE-STUDENT RESEARCH

An important motor to the growth of tele-learning as a scientific area of investigation is the work of graduate students in educational technology who immerse themselves in research relating to some aspect of the domain. Many of the institutions in Johnson's (1995a) AECT inventory have examples of this, particularly as the inventory also gives main research areas of the graduate-faculty members associated with the programs in the inventory, and 58 indicate some aspect of tele-learning as a specialty.

Just as one example of the sort of energy and range of investigation in which graduate students in educational technology can be involved, Box 9.20 lists the titles of a sample of the graduate-research theses and dissertations which I have supervised during 1993–95 in the Faculty of Educational Science and Technology at the University of Twente which relate to tele-learning:

PRACTICE WHAT WE PREACH...

Because the domain of tele-learning is rapidly and continually evolving, its institutionalization in the form of courses in the training- or graduate programs of educational technologists is bound to lag behind its growth in practice. A first step is for educational technologists in their own teaching to evolve both an experience base and a theoretical base about tele-learning. A next step then is to practice what they preach. From the iteration of these two, we will not only see a continuing increment in the number of academic courses relating to "tele-learning as an educational technology" but we will also be better able to model what we are teaching.

Table 9.7 Sample of graduate-degree programs offered via tele-learning, relating to tele-learning

Program and institution	Sample of courses
EdD in Instructional Technology and Distance Education, Nova Southeastern University, US	Impact of technology on leadership and management Integrating technology in education, training, and distance delivery Instructional technology and distance delivery: Strategies for information-age educators (contact Vera Flight at: `flightv@alpha.acast.nova.edu`)
MA in Distance Education, University of London, (UK)	Adult learning and communication in distance education Electronic media in distance education Distance teaching for non-formal education (contact: Training Programmes Manager, International Extension College, Institute of Education, 10 Woburn Square, London, UK, fax: 44-71-323-0325)
Master of Science in Information Technology and Learning, Lancaster University, UK	Learning with interactive media Methods of IT-based learning materials production Open/distance and student-centred learning (Goodyear, 1994; `P.Goodyear@cent1.lancs.ac.uk`)

An excellent example of an educational technologist who does practice what he preaches is Greg Kearsley, an experienced educational technologist at George Washington University in the US (see Heller and Kearsley, 1995, as an example of Kearsley's work). As another example, Kearsley has made available a database he developed summarizing and illustrating 48 major theories of learning and instruction through a WWW site. Not only are the theories conveniently summarized, but hyperlinked to one another, so that interrelationships are brought out:

The Theory into Practice Database (Kearsley, 1995)
URL `http://www.gwu.edu/etl`

Until we, the educational technologists who teach specialist courses about educational technology at the university level, exemplify in our own teaching

> **Box 9.20**
>
> **Sample of graduate projects relating to tele-learning at the Faculty of Educational Science and Technology of The University of Twente**
>
> - Tele-cooperation support tools: Audio-conferencing and shared-workspaces in collaborative learning
> - On-line communication support for the handicapped
> - Integrating television, computer software, computer conferencing and print materials in instructional programming
> - Decision support for the choice of technology for distance education
> - Simulation software for learning about telecommunications use
> - An electronic support environment for support of distance-delivered mathematics courses
> - Designing, moderating, and analyzing the content of computer conferences as professional-development for instructional designers in a distance-education institution
> - Flexibility in course design for pan-European tele-learning
> - The "Remote Classroom"—bringing experts from the field into the vocational-education class
> - Adapting groupware to support distributed learning groups
> - Analyzing the impact of networking as a strategy for teachers' increased use of computers in instructional practice
> - Designing a WWW-based performance support system for teachers wishing to use the Internet for instruction
> - Improving the cross-cultural portability of educational software through computer-communication
> - Designing an interface based on teaching strategies for accessing resources on the Internet
> - Designing a new WWW browser based on learning-style preferences
> - Supporting distributed learners with a desktop multimedia learning environment
> - Designing a WWW environment for community learning
> - Management games via the Internet in a distance-education program in business administration
> - Scenarios for stimulating staff at an institute of technology to use real-time tele-learning technologies in teaching
>
> (Projects supervised by B. Collis in 1993–95)

the utilization of tele-learning as a support for the teaching-learning practice, we are not likely to take the leadership role that we could in the domain of tele-learning. Paraphrasing the advice of Ralph and Yang (1993), in their analysis of the impact of educational technology preparation on subsequent practice in Canada, if educational-technology graduates can be helped to internalize skills of tele-learning, then their faculty "will have contributed to the preparation of knowledgeable [professionals] for the 21st century".

Perhaps this is the most important way that many educational technologists can make a contribution to the tele-learning domain: through providing leadership, modeling, and inspiration to their own students.

INTERFACE 9: LOOK WHAT MY STUDENTS DID

THE WWW AS A LEARNING TOOL

PUTTING IDEAS INTO PRACTICE

I teach various courses in the Faculty of Educational Science and Technology at the University of Twente. One of these courses is an elective course, for students about to begin their Masters'-level final project. The course is called "On-Line and Distance Learning" and was first offered in Spring 1994. The course is scheduled to meet face-to-face for eight two-hour sessions in the Spring Term (March–May), and to include approximately 120 hours of total time for the students. The students have been studying educational technology (not teacher training) for three or four years.

Two sets of beliefs motivated my approach to this course in the Spring Term of 1995: social constructivism, and the potential of the WWW environment as a learning tool. The first belief I hope permeates all my teaching: I support a pedagogical approach where I and the students learn together by working together in a collaborative way. The second approach reflects my own learning with respect to the potential of the WWW as a learning environment: as I began the course in March 95 I wanted to test my own conviction, in practice, as to the potential of the WWW environment as a new type of educational technology.

OBJECTIVES FOR THE COURSE

I set up a distribution list for all the students enrolled in the course, and a week before the course began sent them via the list the course syllabus, planning, and objectives. All of these can be seen at:

URL http://www.to.utwente.nl/
ism/OnLine95/campus/campus.html

The eight objectives for the course included:

1.6 You will be able to use the Internet as a designer of educational resources by:

1.6.1 Collaborating with your classmates on design and execution decisions relating to the WWW site for our course reader

1.6.2 Using appropriate resources to contribute to the further development of the Reader for the course by expanding some aspect of it as WWW pages linked to the other pages in the reader...

The "reader" for the course was mounted on a WWW site. It consisted of the course materials from the 1994 version of the course and the final project created by the students in the 1994 cohort. This final project was a "book" about on-line learning, where each chapter had been written collaboratively by two students in the course and one colleague of my own, all through e-mail and file transfer. The book was written as a reader and subsequently mounted as a WWW site (this was Spring 1994 and I was only learning about the WWW myself). So the reader was content- and history-rich, but did not reflect any exploitation of the learning potential of the WWW. Particularly, there were almost no links, and almost no use of images or layout as learning support.

COURSE ACTIVITIES

The 32 students in the 1995 cohort (which included five exchange students, from Spain and Germany) and I met eight times face-to-face in a computer laboratory, a terrible room for teaching because of lighting, acoustic, and display problems. But there are 16 networked (rather old and slow) PC computers, all connected to our LAN and through that to the Internet. More importantly, each student has an unlimited Internet-access account, and there are many other, newer and faster, machines for them to work on outside of class.

We spent approximately six hours per week on-line in addition to the two hours face-to-face. I would send the students some sort of exploratory activity to do on line, focusing on design aspects of WWW sites and educational possibilities, and in groups of three they would contribute to a weekly computer conference which I monitored, using the FirstClass conferencing environment. In addition, I sent messages to them via the distribution list approximately three or four times weekly—interesting things I was learning, communal comments on their work, etc. (All this is described

within the Course WWW site whose URL was given above, under the link "Course Process".

THE DESIGN PROJECT

After a few weeks of preliminary study, the main project of the course began. Students formed groups of three (with two in a special category as overall design co-ordinators) and choose one of the ten chapters written by the students (and their distance collaborators) in the 1994 class.

The class project began: I set them, and myself, the challenge of how we could convert this material so that it would be a stimulating WWW-based textbook for the following year's class, and how we could integrate all the materials in the course into an overall WWW site which would be not only a course integrator but a learning environment. The two "special category" students took the overall-course aspect; the rest worked in groups of three (with the exchange students divided among five of the groups) and everyone worked in English, for the benefit of the exchange students.

DESIGN ISSUES

Through quite intense use of computer conferencing as well as small-group collaborative work, the students and I identified and confronted a number of important design issues relating to making our WWW environment both a valuable course environment for next year's group, but also an environment on the Internet that could serve as a learning resource for who ever would find it, and a resource for me to use with some students in 1996 who will be taking the course entirely at a distance (from

Bulgaria and Russia) as classmates of the face-to-face group.

Among the design issues the students debated quite vigorously among themselves:

- How much structure should be in each of the chapters? Is our approach to learning one of "instructional design" or of "learner control"?
Chapter 4 reflects a belief that instructional guidance and sequencing is best for learning the complex material in the chapter; Chapter 11 a belief in learner control of paths and choices.
- How important is consistency among the chapters? Does consistency constrain creativity and a best-fit of structure and layout to content?
...We finally agreed on a compromise: Freedom of expression within each chapter, but common use of terms, contribution of index terms to the overall index for the book, and agreement that all include some form of visual overview of the structure of each chapter.
- Should the structure be one of a long page of generally linear information but with a rich use of "example" and "footnote" links (better for studying, for printing out, for coherent development of ideas), or menu-type pages, rich with links to external sources?
...Chapter 3 is an example of the first approach, while Chapter 2 is an example of the second.
- Is this really a book, or something else, and thus will we still need a "real" book in addition to the site? What are the roles of the different technologies of text and distributed hypertext?
...Examples do not show up so much in the on-line site but were dominant points of debate among the students.
- How important are the links and graphics, anyway? Perhaps after all they are superficial and distracting?
...Chapter 8 is an example of a chapter based on a scepticism about the learning value of image features for our target group (senior university students) while Chapter 5 is an example of a group that used the chapter mainly to show hypermedia learning materials that could not be shown in ordinary textbooks.
- What metaphor should we choose for the overall environment?
...We chose that of a "virtual campus" in which we all had personal rooms (i.e., personal home pages), access to a shared set of tools and a shared library, and places to talk and work and debate together. The link "Our Environment" on the homepage expresses decision making relating to this metaphor.

RESULTS AND EVALUATION

The WWW provided a powerful learning environment for this course. The product can be seen via its URL, but more importantly the WWW gave us a rich, common, public, distributed environment on which we could work collaboratively on the creation of a shared product. And the WWW means this product is visible to the world for reaction and comment, as well as next years' students. In my own appraisal, it was one of the most stimulating learning experiences that I have been engaged in for many years. Of course there is always a chemistry of people and circumstance in a course, but the WWW environment gave us a learning tool that stimulated thought and collaborative construction of a problem solution.

It was a wonderful class....

10 Tele-learning: the future?

In this chapter, the tone changes from objective to subjective, from a reporting of current possibilities and issues with respect to tele-learning, to a personal prediction of the near-future (five to ten years from when this book was written, thus 2000–2005). The style of writing will change, from one heavily based on references and examples to one based more explicitly on the author's own ideas and predictions. In places, the chapter may be provocative, but it is never meant to be far-fetched. In the chapter, I look at major trends in technology, both at the transmission-channel level and at the instrumentation level, and focus on "convergence" and "bottlenecks" as two major words. I then translate these trends to the educational and learning landscape. I will try to indicate what I think likely to be the main characteristics of that landscape in the near future and what tele-learning has to do with that landscape. In particular, I give some reflections on the implications of tele-learning for learning, teaching, intellectual work, and even the way we label ourselves. This inevitably moves into implications relative to psychological, social, political, and moral issues; I will also express some views on how these relate to tele-learning in the future.

But I am a professional educational technologist, so I am particularly interested in what tele-learning is going to mean to my profession, the way I teach my students, the way my own work is valued. I end with a very personal thought about what tele-learning is likely to mean to myself and my colleagues in next decade.

▓ **10.1 Convergence and bottlenecks: key words for tele-learning technology in the near future**

▓ **10.2 The WWW as the "killer ap" for tele-learning**

▓ **10.3 Two settings for learning: in and out of school**

▓ **10. 4 A new paradigm for education?**

▓ **10. 5 And the implications for educational technologists?**

Objectives

After this chapter, you should have your own opinions as to the author's predictions about tele-learning in the near-future. Do you agree or not?

These predictions are:

- That keywords for technological developments affecting tele-learning will be "convergence" and "bottlenecks"

- That the next generations of the WWW will become the "killer ap" for tele-learning

- That two major "learning settings" will be operating in society, mostly in parallel to each other and with only some overlap. One will be situated inside existing educational institutions and the other outside of them. Each will have its own dominant uses of tele-learning; each will be based on a different philosophy of learning:
  The first is easy to explain because it has been in place for many years: institutions run courses, students "take" courses, students are finished when they do what they were required to do
  The second is life-long learning, learning at the workplace, just-in-time learning for which the individual takes responsibility, based on her own analysis of her own learning needs, motivated by her contacts with others and with new ideas

- That the most powerful innovations in education and learning will emerge from the overlap of these two learning settings. Tele-learning is a necessity for this overlap area

- That psychological, social, political, and moral forces will impact on the overlap area, mainly to constrain it, but without the validation of these forces the real potential of tele-learning will be much slower to emerge

- That educational technologists in particular face a serious challenge amongst all this opportunity, including how to keep up and grow within all the convergences, how to anticipate and lower the bottlenecks, and how to change their own curricula and ways of teaching in order to be leaders in the science and practice of tele-learning

These propositions will be elaborated and defended in this chapter.

■ 10.1 CONVERGENCE AND BOTTLENECKS: KEY WORDS FOR TELE-LEARNING TECHNOLOGY IN THE NEAR FUTURE

Everyone reading the newspaper and popular magazines in 1995 sees articles about the convergence of data, video and voice through new forms of networking or through existing distribution channels such as cable. The "hot phrase" of 1995 could well be "the information highway" (or its permutations, such as the German "info-autobahn"). Although what the information highway is, or will be, probably varies from reader to reader and differentiating fact from hype is difficult, the general idea of signal convergence is clear.

The information highway metaphor also involves a component set of analogies, these relating not to speed but to bottlenecks. We read about "traffic jams", "detours", "highway under construction", "problems with the entrance ramps", "obtaining a driver's license", "tollways vs highways", and many other such highway-related images, all relating to the problems facing those who wish to travel, full speed, down the information highway to where ever it is that it is leading. In this section, I make two sets of predictions about the technology of tele-learning in the decade spanning the century change, one set relating to convergence and the other to bottlenecks.

■ 10.1.1 PREDICTIONS RELATING TO THE CONVERGENCE OF TRANSMISSION TECHNOLOGIES

It is clear (in 1995) that the technical possibilities for an integration of communication systems are rapidly underway. Gradually telephone systems are handling as much data as voice, and are able, through compression technologies and technologies such as ISDN and ATM, to use their existing wires to handle some integrated signals. The strength of existing telephone systems is that they are switched, symmetrical, and interactive. Their backbones are increasingly digital, although analog copper wires still deliver services the "last link" —from the curb to the private user. It is this weak link especially which will improve in the near future. The suggestion has been put forward to remove this last link from the jurisdiction of the telephone companies and leave it open to private enterprise; perhaps this will speed the process if legislative protection of telephone companies becomes loose enough for this kind of competition. In contrast, many existing cable systems are unswitched and distributive, built on a backbone of analog fiber and satellites, with analog coaxial cables into end-receiver sites.

It does not need a prediction from me to speculate that in the future, these systems in terms of their architectures will be virtually identical. Such predictions appear regularly in the media, both popular and technical:

> ...interconnected signal connection and routing points will feed services via fiber to the neighborhood or curb. From these nodes, data enters homes and businesses on a mix of coaxial cable, copper wire, and fiber to reach set-top boxes, computers, and phones. Both systems [will be] switched and two-way, though not necessarily symmetrical or entirely digital. (Reinhardt, 1994, p. 48)

These networks, at least in their backbones, will be more- and- more fiber-optic cable, and within the next decade commercial and scientific forces together will probably have pushed the convergence of full digital streams of video, sound, and text through a single wire, cable, or fiber (or even through the air via a mobile data network; see Brodsky, for a 1995 analysis of how to connect to the Internet via cellular phone throughout the US). The streams will flow not only through these fibres and cables, but through the mixture of old and new wires going into homes, schools, offices, and businesses. The pipelines that carry these streams of signals will be switched, allowing information to be routed in two directions—in and out.

THE NETWORK COMPUTER

But there is another aspect to signal convergence and more powerful networks. This relates to the future of personal computers, and there is an important debate developing here (Laws, 1995). On one hand are the more-powerful-PC supporters, seeing a constant need to increase memory and speed of personal computers in order to handle the increasing demands of software and operating systems and multi-media and multi-tasking. On the other hand are the "network computer" proponents who see the future moving toward relatively low-memory terminals, mobile screen/keyboard devices with little intelligence or storage in themselves but getting what they need from a network, when it is needed. All software and information is held on remote units, powerful distributed servers.

CLIENT-SERVER CONCEPTS

This trend is already starting. The HotJava browser (see **Interface 3**) allows programmes to be downloaded from the WWW along with data and WWW documents. If you don't have the right software already on your computer to handle the program, Java will determine this, and give it to you without your knowing it as it downloads the requested links and WWW pages. Network computers will perhaps have only four basic packages installed locally: word processing, a WWW browser like HotJava, an e-mail package, and software for desktop video-conferencing. Everything else may come, in client-server fashion, from the network. These network computers can be relatively low cost and truly portable; costs will be based on what one uses from a network. Installation, maintenance, updating of software, will be the task of those managing the network, not of each personal computer user, struggling with updates and installation of massive packages which may only be occasionally used and then, only used in part.

Thus, my first prediction is in Box 10.1.

As a corollary of this prediction and easy to visualize because of what has happened with the WWW in 1995, the number of central sources to which the learner can connect will be vast, and the distinction between being a learner and

---

Box 10.1

Prediction 1. The network computer: an ubiquitous learning-station

Advances in technology—distribution technologies, user-access platforms, and client-server architectures—will make it possible for tele-learners to use the same "learn-station" for both real-time and asynchronous interactions and for their choice of combinations of text, video, sound and graphics. This learn-station will be affordable and portable because it will primarily function as a client or network computer, downloading temporarily what it needs locally but mainly working from network resources.

being a central source will increasingly blur. There is an old joke—On the Internet, nobody knows you're a dog—that has serious implications in a tele-learning context. On the WWW, nobody knows if you are a fool or wise, until they study what you offer.

■ 10.1.2 CONVERGENCE OF SYNCHRONOUS AND ASYNCHRONOUS

Galbreath (1995b) identifies two basic tele-learning applications for networked multi-media: an asynchronous application, such as for store-and-forward delivery of stored material such as video-on-demand requested from a video server; and synchronous for support of real-time interactions among persons such as during desktop video-conferencing. If we look at four basic patterns of communication—tell, ask, respond, discuss—we can see some how these two basic applications for distributed multi-media relate to the basic patterns of communication involved in tele-learning.

TELL MODE

Multiple representation forms and "receiving when desired"
The first pattern is the "telling" mode of communication: a central source disseminates information to some number of subscribers. The central source decides when this dissemination will occur, and to whom it goes. In this pattern, when the subscriber comes to her "learn-station", she will be able to obtain this communication in what ever form the central source has sent it, from text to video. She will be able to choose to receive the communication at a specified time, or retrieve it from the network at a time of her convenience. For the tele-learner, this means not only the bulletin-board type of text-based information-dissemination familiar in the early 1990s, but also "video on demand" possibilities for stored lectures, interviews, documentaries, and other sorts of learning-relevant dispatches. The "learn station" means she doesn't have to go to a different piece of equipment if she chooses to read text-based information or watch a video sequence.

The teacher and the class as "subscribers" in the tell mode
Of course, the learner does not always make these choices in isolation. The learner in a face-to-face classroom where tele-learning is part of the learning experience will not be an individual, but a member of a group or class. Someone, probably the teacher, will make the decision as to what is to be received by the group, in

the same way that the teacher does now with broadcast television. Two other layers of technology will become necessary—some "teacher tools" where the teacher in advance can select what she wishes to receive and to adapt and alter it further for the needs of the local class, and a "local-projection device" so that the screen of the learn station can be viewed by more than one or two persons at the same time. The latter is one of the major bottlenecks for tele-learning development that we discuss later in this section.

ASK MODE

Similar to receiving a message that has been disseminated by a central source, the tele-learner through her learn station will be able to ask or initiate requests in a variety of ways—through her own voice, through typing in requests in natural language, through use of increasingly helpful search tools and agents and robots, and even through video messages. Again the single learn station will technically accommodate multiple representational forms.

As before, these possibilities will be easier to apply when the tele-learner has her own learn-station. For learners in a group setting, human practices as well as technological "request filters" will have to be developed to prevent a collision of requests and questions streaming out from the group at the same time. Perhaps the technology can sort this out (maybe giving each member of the group a "personal request pad" to indicate to the central source that he or she has a question). If the central source is a computer, it can put requests in a queue for processing, but if the central source is a human teacher, there is a much lower limit to the barrage of requests that can be handled. For example, an instructor, speaking to distributed remote learners in real time and getting indications via flashing lights or beeps or icons that a number of learners have personal questions or requests will be like the classroom teacher seeing 25 hands waving in the air for simultaneous attention.

RESPOND MODE

Respond mode is the other side of the coin from ask mode. Client-server technology already makes it possible for one central source to respond in seemingly parallel fashion to many different requests, with different forms of messages (text, video, audio...). Of course, if the central source is a human, then she can only give one sort of response at a time, although she may be able to send this response back to multiple requesters simultaneously, such as she can now do electronically with a distribution list or through broadcasting. With convergent technologies she can speak her response and multi-cast it out, probably quicker and more naturally than typing a response in real time.

DISCUSS MODE

In Discuss mode, the central source organizes in some way the back-and-forth communication of various subscribers. With convergent technologies, this means that the subscribers, through their respective learn stations, may be able to see and talk to each other in real time; to review a real-time discussion that occurred earlier and perhaps make a non-real time follow-up contribution; as well as to participate in familiar asynchronous computer-conferencing discussions. And even the familiar asynchronous computer conference will benefit from the possibility of multiple representational forms through the learner station—the tele-learner may choose to send her contribution by text, by voice, or by video clip; any combination of forms can be stored as a incoming contribution to an asynchronous discussion, waiting to be read, heard, or watched when the other participants come to participate in the discussion.

MEANING FOR TELE-LEARNING?

The meaning of this technical convergence, not only of type of signal, but also in the way the bundled signal can be handled and received, will make an enormous difference to tele-learning. We saw some 1995-vintage examples of technical convergence with desktop multi-media conferencing applications in Chapter 8, but in general, in the mid 1990s, the technical division between television/video-type tele-learning and Internet-type tele-learning is still stark. Once we move to the level of technology where the same portable, affordable network computer can be used to send and receive a variety of signals including high-quality digitized video and those resulting from interaction with a multi-media database and applications accessed through a hypertext information system such as the WWW, then we will make a substantial breakthrough in tele-learning.

■ 10.1.3 WHERE WILL THE EMPHASIS BE? ON RESOURCES OR COMMUNICATION?

At the same time as I feel confident about my prediction about technical convergence and network computers, I am much less confident about predicting the way this convergence will be utilized in the tele-learning marketplace. Thus, I wonder myself about the following (Box 10.2):

WHOSE MARKET WILL IT BECOME?

What I do not have a prediction on is who will have the jurisdiction for this integrated stream of data and its broadband pipelines: the telephone company? the cable company? the provider for celluar mobile telephony? direct-broadcast

> **Box 10.2**
>
> **I wonder... what is going to dominate?**
>
> What will come to dominate the development of services for this technical convergence—Personal communication needs, or needs related to distributed access to quality resources?

satellite service providers? A main software company? This will matter for tele-learning, at least in 2005, for a number of reasons. To begin with, telephone companies bring the strengths and weaknesses of a point-to-point, pay-by-the-tick orientation and a close affinity to communication and information exchange, while cable providers bring an orientation toward point-to-multi-point one-way dissemination, with the user limited to making choices among channels, but with the expectation of a high-quality, attractive, dependable product. The orientation of broadcast television and the cable companies is that the subscriber pays for the opportunity to receive professionally prepared material. The orientation of the telephone companies is that the subscriber pays for the right to send and receive his or her own self-made material (voice or data), and that the subscriber accepts that she or he pays on the basis of time and quantity, not quality.

This very much relates to some of the differences in tele-learning between the television/video type approaches and the networking type approaches that we have been examining throughout this book. Television type tele-learning typically assumes professionals are responsible for the planning, production, and broadcasting of a quality "performance"; learners expect this and even when "free-form" communication is integrated with the delivery, the expectation is still that the course designer and instructor will have prepared and structured this well. In contrast, network-type tele-learning has been very much dominated by the idea of personal, private, communication, perhaps under the structured monitoring of a teacher but perhaps not. The freedom and self-responsibility of meaningful expression is a core motive for CMC-forms of tele-learning, and for the proliferation of self-made WWW pages in 1995.

I see at least two major issues here.

Where do we put the quality emphasis? Video or text?

For me, an important question is: whose standards of quality are going to prevail? In my opinion, the technical attributes needed for most of the tele-learning examples in this book relate more to fast access to a variety of resources than they do to the expectation that a high-quality learning resource ready to download and use in the classroom will be found. Thus to me, and given my own learning philosophy (see Section 10.3), "quality" of service rests more in relating flexibly to the requests of the learner than in presenting structured, quality-made lessons to the learner. To me, then, I am more concerned about having access to a great variety of resources, which I can browse, scan, skip, or study carefully, than I am about the quality of presentation within individual exemplars of these resources. But this of course is a personal opinion, based on my own philosophy of teaching and learning.

Seeing or reading?

One's philosophy of learning also relates to one's perspective on the importance of interaction and the forms that interaction can take. The more important learner interaction of various sorts (beyond clicking choices on a remote control unit) is to one's philosophy of learning, the more important it is in relation to the choice of the dominant service provider for tele-learning. Those who believe a core model for tele-learning is tele-presence and realistic real-time personal interaction will welcome a dominance of television expertise. Those who relate more to asynchronous communication and resource sharing will welcome a dominance of network expertise.

The core issue to me is when do we learn better by seeing and talking to each other in real time, and when do we learn better by reading and reflecting before responding? Most of the (interactive) television-type delivery situations which I have seen feature much less input, in quantity and (arguably) in quality from the individual learner than occurs in a computer conference, and also only involve inputs from some of the learners rather than all. The belief in real-time questioning among many instructors is strong, but not much exploited.

The WWW: breakthrough again...

The WWW is making a remarkable breakthrough here, with respect not only to the convergence of technologies, but more fundamentally to the convergence of mentalities (personal communication vs dissemination of a quality product). For the first time in any practical terms, individuals are able to be publishers and broadcasters, able to communicate in their own way their message to an unknown range of receivers. Receivers can choose a "selection" similar to the way they can choose a media title or a television program, and be engaged with it for enjoyment as well as learning. This is a power of the WWW in 1995: that we can choose to use it for personal expression and communication or can use it as a learning-material resource. The convergence between communication and receiving a quality- prepared message is occurring in WWW environments in a way that I think is remarkable and important. But this is the theme of Section 10.2...

■ 10.1.4 WHAT WILL HAPPEN TO THE INTERNET?

Let us first look more closely at the Internet and in particular the WWW as we know them in 1995 to see if they will be part of the delivery model for convergent-technology tele-learning in the next decade. Here is another place in which I am not sure of a prediction. Box 10.3 expresses my question.

Box 10.3

I wonder...about the Internet?

I wonder if the Internet, as it is now will still be functioning in 2005? Or will it have become the victim of its own success, overburdened and at an extremely high noise:value ratio where it is not commercialized, and a system for tele-shopping where it is commercialized?

The Internet system as we know it in 1995 is growing in usage so rapidly, that predictions have been made in September 1995 that if the current rate of Inter-net-access growth continues, every person on earth will have an Internet account by 2005. How can we control the quality of tele-learning, if everyone can talk to everyone and everyone can publish? (see **Interface 1**)

With the discovery of the Internet by businesses in 1995, the relentless desire of users for multi-media, the need for security for many different sorts of network applications, coupled with these high user-growth factors, it is not clear what the Internet will be like in 2005. The freedom, in 1995, of contacting others, of putting up one's own WWW site, of being able to enter all those sites found by search engines and robots, is already running in conflict with those who want to offer a quality product but need to be paid for its delivery.

"SCREECHING HALT?"

Predictions are increasingly heard about the current Internet system coming "to a screeching halt" (Ashley, 1995), particularly as users have discovered how to send real-time audio and video through the current system. The current Internet system is a point-to-point, or unicasting, system; when real-time video or radio is sent to a group of recipients, the volume of network traffic can quickly overwhelm the available bandwidth, as the unicast system tries to establish individual connections and transmissions with every recipient. Technological developments are doing much to deal with this, including the current "Mbone Internet backbone", better compression algorithms, and broadband network technologies such as ATM. However, the technical capacity of an internetworked system cannot be infinite; the "vision" of everyone learning what they want, when they want, and in the form they want, is nice as a vision but impossible as a realization. And someone has to pay for all these developments. Universities are less and less able, or willing, to invest in research about the Internet, given its high costs and direct payoff not so much to universities but to commercial users.

THE TELE-LEARNING SHOPPING MALL?

My guess is that the current Internet will evolve in a way that is already happening in 1995—toward being a general entry into a "shopping mall" which will serve as a sort of window-shopping corridor with further entry points for "intranet" addresses accessible through the system. From a tele-learning perspective, I see this as a sort of "tele-learning shopping mall" (or bazaar or market, depending on one's cultural frame of reference). One's overall Internet address will let one "window shop" around, browsing among "free samples" of those willing to let browsers drop in for free on their discussions and for (samples) of their services. However, most "shops" in this "tele-learning mall", unlike in a shopping centre, will have a price to enter, and will require a pass to make use of their services. This is because of the nature of information as a commodity, compared to commodities such as the ubiquitous shoes and jewelry of the real shopping mall.

"A TELE-LEARNING SMART CARD"

The mechanism for charging these entry prices may well be some sort of "smart-card" system associated with one's electronic address. A product is already being marketed in the US and France which may show us some aspects of tele-learning in 2005. This product is called the "ActivCard" (interestingly, the vendors of this card do not indicate an e-mail address, only fax numbers[1]). The ActivCard looks like a credit card, and is inscribed with information about the learner-subscriber, including his or her financial status. Under the control of the accompanying software system, card owners can connect into encrypted television broadcasts, can send their comments and assignments to an instructor, can access other sorts of on-line resources, and can even take examinations at home, through a modem connection.

This leads to my second prediction, one I fear is inevitable (see Box 10.4).

---

[1] In the US, ActivCard Networks Inc., Larkspur, CA, fax 1-415-464-1384; In Europe, ActivCard, Issy-les-Moulineaux Cedex, France, fax 33-1-41-08 33 99

> **Box 10.4**
>
> **Prediction 2: Controlled and with a price tag...**

Just as the technology will give tele-learners the possibility of choosing from multiple types of representation forms, choosing among vast numbers of central sources and choosing to make contact with a vast range of human contacts, so too will the technology be used to set up to control access and content of those resources and to provide a uniform way to make learners pay for them.

This model is already functioning with the commercial network organizations, particularly in the US and the UK (see **Interface 5**). It is my prediction that this sort of "validated user" approach will grow quickly, but it will not be uniform in the next decade. "Central Sources" will set up their own closed systems which could be called "Intranets", taking advantage of Internet tools and developments, but setting up firewalls to prevent unauthorized (i.e., non paid for) entry. Tele-learners can access an instructor and course materials in those systems to the extent the tele-learners are validated (i.e., that they have paid for this access). The free samples on the Internet will be just that.

Decisions controlled by administrators

I further predict that the smart-card aspects of this kind of system will be based in the financial administration of an institution, not in the computing centre. This suggests some interesting implications for some of the management problems of circa-1995 tele-learning, particularly problems of persons who contribute disproportionally often to computer-conferences in a tele-learning setting: perhaps the instructor can specify that no one is allowed to make more than a certain amount (by byte?) of contributions, and conversely, that lurkers cannot receive examination questions!

These comments seem factitious, and will be resented by those who believe a major benefit of computer communication is its freedom. But, the problem of manageability of asynchronous group discussions from the perspective of the instructor in the post-secondary setting is already significant, as we have seen in Chapter 6. Perhaps smart-cards can come to be used to even out on-line contributions and other contacts in the way the instructor thinks is pedagogically best?

But an educational rationale for access control will probably not be institutionally organized by 2005, or perhaps ever; enormous efforts will have to be made to get even the most basic information such as "Has the student paid his tuition?" onto these cards and to keep this information up-to-date. Commercial providers will figure billing systems out quickly; but I suspect that most educational institutions will not have this worked out in a sophisticated way by 2005.

■ 10.1.5 "CONNECT IN"...FOR TELE-LEARNING

My prediction is then that by 2005 we will be able to connect to some sorts of worldwide inter-networked "tele-learning shopping malls" as easily as we can in 1995 find a telephone and dial a number. (Perhaps we will some day all have one "address" through which we can be reached for all sorts of contacts including voice contact, video or still-frame contact, or contact with our WWW-based home page and its stationary data storage, but I do not predict this within the next decade.)

It is not clear what the operative verb will be for this making-connections act: log in? dial? select? point your browser at? But whatever the verb to describe what we are doing, the technological reality of it has already begun. In Japan, even in 1995, there are ISDN telephone booths that allow users to plug in a computer and access the Internet at high speed (for this and other examples, see Quittner, 1995). This is a start toward convergence in access to converged data streams. The organization of the "shopping mall services" will come much more slowly, in that this is a human jurisdictional problem. Because it is a human problem, it will take a long time to reach some commonly accepted forms. I cannot predict yet those will be but I think they will have their recognizable roots in the WWW of 1995.

■ 10.1.6 TECHNICAL BOTTLENECKS, OTHER CANDIDATES

But while the major commercial players fight out the technical issues relating to getting us onto their systems, and charging us for it, I encounter, very often, at least three other types of technical bottlenecks which negatively affect my own use of tele-learning. These bottlenecks worry me; they are like mosquitoes that the major commercial players are not considering and yet they have a major constraining effect on what I and others like me do. These are: (a) printer access and costs, (b) unclear sources of support, and (c) projection problems. They may seem trivial problems in relation to the vision of the information superhighway, but they are not to the realities of tele-learning implementation.

PRINTER ACCESS AND COSTS

For many applications of tele-learning, getting a printout for off-screen study and reference is important. Increasingly, this is difficult, as learners are sharing a printer across a LAN or do not have access to a personal printer at their private tele-learning location. In my own institution, we regularly waste time with printer problems and with waiting for printed output. Because of the discovery of the WWW and the ease with which pages can be printed, everyone is doing it, complete with downloaded graphics. The time this takes is substantial, and the print queue usually is long. Also, if I encourage my students to discuss topics via computer conferencing, and I wish printouts for my own reading and reflection and administrative needs, the printer is even busier. Furthermore, our institution also places a ceiling on how much can be printed per student; this ceiling is not adequate for heavy tele-learning use. For example, I have placed an entire course in a WWW site (see **Interface 9**); "paperless" in theory, but its 400 or so associated pages are too much to study without maintaining some printouts. Each student in a class of 30 sending pages to the shared printer is a continual cause of delays and problems for them as well as using up their printing budgets. Before, they only had to buy a book from the bookstore....

And for home tele-learners this printout problem is even worse. The costs of maintaining a good-quality printer at home for tele-learning support are high, and maintenance problems are frustrating. No body makes house calls when the printer stops working...

UNCLEAR RESPONSIBILITIES

One of the incredible aspects of the WWW and its browsers is their compatibility; although layouts can differ among browsers, I still am generally able to look at a properly constructed WWW site from where ever I am, assuming the computer I am working from has Internet access (that of course, is a significant barrier for many people). Generally, they work. In contrast, this is not so with many other new tele-learning technologies, such as ISDN connections and desktop multimedia conferencing. When something goes wrong in the tele-learning setting, it is often not clear where the problem is, or who to call for help. Is the problem in the network? the software? the server? which server? This is especially so the more innovative one tries to be. This kind of problem will only escalate with the escalation of tele-learning in the next decade...in a newly interconnected world, who is responsible for breakdowns in the interconnectivity?

PROJECTION AND VISIBILITY PROBLEMS

As I have pointed out throughout this book, tele-learning often takes place in a classroom or lecture hall—a group of persons needing to see what is coming out of a monitor. While television-type tele-learning can be set up for display on large-size monitors, many classrooms and lecture halls only have individual-sized monitors. Quantity is meant to compensate for size in many situations, in that some number of monitors are mounted in different places around the hall. Even so, monitors looked at from a seat at even a few meters' distance are not appropriate for reading small text or details of graphic displays. Monitors are for pictures and video, not for text beyond titles and labels.

How can a large group see one computer screen?

This is obviously one limitation on what can be shown in the classroom- or lecture-hall type of tele-learning, but it is not much more difficult than the problems faced by the instructor who teaches face-to-face in those settings. More critical is computer-screen output. Computer screens are still oriented to the single user, sitting close up, and reading, at his or her rate. Web applications generally fit this description, as do all tele-learning applications involved textual communication.

As an instructor who wishes to use tele-learning for pedagogical enrichment and re-engineering of my courses, I want to show my students, and discuss with them, resources and results of network searches relevant to tele-learning design and application. I am continually frustrated by the projection problem and now prepare PowerPoint slides of screendumps for use in lectures. (This also circumvents the increasing problem of inability to connect to WWW sites because of high traffic. On-the-spot connectivity cannot be counted on, for teaching situations.)

WHO IS PAYING ATTENTION TO THESE ISSUES?

Unfortunately, I do not see quick progress with respect to the three types of problems I have described here, as these fall in a gray area that will be only slowly harmonized with other aspects of the technical provision for tele-learning. (There is an noteworthy exception to this; in July 1995 in his keynote speech at the World Conference for Computers in Education in Birmingham, UK, Lazarus, an executive in the Microsoft Corporation associated with the education market, predicted that major technical developments in the future by which "schools can harness the coming communications revolution" will include larger storage, broadband media, faster connectivity, and "flat-panel screens to replace blackboards". I like this!)

However, despite Lazarus' predictions, I suspect that in 2005 problems with projection, printing, and support will still confront tele-learning participants, as learners, instructors, or innovators.

Let me turn from points of frustration with regard to technical issues, to a technical development for tele-learning about which I have much enthusiasm.

■ 10.2 THE WWW AS THE "KILLER AP" FOR TELE-LEARNING

Since 1994 I have become increasingly aware of something new and I think important coming into our field of tele-learning: the World Wide Web. As we all know, during 1995 alone technical breakthroughs in WWW technology and WWW browser and editor instrumentation are happening at an amazing rate. And what is further amazing, perhaps unprecedented, is the immediate exploitation of these developments by thousands of persons throughout the world, without "training courses" (although these are starting to be offered), without commercial advertising, without a direct profit motive, and often just by discovering and downloading a freely available tool. As an indicator of how fast WWW technical developments are emerging, in September 1995 alone I encountered the technical advances listed in Box 10.5.

Box 10.5

Technical developments in the WWW relevant to tele-learning, circa September 1995

Using the Java cross-platform, an object-oriented programming language created for the WWW, users can write programs that can be called up from a WWW page

The player for a popular multi-media development system is embedded in the NetScape browser so that, in the same window as users view a Web site, they can also take part in interactive experiences similar to those found now on CD-ROMs

Conversion programs, HTML editors, authoring tools, and Web production environments are rapidly enhancing the way that documents from word processors and data bases (flat and workgroup) can be converted into Web pages, for example:
```
http://www.halcyon.com/Webwizard/welcome.htm
http://www.sq.com/products/hotmetal/hmp-org.htm
http://www.qdeck.com/Webauthor/fact.html
http://www3.primenet.com/
http://w3.com
```

Users can receive both e-mail and HTML responses to the on-line forms that they fill out

Remote users can edit pages

Over 30 server packages are available, including various freeware packages, so an organization can have its own Web server on site

Search engines are evolving into robotic indexers, taking single terms or terms "ANDed" together and returning lists of URLs that even a month earlier took considerably longer to produce. Some of the more than 30 examples I have tried in September include:

`http://www.atext.com` *and* `http://www.verity.com`, *for concept-based searches,*

`http://www.eb.com`, *for an example of natural-language queries handled by a WAIS Inc. server (see also* `http://www.wais.com`*)*

`http://www.lycos.com` *for indexing and abstracting WWW pages*

`http://lib-www.ucr.edu/pubs/navigato.htm` *for a search of evaluations and ratings of thousands of WWW pages*

Agents automatically forward incoming mail as well as search results into folders based on subject

Clickable icons that represent a specific URL can be placed where ever the user wishes on his or her (Windows 95) desktop, inside folders or directories, or as embedded mail objects, and allow the user to click to enter the WWW site when ever he wants (see: `http://www.mcom.com/comprod/mirror/index.html`)

Integration of conferencing-type communication support into a site without needing a Unix-based server is now supported

VRML (Virtual Reality Modeling Language) leads to powerful enhancements in three-dimensional visualization within a WWW page

Software is available to help the user organize and manage WWW site information in "folios", and access the site from the folio in which a reference to the site is stored

Viewers allow the preservation of document design and layout, important with tables and figures

Data bases can be published on the WWW and the WWW environment can support real-time enquiry in those data bases (see Duncan, 1995a, for a good explanation of how to do this)

And this is only what I discovered during September 1995 without specifically trying to locate new developments. All of these have powerful implications for tele-learning. As Wolf (1995) notes, even the current (circa 1995) functionalities of the WWW allow the development of open learning environments for school, work and home that are (see Box 10.6):

> **Box 10.6**
>
> **Circa 1995 capabilities of WWW sites relevant for tele-learning**
>
> - Platform independent and scaleable
> - Multi-user capable
> - Based on an open standard
> - Support a hypermedia structure
> - Allow users to work with free or inexpensive software through the WWW
> - Use a client-server architecture
> - Support communication via a network
> - Support integration with other interactive media
> - Support working with "real-world" applications, such as spreadsheets, data bases, and word processors
> - Allow learners to create their own documents, construct links between documents, communicate with each other , and cooperate and collaborate on their learning (Wolf, 1995, pp. 689–690

■ 10.2.1 THE "KILLER AP"

To me, after 15 years of tele-learning activities as an educational technologist, instructor, and independent learner, the WWW, and its various tools and access technologies which together might be called "Webware" is the "killer application" for tele-learning. Thus my next prediction (Box 10.7) is easy.

> **Box 10.7**
>
> **Prediction 3: "Webware" as the breakthrough technology for tele-learning**
>
> The WWW, circa 1995 and its subsequent generations, is the breakthrough application for many forms of tele-learning—the application that can support and stimulate tele-learning for individual learners, in the teacher-led classroom, in the course-at-a-distance.

■ 10.2.2 TECHNICAL AND PEDAGOGICAL VERSATILITY

Among the versatile aspects of the WWW: it can be used to support the classroom lecture, it can be used for collaborative construction of information by learners working together in the same physical location or at a distance. It is for both real-time interaction, when used as a tool by the instructor or by learners working

---

[2] By the way, for non-native English speakers, please excuse my use of English (and perhaps only North American slang): "Killer ap" is short for "killer application" which in turn comes from the marketing world and implies the one particular product that is associated with a breakthrough and explosive growth in sales

together in traditional settings, as well as asynchronous interaction. It supports creativity and communication at the same time as it supports individual or group access of text-based information. It is remarkably standardized. I can tell you my URL of my home page and you can see it and share it immediately, from whereever you are. The threshold for beginning use and first-time design is low. The sense of energy exuding from its explorers is enormous.

In my opinion, I as an educational technologist have never seen such a rapid development as the WWW in terms of learning media. To me it is already a key tool for tele-learning in 1995 and will become more so during the next decade as the networks through which WWW sites are accessed become increasingly broadband, and the platforms through which the sites are accessed have increasingly fast and powerful processors. Thus as an expansion of Predictions #1 and #3, I venture the following (Box 10.8).

Box 10.8

Prediction 4: The evolving WWW

"Central Sources" for tele-learning will be future generations of WWW servers; subscribers at their "learn stations" will work and communicate through client environments that are extensions of WWW clients of the mid 1990s; multi-media will be supported through this distributed system, particularly by innovations in multicasting; and separate applications ranging from video-conferencing to ftp and computer conferencing will all be entered via a WWW-like hyperlinked structure and a common type of user interface growing out of the browser-look of 1995.

An important part of the evolving WWW will be the parallel existence of "intranet" WWW systems with full WWW functionalities, but secured from open access from public WWW. The WWW will be, like the Internet itself, a web of webs sharing a common protocol.

▧ 10.2.3 THE END OF TELEVISION-TYPE TELE-LEARNING?

Does this mean I do not think there will be (interactive) television-type tele-learning in the next decade? No, it doesn't. There is an important role for television-type learning transmission, both interactive and non-interactive, and it will continue. What I do predict is that this kind of tele-learning will also be accessed through a hyperlinked system that supports not only the real-time television-type interaction, but also at the same time allows participants to link to other resources and tools and persons via the WWW-type common architecture.

What I can't predict is the following (Box 10.9).

Box 10.9

I wonder if...?? The WWW in 2005?

Will the following generations of WWW-type sites and browsers still look like and basically act like those of 1995?

I can't predict this. Browsers are generically similar now in user interface, but evolving so quickly that who can say? But I do think the basic concept of hyperlinked connectivity will remain. Marshall McLuhan said in 1962 that "the medium is the message". Baskin, editor of an international computer trade magazine, says in 1995 that "The computer is the network" (p. 30). Pickering (1995) says that the Web is a medium by which we "unconsciously receive and transmit another message. That message is independence, and that is an education in itself". I say, in a less-lyrical blend of all of these, that "the WWW is the breakthrough ap of tele-learning".

This breakthrough is relatively easy to argue from a technical side. But what about from human and organizational sides? What does the WWW have to do with the established educational system that is in place throughout the world?

So far in this chapter, I have been talking primarily about the technology of tele-learning in the next decade. In the next section, I would like to look instead more specifically at the educational landscape itself. What will "learning" be like in 2005 and what will be the role of tele-learning within that?

■ 10.3 Two settings for learning: in and out of school

In this book, we have looked at tele-learning as both individual learning outside of the formal educational institution (Chapters 3 and 4) and within (Chapters 5, 6 and 7). How will these learning settings evolve during the next decade? What is the contribution of tele-learning to this evolution?

■ 10.3.1 Changes within the educational organization

The educational philosopher Illich, in 1971, said the following, long before the days of the WWW or of layman access to the Internet system:

...I intend to show that the inverse of school is possible: that we can depend on self motivated learning instead of employing teachers to bribe or compel the student to find the time or the will to learn; that we can provide the learner with new links to the world instead of funneling all educational programs through the teacher...'Network' is often used, unfortunately, to designate the channels reserved for materials selected by others... I wish we had another word...a synonym for an 'educational web'" (1971, Chapter 7)

A few years later, in 1973, the French philosopher Teilhard de Chardin predicted that a "web of communication technology" would emerge that would initially work through education, but then later through "human consciousness itself". This prediction, as well as that of Illich, was remarkably ahead of its time. I think they are interesting in that both suggest that if such a technology would emerge, the educational system might change in some of its fundamental characteristics.

CHANGES IN EDUCATIONAL PHILOSOPHY AND PRACTICE?

Now, almost 30 years later, we have the technology suggested by Illich and Teilhard de Chardin, albeit not yet available very much in classrooms: is the educational system also changing? Will it fundamentally change in the next decade? Will tele-learning be associated with such a change? In Table 10.1 some visions for change in the nature and philosophy of "the educational enterprise" are noted, along with their potential relationship to tele-learning.

■ 10.3.2 BUT, ARE EDUCATIONAL INSTITUTIONS REALLY CHANGING?

The visions espoused in Table 10.1 are exciting; all involve some fundamental change in the way we as educational practitioners organize the practice of organized teaching and learning. Tele-learning clearly plays a key role in facilitating these changes. But to what extent are such fundamental changes actually happening in schools and universities and training institutions?

DOING THE SAME THINGS, DIFFERENTLY...

In my opinion, not much. While much is going on, and going on with tele-learning, when the broad picture is looked at the educational system is more likely to "do the same things differently than to do different things" (Thornburg, 1995). Tele-learning is still often equated with "distance education" in its "first-generation model", that of trying to replicate the existing face-to-face classroom as

Table 10.1 Predicted changes in the education enterprise, and tele-learning

Source	Change	Relation to tele-learning
Brown, et al, 1993	Learning as participation in communities of practice, distributed expertise throughout the learning community; learners change from recipients of incoming information to researchers; school activity should be authentic to the real world	Tele-learning allows new communication contacts and new opportunities for being part of a distributed learning group; networks allow the learner access to vast amounts of real-world information which he must learn to access and handle
Jonassen, 1995	Meaningful learning is collaborative and conversational; technology can be an intellectual partner, a tool, and a context	Computer conferencing can support discourse among knowledge-building communities of learners
Lowyck, 1994	Learning should move from being "closed steering" to "open, self regulating" and education is moving from being "stable, fixed" to "changing, flexible"	Tele-learning technology is accompanying a movement in education from being one-way to interactive, linear to a-linear, involving isolated media to integrated media, fixed location to distance, oriented toward the individual to oriented toward networking
Ortner, Graff and Wilmersdoerfer, 1992	Distance education should move from the transport of information to the "transport of personalities"	The move from computer conferencing to audio and video conferencing improves the naturalness of human contact and communication
Jessup and Valacich, 1993	Collaborative group work and learning should be supported by various learning scenarios: any time/any place, culture bridging, just-in-time learning, and "window to anywhere"	Technologies need to be light-weight and portable, such as laptop computers and wireless LANs; technologies to support group "sensemaking" and "tele-presence" are important; ready access to appropriate information is important; videoconferencing needs to be supplemented with tools for group support

Lever, 1991	The learner must engage in the exploration of questions yet to be posed; this requires a "collaboratory" classroom model	Tele-learning technologies combine collaboration made possible through technological connections with an electronic laboratory for exploration and discovery
Pea, 1994	Education should move from transmission and ritual toward transformative, a "quest to expand the ways of knowing	Multi-media computing and communications capabilities need to be integrated; support tools for the co-construction of new representations of knowledge such as annotated video and hypertexts are needed
Itzkan, 1994–95	Technologies should move from a substitution mode in education to a transformation mode	Networks evolve from automated messaging to resource sharing to "educational landscapes; Students evolve from pen pals to "global citizens"
Dede, 1994	Virtual communities will complement face-to-face relationships in learning; customized knowledge utilities will complement the text, the teacher, and databases as major information sources	Networking and the WWW are stimulating these developments

much as possible for students who are not fortunate enough to be there. The assumption is that the face-to-face model, as traditionally practiced, remains the ideal.

In this view of tele-learning, its effects are measured by comparing the learning gains (and the costs) of students in face-to-face situations with those at a distance. In this view of tele-learning (commonly called distance learning in the US or tele-teaching) the assumption is that the teacher teaches, the students are taking a course, and the organization validates and defines what students do and achieve.

Even in second-generation "distance education" such as delivered by the Open Universities in many countries, the assumption is still that students learn through following well-designed courses, with their achievement certified by the faculty of the university based on pre-set criteria.

MOVING TOWARD DOING THINGS DIFFERENTLY?
Can institutions break away from this mould, and support learning of the sort envisioned in the middle column of Table 10.1?

An Electronic University?
It is very difficult. Despite, for example, a number of initiatives relating to "campuses without walls", "virtual universities", and "electronic universities" (see, for example, Alexander and Cutcher, 1992, for results of an investigation supported by the Commission of the European Community), and a few entrepreneurial efforts making use of the Internet (see for example, the *Global Network Academy,* `http://uu-gna.mit.edu/uu-gna/` or the *Virtual Online* University, contact `billp@showme.missouri.edu`), it cannot be said that the nature of course- and institution-based education is much changing in many of its fundamental characteristics.

Administrative bottlenecks
Moore (1993) noted a major administrative problem: "...there is still no agency in North America that has the power, recognition, or authority to provide a certification of independent, individually constructed learning programs that has credibility in the academic and business environment comparable to the degree awarded by a brick-and-mortar university" (p. 6). And even the effort to transfer credits among each others' courses as a step toward more flexible learning opportunities for students is very hard to do.

> *"The agenda... begins with questions about who is to coordinate and regulate electronic courses offered on network or satellite; who is to set standards, especially when nations and universities disagree;...and who is to arbitrate and decide on such matters as degrees and exchange of course credits"*(Rossman, 1993, p. 13).

Institutions would have to change substantially
Collaborative projects do go on in different countries and regions; some collaborations do work; but in general structural change in any educational institution is slow, even torturously slow. Bates (1994) notes that a

> *"21st century electronic educational institution" will not occur from "merely adding on new technologies to the existing structure or schools, colleges and universities...This will just increase costs and marginalize the use of technology....Some organizations will be created from scratch to meet the education and training needs of a networked, multimedia society...[Existing*

institutions will need to go through] a thorough re-examination of their core practices of organization... (pp. 17–18).

The institution must become a "facilitator of learning" whose instructors may not work for the institution, whose students may not even be registered with the institution. The institution may come to serve more as a "multi-media reference library", providing the technological infrastructure for learner access of what they want and need.

Bates is correct that this sort of delivery model is what is needed to realize many of the visions of educational reformers when they think about tele-learning. In my opinion, however, I am pessimistic about Bates' opinion that existing institutions can "re-examine" themselves to evolve into such roles. As Rossman (1993) says, reaching a state of "technical readiness" for a new form of learning institution is easier than reaching a state of curricular and administrative readiness.

■ 10.3.3 BUT GOOD THINGS ARE HAPPENING...

IN POST-SECONDARY...

But because I do not think radical change is occurring in educational institutions does not mean that I do not think any change is happening: this book is full of examples of interesting changes in educational practice within existing institutions through tele-learning. Sometimes these changes involve doing the same thing differently, and better—for example, e-mail contact rather than office hours for the university instructor. Other times new types of learning activities are being made possible, such as the collaborative design of WWW pages as learning materials with co-learners outside one's class, university or even country.

Thus I agree with Dede's predictions about the impact of tele-learning on educational institutions during the next decade, given in Box 10.10.

Box 10.10

Prediction 5: New communities, new knowledge utilities

Two of the most significant changes to education involving tele-learning will be the increasing importance of virtual communities to complement face-to-face relationships in learning, and the increasing use of "knowledge utilities" particularly through the WWW, to complement the textbook and the teacher as major information sources (Dede, 1994).

I also believe that offering and taking courses at a distance will increase, particularly in higher-education institutions, but often this will be in a way that tries to reproduce the face-to-face course over time or space, rather than represents any paradigm shift in educational organization. However, not everything has to be a paradigm shift in order to be valuable!! With tele-learning we can do both the same things differently or better, and do things differently (to use Thornburg's phrase, 1995), but in educational organizations the latter will be harder to accomplish than the former.

AND IN SECONDARY SCHOOLS?

In the previous paragraphs, I have been implicitly talking about higher education. What is my prediction about secondary schools and tele-learning in the next decade? Perhaps a good way to summarize the prediction is indicated in the following sentence:

> *James Gleick, the Pulitzer-prize winning writer about technology, has said "I have seen the future, and it's still in the future"* (reported in Kim, 1995).

Dede's prediction of virtual communities and of supplementing traditional text materials with customized information will have greater difficulty the younger the learner and the more sensitive the teacher and school is to parental, community, and other external standards. For example, the concern in 1995 about students having access to pornographic materials on the Internet has been sufficiently powerful to convince some legislators in the US to believe that the Internet must be "regulated" and controlled. In school systems where success is measured by performance on standardized examinations, the importance of staying with well-structured, examination-tuned learning materials will remain, no matter how many educational theorists call for self-guided learning. The difficulty of secondary school teachers to innovate their existing educational practice is one of the best-documented observations in educational research (see Chapter 7 and 9).

But things are changing, even in secondary schools. Itzkan (1994–95), for example, see networking moving from a "substitution" function, primarily automating messaging, through a "transition function" of resource sharing, to a "transformation" function, where networks will become "educational landscapes". Itzkan sees secondary schools of the future being judged by their degree of "access to the network—what services they are connected to and how many students can utilize them".

My prediction? How will secondary schools be affected by tele-learning in the decade 1995–2005? I suggest the following (Box 10.11).

> **Box 10.11**
>
> **Prediction 6: Secondary school and enrichment**
>
> Teachers, and later on, secondary school students will come to routinely access distributed multi-media resources for resource materials, make occasional contacts with distributed experts for feedback and motivation, and occasion use of 'virtual field trips' will be part of the secondary-school experience.

AND IN ELEMENTARY SCHOOLS?

I furthermore predict very interesting and innovative tele-learning possibilities for younger children, whose teachers are not so bound by rigid curricula and examinations and time-tables as secondary-school teachers, and who are more attuned to multi-disciplinary and explorative activities. Thus, Box 10.12.

> **Box 10.12**
>
> **Prediction 7: Young children and creativity**
>
> When elementary schools are able to get comfortable Internet access, young children and their teachers will make creative use of the WWW and its successors.

AND IN TRAINING?

In training, where cost-containment and efficiency considerations tend to dominate decision making, I see a very interesting dichotomy developing. On one hand, the traditional course, with a well-structured content and approach, a competent instructor, and clear goals and payoff, will continue to be a strong motivator for training decisions. The course as a core for learning will continue, but within this tele-learning possibilities will bring a large number of variations. The TeleScopia Project (1994–95, see Chapter 9), illustrates some of these. Table 10.2 shows how traditional training courses in the TeleScopia Project had been first adapted for tele-learning, by moving away from face-to-face sessions with individual study between the face-to-face sessions, and then how they were further adapted for the TeleScopia Project:

As these example show, there is a steady innovation in professional education and high-level training to move from the restrictions and costs of bringing all learners together to a traditional course setting. One general way in which this evolution has moved, as we saw in Chapter 7, is toward using television-type

Table 10.2 Course variations for training, with tele-learning: examples from the TeleScopia Project (Collis, 1995d)

Courses	1st-Generation change	2nd-Generation change
Language Learning for Professionals	Move from face-to-face sessions to use of e-mail and occasional interactive television sessions	Move to fewer interactive television sessions and more extensive use of computer conferencing
Telematics for Engineers	Face-to-face sessions in a central lecture hall are also distributed to remote classrooms via ISDN; learners indicate they have a question by pushing a button on a console where they are seated	1st-generation changes augmented by use of e-mail for asynchronous personal interactions between instructor and learners outside of the lectures
Greek for Adult Beginners	Video lessons sent by satellite; print and study materials sent by mail	1st generation changes augmented by fax or e-mail for quicker interaction with the instructor and feedback on assignments; learning materials translated into additional languages for pan-European learning
Management Innovation for Business Administration	Interactive television used as focusing event, to bring distributed groups of learners together for discussion of cases	1st generation changes augmented by the use of e-mail and computer conferencing for additional communication, and also by translation of case materials and printed and video-based study materials into additional languages, for pan-European learning range
Environmental Engineering	Materials developed for text-based distance education	Materials adapted into a WWW environment with embedded computer conferencing; occasional videoconferencing sessions used to focus and stimulate collaborative work on assignments
European Aspects of Accounting, for Small Companies	Learning materials (text, software) sent by mail for self-study; occasional face-to-face meetings with tutor at local centre to personalize application of course principles to the learner's own situation	1st-generation changes, but face-to-face sessions done by desktop multi-media conferencing with application sharing so that learners can interact with a tutor even in another country

tele-learning in order to bring the instructor, virtually, to a classroom convenient to the local learners, perhaps even in their own company. This strand of evolution is gradually adding opportunities for asynchronous interaction, usually in terms of provision for questions to the instructor, or for sending and receiving assignments and feedback. The other strand of evolution, to the classic "distance and open learning model" where the learner has a carefully designed package of learning materials and works through them at his or her own time and place, with opportunities of various sorts for questions and local tutoring, is now being augmented by trying harder to increase "tele-presence" with the distant instructor, or to bring the learner into a group-type situation, for discussion or to work together on an assignment. Common in all of these are (a) the approach to learning is still via participating in a course, run by an instructor, and with most expectations of how to complete the course pre-determined by the instructor or his institution; and (b) the learners can stay in their own locality, even building, rather than having to leave work and home to attend a course in a residential setting at another location.

Away from the course, toward the "just-in-time" support model

But I said there were two very different strands of evolution in training, both of which are facilitated by tele-learning. The second strand is similar to the above in terms of (b), in that the learner stays not only in his or her region, but directly in his or her workplace. However, the second strand is different in that the learner probably does not take a course structured by others. Based on his own, perhaps unique, learning need, he turns to tele-learning for just-in-time access to appropriate resources to help him with his problem. The resources may be persons or learning materials, or examples, or even computer-based tutorials. Through tele-learning, he is able to access this range of possibilities from close to his workplace, and have more self-control over how much and what he wishes to study and discuss with experts.

This approach brings many more aspects of flexbility into the learning setting than are possible in pre-structured courses. It also brings more problems with respect to helping the learner make his own decisions about what learning materials are appropriate, how much he needs to learn to solve his problem, and how well he has learned. All of these appraisals are typically done by the educational specialist in the traditional learning situation: in just-in-time learning, learning of the sort we considered in Chapters 3 and 4 of this book, the learner moves more and more to an expectation of self-responsibility for learning decisions. This kind of life-long, "finger-tip" learning can be supported through devices such as "EPSSs" (see Chapter 8) or "network services" (see Chapter 9 and

Interface 5), or organizational services provided by professional societies (see Chapters 4 and 9). The key to just-in-time learning? The sorts of tele-learning possibilities we considered in Chapter 4.

PREDICTIONS ABOUT TRAINING...

What is going to happen in training and professional education? Will one of these paradigms come to dominate? My guess is that both paradigms will continue. The structured course will be appropriate when learners (a) need structure and motivation, (b) need institutional credit and legitimization for their learning, or (c) choose themselves for a course-type experience in order to leave the ordinary workplace and immerse themselves in a learning experience for a certain period of time, cleaning away daily distractions and problems and absorbing not only the course material but the opportunity to interact personally with a group of fellow-students.

Tele-learning faces an uphill battle when learners are motivated by Facet (c). I discovered this in an evaluation I did of a training innovation, where the learners, practicing engineers in various branches of a multi-national corporation, were told that they could eliminate the costly annual training course for two-weeks' updating that occurred in places such as Rome or Paris, and instead have the "same benefits" by interactive television and e-mail right in their own buildings (Collis, 1993a). The management was delighted at all the time and cost that would be saved by avoiding those two weeks in Rome; the engineers were distinctly less pleased, as the two-weeks' experience each year had become a valuable activity for them in a variety of ways, not only for the course itself.

In contrast, the "just-in-time" approach will be an on-going sort of activity, for browsing, for updating one's self as to new developments, for non-disruptive communication with others in one's same field, for occasional targeted questions, for motivation, for hints. As professionals are more and more specialized, it will be less- and-less possible to find a "course" adequate for their own needs, or an appropriate instructor; tele-learning through interaction with one's peers and through access to targeted reports and research results will be more and more the way professionals learn. Thus the next prediction, in Box 10.13.

Box 10.13

Prediction 8: Training and pedagogical re-engineering

Training departments in businesses will lead the way in increased use of multi-media networks for more-efficient one-to-one tutoring and access to multi-media training materials, on the job and just-in-time.

AND OVERALL?

Thinking of the current and future deployment of tele-learning in four different levels of organized educational delivery—elementary schools, secondary schools, higher-education institutions, and training departments, therefore, I make the following overall predictions for the decade 1995–2005 (Box 10.14):

Box 10.14

Prediction 9: The tele-learning landscape overall...

- In higher-education, the use of the WWW and other forms of networking will increase both qualitatively and imaginatively. Video-on-demand will have some creative educational applications
- Elementary schools will make use of tele-learning for creative enrichment; secondary schools will make use of tele-learning to extend learning opportunities but without substantial re-engineering of instruction
- It will be in various training and professional development settings that the most radical pedagogical re-engineering will take place, toward just-in-time learning and learning on the job and away from the course structure
- Institutions who already support (interactive) television-type tele-learning (predominately large training institutions, some higher-education institutions, and schools), will continue to do so, with little change in their educational practices and philosophies. All institutions will maintain some level of network infrastructure; tele-learning as pedagogical re-engineering will be most associated with improvements in network acces and capability.

Some further comments...

- Those who want and need structured, instructor-led courses will welcome the increased interaction possibilities made available by "network computers" and by the new generations of television/video-type tele-learning technology. Video-on-demand will make much more course content available to learners, but at the cost of peer interaction and group participation. The pedagogy for this type of learning will continue to evolve, but with its roots clearly in the premise that "the best" learning would have been in the classroom with the teacher, had this been possible.
- In higher education, I predict courses will still be the norm in 2005, with familiar aspects such as number of credit hours, semester being offered, and pre-requisites still operating. Although getting credit for courses taken outside one's home institution will be increasingly common, the student will still have a home institution, to whom he pays his fees and from whom he receives his diploma and its associated accreditation.

- However, the WWW and its successors will make the concept of integrated and hyperlinked access to a wide range of learning materials an increasing aspect of course participation. Either as supplements to traditional texts or replacements, learners and instructors will more and more expect to search for and evaluate the relevance of resources, cases, and other learning materials.
- Collaborative learning and projects will be much more common in higher-education than in 1995, as learners will have increasingly attractive and powerful ways to access shared materials and to communicate and collaborate via networking.
- Lectures will more and more be available electronically, in both text and video form, for time-independent study and to provide more depth and content than possible in the time-bound lecture setting.
- Instructors themselves will be more and more identified in terms of their distributed professional communities, rather than their departments or physically immediate colleagues. Research projects will be done not by peers in the same hallway or department or faculty, but in collaborative teams representing many different organizations. The learning that accrues from this will be strong and stimulating; however, finding a way to re-cycle it in one's own institution will remain difficult.
- The faculty member's one "home page" (or its 2005 equivalent) will not only be a multi-media curriculum vita, but also an important way to substantiate and share one's growing knowledge and accomplishments with peers (and review and promotion committees).

Thus, will schools and higher-education institutions and training centres disappear by 2005? My response to this (Box 10.15) is in the sense of certainty rather than prediction.

Box 10.15

Prediction 10: Not a radical change...

Schools and higher-education institutions and training centres will be operating in 2005, structurally, in ways similar to what they do in 1995, with a variety of extensions and enrichments of existing practice, and some new habits.

The new habits will be most strongly seen in higher education, where:

- Communication with one's instructor via e-mail and one's learning group via computer conferencing will be routine practice

- Integration of course materials, including videos of lectures, in a hyperlinked WWW-successor environment will be routine practice
- Group and collaborative learning will be common, facilitated by electronic shared-workspace tools and access to shared resources
- Assignments will be typically available for all to see, as part of the growing WWW-successor environment for a course
- Textbooks will be less central as study material, as effective use of customized searches for relevant sources and examples will be expected of learners as part of the learning process
- Lectures will still occur, as focusing events and as opportunities to stimulate the group chemistry of the participants in the course, but the quantity of lectures will decrease to balance the increased amount of time the instructor will be interacting on-line with individual and groups of learners
- Assigning grades will become more and more problematical as learners will move in less-and-less common ways through a course
- The strain and demands on the instructor will increase, not decrease, as she tries to manage all the communication and diversity of resources that will be contributed by learners.

In secondary and elementary schools, the new habits will be less pervasive than in higher education, and more optional. The creative teacher will have more tools and possibilities to bring the world into her classroom and to send her students out in the world for contacts and feedback and resources. How much the less-inspired teacher will make use of these opportunities remains to be seen, but my prediction is, not too much and only slowly during the next decade. Television-type tele-learning that can be channeled directly into the classroom and is accompanied by various sorts of learning materials and opportunities for communication, learning-support experiences that are available via networking and network services organized in WWW-successor environments accessible through the same "learn station" as the broadcast materials, will in my prediction, be the "way in" for tele-learning in the typical school classroom during the period 1995–2005.

▦ 10.3.4 LEARNING OUTSIDE OF THE EDUCATIONAL INSTITUTION

In the previous section, we generally focused on learning within an educational institution, although the just-in-time example relevant to professional development was different. And I think that difference is very important. As we saw in

Chapters 3 and 4 of this book, an increasing amount of learning is going on, even in 1995, outside of the traditional educational institution. Of course, this has always been the case; people learn from their families, their friends, their cultural myths and their religious leaders. People learn from books and magazines and from public lectures and self-teaching materials. People learn from watching documentaries on television and from listening to informed debate on both television and radio.

People learn, and learn a great deal outside of school. What they don't get is formal acknowledgment for this learning; it usually "doesn't count" in terms of grades, and examinations, and diplomas and degrees and salary scales. Informal learning may make a person wise or well-informed or even rich, but traditional educational institutions do not accredit it. Within the walls of the institution, the instructor is the authority; the instructor (and/or the institution) decides what qualifies as adequate for the "stamp of approval" of course completion. The assembly-line, or Fordist model, of education is efficient and predictable; but by definition deviations are not efficient, not comfortable, or even not often allowed.

One reason is that society expects its products, be they cars or MAs, to have to meet some uniform quality standards and to function in predictable ways. Another reason is that those responsible for the operation of the system are held accountable for the quantity, and often conformity, of those emerging from it. "League tables" comparing institution (or teacher) performance is becoming part of accountability movements in many countries. "Raising test scores" is a measure of success.

In parallel to, or contrast to, the educational institution, I think what is happening with tele-learning, particularly the WWW-type and certain types of CMC, is a movement toward some kind of breakthrough with respect to the dominance of the educational institution in determining and recognizing what is legitimate learning achievement. We have already in 1995 seen an erosion in the teacher's role as an "authority" compared to what it had been a generation earlier. People, students and parents alike, turn to 24-hour news programs for the interpretation of world events, not to their teachers. People, students and parents alike, turn to on-line help and discussion groups, not the school teacher, for many different sorts of problems, such as those related to handling new technologies. People, students and parents alike, are even in 1995 creating and exchanging materials over the Internet, without any involvement of a classroom teacher. And slowly, specialist courses are coming available, either via the current forms of Internet environments, or video-on-demand sorts of possibilities, both of which will become integrated and available in both home and school during the next decade. These courses will be chosen by learners themselves or their parents, often without a gate-keeper role for the classroom teacher. Bit by bit, students will come to expect to take some specialist courses via tele-learning, outside of the school and teacher making the decision (as is now the case in most institutional settings). Society will respond to these courses, to compensate for local deficiencies in education, to give learners a better chance and more possibilities. A new market will emerge, competing for course delivery. Parents will insist on school accreditation for such courses on more say in what courses their school-age children should be taking, and in what format, and from what source. And schools themselves will compete more with each other for students: because of tele-learning a learner can stay in her own home and yet be a student at a "wonderful" and innovative school in another city or region, or part of the country.

Thus I predict something powerful is starting that may already have an impact by the year 2005 (Box. 10.16).

Box 10.16

Prediction 11: Competition for established education

Gradually, schools and educational institutions will compete with each other and with market-place course providers in course delivery and for student enrollment. Schools will still function as they do now, but students will increasingly pick and choose where and what they learn, and from whom.

This will start even with very young children, as parents will fear that their children are "missing out" on best-quality experiences. The local school will remain, but be under heavy competitive pressure. Students will congregate at the school for learning and communicating and socializing purposes, and for administrative reasons, but will increasingly opt out of at least some kinds of face-to-face classes for tele-learning alternatives. An early candidate will be (foreign) language courses.

The importance of the teacher in providing the personal support and even charismatic motivation to keep students "in" will place heavy demands in teachers. Education, probably not so much in the decade 1995–2005 but I think beyond this, will be much more of a competitive marketplace, facilitated by the evolution of tele-learning. Much of what we hold central in educational organization, such as teacher security and tenure, cannot go on in such a competitive system. Schools must run more like companies, and re-organizations that involve the loss of jobs will have to start to occur. Political pressure will build to give parents and learners freedom of choice, and to take their tax vouchers and subsidized choices to providers of their own selection. The place of the educational institution as the arbitrator of educational success and progress will change, as surely as it changed when the book moved teaching and knowledge out of the hands of the few priests and wealthy and into the hands of the masses. I predict that, some day, but not in the next decade (Box 10.17):

Box 10.17

Prediction 12: Toward a new paradigm...

Tele-learning, connecting to resources and people via telecommunications, will be an important instrument of a new paradigm of educational organization and of a new social conception of learning, in ways similar to the paradigm shifts accompanying the printing press and the popularization of books some centuries before.

Of course, the book did not replace the expert-as-teacher, but changed mightily the quantity and definition of those who were experts. With well-designed books and other learning materials, the non-expert teacher has been able to function as an "expert". Teachers who are not scientists teach science, teachers who are not mathematicians teach mathematics; the book and other media extended the skills of the teacher.

Similarly, in the future, I think we will see two interesting and competing phenomena: first, teachers can be less- and less experts themselves, because of having access to a wider range of resources and even "guest lecturers" for their classes. Teachers will be "guides" to resources, rather than experts.

But the competing phenomena is that, while the ordinary instructor will not be expected in herself to be an expert, she more and more will be expected to know where to go, via tele-learning, to put her students (and herself) in contact with a real expert. The "expert" will not so much be captured in a book for dissemination, but will be disseminating his expertise via tele-learning. The expert may still try to capture her expertise in a book, but the book will not be expected to stand by itself; she will incorporate it as a resource in her own "learning site", a site that will feature her own contacts and communication with subscribing learners as much as what she has written.

■ 10.4 A NEW PARADIGM FOR EDUCATION?

I see this is an interesting full circle, when I think of the evolution of technology in education in a very global way (Collis, 1991). Let me sketch this by indicating what I see as the previous four paradigms of education, with the role that technology plays in each:

THE FIRST PARADIGM: ONE-TO-ONE MODELING

I see the first educational paradigm to have been one of one-to-one modeling, learning by watching and doing, by apprenticeship with one's own parents and tribe. The interaction was close and personal, in that the on-going emergence of the child as a member of the tribe or community was continuously being evaluated, and rewarded or punished, by all those around. But while this learning was personal, it was not much personalized: the young girl learned to cultivate and prepare food and clothes and care for younger children, if she liked it or not. The technology here was one of direct use of tools, and of modeling. The skills needed by the learner were primarily those of observing and practicing.

THE SECOND PARADIGM: GOING AWAY, TO AN EXPERT

After some time, as existence became stable enough to allow for the occasional member of the tribe or community to leave its immediate web of survival activities, a second paradigm for learning emerged, not at all replacing the first but developing parallel to it, for a lucky few. Probably the first experts to whom one went away were religious figures, priests with special skills not to be found or modeled in the family or tribe. Often these skills would probably include both observable behaviours and less-tangible attributes, better expressed by word and preaching than by skill modeling. The technology of instruction became more and more the voice. More than one learner could benefit at the same time from one expert, as many as could hear him. Desirable learning skills moved toward listening and remembering. Personal feedback could still occur, but less so than in a one-to-one situation. And not everyone went to the expert: those who could be spared and those who were chosen.

I see this second paradigm as qualitatively different from the first, although incorporating some of the attributes of the first. Learners, those selected for the experience, were no longer bound to the fate of those to whom they were born. Away from the tribe new perspectives were acquired, new ways of doing things introduced that in turn were re-infused back to the tribe and family. Sitting quietly and listening became important; speaking effectively to an audience became more and more the mark of a skilled teacher. And as the size of the audience increased, the range of physical behaviours that could be modeled decreased, and the need to express what one wanted to convey through words rather than actions developed.

THE THIRD PARADIGM: THE EXPERT AT A DISTANCE VIA PRINT

Gradually, the restriction of having to be within hearing radius of the expert to gain from his knowledge was lifted, through the medium of text or written records. Now the expert could be captured, his wisdom disseminated to those beyond physical and temporal proximity. But such a process required either the skill to translate the written record, which few had, or intermediaries who were not the expert himself, but could read, and could qualify in some way to communicate the expert's words. The expert was represented by a secondary layer of communicators, but the ordinary learner still needed to go to someone in this secondary layer, and listen and accept.

I do not see this development as a paradigm shift, but rather a paradigm expansion. Technology and reading skills were needed for the secondary layer of communicators to function in that they usually needed to read and interpret the stored words of the distant expert. Also, what was stored needed to be more and more complete the farther it went from the elucidation of the expert himself, so that skills of written communication also increased.

However, it was the technology of print and the printing press which brought about the next paradigm shift. With reproducible and relatively cheap copies of print, more and more ordinary people wanted to see for themselves, and read for themselves, the words of the distant master. With transportable print materials, ordinary persons could stay with the family or community, and still learn from a distant expert—it they were able to read. The availability of things to read fed the desire to read, and more and more persons became qualified both to read and teach others to read.

Learning was still not just a matter of reading the words of the distant expert; many times these words were difficult to understand in their meaning, even if read, and still required filling-in and interpreting. The role of the teacher broadened, from transmitting to transmitting and helping to interpret or even telling how the words of the expert were intended to be interpreted, if the learner seemed to be forming an opinion different from that of the teacher. But the role of the teacher also contained its own ambiguities: as the learner himself learned to read, his interpretations could sometimes be argued to be as accurate if not more so than those of the teacher.

The technology critical to all this was print: cheap, easily reproducible, easily replaceable, easily disseminated copies of the original, as well as supplementary print materials to support and interpret the originals. The evolution of support media for learning took some of the tasks of the teacher away, and at the same time gave the teacher an extra burden: she had to read and study the support media as well as the original material to continue in her role as interpreter and guide of her students. By this time there were many layers of persons, interpretations, time and distance between the learner and the original expert. And perhaps the original expert could no longer be found, given the plethora of interpretations which had developed around his words.

Thus we see more and more people learning, from reading, with some listening. The process of learning was one of dealing with words; learners modeled their teachers in the use of books and writing and language. The original expert was farther and farther away: many intermediary "experts" came between the learner and the original source.

THE FOURTH PARADIGM: THE ASSEMBLY-LINE

While the third paradigm was effective in terms of its multiplier effect in reaching many more persons than could be reached by an expert's voice directly, the many different layers of local experts, many of whom were far from being expert in any way beyond having read a book, may have gradually stimulated the need for some kind of uniformity to compensate for local variability. Being a prisoner of one's local fate was a dominate feature of the first paradigm; while books and print allowed a wave of expertise to come to the individual, one's local circumstances still largely shaped what one could or would do in response to the possibilities of such (word-bound) knowledge.

I suspect that somewhere during the industrial revolution in society, made possible by technological advances, a parallel phenomenon begin to occur with education. Bringing raw materials together and processing them in a repetitive, carefully monitored way brought enormous benefits to the productivity of society. Much more could be produced, at a much higher consistency of quality and predictability of functionality, and thus at lower cost, than before. The assembly line brought large quantities of goods on the market, with an assurance of their similarity and guarantee of their satisfactory performance.

A similar model occurred in educational delivery: the technology of the school and curriculum, of the examination, and grade and course evolved. Unpredictability and variation in local teaching was gradually supplanted by the guarantee to society that a learner, going into the process on a certain day would emerge with satisfactory functionality a specified number of days later. Deviations to this plan were failures, both as teachers and learners. All possible should be done to fit everyone into the process, so that learners can emerge, as a group, diplomas in hand, on the appointed date of "completion".

For this paradigm, aspects of the three previous paradigms are all present. Modeling takes place, via the teacher, of certain skills but more globally of acceptable standards of behaviour and bearing as "educated persons". Teachers function as local experts, and in some cases are, but in most cases, are many layers of time and distance removed from the "experts" who originated the ideas and materials to be learned. The efficiency of the school and curriculum and examination routine means a large number of units can be processed, at a consistent quality, bringing more and more expertise to more and more persons than ever before. And the core skills of thinking and reading and writing and problem-solving which were to be absorbed directly and indirectly during the overall process would translate into human capital for the betterment of society, as an end result of the process.

In my opinion this is the paradigm in which organized education still is defined. Many technologies are involved, but central to the use of most of them is the core idea that the experts should be specifying to the learners how and what to learn, and indicating their approval of the rite of passage before the learner can emerge as "finished". There are many layers of experts, almost none of whom are the original subject-area experts, but instead layers and layers of curriculum developers, measurement specialists, textbook authors, learning-material creators, and teachers themselves. Consistency remains hard to achieve, but the urge toward it, and the desire for it in society is still strong. Schools must be accountable; test scores must increase; mastery levels must raise; entry to higher education and to funding support for higher education will be gauged on the basis of finishing ahead of others in a well-defined system. Completion depends on amassing the requisite number of marks or credits, which in turn are specified by a certified institution and its gatekeepers. Although we recognize the value of independent thinking, of creativity, of critical thought, we reward passage through most educational institutions in 1995 in terms of indicating to the teacher that the student has learned what the teacher said should be learned.

I am painting the picture bleakly, but as someone whose life is spent within it, I also recognize its benefits. For one, society needs labels and validation, as we increasingly must rely on strangers for our life-and-death needs. When I go to a doctor or take an aspirin or drive my car, I need to be assured that those who produced these are valid in their skills. I cannot tell by personal knowledge, as I might have been able to do generations ago in a small community where one's reputation, for better or worse, would be known to the recipients of one's services. And the more I believe in equal opportunity for all, to remove us from the tyranny of circumstance, the good or unlucky fortune of birth which makes life so unfair and unequal among us, the more I realize that mass accommodation needs a system, needs management, needs efficiency. Books, print, media, and the efficient organization of school and curriculum are powerful tools to bring something closer to equitable access to distant expertise to large numbers of people.

However, there are weaknesses. In our quest for efficiency and standard quality, we may go too far in telling learners what to read and how to think. Paradoxically, the more books and media that are available, the smaller the proportion of them that make it into the system. The need to standardize them, to measure student achievement of their content, means a severe filtering process, not in the hands of the learner but of the institution. We as local experts are farther and farther from "real experts", real scientists, real mathematicians, real artists, real authors. We teach about them; we read what they say, or more typically what others say about them; we never have the chance to communicate with real experts ourselves. Or even with their interpreters. The demands of the system and curriculum must take precedence over our own ideas of what and how to learn. And in a world of explosive growth in new knowledge, we as local experts will be farther and farther away from being adequate translators and guides for our students.

In this context, I predict an inexorable move in education, a new, fifth, paradigm change, that, like those before it will not replace but join and extend those before it as well as adding its own new features. And like the others, technology will be integral to the change, both to making it available and to defining competency within it.

THE FIFTH PARADIGM: INTERCONNECTIVENESS

The core of what I predict as a future paradigm for education is interconnectiveness. Being able to connect to human experts, to customized resources, beyond one's own local possibilities. Like the 1st Paradigm, we will be able to have occasional one-to-one intellectual modeling with experts, but unlike Paradigm 1, we are not limited to experts in our personal setting. Through virtual communities and contact with experts independent of one's place and circumstance, we have a new possibility for one-to-one learning. And, expertise is a matter of degree. There can be more than a handful of experts, what is an expert for one learner need not be the same as what is needed as an expert for another learner. Like the 2nd Paradigm, experts will increasingly be consulted, but unlike the 2nd Paradigm, experts will increasingly be recognized not by validation of a church or institution, but by what they offer to those who wish to learn.

And not only will interconnectivity increase our access to experts and the way that experts are defined, interconnectivity is also changing our opportunities for access to learning resources. The textbook, the curriculum guide, will only be several of a vast number of ways to learn about a topic, many of which are much more responsive to changes in knowledge and insight than institutionally accepted curriculum materials can ever be. Through interconnectivity, we can not only access emerging perspectives on a topic, but also alternative perspectives on that topic, not only those chosen by our "local experts". Even more powerfully, we can access the authors themselves, casually, instantaneously, we can initiate a communication. We can sit ourselves at the feet of a master, in the way of disciples in the 2nd Paradigm, limited not by the radius of her voice, but her willingness to return an e-mail message.

But all this opportunity has its price. Standardization is the first item at risk. The authority of the local leader as a content expert and determiner of "mastery" also comes under great, even unbearable strain. The textbook as a static source of knowledge will become redefined, relative to its harmonization with an unpredictable number of interconnected resources that will compete with it for comment and insight. The sense of who is an expert will continue to evolve, as it has through the 2nd, 3rd and 4th Paradigms; the technology through which the expert transmits her expertise will be a mixture of personal and impersonal communication, of writing and speech, and of something new—a skill at finding a way to link one's message to the web of interconnective resources available to the learner.

Critical to this 5th Paradigm is what I have been calling tele-learning. As I indicated earlier, I see this new paradigm emerging first in professional and higher education. I am not alone in this prediction. In a European meeting, in 1994, to predict the ways that communication technology will change learning in universities in 1998, the points in Box 10.18 were agreed upon by the participants (all faculty members themselves in higher education and many of them professional educational technologists).

OTHER PREDICTIONS OF EVOLUTION?

How tele-learning will evolve in its technology is still as unknown as the format of 1995's multi-media encyclopedia would be unknown to the early users of the printing press. How tele-learning will evolve in its organization is still as unknown as the current examination and course-driven school and university and training enterprise would be to the coming-to-an expert assemblages in temples and guildhalls of the centuries past. How tele-learning will evolve in terms of the role of the teacher is also not clear, but I am confident of at least one prediction (Box 10.19).

The more there is to choose from, the more we will occasionally crave someone to help us with decisions. The more we move to self-choice and personal decision making about learning, the more we will occasionally desire external reward and feedback for our work and achievements. The more we can talk to anyone, the more we will crave having a special person to talk to that really knows us and our history and our needs.

> **Box 10.18**
>
> **Changes in higher education, circa 1998, European predictions in 1994**
>
> - There will be subject-centred groups of instructors who will communicate over the network
> - Communication between instructors, and between students, on a world-wide basis will be normal
> - Courses will be available on a logging-in basis to large groups of persons
> - It will be easy for instructors to collaborate with colleagues on the same demonstration materials
> - Graphics and image databases will be available over wideband networks and will be used heavily in teaching
> - Time and space-independence will apply as much to local students as it does to distance-learning students
> - Many students will work on the basis of short, intensive courses interwoven with longer periods of independent work
> - The networks will make multi-media material available everywhere
> - Lectures will be available as video on demand
> - There will be much more use of globally available material accessed distributed information systems
> - Research publications will be largely electronic and accessed from national or international repositories via the Internet
> - However, instructors will not have much changed their teaching approach, lectures will still continue, the "not invented here" syndrome will not have disappeared
>
> (Rowland, 1994, p. 79)

The difference between the teacher of the future, and the teacher of the present is, I think, that the teacher of the future will increasingly be someone we select, via tele-learning experiences, as good for us, both in terms of what we feel we need, content wise and subjectively. Less and less will the learner be consigned to a teacher he does not want to work with; more and more a market will develop from which one can choose one's mentor, one's interpreter, one's learning guide.

Of course, the liberating potential of tele-learning, in its future versions, is also its terrible risk. Will learners choose wisely? What will they use as criteria for choice, of expert or materials? How can society tolerate freedom of choice in learning for its doctors, bridge builders, voters or plumbers? What is to counter the voice of the zealot, of the demagogue, if that voice is attractive and apparently offers what the learner wants to hear?

Thus, I predict the paradox stated in Box 10.20.

However, I also predict a cluster of important changes, in line with the evolution to Paradigm 5 (Box 10.21).

Box 10.19

Prediction 13: The teacher stays central

Especially in the 5th Paradigm, teachers will be still be important to tele-learning.

Box 10.20

Prediction 14: Paradox..

The organization of education as we now know it, in its Paradigm 4 form, will continue; society will demand common standards and legitimization at the same time that society demands life-long learning and competence among its citizens in terms of universal access to interconnectivity for learning purposes. This contradiction will cause great tensions.

Box 10.21

Prediction Cluster 15: Some important changes...

- Tele-learning will blur the distinction between expert and non-expert
- Tele-learning will support competition and diversity in course and teacher selection
- Tele-learning will lead to a break with the dominance of the textbook and curriculum toward an expectation that part of learning is to sort between a wide range of resources, extracting and synthesizing from many sources rather than mastering what one person or team has written
- Assessment and evaluation will have to evolve to handle discoveries that are not known to the test developer
- And being an effective teacher in a tele-learning world will require skill and insight into linking: linking of persons, of ideas, of concepts, and of helping one's students, and one's self, see an idea or person as part of a web whose boundaries are continually changing, and whose attributes vary depending on one's vantage point

This is what I find important about tele-learning, circa 1995. I see it as a mixture of technology and human development, as a reflection of inexorable trends in society which will affect us, or more likely which will affect our children, in radical ways. Our sense of identity, so very much rooted in who we belong to as a community, is already changing for many people, through the combination of increased mobility in society, decreased family cohesiveness, and increased access to communication technologies. Our sense of identity as learners and teachers will be affected in a similar way. Our sense of certainty about facts and skills, and pride in our development of accomplishment, is always under serious strain due to the rapid change in the nature of skills required in the workplace, and the sudden obsolescence of so many of us through re-organizations and redundancies, our skills of a lifetime no longer visible in the avalanche of new knowledge, new methods, new technologies.

Thus, although in some ways change is slow, and change in educational institutions and practices is even slower, in the broader perspective I think change is already accelerating. I see tele-learning as critical to the change, because tele-learning as I define it is interconnectivity for learning, and this interconnectivity is technical, human, and strategic.

■ 10.5 AND THE IMPLICATIONS FOR EDUCATIONAL TECHNOLOGISTS?

A major purpose of this book is to stimulate those in my own professional community—educational technologists involved in education of new generations of educational technologists—to consider carefully what tele-learning can mean to our own practice, to how we teach, to what we teach, and to how we work with and guide our students. In Japan, where curriculum is organized centrally, a new qualification called "education engineering" is being introduced (Sakamoto and Miyashita, 1994) with the following main themes (Box 10.22):

Box 10.22

Educational engineering as a new perspective on educational technology in Japan

- Skills for designing another person's lessons
- Skills for educating others in knowledge and techniques relative to educational engineering
- Skills for making effective media presentations and for communication
- Skills for making high-quality educational materials, such as multi-media materials for network distribution. (Sakamoto & Miyashita, 1994)

I believe that tele-learning will call for educational technologists to have these sorts of core skills for educational engineering but also to be involved with pedagogical re-engineering parallel to the more technology-specific aspects of tele-learning.

And I believe that a philosophical perspective should gain more attention in the education of educational technologists, not only for tele-learning but for our professional functioning in general. In Canada, Hlynka and Chinlen (1990) call for a "post-modern" approach to educational technology in which the "educational technologist would explore the incongruities of different technologies, different goals, opposing social/cultural needs, and their juxtaposition" (p. 77), focusing on the linkages between language, meaning, media representation, and reality. I believe that tele-learning through its increasing possibilities for interconnectivity—among persons, cultures, media, and contexts—will require increased sensitivity to new philosophical conceptions of learning among its educational technologists. I am, in a way, calling for a post-modern approach to educational technology.

I also believe that increased development in the profession of educational technology requires increased attention to social concerns and broader issues relating to the function of education in society. Equity of opportunity is a dream and motivator in most of our societies; such equity can be powerfully served by educational technology, and particularly by tele-learning, but much must occur in terms of affordable and equitable access to a tele-learning infrastructure; to the development of the literacy skills, both technical and meta-cognitive, to make equitable use of the possibilities of interconnectiveness once they are available; and the new structures of responsibility and quality control that must emerge to prevent the pollution of tele-learning by those who would dominate its reach for their own purposes. Weisberg and Ullmer (1995) capture this well when they comment that for universal access to tele-learning resources to be meaningful:

> *It is not adequate simply for technology to provide high tech conduits for transferring information. The content traversing the conduits must be of high quality and relevant...The end user in turn must possess an abiding purpose for accessing, retrieving and utilizing the information, and most importantly, fundamental literacy and information technology skills"(p. 644).*

Somehow, we as educational technologists must combine both educational and pedagogical re-engineering skills with a post-modernist approach to educational and social complexity, to help both the quality of the content and communication that take place via tele-learning and the insight, literacy, and skills of the participants in making use of these tele-learning possibilities. As earlier educational paradigms required skills of modeling, listening, reading, and learning for tests, the 5th Paradigm will require that:

> *...schools must prepare, develop, and graduate sophisticated scanners, integrators, and communicators...*

Scanners: Must be able to gain access to information and sift through it rapidly. Scanners must be excellent readers.

Integrators: Must absorb a great deal of information in a disciplined fashion, be able to discard the irrelevant, to know wheat from chaff. Above all, integrators must cogitate with competence: primarily, integrators must be rigorous thinkers.

Communicators: Must be able to present informed ideas and information clearly, to bring together and carry forward what the scanner and integrator have accomplished, and transmit it with persuasive precision. Communicators must be first-rate writers..." (extracted from Donlevy and Donlevy, 1995, pp. 3–4)

The educational technologist must not only have scanning, integrating, and communicating skills, but must learn how to design learning materials that develop these skills in others. Such instructional design will build on our current methods, but will require extension and revision of them in a tele-learning context. Gustafson (1993) has made the following comments about the need for change in approaches to instructional design which I think are also appropriate more generally to educational technology and tele-learning:

...the underlying paradigm [of the field], tools employed to apply that paradigm, instructional models, and delivery technologies, are all being influenced by powerful and continuing forces from outside the field. ...it is not that our present knowledge and skills are wrong and should be abandoned. They are just incomplete and inadequate for facing many of the challenges of the next decade and the coming millennium. Like all professions, we must constantly learn, grow, and change to meet changing conditions...There is a pioneering spirit in our heritage, and we will use it again now that it is needed. We are professional change agents who must now apply these same change principles to ourselves. We know how to promote change, and we understand the psychology of its process. Now we are on an equal footing with many of our clients, who are also experiencing rapid change, and we may be better able to enjoy the voyage since we have so much company. (p. 31).

This book has been my invitation to join me, and so many others, on the tele-learning voyage.

Source materials

1. References and sources for the Interface sections

2. Glossary

3. Overall Reference list

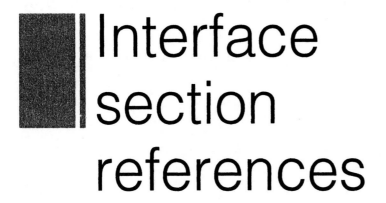

Interface section references

INTERFACE 1: THE INTERNET

WEB SOURCES

Among a huge number of possibilities:

The Internet Index Home Page:
URL http://www.openmarket.com/intindex/
Internet Domain Survey:
URL http://nw.com/zone/WWW/report.html
Internet Country Codes from ISO 3166:
URL http://www.nw.com/zone/iso-country-codes
Internet Society Statistics:
URL http://www.isoc.org
InterNIC:
URL http://www.internic.net/
Netcraft Survey:
URL http://www.netcraft.co.uk/survey/
The Commercenet/Nielsen Internet Demographics Survey:
URL http://www.commerce.net

Hobb's Internet Timeline:
URL `http://offworld.wwa.com/timeline.html`

PRINT SOURCES
Consistently good magazine sources:

Internet World, Meckermedia, Artillery House, Artillery Row, London SW1P 1RT, UK
URL `http://www.internetworld.com/`
PC Magazine, Ziff-Davis Publications, One Park Avenue, New York, NY 10016, USA
URL `http://www.pcmag.com`

BOOK:
The Internet Unleashed (C. Morrow, Ed.), (1995). SAMS Publishing, 201 W. 103rd Street, Indianapolis, IN 46290

INTERFACE 2: THE WORLD WIDE WEB: TECHNOLOGIES AND METAPHORS

WWW SITES
Numbers of WWW Servers

URL `http://www.w3.org/hypertext/DataSources/WWW/Geographical.html`
URL `http://www.mit.edu/people/mkgray/growth/`

Catalogues of WWW Sites
URL `http://www.yahoo.com/Computers_and_Internet/Internet/World_Wide_Web/Statistics_and_Demographics/`
URL `http://www.einet.net/galaxy/Reference-and-Interdisciplinary-Information/Internet-and-Networking.html`

History and Evolution of the WWW
URL `http://www.w3.org/hypertext/WWW/History.html`
URL `http://www.w3.org/hypertext/WWW/TheProject.html`

General Information on the WWW
URL http://www.earth.com/server/doc/web-info.html
URL http://www.eit.com/web/www.guide
URL http://www.w3.org/pub/Conferences/WWW5/Welcome.html

Search Engines
URL http://webcrawler.com
URL http://www.lycos.com
URL http://wwwmcb.cs.colorado.edu/home/mcbryan/WWWW.html
URL http://www.home.mcom.com/home/internet-search.html

MAGAZINES:
Same recommendations as for **Interface 1**.

BOOK:
Teach Yourself Web Publishing with HTML in a Week (1995). (Laura Lemay, Sams Publishing, 201 W. 103rd Street, Indianapolis, Indiana 46290). Although predominately focused on making Web pages, also a good, simple-to-understand overview of the WWW itself.

INTERFACE 3: THE WORLD WIDE WEB:
NEW DEVELOPMENTS

WEB SITES
Technical Advances

URL http://www.adobe.com/acrobat/
URL http://java.sun.com/
URL http://www.w3.org/hypertext/WWW/Style/
URL http://www.sgi.com/Products/WebFORCE/WebForceSoft.html
URL http://hyperg.iicm.tu-graz.ac.at/hyperg;sk=9F0774D9
URL http://info.webcrawler.com/mak/projects/robots/
robots.html

Editors and Link Checkers
URL http://www.ics.uci.edu/WebSoft/MOMspider/
URL http://www.yahoo.com/Computers/World_Wide_Web/
HTML-Editors/

```
URL http://www.ugrad.cs.ubc.ca/
spider/q7f192/branch/checker-man.html
```

General Sources of Tools and Information
```
URL http://www.pcweek.com/archive/45/pcwk0033.htm
```

HTML 3.0
```
URL http://www.hpl.hp.co.uk/people/dsr/html3/
CoverPage.html
```

Tools for Educational Authoring
```
URL http://www.west.ie/home.html
URL http://lglwww.epfl.ch/Ada/Tutorials/
Lovelace/userg.html
```

MAGAZINES:
As in **Interface 1** and **2**; also computer-science journals such as:
Communications of the ACM, and Interactions of the ACM, Associations for Computing Machinery, 1515 Broadway, New York, NY 10036-5701, USA.

INTERFACE 4: READ/WRITTEN A GOOD BOOK LATELY? NEW FORMS OF PUBLICATION

BOOKS:
Brand, S. (1987). *The Media Lab: Inventing the Future at MIT.* New York:Penguin Books.
Dennings, P.J., & Rous, B. (1995). The ACM Electronic Publishing Plan. *Communications of the ACM, 38*(4), 97–103.

INTERFACE 5: PROVIDING AN ON-RAMP: NETWORK SERVICE ORGANIZATIONS

MAGAZINES
Computer magazines or information from local providers.

INTERFACE 6: DOING IT IN STYLE: DESIGN GUIDELINES FOR WWW ENVIRONMENTS

WWW SITES
List of Style Guides
URL `http://union.ncsa.uiuc.edu/HyperNews/get/www/html/guides.html`
URL `http://WWW.Stars.com/`

Specific Design Guidelines
URL `http://www.matterform.com/mf/hypermedia/hypermediahome2.html`
URL `http://cast.stanford.edu/cast/www/donts.html`

HTML CyberClass
URL `http://www.ib.be/ib/outline.html`
. . . *Class occurs every two months, except July and August. Class operates through a private discussion list as well as a public WWW site. The course is for persons beginning to develop WWW sites and focuses on the effective development and use of homepages. Discussion groups in the May and June 1966 round of the course will be in English, German, or French. There is a fee for participation in the course.*

BOOKS:
From **Interface 2**, also:

Aronson, L. (1995). *HTML Manual of Style*. Emeryville, CA: Ziff-Davis.
Cox, K. ,& Walker, D. (1993). *User-Interface Design*. New York: Prentice Hall.
Shneiderman, B. (1993). *Designing the User Interface*. 2nd Edition. Reading, MA: Addison Wesley.

INTERFACE 7: THE INTERNET FROM A GLOBAL PERSPECTIVE: CULTURE, CIRCUMSTANCE AND TECHNOLOGY

NEWSLETTER:
FID News Bulletin
FID is the Federation for Information and Documentation. Founded in 1885, it is the leading international organization in the information sector. Contact FID Secretariat, PO Box 90402, 2509 LK The Hague, The Netherlands, `Secretariat@FID.nl`

INTERFACE 8: MEET YOU ON-LINE: BEING A LEARNING GROUP AT A DISTANCE

WWW SITES
WWW Collaborative Projects: A List of Resources
URL `http://union.ncsa.uiuc.edu:80/HyperNews/get/www/collaboration.html`

Human Computer Interaction Archives
URL `http://www.lpac.ac.uk/SEL-HPC/Articles/HciArchive.html`

Human Computer WWW Virtual Library HCI Page
URL `http://www.cs.bgsu.edu/HCI/bin/people`

HCI Resources
URL `http://www.cis.ohio-state.edu/~perlman/readings.html`

BOOKS:

Harasim, L. M. (1993b). *Global networks: Computers and international communication.* Cambridge, MA: MIT Press.

Heeren, E. (1995). *Technologies for collaborative distance learning.* Doctoral dissertation. Faculty of Educational Science and Technology, University of Twente, Enschede, The Netherlands.

Jones, S. G. (1995). Understanding community in the information age. In S. G. Jones (Ed.), *Cybersociety: Computer mediated communication and community* (pp. 10–35). Thousand Oaks, CA: Sage Publications.

Schnase, J. L. & Cunnius, E. L. (Eds.) (1995). CSCL 95: Computer support for collaborative learning. Mahwah, NJ: Lawrence Erlbaum.

INTERFACE 9: LOOK WHAT MY STUDENTS DID: THE WWW AS A LEARNING TOOL

WWW SITES
On-Line and Distance Learning
URL `http://www.to.utwente.nl/ism/OnLine95/campus/campus.html`
URL `http://www.to.utwente.nl/ism/online96/campus.htm`

Tele-learning technologies: glossary of selected terms

Account A business arrangement between a network and a network user that gives the user a unique name and password through which to access the network.

Address A unique name or number that identifies a computer user or computer; used in network communications to transmit messages to a particular person or machine.

Analog signal Information represented by a continuous electrical signal.

Anonymous FTP site An Internet host computer that makes certain of its files available to those who log-in as "anonymous", and give their e-mail address as a password. The files usually found at anonymous FTP sites are software packages for various systems, utilities, information, mailing list or usenet group discussion archives. At most FTP sites, the resources are organized hierarchically in directories and subdirectories.

ASCII (American Standard Code for Information Interchange) A standard method for encoding characters; includes codes representing upper- and lowercase letters, numerals, and punctuation.

Asynchronous In the tele-learning context, asynchronous interaction is where two or more parties communicate via e-mail or related technologies in a time-independent matter.

ATM A network technology to increase data flow in order to restrict multimedia traffic and bandwidth.

Audiobridge A method of connecting a small number of telephone lines, and equalizing noise distortion and background noise for a live audioconference.

Audioconferencing Telephone contact between two or more sites, usually connected by means of an audio-bridge and via speaker phones. Unless video phones are used, there is no visual communication.

Audiographic systems Combination of an audio conference used with graphic support, such as an electronic blackboard, writing tablet, still video, or computer generated visual material. There is two-way audio interactivity and two-way visual exchange of electronic text and/or graphics.

Bandwidth The range of frequencies required to transmit a signal. For example, voice over the telephone network requires a bandwidth of 3 kHz while uncompressed video requires a bandwidth of 6 mHz.

Broadcast television Transmission of picture (video) and sound (audio) over standard UHF and VHF television channels.

Browser Any program used to view material prepared for the WWW; Mosaic, Lynx and Netscape are examples of browsers. Browsers can interpret URLs and HTML and understand several Internet protocols, such as http, FTP and Gopher.

Bulletin Board System (BBS) An electronic storage area for related e-mail messages, organized so that subscribers may read or post messages.

Cable television A broadband distribution network, using coaxial or fiber-optic transmission technology, which carries multiple television channels to domestic and business subscribers within a franchise area. Cable television networks can also carry telephony and information services.

Chat An option that makes it possible for users to communicate in real-time. The "chatting" is not vocal; the information is typed into each computer and immediately displayed on the other computers.

Client-server system A relationship among networked computers whereby software on a client computer can send requests to an associated server computer, which executes the request and then sends back the appropriate data, to the client.

Coaxial cable A metal cable consisting of a conductor surrounded by another conductor (as in "cable TV"), which can carry video, audio, and data signals from point to point.

CODEC COder-DEcoder. Converts analog data into a digital signal for transmission and re-converts after reception. Two CODECs are required, one at each end of a channel.

Compressed video Processing technique to reduce the bandwidth required to transmit video frames over a telecommunications channel. This results in a reduction in transmission time.

Compressed digital video Video which has been reduced, usually from broadband to narrowband form, by a digital compression process.

Computer conferencing (software) A development of electronic mail with features specifically designed to help in the organization, structuring and retrieval of messages. Messages can be linked to each other and organized in different databases accessible to all with access privileges.

Computer network A group of computers linked in such a way so they can send information back and forth between themselves.

Conferencing In the tele-learning context, a discussion among persons via a multi-party telephone call, especially equipped and networked video equipment, or networked computers each running appropriate software.

CSCW Computer Supported Cooperative Work

Database A collection of information organized to allow users to search and retrieve contents that interest them.

Digital The representation of data or physical quantities by means of digits (discrete elements).

Direct Broadcast Satellite (DBS) Full-motion television programming transmitted via satellite directly to the user, who receives video and audio information using a satellite antenna or receiver dish.

Distributed network (system). A system where resources are spread among many computers, instead of being stored in a single location.

Distribution list A facility in electronic mail systems to enable a large number of subscriber mail addresses to be reached through a single (list) name.

Downlinks The ground equipment used to receive signals from a satellite.

Download Receiving and saving a file through a telecommunications system.

E-mail address Electronic mail address, following a common format.

Electronic mail (e-mail, email) Messages sent from one individual or group to another through a computer network.

Facsimile A technique for transmitting printed information over the telephone network.

Fiber optics A medium that transmits voice, full-motion video, and data by sending light impulses through ultra-thin glass fibers. Fiber optics permits two-way, full motion video and two-way audio interaction between participating sites.

File(s) In the tele-learning context, a set of associated data readable by a computer with a unique identifying name.

File server A computer used primarily to store files and provide network users with access to those files.

File transfer The exchange of files from one computer to another over a network.

Freeze frame/slow scan Transmission of still pictures over regular telephone lines. So that the visuals are received in a "slow-scan" format—that is, a new picture can be replaced in regular intervals of a certain number of seconds.

FTP (file transfer protocol) A protocol allowing a user linked to one Internet host to access and transfer files with another host over a network.

Full duplex A communications channel which allows conversation to take place interactively and simultaneously between various parties.

Gateway A computer that connects two or more networks using different protocols.

Gopher Client/server software to provide flexible access to resources such as databases in distributed information systems; most frequently associated with Internet access.

Groupware General term for network software that allows designated users access to common databases as well as use of a mail system and other tools to facilitate distributed groups.

Half duplex A communication channel which allows conversation to take place in only one direction at a time.

Home Page The intended introductory page of a WWW site; usually provides an introduction to the site, along with hypertext links to other pages in the site.

Host A computer offering resources and services that an individual user may access through application programs such as telnet and FTP.

HTML Hypertext markup language; the language used to code Web pages.

Http Hypertext Transfer Protocol, conventions to transfer information in Web systems.

Hypertext link Connection between one hypertext document and another.

Information networks Channels through which narrowband, wideband, and broadband transmission-switching capabilities enable information to be transported locally, nationally, and internationally, via networks.

Infrastructure The physical equipment (hardware and software) that enables a network to function.

Interface (user) In terms of the user, the way in which a system such as a piece of software presents itself.

Internet (The Internet) A world-wide network of networks based on the TCP/IP protocol.

ISDN Integrated Services Digital Network, a set of international switching standards whereby the telephone system is used to offer integrated forms of telecommunication (voice, computer-readable data, facsimile, video image) all in digital form, to subscribers.

Kbits/s A digital data rate expressed in 1/1000s bits per second.

Leased lines The rented use of a dedicated circuit which runs from one point to another. The circuits can be analog or digital, and can use fiber optics, telephone lines, microwave or other transmission systems.

Listservs Also known as Listserv Discussion Groups, distribute e-mail (messages) to members on a specific address list.

Local Area Network (LAN) A group of computers linked together within a limited physical space, usually to share printers and software.

Modem Stands for MOdulator-DEModulator, devices that enable computers to transmit information over telephone lines.

Moderated conference An audio, video or computer conference with a moderator, a person who functions as a leader of a discussion or chairman.

Multi-media Various media (text, diagram, image, audio or video), eletronically integrated.

Multi-media desktop conferencing Interconnected computers with specialized software allowing partners to exchange and view various combinations of video, voice, images and data and/or jointly edit files and share applications while in audio and video contact; requires adequate network connections.

Netscape A graphical WWW browser.

Network A group of computers that communicate electronically through a physical connection and a shared protocol.

Network Services Voice, data text, image, graphic, and video services that enable information to be organized and accessed in individual or multimedia forms, over narrowband, wideband, or broadband facilities.

Newsgroup(s) A form of computer conference organized to support a continuing discussion over a period of time.

Node A single computer within a network.

Off-line Refers to performing an operation with a computer while it is not making use of a connection to a communication network.

On-line Connected to a remote system.

On-line services (network services) Information resources such as news or databases available through a network to computers equipped to access the services.

Protocol The rules governing network interaction; determining where, when, how, and in what format information is transmitted.

Real-time In the tele-learning context, interaction among participants communicating at the same time with each other

Remote access To connect to a computer other than one's local computer by using an identifying name and a password.

Resources Information sources available electronically on local or remote computers.

Satellite An electronic transmission device, normally placed in orbit about the earth, for the purpose of receiving and retransmitting electromagnetic signals.

Scanner A device for digitizing text, drawings or photographs (anything in paperform).

Synchronous Synchronous interaction is where two or more parties are communicating at the same time, though not necessarily in the same place.

TCP/IP (Transmission Control Protocol/Internet Protocol) A common designation for the Internet suite of protocols.

Tele-learning Making connections among persons and resources via communication technologies for learning-related purposes.

Telecommunications The exchange of information (voice, video or data) using electromagnetic signals, in digital or analog form.

Telepresence In conferencing situations, the use of communication technology to provide each user with the feeling that users at other sites are physically present.

Telnet An Internet protocol enabling a user at one site to gain access to the commands and programs of a host at another site; also used to refer to the program that allows this remote login.

Tool Specific software applications.

Uplink An earth station transmitting signals up to a satellite.

Upload The process of sending a file from a host computer to another.

URL Uniform Resource Locator; a scheme used to address Internet resources on the WWW.

Video-conferencing The combination of audio and visual media to provide interactive communication between two or more sites.

VSAT (Very Small Aperture Terminal) A small-size earth station terminal, usually portable and designed to handle data transmissions.

Wide Area Network (WAN) A long-distance computer network that enables computers not physically linked to communicate with each other through modems.

World Wide Web (WWW) A hypertext information and resource system based on client-server architecture; "the" WWW, or "the" Web refers to the system accessible via the Internet. (WWW systems can also run locally)

# References

Abel, I. (1995). Open learning services and infrastructures for SMEs. In P. Held & W. F. Kugemann (Eds.), *Telematics for education and training* (pp. 114–117). Amsterdam: ISO.

Acker, S. R. (1995) Space, collaboration, and the credible city: Academic work in the virtual university. *Journal of Computer Mediated Communication*, **1**(1). [WWW document]. URL `http://cwis.usc.edu:80/dept/annenberg/vol1/issue1/`

Ahern, T. C. (1993). The effect of a graphic interface on participation, interaction and student achievement in a computer-mediated small-group discussion. *Journal of Educational Computing Research*, *9*(4), 535–548.

Ahern, T. C., & Repman, J. (1994). The effects of technology on online education. *Journal of Research on Computing in Education*, *26*(4), 537–546.

Albright, M. J. (1994). Computer networking and college media centers. *College and University Media Review, Summer*, 7–24.

Alexander, G. (1992). Designing human interfaces for collaborative learning. In A. R. Kaye (Ed.), *Collaborative learning through computer conferencing* (pp. 210–210). Berlin: Springer Verlag.

Alexander, G., & Cutcher, M. (1992). Communications-centred multi-media learning systems. In S. A. Cerri & J. Whiting (Eds.), *Learning technology in the European Communities* (pp. 79–90). Amsterdam: Kluwer Academic Publishers.

Alexander, G., Lefrere, P. & Matheson, S. (1994). Towards collaborative learning at a distance. In M. F. Verdejo & S. A. Cerri (Eds.), *Collaborative dialogue technologies in distance learning* (pp. 65–77). Berlin: Springer-Verlag.

Ambach, J, Perrone, C., & Repenning, A. (1995). Remote exploratoriums: Combining network media and design environments. *Computers & Education, 24*(3), 163–176.

Amodeo, A., & Bullowa, J. (1995). Distance education without high co$t$. *Learning and Leading with Technology, 22*(8), 12–13.

Andres, Y. M. (1995a). *The Global Schoolhouse Project.* [WWW document]. URL `http://www.gsn.org/`

Andres, Y. M. (1995b). *Scientist on tap: Video-conferencing over the Internet.* [WWW document]. URL `htpp://gsn/article.sot.html`

Andres, Y., & Rogers, F. (1995). *How to design a successful project.* [WWW document]. URL `http://gwww.gen.org`

Andrews, K., Kappe, F., & Maurer, H. (1995). *Journal of Universal Computer Science, 1*(4), 206–220.

Arav, T. (1995a). *Distance education: From within traditional education.* Masters thesis, Faculty of Educational Science and Technology, University of Twente, Enschede, The Netherlands.

Arav, T. (1995b). *The Remote Classroom: Telematics in the traditional classroom.* Faculty of Educational Science and Technology, University of Twente, Enschede, The Netherlands.

Aronson, L. (1994). *HTML manual of style.* Emeryville, CA: Ziff-Davis Press.

Ashley, C. (1995). Internet: An information superhighway? *ATM Digimedia,/NAB '95*, pp. 8–12. (Newsmagazine for Advanced Television Markets, 53–533 Kings Road, London SW 10, UK)

Ayre, R., & Reichard, K. (1995, February 7). The Web untangled. *PC Magazine*, pp. 173–196.

Bacsich, P. (1994). ISDN- strategic issues. In R. Mason & P. Bacsich (Eds.), *ISDN applications in education and training* (pp. 39–62). London: The Institute of Electrical Engineers.

Baker, B. T., & Davis, B. (1995). *Designing a server with a K-8 school in mind.* [WWW document]. URL `http://www.ncsa.uiuc.edu/SDG/IT94/Proceedings/Educ/thurber/thurber.html`

Baloian, N, A., Hoppe, H. U., & Kling, U. (1995). Structured authoring and cooperative use of instructional multimedia for a computer-integrated classroom. In H. Maurer, (Ed.). (1995). *Educational multimedia and hypermedia, 1995* (pp. 81–87). Charlottesville, VA: AACE.

Barker, B. O. (1992). *The distance education handbook: An administrator's guide for rural and remote schools.* Charleston, West Virginia: ERIC Clearinghouse on Rural Education & Small Schools.

Barker, B. O., Bannon, J. E., & Miller, P. (1994). The Hawaii Kidscience Teleschool Program: A description and evaluation. *DEOSNEWS, 4*(10). [Internet journal] (contact: `ACSDE@PSOVM.PSU.EDU`)

Barker, P., & Banerji, A. (1995). Designing electronic performance support systems. *Innovations in Education and Training Internation, 32*(1), 4–12.

Barker, B. O., & Hall, R. F. (1993, October 14–17). *A national survey of distance education use in rural school districts of 300 students or less.* Paper presented at the Annual Conference of the National Rural Education Association, Burlington, Vermont.

Baskin, R. (1995, July). The killer ap connection. *Byte*, p. 30.

Bates, A. W. (1984a). *Broadcasting in education: An evaluation.* London: Constable.

Bates, A. W. (1984b). *Selecting and designing low-cost media for distance education.* Hegan, Germany: Zentrales Institut für Fernstudienforschung.

Bates, A. W. (1994, November 24). *Strategies for the future.* Paper presented at Telematics for Education and Training, Düsseldorf, Germany.

Bates, A. W. (1995). *Technology, open learning and distance education.* London: Routledge.

Bates, P. (Ed.) (1995). *Telematics for flexible and distance learning (DELTA): Final report.* Brussels: Commission of the European Communities DG XII.

Baumbach, D., Eason, M., Bird, M., & Brewer, S. (1995, July 24). *A multifaceted approach to technology training and support for teachers.* Paper presented at the World Conference For Computers in Education (WCCE '95), Birmingham, UK.

Beazley, M. (1988). In the beginning...The birth of the Computer Pals Around the World Project. In R. Czerniejewski (Ed.), *Sharing in a global classroom* (pp. 6–11). Alice Springs, Australia: Alice Springs Educational Computing Association.

"Bell Atlantic.." (1995). Bell Atlantic awarded multi-million dollar contract to build 'Virtual Campus' at George Mason University. *Techtrends, 40*(3), p. 5.

Bell, P., Davis, E. A., & Linn, M. C. (1995). The Knowledge Integration Environment: Theory and design. In J. L. Schnase & E. L. Cunnius (Eds.), *CSCL 95: Computer support for collaborative learning* (pp. 14–21). Mahwah, NJ: Lawrence Erlbaum Associates.

Bell, T. C., Moffat, A., Witten, I. H., & Zobel, J. (1995). The MG Retrieval System: Compressing for time and speed. *Communications of the ACM, 38*(4), 41–42.

Bentley, D., Bentley, S. C., Drobinski, P. N., & Watts, M. (1992). Learners deserve better: Improving the quality of educational television. In M. Meyer (Ed.), *Aspects of school television in Europe* (pp. 322–328). München: K. G. Saur.

Berg, J. van (1995, September 29). WEB World Receiver completes the "World News". *The Volkskrant*, pp. B-12. See also [WWW document] URL http://www.vpro.nl/www/vpro-dogotaal/web-world-receiver

Berge, Z. L. (1995). Facilitating computer conferencing: Recommendations from the field. *Educational Technology, 35*(1), 22–30.

Berge, Z. L., & Collins, M. (1995). Computer-mediate scholarly discussion groups. *Computers & Education, 24*(3), 183–189.

Berger, B. (1995, July). Does God need a Web page? *Netguide*, pp. 22–26.

Berlin, E. (1995, November). The virtual tycoon. *Internet World*, pp. 136–138.

Bieber, M., & Isakowitz, T. (Eds.). (1995). Special Issue on Hypermedia. *Communications of the ACM, 38*(8).

BIS Mackintosh (1990, January). *Distance learning: Inhibiting factors and the creation of a favourable environment.* Paper presented to the Conference on Telecommunications Based Training Systems in the 90s, Madrid, Spain.

Blanch, G. (1994). Don't all faculty want their own TV show? Barriers to faculty participation in distance education. *DEOSNEWS, 4*(1). [Internet journal]. Contact ACSDE@PSUVM.PSU.EDU

Blumberg, R. B. (195). *MendelWeb: An electronic science/math/history resource for the WWW.* [WWW document]. URL http://www.ncsa.uiuc.edu/

Boaz, M. H., & Hardy, D. W. (1993, November 11). *From autonomy to team work: The real distance education challenge.* Paper presented at Teled '93: Global Connections, Dallas, TX.

Bork, A. (1995). *Distance learning and interaction: Toward a virtual learning institution.* Irvine, CA: Educational Technology Center, University of California.

Boroughs, D. L. (1995, June 5). A high-technology meeting of minds. *U.S. News & World Report*, pp. 46–48.

Bos, E., Kikstra, A., & Morgen, C. (1996). *Multiple levels of use of the Web as a learning tool.* Paper presented at ED-TELECOM '96, Boston, MA.

Braatane, K. (1993). Teachers in network. In G. Davies & B. Samways, (Eds.), *Teleteaching '93* (pp. 123–132). Amsterdam: North-Holland.

Brand, S. (1987). *The Media Lab: Inventing the Future at MIT.* New York: Penguin Books.

Brodsky, I. (1995, July). Wireless world. *Internet World*, pp. 34–41.

Brown, A. L., Ash, D., Rutherford, M., Nakagawa, K., Gordon, A., & Campione, J. C. (1993). Distributed expertise in the classroom. In G. Salomon (Ed.), *Distributed cognitions: Psychological and educational considerations* (pp. 188–228). Cambridge, UK: Cambridge University Press.

Browning, P., & Williams, J. (1995, July). The geology@bristol experience. *Active Learning, 2,* 34–38.

Bruce, M. A., & Shade, R. A. (1995). Effective teaching and learning strategies using compressed video. *Techtrends, 40*(4), 18–22.

Bruce, M. A., & Shade, R.A. (1994). Teaching via compressed video: Promising practices and potential pitfalls. *DEOSNEWS, 4*(8). [Internet journal]. Contact: ACSDE@PSUVM.PSU.EDU

Bruder, I. (1993, October). Technology in the USA: An educational perspective. *Electronic Learning*, pp. 20–28.

Bruntlett, S. (1995, July). *The development of MOSAIC-based multimedia museum resources for secondary art and design education.* Paper presented at WCCE '95 (World Conference in Computers in Education), Birmingham, UK.

Brusilovsky, P. (1995). *Intelligent tutoring systems for the World-Wide Web.* [Internet document]. Contact `plb@cogpsy.uni-trier.de`

Bull, G. (Ed.). (1993). *Student owned computing: The issues for higher education management.* Paris: Organization for Economic Cooperation and Development (OECD).

Bull, G. L., Cooper, J. M., & Davis, N. (1994, April). *The Teacher Education Internet Server (TEIS).* Presentation at the Annual Meeting of the American Educational Research Association, San Francisco.

Burge, E. J., & Frewin, C. C. (1989), Self-directed learning in distance education. In M. Eraut (Ed.), *The international encyclopedia of educational technology* (pp. 291–293). Oxford: Pergamon.

Burgoyne, J. (1992, April). Creating a learning organization. *RSA Journal,* pp. 321–332.

Business Week. (1995a, February 13). Europe goes online. *Business Week,* p. 91.

Business Week. (1995b, February 27). The ever-widening Web. *Business Week,* p. 78.

Carnegie Mellon University (a.k.a. fuzzy@cmu.edu) (1995, June 14). *Carnegie Mellon Lycos: The catalog of the Internet.* [WWW document] URL `http://www.lycos.com/`

Carvin, A. (1995). Introduction: K-12 publishing on the upswing. *International Journal of Educational Telecommunications, 1*(1), 105–109.

Cervantes, R. (1993, April). *A situated evaluation of electronic computer networking in four classroom settings.* Paper presented at the Annual General Meeting of the American Educational Research Association, Atlanta, GA.

Chapman & Hall. (1995). *Journals 1996 Publications list, with Internet distribution.* 2–6 Boundary Road, London, SE1 8HNUK.

Charp, S. (1994). Delivery systems around the world. *T.H.E. Journal, 21*(9), 6, 8.

Chatterjee, R., Gupta, S., & Pitkow, J. (a.k.a Hermes). (1995, July). *A research project on the commercial uses of the World Wide Web.* [WWW document]. URL `http://www.umich.edu/~sgupta/hermes/`

Chavkin, N. F., Kennedy, P. A., & Carter, M. (1994). Distance learning partnerships for underserved learners. *Tech Trends, 39*(5), 30–38.

Chico State University. (1995). *Newsrelease: Chico State University, Chico: A leader in distance education.* Center for Regional and Continuing Education, California State University Chico, Chico, CA 95929–0250.

Cirtin, A. (1995). The MBA degree on television: Distance education for the upwardly mobile. *DEOSNEWS, 5*(3). [Internet journal]. Contact: `ACSDE@PSUVM.PSU.EDU`

Cisco Systems. (1995). *CyberFair: "Share and Unite" Schools and Their Communities.* [Internet listserv document]. Contact `cyberfair@gsn.org`

Clement, G. P. (1994, September). Library without walls. *Internet World,* pp. 60–64.

CNAM. (1995). *The CNAM Remote Teaching Network in the Pays de la Loire area.* Nantes, FR: Conservatoire National des Arts et Métiers.

Cohen, M., & Riel, M. (1989). The effect of distant audiences on students' writing. *American Educational Research Journal, 26*(2), 143–159.

Collins, D., & Bostock, S. J. (1993). Educational effectiveness and the computer conferencing interface. *ETTI, 30*(4), 334–342.

Collins, L. J., & Pawloski, B. (1995). Telecomputing, distance learning, and environmental science: A match for the 21st century. *Learning and Leading with Technology, 22*(8), 33–35.

Collis, B. (1991, November). *New paradigms for education through networking.* Paper presented at ADCIS, St. Louis, USA.

Collis, B. (1992a). Supporting educational uses of telecommunications in the secondary school: Part I: An overview of experiences. *International Journal of Instructional Media, 19*(1), 23–44.

Collis, B. (1992b). Supporting educational uses of telecommunications in the secondary school: Part II: Strategies for improved implementation. *International Journal of Instructional Media, 19*(2), 97–109.

Collis, B. (1993a). Evaluating instructional applications of telecommunications in education. *Educational Training and Technology International, 30*(3), 266–274.

Collis, B. (1993b). Telecommunications applications in education: A research taxonomy. *Australian Educational Computing Journal, 8*(2), 1–11.

Collis, B. (1994). Triple innovation in The Netherlands. *Journal of Computing in Teacher Education, 11*(1), 12–18.

Collis, B. (1996). The evolution of educational software portability. *Educational Media and Technology Yearbook,* (pp. 76–97). Englewood, co: Libraries Unlimited.

Collis, B. (1995a). Networking and distance learning for teachers: A classification of possibilities. *Journal of Information Technology in Teacher Education, 4*(2), 117–136.

Collis, B. (Ed.). (1995b, June). *On-Line Learning.* [WWW document]. URL `http://www.to.utwente.nl/ism/online95/campus/campus.html`

Collis, B. (1995c). Societal and organizational influences on integration: What about networking? In D. Watson & D. Tinsley (Eds.), *Integrating information technology into education* (pp. 249–262). London: Chapman-Hall.

Collis, B. (Ed.). (1995d). *The TeleScopia Courses: Experiences with the adaptation process for trans-European tele-learning.* Deliverable UT/DL1001/WP3/3. Bonn, Germany: Deutsche Telekom AG, Generaldirektion.

Collis, B., & Anderson, R. (1994). Computer literacy for the 1990s: Theoretical issues for an international assessment. *Computers in the Schools, 11*(2), 55–72.

Collis, B., & Carleer, G. (1993). *Technology-enriched schools: Nine case studies with analysis.* Eugene, OR: ISTE.

Collis, B., De Diana, I., & Sterk, E. (1993). *Communication and information services for the educational system: An overview of the CISO Project.* Report under contract to the CISO Project. The Hague, NL: PTT Telecom.

Collis, B., & De Vries, P. (1991). *Telematics in education.* Hoevelaken, NL: PRINT VO (Ministry of Education).

Collis, B., & De Vries, P. (1993). *The emerging trans-European network for education and training.* Report No, 92–001-NIT-109/NL. Brussels: Commission of the European Community, Task Force Human Resources, Education, Training, and Youth.

Collis, B., & De Vries, P. (1994). Telecommunications in education and training in Europe: An analysis of research and practice. *Journal of Machine-Mediated Learning, 2*(2&3), 187–201.

Collis, B., & Moonen, B. (1995a). *The PIT Project: Final evaluation report.* Hoevelaken, NL: PRINT-VO, Ministry of Education and Science.

Collis, B., & Moonen, B. (1995b). Teacher networking: A nationwide approach to supporting instructional use of computers in the Netherlands. *Australian Educational Computing Journal, 10*(2), 4–9.

Collis, B., & Muir, W. (1986). A survey of computer education courses in Canadian faculties of education. *The Canadian Journal of Higher Education, 16*(1), 61–72.

Collis, B., Nikolova, I., & Martcheva, K. (Eds.). (1995). *Communication and information technologies for teacher education: Issues and experiences for countries in transition.* Paris: UNESCO.

Collis, B., Parisi, D., & Ligorio, B. (1995). Adaptation of courses for trans-European tele-learning. *Journal of Computer-Assisted Learning, 12*(1), 47–62.

Collis, B., & Smith, C. (1995). Desktop multimedia conferencing environments to support collaborative distance learning. CTTT Technical Report series, No.96–04. Centre for Telematics and Information Technology, University of Twente, Ensched, The Netherlands.

Collis, B., Van Holstein, M., Rikkerink, E., & Woerts, G.(1994). *An evaluation of SLO-Lijn: Users and usage.* Enschede, NL: National Institute for Curriculum Development (SLO).

Collis, B., Veen, W., & De Vries, P. (1994). *The CISO Project: Toward a communication and information system for The Netherlands.* Den Haag: PTT Telecom.

Collis, B., & Verwijs, C. (1995). A human approach to electronic performance and learning support systems: Hybrid EPSSs. *Educational Technology, 36*(1), 5–21..

Collis, B., Vingerhoets, J., & Moonen, J. (1995). *Flexibility as a key construct in European training: The TeleScopia Project.* Report 1.2a of Workpackage 1.2, The TeleScopia Project. Bonn, Germany: Deutsche Bondpost Telekom.

Comes, J. F., & Kirkwood, J. J. (1992). Electronic information files and resources assist students and teachers: One day to organize and present a topic. In N. Estes & M. Thomas (Eds.), *Proceedings of the Ninth International Conference on Technology and Education* (pp. 1334–1336). Austin, TX: Morgan Printing.

Commission of the European Community. (1994). *The Luxembourg Link: A conference about the users' needs and views on a European Electronic Network for education and training.* Luxembourg: CEC, Task Force Human Resources, Education, Training and Youth, and Ministry of Education, Luxembourg.

Cookson, P. S.(1995). Audioconferencing: Instructor and participant responses to critical conditions. *Techtrends, 40*(4), 23–25.

Cotton, C. (1995). Time-and-place independent learning: The higher education market for distance learning emerges. *Media Newsletter, 8*(5), 37–39.

Cowick, D. (1995). *Letters to Santa—11th year for this highly successful project.* [Internet listserv message]. Contact santa@gsn.org

Cox, K., & Walker, D. (1993). *User-Interface Design.* New York: Prentice-Hall.

Crawford, D. (1995). Editorial pointers. *Communications of the ACM, 38*(4), 5.

Croft, W. B. (1995). NSF Center for Intelligent Information Retrieval. *Communications of the ACM, 38*(4), 42–43.

Curran, C. (1993). *The Review Board Report on information and telecommunication technologies applied to education and training.* Brussels: Commission of the European Community, DG XIII, DELTA Office.

Cyrs, T. E., & Smith, F. A. (1990). *Teleclass teaching: A resource guide.* Center for Educational Development, College of Human and Community Services, New Mexico State University, Las Cruces, NM 88003

D'Ignazio, F. (1995a). Multimedia authoring programs: Preparing students for publishing on the Internet. *Learning and Leading with Technology, 23*(1), 58.

D' Ignazio, F. (1995). The One-Minute Guru. *Learning and Leading with Technology* (formerly The Computing Teacher), *23*(8), 51–52.

Davis, A. W. (1995, October). Face to face. *Byte,* pp. 69–72.

Davis, J. R., & Huttenlocher, D. P. (1995). Shared annotation for cooperative learning. In J. L. Schnase & E. L. Cunnius (Eds.), *CSCL 95: Computer support for collaborative learning* (pp. 84–88). Mahwah, NJ: Lawrence Erlbaum Associates.

Davis, N. (1994). ISDN technology in teaching. In R. Mason & P. Bacsich (Eds.), *ISDN applications in education and training* (pp. 161–178). London: The Institution of Electrical Engineers.

Davis, N. (1995a). Cooperative work between schools and a university with ISDN multimedia. In B. Collis & G. Davies (Eds.), *Innovating adult learning with innovative technologies* (pp. 123–128). Amsterdam: Elsevier Science B.V.

Davis, N.(1995b). Telecommunications in teacher education: Design issues for the global information highway. *Journal of Information Technology in Teacher Education, 4*(2), 105–116.

Davis, S., & Elliott, C. S. (1992). Whose job is teleconference reception? In M. G. Moore (Ed.), *Distance education for corporate and military training* (pp. 31–44). American Centre for the Study of Distance Education, The Pennsylvania State University, College of Education, University Park, PA

December, J. (1993, October 2). (Release 2.98). *Information sources: The Internet and computer-mediated communication.* [WWW document]. URL http://ccadfa. cc.adfa.oz.au/cmc.htm

Dede, C. (1994, April). Swimming in a sea of information: The future of education in the information age. *Inventing Tomorrow's Schools,* Newsletter of The Global Village Schools Institute, PO Box 22075, Alexandria, VA 22304, pp. 14–19.

Denning, P. J., & Rous, B.(1995). The ACM Electronic Publishing Plan. *Communications of the ACM, 38*(4), 97–103.

Derfler, F. J. (1990, February 13). Is ISDN tomorrow's interoffice network? *PC Magazine,* pp. 229–254.

Derycke, A. (1992). Toward a hypermedium for collaborative learning? In A. R. Kaye (Ed.), *Collaborative learning through computer conferencing* (pp. 211–224). Berlin: Springer Verlag.

Deutsche Telekom. (1994). *FUNLINE: Systematic overall solultion for computer-assisted learning.* Bonn: Deutsche Telekom AG. Generaldirektion.

De Vries, L. (1994). *Design considerations and the application of a qualitative content evaluation to a tele-seminar at the Deistance Education Centre, Toowoomba, Australia.* Masters thesis, Faculty of Educational Science and Technology, University of Twente, Enschede, The Netherlands.

De Vries, P., & Collis, B. (1993). Software for educational communications. In B. Samways & G. Davies (Eds.), *Teleteaching '93* (pp. 915–924). Amsterdam: North Holland.

Donlevy, J. G., & Donlevy, T. R. (1995). Teachers, technology, and training. *International Journal of Instructional Media, 22*(1), 1–4.

Doyle, C. (1992). *Information literacy in an information society: A concept for the information age.* Syracuse, NY: ERIC Clearinghouse on Information & Technology.

Duffy, C., Arnold, S., & Henderson, F.P. (1995, July). NetSim: Electrifying under-graduate seminars. *Active Learning, 2,* 42–48.

Duncan, R. (1995a, August). Publishing databases on the World-Wide Web. *PC Magazine,* pp. 409–412.

Duncan, R. (1995b, May 16). Setting up a Web server. *PC Magazine,* pp. 273–280.

Duning, B. S., Van Kekerix, M. J., & Zaborowski, L. M. (1993). *Reaching learners through telecommunications.* San Francisco: Jossey-Bass, Inc.

Durham, M. (1995, February 9). *The final frontier: An EPSS helping teachers utilize NASA resources.* Paper presented at the annual meeting of the Association for Education and Communication Technology (AECT), Anaheim, CA.

Dybvik, P. E., & Lie, H. W. (1995). *Combining WWW/Mosaic with realtime multimedia conferencing in distance education.*

EADTU. (1994a). *EADTU News.* Newsletter of the European Association of Distance Teaching Universities. Secretariat, Open University, P.O. Box 2960, 6401 DL Heerlen, The Netherlands.

EADTU (1994b). *EuroStudy Centres: Development and implementation.* Heerlen, The Netherlands: European Association of Distance Teaching Universities.

EADTU (1995). *The EuroStudy Centre concept within the development of the European Open University Network.* EADTO, PO Box 2960, 6401 DL Heerlen, The Netherlands. [see also WWW document]. URL `http://www.ouh.nl/eadtu/homepage.html`

Edelson, D., & O'Neill, K. (1994). The CoVis Collaboratory Notebook: Supporting collaborative scientific enquiry. In D. Foster & D. Jolley (Eds.), *Proceedings of the National Educational Computing Conference 1994* (pp. 146–151). Eugene, OR: ISTE.

Eidgahy, S. Y., & Shearman, J. P. (1994). Keiretsu approach to educational technologies in distance education. *Tech Trends, 39*(5), 21–28.

Eijkelenburg, K. van, Heeren, E., & Vermeulen, L. (1992). *ECOLE as a computer supported cooperative learning device: Technological possibilities for telecommunications-mediated interactive learning.* Report ITB-IN-1543. Groningen, NL: Institute for Applied Social Science, PTT Research.

Eisenstadt, M. (1995). *Virtual Summer School.* [WWW document]. URL `http://kmi.open.ac.uk/kmi-misc/virtualsummer.html`

Ellermann, H. H., Husiman, W. H. T., Schellekens, A. M. H. C., Zwaneveld, G., & Berns, R. M. (1992). An experimental network-mediated study support system. *Journal of Computer Assisted Learning, 8,* 186–192.

Ellis, A., Debreceny, R., & Crago, R. (1995). Audiographics in transition: Changing technologies and patterns of usage. *Journal of Education and Information Technologies, 1*(1), 21–41.

Ellsworth, J. (1994). *Education on the Internet*. Indianapolis: Sams Publishing. [See also WWW document]. URL http://www.nova.edu/Inter-Link

Elmer-Dewitt, P. (1993, April 12). Take a trip into the future on the electronic superhighway. *Time*, pp. 50–55.

Emmons, D. (1990). Using CoSy in a social science policy course. In *Conferencing in our classrooms: The CoSy Project* (pp. 3–5). Stockton State College, College Drive, Pomona, NJ.

Enkvist, I. (1992, November). *The video-conference technology in foreign language teaching*. Paper presented at the International Council for Distance Education 16th Annual Meeting, Bangkok, Thailand.

Eschelbeck, G. (1995). An architecture for multimedia communication in a distributed education environment. H. Maurer, (Ed.). (1995). *Educational multimedia and hypermedia, 1995* (pp. 217- 222). Charlottesville, VA: AACE.

Eurich-Fulcher, R. , & Schofield, J. W. (1995). Wide-area networking in K-12 education: Issues shaping implementation and use. *Computers & Education, 24*(3), 211–220.

Evans, T., & Nation, D. (1989). *Critical reflections on distance education*. London: Falmer Press.

Everett, D. R., & Ahern, T. C. (1994). Computer-mediated communication as a teaching tool: A case study. *Journal of Research on Computing in Education, 26*(3), 336–357.

Falten, D. (1994, November/December). Curriculum related ITV programs: What's new, what's hot. *Media & Methods*, pp. 12 - 13.

Farnes, N. (1993). *Evaluation of an online education and training course (OET 93)*. SRC Report No. 83. Student Research Centre, Institute of Educational Technology, The Open University, UK.

Feller, G. (1995, March). East meets West- Online. *Internet World*, pp. 48–50.

Fields, H. (Ed.), (1995). Survey shows half of American homes have computers or will buy one soon. *Educational Technology News*, Sample Issue, Business Publishers Inc., 951 Pershing Dr., Silver Spring, MD 20910–4464. (e-mail: fields@access.digex.net)

Fine, C. S. (1993). CAWP On-Line: Enhancing collaboration through technology. In G. Davies & B. Samways (Eds.), *Teleteaching* (pp. 239–248). Amsterdam: North Holland.

Flaskerud, G. (1994). The effectiveness of an interactive video network (IVN) extension workshop. *DEOSNEWS, 4*(9). [Internet journal]. Contact: ACSDE@PSUVM.PSU.EDU

Florini, B. M. (1989). *Computer conferencing: A technology for adult education*. Syracuse, NY: Syracuse University Kellogg Project.

Fluck, A. E. (1995, July 27). *Managing the Net - in the classroom.* Paper presented at the World Conference of Computers in Education (WCCE '95), Birmingham, UK.

Flyndal, E. (1995). Co-operative work within habilitation through videophones and computers: Simple technology, great visions and some experiences. In B. Collis & G. Davies (Eds.), *Innovating adult learning through innovative technologies* (pp. 137–154). Amsterdam: Elsevier Science BV.

Foley, M. (1995). Satellite broadcasting and the European Training Network: From research to implementation. In P. Held & W. F. Kugemann (Eds.), *Telematics for education and training* (pp. 135–139) . Amsterdam: IOS Press.

"Ford links..." (1994, May 9). Ford links dealers'offices via satellite. *Investor's Business Daily*, p. A4.

Forsslund, T. (1992). European school television research in the 80s: A literature review of current directions and central issue. In M. Meyer (Ed.), *Aspects of school television in Europe* (pp. 445–476). München: K. G. Saur.

Foster, D., & Jolley, D. V. (Eds.). (1993). *Proceedings, Teled '93: Global Connections.* Austin, TX: SEDL.

Fox, E. A., Akscyn, R. M., Furuta, R. K., & Leggett, J. L. (Eds).(1995). Digital libraries. Special Issue of the *Communications of the ACM, 38*(4), 23–96.

Friedman, E. D., Haefele, L., Keating, K. M., Mullen, M., Patrick, M., Plotkin, D., & Strenski, E. (1995). An electronic discussion list in an undergraduate writing course. *Computers in Education, 24*(3), 191–201.

Fries, C. (1995). Learner needs in a corporate teletraining environment: Evaluation findings in the MTS Project. In P. Held & W.G. Kugemann (Eds.), *Telematics for education and training* (pp. 351–354). Amsterdam: IOS Press.

Fritz, J. (1995, September). You can take it with you. *Byte*, pp. 41–48.

Fullan, M. (1982). *The meaning of educational change.* Toronto, ON: OISE Press/ The Ontario Insititute for Studies in Education.

Fullan, M. (1991). *The new meaning of educational change.* London: Cassell Educational Ltd.

Fullan, M. G., Miles, M. B., & Anderson, S.E. (1988). *Strategies for implementing microcomputers in schools: The Ontario case.* Toronto, ON: The Queen's Printer, Ministry of Education, Ontario.

Furht, B. (1994). Multimedia systems: An overview. In B. Furht & M. Milenkovic (Eds.), *A guided tour of multimedia systems and applications,* (pp. 47–59). Los Alamitos, CA: IEEE Computer Society Press.

Fyock, J. J., & Sutphin, H. D. (1995). Students' perceptions of the effectiveness of two-way interactive television. *DESONEWS, 5*(4). [Internet journal] Contact: ACSDE@PSUVM.PSU.EDU

Gaede, O. F. (1995). Internet information tools developed by the Florida Schoolyear 2000 Initiative. In H. Maurer, (Ed.). (1995). *Educational multimedia and hypermedia, 1995* (pp. 235–240). Charlottesville, VA: AACE.

Gaffin, A. (1993, November-December). U.S. Government information available via the Internet. *Internet World,* pp. 24–31.

Galbreath, J. (1993). Multimedia: Beyond the desktop. *Educational Technology, 33*(5), 27–32.

Galbreath, J. (1995b). Multimedia on the network: Has its time come? *Educational Technology, 35*(4), 44–51.

Galbreath, J. (1995a). Compressed digital video-conferencing: An overview. *Educational Technology, 35*(1), 31–38.

Gallo, M. A., & Horton, P. B. (1994). Assessing the effect on high school teachers of direct and unrestricted access to the Internet: A case study of an East Central Florida high school. *ETR & D, 42*(4), 17–39.

Garcia Alcocer, J., & Ribera i Górriz, N. (1994). Literary analysis in the telematic classroom. In W. Veen, B. Collis, P. de Vries, & F. Vogelzang (Eds.), *Telematics in education: The European case* (pp. 209–220). De Lier, NL: Academic Book Centre.

Gardiol, C., Boder, A., & Peraya, D. (1993). The JITOL Project and model (Just in Time Open Learning). In B. Samways & G. Davies (Eds.), *Teleteaching '95* (pp. 269–286). Amsterdam: North Holland.

Garito, M.A. (1995). The role of television in teaching and learning processes. In M.A. Garito, (Ed.), *Multimedia and distance learning for science and technology.* (pp. 239–272). Rome: Garamond.

Garito, M. A., Parisi, D., Hediard, M., & Natali, E. (1995). La Sept/Arte, Innovation Management. In B. Collis (Ed.), *The TeleScopia Courses: Experiences with the adaptation process for trans-European tele-learning* (pp. 32–36). Deliverable UT/DL1001/WP3.3. Bonn, Germany: Deutsche Telekom AG, Generaldirektion.

Gay, G., & Lentini, M. (1995). *Use of communication resources in a networked collaborative design environment.* [WWW document]. URL http://cwis.usc.edu/dept/annenberg/vol1/issue1/

Gilster, P. (1993). *The Internet navigator.* New York: John Wiley & Sons.

Gleick, J. (1995). Quoted in A. Kim, "Cyberspace Invader", *Time,* September 18, 1995, p. 24.

GNA (Global Network Academy). (1995). *The Global Network Academy.* [WWW document]. URL http://uu-gna.mit.edu:8001/uu-gna/index.html

"Going the distance..." (1995, August 4). Going the distance with PBC. *Chronicle of Higher Education,* p. A15.

Goldman, S. V., & Newman, D. (1992). Electronic interactions: How students and teachers organize schooling over the wires. *Interactive Learning Environments, 2*(1), 31–44.

Goodlad, J. (1983). A study of schooling: Some implications for school improvement. *Phi Delta Kappan, 64*(8), 552–558.

Goodyear, P. (1994, July). Telematics, flexible and distance learning in postgraduate education. *The CTISS File, 17,* pp. 14–19.

Gray, A., & O'Grady, G. (1993). Telecommunications pedagogy for effective teaching and learning. In B. Samways & G. Davies (Eds.), *Teleteaching '93* (pp. 307–316). Amsterdam: North Holland.

Gray, A., & O'Grady, G. (1994). Interactive television: Expanding established skills or new experiences for old? In M. Ryan (Ed.), *Proceedings of APITITE 94, Vol. 2,* (pp. 665–670). Murray Hill, NSW, Australia: Australian Computer Society.

Greenbowe, T. J., & Burke, K. A. (1995). Distance education and curriculum change in introductory chemistry courses in Iowa. *Techtrends, 40*(5), 23–25.

Gunawardena, C. N., & Heeren, E. (1993, 4 August). *Design and analysis of global cooperative learning through computer conferencing.* Paper presented at the Ninth Annual Conference on Distance Teaching and Learning, Madison, WI.

Gustafson, K. L. (1993). Instructional design fundamentals: Clouds on the horizon. *Educational Technology, 32*(2), 27–32.

Gutwin, C., & Greenberg, S. (1995). Support for group awareness in real-time desktop conferences. In *Proceedings of the Second New Zealand Computer Science Research Students' Conference.* Hamilton, New Zealand: University of Waikato.

Hackman, G., & Montgomery, J. (1995, July). One-click Internet. *PC Computing,* pp. 114–124.

Hackman, M. Z., & Walker, K. B. (1995). Perceptions of proximate and distant learners enrolled in university-level communication courses: A significant nonsignificant finding. *International Journal of Educational Telecommunications, 1*(1), 43–51.

Hafner, K. (1995, February 6). Wiring the ivory tower. *Newsweek,* pp. 44–46.

Hakes, B. T. (1995). Vendor selection: Judging the alternatives and who really is the vendor? In B. T. Hakes, J. Cochenour, L. L. Rezabek, & S. G. Sachs (Eds.), *Compressed video for instruction: Operations and applications* (pp. 85–108). Washington, DC: AECT.

Hakes, B. T., Cochenour, J., Rezabek, L. L., & Sachs, S. G. (Eds.). (1995). *Compressed video for instruction: Operations and applications.* Washington, DC: Association for Educational Communications and Technology

Hall, G., Loucke, R., & Rutherford, W. (1977). *Measuring stages of concern about the innovation.* Austin, TX: University of Texas Research and Development Center for Teacher Education.

Hammerschmidt, C. (1993, July). Learning over networks. *Byte,* pp. 23–26.

Harasim, L. (1993a). Collaborating in cyberspace: Using computer conferences as a group learning environment. *Interactive Learning Environments, 3*(2), 119–130.

Harasim, L.M. (1993b). *Global networks: Computers and international communication.* Cambridge, MA: MIT Press.

Harasim, L. (1993c). Learning to teach online. *T.I.E. News,* Newsletter of the SIG-TIE (Telecommunications in Education), Volume 5, Number 1, pp. 22–28. ISTE, 1787 Agate Street, Eugene, OR.

Harasim, L., & Teles, L. (1994). *Developing the Virtual Interactive Environment for Workgroups: An example of a CANARIE applications initiative.* Internal report, School of Communication, Simon Fraser University, Vancouver, British Columbia, Canada.

Hardy, G., McConnell, D., Hodgson, V., & Reynolds, M. (1991). *Computer mediated communication for management training and development.* Lancaster, UK: Centre for the Study of Management Learning, Lancaster University.

Harris, J. (1994a). Information collection activities. *The Computing Teacher, 21*(6), 32–36.

Harris, J. (1994b). *The way of the ferret.* Eugene, OR: ISTE Publications.

Harris, J. (1995a). Educational telecomputing activities: Problem-solving projects. *Learning and Leading with Technology (formerly The Computing Teacher), 23*(1), 59–64.

Harris, J. (1995b). *"Matches" with experts now available.* [Internet listserv message]. Contact jbharris@tenet.edu

Hartwig, R. L. (1990). *Basic TV technology.* Boston: Focal Press.

Hasebrink, U. (1992). School television in Northern Germany: Some results of a utilization and acceptance study. In M. Meyer (Ed.), *Aspects of school television in Europe* (pp. 485–495). München: K. G. Saur.

Hauke, H. (1992). Acceptance and utilization of school television in South-West Germany. In M. Meyer (Ed.), *Aspects of school television in Europe* (pp. 496–506). München: K. G. Saur.

Hawkridge, D. (1991). Machine-mediated learning in third-world schools? *Machine-Mediated Learning, 3,* 319–328.

Hedberg, J. G., & Harper, B. (1993). Supporting and developing teachers through telecommunications. *Educational Media International, 30*(2), 88–93.

Heeren, E. (1995). *Technologies for collaborative distance learning.* Doctoral dissertation. Enschede, NL: Faculty of Educational Science and Technology, University of Twente.

Held, P., & Kugemann, W. G. (Eds.), (1995). *Telematics for education and training.* Amsterdam: ISO.

Heldman, R. K.(1994). *Future telecommunications: Information applications, services, & infrastructure.* Washington, DC: McGraw Hill, Inc.

Heller, R., & Kearsley, G. (1995). Using a computer BBS for graduate education: Issues and outcomes. In Z. Berge & M. Collins (Eds.), *Computer-mediated communication and the online classroom in distance learning* (pp. 129–139). Cresskill, NJ: Hampton Press, Inc.

Henri, F. (1991). Computer conferencing and content analysis. In A. R. Kaye (Ed.), *Collaborative learning through computer conferencing* (pp.117–136). Berlin: Springer-Verlag.

Heppel, S. (1995). *Welcome to Schools OnLine.* [WWW document]. URL http://www.ultralab.anglia.ac.uk/

Herring, M., Smaldino, S., & Thompson, A. (1995). Preservice teacher education: Innovative applications of interactive television. *Techtrends, 40*(5), 16–18.

Hesse, B. W., Sproull, L. S., Kiesler, S. B., & Walsh, J. P. (1993). Returns to science: Computer networks in oceanography. *Communications of the ACM, 36*(8), 90–101.

Hettinga, M. (1995). *Greenpeace World Wide Web: Lesson materials about Greenpeace on the Internet.* Hengelo, NL: PTT Telecom.

Hill, J.W., & Judd, M. F. (1995, February). Fiber optics illuminate our future. *Electronic School,* pp. 37–38.

Hillman, D. C. A., Willis, D. J., & Gunawardena, C. N. (1994). Learner-interface interaction in distance education: An extension of contemporary models and strategies for practitioners. *The American Journal of Distance Education, 8*(2), 30–42.

Hiltunen, J., Sjöman, I., & Martinmäki, H. (1994). *Experiences from satellite based video-conferencing in distance education.* Internal Report. Centre for Educational Technology, University of Oulu, Finland. (contact: hiltunen@oyt.oulu.fi)

Hiltz, S. R. (1990). Collaborative learning: The Virtual Classroom approach. *T.H.E. Journal, 17*(10), 59–66.

Hiltz, S. R. (1993). Correlates of learning in a virtual classroom. *International Journal of Man-Machine Studies, 39,* 71–98.

Hiltz, S. R. (1995, March). *Teaching in a Virtual Classroom.* Paper presented at the 1995 International Conference on Computer-Assisted Instruction, Taiwan. [Also WWW document]. URL http://ww.njit.edu/cccc/vc/Papers/

Hiltz, S. R., & Turoff, M. (1993). *The network nation: Human communication via computers.* Cambridge, MA: MIT Press.

Hirumi, A., Harmon, S., & Palumbo, D. (1994). TEA^{3}M: A system for infusing technology into teacher education. In M. R. Simonson, N. Maushak, & K.

Abu-Omar (Eds.), *16th Annual Proceedings of Selected Research & Development Presentations, AECT* (pp. 259–276). Ames, IW: Iowa State University.

Hlynka, D., & Chinlen, C. (1990). Technological visions in education. *Journal of Thought, 25*(1/2), 66–80.

Hoebel, M., & Mussio, J. (1990). *Educational reform and tools for change.* Victoria, British Columbia: Education Technology Centre.

Holte, J. (1995a). Electronically connecting your community and schools: Why should you? *Learning and Leading with Technology, 22*(8), 43–46.

Holte, J. (1995b). Making network connections: The St. Louis Park Schools Story. *Learning and Leading with Technology, 22*(7), 34–36.

Holyfield, S., & Liber, O. (1995). Using the World Wide Web for the management of online learning resources. *Active Learning, 2,* 30–33.

Honey, M. (1993a). *The Mathematics Learning Forums Project.* Internal report. Bank Street College, New York, NY.

Honey, M., & Henríquez, A. (1993b). *A national survey on K-12 teachers' use of telecommunications systems.* Center for Technology and Education, Bank Street College of Education, 610 W. 112th St, New York, NY 10025.

Honey, M., & Henríquez, A. (1993). *Telecommunications and K-12 education. Findings from a national survey.* Center for Technology in Education, Bank Street College of Education, 610 West 112th Street, New York, NY, 10025.

Honey, M., & McMillan, K. (1994). NII roadblocks: Why do so few educators use the Internet? *Electronic Learning, 14*(2), 14–15

Horsley, M., & Beazley, M. (1993). Training teachers to use computers in communication: Lessons in orchestration and harmony. In G. Davies & B. Samways (Eds.), *Teleteaching '93* (pp. 401–409). Amsterdam: Elsevier Science B.V.

Horton, L. (1994). A distance education and training network. In M. Ryan (Ed.), *Proceedings of APTITE 94* (Vol. 2) (pp. 747–754). Murray Hills, NSW: Australian Computer Society.

Huntley, M. (a.k.a. National School Network Testbed). (1995, July). *National School Network Testbed. [WWW document]* URL `http://copernicus.bbn.com:70/testbed2/TB2home.html`

Hutchinson, H., & Koplin, M. (1995). *The impact of technology on the teaching of Grench at tertiary level in Australia: A comparison of TV open learning and alternative modes of study.* School of Modern Languages, University of New England, Armidale, NSW, 2351 Australia (paper submitted for publication). `hutchinson/CHRISR.html` or contact: `chrish@isys.kingston.ac.uk`

Hutchison, C. (1995). *The 'ICP OnLine': Jeux sans frontières on the CyperCampus.* URL `http://cwis.usc.edu/dept/annenberg/vol1/issue1/`

IHAC (Information Highway Advisory Council, Canada). (a.k.a.

bdgraham@achilles.net) (1995, September). *Canada's Information Highway Advisory Council Final Report.* [WWW document]. URL http://info.ic.gc.ca/info-highway/

Illich, I. D. (1971). *Deschooling society.* London: Calder and Boyars.

Individual, Inc. (1995). *NewsPage: An information service from Individual, Inc.* [WWW document]. URL http://www.newspage.com/

"Internet ABCs..." (1994, April 14). Internet ABCs essential. *Investor's Business Daily,* p. 4.

Investor's Business Daily. (1995, September 28). Amazing shrinking Internet. *Investor's Business Daily,* p. A8.

ISSUE Consortium (1994). *Human factors guidelines for videotelephony.* RACE Project 1065. HUSAT Research Institute, Loughborough University of Technology, Leicestershire, UK.

ISSUE Consortium. (1995). *Video-conferencing: Guidelines for user organizations and service providers.* RACE Project 1065. Volume I. HUSAT Research Institute, Loughborough University of Technology, Leicestershire, UK. (Contact: A.M.Clarke@lut.ac.uk)

Itzkan, S. J. (1994–95). Assessing the future of telecomputing environments. *The Computing Teacher, 22*(4), 60–64.

Jacobs, G. (1994). ISDN: Theoretical specification, practical potential. In R. Mason & P. Bacsich (Eds.), *ISDN applications in education and training* (pp. 1–24). London: The Institution of Electrical Engineers.

Jegede, O. (1995). From talking drums to electronic networking: Africa's snailmobile through the Cyberspace. *FID News Bulletin, 45* (7/8), 218–224.

Jelley, C. (1992). "Scientific Eye"- A new way of science education. In M. Meyer, (Ed.), *Aspects of school television in Europe* (pp. 275–281). München: K. G. Saur.

Jessup, L. M., & Valacich, J. S. (1993). Future directions and challenges in the evolution of group support systems. In J. M. Jessup & J. S. Valacich (Eds.), *Group support systems: New perspectives* (pp. 311–318). New York: Macmillan.

Johnson, J. K. (Ed.). (1995a). *Degree curricula in educational communications and technology.* Washington, DC: Association for Educational Communications and Technology.

Johnson, J. K. (1995b). The third degree: Survey of degree programs in educational communications and technology. *Techtrends, 40*(4), 27–29.

Johnson, L. (1994). Characteristics of media service departments at mid-size universities. *Tech Trends, 39*(1), 20–24.

Jonassen, D. (1995). Supporting communities of learners with technology: A vision for integrating technology with learning in schools. *Educational Technology, 35*(4), 60–63 .

Jones, A., Kirkup, G., & Kirkwood, A. (1994). *Personal computers for distance education: The study of an educational innovation.* Milton Keynes, UK: St. Martin's Press.

Jones, G., & Knezek, G. (1995). Categorizing distance learning systems: Discovering successful ingredients. In J. D. Tinsley & T. Van Weert (Eds.), *World Conference on Computers in Education VI* (pp. 243–249). London: Chapman & Hall.

Jones, S. G.(Ed.). (1995). *Cyberspace: Computer-mediated communication and community.* Thousand Oaks, CA: Sage Publications.

Jones, T. (1995, June). *The Human-Languages Page.* [WWW document]. URL http://www.willamette.edu/tjones/Language-Page.html

Jordahl, G. (1991, February). Breaking down classroom walls: Distance learning comes of age. *Technology & Learning,* pp. 72, 74, 76–78.

Jussila, T. (1994, September 7). *A distance learning environment with automatic telephone service.* Paper presented at the Distance Education Conference, Univ. Estatel en Distancia, Costa Rica.

Kaye, A. (1989). Distance learning systems. In M. Eraut (Ed.), *The international encyclopedia of educational technology* (pp. 286–291). Oxford: Pergamon Press.

Kaye, A. (Ed.).(1992a). *Collaborative learning through computer conferencing.* Berlin: Springer Verlag.

Kaye, A. (1992b). Learning apart together. In A. R. Kaye (Ed.), *Collaborative learning through computer conferencing* (pp. 1–24). Berlin: Springer Verlag.

Kaye, G. R. (1993). Electronic campus—UK. In B. Samways & G. Davies (Eds.), *Teleteaching '93* (pp. 487–501). Amsterdam: North Holland.

Kearsley, G. (1995). *Explorations in learning and instruction: The Theory into Practice Database.* [WWW document]. URL http://www.gwu.edu/etl.

Kegel, D. (1996). Dan Kegel's ISDN Page. [www document]. URL http://www.alumni.caltech.edu/|dank/isdn/

Kendall, J. R., & Oaks, M. (1992). Evaluation of perceived teaching effectiveness: Course delivery via interactive video technology versus traditional classroom methods. *DEOSNEWS* 2(5). [Internet journal]. Contact: ACSDE@PSUVM.PSU.EDU

Kent, P. (1995, April). Browser shootout. *Internet World,* pp. 46–59.

Keskinen, R. (1995). ENIC, Introduction to networks. In B. Collis, (Ed). (1995). *The TeleScopia Courses: Experiences with the adaptation process for trans-European tele-learning* (pp. 21–24). Deliverable UT/DL1001/WP3.3. Bonn, Germany: Deutsche Telekom AG, Generaldirektion.

Khan, B. H. (1995). Obstacle encountered during stages of the educational change process. *Educational Technology, 35*(2), 43–46.

Kiernan, K. (1995). *The Electronic Beowulf.* [WWW document]. URL `http://service/uky/edu/ArtsScience/English/Beowulf`

Kiesler, S. (1990). Talking, teaching, and learning in network groups. In A. Kaye (Ed.), *Collaborative learning through computer conferencing* (pp. 147–166). Berlin: Springer-Verlag.

Kimeldorf, M. (1995). Teaching online: Techniques and methods. *Learning and Leading with Technology, 23*(1), 26–31.

Kirby, R., McAndrew, P., Kilgour, A., Taylor, H., & Mayes, J. T. (1995). ELF: The Electronic Learning Facilitator. *Advanced Learning Technologies Journal (ALT-J), 3*(1), 69–74.

Kirkwood, A. (1993). Screens and their surroundings: Learning at home with information and communication technologies. In G. Davies & B. Samways (Eds.), *Teleteaching '93* (pp. 503–512). Amsterdam: North- Holland.

Kitchen, K., & Hughes, M. (1992). *Interactive television for distance learning: From plan to practice.* National School Boards Association, 1680 Duke Street, Alexandria, Virginia 22314–3493

Klemm, W. R., & Snell, J.R. (1994). Teaching via networked PC s: What's the best medium? *T.H.E. Journal, 21*(10), 95–98.

Koch, D. B. (1995). Interactive network tools for international collaborative teaching. In H. Maurer (Ed.), *Educational multimedia and hypermedia* (pp. 378–383). Charlottesville, VA: AACE.

Koster, M. (a.k.a. NEXOR) (1995, June). *World Wide Web robots, wanderers and spiders.* [WWW document] URL `http://www.nexor.co.uk/mak/doc/robots/robots.html`

Kovacs, R. E. (1993). The overselling of fiber optics. *Tech Trends, 38*(5), 15–17.

Kraut, R. E., Edigo, C., & Galegher, J. (1990). Patterns of contact and communication in scientific research collaboration. In J. Galegher, R. E. Kraut, and C. Edigo (Eds.), *Intellectual teamwork: Social and technological foundations of cooperative work* (pp. 23–61). Hillsdale, NJ: Lawrence Erlbaum Associates.

Kristiansen, T. (1993). *Five years of research into the use of telecommunications in distance education.* Report TF R 29/93. Oslo: Norwegian Telecom Research Institute.

Kugemann, W. F. (1993). Learning-systems delivery: Options, costs, chances for implementation. *ALT News,* Issue 02/93, pp. 8–9, 12.

Kurshan, B. L., Harrington, M. A., & Milbury, P. G. (1994). *An educator's guide to electronic networking: Creating virtual communities.* ERIC Clearinghouse on Information & Technology, Syracuse University, Syracuse, NY.

Labriola, D. (1995, April). Desktop videoconferencing: Candid camera. *PC Magazine,* pp. 221–254.

Lafford, A. (1994). NISS: Sources for courses? *The CTISS File, 17*, 43–45.

Lafon, J. L. (1995). *Tuttelvisio: Tools for distant learning*. ENIC, Rue Marconi, Cité Scientifique, 59650 Villeneuve d 'ASCQ, France.

Lampikoski, K. (1993). Implementing computer-mediated communication as an innovation by change management: The project leader perspective. In G. Davies & B. Samways (Eds.), *Teleteaching '93* (pp. 529–535). Amsterdam: North-Holland.

Landry, P. (1994). Corporate steps to new learning. In TRIBUTE Consortium (Eds.), *Insights on policy impact: Policy making and monitoring of OFDL development*. TRIBUNE Report 6 (pp. 67–70). Zirndorf, Germany: Bollmann-Druck GmbH.

Lange, L. (1995, July 17). The Internet: Where's it all going? *Information Week*, pp. 30–32, 34, 36.

Larsen, I. B., & Malmberg, A. C. (1991). *LEARN Network: Education via networks*. Copenhagen: Royal Danish School of Educational Studies.

Latchem, C., & Rapley, P. (1992). Trial by satellite: Videoconferencing for continuing education for rural area nurses. *Distance Education, 13*(1), 118–130.

Laws, M. (1995, 12–18 October). Will networks pull the plug on PCs? *The European*, p. 21.

Layton, T. (1995). *CyberSchool*. [WWW document]. URL http:// Cyberschool.4j.lanc.edu/CyberSchool.html

Lazarus, J. (1995, July 24). *How schools can harness the coming communication revolution*. Keynote presentation at the World Conference for Computers in Education (WCCE '95), Birmingham, UK.

LeBaron, J.F., & Bragg, C. A. (1994). Practicing what we preach: Creating distance education models for the twenty-first century. *The American Journal of Distance Education, 8*(1), 5–17.

LeBlanc, G. (1993). A faculty and staff support program at the University of Maine at Augusta. *DEOSNEWS, 3*(5). [Internet journal]. Contact ACSDE@PSUVM. PSU.EDU

Lee, D. (1992). Ears to the ground: Independent television's liaison activities with the school audience. In M. Meyer (Ed.), *Aspects of school television in Europe* (pp. 167–195). München: K. G. Saur.

Lemay, L. (1995). *Teach yourself Web publishing with HTML in a week*. Indianapolis, IN: SAMS Publishing.

Lepeltak, J., & Collis, B.(1993). Multimedia resources and their effective use in distance education. In B. Schriven, R. Lundin, & Y. Ryan (Eds.), *Distance education for the Twenty-First Century: Selected papers from the 16th World Conference of the International Council for Distance Education* (pp. 292–294). Oslo: International Council for Distance Education.

Lever, J. C. (1991, August). *Distance learning: An alternative approach to education in the Information Age.* Internal report, Director of Instructional Technology, Miami-Dade Community College, Homestead Campus, Miami, FL.

Levin, J., Waugh, M., Brown, D., & Clift, R. (1994). Teaching teleapprenticeships: A new organizational framework for improving teacher education using electronic networks. *Journal of Machine-Mediated Learning,* 4(2/3), 149–162.

Lewis, D. (1994, May). 10 commandments for distance learning. *Education at a Distance, 5,* 20–21.

Lewis, R. (1995). *JITOL concepts: Perspectives and futures.* DELTA Deliverable D2015/WP7. Neurope Lab, Le Forum, International Business Park, 74166 Archmaps, France.

Lewis, R., & Collis, B. (1995). Virtual mobility and distributed laboratories: Supporting collaborative research with knowledge technology. In B. Collis & G. Davies (Eds.), *Innovating adult learning through innovative technologies* (pp. 163–176). Amsterdam: Elsevier Science BV.

Li, J. & Mantei, M. (1992). *Working together, virtually.* Department of Computer Science, University of Toronto. Paper presented at Graphics Interface '92, Vancouver.

Libotton, A. (1994). Computer networks in teacher education: Realization in the framework of the PLUTO Project In B. Collis, I. Nikolova & K. Martcheva. (eds.), *Communication and information technologies in teacher education: Issues and experiences for countries in transition* (pp. 84–92). Paris: UNESCO.

Lieberman, J. A., & DiVito, N. (1994). *WILT: A WWW based interactive language teaching tool.* [WWW document]. URL http://www.ncsa.uiuc.edu/ SDG/IT94/Proceedings/Educ/lieberman/lieberman.html

Long, G., Pence, H., & Zielinski, T. J. (1995). New tools vs old methods: A description of the CHEMCONF '93 discussion. *Computers & Education,* 24(4), 259–269.

Lowry, M., Koneman, P., Osman-Jouchoux, R., & Wilson, B. (1994). Electronic discussion groups: Using email as an instructional strategy. *Tech Trends, 39*(2), 22–24.

Lowyck, J.(1994,March). Increasing access and participation: The use of new educational methods, media and technology for course participation and for student support. *EADTU News, 16,* 36–37.

Luther, A. C. (1991). *Digital video in the PC environment.* New York: McGraw-Hill, Inc.

Maddox, J. (1995). *Commentary on Art.* [WWW document]. URL http:// salazar.aa.psu.edu/courses/art122w/122WHome.htm

Maly, K., Overstreet, C. M., Abdel-Wahab, H., & Gupta, A. K. (1994). Melding television, networking and computing for interactive remote instruction: Exploiting potential. In T. Ottman & I. Tomek (Eds.), *Educational multimedia and hypermedia 1994* (pp. 367–372). Charlottesville, VA: AACE.

Marchionini, G. (1995). The costs of educational technology: A framework for assessing change. In H. Maurer (Ed.), *Educational multimedia and hypermedia* (pp. 33–38). Charlottesville, VA: Association for the Advancement of Computing in Education.

Marchionini, G., & Maurer, H. (1995). The roles of digital libraries in teaching and learning. *Communications of the ACM, 38*(4), 67–75.

Marcinkiewicz, H. R., & Wittman, T. K. (1995). Tracking teachers' personal variables and computer use: Phase Two. In M. R. Simonson & M. L. Anderson (Eds.), *17th Annual Proceedings of the Selected Research and Development Presentations AECT* (pp. 399–402). Ames, Iowa: Iowa State University College of Education.

Markoff, J. (1995, July 10). New Internet feature will make voluntary ratings possible. *The New York Times*, p. 25.

Marriott, A., Currie, R., & Smith, T. (1995). Teletutoring - laying a firm foundation. Critical factors in planning and implementing effective telematics-based tutorial support in further and higher education. In G. Davies & D. Tinsley (Eds.), *Open and distance learning critical success factors* (pp. 143–145). Erlangen, Germany: FIM.

Marshall, A. D. (1995). Developing hypertext courseware on the World Wide Web. In H. Maurer (Ed.). *Educational multimedia and hypermedia, 1995* (pp. 418–423). Charlottesville, VA: AACE.

Mason, R. (1989). An evaluation of COSY on an Open University course. In R. Mason & A. Kaye (Eds.), *Mindweave* (pp. 115–145). Oxford: Pergamon.

Mason, R. (1994). *Using communications media in open and flexible learning.* London: Kogan Page.

Mason, R., & Bacsich, P. (Eds.), (1994). *ISDN applications in education and training.* London: The Institution of Electrical Engineers.

MathSoft. (1995). *Mathcad 6.0.* MathSoft, Cambridge, MA. [See also, WWW document]. URL http://www.mathsoft.com.

Matusevich, M. (1995). *Montgomery Country Public Schools: Projects.* [WWW document] URL. http://pixel.cs.vt.edu/melissa/projects.html

Maurer, H., & Schneider, A. (1995). Conferencing: Doing it the hypermedia way. In H. Maurer (Ed.), *Educational multimedia and hypermedia* (pp. 436–441). Charlottesville, VA: AACE.

Mayes, T., & Neilsen, I. (1995). Learning from other people's dialogues: Questions about computer-based answers. In B. Collis & G. Davies (Eds.), *Innovating adult learning through innovative technologies* (pp. 31–48). Amsterdam: Elsevier Science BV.

McConeghy, G., & McConeghy, J. (1990). Higher education media management in the 90s: Administration of Media Centers. *Techtrends, 35*(5), 54–57.

McCreary, E., & Brochet, M. (1990). Collaboration in international online teams. In A. Kaye (Ed.), *Collaborative learning through computer conferencing* (pp. 69–85). Berlin: Springer-Verlag.

McGreal, R. (1993). Exemplary programs of secondary distance education in Canada. *DESONEWS, 3*(6). [Internet journal]. Contact ACSDE@PSOVM.PS.EDU

McKenna, P. (1994). The National Information Technology in Education Centre (NITEC) Project. In W. Veen, B. Collis, P. de Vries, & F. Vogelzang (Eds.), *Telematics in education: The European case* (pp. 93–106). De Lier, NL: Academic Book Centre.

McKenzie, T. (1995, September). *Home sweet home: Creating WWW pages which deliver.* [WWW document]. URL http://www.pacific.rim.net/~mckenzie/homesweet.html

McKinley Group. (1995). *Magellan: Mckinley's Internet directory.* [WWW document]. URL http://www.mckinley.com/

McLuhan, M. (1962). *The medium is the message.* London: Penguin.

McLuhan, M. (1964). *Understanding media: The extensions of man.* New York: New American Library.

McMillan, K. (1993, April). Telecommunications in a small community. *Newsletter from the Center for Children and Technology*, Bank Street College of Education, 610 West 112th Street, New York, NY, p. 4.

Meisner, G.W., & Hoffman, H.M. (1995). Technology tools and the Curie Internet delivery system. In J. D. Tinsley & T. van Weert (Eds.), *Proceedings of the World Conference on Computers in Education VI* (pp. 1069–1078). London: Chapman & Hall.

Mello, C. de (1995, June 25). *College and university home pages: Alphabetical listing.* [WWW document]. URL http://www.mit.edu:8001/people/cdemello/univ.html
MendelWeb94.blumberg.html

Merrill, D., Parker, N., Gey, F., & Stuber, C. (1995). The University of California CD-ROM Information System. *Communications of the ACM, 38*(4), 51–52. [Also WWW document]. URL http://cedr.lbl.gov/cdrom/doc/cdrom.html

Meyer, M. (1992). On the situation of school television in Western Europe: Summary of results of a survey. In M. Meyer, (Ed.), *Aspects of school television in Europe* (pp. 17–54). München: K. G. Saur.

Miller, G., & Doerfert, D. L. (1995). Teaching through fiber-optics telecommunications technology: Possibilities and priorities for agriculture. In M. R. Simonson & M. L. Anderson (Eds)., *17th annual proceedings of selected research and development presentations, AECT* (pp. 432–431). Ames, Iowa: Iowa State University College of Education.

Milner, H. (1995). Increasing access to higher education using ISDN conferencing to create a virtual classroom: A model from the University of Sunderland. In B. Collis & G. Davies (Eds.), *Innovating adult learning with innovative technologies* (pp. 201–206). Amsterdam: North Holland.

Mollgaard, T., & Sides-Gonzales, K. (1995) Stockbroker of the technological curriculum. *Techtrends, 40*(5), 28–30.

Moonen, B. (1995a). *A case study of the PIT Project in nine schools.* Masters thesis, Faculty of Educational Science and Technology, University of Twente, The Netherlands.

Moonen, B. (1995b). *Is there a future for educational software? Perspectives from the eye of the software publisher.* Masters thesis, Faculty of Educational Science and Technology, University of Twente, Enschede, The Netherlands.

Moonen, J. (1994). How to do more with less? In K. Beattie, C. McNaught, & S. Wills (Eds.), *Interactive multimedia in university education: Designing for change in teaching and learning* (pp. 155–164). Amsterdam: Elsevier.

Moonen, J. (1995). Prototyping as a design activity. In T. Husén & N. Postlethwaite (Eds.), *International Encyclopedia of Education, Vol.10,* (pp. 4799–4803). Oxford: Pergamon.

Moonen, J., & Kommers, P. (1995). *Implementation of computer use in the school.* Report done under assignment to the Ministry of Education and Science, The Netherlands. Enschede: Faculty of Educational Science and Technology.

Moore, M. G. (1993). Free trade in higher education. (Editorial). *The American Journal of Distance Education, 7*(3), 1–7.

Morel, R. (1995). *Operation "Success Stories".* Version 2.0. Geneva, Switzerland: Centre Informatique Pédagogique.

Morrow, C. (Ed.)(1995). The Internet unleashed. Indianapolis, IN: SAMS Publishing.

Moses, D., & Croll, P. (1992). *School television in use.* London, UK: BBC Broadcasting Research Unit.

Mountain, L. (1992). Doing homework on a telecommunications network. *Journal of Educational Technology Systems, 21*(2), 103–107.

Mueller, B. (1995). *Using World Wide Web as an information system to reduce the average period of study by better information providing and to relieve administration.* [WWW document]. URL `http://www.ncsa.uiuc.edu/SDG/IT94/Proceedings/ Educ/mueller/Paper.html`

Murray, R. (1994, November 21). Interactive employers switch over to satellite. *The Telegraph,* (UK), p. 33.

Nakabayashi, K., Koike, Y., Maruyama, M., Touhei, H., Ishiuchi, S., & Fukuhara, Y. (1995). An intelligent tutoring system on World-Wide Web: Towards an integrated learning environment on distributed hypermedia. In H. Maurer, H.(Ed.). *Educational multimedia and hypermedia, 1995* (pp. 488–493). Charlottesville, VA: AACE.

Nasta, T. (1994). *Change through networking in vocational education.* London: Kogan Page.

Nielsen, J. (1993). *Usability engineering.* Boston: Academic Press.

Netguide. (1995, July). Contributors: Creating a space where rookies and experts all can feel welcome. *Netguide,* p. 8.

Network Wizards (1995, July). *Internet Domain Survey* [WWW document]. URL http://www.nw.com

"Networking is..". (1995, 12–18 October). Networking is the key to survival in a changing profession. *The European,* p. 29.

Newman, D., Bernstein, S. L., & Reese, P. A. (1992). *Local infrastructures for school networking: Current models and prospects.* BBN Report No. 7726. Bolt Beranek and Newman, Inc., Boston, MA. [See also the WWW document for BBN]. URL http://www.bbn.com/

Ng, J. M., Chan, E., & Tsang, P. H. H. (1993). MITS: A multimedia interactive tutoring system. In T. W. Chan (Ed.), *Proceedings of the 1993 International Conference of Computers in Education* (pp. 270–275). Taipei, Taiwan: National Central University.

Nicholson, P. (1993). Facilitating changes in learning with electronic communications. In D. C Johnson & B. Samways (Eds.), *Informatics and changes in learning* (pp. 23–26). Amsterdam: North Holland.

Nipper, S. (1989). Third generation distance learning and computer conferencing. In R. Mason & A. Kaye (Eds.), *Mindweave* (pp. 63–73). Oxford: Pergamon.

Noack, D. R. (1995, October). Visiting museums virtually. *Internet World,* pp. 86–91.

Norrie, D. H., & Gaines, B. R. (1995). The Learning Web: A system view and an agent-oriented model. *International Journal of Educational Telecommunications, 1*(1), 23–41.

Novick, D. G., & Fickas, S. (1995). Collaborative networked hypermedia education: Lessons from the Nero Project. *Computers in Education, 24*(3), 157–162.

O'Neill, D. K., & Gomez, L. M. (1995). *The Collaboratory Notebook: A networked knowledge-building environment for project learning.* [WWW document]. URL http://www.covis.nwu.edu/

Oliver, R. & Reeves, T. (1995). *Telematics in rural education.* Mt Lawley, Western Australia: Edith Cowan University.

Ortner, G. E., Graff, K., & Wilmersdoerfer, H. (Eds.). (1992). *Distance education as two-way communication.* Frankfurt am Main: Peter Lang.

Oscheske, T. J., Klus, J. P., Stremikis, J., & Hoyman, D. (1995). *A guide to delivering independent learning materials on the Internet.* [WWW document]. URL `http://epdwww.engr.wisc.edu osl/aad/aadclass/studentparent.html`

Paquette, G., Bergeron, & Bourdeau, J. (1993). The Virtual Classroom revisited. In B. Samways & G. Davies (Eds.), *Teleteaching '93* (pp. 639–647). Amsterdam: North Holland.

Palme, J. (1992). Computer conferencing functions and standards. In A. R. Kaye (Ed.), *Collaborative learning through computer conferencing* (pp. 225–246). Berlin: Springer Verlag.

Pals, N., Mulder, J. A., Nelissen, P., Wolswijk, P. C., & Bruining, J. (1995). *Field trial evaluation report: "Cross Cultural Communication" course.* ECOLE: DELTA Deliverable 42. ITB-RAP-95-107. Groningen, NL: PTT Research Institute for Applied Social Science Research.

Paquette, G., Ricciardi-Rigault, C., Bourdeau, J., & Liégeois. (1995). Modeling a virtual campus environment for interactive distance learning. In H. Maurer, H.(Ed.). *Educational multimedia and hypermedia, 1995* (pp. 523–528). Charlottesville, VA: AACE.

Parker, T. L. (1994, June). *The Internet and schools: A survey of networking activities.* Paper presented at the Internet Society INET '94 Conference, Prague. (contact: `tparker@cisco.com`)

Pasos, L. (1995). *"Where on the globe is Roger?"* [Internet listserv message]. Contact `roger@gsn.org`

Pastor, E., Sanchez, G., & Alvarez, J. (1994). Distributed multimedia environment for distance learning. In M. F. Verdejo & S. A. Cerri (eds.), *Collaborative dialogue technologies in distance learning* (pp. 258–269). Berlin: Springer Verlag.

Paulsen, M. (1995). *The online report on pedagogical techniques for computer-mediated communication.* [WWW document]. URL `http://www.nki.no/morten/cmcped.htm`

Paulsen, M. F., Barros, B., Busch, P., Compostela, B., & Quesnel, M. (1994). A pedagogical framework for CMC programmes. In M.F. Verdejo & S. A. Cerri (Eds.), *Collaborative dialogue technologies in distance learning* (pp. 11–20). Berlin: Springer-Verlag.

Pea, R. D. (1994). Seeing what we build together: Distributed multimedia learning environments for transformative communications. *The Journal of the Learning Sciences, 3*(3), 285–299.

Pelgrum, W. J., Janssen Reinen, I. A. M., & Plomp, Tj. (1993). *Schools, teachers, students and computers: A cross-national perspective.* The Hague: IEA.

Phelan, A. (1995). Satellite television and interactivity. In P. Held & W. F. Kugemann (Eds.), *Telematics for education and training* (pp. 140–144). Amsterdam: IOS Press.

Pickering, J. (1995). Teaching on the Internet is learning. *Active Learning, 2,* 9–12.

Piller, C. (1994, October). Dreamnet: Customers want more than tv overload from the information highway. *MacWorld,* pp. 96–105.

Pilon, D., Raymond, J., & Raymond, P. (1995). Software tools for improving classroom interaction. In H. Maurer (Ed.), *Educational multimedia and hypermedia, 1995* (pp. 538–543). Charlottesville, VA: AACE.

Pincas, A. (1995). The learning benefits of well-designed computer conferencing. In P. Held & W. F. Kugemann (Eds.), *Telematics for education and training* (pp. 277–280). Amsterdam: IOS Press.

Pioch, N. (1995). *The WebMuseum.* [WWW document]. URL `http://mistral.enst.fr/~pioch/louvre`

Pohjonen, J. (1994). *On media selection.* Oulu, Finland: University of Oulu, Continuing Education Centre, Centre for Educational Technology.

Poole, L.(1992, February). Digital data on demand. *MacWorld,* pp. 224–227.

Posner, B. Z., Danielson, R. L., & Schmidt-Posner, J. (1992–93). *Journal of Educational Technology Systems,* 21(1), 5–19.

Pozzi, S., Tancredi, A., & Tisato, F. (1994). An integrated environment for distance educaiton supporting multiple interaction styles. In T. Ottman & I. Tomek (Eds.), *Educational multimedia and and hypermedia* (pp. 450–455). Charlottesville, VA: AACE.

Preece, J., Rogers, Y., Sharp, H., Benyon, D., Holland, S., & Carey, T. (1994). *Human-computer interaction.* Wokingham, UK: Addison-Wesley Publishing.

Pugh, H.L., Parchman, S. W., & Simpson, H. (1992). Video telecommunications for distance education: A field survey of systems in US public education, industry and the military. *Distance Education, 13*(1), 46–64.

Pugh, S. (1993). Using case studies and collaborative computer-assisted communication to support conceptual learning in a teacher-education course on critical reading. *Educational Technology, 33*(11), 30–38.

Quittner, J. (1995, July 17). Wiring the world. *Time Magazine,* pp. 52–53.

Ralph, E. G., & Yang, B. (1993). Beginning teachers' utlization of instructional media: A Canadian case study. *Educational Training and Technology International, 30*(4), 299–318.

Rannebo, S. (1994, May). *The Nordic Schools Network.* Presentation at the Conference "The Luxembourg Link", Luxembourg City, (Commission of the European Community, DG XXII).

Rao, R., Pedersen, J. O., Hearst, M. A., Mackinley, J. D., Card, S. K., Masinter, L., Halvorsen, P.-K, & Robertson, G. G. (1995). Rich interactions in the digital library. *Communications of the ACM, 38*(4), 29–39.

Rebelsky, S. A. (1994). *A web of resources for introductory computer science.* [WWW document]. URL http://www.uiuc.edu/SDG/IT94/Proceedings/Educ/rebelsky/rebelsky.html

Reeves, T. (1995). Questioning the questions of instructional technology research. In M. Simonson & M. Anderson (Eds.), *Selected research and development presentation 1995 National Convention of the Association for Educational Communications and Technology* (pp. 459–470). Ames, Iowa: Iowa State University and AECT.

Reif, L. (1995). The integration of telematic-based training in international enterprises. In P. Held & W. F. Kugemann (Eds.), *Telematics for education and training* (pp. 129–132). Amsterdam: IOS Press.

Reinhardt, A. (1994, March). Building the data highway. *Byte*, pp. 46–74.

Reisner, R., & Gagné, R. M. (1982). *The selection of media for instruction.* Englewood Cliffs, NJ: Educational Technology Publications.

Resnick, R. (1995, April). Olé: Latin America's Net presence is growing. *Internet World*, pp. 88–90.

Rezabek, L. L., Cochenour, J. J., Bruce, M. A., & Shade, R. A. (1995). Effective use of compressed video for teaching and learning. In In B. T. Hakes, J. Cochenour, L. L. Rezabek, & S. G. Sachs (Eds.). (1995). *Compressed video for instruction: Operations and applications* (129–140). Washington, DC: Association for Educational Communications and Technology.

Rézeau, J. (1994). Integrating telematics data into CALL packages. *Computers & Education, 23*(1/2), 159–164.

Rheingold, H. (1993). *The virtual community: Homesteading on the electronic frontier.* Reading, MA: Addison-Wesley.

Rief, L. (1995). The integration of telematics-based training in international enterprises. In P. Held & W. F. Kugemann (Eds.), *Telematics for education and training* (pp. 129–132). Amsterdam: IOS Press.

Riel, M. (1990). Cooperative learning across classrooms in electronic Learning Circles. *Instructional Science, 19*, 445–466.

Riel, M. (1992). A functional analysis of educational telecomputing: A case study of the learning circles. *Interactive Learning Environments, 2*(1), 15–29.

Riel, M. (1995). *Passport to Knowledge Newsletter.* [Internet listserv document]. Contact mriel@weber.ucsd.edu

Riel, M., & Levin, J. (1990). Building electronic communities: Success and failure in computer networking. *Instructional Science, 19*, 145–169.

Riel, M., Levin, J. A., & Miller-Souviney, B. M. (1987). Learning with interactive media: Dynamic support for students and teachers. In R. Lawler & M. Yasdani (Eds.), *Artificial intelligence and education: The broad view* (117–134). Norwood: Ablex.

Rifkin, G. (1995, July 3). Waiter, oh, waiter! Excuuuse me, but there's a mouse in my coffee! *The New York Times*, p. 25.

Rikkerink, E. (1995). *Examples of Internet courses*. Internal report. Faculty of Educational Science and Technology, University of Twente, Enschede, The Netherlands.

Ring, J., Watson, T., & Ring, G. (1994). The Edith Cowan University Virtual Campus Project. In M. Ryan (Ed.), *Proceedings of APITITE '94* (pp. 957–962). Murray Hill, NEW: ASCILITE.

Robin, B., & Miller, R. (1995, March). *Developing an electronic infrastructure to support multimedia telecomputing resources*. Paper presented at the CAL '95 Conference, Cambridge, UK.

Rogers, E.M. (1983). *Diffusion of innovations*, 3rd Ed. New York: The Free Press.

Rolland, J. (1995). The CNAM Remote Teaching Network. In P. Held & W. F. Kugemann (Eds.), *Telematics for education and training* (pp. 118–120). Amsterdam: IOS Press.

Romiszowski, A. (1993). *Telecommunications and distance education*. ERIC Digest EDO-IR-93-2. Syracuse, NY: ERIC Clearinghouse on Information Resources, Syracuse University.

Romiszowski, A. J., & Chang, E. (1995). Hypermedia networks for case-study discussions in distance education. In H. Maurer (Ed.), *Educational multimedia and hypermedia* (pp. 562–566). Charlottesville, VA: AACE.

Ross, J. A., & Regan, E. M. (1993). Sharing professional experience: Its impact on professional development. *Teaching & Teacher Education, 9*(1), 91–106.

Ross, P. (1995). Relevant telecomputing activities. *The Computing Teacher, 22*(4), 28–30.

Rossman, P. (1993). *The emerging worldwide electronic university: Information age global higher education*. Westport, CT: Praeger.

Rowland, F. (1994). In what ways will communication technology change learning? In J. Martin, J. Darby, & B. K. Kjöllerström (Eds.), *Higher education 1988 transformed by learning technology* (pp. 78–80). Oxford, UK: CTISS Publications.

Rueda, J. (1990). Collaborative learning in a large-scale computer conferencing system. In A. Kaye (Ed.), *Collaborative learning through computer conferencing* (pp. 87–102). Berlin: Springer-Verlag.

Rumble, G. (1993). *Definitions of 'What are we talking about?'* Deliverable, DELTA Project, Report D2104. Brussels: Commission of the European Community, DG XIII.

Ruopp, R., Gal, S., Drayton, B., & Pfister, M. (1993). *LabNet: Toward a community of practice*. Hillsdale, NJ: Lawrence Erlbaum.

Rush, P. (1991, January). *Education via satellite: Technology in the boardroom and in the classroom*. Paper presented to the Conference on Telecommunications Based Training Systems in the 90s, Madrid, Spain.

Søby, M. (1992). Waiting for Electropolis. In A. R. Kaye (Ed.), *Collaborative learning through computer conferencing* (pp. 39–49). Berlin: Springer-Verlag.

Sachs, S. G. (1995a). Compressed video: A technical overview. In B. T. Hakes, J. Cochenour, L. L. Rezabek, & S. G. Sachs (Eds.). (1995). *Compressed video for instruction: Operations and applications* (11–22). Washington, DC: Association for Educational Communications and Technology.

Sachs, S. G. (1995b). Compressed video facilities. In In B. T. Hakes, J. Cochenour, L. L. Rezabek, & S. G. Sachs (Eds.). (1995). *Compressed video for instruction: Operations and applications* (51–61). Washington, DC: Association for Educational Communications and Technology.

Safdar, S. J. (1995). *Internet parental control frequently asked questions (FAQ)*. [WWW document]. URL `http://www.panix.com/vtw/exon/index.html`

Saga H. (1993). Students' perceptions of media and teachers as related to the depth of their learning. *Educational Media international, 30*(3), 158–167.

Saiedian, H. (1992–93). An interactive computer-based conferencing system to accommodate students' learning process. *Journal of Educational Technology Systems, 21*(2), 109–123.

Sakamoto, T. & Miyashita,K. (1994, October). Social and political influences on the integration of informatics into Japanese education. In D. Tinsley & D., Watson (Eds.), *Integrating information technology into education: Pre-conference proceedings, IFIP WG 3.1 Working Conference* (pp. 255–264). Barcelona, Spain: Generalitat de Catalunya, Departament d'Ensenyament.

Salamone, S. (1995, August). Video-conferencing's Achilles' heels. *Byte*, pp. 24–26.

Salomon, G. (1983). Television watching and mental effort: A social psychological view. In J. Bryant, & A. Anderson (Eds.), *Children's understanding of television: Research on attention and comprehension* (pp. 181–198). New York: Academic Press.

Salomon, G. (1990, April). *What is so special about the study of computer-mediated communication?* Studying the flute and the orchestra. Paper presented at the Annual Meeting of the American Educational Research Association, Boston, MA.

Salomon, G. (Ed.). (1993). *Distributed cognitions: Psychological and educational considerations*. Cambridge, UK: Cambridge University Press.

Samuelson, P. (1995). Copyright and digital libraries. *Communications of the ACM, 38*(4), 15–21, 110.

Samways, B., & Davies, G. (1993). *Teleteaching '93*. Amsterdam: North Holland.

San Chee, Y. (1995). Mind Bridges: A distributed multimedia learning environment to support collaborative knowledge construction. In H. Maurer (Ed.), *Proceedings, Educational Multimedia and Hypermedia '95* (p. 151–156). Charlottesville, VA: AACE.

Sanchez, R. (1995a, September). The digital press. *Internet World*, pp. 58–60.

Sanchez, R. (1995b, October). A wired education. *Internet World*, pp. 71–74.

Schellekens, A. (1995). StudieNet: A telematic study support system. In P. Held & W. F. Kugemann (Eds.), *Telematics for education and training* (pp. 85–90). Amsterdam: IOS Press.

Schlosser, C. A., & Anderson, M. L. (1994). *Distance education: Review of the literature*. Washington, DC: Association for Educational Communications and Technology.

Schnase, J. L., & Cunnius, E. L. (Eds.). (1995). *CSCL 95: Computer support for collaborative learning*. Mahwah, NJ: Lawrence Erlbaum, Associates.

Schneider, D., & Block, K. (1995). The World Wide Web in education. *ANDREA* 2(5). [Internet journal]. Contact andrea@nki.no

Schoenmaker, J. (1993). Linking new applications to new design paradigms . *Computers & Education*, 21(1/2), 181–192.

Schramm, W. (1977). *Big media, little media*. London: Sage Publications.

Schrum, L. (Ed.). (1994). *Directory of educational telecommunications services*. Eugene, OR: ISTE.

Schrum, L. (1995). Educators and the Internet: A case study of professional development. *Computers in Education*, 24(3), 221–228.

Schuler, D. (1994). Community networks: Building a new participatory medium. *Communications of the ACM*, 37(1), 38–51

Schuler, D. (1995, December). Public space in cyberspace. *Internet World*, pp. 89–95.

Schuster, J. (1995). Five things you should know about districtwide networking. *Electronic Learning*, 14(5), 32–36, 41–42, 44, 46.
SDG/IT94/Proceedings/Educ/blumberg.mendelweb/

Seels, B. B., & Richey, R. C. (1994). *Instructional technology: The definition and domains of the field*. Washington, DC: Association for Educational Communications and Technology.

Seltzer, R. (1995, October). Picture power. *Internet World*, pp. 84–87.

Seymour, J. (1995, June 13). Small-office power. *PC Magazine*, pp. 102–121.

Shannon, C. E., & Weaver, W. (1949). *The mathematical theory of communication*. Urbana: University of Illinois Press.

Shapiro, A., Heck, J., & Freedenberg, P. (1992). The planning, design, and implementation of a statewide distance learning system. *Educational Technology*, 32(7), 28–32.

Sharples, M. (1993). A study of breakdowns and repairs in a computer-mediated communication system. *Interacting with Computers, 5*(1), 61–77.

Shepherd, D., & Bowser, D. (1992, November). *Students' attitudes and preferences to the use of electronic technologies in the delivery of courseware: A case study.* Paper presented at the International Council for Distance Education 16th Annual Meeting, Bangkok, Thailand.

Sherry, L. C., & Morse, R. A. (1995). An assessment of training needs in the use of distance education for instruction. *International Journal of Educational Telecommunications, 1*(1), 5–22.

Shneiderman, B. (1993). *Designing the user interface.* 2nd Edition. Reading, MA: Addison Wesley

Shneiderman, B., Alavi, M., Norman, K. & Borowski, E.Y. (1995). Windows of opportunity in electronic classrooms. *Communications of the ACM, 38* (11), 19–24.

Sholdt, G. P., Zhang, S., & Fulford, C. P. (1995). Sharing across disciplines: Interaction strategies in distance education. In M. R. Simonson & M. L. Anderson (Eds)., *17th annual proceedings of selected research and development presentations, AECT* (pp. 533–541). Ames, Iowa: Iowa State University College of Education.

Silberman, S. (1995, July). Home sweet home page: The missing link is yours. *Netguide,* pp. 52–59.

Simón, C. (1992). Telematic support for in-service teacher training. In A. R. Kaye (ed.), *Collaborative Learning Through Computer Conferencing* (pp. 29–37). Berlin: Springer-Verlag.

Simonson, M., & Schlosser, C. (1995). More than fiber: Distance education in Iowa. *Techtrends, 40*(5), 13–15.

Sippel, F. (Ed.). (1994). *Implementation and management of teletraining.* Report Nr. 123. Bad Honnef, Germany: Wissenschaftliches Institut für Kommunikationsdienste.

SITN, (1995). *Information about the Stanford Interactive Television Network SITN.* 401 Durand Building, Stanford CA 93305–4036, `e-mail: na.itv@forsythe.stanford.edu`. [Also WWW document]. URL `http://www-sitn.stanford.edu/sitn.html`.

Sligte, H., & Meijer, P. (1993). Evaluating teletrips within the Educational Schools Project. In B. Samways & G. Davies (Eds.), *Teleteaching '93* (pp. 797–808). Amsterdam: North Holland.

Slovacek, S. P., & Doyle-Nichols, A. R. (1992). Enhancing telecommunication in teacher education. *Journal of Research on Computing in Education, 24*(2), 254–264.

Smeaton, C., & Slater, A. (1994). *Integrating simulations and W3 courseware.* [WWW document]. URL `http://www.ncsa.uiuc.edu/SPG/IT94/Proceedings/`

Smeaton, C., & Slater, A. (1995). *Integrating simulations and W3 courseware.* [WWW document]. URL http://www-interact.eng.cam.ac.uk/TLTP_EXHIB/ DEMOS/index.html

Smith, C. (1995). Measuring the usability and effectiveness of advanced learning technologies. In P. Held & W. F. Kugemann (Eds.), *Telematics for education and training* (pp. 328–335) . Amsterdam: IOS Press.

Smith, R. (1995). *Map-Extra: Guest lecture.* [WWW document]. URL http://www.brandonu.ca/ennsnr/Resources/Roadmap/guest.html

Soloway, E. (1995). Beware, techies bearing gifts. *Communications of the ACM, 38*(1), 17–24.

Somekh, B. (1989). The human interface: Hidden issues in CMC affecting use in schools. In R. Mason & A. Kaye (Eds.), *Mindweave* (pp. 242–246). Oxford: Pergamon.

Sorenson, C. K. (1995). Evaluation of interactive television instruction: Assessing attitudes of community college students. *DEOSNEWS, 5*(9). [Internet journal]. Contact ACSDE@PSUVM.PSU.EDU

Spencer, S. M., Nibert, M. L., & Sgro, J.-Y. (1994). *Communicating information about virus structure and biology via the World Wide Web.* [WWW document]. URL http://www.ncsa.uiuc.edu/SDG/IT94/Proceedings/Educ/ spencer/spencer.html

Spenciner, L. J., & Squibb, B. (1994). Preparing practitioners at a distance: Use of telecommunications in an introductory early childhood special education course. *DEOSNEWS,* 4(2). [Internet journal]. Contact: ACSDE@PSUVM.PSU.EDU

Spitzer, W., & Wedding, K.(1995). LabNet: An intentional electronic community for professional development. *Computers & Education, 24*(3), 247–255.

Squires, D. (1990). The design of network-based multi-user CAL. In A. McDougall & C. Dowling (eds.), *Computers in education* (pp. 201–206). Amsterdam: North Holland.

Stacy, E. (1995). Teaching and learning with aduiographics: Developing positive attitudes and effective pedagogy. *DEOSNEWS, 5*(10). [Internet journal]. Contact DEOSNEWS@PSUVM.PSU.EDU

Stahl, G., Sumner, T., & Owen, R. (1995). Share globally, adapt locally: Software assistance to locate and tailor curriculum posted to the Internet. *Computers & Education, 24*(3), 237–246.

Stahmer, A., Bourdeau, J., & Zuckernick, A. (1992). *Technologies and life-long learning.* Ottawa, CA: Department of Communications, Prosperity Secretariat.

Stallings, W. (1992). *ISDN and broadband ISDN.* New York: Macmillan Publishing Company.

Stanley, N. (1991). Networks for teacher training. *The CTISS File, 11,* 32–33.

Steeples, C. (1993). *A computer-mediated learning environment for adult learners: Supporting collaboration and self-direction.* JITOL Project Report. CSALT, Department of Educational Research, Lancaster University, Lancaster, UK.

Steinberg, E. R. (1992). The potential of computer-based telecommunications for instruction. *Journal of Computer-Based Instruction, 19*(2), 42–46.

Stockton State College. (1990). *Conferencing in our classrooms: The CoSy Project.* Internal Report. Stockton State College, College Drive, Pomona, NJ.

Sturm, C. N.(Ed.). (1995, March). Managing the Internet at your school. *Classroom Connect Newsletter,* pp. 1, 4. [Also WWW document]. URL http://www.wentworth.com

Supovitz, J. (1991). *Tuning in on current events: The uses and effects of video news programs in high schools in Mississippi and North Carolina.* Southeastern Educational Improvement Laboratory, Research Triangle Park, NC.

"Survey results...". (1995, August 28). Survey results. *EDUCOM Update.* [Internet newsletter]. Contact educom@elanor.oit.unc.edu

Swadley, R. K. (Pub.). (1994). *The Internet unleashed.* Indianapolis, IN: SAMS Publishing.

Swain, M. (1995, October). Selective surfing. *MacUser,* p. 141.

Tanski, C., Riel, M., & Hodas, S. (a.k.a. webmaster @quest.arc.nasa.gov). (1995, May). *Live from Antarctica.* [WWW document]. URL http://quest.arc.nasa.gov/Livefrom/Livefrom.html

Taukojärvi,S., & Jarvilehto, P. (1995). UETP-EEE Environmental Management. In B. Collis (Ed.), *The TeleScopia Courses: Experiences with the adaptation process for trans-European tele-learning* (pp. 43–51). Deliverable UT/DL1001/WP3.3. Bonn, Germany: Deutsche Telekom AG, Generaldirektion.

Taylor, D. (1995, March). Yahoo! A hotlist cornucopia. *Internet World,* pp. 24–25.

Taylor, J. (1992). *Technology, distance education and the tyranny of proximity.* Distance Education Centre, University of Southern Queensland, Toowoomba, Australia. Teaching.html.

Teles, L., & Duxbury, N. (1991). *The networked classroom: An assessment of the Southern Interior Telecommunications Project.* Vancouver, BC: Faculty of Education, Simon Fraser University.

TENET (a.k.a. web-master@tenet.edu). (1995). *Texas Educational Network.* [WWW document]. URL http://www.tenet.edu/

TERC. (1993). *NGS Kids Network/Middle Grades.* Curriculum units available from TERC Communications, 2067 Massachusetts Avenue, Cambridge, MA 02140.

Thach, E. C., & Murphy, K. L. (1995). Competencies for distance education professionals. *Educational Technology Research & Development* (ETR&D), 43(1), 59–79.

Thornburg, D. D. (1995). Welcome to the communication age. *Internet Research*, 5(1), 64–70. (Also at WWW document URL http://www.mcb.co.uk/)

Thorpe, M. (1989). *The tutor perspective on computer mediated communication in DT200: Introduction to Information Technology*. CITE Report No. 76. Milton Keynes, UK: Institute of Educational Technology, Open University.

Tiene, D. (1993). Exploring the effectiveness of the *Channel One* school telecasts. *Educational Technology, 33*(5), 36–42.

Tiene, D., & Whitmore, E. (1995). Beyond *Channel One*: How schools are using their schoolwide television networks. *Educational Technology, 35*(3), 38–42.

Tiffin, J. (1989). The failure of success and the success of failure. *Educational Training and Technology International, 26*(2), 136–140.

Traw, R. (1994). School/university collaboration via e-mail. *Tech Trends, 39*(2), 28–31.

Treese, W. [a.k.a.treese@OpenMarket.com] (1995, April 28). *The Internet Index* (Number 7) [WWW document]. URL http://www.openmarket.com/intindex/

Tremblay, W. (1992). Telecourse utilization in American research universities: Institutional context and instructional innovation. *International Journal of Instructional Media, 19*(3), 197–207.

Turner Educational Services, Inc. (1995). *CNN Newsroom* [Service available through *America On-Line*]. Atlanta, GA.

Turoff, M. (1991). Computer-mediated communication requirements for group support. *Journal of Organizational Computing, 1*, 85–113.

Turoff, M. (1995, March). *Designing a Virtual Classroom*. Paper presented at the 1995 International Conference on Computer-Assisted Instruction, Taiwan. [Also WWW document]. URL http://ww.njit.edu/cccc/vc/Papers/Design.html.

Tykwinski, J. R., & Poulin, R. C. (1995). A practical guide to teleconferencing and distance education. In In B. T.Hakes, J. Cochneour, L. L. Rezabek, & S. G. Sachs (Eds.), *Compressed video for instruction: Operations and applications* (pp. 433–456). Washington, DC: AECT.

Ubois, J. (1995, October). The great facilitator. *Internet World*, pp. 62–66. URL http://salazar.aa.psu.edu/courses/art122w/

US Congress Office of Technology Assessment. (1990). *Worker training: Competing in the new international economy*. OTA-ITE-457. Washington, DC: US Government Printing Office.

US Congress Office of Technology Assessment. (1993). *Adult literacy and new technologies: Tools for a lifetime*. OTA-SET-550. Washington, DC: US Government Printing Office.

US Congress Office of Technology Assessment. (1995). *Teachers & technology: Making the connection.* OTA-PHR-616. Washington, DC: US Government Printing Office.

Vacca, J. R. (1995, October). CU on the Net. *Internet World*, pp. 81–82.

Van den Brande, L. (1993). *Flexible and distance learning.* Chicester, UK: John Wiley.

Van Haalen, T., & Miller, G. (1994). Interactivity as a predictor of student success in satellite learning programs. *DEOSNEWS, 4*(6). [Internet journal]. Contact: ACSDE@PSUVM.PSU.EDU

Vaughan-Nichols, S. J. (1995, August). BBSs to provide local Web access. *Byte*, p. 30.

Veen, W. (1993). How teachers use computers in instructional practice: Four case studies in a Dutch secondary school. *Computers & Education, 21*(1&2), 1–8.

Veen, W., Collis, B., De Vries, P., & Vogelzang, F. (1994). *Telematics in education: The European case.* De Lier, NL: Academic Book Centre.

Veen, W., Van der Neut, I., Spoon, P., & Vogelzang, F. (1991).*The reality of computer use in the classroom: Four case studies from a secondary school.* De Lier: Academisch Boeken Centrum.

Vergés I Trias, M., Castells I Prims, J., & Ruiz I Tarragó, F. (1994). Experience in the use of telecommunications in Catalan schools. In W. Veen, B. Collis, P. de Vries, & F. Vogelzang (Eds.), *Telematics in education: The European case* (pp. 191–202). De Lier: Academic Book Centre.

Vetler, R. J., & Du, D. H. C. (1993), February). Distributed computing with high-speed optical networks. *Computer*, pp. 7–18.

"Virtual colleges...". (1995 May 18). Virtual colleges provide on-line learning. *Investor's Business Daily*, p. A1.

Wagner, E. D. (1990). Looking at distance education through an educational technologist's eye. *The American Journal of Distance Education, 4*(1), 53–68.

Wagner, E. D. (1992). Separating myth and reality in distance education. *Educational Technology, 32*(10), 42–45.

Ward, J. (1990). Landline two-way video: Being there—and here. *T.H.E. Journal, 17*(9), 59–61.

Ward, P., & Davis, K. (1994). *Empowering students in the information age.* [WWW document] URL http://www.ncsa.uiuc.edu/SDG/IT94/Proceedings/Educ/Ward/Ward.html

Ward, R. (1995, July). A HTML-based case scenario for teaching business computing skills. *Active Learning, 2*, 49–50.

Watabe, K., Hamalainen, M., & Whinston, A. B. (1995). An Internet based collaborative distance learning system: CODILESS. *Computers in Education, 24*(3), 141–155.

Waugh, M. L., Levin, J., & Smith, K. (1994). Organizing electronic network-based instructional interactions: Successful strategies and tactics, Part I. *The Computing Teacher, 21*(5), 21–22.

Weidemann, S. (1994). Schools Database Service (SDBS). In W. Veen, B. Collis, P. de Vries, & F. Vogelzang (Eds.), *Telematics in education: The European case* (pp. 25–30). De Lier, NL: Academic Book Centre.

Weisberg, M., & Ullmer, E. J. (1995). Distance learning revisited: Life-long learning and the National Information Infrastructure. In M. R. Simonson & M. Anderson (Eds.), *Selected research and development presentations at the 1995 National Conference of the Association for Educational Communications and Technology* (pp. 628–647). Ames, IA: AECT.

Welz, G. (1995, March). New dimensions: A multimedia revolution is unfolding on the Net. *Internet World,* pp. 31–36.

Wetzel, C. D., Radtke, P. H., & Stern, H. W. (1994). *Instructional effectiveness of video media.* Hillsdale, NJ: Lawrence Erlbaum Associates.

Whalley, W. B. (1995, July). Teaching and learning on the Internet. *Active Learning, 2,* 25–29.

Wheeler, B. C., Valacich, J. S., Alavi, M., & Vogel, D. (1995). *A framework for technology-mediated inter-institutional telelearning relationships.* [WWW document]. URL `http://cwis.usc.edu/dept/annenberg/vol1/issue1/wheeler/` Also [Internet journal]. *Journal of Computer-Mediated Communication, 1*(1).

Whittle Communications Corporation, (1992). *The Whittle Educational Network. Information package.* 706 Walnut Street, Knoxville, TN 37902 USA.

Wiggins, R. W. (1995a, July). Presentation in a box: Don't risk disaster by relying on a live connection. *Internet World,* pp. 64–65.

Wiggins, R. W. (1995b, November). The unfolding Net. *Internet World,* pp. 42–45.

Wighton, D. J. (1993). Telementoring: Examining the potential for an educational network. *T.I.E. Newsletter, 4*(3), 13–16.

Wild, R. H., & Winniford, M. (1993). Remote collaboration among students using electronic mail. *Computers in Education, 21*(3), 193–203.

Williams, M. (1994). Telecommunications and Australian schools: Retrospect and prospect. In M. Ryan, (Ed.), *Proceedings of APITITE '94,* Vol. 1 (pp. 187–193). Murray Hills, NSW: Australian Computer Society.

Willis, B. (1993). *Strategies for teaching at a distance.* ERIC Clearinghouse on Information Resources, Syracuse University, School of Education, Syracuse New York 13244–2340

Willmott, D. (1995, July 14). PC Magazine guided tour: 100 WWW site. *PC*

Magazine, pp. 124–139. [WWW version] at URL `http://www.zdnet.com/pcmag/1407/07w3_edu.htm`

Wilson, V. (1994). Developing the adult independent learner: Information literacy and the remote external student. *Distance Education, 15*(2), 254–278.

Windley, P. J. (1995). *Using WWW to augment classroom instruction.* [WWW document]. URL `http://lal.cs.byu.edu/people/Windley/using.www.to.teach.html`

Winrich, L. (1995). *SIGTEL Exemplary Project MATH PEN PALS.* [Internet listserv document]. Contact `lwinrich@quest.arc.nasa.gov`

Wolf, K. D. (1995). The implementation of an open learning environment. In H. Maurer, H. (Ed.). *Educational multimedia and hypermedia, 1995* (pp. 689–694). Charlottesville, VA: AACE.

Wolff, M. (1995a, September 21). The Internet is about information emplowerment. *Investor's Business Daily,* p. A8.

Wolff, M. (1995b, March). *Ki Net: The art of integrated living and working. Competitive and collaborative edge through virtual organization.* [WWW document]. URL `http://www.ki-net.co.uk/netinnov/ki-net/index.html`

Wong, K. Y. P., & Lam, A. S. Y (1995, March 8, Version 1.5.3). *CU_HTML.DOT* (Version 1.5.3). [WWW document]. URL `http://www.cuhk.hk/csc/cu_html/cu_html.htm`

Wood, J. (1995, July). Work in progress at the Virtual Monash. *Active Learning, 2,* 13–18.

Wood. J. (1993). The professional development of teachers as facilitators of computer mediated collaborative learning. In T. Nunan (Ed.), *Distance education futures* (pp. 93–104). Adelaide, Australia: Australian and South Pacific External Studies Association.

Wray, R. E., Chang, R., Philips, J., Rogers, S., Walsh, W., T Laird, J. (1994). **Organizing information in Mosaic: A classroom experiment**. [www document]. URL `http://www.nesa.uiuc.edu/SDG/IT94/Proceedings/Educ/Wray-experiment.mosaic94.html`

Yakimovicz, A. D., & Murphy, K. L. (1995). Constructivism and collaboration on the Internet: Case study of a graduate class experience. *Computers & Education, 24*(3), 203–209.

Yarnoff, S. (1995 July 16). *Special Internet connections.* [WWW document]. URL `http://www.uwm.edu/Mirror/inet.services.html`

Zariski, A. (a.k.a. zariski@csuvax1.murdoch.edu.au) (1995). *Course Outline and Study Guide for the course 'Legal Practice and Documentation'.* [Gopher document]. URL `gopher://infolib.murdoch.edu.au`

Zhang, S., & Fulford, C.P. (1994). Are interaction time and psychological interactivity the same thing in the distance learning television classroom? *Educational Technology, 34*(6), 58–64.

Zinck, R. A. (1989). Distant dialogs: Telecommunications in teacher training. In *Proceedings of NECC '89* (pp. 256–260). Eugene, OR: ISTE.

Zwart, C. (1995, September 8). Surfnet popular in the university world. *Computable,* pp. 5, 12.

Index